The Urban Web

The City. Fernand Leger (French, 1881–1955). 1919. Oil on Canvas. 90¾″ × 117¼″.
Philadelphia Museum of Art, A.E. Gallatin Collection.

THE
URBAN WEB

Politics, Policy, and Theory

Lawrence J.R. Herson
The Ohio State University

John M. Bolland
The University of Alabama

NELSON-HALL SERIES IN POLITICAL SCIENCE

Consulting Editor: Samuel C. Patterson
The Ohio State University

Nelson-Hall Publishers/Chicago

Project Editor: Dorothy Anderson
Text Designer: Tamra Campbell-Phelps
Illustrator: Bill Nelson
Text Compositor: Interface Studio
Manufacturer: Bookcrafters
Cover Painting: Matthew Schaefer, *Rush St. Cafe,* oil on canvas.

Library of Congress Cataloging-in-Publication Data

Herson, Lawrence J. R.
    The urban web : politics, policy, and theory / Lawrence J.R.
Herson, John M. Bolland.
        p.   cm.
    Includes bibliographical references (p.   ).
    ISBN 0-8304-1078-3. — ISBN 0-8304-1220-4 (pbk.)
    1. Cities and towns—United States. 2. Cities and towns—United
States—Growth. 3. Municipal government—United States. 4. Urban
policy—United States. 5. Sociology, Urban—United States.
I. Bolland, John M. II. Title.
HT123.H47   1990
307.76'0973—dc20   89-28887
                                                                              CIP

To our wives and children

Libby D. Herson
&
Eric, Viktoria, and John

and

Kathleen A. Bolland
&
Anneliese

*May they always know the
pleasure of travel to far-off cities*

Contents

Contents

___ Preface

Books, like rivers, have many sources; but unlike rivers, a book may have more than one destination. Among the sources that feed our book are several excellent textbooks now in print on urban politics. We acknowledge our debt to the conceptual frameworks provided by Charles Adrian and Charles Press (1977), John Harrigan (1989), Bryan Jones (1983), Dennis Judd (1988), Robert Lineberry and Ira Sharkansky (1978), and Clarence Stone, Robert Whelan, and William Murin (1986).

Another source for this book is our own research on the politics of several small cities in Alabama, Kansas, Ohio, Colorado, Montana, and the state of Washington. In addition to instilling in us a good deal of respect for the political process in small-town America, our research also afforded insight into the manner in which policy and politics vary according to city size and geographic region. Thus, in writing this book, we have attempted not to slight small cities nor presume that only big cities have significant problems.

A third source for this book is our preoccupation over several years with the American value system and American political theory. This preoccupation has led us to attempt a stance of ideological neutrality in discussing matters of market economics, zoning, race, poverty, service delivery, and central-city decline. Our purpose is to enlighten and explain, not to convert the reader to an ideological point of view. But we are also mindful of the difficulties of keeping this stance. As a professor of literature recently reminded us: No student of human affairs can escape his or her own involvement with the subject being studied.

Both of us are city-travellers. We visit great cities as often as we can, taking pleasure in their architecture, their energy, their historic role as creators and transmitters of culture. In writing this book, we have attempted to convey some sense of this pleasure, along with what Kevin Lynch (1960) calls "the image of the city."

A book may have several destinations. We have set our compass by the polestar of social science theory, hoping thereby to set our book apart from most others by its attention to theory. Our goal throughout has been to make explicit the theories that organize our knowledge about urban politics and that, accordingly, do most to explain those politics.

We have also attempted to steer toward the reader whose educational home is in the liberal arts. Our goal has been to work toward a triad of liberal arts traditions: To see how the past flows into the present, to see that all social processes are interconnected, and to understand that abstract ideas have real-world consequences.

In attempting to lay bare the real-world consequences of abstract ideas—especially those that nest inside ideologies—we are mindful that most of our readers will have had first-hand experiences with cities and city life. Our book is thus an attempt to put those experiences in perspective, to offer a theoretical framework within which our readers may better understand their own urban experiences, and to provide them with intellectual tools that will sharpen their judgment about present and future urban problems and policies.

But of all the goals that guide our book, none is more important than the one we take from the distinguished historian of art, Kenneth Clark (1956). Like him, we have done our best to "look with fresh eyes on a subject tarnished by familiarity."

We owe much to several persons for their encouragement and for their critical reading of our book in manuscript state.

Professor Emeritus Richard C. Snyder, the former Director of the Mershon Center of The Ohio State University, was first to encourage and support the collaboration that brought about the book. The present Director of the Center, Professor Charles F. Hermann, has generously assisted Lawrence Herson's several years' study of American political theory, and Professor Philip B. Coulter, Director of the Institute for Social Science Research of The University of Alabama, has given generous assistance to John Bolland's research into local politics and administration.

Several friends and colleagues read our manuscript in its entirety, offering precise and helpful criticism: Professor James Clingermayer (Texas A&M

University); Professor Samuel C. Patterson (The Ohio State University; also, political science editor for Nelson-Hall Publishers); Professor Craig Rimmerman (Hobart and William Smith Colleges); Professor Clarence N. Stone (The University of Maryland); and with special concern for style, linguistic usage, and common sense, Kathleen A. Bolland (College of Education, The University of Alabama) and Viktoria Herson (Department of Slavic Languages and Literatures, The Ohio State University).

Several others have been generous in reading and criticizing portions of the manuscript: Professors Lawrence Baum, John Champlin, and Randall B. Ripley (all of The Ohio State University); Professor Joan E. Crowley (New Mexico State University); and John Selby (The University of Alabama). And still others assisted greatly in the research that underpins our book: Cheryl Wilson, Scott Clark, and Paul Mego (all of The University of Alabama).

To all these, we offer our sincere thanks. They have made our book far better than it might have been, but we remain fully responsible for the book's failings and omissions.

Part One

The Urban Web

Old and New New York. Alfred Stieglitz. 1910. Photogravure. The Alfred Stieglitz Collection. 1949.845. © 1989 The Art Institute of Chicago, All Rights Reserved.

The Urban Web: _____ 1
An Introduction _____

...experience has shown that a very populous city can rarely, if ever, be well governed.... For law is order and good law is good order, but a very great multitude cannot be orderly.
  Aristotle
  The Politics

Inquiries Old and New

This book is an inquiry into the politics of contemporary American cities, but it is inquiry built on foundations that are at least two thousand years old. As long ago as classical Greece, reflective minds attempted to unravel the puzzles of the city. How do cities get established and who comes to live there? Why do some cities grow large while others remain small? What kind of government is best for cities? Why is it that large cities are less easily governed than small cities? And why is it that some cities seem to bestow happiness on those who live there, while others seem forever bound in misery?

These are ancient questions, but they fit the present because the ancients understood the city to be more than a unit of government. A city is also an urban place—marked by a relatively dense population and by lifestyles that set city dwellers apart from country dwellers. A city is also a sociological entity, a collection of strangers who relate to each other by means of an elaborate network of formal roles. And a city is an economic enterprise, groups of people who make, sell, and exchange goods and services.

What the Greeks knew about cities and what we also know about

3

cities is a set of ideas that serves as the framework for this book. First, each city is a unit of government. Second, as a unit of government, a city is also a triad of related enterprises: an arena of politics, a creator of public policies, and a provider of public services. Third, what a city does as a unit of government is very much affected by its other attributes; it is an urban place, a sociological network, an economic activity. And fourth, what a city does as a unit of government can also have consequences for its sociology and its economics.

In essence, our framework of ideas means that each city is a web of interconnecting attributes; it is a government, an urban place, a sociological network, and an economic enterprise. The strands of the web connect, so that activity in any one part of the web affects every other part.[1]

It is the essence of a web that every strand connects with every other strand. Pull or twist even a single strand and all others are affected. At any point in the web, begin to trace any single strand and, sooner or later, the tracing travels across every other strand.

Those familiar with the literature of the social sciences will know that our definition of web has parallels to the concept of system. Quite deliberately, we do not use that concept so as to avoid its extensive (and for our purposes, limiting) terminology—for example, input, output, throughput, boundary-maintenance—and to avoid what may be its conceptual biases—for example, equilibrium as opposed to disequilibrium. We, of course, as students of political science, concentrate our attention on one part of the urban web, that which deals with government and the enterprises of government—politics, policy, and public services. But to concentrate our attention there does not mean that we ignore other strands of the web. Quite the contrary. We will, for example, examine the relationship between city politics and urban poverty, and, for another example, the relationship between city politics and city size. And we will also be mindful of the fact that the urban web does not stand alone. It is connected to other levels of American government and to their politics and policies. This is so because in the United States every city is a unit of government, but no city is an autonomous unit of government. Each city is affected and controlled by the activities of the national government, by the state in which the city is located, and by the presence of other, nearby cities. Thus, the urban web is anchored to the larger web of government in the United States. But if we are to keep the idea of an urban web fairly discrete, it will be useful to retrace some of our ideas, by better defining our terms, and by paying further attention to one of the oldest puzzles of urban life: How is it possible that

1. The dictionary offers several definitions of *web*. As a noun, a web is defined as any complicated arrangement; as an arrangment of interwoven or interconnected parts, for example, a woven cloth. As a verb, to web means to entangle or envelop, as in a spider's web.

a collection of strangers—and the city is mostly a collection of strangers—can live in close physical proximity in a reasonably cooperative manner, without doing each other violence and harm?[2]

Urban and City Defined: The City in History and Logic

> The City is the People.
> Shakespeare
> *Coriolanus*

Although the words *urban* and *city* are nowadays used almost interchangeably, there is more than a shade of difference between them, a difference that can be traced to their original meanings. The noun *city* incorporates the idea of government and administration, while the adjective *urban* carries the idea of a densely populated place and the lifestyles of those who live there. Urban comes from the Latin, *urbs*. The word derives from the palings or palisades that were once used to surround and protect a settled place from intruders. From the earliest of times, those who lived in settled, protected places developed a characteristic way of life associated with a non-agricultural, non-nomadic existence. Our English word *urbane* came into the language about 1500, and with it came a sense of the qualities of life and mind that are traditionally associated with lives lived in an urban setting.

The word *city* is also Latin in its derivation. *Civitas*, to the Romans, carried in its meaning the idea of citizenship and the rights and privileges of those who were citizens. The rise of cities as self-governing places began in Europe with the Greek city states and continued until the end of the Roman Republic (about the last century B.C.). During the Roman Empire and through the successive stages of feudalism, European cities continued as walled enclaves, but not usually as self-governing entities. Then, sometime in the eleventh century, the city as a self-governing place came into being again. Feudal rulers bestowed certain degrees of self-government on their cities, largely as a result of the insistence of local craft guilds that they be free to conduct guild business, including the right to enforce contracts, conditions of work, and standards of craftsmanship. Cities as we now know them thus began with the granting of *charters* from their feudal overlords that bestowed on them a measure of self-government (Pirenne 1925). It was this tradition of the city as a group of citizens with a charter for self-rule that was carried into the New World when the first settlers came to build cities in the American wilderness.

---

2. Finley (1966) and Kitto (1951) explore this puzzle as it applies to the lives of the ancient Greeks.

Thus, the meanings that attach to the word *city* have mostly to do with its legal and governmental status, while the meanings that attach to the word *urban* have to do with what is commonly called the culture of cities: their architecture, lifestyle, sociology, and economics. But the two sets of meanings meet and mingle. The reasons are not hard to find. Every city is an urban place and every urban place—if it has legally defined boundaries and a charter from its state—is a city.[3]

But despite this mingling, it will be useful to play out the differences between city and urban a little longer. Doing so will permit us to see more clearly how the activities of a city's government are a response to a city's urban qualities. We begin, then, with a sketch of urban attributes by historian Howard Chudacoff (1975).[4]

The city as an urban place, says Chudacoff, is characterized by "communities of concentrated populations that coordinate and control large-scale activities."

> This phrase implies four major criteria: (1) that population density is a necessary characteristic; (2) that cities are focal points, or nodes that centralize and disperse goods, services, and communications; (3) that complex and specialized relationships characterize social life; and (4) that urban dwellers display particularly 'urbane' habits and shared interests. (P. vi)

Rural communities, in contrast, he says, are "less dense, contain lower proportions of wage earners, promote simpler, more close-knit social ties, and are less cosmopolitan in their outlook." These four characteristics (urban density, urban functions, urban society, and urban attitudes) set in motion those other qualities we associate with urban life and with the word *urbane*: cities as centers of human culture and creativity. What is more, by bringing "together people and resources, cities have encouraged the specialization that in turn has been responsible for economic and technological progress" (Chudacoff 1975, vi).

But if these are the urban qualities of the city, what is it that connects them to the government of the city? Broadly speaking, what do city governments do that reflects an "urban presence?" Our answer begins with the fact of urban density—the presence of large numbers of persons living in close physical proximity. By the logic of urban life, places of residence are divorced from places of work. That is so because the urban dwellers do not farm surrounding land, nor cut timber, nor take minerals from the ground. Instead, the

3. This mingling of governmental functions and the culture of cities is examined historically in several books by Lewis Mumford (especially, 1938 and 1961).
4. Chudacoff and most others who examine the city in socioeconomic terms draw on the seminal work of Louis Wirth (1938, 1964).

urban dweller trades things, makes things, transports things. And if he or she does not deal with material things directly, the urban dweller earns a livelihood by providing services for those who do. As a maker and dealer in goods and services, the urban person tends to earn a living as a member of a specialized group or organization whose logic of production requires that work be carried on in special buildings and specialized geographic areas.

This said, let us take the explanation one step further. The larger the urban population, the more it is likely that the urban place is a place of strangers, whose capacity for existing in a reasonably safe, comfortable, and healthy environment only partially can depend on the cooperation of friends and family and on the self-restraint imposed by a sense of shared existence.[5] To achieve a safe and comfortable life, the urban person relies on the services provided by the city's government, for it is government that (for example) uses a police force to keep the peace and restrain what society generally regards as harmful behaviors. It is city government that maintains the streets that carry the city dweller from place to place and from home to work. City government brings safe water to buildings where people live and work, and it builds and maintains the pipes and sewage plants that carry waste materials away. City government lays down standards for the safe construction of buildings and protects them from the hazards of fire. It supervises the sanitary conditions under which an urban population lives, and it performs a thousand other tasks that make life lived among strangers possible.

Politics and Public Policy

This, then, is what city government is all about, and this , then, is the connection between the city as government and the city as an urban place: rules that direct and constrain behavior on behalf of the collective good; services that make collective living possible; and money—raised through taxes—that pays the people who enforce the rules and provide city services.[6]

And here, too, is a working definition of *public policy*: the rules and services of government directed toward some specified end or purpose that is intended to serve the common good. And here, too, is the threshold of a definition of politics—for people quarrel over which rules are to be enforced,

---

5. This quality of self-restraint that derives from a sense of shared existence is seen by many, and sorrowfully, as on the wane in contemporary American urban society (e.g., Bellah, et al. 1985). Some also attribute to this waning the now-pervasive presence of urban street crime and vandalism (e.g., Oldenquist 1986).

6. As disciplines, political science and economics are concerned with a common phenomenon: the allocation of scarce resources. This commonality can be extended by noting that government functions to bring order to otherwise random and dysfunctional social behaviors, while the market (and market exchanges) serves to bring order to otherwise random and dysfunctional economic behaviors.

what services are to be provided, how much money is to be spent, and what (after all) is the common good?[7] These terms deserve further elaboration.

Public Policy

In simple terms, public policy is what government does or does not do. Public policy consists of the laws, judicial decisions, and administrative rules that determine the benefits and constraints that come from government. Thus, an inquiry into public policy not only looks at benefits and constraints, it also looks to see which persons and which groups are helped and hurt by those benefits and constraints. Of course, not every law, decision, or ruling is public policy. Common sense will suggest that while one police officer's decision to write a parking ticket is not public policy, the law under which the ticket is issued is public policy. Common sense will also suggest that the clerk who issues a building permit is not engaged in policy-making, but that the ordinance that defines who may build what kind of building (and where) *is* public policy.[8]

Public policy is thus understood to apply to a broad class of things, events, or persons. It is intended to be consistent over time and is generally said to be purposeful; that is, those who urge it and those who create it are expected to understand and anticipate its consequences. Every level of government creates public policy; but public policy in the city is a direct consequence of urban life. It is policy created by city government's need to make collective living possible within a densely populated environment.

Politics

In its oldest and most general sense, *politics* refers to the art and craft of governing. Used in this way, the word directs our attention to the broad purposes of government. In democratic societies, these broad purposes have to do with creating public policy in furtherance of the public good, and as determined by popular will and public demand. Used in this way, politics also directs our attention to competing definitions of the public good and to the values and arguments that underlie those competing definitions.

Another definition characterizes politics as the struggle to dominate government and determine its policies. This definition assumes that competing definitions of the public good, along with contending values and philosophic arguments, are all part of the struggle for dominance. And this

---

7. As will be noted, any definition of the public good invites a quarrel (a cornerstone of the struggle that is politics). And as will be noted, quarrels over the definition of the public good are inescapably shaped by individual and collective values and beliefs (the essence of an ideology).

8. Later, in chapters 11 and 17, the role of the individual bureaucrat in the policy process is further elaborated and the previous generalizations are tempered somewhat.

8

same definition also includes the more ordinary, garden-variety politics—activities that turn on running for public office.

Harold Lasswell did much to bring this second definition into widespread use. Politics, as he defines it in a celebrated book title, is *Who Gets What, When, and How* (1936). Within this definition, politics can be found everywhere in human affairs, and recent years have seen a spate of books that describe church politics, family politics, even sexual politics. But the politics we are concerned with is the politics of city government. City politics thus deals with what city governments do and do not do—in short, with their policies. Politics in the city deals with the behaviors, strategies, resources, and ideas of those who seek to influence city policies. It deals with the timing of those policies—for today's decision is an accomplished fact, while next year's decision is at best a hope and at worst a promise unfulfilled. And politics also deals with long-term outcomes—the ultimate consequences of city policies (e.g., Pressman and Wildavsky 1973; Levy et al. 1974).

Within this extended definition, city politics becomes inseparable from its urban anchorage. To understand city politics, it becomes important to pay attention to the sociology of the city, to see who among Chudacoff's "communities of concentrated populations" gets what, when, and how. Public policy affects nearly everyone in the city, but some groups are affected for the better, while others become worse off. Thus, to understand city politics, we need to ask which groups emerge better off from the struggle that is politics, and we also need to ask which groups emerge worse off. In short, to understand city politics, we need to see it as the knot that ties together the sociological, economic, and governmental strands of the urban web.

Choice, Change, and Constraints

If politics is part of governing, then governing is an exercise in choice. To govern is to choose among alternative courses of action. And unless the choice favors the status quo, choice results in change. But choices in government, as in private life, are neither free nor unlimited. Choices are almost always constrained by a clutch of considerations. As individuals, we choose among alternatives only in accordance with our ability to invent, imagine, or borrow those alternatives. We are further constrained in our choices by our values, those things and ideas and states of being that we prize and prefer (e.g., peace, liberty, low taxes, or an extension of the welfare state). The feasibility and practicality of a course of action is another constraint. So, too, are the costs and benefits we think will accompany any particular choice. And to these constraints, we need to add the constraint of resources (we are less likely to choose that which we cannot afford), along with constraints that come as we adjust what we choose to what we anticipate others will be choosing and doing.

These constraints upon private decisions are multiplied many times over

9

for those who make decisions for city governments. Four sets of constraints operate with special force on cities. First come constraints that result from the legal status of cities: cities are units of government, but not autonomous units. Any policy that a city may choose must conform to the policies of its state and also to the policies of the national government. Thus, no city may borrow money, nor hold elections, nor do anything else if what it does is not in accordance with the general policies of its state government or the national government. For example, no city may attempt to keep down the costs of providing services by forbidding the poor to settle there. No city may censor books or movies if they have been held by the courts to fall under the protection of the First Amendment. And no city may attempt to segregate persons by race. Cities are forever required to operate under the policy umbrellas of higher levels of government.

A second set of constraints involves money. Cities are among the governmental poor. They depend for income largely upon property taxes. Some also raise revenue by means of an income tax. But property taxes are slow to adjust to inflation. Upward adjustments are limited by state law to a fixed percentage of property values. And city income taxes are also limited by state laws which commonly require that city income taxes be approved by popular vote rather than by the city council.

Cities vary enormously in their taxable wealth. A few (mostly suburbs with expensive homes and high personal incomes) have revenues adequate to their policy desires. Most cities, particularly the largest cities, are revenue poor. These, as a rule, are also cities of slums, urban decay, and personal poverty. And these, also as rule, are cities with the greatest revenue needs.

A third set of constraints is socioeconomic. Ancient and medieval cities were walled cities, whose walls served not only for defense, but to keep out those whom the urban governors did not approve of (Long 1972). Since at least the eighteenth century, people have moved freely in and out of American cities. In fact, the freedoms to choose one's form of livelihood and one's place of abode—with the troubling exception of blacks, American Indians, and other minorities—have been regarded traditionally as two of the freedoms implicit in our constitutional system (Herson 1984). What this means is that the size and composition of a city's population is very much a matter of individual and private choice: A city's population is the sum total of all those who choose to move in, move out, or stay in that city. Accordingly, those who make city policy must be constantly mindful that any policy that adversely affects a significant group in the city may cause members of that group to move elsewhere, "to vote with their feet."[9]

_____

9. Economist Albert Hirschman (1970) offers an elegant theory of political and market choices, neatly framed in his book's title, *Exit, Voice, and Loyalty: Responses to Decline in Firms, Organizations and States,* which says that critics and the dissatisfied can leave, voice dissent, or give their leaders loyalty. For an application to local politics, see Orbell and Uno (1972).

Conversely, any policy that bestows significant benefits on any group may cause persons of similar social and economic circumstances to migrate to that city. Thus, policymakers are constrained to make policy that will keep in residence those who are regarded as desirable citizens, usually those whose affluence and education can contribute to civic leadership and the city treasury. And policymakers are also constrained by the prospect that some policies, however humane, may attract to their city a new group of urban poor, for the poor are those most likely to put the greatest burden on already-strained urban revenues and services (P. Peterson 1981, Clark and Ferguson 1983).

A final set of urban policy constraints has to do with national economic conditions. The prosperity of every city is tied to the prosperity of the country as a whole. It is true, of course, that some cities (and regions) are less severely affected by economic downturns. And it is also true that some cities benefit less than others from periods of rising prosperity. But by and large, it is true that economic good times and economic bad times are in the city *but not of the city*. There is relatively little that cities can do to offset general economic conditions, and though many cities become desperate to invent policies that will bring them prosperity (for example, building a sports arena or a convention center), the hard truth is that only the national government has resources sufficient to grapple with widespread economic distress. Cities are constrained to operate on the margins of policies created by other levels of government. And they are also constrained by the knowledge that a policy intended to give any city an economic edge over neighboring cities—say, the building of a convention center or granting tax rebates to new industry—invites retaliation by those neighboring cities.

Thus, every city is part of an urban web. Its strands are many—economic, sociological, governmental. Political and policy choices and constraints are all part of the web. If we follow any single strand, sooner or later that strand will be seen to connect with every other strand.

Grand Canal. George Geerlings. 1933. Drypoint. Gift of the Chicago Society of Etchers. 1976.487.

An Almanac of Cities ———— 2

To most people, the vision of a great city is that of streets, parks, rivers, bridges, and endless and bustling crowds . . . but the idea which weighs on me . . . is that of a vast unexplored interior with a million forms of hidden life.

J.A. Spender
The Bagshot Papers

Patterns and Variety

Thus far we have defined the American city in fairly simple terms: an urban place with a charter for self government. But embedded in this definition is a set of rich and complex ideas. The word *urban* implies population density, a style of life, a network of social roles, and a variety of economic activities. And the term *self-government* implies an arena of politics and the institutions of government—both operating within the norms and values of democracy.

This definition helps identify patterns that are common to every American city. And it helps fix attention on the importance of cities to the American way of life, for the urbanized areas of the United States account for:

1. more than 80 percent of savings and loan deposits in the United States,
2. about 80 percent of all bank deposits,
3. about 75 percent of the value added to our economy through manufacturing,
4. about 75 percent of the nation's personal income,
5. about 70 percent of all retail sales,
6. about 70 percent of the value of all assessed property in the U.S.[1]

13

But in identifying these common patterns, this definition draws attention away from the great variety of urban places and the many varieties of urban politics. There are approximately twenty thousand cities in the United States, and each is unique. Every city occupies a singular territory. No two cities have precisely the same population demographics (age, gender, wealth, occupations, and so on). Each city is set within a distinctive geographic context. Every city has its own array of economic enterprises that provide jobs for its inhabitants and taxes for its government. And every city has its own history, a collective memory that helps mold and shape the conduct of its politics. Thus, endless variety forms the mosaic of American cities. How, then, shall we put them into classes and groups?

The Statistical City

Keeping track of American society is the job of the U.S. Bureau of the Census. It does so by gathering information and arranging data according to classes and categories. The United States was first described as an urban nation in the census enumeration of 1920. As of that date, more than half the population was reported to be living in urban (as distinguished from rural) places. Today, the proportion of urban dwellers stands at about 75 percent of the total population. We have thus become a nation of urban places and urban dwellers. The Bureau provides further details: An urban place is a geographic area with a population of at least 2,500. An urbanized area consists of a central city (or two central cities) with a population of at least 50,000—plus densely settled adjacent areas.

A metropolitan statistical area (MSA) contains a central city (or two or more central cities) of at least 50,000 persons along with surrounding counties that are socially and economically dependent on the central city.

Of course, an urban place of 2,500 is not what usually comes to mind when we use the term city. Closer to the popular image is an urban place with at least 50,000 people. And closest of all is the MSA. The MSA is what is usually meant by a city: a large urban area dominated by a central city set inside a ring of smaller satellite cities.

At present, there are 318 MSAs in the United States, the largest in population being New York (17,677,042 people) and the smallest Meriden, Connecticut (57,118 people). In area, the largest MSA is Los Angeles, containing 464.7 square miles. The smallest again is Meriden, with only 23 square miles. As was said earlier, the MSA fulfills the popular image of the city and is the most complete expression of what was earlier defined as an urban place: densely populated, marked by a great variety of social

1. Adapted from Lineberry and Sharkansky (1978, 67).

roles and an extensive specialization of labor—all linked by road, bus, and (often) rail networks.

The MSA's central city is generally home to what is often called the urban problem: slums, poverty, traffic snarls, a high crime rate, and racial tensions. And in many places the MSA's satellite cities are the suburbs of an affluent America—racially white, upwardly mobile, well-educated persons; the suburbs of expensive, single-family homes, large lawns, and backyard patios. But generalizations can mislead: The MSAs also contain pockets of suburban poverty as well as enclaves of dazzling central-city wealth.

As figure 2.1 suggests, most MSAs are located in the Northeast quadrant of the United States. That is the area of our first urban settlements and hence, our oldest cities. The newer MSAs are located in the southwest quadrant of the United States—"sunbelt cities"—and their newness reflects the recent shift of population southward and westward (see chapters 15 and 18; also see Perry and Watkins 1977, Sale 1975). Generally speaking, it is the older, central cities of the Northeast that evoke the image of cities in crisis while sunbelt cities are perceived, if not always correctly, as cities that are free from crises and therefore good cities to live in.

Central cities on the Bureau's list of MSAs are also the urban places that give us our sense of America as a nation of great cities. These are the creators and curators of the American urban lifestyle. But significantly, only about 30 percent of Americans live in MSA central cities and only about 40 percent of the population live in metropolitan areas defined by large central cities (those with over 300,000 people). Taken together, these two facts suggest that most Americans live in middle-to-small-size cities.

The Sociological City

The essence of the city as an urban place is its variety of lifestyles: the larger the city, the more varied the lifestyles. Equally important, the larger the city, the greater the likelihood that among its lifestyles will be "problem lifestyles": lives that labor under poverty, limited education, substandard housing, high rates of unemployment and crime, and racial and ethnic discrimination.

Lifestyle is hardly a precise term, but a sense of lifestyle variety and lifestyle problems can be captured by comparing a number of logically derived "lifestyle indicators" for central cities, suburbs, and nonmetropolitan areas. Table 2.1 shows these comparisons.

Good Cities and Bad

The Census Bureau does not classify cities subjectively. But scholars and journalists do. One such ranking was recently offered by *Money* magazine (August

15

FIGURE 2.1: The Location of MSAs in the United States

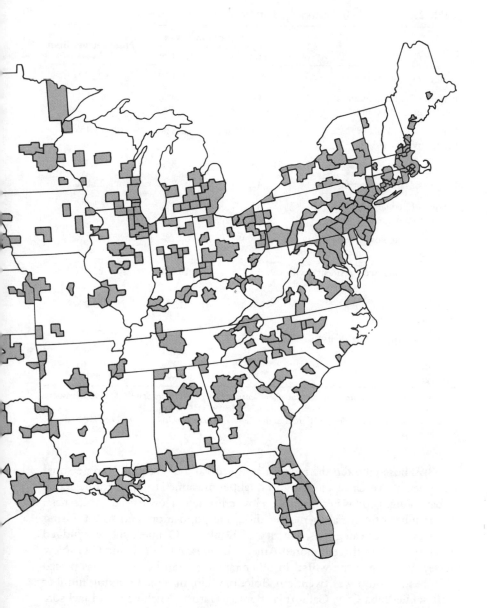

Table 2.1 Lifestyle Indicators for Different Types of Cities

	Metropolitan Areas		Nonmetropolitan Areas
	Central Cities	Urban Fringe	
Median family income[a]	$25,369	$33,038	$22,124
Percent of families living in single-family dwellings[a]	44.5%	62.9%	68.1%
Percent of households headed by females[a]	23.7%	12.5%	13.4%
Percent of living in poverty[a]	15.9%	6.8%	14.7%
Percent of families renting[a]	42.4%	22.2%	22.8%
Percent of people (over 25) with high school degree[c]	64.9%	74.1%	63.0%
Percent of employed residents with "managerial and technical" positions[c]	56.4%	60.1%	49.1%
Percent of employed residents with production or laboring positions[c]	17.1%	15.0%	20.4%
Percent of families living in subsidized housing[a]	6.4%	1.5%	3.2%
Crimes per 100,000 residents[b]			
assaults	3,081	2,421	1,862
robberies	1,075	470	261
burglaries	8,696	5,596	5,296

a. U.S. Department of Commerce, Bureau of the Census, *Poverty in the United States 1985* (1985 statistics).
b. Fanagen and McGarrell, *Sourcebook on Criminal Statistics* 1985 (1984 statistics).
c. U.S. Department of Commerce, Bureau of the Census, *Detailed Population Charactistics,* 1980 census (1980 statistics).

1988). Those who did the ranking assigned variable weights (and personal judgments) to each of a number of qualities presumed to make for desirable urban living: good water, clean air, a low crime rate, a low level of joblessness, the number of cultural events per thousand population, and so on. Using these and other categories, the city of Danbury, Connecticut was judged to be the best of three hundred American cities, while Atlantic City, New Jersey was judged the worst! In other rankings, San Francisco was placed fifth best, Boston was twentieth, Toledo, Ohio, occupied ranking number 150, while Yuba City, California, Benton Harbor, Michigan, and Jackson, Michigan carried the dubious honor of jostling for rankings number 297, 298, and 299.[2]

2. Another well-known attempt to rank the quality of life in the United States metropolitan areas was carried out by Boyer and Savageau (1985). The subjectivity of selecting and weighting

The Legal and Corporate City

The sociological city is defined by the character of its population, and good and bad cities by their quality of life; but legislatures and courts define the city differently. Legal definitions of the city begin with a curious historical fact: Both the modern business firm and the contemporary city descend from a common ancestor—the corporation. A corporation, says *Black's Law Dictionary,* is a group of persons united under a common name, the members of which succeed each other so that the corporation continues always the same, notwithstanding the change of individuals who compose it.

For certain purposes, a corporation is also considered a "natural person." As a "natural person," a corporation has the right to buy and sell property, sue and be sued, and to make rules governing its affairs. English corporations were created by a grant (a charter) from the Crown, and, prior to the eighteenth century, were used for three general purposes: for foreign trade and colonization, for charitable and educational enterprises, and for local government. The earliest English settlements in North America began their existence as corporations that combined all three corporate purposes, with governmental purposes only gradually coming to dominate (Scott 1910-1912; Lucas 1917). These first settlements took the form of villages (the better to achieve mutual assistance and common defense). However, the charter of incorporation was not to any single village, but to an entire territory or colony. Within a colony, as population increased, or as people grew unhappy with life in the settlement, new villages were founded, but they were still considered to be part of the original chartered colony.

At the time of the American Revolution, the laws of urban incorporation were only beginning to assume their present form (Frug 1984). Only about twenty cities possessed charters of incorporation. All the rest based their authority to exist and to govern on a patchwork of sources: on the authority for self-government given the original colony; on the rules of the craft guilds and merchant organizations in the former colony; and on a presumption of self-rule asserted by the pioneers who had come to build a city in the wilderness (Bridenbaugh 1938, 1955, Schlesinger 1933).

At the signing of the Declaration of Independence, all the powers of the colonial governments were presumed to have passed to their successive state governments. And the laws of urban incorporation began shifting toward their present form. Just as the king had once granted a charter of incorporation to a colony, the state governments now began granting charters of incorporation to cities and towns within their jurisdiction. And by about 1840, the laws and

---

quality-of-life indicators is demonstrated by the variability between their rankings and those of *Money.* For example, Boyer and Savageau ranked Danbury as 55th among the 329 metropolitan areas they considered; Atlantic City was 165th.

practice of urban incorporation were becoming everywhere the same. Henceforth, every new city would receive a charter of incorporation from its state government (Frug 1984).[3]

The consequences of the laws of urban incorporation are considerable. They run like luminous threads through every aspect of city government and politics.

Cities as Agents

To understand this consequence of incorporation requires understanding a proposition grounded in both law and logic: those who bestow a charter are superior to those who receive it. Thus, every city is held to be subject to the government that grants its charter, the state. Every city (says a legal maxim) is both a creature and an agent of its state. No city (under the law of agency) may do anything contrary to the best interests or the expressed commands of its "principal," the state. Hence, every city is a unit of government, but not an autonomous government. Each city is subject to control by its principal— the state. And the history of American cities is a history marked by struggles for greater city autonomy from state government.

In the nineteenth and early twentieth centuries, cities were subject to continuous supervision by their state legislature, which often appointed and removed mayors, passed city laws, and granted street paving contracts. Sometimes this supervision (meddling, said city dwellers) was a result of rural legislators' distrust of city people and their urban lifestyle. More often, it was the result of legislators' attempts to use the city (its offices, its purchasing authority, its revenues) to aid political friends and punish political enemies. Home Rule thus became a rallying cry for the cities as well as a reform movement that was to bring greater self-management and independence from legislative interference to the cities. Episodes of crisis (such as the recent near-bankruptcy of New York City) tend to bring a reassertion of state control over problem-swamped cities.[4] But overall, under terms of home-rule, most states now permit their cities a good deal of leeway in managing their affairs—providing they conform to state laws and general state policies.

Cities and Courts

Still another consequence of urban incorporation is juridical. Because a city is required to conform to the terms of its charter as well as to state laws

---

3. *Municipal* is the word most used in law to designate an urban place having a corporate charter. Thus, state statutes refer to "municipalities," "municipal law," and so forth. (*Municipal,* from the Latin, indicating a person with local citizenship.)

4. For a discussion of New York's near-bankruptcy, see chapter 16.

and the general tenor and purpose of state policy, cities are constantly subject to challenge in the courts. Cities, of course, enact their own laws (usually called ordinances), but every city law is subject to courtroom challenges, whereby judges decide whether city laws conform to the principles of agency and the court's interpretation of the city's charter. Eternal litigation, it is often said, is the price cities must pay for their incorporation.[5]

The Metropolitan Patchwork

Another consequence of city incorporation connects to the long-standing American tradition that local populations are to be encouraged to undertake self-rule. Generally speaking, state legislatures have made urban incorporation fairly easy. And once accomplished, it is nearly impossible to undo. This tradition of easily accomplished incorporation is not only sustained by the American ideal of grassroots democracy, but is also nurtured by a tradition that looks with favor on the idea of America as a congeries of "republics in miniature" (Jefferson's felicitous phrase; see Wood 1959; Tocqueville 1945). But these republics in miniature, scattered across the landscape, and often crowded side-by-side (which is the essential definition of an MSA) make for the patchwork of jurisdictions that spring up all around large central cities. No city may intrude into the affairs of another city. More to the point, however much the central city may need to expand (to acquire new territory, to gain access to the taxable wealth of nearby communities), it may not do so if adjacent areas have previously been given separate charters of incorporation.[6]

The City as Proprietor

A last consequence of incorporation connects to the long-ago business and commercial aspects of city charters. All through the eighteenth, nineteenth, and early twentieth centuries, the activities of state and national governments were strictly limited. Government was very much in the style of what has been called "protective democracy" (Macpherson 1977), using its powers to protect life and property, but doing very little to provide services and amenities for its citizens. However, the cities were the notable exception to this style of protective democracy. The city was regarded as having proprietary powers—the powers of a corporation to do whatever its proprietors might decide would best serve the interests of the corporation. Accordingly, long

---

5. Technically, city laws are called municipal ordinances to convey three attributes: their limited, local jurisdiction, the fact that they are subordinate to state laws, and the fact that in giving cities power to pass ordinances, the state has not parted with its overall and superior law-making powers.
6. See the discussion of annexation in chapter 13 for exceptions to this general rule.

before states and the national government were offering amenities and welfare services to the public, city governments were doing just that.

Today, we think of government services as proper and legitimate and quite ordinary. But in the nineteenth century, cities were the pioneers of service government. Cities built roads and streets to be used without charge. Cities provided water and sewage services and police and fire protection. Some cities even built gas works and electric generating plants. (Gas and water socialism, the critics cried.) And occasionally, cities carried their "business enterprises" to what must have seemed strange and wondrous domains: They built and operated zoos and art museums, established municipal colleges, funded symphony orchestras, and operated hospitals and food kitchens for the poor. (See Howe, 1905, for a reformer's plea for more urban proprietary enterprises.) In essence, the city's voters were seen by courts and state legislatures as possessing a business firm's powers, with city officials being the corporation's proprietors, able to do things ordinarily beyond the powers of other levels of government.[7]

Cities, Towns, and Villages

A final way of classifying cities is by size.

The Village

In every one of the fifty states, the village is the smallest incorporated place. The number of persons required for incorporation varies from state to state. In Arkansas and North Dakota, for example, no minimum population is set for incorporation, while Alabama requires seventy-five people to petition for and receive a charter of incorporation. In a number of other states (e.g., Colorado, Massachusetts), well over a thousand residents are required before incorporation will be considered. In most states when a village attains some specified population (determined by the state), it is required to accept a charter incorporating it as a town.

As befits its small size, charter provisions for village government are fairly simple. Most villages elect a fairly small legislature, the village council, of from five to seven persons. Villagers traditionally also elect an executive officer, the mayor, who is usually given authority to appoint a law-

---

7. A generation ago, no textbook on municipal government (as the subject was then generally known) was considered complete without extensive discussion of the law of municipal torts: legal liabilities that followed from a city's use of its proprietary powers. (See, for example, Munro 1923, Herson 1957.) A city using its corporate (governmental) powers was generally held to be acting as an agent of state government, and therefore not to be sued. But a city using its proprietary powers was held to be acting in its "private, business" capacity, and thus open to lawsuits for wrongful and negligent actions.

enforcement officer, the village constable. Some village charters provide for the appointment of a village clerk who often serves as treasurer also.

The Town

Town government is likely to be more elaborate. Each state has its own population requirement for towns, and like villages, these requirements are highly variable from state to state. The town council is usually small (from five to seven members), but a town charter may require a larger and more complex administration. In many states, town voters may choose between a council-mayor charter or a council-manager charter. In the latter, the council appoints a nonelected administrator to head such town-government departments as police, fire, streets, and sanitation.

The City

The larger the urban population, the greater its need for the services that make urban living safe and convenient. And the more such services are needed, the more elaborate will be the city charter's provisions for elected and nonelected officials. City councils vary greatly in size. While most cities have councils consisting of five or seven members, Chicago's city council consists of half-a-hundred aldermen. Some city charters invest their mayor with considerable power, authorizing the mayor to hire and fire the heads of city agencies (police chiefs, fire chiefs and the like), while other charters reduce the mayor's powers to the ceremonial: presiding over council meetings and serving as host to visiting dignitaries.

Later chapters will explore these types of organizational arrangements, but for now let us conclude our overview of the varieties and types of urban places by fixing attention on the diversity of cultural experiences that mark big cities, using New York as the yardstick against which all other cities tend to be measured.

The Big Apple

Within its population of 7 million, New York, in effect, is many cities in one. It is, in an area called the South Bronx, a city of fearsome devastation, a place of burnt-out buildings, high crime, and grinding poverty. Block after block of rubble-strewn ground lie as reminders of the buildings that once stood here. This is the city that calls forth the description common to other large cities with a burnt-out, abandoned core—a donut city.

Elsewhere in New York, there is another "city": Spanish Harlem, a racially mixed area that is home to immigrants from Puerto Rico and elsewhere in the Caribbean, redolent of the sights, sounds, and smells of a third-world country. In the Queens area, New York is a city of small, two-family homes, jealously guarded against racial and ethnic intruders by their white, working-class owners. And from Queens, the view is across the East River to the island of Manhattan, the city of affluence and elegance, high-rise apartments, powerful banks, Wall Street law firms, stock brokers, museums of science and art, concert halls, and shops that cater to the tastes of a rich, consumer society. Here, too, is the New York that rightfully claims its place as America's center of culture. More art, music, dance, and drama is played and exhibited here in a single day than may appear in other cities in a year. Even an abbreviated list of a week's worth of entertainment and cultural events offers insight into one of the powerful dynamics of Western history: that cities—especially big cities—are the creators and repositories of much of humankind's artistic and cultural achievements (Mumford 1938). By way of examples, there are about seven hundred galleries and museums in New York that display and sell visual works of art. And for a typical week in the spring of 1989, *New Yorker* magazine in its "Goings on About Town," lists sixteen opera performances, fifteen symphony and recital performances, forty-six plays and musicals, twenty-one dance and ballet performances, and (in addition to several dozen movie houses featuring Hollywood films) twenty-three movie houses dedicated to showing noncommercial and classic films.

Cities as Opportunity for the Chance Encounter

Lewis Mumford, a distinguished student of cities, once remarked that the sense of excitement we experience in big cities springs from their ever-present opportunities for the chance encounter. We walk the streets of a city never quite knowing what or whom we will meet or see. The city's size is such that much of what happens seems unpredictable. And yet, beneath the happenstance are patterns that can be understood by those who study the city and take note of the theories that explain the patterns. Accordingly, and if we are to peer beneath and beyond the variety of twenty thousand cities, it is to theories of the city that we must now turn.

24

Joliet, Illinois. Rhondal McKinney. Photograph. 1987.

Theories of Urban Politics ____ 3

Every why hath a wherefore.
Shakespeare
Comedy of Errors

Behold! An Inner Logic

Every book is built around two sets of ideas: an external outline and an inner logic. The external outline organizes the book's topics and sets out the order of their presentation in the table of contents. The inner logic gives the outline its coherence and makes the order of presentation cumulative. With a fair amount of effort, the inner logic can be deduced from a book's index, but it appears in nothing so handy as a table of contents.

A book's inner logic comes out of the authors' views on how the world works and why things happen. And it is no accident that an inner logic is part of the enterprise called theory, for the idea of theory has the same roots as the word *theatre,* which in its original Greek meant "to behold."

The inner logic of this book is built around theories of the city. And to better understand the idea of theory, it may be useful to examine an incident in the history of the theater.

27

Theory as Compressed Knowledge

For more than three hundred years, playgoers have delighted in the antics of Monsieur Jourdain, who rollicks through a play by Moliere and eventually announces in a voice overcome by astonishment that he has made an amazing discovery. Without even knowing it, he has been speaking prose all his life! The audience, of course, finds this funny. Imagine not knowing so obvious a fact of everyday life! Or funnier yet, imagine that anything has been changed merely by giving an everyday occurrence an elegant-sounding name. Yet, everyday occurrences do take on different meanings when given different names. (Think of the car dealer who calls his cars "previously owned" instead of used, or the member of Congress who avoids talking about new taxes by using the words "revenue enhancements.") All through the preceding pages, we have been using a special sort of language—the language of social science theory. Of course, theory is an everyday activity. Theoretical language is what we use when we try to explain the world around us. It is often the language we use when we want others to change their ways, or do as we say. Theory gives us an understanding of the whys and wherefores of behaviors and events. Theory connects and relates means to ends, antecedents to consequences, and causes to effects. Theory thus tells us how and why things happen; and in doing so, theory explains.[1]

A simple definition of theory is framed in terms of connections and relationships: Theory is a set of logically connected, experience-grounded observations. Sometimes these observations are of a prescriptive or normative variety (i.e., norms, standards, values). If you wish to achieve justice, we may say, then you should—you ought to—treat in like manner all persons accused of the same crime. Thus, prescriptive theory speaks to the world as we wish it to be and to the ideals and goals we wish to achieve.

At other times, these relational observations are of a descriptive variety. The larger the city, we may say, the more likely it is to contain a sizable number of economic enterprises. (In this theory, the number of economic enterprises connects to—is an outcome of—city size.) Descriptive theory is a statement about things as they are now or as they were in the past. Descriptive theory also has potential for dealing with things as they may become. It has predictive capacity when framed in an "if. . .then" manner: If Genoa City continues to grow (we may theorize), then it is likely to contain an increasing number of economic enterprises.

Descriptive theory deals with the world of our experience, and accor-

---

1. Given the importance of theory to all branches of knowledge, and as might be anticipated, the literature of theory is extensive. Works of importance in framing this chapter include Herson (1984), Gibson (1960), Bernstein (1961), Meehan (1965), Taylor (1967), Fay (1975), Popper (1963), and Hanson (1985).

dingly is also called *empirical* theory (from the Greek word for "experience"). More important, descriptive theory is an assertion of cause and effect.[2] Improve the schools, we may theorize, and new factories, attracted by the availability of an educated work force, will come to our city.

Fulfilling a single prediction is a common form of validation. But for the social sciences, a more reliable form of validation involves a pattern of covariance: When a change in one factor is generally associated with a change in another factor, providing that coincidence can be ruled out, then the theorist is privileged to assert the cause that lies behind the change (e.g., Popper 1959, Cook and Campbell 1979).

Causation is an everyday term, but is philosophically elusive. Philosophers agree that causation is not some mechanical force that pushes and bumps things and behaviors in and out of place. Causation is better defined as patterned, rule-following behavior, expressed as co-variance across time and differing conditions and/or as a consistent set of antecedent and subsequent conditions, behaviors, and events.

Prescriptive and descriptive theory can be separated in logic, but in everyday use they tend to blur at the edges. Take, for example, a much-used theory of crime: As poverty increases, an increase in crime is likely to follow. But those who hold this theory may, in fact, have more in mind than merely explaining the connection between poverty and crime. They may also have in mind a normative and prescriptive concern, subtly (or not so subtly) suggesting that since crime is undesirable, a useful and desirable way of combating it will be by reducing poverty.

Often, prescriptive theory (which is the bedrock of most political argument) is expressed as a simple set of means-to-desired-ends relationships: If we want our city to grow (we may theorize), then we must improve our schools. But, to prescribe improving the schools may require that we use some component of descriptive theory. City growth (it has been previously observed) may take place under certain specified conditions—for example, as an outcome of having schools of sufficiently high quality to attract settlers with young children. Thus, when we say, "If we want our city to grow, we must improve the schools," we have built our prescriptive theory on foundations of descriptive theory.

Theory can be as short as a single sentence: For example, the older the urban neighborhood, the higher its insurance rates are likely to be. And theory can also consist of an elaborate arrangement of logically connected theories,

---

2. In the social sciences as well as the natural and physical sciences, those who frame theories also seek to validate them. To assert that X is the cause of Y (and that Y is the consequence of X) may give us insight into the cause of things, but theory does not truly advance knowledge until we attempt to validate it, that is, subject the theory to various tests that increase our confidence that X is indeed the cause of Y.

as do those that connect poverty to such factors as racism, level of education, job opportunities, and general economic prosperity, and then further connect the resulting poverty to illness, loss of self-esteem, and families marked by domestic violence.

These more complex theories usually consist of a number of fairly short, concise theories that converge around a central idea or explanation. Accordingly, we shall call them *convergent theories*.[3] In the example of the preceding paragraph, the convergence is on the many consequences of poverty. But whether short and direct, or complex and convergent, theory speaks to the how, why, wherefore, and whence of the world around us. In short, theory tells us how the world works or how it ought to work; and in so doing, theory not only explains, it organizes knowledge and compresses it, and thus makes knowledge comprehensible.

Convergent Theories as Organizing Theories

The two preceding chapters contain a number of convergent theories. For example, a theory of politics converges around the ideas of conflict and competing wants. A theory of governmental functions converges around the idea that strangers are not likely to provide the services necessary for collective living. And a theory of the urban place converges around the idea of the city as a spatial area in which places of residence are separated from places of work.

What is more, convergent theories are often strung together, like links in a long chain. Thus, a theory of the urban place converges on still another theory: The city is a place given to specialized economic activities that (as a consequence) attract a growing population that (as a further consequence) calls forth such specialized government activities as water, sewage, and sanitation services, and building inspection.

A considerable number of theories of the city are widely understood and easily grasped. Others are not so self-evident. They are, however, sufficiently important to require spelling out. As we do so, we will also lay bare the inner logic of this book and the way in which we see and explain the workings of the urban web. In the following paragraphs, we will outline a few of these theories. Later on, we will fill in the details.

---

3. Other terms for convergent theories are *organizing* and *concatenated* theories: "A network of relations...[framed] so as to constitute an identifiable configuration or pattern. Most typically, they converge on some central point.... The 'big bang' theory of cosmology, the theory of evolution, and the psychoanalytic theory of neuroses, may all be regarded as of this type" (Kaplan 1964, 298). Because they deal with a broad range of phenomena, organizing theories give us a broad understanding of the world around us. In contrast, *precision theories* deal with a fairly limited range of behaviors and events. Precision theories specify *determinate relationships* (for example, 1 percent increase in the consumer price index results in a specified decrease in the number of new houses built). Thus, well-framed precision theories lend themselves fairly readily to validation or falsification. Generally speaking, such validation helps give credence and validity to the broader organizing theory of which they are part.

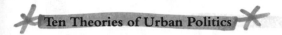

Ten Theories of Urban Politics

1. Grass Roots Democracy: A Prescriptive and Descriptive Theory

The American political culture places great emphasis on the importance of local self-government. We value that government and often make elaborate claims for its supposed sensitivity to citizen wants and needs and for its usefulness as a training school for citizenship. The average man or woman, the argument usually asserts, can know little of such matters as nuclear defense, monetary (as opposed to fiscal) policy, and so on, but he or she knows if garbage gets picked up and whether or not the fire department is on instant call. Hence, Mr. and Ms. Citizen are sufficiently knowledgeable to participate effectively in city affairs. And by participating in city affairs, they get educated to take part in the affairs of higherlevel, more complex government.[4]

It may be that our attachment to local government is also rooted in our experience as a frontier society when local government was the most meaningful and effective government. And it may also be that our attachment to local government is rooted even further back in our history, for the United States was first settled as a thinly stretched string of small villages. But whatever the source of the attachment, our society is strongly imprinted with the idea that local government is virtuous government. As previously noted, the consequences for urban politics are significant.

States have traditionally made it easy for any settled place to obtain a charter of incorporation. And once incorporated, that place, without its voters' express consent, may not be annexed to any neighboring city. Here, then, is explanation for the mosaic of towns, cities, and villages that make up the metropolitan area. And here, too, is explanation for many of the problems that beset the metropolitan area as a dozen (even a thousand) local governments struggle to co-exist in the same area. Where the problems of the area might be better solved by one single, overall government or by local government cooperation, the usual pattern is that of multiple local governments and sharp competition and rivalry among them. For example, much of the politics of affluent suburbs is dedicated to a strategy of exclusivity—devising ways (through zoning laws, building codes, and the like) to discourage the central city's poor from settling in the suburban ring. And central cities, though they may provide jobs and offer cultural enrichment for those who live in suburbs, as a general rule cannot require that the suburbs help pay the costs of central-city government.

---

4. The perceptive reader will see here a blending of prescriptive and descriptive theory. A premise to the argument is the value of (preference for) citizen participation in government and knowledge of its workings. How else is democracy's self-rule to be realized? The argument (in theoretical terms) then proceeds to connect local government to democracy's success, that is, to assert that participation in local government is one of the factors ("causes") of democracy's success.

2. The Unwalled City: A Theory of Permeable Boundaries

Suburbs may seek strategies for excluding those whom they view as undesirable, but central cities have no such tradition of exclusivity. They accept whoever chooses to settle there. They are cities without walls—either physical or legal (Long 1972). Their boundaries are permeable. Following the great in-migration that began in the 1950s (as Southern and Puerto Rican poor people moved northward to seek a better life), central cities in the Northeast increasingly became home to a social and economic underclass. (In an earlier time those same cities were host to a social and economic underclass of newly arrived immigrants from Europe.) And with the arrival of this underclass (paralleled by the outward flight of an affluent middle class) came an increase in the problems we have come to regard as urban pathologies: crime, poverty, racial tensions, slums, drugs, disease, and the homeless.

Thus, a theory of permeable boundaries converges on the proposition that central cities are marked by stubborn social problems that are *in* the city but not *of* the city—which is to say, not of the city's making. Their sources and causes (whatever they may be) lie elsewhere in the larger society. This being so, the theory converges on still another proposition: City policies that try to grapple with urban pathologies usually will be outmatched and overcome by these urban ills. Central cities, it is often said, can attempt to cope with their poverty-rooted problems. But without state or federal assistance, they are not likely ever to solve them.

3. A Theory of Social Learning: How Not to Solve City Problems

Communities, like individuals, learn from experience. When new problems appear, the rationally minded may propose that we seek new solutions for those new problems. But a theory of social learning converges on the idea that societies, like individuals, generally try to apply old solutions to new problems (Lindblom and Cohen 1979, Brewer and de Leon 1983). Perhaps this preference for the tried and familiar springs from an all-too-human yearning for continuity; or perhaps, this quality springs from the fact that new solutions are hard to come by. But whatever the source, this theory converges on the proposition that urban policymakers rarely attempt policies that redistribute wealth, or disturb the economic status quo, or attempt a full-scale assault on urban poverty (P. Peterson 1981). Past experience has taught them that the size of the problem is likely to outstrip a city's financial resources. Policymakers have also learned from past experience that redistributive policies may motivate affluent residents to seek the financial safety of nearby suburbs. And some policymakers also profess to have learned that solicitous concern for the poor will bring still more poor flooding into their city, shopping for a city with the most generous welfare benefits.

This theory of social learning links to a theory of permeable boundaries: Given the fact that the city is open to all who choose or can afford to settle there, practical considerations and past experience teach a city's policymakers that an assault on the economic status quo is a perilous policy option.

4. The Commodification of Land and Buildings: A Theory of Market Externalities

Our society is deeply committed to an economic system that in ideal form would leave economic transactions solely to buyers and sellers. Our philosophic commitment to freedom of the marketplace has deep historical roots, and most Americans grow up convinced of the truth of the proposition (itself a theory) that liberties of everyday life find their greatest protection in a market economy: One's freedom to work, choose an occupation, pursue an education, settle on a place to live, and even select a spouse are all bound up with the freedom to buy and sell. Indeed, what is an intuitive truth for most Americans is, in fact, historical truth: Liberal, democratic societies grew up in and around—some would say, are inseparable from—the freedom of contract that is at the center of market economies. And what is more, most Americans are also convinced that a market economy (in contrast to what is sometimes called a command, or government-controlled, economy) is the most efficient and best arrangement for setting wages, prices, production, and distribution schedules (Friedman and Friedman 1981, Lindblom 1977).

A pure market economy has always been more an ideal than a reality, for market economies traditionally have been burdened by severe problems: overproduction, cycles of boom and bust (good economic times followed by bad), monopolies that can drive prices skyward, harsh conditions of work, and for many workers, low or inadequate wages. As a consequence, most Americans accept the idea that a market economy must never exist without some form of government regulation. How much? and for whose benefit? are questions that help define contemporary Liberals and Conservatives. Thus, a fully operative market economy has been a lesser reality in the United States for the past half-century—ever since the rise of the welfare state in the 1930s, whose precepts and laws include government-set minimum wages, workplace health and safety regulations, unemployment insurance, old-age pensions, and a host of other market interventions (Lowi 1969a, Miles 1976, Herson 1984, Dahl and Lindblom 1953).

But whatever the gap between the ideal and the reality, the bedrock of a market economy is private ownership of property. Thus, the logical outcome of private ownership of property is that land and buildings are regarded as commodities to be freely bought and sold. With this fact of everyday life, the strands of our theory converge on a major explanation of urban politics: Policies that seek to curb the buying and selling of property are only carefully

33

and cautiously attempted by American city governments. Much more important, a city's physical form is in very large measure the consequence of countless
private-market (as distinguished from government) decisions—to buy and
sell land, to build buildings, and to rent, exchange, and tear them down. Of
course, decisions of government do affect the physical form of cities. Road
location and freeway construction, for example, contribute to urban sprawl;
and tax policies, for another example, may make it profitable to build high-
rise office spaces downtown or restore old buildings in the city's inner core.
But however much government policies may animate and affect private market
decisions, it is the private market that ultimately shapes the city's physical form.
Thus it stretches the point only slightly to say than a city's physical form *is*
market decisions cast in wood, steel, and concrete. Where the buildings go,
people come, roads and streets get built, and specialized economic activities follow.

To carry the theory one step further requires that we define market externalities. In short, a market externality is nothing more than the consequences
for others of a single market decision. To take just one obvious example: the
high price that I may pay for land in the downtown business district has nothing to do with any intrinsic qualities of that land, but everything to do with
the fact that people who do not own it gather nearby, in stores, offices, and
traffic intersections. Land values downtown are thus a consequence of population densities and overall commercial use which, in turn, are the consequence
of hundreds and hundreds of other market externalities.

In another example, I may decide that the expense of maintaining my
apartment building, with taxes, repairs, and low rents, makes it unprofitable
to keep it in good condition. I may even decide to let the building deteriorate
to the point where it can never again be profitably restored to good condition. What takes place is a market decision between me and my accountant
or between me and my tenants. But the social consequences are external to
the decision. They fall on the entire community. And thus the market externality of what is essentially a private decision helps to create a slum.

Of course, one property owner's decision does not create a slum. But often,
one decision feeds others until an entire neighborhood begins its downhill slide.
In fact, much of urban politics has to do with responding to, heading off, or
challenging the consequences of market decisions and market externalities. Land-
use laws, zoning, slum clearance, building inspections, traffic routes, traffic and
parking control, and street building are all issues that flow from market externalities, and they are at the center of much of urban politics and policy.

5. Looking for Mr. and Ms. Big: A Theory of Influence

Power in politics, as in everyday life, is sometimes defined as the capacity to
influence the behavior of others—to get them to do what you want. The
sources of political influence are numerous: wealth, status, organizational

34

position, the gift of persuasion, and a commanding personality. In an ideally working democracy, power ought to be widely distributed and it ought to pass easily from person to person (a normative theory of power). Social scientists have worked diligently to discover the realities of power in America—to construct and validate a descriptive theory of power: Who has it? How widely is it distributed? Is it passed around? What do those who have power do with it? A fully descriptive theory of power in America has yet to be validated, but careful observers of the city are drawn to the conclusion that influence in urban politics is one of the spin offs or consequences of the commodification of land and buildings.

This theory of influence is far from being an unvarnished Marxian postulate that political power is only economic power in disguise. But the theory does converge on the proposition that business leaders—especially those of importance in the downtown business district and in outlying shopping malls and apartment complexes—command the very respectful attention of political leaders and other governmental policymakers. "Business gets what business wants," is a common saying; and the suggested truth behind the aphorism is that large-scale property owners and developers, and managers of large-scale corporate enterprises not only have a disproportionate influence on what cities do—they are also able to assert a veto on programs that they think the city should not undertake.

6. A Theory of Lifestyle and Territory

Our theories of politics, power, permeable boundaries, and commodification all link to still another theory: lifestyle and territory. In a market society, most urban housing is privately owned. The house we buy and the rent we pay for space in somebody else's building represents more than cash payment for a domicile. It is cash payment for a style of life—a lifestyle that is maintained and protected as persons of like social status, like values, and comparable incomes establish themselves in neighborhoods and suburbs. A neighborhood is thus more than a fact of geography; it is lifestyle territory (Cox 1973).

Urban politics is never far removed from lifestyle. Recall that politics is the struggle over outcomes; but outcomes are not limited to who wins an election or who gets what government job. Outcomes also include policy, and few outcomes in urban politics are as important as policy aimed at protecting a territory's lifestyle. In everyday language, this is the politics of turf.

Zoning struggles are one form of turf politics. So too are many of the debates over city services—such as the distribution of police and fire protection and the money that is to be spent on schools. And so too are the occasional outbursts of violence that flare forth in older, central-city neighborhoods where residents see themselves threatened by the incursion of persons of different race, ethnicity, or, most important of all, different social status.

7. The Style of Urban Politics: A Theory of Size, Affluence, and Heterogeneity

Our previous theories now converge on a theory of the style of urban politics. In middle-class and affluent suburbs, political activity tends to concentrate in the hands of amateur politicians, persons much more concerned with national than local political issues (see Wilson 1962). For them, issues that turn on the delivery of city services are better entrusted to career administrators. But local issues having to do with lifestyle arouse their concern and bring them full tilt into the political process.

In big cities, holding political office is often a lifetime career, and the style of politics there is dominated by the outlook of those whose livelihood depends on winning elections. Quite often, the delivery of adequate city services is the key to winning elections. For example, a paralyzing snowstorm, and the city's subsequent failure to clear the streets, is thought to have cost Mayor Michael Bilandic the Chicago primary election of 1979; and Mayor John Lindsay of New York found his political career derailed by a series of city-crippling strikes by transit workers, sanitation workers, and so forth. (It was during Lindsay's term of office that popular wisdom had it that New York had become "ungovernable.")

Where a city's population is racially and ethnically mixed, elected officials are expected to champion the causes and concerns of important racial and ethnic groups. Election slates are drawn up with a concern to "balance the ticket"—making certain that important racial and ethnic groups are represented on the ballot.

Lifestyle issues, especially when they turn on protecting territory from racial or ethnic incursion, can easily turn bitter and acrimonious. For example, for more than a decade (from 1974 to 1985) school integration was the explosive issue of Boston's politics, and for a good part of that time the style of its politics was that of turmoil, anger, and resistance to court-ordered integration. At least one mayoral election turned on the candidates' challenging each other as to which would do more to resist school busing. (The effect of school integration upon Boston politics and on the lives of Bostonians is examined by Lukas 1985.)

8. A Theory of Urban Reform

A theory of urban reform turns on the pervasive corruption that marked big-city politics through the nineteenth to the mid-twentieth century. The theory connects with the social and economic conditions that helped produce that dishonest politics. And ultimately, a theory of urban reform converges on the lasting consequences of the reformers' attempts to clean up city politics.

One such consequence is to be found in the dispersal of governmental authority in many big cities. In an attempt to take power away from then-corrupt mayors and city councils, reformers in several cities established independent boards and commissions and gave them an independent authority to run selected units of city government. (Independently elected school boards are one example; police commissioners whose terms of office extend beyond that of the mayors who appoint them is another.) And while this dispersal of authority in some cities went a considerable distance in reducing the power of political bosses, this same dispersal has made it difficult for many present-day mayors to do the job they were elected to do: run their cities with a reasonable degree of authority and control.

Still another consequence of urban reform has been to bring to a number of cities an alternative to the usual pattern of American government. That usual pattern is the separation of powers (along with checks and balances) enshrined in the national Constitution and replicated in the constitutions of the fifty states. Under separation of powers, each branch of government is separate and independent of the others. Each elected official has an independent tenure, and each branch of government is expected to have a will of its own, checking and balancing the other branches (Herson 1986).

Reformed cities, however, are different. There, the inspiration for government organization is not the U.S. Constitution but the business firm. The city council (likened by reformers to a corporation's board of directors) makes general policy and, in addition, chooses a city manager to administer that policy. The manager is not elected; he or she is thus not independent of the council, but serves at its pleasure. Moreover, the manager is not expected to take part in the political process. Instead, he or she is expected to be a professional administrator, outside politics, whose job is to bring to city government the benefits of businesslike efficiency and economies.

9. A Theory of Urban Administration: Street-Level Bureaucrats

However much urban reformers long to bring efficiency and economy into city government, a city is not a business. Mayors and managers may strive to make delivery of city services efficient and economical, but it may be that city services can never be measured against what businesses do, if only because cities do things that business cannot be expected to do, such as provide police and fire protection in high-risk, dangerous situations. Equally important, cities are less likely to achieve the economies of private business because city services are distinctive. For the most part, they are labor intensive, which is another way of saying that their performance requires a high ratio of human labor to that performed by machines. And human labor, by its nature, is relatively expensive. City services are performed by people interacting with other people: the teacher in the classroom, the fire fighter in the burning

37

building, the police officer on the beat, the sanitation workers bringing trash from curbside to truck.

What is more, labor-intensive service involves a process that is loaded with opportunities for service deliverers to exercise a considerable degree of personal initiative and judgment. (Should the police officer give a ticket to a driver going through an amber light, or let the driver off with a warning? If the door to a restaurant storeroom is locked, should the health inspector come back another day? Or should he or she base inspection only on what can be observed directly?) In a word, cities are administered by what Michael Lipsky (1976, 1980) calls street-level bureaucrats: persons who are involved in the day-to-day delivery of urban services, and who must interpret policy guidelines in their day-to-day decisions.

Thus, a theory of urban administration not only takes account of the costs and the style of service delivery, it also converges on the proposition that services that require a high degree of in-the-street, on-the-site human interaction will never be managed easily from some central headquarters. Nor will such services ever be uniform all across the city. Nor will these services ever be without opportunity for bias, favoritism, and corruption (Yates 1977, Lipsky 1976, 1980).

10. A Theory of Ideology and Interpretations

The nine theories discussed above are the basic theories of urban politics, theories that help us to see and understand overall patterns. But one more theory must be invoked, a theory drawn from the overlapping realms of psychology and politics; a theory of ideology and conflicting interpretations.

We can, for the present, postpone an extended definition of ideology and postpone as well an explanation of the two major ideologies of American political life, Liberalism and Conservatism. What we need to do, however, is take note of two ideas: First, ideologies consist of those important values and beliefs we carry in our minds and hearts; and second, these values and beliefs serve as a lens (or screen) that blocks from our minds facts and ideas that contradict those basic values and beliefs. Said somewhat differently: An ideology is self-reinforcing. It is a pattern of values and beliefs so strong and persistent that each of us achieves a measure of psychological peace by blocking from our minds messages that challenge those values and beliefs.

Based on this provisionally sketched theory of ideology, we can expect that much of what we are likely to observe about cities is subject to being altered and interpreted by the ideology we hold. For example, what shall we make of an economically depressed, older city, with its high unemployment, its closed and obsolescent factories, its pervasive sense of social despair? For some, ideology leads to the belief that government has an obligation to intercede in the economy, to take care that none in our society are to suffer unduly, to set things gone wrong to right. These are the persons likely to "see" that the problems common to an old and failing city are society's problems (not the city's), and that the national government should pursue a vigorous program that will restore and reinvigorate cities in trouble.

But an opposing ideology leads others to resist government intervention in the economy, to believe that the national government is far too big and involves itself in too many tasks, or to believe that each of us is responsible for our own successes and failures. These are the persons likely to "see" an older city as a place whose problems are best solved locally—by those who live there.

In this fashion, a theory of ideologies helps us understand that what we "see" is often a consequence of the ideas (the values and beliefs) we carry to our field of vision, and this theory of ideologies also helps us understand that policies aimed at solving urban problems are also molded and shaped as well by the ideologies of those who invent and propose such policies.[5]

Next Steps

With these ten theories of urban politics now in place, the next step as we thread our way through the urban web is to place these theories within their historical context, examining how the past has shaped the present.

5. The possibility that reality—what we perceive to be true—is a social construction, fundamentally affected by those with whom we share values and experiences, is explored by Berger and Luckman (1967).

Part Two
A Backward Glance

Wake on the Ferry. John Sloan. Etching. Gift of Mr. and Mrs. John Estabrooks. 1960.36. © 1989 The Art Institute of Chicago, All Rights Reserved.

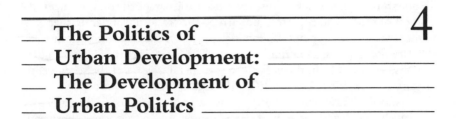

The Politics of Urban Development: The Development of Urban Politics

4

Nothing which has entered into our experience is ever lost.
  William Ellery Channing
  Notebook

Cities Moving West

In the popular imagination, abetted by novels and movies, the pioneers who settled the United States were a brave and heroic people who fought with Indians, moved westward in wagon trains, and built farmsteads in the wilderness. It is the story of men and women alone or in tiny bands living in remote isolation on the frontier.

The historian's truth is somewhat different. It is no less dramatic, no less heroic, but perhaps a touch less romantic. The historian's truth is this: America was settled as a long, thin line of urban places, scattering outward and westward from the Atlantic seaboard. The popular imagination has it that farmers came first and villages later. The historian's truth is that villages and towns came first, pulling farmers along to settle the land around and between urban settlements.

It is important to discard the image of expanding agricultural settlement bringing the towns along behind it.

In the first English settlement of the country, towns were the necessary bases from which farmers could move out and begin to subdue the new land to their purposes. . . . Indians and the problem of security alone would have dictated

43

some kind of concentrated settlement before agricultural settlement could safely begin. (Glaab and Brown 1976, 24)

To offer this amended view of history is not to disparage the bravery or stead-fastness of those who explored and farmed the western frontier. Rather, it is to make an important point: Urban life, and hence urban politics, came with the very first settlers, and present-day urban politics is part of a pattern that extends backward from the present to the opening years of the seventeenth century (Green 1957, Warner 1972, Bridges 1984).

Added to this is another important point, the point of paradox: How-ever much cities have been important to creating American society, the overall pattern of our politics has been mistrustful of our cities (White and White 1977). Thomas Jefferson gave voice to an early expression of this mistrust, saying that cities were a cancer on the body politic; and in our own times, especially after the urban riots of the 1960s, cities have been widely regarded as the seeds and seats of our disorder (Shefter 1984). As we look to the sources and consequences of this mistrust, we find in our past both a continuing con-cern for the impact on our society of those who live "huddled in cities" and a recurring concern on the part of states and the national government to impose varying forms of social and political controls over the cities.

But to make these ideas comprehensible, it will be useful to divide America's urban development into historic epochs. We can start with the period that runs from the first decades of the seventeenth century to the last of the nineteenth, for that was the great time of city-founding in the United States. Jamestown, Virginia was founded in 1609; the Massachusetts Bay Colony in 1620. And 1890 marks the decade that closes the epoch of city-founding:

> With the exception of an occasional city such as Miami, Florida which sprang up after a railroad was built along the east coast of Florida in 1896, or Tulsa, Oklahoma, located at the site of an oil discovery, most American cities destined to achieve even moderate size had been founded by 1890. (Glaab and Brown 1976, 100)

But to cut so wide a swath over three hundred years mows down too much. To better understand the politics of urban development, still finer cuts are needed. Thus, we look first at the Colonial period (1609-1776), then to the period of the early republic (1776 to the Civil War), and then to several suc-ceeding stages of city development. In each period, cities attempted to solve the problems of their day, and in each period—consonant with the theory of social learning advanced in the previous chapter—the problem solvers made use of the past to solve the problems of the present.

44

The Colonial Town

English colonists, in what was to become the United States, moved outward and westward from two regions, Virginia and Massachusetts. Towns came first, hiving off one from the others, farmsteads spreading between the towns. Thus the beginnings of our country are to be found in its urban experience.

Immigrants came to the new world for a wide variety of reasons: trade, adventure, opportunities to live a better life, the quest for personal wealth, the search for religious freedom. The early colonists came mostly from the English "middling class" (Tocqueville's term), neither the richest nor the poorest of English society, but even so, they brought with them a well differentiated social structure (Warner 1972). What began as a few hundred settlers in the years around 1600, by 1700 had become a New World of 250,000 Europeans. And by 1775, the Thirteen Colonies had grown a thousand percent—to an astonishing 2.25 million. (The population doubled again in the following twenty-five years, so that by 1800 the European-descended population of the new United States was estimated to be something on the order of 5.3 million; see Kelley 1982).[1]

The Colonial period was thus a period of prodigious town founding and an even more prodigious time of town growth. By 1770, the territory that was to become the United States had become a nation of towns that included:

- in the New England colonies—Falmouth, Portsmouth, Boston, Hartford, New Haven, and Newport;
- in the Middle Colonies—New York, Perth Amboy, Philadelphia, (and in the then far west) Pittsburgh;
- in the Southern Colonies—Baltimore, Alexandria, Stanton, Richmond, Williamsburg, Norfolk, Salem, Camden, Charleston, and Savanna.

As to population, Boston held 7,000 people in 1670 and 13,000 in 1730. New York had reached 7,000 by 1730 and Philadelphia's growth was startling: From 4,000 at the beginning of the century, it grew to 10,000 by 1720 and more than 30,000 by 1774. Next to London, it was the largest city in the English-speaking world (Kelley 1982,70).

The circumstances of the founding and growth of American towns varied widely. Boston, New York, Baltimore, and Charleston came into being as trading centers and ports. Williamsburg was both trading center and capital of colonial Virginia. Philadelphia sprang from the vision of its Quaker founder, William Penn, as the place where a religiously inspired social order might

---

1. Some sense of population scale can be gained by noting that in 1720 England had an estimated population of something over 5 million, increasing to about 6.5 million on the eve of the American Revolution.

flourish—and even more to that purpose were the Pilgrim towns of New England. This is not the place to recount these early town histories, but from them can be distilled a number of patterns all pertinent to the politics of present-day American cities.

Economic Patterns

Even at a glance, three economic patterns make themselves visible. First, and almost without exception, colonial towns were founded for purposes of economic profit. Even where the search for religious freedom was dominant, the economic motive was never far behind. Towns came into being as centers of trade and commerce, places where their inhabitants were to make money. They were thus linked to a set of social forces as old as recorded history— urban settlements as places of economic enterprise (Jacobs 1970).

As places of economic enterprise, public and private goals were mixed and mingled. Settlers, as individuals, would come to the town for private and personal reasons, but in coming they became part of the town's collective purpose, that of creating a prosperous economic enterprise. What is more, as public and private purposes mingled, it was the general pattern that political and social leadership fell to those who exercised economic leadership (Warner 1972, Thernstrom 1964, Bridges 1984). All leadership, political, social, economic, tended to collect in the same set of hands. Thus, the political role of "economic dominants" that so much characterizes present day cities traces very directly to the earliest history of American urban settlements. (Perhaps it is the case that patterns once set become exceedingly hard to change.)

Self-Rule

A second pattern that marks the colonial town has been noted in previous pages: self-rule. From their beginnings (and especially because of their isolation from each other and from England), colonial towns enjoyed a considerable measure of self-rule. By present standards, this self-rule was far from democratic. Participation in public decisions was usually limited to persons owning property, and town-government itself was subordinated to the rules of the commercial corporation that had founded the town. (In the later colonial period, town government became subordinated to the rule of royal governors and the British parliament.) But however limited the scope of self-rule, it was there. Where the rest of the world was governed by autocrats and aristocrats, inhabitants of American colonial towns commanded a considerable degree of freedom in their own local affairs (Tocqueville 1945).

46

Property Rights as Civil Rights

A third, and perhaps most important, pattern that marks the colonial town has to do with property and property rights. In the New World, land was available for the taking. (At least, provided that it could be bought, traded, or forcefully taken from the Indians.) Conceivably, the towns could have entered into a collective way of life. They could have held their land, and the buildings on them, as common property, belonging to the town, dedicated to common purposes and benefits. They did not. Real estate was personal, privately owned, to be kept, to be bought and sold for profit. And with this commodification of land and buildings, there was set into place the pattern of property rights and the role of the property entrepreneur that have dominated American city politics for nearly four hundred years. As Howard Chudacoff (1975, 102) notes: "Americans have always considered the management and disposal of land and buildings as a sacred civil right."

Corporate and Political Patterns

With very few exceptions colonial settlements first came into being by means of a corporation charter. In the seventeenth and eighteenth centuries European statecraft was committed to founding colonies all around the world. Colonies for the English, Dutch, and French were begun by private persons (merchant adventurers, they were usually called) whose private intent was to turn a profit for those running the corporation and subscribing its capital. The public purpose behind such undertakings was to enrich the mother country by providing it with raw materials (gold, timber, furs, sugar cane, and the like).[2] Thus, those who dominated the economic life of the colony (merchants, traders, shipowners) were much favored by the mother country and encouraged (if, indeed, such encouragement was ever needed) to dominate the political life of the colony. Even more important, government in colonial towns was commonly put into the service of the town's economic enterprises.

> When, in 1644, three New Haven entrepreneurs proposed to deepen the channel of a creek, the authorities gave them four days of work from each male resident between the ages of sixteen and sixty. On another occasion, Newark offered three days of work from every able-bodied resident to assist anyone who undertook to set up a corn mill. (Glaab and Brown 1976, 4)

---

2. *Mercantilism* is the term used to describe this statecraft, using the "strength of the economy to defend the power of the state" (Lee and Passell 1979, 28).

47

Patterns of Social Control

In colonial towns, social and political controls took many forms and had many faces. And they were tied, one to the other. Some towns, for example, attempted to keep paupers and beggars out. Other towns tried to recruit workers with needed skills (shipwrights and millers, for example). And everywhere, in the interest of public morals and safety, colonial towns tried to control the behavior of their inhabitants. Then as now, crime against persons and property and offenses against the prevailing moral code were the special concerns of urban legislation (Glaab and Brown 1976, 14).

- In New Amsterdam, New York, in the seventeenth century, laws were promulgated to assure that the town authorities knew the name and whereabouts of everyone who came into the city.
- In Newport, Rhode Island, bond had to be posted for all newcomers before they could be admitted to the city.
- Beginning in 1705, Philadelphia adopted regulations (similar to those of New Amsterdam) requiring registration by name and domicile of all those entering the city.

The most pervasive and stringent social controls were asserted by the Puritan towns of New England. As Michael Walzer (1965, 209) observes,

> with the intense moral discomfort of the righteous and high minded, Puritans sought desperately to separate themselves from the chaotic sinfulness that they imagined to surround them. . . . [They wished] to create a society in which godly order would be the rule and sin not a possible activity.

These Puritan towns regulated matters of worship, work, dress, speech, and every conceivable aspect of social intercourse. And while the Puritans and their towns were never numerous, they helped create at least one legacy that is still very much part of the urban scene: the city as guardian of morals and promoter of citizen virtue. Present-day cities derive their powers to monitor morality from the *police powers* of their state. This term is not be confused with administering a city police force (though the city's police force is legally based on the city's role as agent of the state). Judicially, police powers are the state's inheritance from English common law: the responsibility of the king as guardian of his subjects to regulate social life in the public interest, primarily in matters of health, welfare, morals, safety, and public convenience (Gunn 1969). Thus, cities attend to regulating manners and morals, and to "keeping the peace," and their vigor in doing so can be interpreted as a partial inheritance from Puritan towns.

Perhaps a second legacy of the Puritan town is our continued yearning for a sense of community. By present values, the Puritan town seems a costive and meddlesome place. But for all that, it was a town with a fierce sense of belonging, a sense of community. The essence of community is an urban place that is more than a place to live and work. It is a place of shared values that are to be nurtured and protected. It is a sense of "we fortunate few" against all outsiders (Stein 1960, Bellah, et al. 1985). Today, of course, it is the small town that most embodies the sense of community. But it is the longing for community that continues to animate much of urban politics—the small town that tries to limit growth and development, the metropolitan-area suburb that tries to fend off apartment-house builders and industrial-plant developers; and the central-city neighborhood that draws its residents into fierce resistance against the intrusion of would-be settlers from outside. This legacy of community thus appears in modern dress as the theory of lifestyle and territory.[3]

The Early Republic (1789 to the Civil War)

The early years of the republic were profoundly important to urban development. It was the period that saw the rise of cities as units of economic specialization. It was the period that ushered in the rise of the industrialized city—the place of tall smokestacks, soot and grime, and of "dark, satanic mills." It was a time that brought a politics of class conflict to the cities, and a time of spreading slums and urban congestion. It was also a period of growing resentment by white, native-born, "old Americans" against foreign immigrants, a resentment that brought the first waves of violence against the city's ethnic and religious minorities.

Urban Growth

At the center of these developments was the growth of older, established cities and the rapid founding of new towns. The older cities expanded their populations almost exponentially, so that by 1830 (to take an illustrative date) New York had grown to more than 202,000 and Philadelphia to more than 161,000. Equally important, this was the period in which the logic of a market economy moved cities toward economic specialization. The availability of nearby (and therefore cheap) water power created the thread-weaving, textile-spinning towns of New England. Boston, New York, and Philadelphia, as major seaports, drew into their maritime trade shippers, brokers, wholesalers, and those important suppliers of money and credit, bankers and banks. New

---

3. Two portraits of small towns desperately trying to fend off the incursions of the outside world are provided by Vidich and Bensman (1958) and Baskin (1976).

Orleans and Charleston prospered as trading centers that specialized in southern cotton. Thus the logic of the market (in its drive for efficiency that brings
related enterprises into close proximity) set the stage for what in the late nineteenth and early twentieth centuries were to be cities of manufacturing
specialization—Detroit as the center of automobile-making, Pittsburgh as the
center of iron and steel, and the stockyards of Chicago and Kansas City as
"butchers to the nation" (Green 1957, Chudacoff 1975, Warner 1972).

The City as a Symbol of Progress; The City and Land-Use Economics

Following the War for Independence (and later, with the Louisiana Purchase),
the entire continent beckoned those who aspired to establish new towns and
cities. New settlements sprang into being all across the receding frontier, and
Americans took considerable pride in the rapidity with which new towns were
established and even greater pride in the capacity of their new towns to bring
civilization to the wilderness.

Here, for example, is what an early president of Yale had to say
concerning his travels (in the early 1800s) through New England and upstate
New York.

> The colonization of a wilderness by civilized man, where a regular government,
> mild manners, arts, learning, science, and Christianity have been intertwined
> in its progress. . .is a state of things of which the record of past ages has fur-
> nished neither an example nor a resemblance." (Quoted in Rifkind 1977, 3)

Thus, early on, Americans came to regard city building and urban development as the very essence of the American gift for progress and to see nothing
but good in the city's intrusion on the countryside.

The new towns that sprang up on the frontier followed precedents laid
down in Colonial times. They came into existence as an enterprise in the private
ownership of property, but with this difference: Most new towns were not
developed by settlers coming to untitled and previously unowned land
(unowned, that is, by Europeans). They came, instead, to land that was owned
by land-development companies. These land-development companies were,
in effect, wholesalers of land. That the western lands should be settled was
national policy, and Congress sold these lands in great blocks to privately
owned land companies with an understanding that the companies, in turn,
would re-sell to small buyers.

In principle, Congress could have given the land free to settlers (as was
done under the Homestead acts that followed the Civil War), or, alternatively,
Congress could have sold unsettled land plot-by-plot to individual settlers.
With few exceptions, neither course was followed. Instead, the land was sold
in huge tracts to land wholesalers (land companies) that, in turn, resold it (at

considerable profit) to individual buyers. Thus, land company employees surveyed the territory, laid out sites for new towns, and established land offices on the new sites (or in cities back East) from which lots and plots and blocks of land could be sold.

Settling new towns was big business and great fortunes were made in that business all through the nineteenth and early twentieth centuries. After the Civil War, companies dealing solely in land were superceded by railroad companies that repeated the wholesaling process: platting streets and selling lots in towns that would be built along the railroad's right of way (Swisher 1954). But whether new towns were organized by land companies or railroad companies, the economics of settlement was much the same: Land was a commodity to be sold at a profit. More important, the future value of any particular piece of urban land was contingent upon market externalities—upon future population density. Consequently, urban development, then as now, was tied to civic boosterism and the psychology of land speculation. Then, as now, the slogan, "Come grow with us" was the key to the economics of urban development.

> Would you make money? [asked an advertisement luring settlers to Columbus, Nebraska] . . . . Find then the site of a city and buy the farm that it is to be built on. How many regret the non-purchase of that lot in New York, that block in Buffalo, that quarter section in Omaha? Once these properties could be bought for a song . . . . fortunes [are to be made] that way. (Quoted in Glaab and Brown 1976, 108).

Social and Political Consequences of Industrialization

While new towns sprang to life, older cities expanded their commercial and industrial development. And profound political consequences followed. Cities grew in population and physical size, and they accelerated what had been the steady drift toward separation of places of work from places of residence. In colonial and post-colonial times, those who owned workshops and warehouses usually lived in or above their places of work. Businesses were small, and employees often lived with their employers or in lofts and odd rooms nearby. The sense of community was strong, and the interests of business owners were more often than not shared by their workers (Handlin and Handlin 1975). But with industrialization, the interests of owners and workers drifted far apart and a politics of social and economic class grew stronger. What is more, persons of wealth began shifting their places of residence outward and away from the commercial districts, and the first tracings were to be seen of what was to become in the twentieth century the city of concentric rings: a commercial and factory district in the oldest part of town, workers' housing in a ring around the old town, and homes for the middle class set in wide circle outward and apart from the ring of working–class houses.[4]

As industry grew, the gap between rich and poor became wider and deeper. And housing for the poor became oppressive and unsanitary. The age of the slum had arrived. In 1843, a survey found 7,196 people living underground in New York.

> Within seven years as immigration expanded during the decade, the cellar-dwelling population had increased to 29,000. . . . A Cincinnati board of health report of 1865 told of a two-story tenement which housed 102 people for whom only one privy had been provided. (Glaab and Brown 1976, 69, 76).

Dust and mud and garbage in the streets marked the cities of the nineteenth century. Sanitary facilities and water supplies were provided mostly by backyard wells and earth-toilets, supplemented by privately owned water carriers and waste removers (often with the same contractor doing both jobs). Small wonder, then, that periodic epidemics swept the cities. Yellow fever, typhoid, and cholera were recurring urban diseases. Crime, too, was rampant, and as historians of urban violence frequently note, organized street gangs operated openly and with impunity, making life difficult and dangerous for rich and poor alike (Silberman 1978).

Housing laws and city-supervised housing standards were almost nonexistent. In 1867, New York pioneered the setting of standards for tenement construction. But municipal water works and city police came earlier. Philadelphia was the pioneer of the city-owned water supply. (It completed the Fairmont Water Works in 1822; New York began building its aqueduct water system in 1835.) Nine years later (in 1844), New York replaced the then-prevalent system of private watchmen with the nation's first city police force—eight hundred strong (Glaab and Brown 1976).

But even as the populous cities of the east were taking their first hesitant steps toward coping with problems of crime, public health, and sanitary housing, they were further beset with the problem of recurring crowd violence: All through the nineteenth and early twentieth centuries, the growth in urban populations came primarily from foreign immigrants, newly arrived to seek the promise of American life.[5] But as immigrant ranks swelled, white, native-born Americans grew increasingly resentful of those with different cultures, customs, and languages. Resentment turned violent, and the 1830s were marked by what would become a recurring pattern of violence against racial, ethnic, and religious minorities.

---

4. This demographic pattern was given its classic formulation in 1925 by University of Chicago sociologists Robert E. Park and Ernest Burgess (reprinted in 1967). For a study of population mobility in a single city, Boston, between 1830 and 1860, see Knights (1971).

5. Immigrants and their importance to urban politics will be discussed in chapter 5.

> Anti-Catholicism first became a disturbing factor in American life in the 1830s when Protestant leaders began to declare that the Roman Catholic hierarchy was conspiring to win complete control of the United States. . . . The crusade resulted in several outbreaks of rioting; an Ursuline convent was burned by a mob in 1834, ten years later several Catholic churches were destroyed by a three-day riot in Philadelphia. (Parkes 1959, 263-64)

Thus, cities had become at one and the same time the focus of an anti-immigrant agitation and the places in which mob violence might be expected to flare forth. Those who lived in rural areas had their dislike of cities, with their foreign ways and foreign people, intensified; and those who lived in cities became part of a rapidly expanding population of foreign-born and newly arrived immigrants.

The Age of the Common Man

In the 1830s, a new spirit and style entered American political life—signalled by the election of Andrew Jackson (1832). The slogan of Jacksonian politics, "To the victor belongs the spoils," announced that henceforth the jobs and rewards of government would be handed to friends and supporters of those who won elections. In unmistakable terms it also announced that politics itself would belong to those who could organize with sufficient numbers and discipline to capture public office. Political participation would no longer be the restricted preserve of the literate and the wealthy; suffrage would continue to expand to include (in growing numbers) "the common man" (Schlesinger 1945).

Consonant with this style and spirit, a new form of political organiza-tion came to the cities. This new form frequently centered around volunteer fire departments. As organizations, they offered fellowship and social recogni-tion to their members. Owing to the rapid growth of cities and the crowding of wooden buildings on narrow lots, the volunteer fire departments performed an increasingly important public service. Equally important (for political pur-poses) they were built around the efforts of the working classes. They thus provided the framework for a new type of political organization that would soon dominate big city politics. Mass-based and egalitarian in outlook—operating in hierarchical fashion, with leaders at the top and followers ready to take orders—this new type of political organization was called the *machine*,[6] and it carried into cities a politics of numbers, organizational discipline, egalitarianism—and corruption (Frug 1984; Bridges 1984; Bryce 1889). In the decades ahead (especially after the Civil War) it would come to dominate totally the politics of most big cities.

___

6. The origin of the term is obscure. That great student of American slang and usage, H.L. Mencken (1963), thought that the term was first coined by Aaron Burr to describe Burr's own political organization in eighteenth-century New York. Whatever its origins, it nicely fits the American fascina-tion with mechanical contrivances.

Subway Excavation. Philip Cheney. Lithograph. Lent by the WPA. 667.1943.
© 1989 The Art Institute of Chicago, All Rights Reserved.

A Backward Glance Continued: From the Civil War to the New Federalism _____ 5

I want to say that I don't own a dishonest dollar. If my worst enemy was given the job of writin' my epitaph when I'm gone, he couldn't do no more than write, "George W. Plunkitt. He seen his opportunities, and he took 'em."

George Washington Plunkitt
quoted in William Riordan,
Plunkitt of Tammany Hall

The Industrial Age

The decades after the Civil War were a period of unprecedented industrial, and therefore, urban expansion. Railroad building proceeded with astonishing speed. Before the war (in 1850) the United States had fewer than 9,000 miles of railroad, mostly in New England. Between 1860 and 1900, 163,000 miles of track were laid down. Big cities now had the ability to enter and then dominate the markets and economics of an entire region, and even smaller cities and towns were linked to regional, national, and even international markets. Capital invested in manufacturing rose from $1 billion in 1860 to $10 billion in 1890. During this same period, the number of industrial workers rose from something over 1 million to more than 5 million, and the "value of [their] annual product from less than $2 billion to more than $13 billion" (Parkes 1959, 395).

Immigration into the United States also shot skyward and cityward. From 1870 to 1900, it is estimated that nearly 12 million immigrants entered the country, some to take up rural life, but by far the greatest number to settle in the cities. There, those who arrived with limited work skills, little money, and scant command of the English language could hope to find jobs, housing, and the comfort and guidance of fellow countrymen who had arrived earlier.[1]

But none of this change and expansion was without social cost. The industrial city made it possible for an entrepreneurial few to make great fortunes and to display those fortunes in the imposing townhouses and mansions that stood in private parks and along avenues of urban opulence.[2] For the less fortunate many, life in the industrial city was considerably harder. Factory labor was monotonous. The workday was long, often ten, twelve, even fourteen hours. Wages were low, and loss of one's job because of an economic downturn was frequent. Industrial accidents were commonplace. (In 1900, for example, it is estimated that they caused twenty thousand deaths and 1 million injuries.) Under the legal doctrine of the time, neither victims nor their families were entitled to compensation. Little by way of public welfare existed, and aid to the poor, to orphans, and to the injured and the sick was almost completely a matter for private charity.

Some sense of life among the city poor can be gotten from Jacob Riis (1957, 36, 47, 124, *passim*), a pioneer photojournalist who took his camera to record lives of poverty in New York in the early 1900s.

> A Seventh Ward tenement was typical. . . . There were nine in the family; husband, wife, six children, and an aged grandmother. . . . All nine lived in two rooms, one about ten feet square that served as parlor, bedroom, and eating room, the other a small hall-room made into a kitchen. . . . Here, in this tenement, . . . fourteen persons died last year, and eleven of them were children . . . With the first hot nights in June, police dispatches . . . record the killings of men and women rolling off roofs and window-sills while asleep. . . in hot weather, when life indoors is . . . unbearable.

This, then, is the social context of the industrial city. It is also the context for the politics of the machine.

The Industrial Age and the Machine

In 1889, when James, Viscount Bryce, sometime British ambassador to the United States, published his monumental study of American government (Bryce 1889), nothing dismayed or saddened him more than the governance of American cities.[3] His research and observations were extensive. He had traveled to cities all across the country, read their newspapers, corresponded

---

1. The classic study on the immigrant experience is Handlin (1951, revised 1973); for its significance for urban politics, see Harrigan (1985).
2. Some sense of the lives of the urban rich in the Industrial Age can be gotten from Thomas Beer (1961) and Edward Lucie-Smith and C. Dars (1976).

with their leading citizens. Chicago, New York, Baltimore, New Orleans, San Francisco, Philadelphia, Cincinnati, Louisville, Minneapolis, Albany, Cleveland, and St. Louis were all part of his study. And everywhere, the story was the same: corruption, graft, dominance by a political boss or a small group of bosses ("the ring ") who manipulated elections, sold city services, accepted bribes, stole public money, and controlled a cadre of appointed city workers and elected public officials. What Bryce saw was a style of political organization everywhere called the machine, and whatever else might be said of American political life, Bryce concluded, "there is no denying that the government of cities is the one conspicuous failure of the United States" (Bryce 1889, vol. 1, 608).

In attempting to explain this failure, Bryce searched for its causes. He found no fewer than seven. Three of the causes were legacies of Jacksonian politics and an outlook that (since the 1830s) had equated successful democracy with the greatest possible participation in political life: frequent elections, universal suffrage, and numerous elective offices. A fourth cause was an absence of stimulating issues, a consequence, said Bryce, of the fact that while national politics involves matters of war, peace, and prosperity, local issues are of the humdrum sort—street paving, housing inspection, and water-line locations. As a fifth cause, Bryce concluded, "the leading men are all intensely occupied with business," by which he meant that business leaders had little time for politics. They were too busy making money. Sixth, Bryce found "communities are so large that people know little of one another, and . . . the interests of each individual in good government is relatively small." Finally, he noted that the United States has

> a vast population of ignorant immigrants. . . . They know nothing of the institutions of the country, of its statesmen, of its political issues. . . . Incompetent to give an intelligent vote, but soon finding that their vote has a value, they fall into the hands of the party organizations, whose officers enroll them in their lists and undertake to fetch them to the polls.[5]

Even after a hundred years we can sense the moral indignation that Bryce poured into his assessment of cities. But how correct was that assessment? How close to the mark had he come? By every test, his reporting was accurate. The machine existed to enrich its members, and their concern for the public interest always ran a poor second to opportunities for members' personal

---

3. This two-volume work went through several editions, and for several generations was the standard "textbook" on American government and political life.

4. The Jacksonian ideal that politics was to be open to all meant, in effect, that popular control over government would be achieved by letting the people vote and vote often. It also meant that the more offices that were to be filled, the greater the opportunities for the ordinary citizen to fill them.

5. All quotations are from Bryce (1889, vol. 2, 95).

enrichment. Legislation was exchanged for bribes, and contracts and city services were sold openly. City jobs went to those loyal to the machine, and those on the city's payroll used their jobs—and the promise of still more jobs—to turn out loyal voters at election time. Those who stood near the apex of the hierarchy often became exceedingly rich.

But what about Bryce's explanation (his theories) of the causes that lay behind the machine's power? With a century's hindsight, we can now see that many of Bryce's explanations were clouded by the bias of his own social class. (Like most others, he worked within the confines of an ideology and what we have previously discussed as a theory of ideological interpretation.) He felt strongly that persons of intellect and wealth were best suited to manage public affairs. He never quite saw that business leaders—the "better men" as he called them—were often the strongest supporters of the machine and the largest givers of the bribes that kept the machine rich. And he failed completely to understand that the loyalty of the immigrants to the machine was not a loyalty born of ignorance, but an act of considerable rationality and well-understood calculation.

Businessmen and the Machine

James Bryce's world is considerably removed from our own. His was a time in which the hard-fisted, scheming businessman was far closer to folk hero than villain. In Bryce's world the ultimate success story was the poor child who climbs from rags to riches up the rungs of the business ladder. Bryce's time was one of a pervasive public philosophy—loosely adapted from Darwin's theory of evolution—that saw success in business as tantamount to the survival of the fittest, and equally, saw poverty as the mark of personal defect and moral failings.[6]

Given the spirit of those times, and given the idea (as was often said) "that profits need no justification," it perhaps becomes understandable that bribery of public officials by business firms was an accepted and common activity. In fact, those who bribed city officials could and did take instruction from what went on in Congress and the state legislatures. The Industrial Age was the great age of railroad building; and railroad lobbyists were often the most influential nonelected actors in state politics and the national legislature. Scandals were frequent as railroad lobbyists exchanged money (and sometimes shares of stock) for free grants of land and for favorable rights-of-way.

The pattern in cities was similar. There it involved monopolies (fran-

---

6. Among the best accounts of the influence of social Darwinism on American politics and social life is Richard Hofstadter (1955b).

chises, they were usually called) for street railway lines. Again, the potential for profits was enormous. As cities grew in physical size, as their populations increased, and as workplace and residence grew farther apart, the commuting age arrived. Even before the electric streetcar, in the 1880s, steam trains were pulling passenger cars across the city; and before them, the horse trolley was commonplace. "In New York alone (the year was 1858) five principal [horse-drawn] street railways...were carrying 35 million passengers a year" (Glaab and Brown 1976, 141).

In addition to granting streetcar franchise, cities had other prizes that could tempt the business community into corrupt alliance with the machine: Franchises to build and operate gasworks, and gas-lines (for heating and lighting) were every bit as profitable as owning a streetcar company. The same held true for privately owned water and sewage systems. And it was no less true for contracts to pave streets, build city buildings, furnish coal, make policemen's and firemen's uniforms, and even haul bodies to a pauper's grave.

But to see the alliance of bosses and business as cemented only by the profits derived from franchises and city purchases is to see too little. To see still more, an important idea will need to be elaborated. One of the legacies of Jacksonianism was to overload the city with elected officials: a large city council, a mayor, perhaps an elected chief of police, and such other elected officials as a commissioner for streetcars, a commissioner for taxicabs, a commissioner (or board of commissioners) for water, gas, sewers, and so on.

Consider the ambitious business person who, for example, wishes to build a factory. Quite possibly, that factory will require a railway spur to ship its goods, a water line to run its steam boilers, an extension of the streetcar line to bring its workers, and dozens of building permits even before the first shovel of earth is turned.

Consider again, that in a government with a multitude of elected officials, each of whom might have to be persuaded—or even bribed—in order for construction to proceed on schedule, or even proceed at all, it may well be that our contemplated factory would never be built. But now, suppose that all these independently elected officials were not truly independent (each with an independent mind, purpose, and electoral mandate), but instead were all part of a common organization, taking instruction from one political leader (the boss) or a small group of political leaders (the ring). And suppose that the business person had only to persuade—or bribe—that one leader or that small group of leaders. The costs of bribery would be known in advance and could be figured into the overall construction costs. The boss or ring could be counted on to keep its word. There would be little or no construction delay. And the factory would be built. Small wonder, then, that in many cities the business community was an enthusiastic, self-interested, and rational supporter of the machine.[7]

The Business of Politics

But getting on with the business of business was not confined to the business community alone. The business person and the politician shared a common outlook that, since the age of Jackson, has been a cornerstone of all American politics at every level of government: Politics is a vocation, an income-producing job, and not a part-time activity to be indulged in by an affluent class moved by a sense of public service and civic obligation.[8]

Thus, the machine was run by "vocationalists," professionals for whom politics was a job and a business. And those who were in it had no reason to set their ethical standards on a higher or more moral plane than that which was everywhere common to business. If the business community could use money to buy what it wanted from government, then the machine's "business men" who were the government could surely take that money.

Listen, for example, to George Washington Plunkitt, boss of Tammany Hall (the machine that ran New York at the turn of the century):

> There's honest graft, and I'm an example of how it works. I might sum up the whole thing by sayin': I seen my opportunities and I took 'em. Just let me explain by examples. My party's in power in the city and it's goin' to undertake a lot of public improvements. Well, I'm tipped off, say, that they're goin' to lay out a new park at a certain place. I see my opportunity and I take it. I go to that place and buy up all the land I can in the neighborhood. Then the board of this or that makes the plan public, and there is a rush to get my land which nobody cared particular for before. Ain't it perfectly honest to charge a good price and make a profit on my investment and foresight? Of course it is. Well, that's honest graft. (Quoted in Conlin 1984, 234)

Immigrants and the Machine

What, then, of Bryce's views of the immigrants? In the main, he was correct in asserting that immigrant families provided the machine's voting strength. But every generalization has its exceptions. Milwaukee, for example, had a considerable concentration of German immigrants (it was often called Rhineland on Lake Michigan), and it was a model of good, clean innovative government (Buenker 1973). Kansas City, in contrast, had a mostly second and third generation, native-born population, but it was notorious as a stronghold of machine corruption (Zink 1930).

---

7. Those who study politics in third-world countries suggest strong parallels between the nineteenth century American political machine and economic and political development in developing countries. There one-party, strong-man government is often the primary instrument for suppressing ethnic and tribal loyalties, for bringing a degree of discipline to a dispirited and incompetent bureaucracy, for assuring the political stability necessary for capital investment. See, for example, Naipaul (1979).

8. See the comments by the early twentieth-century German sociologist Max Weber (1946).

But was Bryce misinformed when he described the alliance between immigrants and the machine as an alliance of the corrupt leading the ignorant? In fact, he was misinformed, for the immigrants were trading votes for social and economic assistance. Workers for the machine assisted the newcomers to America in countless ways. They often posted bond and provided medical assistance for those who needed help in meeting immigration rules. They assisted the newly arrived in finding housing and jobs. They served as interpreters for those who had yet to learn the English language. In an age when welfare was private charity, it was often the machine that ran the best-organized and most generous charity in the city (Merton 1957). It gave food and money to the poor, and coal to heat their stoves. It provided legal assistance to those would could not afford lawyers, and it softened the harshness of the law for those who broke it. In short, the machine was an enterprise in social service, an activity best expressed by Martin Lomassy, the once political boss of Boston: "I think there's got to be in every ward somebody that any bloke can come up to—no matter what he's done—and get help. Help, you understand; none of your law and justice, but help."[9]

Beyond social service, perhaps the greatest contribution of the machine to the immigrants was to set them on the ladder of social and economic success and upward social mobility. The machine served as a kind of employment agency, letting the business community partially "pay" the machine by way of jobs in stores and factories. The machine also recruited into its own ranks ambitious young persons from immigrant families. And once on the ladder of politics, those with ambition moved up. Many (with help from political friends) started small businesses. For example, some whose jobs had begun as manual labor on construction sites (jobs originally found through the machine) ventured to begin their own construction companies. Their children went to school, and within a generation these children began to enter the professions. The details varied, but overall the pattern was the same: The machine offered opportunities and assistance in moving great numbers of immigrant families along "the tenement trail"—upward and outward to middle class status and success.[10]

9. Quoted by Lincoln Steffens (1931, 618). Steffens was a tireless crusader against the machine.
10. The "details" would also stress the fact that all through the nineteenth century and well into the twentieth, immigrants and their descendants lived in compacted urban areas. Every city had its "Warsaw," its "Little Serbia," its "Bohemia," its "Little Italy," and so on; each served by its own foreign language newspaper, often its own foreign-language theater (and later, cinema), its ethnic restaurants. Churches and synagogues offered services in the language of the neighborhood, and in these and comparable ways, ethnic identities were reinforced. The term "tenement trail" is Lubell's (1956). For a recent assessment of the relationship between machine and immigrant and the role of the machine in bettering the immigrants' lives, see Harrigan (1985); and for an early assessment, see Riordan (1963). A splendid account is provided by Handlin (1973, especially chapter 8).

Urban Reform

Political reform is a periodic feature of American politics, like waves that come crashing across a swelling sea. One theory to account for waves of reform asserts that they arise from the clash of the "is and the ought"—the tension between our professed ideals and our everyday political practices—as, for example, in the civil rights revolution of the 1960s, between the lip service paid to "liberty and justice for all" and the treatment of blacks in our society (e.g., Herson 1984, chs. 1, 15). Another theory explains periodic reform as part of a recurring clash between the professional politicians (the vocationalists) who run our government and the amateurs of politics: those who are moved by a sense of public duty, a call to ideology, and a moral desire to set wrongs to right (Wilson 1962). The amateurs of politics are often moved to action during times of crisis, when unsolved problems seem beyond the control of ordinary, everyday politicians. But for the amateurs, politics is an avocation, not a vocation. Their perseverance and persistence is usually limited. The professional politicians (the "pros") sometimes call the amateurs the "goo-goo's" (short for good government) and the pros have long known that the energy and attention span of the goo-goo's is usually short—resulting in quick bursts of reform followed by long periods of inattention.

Both theories of reform find easy harbor (and dozens of examples) in the period roughly from 1900 to 1920. During that time, urban reform was part of a larger, more widespread drive for changes on all levels of government (Hofstadter 1955a). Leadership of the reform movement was primarily middle and upper class, a loosely connected coalition of mostly amateur politicians who called themselves Progressives and marched under the banners of Progressivism.[11]

The agenda of the Progressives was piled high with proposals for reform. On the national level, they pushed for an income tax, for legislation to curb business monopolies, to outlaw child labor, and to improve conditions in shops and factories. On the state level, they proposed to give the electorate a more direct voice in government, using the initiative, referendum, recall, and direct primary.[12] And to give the electorate greater opportunity to hold their elected

---

11. Among the best studies of Progressivism are those conducted by Schlesinger (1957), Hofstadter (1955a, 1968), and Hays (1964). For the flavor of a Progressive writing in his own time, see Croly (1909).

12. Jay Shafritz (1988) provides definitions of these key terms:

Initiative: a procedure that allows citizens, as opposed to legislators, to propose the enactment of state and local laws.

Referendum: A procedure for submitting proposed laws or state constitutional amendments to the voters for ratification.

Recall: A procedure that allows citizens to vote officeholders out of office between regularly scheduled elections.

Direct primary: [An election] in which political party nominees are selected directly by the voters.

officials accountable, Progressives also tried to concentrate governmental authority by decreasing the number of elected officials.

Progressives and the City

Political reform is rarely, if ever, easy. Reform, after all, is an assault on power and privilege. The urban reformers could argue that they were seeking to act in the name of democracy to clean up government, to make it better, to give power back to the people. But in machine cities, the people already had significant power: With the help of the machine, they could get favors and services from their government. Thus, great numbers of those in the city did not want any change in the status quo.

As Hofstadter (1955a) and others persuasively argue, proposals for city reform often came down to nothing less than a clash of lifestyles, cultures, and ways of looking at the world (ideologies). On the one side were the reformers, mostly old-stock Americans who were animated on an ethical plane by democracy's abstract values, but were often moved (if the truth be known) by resentment and downright dislike of foreign-born Americans. Many of the reformers were fearful of what was much talked of in academic and intellectual circles: the oncoming demise of traditional, "Anglo-Saxon," Protestant, and west-European culture, soon to be swamped by tides of immigration from eastern and southern, Catholic and Jewish Europe (e.g., Grant 1916).

On the other side were the immigrants. Many had come from societies built around kinship systems and personal loyalties, societies in which personal dealings and personal favors were the norms. Coming from places in which feudalism was a living memory, immigrants from southern and eastern Europe had no difficulty in understanding the machine to be an American version of a society built around the patron and the personal protector. Most were untroubled by the idea of giving loyalty to their protectors. And most were equally untroubled that they preferred a machine system that delivered immediate and personal benefits instead of something as abstract and intangible as good government and the public interest.[13]

The Reform Package

At heart, the Progressive reformers were prescriptive theorists, striving to bring better government to the cities. But as is often the case with prescriptive

---

13. James Q. Wilson and Edward Banfield (1964) attempt to validate the Hofstadter thesis for contemporary politics by examining issue voting in urban ethnic wards, using the concepts of "private regarding" (i.e., personal benefits) versus "public regarding" (i.e., the public interest). But a number of critics (e.g., Hennessey 1970) have challenged their findings.

theorists, they were confronted by the dilemma of practicality, in this case, how to make the cities more democratic—which is to say, give power to the people—and, at the same time, keep the people from continuing to hand over that power to the machine.

Since "the people" were strong supporters of the machine, the reformers set their sights on changes designed to undercut the institutional foundations of the machine. The machine was to be brought down by means of no fewer than five reform measures that constituted the urban reform package.[14]

First, the reformers attempted to introduce the merit system and civil service appointments in city government. Under a merit system, appointment to city jobs would be based on written examinations and thus (it was reasoned) the city would be served by better-educated employees, better able to resist the temptation of bribery, and more determined to resist being manipulated by political bosses. Under civil service, jobs once gained would be permanent, not subject to dismissal (except for incompetence), and thus removed from control by politicians.

Second, detailed accounting procedures were to be instituted so as to thwart theft of public funds. In a related move, legislation was to require that cities use competitive bidding in awarding contracts to buy and build.

Third, where it was decided that dispersed authority might better insulate an area or activity of government from boss control, provision was made for an independently elected board or commission. The independently elected school board continues as the most frequently used example of this third reform. Then, as now, its justification is that an independently elected school board "keeps the schools out of politics and politics out of the schools."

Fourth, and most significant, attempts were made to scale down the size of city councils and, even more to the point of reform, to do away with election by districts (usually called wards) and to substitute a city council elected at large—each council person chosen by all the city's voters. Much thought and planning went into this fourth reform. Its logic was as follows: for each district to have its own elected representative is to encourage a system of direct, visible personal leadership and followship. District-elected council persons know their constituents personally. To those they thus know and trust, they can offer favors, patronage, and a variety of social services. They can know who turns out to vote; and they can more or less know if that turned-out vote is a return for past favors.

What is more (the reformers reasoned) representation by districts favors ethnic representation. Everywhere (or so it was not so many years ago) immigrants lived in their own tight communities. Ethnic representation (the

14. To grasp the magnitude of their task, as well as their successive disappointments, see the autobiographies of urban reformers (e.g., Whitlock 1914; Childs 1952; Steffens 1931). On the program of the reformers, see Stewart (1950). The term "reform package" is used by Davis and Weinbaum (1969).

reasoning continued) feeds machine politics not only because the machine organizes the voters block by block and house by house, but also because the machine uses ethnic leaders as ward and community workers. Thus, to take machine politics out of the city council, take city council members out of districts.

Perhaps even more important for the better government envisioned by the reformers, an at-large council would be less involved in the affairs of immigrant ethnic groups. The ethnic immigrants might then lose interest in city affairs and perhaps stop voting. But not so the upper and middle class. Control over cities' affairs would then pass to them, for they could be counted on to vote and, by their votes, to demand that the public good be more important than favors for friends or supporters.

Fifth, and perhaps most radical in its departure from the traditions of American government, the reformers proposed to do away with an elected chief executive, the mayor, and to substitute an appointed executive, the city manager, who, as a professional administrator, could be counted on to resist the tugs and pulls of politics.

In this fifth reform, the proponents of change had an important ally in many from the business community. For them, the city-manager plan had a real-world appeal. It reflected their own experiences and appealed to their deep-seated belief that if government was to be made better, it would need to be more like business—removed from popular whim and from the popularity contests of elections. In short, cities would do better by having a competent manager in command.[15]

The Demise of the Machine

Whether the urban reform package accomplished its purposes is difficult to say. What we know now, with more than sixty years' distance from the days of the Progressives, is that what we have previously called a theory of urban reform has taken hold in cities. First, the idea that cities are to be run with regard for efficient and honest use of their resources is now the norm for city government. Second, several parts of the reform package are everywhere in place today—civil service appointments, competitive bidding on city contracts, and careful keeping of public records, all open to public scrutiny. Third, a considerable number of cities make use of small city councils, elected at large. And fourth, well over two thousand cities have adopted the manager plan.

But whether any parts of the reform package or any of the reformers' agitation was directly responsible for driving out the machine is difficult to say. Machine politics continued to dominate large eastern and southern cities

15. For critiques of this reasoning, see Waldo (1948) and Herson (1957, 1973).

until well after the Second World War. The last of the great machines, no doubt, was in Chicago. Its machine did not go down until the death of its last boss, Mayor Richard J. Daley, who died in 1976.[16] And with the election of his son, Richard M. Daley, to the office of mayor in 1989, the machine threatens to reassert itself in Chicago politics.[17] Why and how the machines disappeared is not so much a mystery as a consequence of social forces that may have had nothing to do with the work of the urban reformers. Among these forces were:

- A rising tide of anti-immigrant sentiment that sharply reduced the flow of European immigration in the years that followed 1920;
- The Great Depression of the 1930s and the subsequent rise of the welfare state, which freed the urban poor from dependence on machine-sponsored charities;
- A general economic prosperity in the years following World War II and the rising affluence of once-immigrant families (combined with their geographic dispersal into the suburbs) deprived the machines of their former ethnic loyalists;
- The postwar, general economic prosperity may have brought a rising standard of living to the urban blue-collar class sufficient to make jobs on the city payroll less and less attractive.

But even if the old machines are gone as tightly disciplined organizations of bosses and followers, the style of machine politics continues to haunt many cities. To a considerable degree, the fact that in many places city employees are still open to being bribed (and city services bought and paid for) is a consequence of the on-the-site nature of city service delivery. *[Recall: the theory of urban administration.]*[18] But in addition, machine-style politics in some cities may also be a cultural norm, a style of politics traditionally practiced in the Northeast, in the South, and in a scattering of cities along the Mississippi and Ohio rivers (Wolfinger 1972, Riedel 1964). In all these places, judges are commonly open to being bribed, probate courts award lucrative cases to lawyers who are part of a select ring of political "cronies," housing and health inspectors still accept "under the table" money, and city workers are still required to contribute a portion of their salaries to the election campaigns of party leaders. The machine as organization may be gone, but many of its practices remain. Though Viscount Bryce would no doubt be pleased

16. On Boss Daley and his machine, see Rakove (1975) for a sympathetic account, and Royko (1971) for a scathing indictment.

17. On Chicago politics between the Daleys, see Gove and Masotti (1987).

18. Here, and elsewhere, discussion is tied to the theories of urban politics outlined in chapter 3 by bracketed, italic references.

by the enormous overall improvement in the honesty of city government, he would probably insist that many cities still have a long way to go.[19]

The Great Depression and Beyond

The economic hard times that began with the stock market crash of 1929 were of a scale never before experienced in the United States. Millions were out of work, and for those lucky enough to have jobs, wages tumbled below living costs. By 1932, the Pennsylvania Department of Labor reported

> Wages had fallen to five cents an hour in saw-mills, 6 cents in brick and tile manufacturing. . . . In Malvern, Arkansas, lumber workers received 10 cents an hour; women in Tennessee mills were paid as little as $2.39 for a 50 hour week. (Schlesinger 1957, 249)

Hunger was widespread, and yet farmers found no markets for their crops. "Some found it cheaper to burn their corn than sell it and buy coal. On every side, notices of mortgage and tax sales were going up" (Schlesinger 1957, 175). The urban poor suffered no less severely. "There is not a garbage dump in Chicago which is not diligently haunted by the hungry," wrote one reporter.

> Last summer, in the hot weather, when the smell was sickening and the flies were thick, there were a hundred people a day coming to one of the dumps, falling on the heap of refuse as soon as the truck pulled out and digging in it with sticks and hands. (Wilson 1958, 462)

The Great Depression, said that reporter, was an American earthquake. It knocked over the political party alignments that had governed the country since the Civil War and it leveled the American reluctance to create national welfare programs. It broke open the American style of federalism that had previously separated spheres of government responsibility—the national government attending almost exclusively to foreign trade, diplomacy, and national security; the states having charge of health, welfare, education, morals, and public safety (Herson 1984).

19. Two large cities, New York and Chicago, continue to provide ample instruction in machine-style corruption. Not long ago, one of Chicago's newspapers secretly established a retail business and kept records of the bribes and shakedowns demanded by city officials if the business was to escape being closed down. Fire inspectors, building inspectors, health inspectors, and police on the beat all came regularly to partake of the business' profits. And in New York, for several years the administration of Mayor Edward Koch was buffeted by recurring scandals. For example, in November, 1985, four city officials (including the heads of the Democratic party in Queens and the Bronx) were found guilty of "having turned a city agency into a racketeering enterprise for their own enrichment." The racketeering centered on a contract with the city, for $22.7 million, for "equipping the city's Parking Violations Bureau with hand-held computers for traffic agents to use in writing parking tickets" (Andy Logan, *New Yorker,* Jan. 5, 1987).

A new style of federalism emerged, one in which the national government dominates. Under this new federalism, the national government has come to assume responsibility for managing the nation's economy, supervising civil rights, regulating conditions of employment, protecting the environment, establishing safe standards for consumer products, and building a welfare society (Herson 1984; Miles 1976).

Under this new federalism, the national government has become increasingly involved with cities and with the people who live in them. Under the old federalism, cities were viewed by Congress and the courts as no more than creatures of the state, and the national government had almost no direct dealings with the cities. But since the 1930s and the new federalism, the national government has become an active participant in the government and politics of cities. Conversely, cities have become active participants in the workings of the national government.

This relatively new set of relationships between cities and the national government will be described in chapters that lie ahead. For now, it is useful to ask: What happened in the Great Depression to bring about these new relationships?

With the onset of economic hard times, the electorate followed its intuitions and acted out its traditional response to hard times. It voted the party in power out of office and swept a new party into power. From the Civil War onwards, the Republican party had been the dominant party in American political life. Now, it was the Democrats' turn to govern. The election of 1932 brought a revitalized Democratic party to the center of the national political stage. That party drew its new strength from a new coalition. It was a fusion of traditional Southern, Protestant, (and mostly rural) democrats and the voters of the big cities—blacks, Jews, Catholics, blue-collar workers, and the children and grandchildren of former immigrants.[20]

From now on, the key to winning the presidency would lie in the hands of voters in a dozen or so of the biggest cities. Their voting strength would nearly dominate the Electoral College, and thus, those aspiring to be president would be forced to pay close attention to urban needs and urban demands. Henceforth, the problems of the city would make their way onto the agenda of the national government.

The Past Becomes the Present

Americans have always been ambivalent about their cities. The larger the city, the greater the ambivalence, the more divided the perception. We see the city

20. "Critical election" is the term coined by V.O. Key (1955) to describe the party realignments of 1932. Also see Burnham (1970).

as an instrument of progress and as creator of industrial and commercial wealth, a place of economic opportunity and a place that nurtures the arts. At the same time, we also see the city as a haven for crime, a place of congestion and physical decay, and a place whose scale and impersonal dealings are destructive of the human spirit.

These contradictory visions have a long history. To the Pilgrims and Puritans who came to the New World, all America was opportunity to build a New Jerusalem. "Come hither," preached Cotton Mather, "and I will show you an admirable spectacle! 'Tis a Heavenly City. . .a city to be inhabited by. . . Spirits of Just Men. . . . Oh! America, the Holy City!" And yet, negative thoughts about the city have also been long with us. Some part of this wariness may come from our religious traditions, for cities in the Old Testament are depicted as places of depravity and sin. Another source of distrust may come from our own history. Several of the founders of the American republic were mistrustful of the cities. Even as they framed the Constitution, they could not forget that previous republics had been city-states and, as Hamilton put it in *Federalist* 9, violence and political unrest in the city are always to be feared:

> It is impossible to read the history of the petty republics of Greece and Italy without feeling sensations of horror and disgust at the distractions with which they were continually agitated, and at the rapid succession of revolutions by which they were kept in a state of perpetual vibration. . . (1961,71)

Thomas Jefferson helped further this negative view of the city, for his vision for a future America was one in which the farmer, working mostly alone and always attuned to nature, would be calm and independent in his political judgement, while city dwellers—too easily swayed by the opinions of others and without property to give them a stake in the status quo—would constitute a threat to the stability of our democracy (Griswold 1948, ch. 2, Ford 1904, vol. 4). Thus, as Lucia and Morton White (1977, 1) have said, we are nurtured in an intellectual tradition that is notable for its anti-urban bias. "We have no persistent or pervasive attachment to the city in our literature or in our philosophy."

No complex set of social and political forces ever has a single cause, yet, it is difficult not to conclude that our ambivalence toward cities (what we might call a "theory of ambivalent regard") contributes greatly to the dynamics of urban and suburban change: If our views and our emotions about cities are mixed, then there is no consensus on what, if anything, we should do to save them, and whether we should resist the constant tearing down of central cities—sometimes in the name of progress, sometimes in the cause of economic profits—and the shift of business and people outward to the ever-spreading suburbs. It is this same ambivalent regard that serves as backdrop for the next chapter's exploration of urban politics. In that chapter, as in all the chapters to follow, we shall see again how the past continues to shape the future.

Part Three
The Rulers and the Ruled

From Window #29. William Schwartz. Lithograph. Lent by the WPA. 154.1941. © 1989 The Art Institute of Chicago, All Rights Reserved.

Political Rules and Political Realities in the City   6

Politics in America is the binding secular religion.
Theodore H. White
Breech of Faith

All politics is local politics.
Thomas P. (Tip) O'Neill
Man of the House

An Extended Definition of Politics

As students of language know, the more important a word is in the lives of its users and the more frequently it is used, the more meanings it will acquire. *Politics* is a case in point. As noted in chapter 1, the term has acquired two long-standing meanings: the art and science of governing; and the struggle to dominate government and determine policy. These two meanings convey a variety of ideas, suggesting that politics is a process involving people, struggles, power, domination, and policies. Taken together, these terms convey an extended definition of politics as *a process or activity that has direct public consequences and that directly affects the public good.* The exact line dividing public and private good is difficult to pinpoint, and for guidance to its placement we turn to several contextual definitions of politics.

Webster's New Collegiate Dictionary (8th ed., 1979) defines politics in its first entry as "the art and science of government." Although this legalistic definition long dominated political science,[1] it has given way to a more

---

1. Even as late as 1957, Lawrence Herson's article arguing that the study of urban politics should entail something more than the study of municipal government (Herson 1957) met considerable

anthropomorphic view of politics (e.g., de Grazia 1965, Isaak 1984). More consistent with this changing view is another definition from *Webster's* which views politics as "the total complex of relations among men in a society." This definition, although too broad for our purposes, nonetheless has much to recommend it, for it implicitly recognizes that the process by which decisions are reached, whether by a family, a business firm, or a city council, is much the same. In each case, individuals interact, each attempting to persuade others to accept his or her position on an issue. And this process of interaction has four components that are central to an extended definition of politics: its human quality, its motivational basis, its ties to conflict, and its reliance on power.

Four Components of an Extended Definition of Politics

The human quality of politics. By emphasizing the importance of the individual in politics, definition moves beyond the conception that politics primarily reflects governmental institutions or laws. This emphasis does not suggest that individuals do not function politically as institutional representatives; as we will see, this is an important part of urban politics. Nor does it suggest that the institutional or legal resources used by individuals in their political activity are unimportant. Rather, it suggests that we may miss the essence of politics if we *simply* consider institutions without acknowledging the importance of the individuals who constitute them, or if we consider laws without acknowledging the importance of the individuals who pass and implement them (e.g., Van Dyke 1960).

Motives for political action. Emphasis on the individual leads to a consideration of the motives that underlie his or her political activity. Political activity never occurs in a vacuum. Rather, it is motivated by intertwined human needs and desires. A corollary of this proposition states that political activity is therefore purposive and usually rational. To understand its underlying rationality, however, we must understand the motives that drive an individual's political behavior. For example, the behavior of a mayor who denigrates his or her city may seem irrational if we assume a re-election motive; but it may be perfectly rationale if he or she aspires to a higher political office (e.g., governor). And many seemingly irrational actions from an institution make perfectly good sense when examined in terms of the individuals who constitute that institution (e.g., Snyder, et al. 1962).

---

resistance. About the same time, Charles Hyneman (1956, 26) stated that politics ". . . is that part of the affairs of state which centers in government, and that kind or part of government which speaks through law."

Politics as conflict. A treatment of politics as conflictual (e.g., Wright 1950, Van Dyke 1960) implies that different individuals have different positions on any issue. This interpretation builds on the two previous components of politics, individuals and motives. Individuals, who are the essence of politics, come from different backgrounds and have different experiences, giving them different views of the world. *[The theory of ideology]* Since their political behavior is purposive, that is, motivated by these different views, politics necessarily involves conflict.

Politics as the exercise of power. Our definition also treats politics as the exercise of power. Whenever conflict arises, power is necessarily involved in its resolution. This exercise of power may be subtle, as in the process of convincing others of the merit of one's own position. It may involve the legitimate ability to enforce compromise or call for a vote; or it may involve the invocation of formal authority (e.g., police, courts). It may be more blatant, involving coercive threats of physical or fiscal punishment or reward. But whatever its form, power is an inherent feature of human commerce. Since the Greeks, the concept of power has intrigued those who study politics, and it has found a place in many modern definitions of politics (e.g., Lasswell 1936, Easton 1953).

Public versus Private Action: The Zone of Demarcation

These definitions suggest that political activity does not differ from non-political activity in form (i.e., individuals with various motives conflict and exercise power in both the public and the private sectors). However, political and nonpolitical activity differ in three *substantive* ways. First, political activity tends to be motivated by a desire to achieve a substantial reallocation of resources within some segment (or between segments) of society. Second, political activity tends to be systematic rather than random. And third, political activity affects (or at least has the potential to affect) the lives of the many rather than the few. Taken together, these three criteria form a *zone of demarcation* that separates private from public actions.

Resource allocation. The first criterion is the motivation underlying political activity: Politics is motivated by the desire to allocate or reallocate resources in society. The most obvious resource is money, and all activity involving public taxing and spending is clearly political. Other resources include knowledge, freedom, power, health, historical heritage, opportunity, and so forth. Based on this criterion, a number of activities typically associated with the private sector are political, including the following:

• The director of a community art center solicits contributions for art workshops.

- A neighborhood association protests the nearby location of a large factory.
- Concerned citizens protest the proposed demolition of an historic building.
- A private school board votes to fire a gay teacher.

Each of these cases represents the reallocation of an important public resource, and the action, no matter how private its intent, enters the public domain.

Systematic action. The second criterion holds that these actions must be systematic (i.e., part of a larger whole) rather than random. For example, we can imagine a number of actions that would seem to be guided by a logic of their own rather than by a systematic policy. A community garden club may decide to visit the gardens around Philadelphia rather than those around New York City, reflecting members' current preferences, based, for example, on a recent article about Longwood Garden in a national gardening magazine. By the same token, a local business firm may hire a white male instead of a black female for a particular job because he is better qualified. But if these decision rules become systematic policies, they *may* become political. For example, the Midwest Political Science Association's decision in the early 1980s to hold its annual meetings in Cincinnati and Milwaukee rather than Chicago may seem, on the face of it, to be no different from the garden club's decision to travel to Philadelphia. But the former was motivated by the systematic policy to boycott those states that had not ratified the Equal Rights Amendment (ERA), while the latter lacked any systematic rationale. By the same token, an employment policy giving preference to white males over females and minorities is systematic and therefore qualifies as political, whereas a single incident may be random and does not meet this criterion.

Size of impact. The third criterion for political activity is that it must directly affect the lives of a substantial segment of the population. This precludes a family's vacation decision, even if it is based on a systematic effort to distribute resources in society (e.g., "We will avoid Chicago because Illinois has not ratified the ERA"), or a builder's decision to construct a house of substandard material. But a builder's decision to construct an entire subdivision using substandard material may fall into the political realm because of its larger impact, its systematic character, and its impact on the distribution of public resources (e.g., safety). And the decision to locate a new retail shoe outlet in a community may not be political, but the decision to build a shopping mall is likely to be.

Rules of the political game: An introduction. Each of these criteria is somewhat fuzzy, and even when taken together, they provide only an approximate zone of demarcation between the political and the nonpolitical. But the distinction is important, for as activities or events, ostensibly private in nature, enter this zone, they are subject to a number of informal constraints, derived from democratic theory, that represent the "rules of the political game" (e.g., Truman 1945). Exactly how these norms were derived is unclear, although they appear to precede the founding of the republic (e.g. Tocqueville 1945, Dahl 1961, Dye and Zeigler 1975, Herson 1984). Their enforcement seems to be by "gentleman's agreement": Most people abide by the rules, and those who do not incur the wrath of other participants (and occasionally, of the entire society). Most of us have accepted these norms, and our adherence to them has allowed democracy to flourish in the United States for over two hundred years.

The fact that these norms have guided politics in our society for more than two centuries does not, of course, mean that they have never been violated, for scandals are also a part of our political history. And as was noted in chapters 4 and 5, cities are generally regarded as having violated our democratic norms the most. In the following sections, we will examine these informal norms in greater detail, exploring their role in urban politics. Through this examination, we will explicate the *theory of urban political style* outlined in chapter 3.

Rules of the Political Game

Although a number of rules governing political behavior have been observed, we will concentrate on five, each with a long-standing tradition in American politics and each tied at least indirectly to democratic theory. These five norms are majority rule, protection of minority rights, participation, peaceful management of conflict, and the widespread distribution of political benefits.

Majority Rule

Majority rule is the best known and most sacred of our political norms. Democracy, by its nature, is rule by the people (from the Greek *demos,* meaning people, and *cracy,* meaning rule). Democracy carries in its meaning the idea that all who participate in a decision shall participate on equal terms. Arguments must be settled and choices made by the one formula that provides for equal counting and the least contention concerning the terms and conditions of equal counting. That formula is majority rule.

Almost without exception, all voting and all public decision making in the United States are conducted through majority rule. Not only is the United States the oldest continuing democracy, it is also the one in which its citizens are asked to vote most often.[2] We elect public officials at every

every level of government—city, county, state, and national. Also, at the local level, we vote for bond issues and tax levies, and through the recall and referendum, the majority is able to dispose of unpopular legislators and legislation.

Minority Rights

Majority rule by itself cannot convey the full intent and meaning of democracy. Majorities can and do harm the minority that loses an election. The protection of minority rights is thus an equally important democratic norm. For example, the Declaration of Independence argues that humans are "endowed by their Creator with certain Unalienable Rights" that may not be infringed or curtailed by the majority.

Our political system attends to minority rights on every level of government. The U.S. Constitution, as well as those of the states, attempts to guarantee these rights. They provide for freedom of speech and press; they provide procedural safeguards for those accused of crimes; and they guarantee equal protection of all citizens under the law. If for no other reason, minority rights are important to a system of majority rule because a democracy does not consist of a single majority ruling for all time. It requires open and freely forming majorities, coming together and breaking apart on various issues. The only way to ensure that today's minority may become tomorrow's majority is to ensure that it has the opportunity to speak, argue, vote, and otherwise peacefully convince others to join it (e.g., Herson 1984).

Peaceful Management of Conflict

The distinction between private violence and public violence has been maintained reasonably well in the United States for more than two centuries. On the private side, the violence of person against person is a common characteristic of American life, perhaps tolerated as an extension of our cultural commitment to individualism. Perhaps its roots lie in our history as a frontier society, in which western expansion was accomplished through conquest and war against the Indians, or perhaps these roots are located in the violence that was part of slaveholding and slavery. Whatever the reason, more murders per capita are committed in the United States than in any other western industrialized society.[3] On the public side, however, the use of violence for political ends is generally unacceptable. Throughout our history, rebellions

---

2. At the national level, the United States selects representatives to the lower house of Congress every 24 months, compared to an average of 28.8 months in Australia, 40.6 months in the United Kingdom, and 60 months in India. See Crewe (1981) for a discussion and other examples.

3. Kurian (1984) reports 9.6 murders per 100,000 people in the United States, followed by 7.15 in the Netherlands and 5.25 in Luxembourg. Among *all* countries in the world, the United States ranks eleventh in murders per capita.

have been met with swift and decisive resistance, though the Civil War ground on through four terrible and bloody years.

Participation

Participation in politics is essential to any democratic system: How else can new majorities form, the consent of the governed be realized, or representatives be informed about public wishes and desires? Participation in politics is celebrated as a civic virtue and an obligation of citizenship, and we are constantly reminded of that obligation.

In addition to overtly political participation (like voting), participation in civic activities is constantly solicited. Many urban residents are asked to volunteer time for a variety of community projects, including United Way campaigns, March of Dimes, and so forth. Significantly, many of those who enter local politics are attracted by their volunteer experiences in such community activities; more significant still, political candidates are often recruited from the ranks of those volunteers.

Widespread Distribution of Benefits

Unlike the legal and constitutional guarantees of majority rule and minority rights, this norm is an informal but nonetheless important component of our politics. It connects to the norms of minority rights (e.g., no loser ought to lose completely), and it probably derives from our traditions of a market society (business as an arrangement of freely negotiated contracts in which people are free to pursue their own interests to the best of their abilities).[4] In turn, this norm also connects to the norm of majority rule: Majorities form through coalitions and compromises, ensuring that all sides to a political issue emerge with some sense of benefit.

Of course, the norm of distributed benefits also connects to the peaceful management of public conflict, in that mollified participants do not usually engage in acts of violence. And it helps promote the expectation that politics involves fair play, which is achieved when all participants emerge from the political process better off for having participated.[5]

Rules of the Political Game Applied to Urban Politics

In several respects, the city is the place where democracy in America *ought to* flourish, and where these norms *ought* to receive greatest adherence. *[The*

4. In their defense of market economies, Friedman and Friedman (1981) argue that the liberty of economic contracts has been the historical source of democracy.

5. A variant of this logic has been formalized in economic and decision theory as *Pareto optimality:* A policy is Pareto optimal if it leaves no one worse off and at least one person better off.

theory of grass-roots democracy] After all, democracy had its earliest American beginnings in the Pilgrim settlements of colonial New England, and subsequently in New England town meetings (Boorstin 1974, Tocqueville 1945, Mansbridge 1980). Moreover, urban government governs over a relatively small territory whose inhabitants often know through firsthand experience the issues of government and how those issues affect their daily lives. Democracy and democratic norms *ought to* flourish in the city if for no other reason than the fact that city voters have considerable opportunity to know both their officials and their fellow voters as neighbors.

But contrary to this expectation, the city is not the place where democracy has flourished in America. The style of city politics is different from the style of politics practiced at other levels of government; this difference springs largely from the fact that the rules of the political game are practiced differently in the city.

Most obviously, machine politics flourished for a very long time in our largest cities. Chapters 4 and 5 recounted the origins of that tradition—immigrant populations, their use of politics as a ladder to economic betterment, opportunities to use government spending for private advantage, and the ability of politicians to turn high population densities to their advantage through block-to-block and apartment-to-apartment control over voting.

And, historically, both large cities and small towns have violated what may be the most important democratic norm of all, that involving public violence. Riots, lynchings, and other forms of vigilantism—especially when intertwined with racial and ethnic repression—have been a recurring theme of urban and small-town history. Traditionally, these were treated as local problems and usually as acts of private violence. But in the 1960s, a rising public conscience combined with several long hot summers of urban violence to change the dominant view. Americans began to view such violence as public, bringing to bear not only condemnation but the full attention of the national government (National Advisory Commission on Civil Disorders 1968).

Other, more contemporary factors also help explain the unique style of politics in the urban place. First, urban politics primarily addresses quality of life issues, about which most of us have strong opinions not readily subject to compromise. Partially because of the importance of these issues to our daily lives, urban conflicts are often emotional and bitter. Second, through voluntary, civic, and business associations, urban politics offers more avenues for political participation than those available at other levels of government. Third, the city is the level of government at which politics is usually practiced on a part-time basis. Fourth, and because of the part-time quality of urban politics, urban government has become government by administration. Fifth, power in the city tends to be concentrated in the private rather than the public sector. And finally, the city is comparatively less financially sound than are its state or national counterparts. We will now consider more closely these contemporary factors.

Quality of Life Issues

Even a cursory reading of the local section of most newspapers suggests the kinds of issues likely to concern most community residents. Typically, an article discusses the local school district. Another may concern the local police or fire department, or public parks. Particularly in smaller towns, a list of hospital admissions and discharges, as well as births and deaths, appears. Often these lists are accompanied by a story about newly acquired hospital equipment or new strategies in fighting disease. New businesses or industries that move to town always rate a story, often with a picture of the ribbon-cutting ceremony. Each week, a list of programs sponsored by the library, art center, or recreation department appears. And any contemplated zoning change or ordinance generates headlines.

The newspaper's repertoire of local articles is a reflection of residents' lives. While state, national, or international events are often of great interest and generate widespread debate, they seldom touch residents' lives *directly*. But local events are different, for they do affect the quality of residents' lives directly. Issues of local education directly affect their children's opportunity to get ahead in life, and many may feel the curriculum (e.g., evolutionary theories of biology, sex education) is contrary to religious beliefs or family structure. The quality of local health care affects the life and death of urban residents, as may the quality of the local fire and police department. Leisure time may be spent in a park, at local theaters or concert halls, at the public library, or shopping at a mall. Residents spend hours each week driving on roads they expect to be well maintained, negotiating traffic they expect to be well regulated. Their livelihoods depend on local jobs. And the biggest investment of their lives—their house—is protected by zoning regulations that prohibit apartment buildings, trailer parks, light industry, or shopping malls from being constructed next door.

In short, urban dwellers depend on the many things that urban life provides for them, and this very dependence tends to make them intolerant of change that might adversely affect the quality of their lives. *[The theory of lifestyle and territory]* Given the importance of these issues, convictions are strongly held, and compromise is difficult to achieve. Compromise may work well in homogeneous cities, where opinions about quality of life issues are shared. But politics becomes more difficult, and conflict more rancorous in heterogeneous cities where diverging views about what constitutes quality of life clash.[6]

6. Note how this formulation contrasts with Bryce's view, discussed in chapter 5, that local politics is boring.

Community Conflict

Students of urban politics note that a great deal of rancor often surrounds community conflicts. In one study, Robert Crain and his colleagues (1969) chronicled municipal decisions to fluoridate (or not fluoridate) water supplies. While this seems a tame issue today, it was anything but tame during the 1950s and 1960s, and it evoked hard-fought quality of life concerns. For the profluoridation forces, the concern was one of physical well-being: Parents wanted their children to have better teeth with fewer cavities. For the antifluoridation forces, concerns were more complex. One concern was philosophical, centering on the right of government to intrude into the daily lives of its citizens. Another concern was the potential risk of tampering with the city's water supply: Since a foreign substance was being introduced into the water, it would be easy for anyone who wanted to destroy the city (e.g., foreign agents or terrorists) to substitute some type of toxin for the fluoride, thus poisoning its inhabitants. A third concern was that fluoride is itself toxic, and that those drinking fluoridated water would suffer the physical and mental consequences of fluoride poisoning. Lewis Thomas (1983, 140), a noted medical critic and a member of the New York City Board of Health in the 1950's, views the fluoride debate from this perspective:

> The [public health] department viewed the prospect of fluoridation with zeal, for there was an opportunity to be professionally useful. The Board of Health passed the *pro forma* resolution mandating the installation of fluoridation, the mayor concurred, and then the roof began falling in. Public hearings were demanded by one after another civic group and their lawyers, protesting what was called an attempt to poison the public. . . . In its early stages and throughout the debates, the issue took on an ideological aspect which became increasingly bitter. At one long hearing, . . . the members of the Board of Health were accused by impassioned speaker after speaker of being Communists or tools of Communism. In many parts of America, fluoridation was seen as a foreign plot to weaken the country, possibly by setting loose an epidemic of cancer.

It is easy to imagine how debate over the issue of fluoridation, which may have begun quite rationally, could have digressed into shouting and name-calling. For each side, the stakes were too high to acquiesce without a fight, and fights often followed.

An analysis of other major urban conflicts during the past four decades shows a similar pattern. Consider, for example, the stakes involved in controversies about suitable school textbooks or library books. On one side are parents (and other concerned citizens) who are offended that their children are subjected to what they view as pornographic or unpatriotic material, or material that runs contrary to their moral or religious values (e.g., biology texts that stress theories of evolution over those of creationism or novels, such as Steinbeck's *The Grapes of Wrath,* that use profanity). On the other side are those parents (or concerned citizens) offended by the intrusion of religious teachings into public education, or who desire to offer their children a wide range of literary experiences. The image of books being thrown into bonfires suggests the emotions that run rampant around this issue and of the unwillingness of either side to compromise.

Court-ordered school busing is another issue on which emotions run high (adults in South Boston tossing stones at a school bus loaded with children suggests the height of the emotions; see Lukas 1985). So, too, is the construction of group homes for the mentally retarded or the mentally ill in neighborhoods, or the construction of low-cost housing for the poor in middle-class neighborhoods. Even seemingly noncontroversial issues, like the construction of a shopping mall, can create considerable and bitter conflict, with each side accusing the other of attempting to destroy the community as a viable shopping area.

Coleman's model. The importance of the issues does not by itself account for the dynamics of community conflict. James Coleman (1957) recognizes the complexity of conflict escalation with his conflict model (see figure 6.1). The strength of conviction with which political participants hold opinions moves an issue through the initial stages of conflict. For example, the act of burning books, stoning a school bus, or even writing letters to the editor of the local newspaper may polarize the community, disturbing friendships and generally disrupting the social commerce that is so important in the community. But it is the proximity of individuals in a community, and their familiarity with one another, that allows previously suppressed issues to surface and the conflict to escalate (from stage 2 of the model to stage 3.)

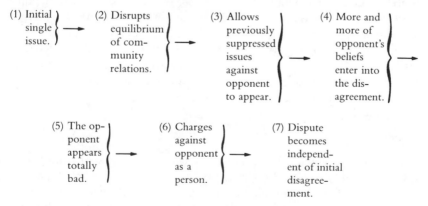

FIGURE 6.1: The Progression of Community Conflict

Unlike national or state politics, where participants change from issue to issue, local issues tend to be characterized by *overlapping issue coalitions.* Over time, as individuals share ideas and concerns, they discover others in the community who share similar ideas and whose judgments they trust. As individuals activate these relationships in response to new issues, *issue networks* emerge on the various sides of the issue. In the aggregate, these issue networks represent coalitions of political participants who share values and beliefs, and often class status. For example, economic issues tend to elicit participation by a common core of individuals, on both sides, regardless of their exact substantive content. Even more important, issue networks that respond to economic issues may become sensitized over time to the economic ramifications of virtually all policy debates. As issue networks are mobilized over time and across issues, their members become stereotyped. They become associated with specific types of issues and issue positions, and their rhetoric becomes predictable.

Just as familiarity is said to breed contempt, predictability breeds cynicism as opponents look for other personal characteristics that may also be predictable. Again, it is close proximity that makes these personal habits and characteristics so visible as conflict escalates further (to stage 4). For example, an individual who opposes industrial expansion may be viewed as antigrowth. If he or she does not maintain a well-trimmed lawn or drives an old automobile, opponents may view this as part of the antigrowth pattern. By the same token, an individual who favors industrial expansion may be viewed as excessively commercialist; a well-maintained yard in a new subdivision may foster this view among his or her opponents. As participants in an ongoing issue become stereotyped, conflict escalates (through stages 5 and 6), taking on personal overtones.

During this process, ambiguity about the issue grows, causing issue networks to contract and become more cohesive and defensive (Bolland 1985a), further limiting the potential for nonrancorous issue resolution. By its final stages, the conflict has little to do with the original issue; rather, it has taken on a life of its own, and arguments have become increasingly personal and acrimonious. The battles between Harold Washington, mayor of Chicago until his death in 1987, and Edward Vrdolyak, chairman of the Cook County Democratic party (the machine) are a case in point, reaching a point where they literally did not speak to one another.

Participation

A third area in which urban politics is qualitatively different from that of other levels of government is the opportunity for, and the level of, political participation. On the one hand, the city offers an abundance of opportunities for the individual to participate. In a study of participation in a twenty-square-block area of Manhattan's lower east side, for example, Yates (1977) found no fewer than two hundred different participatory organizations such as churches and social clubs (see chapter 8 for further discussion). Even in less populous places, the typical citizen may participate in local politics through such organizations as Rotary or Kiwanis, political parties, neighborhood associations, various ad hoc citizen groups, formally constituted citizen advisory committees, and by voting. In view of these opportunities, individuals with very little political ambition may find themselves in positions of local leadership and be recruited to run for local political office (city council, school board). In contrast, participation in state and national politics is limited for most people to voting and to signing petitions.

In spite of these opportunities to participate, however, political participation in most cities falls far short of its potential. Voter turnout in local elections typically is far lower than in state and national elections. While something over 50 percent of registered voters turn out in presidential elections, probably no more than one third of registered voters actually vote in nonconcurrent local elections (Lineberry and Sharkansky 1978). Further, a number of nationwide trends and social forces reduce the proclivity for urban political participation (Bolland 1984). Consider the following changes in urban life.

Social trends affecting urban political participation. First, the average family has turned inward. Since the 1950s, television has become an important part of most people's lives, and the time the "typical American" spends in front of the TV has risen to nearly seven hours daily.[7] For many people, television has become a substitute for interaction with neighbors as well as participation in community activities. This withdrawal is accentuated by the changing style of urban residential architecture. Houses built before World War II typically displayed large front porches that looked out onto the sidewalk and its pedestrian traffic. But since the Second World War, the privacy of the back patio has replaced the public accessibility of the front yard.

Second, the growing fear of crime has also caused people to turn inward. We are all familiar with the stories, whether apocryphal or not, about the "old days" when homeowners left their homes unlocked when they went away for the weekend. Today, those same people express concern about walking outside at night for fear of being mugged. Objective measures of crime tell only part of the story, although the story they tell is revealing: The crime rate has increased sixfold since 1960. More important, fear of crime is increasing at an even more rapid rate. This fear, which has become an obsession for many urban residents, breaks down trust among neighbors and turns residents inward rather than outward toward their community (Wilson 1975).

---

7. This, and other unattributed statistics reported in this section are taken from the *Statistical Abstract of the United States.*

Third, more women participate in the labor force than ever before. In 1960, only one third of married women participated in the labor force, compared with nearly one half in 1980. This increase is most dramatic for women with children under six years of age, leading American families to change childcare patterns. Not only do more children need day care, but care is more frequently given outside the home (Lueck, et al. 1982). In 1958, more than half the children of mothers with full-time paying jobs were cared for in their own homes; by 1977, that figure had declined to 25 percent. In the past, mothers and children provided the social glue that held neighborhoods together, creating the opportunity for contact and social support. But today, fewer women are around the neighborhood by day, and working parents are often too preoccupied to venture away from home at night. The result is the deterioration of the neighborhood as a cohesive social unit in urban America.

Fourth, the out-migration from the inner city to the suburbs, a trend that actually began in the nineteenth century, continues unabated. The two-car garage is as much a cliche of suburbia as the split-level house, and with good reason: Virtually nothing is within walking distance, and most suburbs are poorly served by mass transit. As a result, suburbanites drive wherever they go, substantially reducing the opportunity for social contact among neighbors.

Fifth, the American family has undergone a great transition during the past two decades. A high divorce rate and the rise of alternative living arrangements have generated a sense of informality and transience in many households. In 1960, nonfamily households accounted for only 15 percent of all households; by 1980, this figure had risen to over 25 percent. This trend is accompanied by a substantial decline in the number of traditional (husband-wife) households, down from 74 percent in 1960 to 62 percent in 1978. The reduced stability of the typical household attenuates its attachment to the neighborhood and community and reduces participation in the community.

Sixth, the pattern of ownership of commercial retail businesses has changed dramatically since 1960. In the early 1960s, nationally franchised fast-food restaurants were built in virtually every American city, rapidly followed by nationally owned discount department stores. During this period, the suburban shopping mall also caught the fancy of the American shopper, and literally thousands were built across the United States by 1975; typically only a third of the stores in these malls are locally owned, with the remainder being regionally or nationally owned chains.[8] This shift has resulted in a reduced commitment among a city's economic sector to the social well-being of the community, and a reduced tendency for that sector to become involved in local politics.

8. This rough estimate was derived with the assistance of the chambers of commerce in several cities.

These trends toward nonparticipation are, no doubt, more pronounced in some areas of the country than in others. Their effect is likely to be greatest in suburban areas and middle-sized cities. Given the demographic trend toward suburbanization, nonparticipation is likely to become even more common.

Part-Time Politics

Part-time politics is another distinguishing characteristic of urban political life. At the national and state levels, the chief executive and legislators hold full-time (or at least part-time) salaried positions. But with the exception of perhaps only several dozen cities, mayoral and city council positions carry only a nominal salary. Elected officials must also hold full-time jobs. In small and middle-sized cities, the mayor may be a lawyer, a banker, a physician, a hardware salesperson, or a land developer. Members of the city council typically have similar jobs. As a result, even the most civic-minded members of the governing body cannot commit themselves completely to the task of governing. Instead, they rely on the city staff, and in reformed cities on the city manager, to provide them with information and implement their decisions.

In principle, the manager or administrator is subordinate to the governing body, and serves at its pleasure. But seldom is the distinction between politics and administration as clear-cut as this principle presupposes. In reality, the city administrator typically has considerable influence in formulating policy, often more than that of the council he or she serves. Two factors account for this discrepancy between principle and practice. First, as a full-time employee, the administrator develops an expertise concerning the intricacies of city government that dwarfs that of council members; this leads them to defer to his or her judgment about the soundness and appropriateness of many policies. Second, in the implementation of policies handed down by the council, the administrator typically is given considerable discretion. This allows the administrator to interpret policies in accordance with his or her preferences. These factors are discussed in greater detail in the next chapter. In the interim, however, we will consider briefly the asymmetry of the relationship between the administrator (or city manager) and the council.

Administrative expertise and discretion. As head of the municipal bureaucracy, the city administrator is its most visible employee. Local newspaper articles often quote the administrator as a city spokesperson, and he or she is often visible at public events. Although this may prove time-consuming for the administrator, it also provides a window to the city that council members often lack. And citizens often contact the city administrator rather than council

87

members about municipal problems, such as garbage collection. As a result, the administrator develops a much better understanding of the community, its aspirations, and its concerns than does the council elected to serve it. In addition, many administrators have graduate degrees in public administration or management science, providing them with a foundation in budgeting, personnel management, and other management skills (e.g., cost-benefit analysis). This background, coupled with frequent discussion with department heads, allows the administrator to gain expertise about the city and its government rapidly.

This expertise provides the administrator with considerable influence in urban policy making, for council members typically defer to him or her for information, advice, and ideas. Although the council has the final say on policy issues (including whether or not to retain the administrator), the administrator typically sets the agenda by identifying the problems that need to be addressed by the council. And, in turn, the administrator typically provides the council with background information, possible solutions, and other advice concerning these issues. In short, all that is left to the council is action on the administrator's recommendations.

Even if the city council takes a more active role in formulating policy, the administrator retains considerable influence in the policy process, due largely to the discretion typically accorded him or her by the council in implementing its decisions. *[The theory of urban administration]* Consider, for example, the council's decision to issue industrial revenue bonds (IRBs) as a means of attracting new business and industry to the city. The council may go so far as to specify the kind of industry it wishes to attract (e.g., non-polluting, high-tech). But the administrator and his or her staff must implement the policy, and in so doing, he or she exercises discretionary power. The administration typically decides, for example, whether local industries wishing to expand qualify for IRB money. It may specify certain areas of the city where incoming industries must locate to quality for IRB money. It decides in which publications the availability of IRB money will be advertised, and which parts of the country it will travel to to solicit new industry. This, in effect, allows the administrator to pick and choose exactly which types of new industries are likely to move to the city. And the administration typically decides, on a case-by-case basis, which applicants qualify for how much IRB money.[9]

Government by Administration

A change in the style of governance has accompanied the increasing power acquired by full-time urban administrators. The natural metier of the full-

---

9. Briefly, IRBs offer tax advantages to those who buy them and lower interest rates to businesses that borrow money made available through IRB-financed loans. Thee subjects are further elaborated in the discussion of public policy in chapters 10 and 11 and in the discussion of service delivery in chapter 17.

time politician is the provision of individualized services to those in need, often in implicit exchange for votes. (During the days of the machine, this involved provision of food, clothing, and shelter to new immigrants.) At the national and state levels, this provision of services involves finding ways to accomplish feats that are beyond the ability of the individual constituent. But this style of politics is time consuming, and the politician must either have time to spare or a staff able to perform these services. In today's city, most politicians have neither. As part-time politicians and full-time professionals (or salaried employees), they have little residual time to help needy constituents. And while the city government does hire a staff, staff members typically report to the full-time administrator (who has no need to garner votes through the delivery of personalized services) rather than to the elected officials.[10] As a result, the style of service delivery has changed in important but not altogether anticipated ways.

The first change has been in the direction of collective benefits. Cities have moved toward the provision of services designed to benefit the *typical* city resident rather than those that benefit specific, identifiable residents. For example, services such as recreation, education, public safety, and street maintenance provide benefits to all residents in roughly equal amounts. In contrast, the provision of food and shelter to the poor, political opportunity to the newly arrived, and jobs to the unemployed (all of which the city once delivered through the political machine) imparts benefits to selected individuals (or at least selected classes). In later chapters, these different approaches are discussed as *distributive* and *redistributive*, respectively.

The second change has been in the direction of greater economic efficiency. This should not be surprising, given the academic backgrounds of many city administrators: They are taught to run the city as a business. Nor is it surprising, given the financial straits in which most cities find themselves (the urban fiscal crisis is discussed more fully in chapters 15 and 16). The dominant model governing economic efficiency is cost-benefit analysis, wherein a policy is deemed effective if its derived benefit outweighs its total cost. In the absence of a better unit of measurement, administrators often weigh costs and benefits in monetary terms. Thus, policies are designed to maximize the return on investment, or to use a popular political phrase, to provide the "biggest bang for the buck." For example, in deciding where to locate a new crosstown highway, decision-makers may attempt to maximize flow of traffic per dollar spent on construction. By considering monetary factors in assessing traffic flow and construction costs, decision makers are likely to discover that the most economical distance between two points is a straight line along which

10. In some larger cities, this seems to be changing somewhat, with staff assigned to council members (see chapter 10). But in the vast majority of cities, this generalization remains true.

(a) the most people with the highest incomes can get to work most quickly and (b) the cost of condemning land is least expensive. As a result, new commuter highways are typically constructed through older, low-income neighborhoods, with a great social cost to these neighborhoods but a collective economic benefit to the city. Further, new highways are likely to be constructed so as to provide easy access to more affluent neighborhoods, since the salaries of residents in these neighborhoods (and their costs of commuting) are larger than those of residents in low-income neighborhoods. In short, politics by administration carries with it a middle- and upper-class bias that potentially threatens the protection of minority rights.

Private Power versus Public Power

Another distinction between urban politics and politics at the state and national levels involves the *locus* of political power. *[The theory of influence]* In creating this distinction we enter a domain of considerable controversy. Put in its baldest form, the controversy involves a single question: Is power distributed equitably among the electorate, or is it concentrated in the hands of an elite few? An entire book could be devoted to this question, for it has generated a considerable literature, and its implications for democratic theory are profound. For now, we will merely touch on the issue of power; but we shall return to it in greater depth in chapter 9. Our conclusions can be summarized as follows: Whereas state and national power tends to be concentrated in the hands of those who hold public (and quasi-public) positions, local power tends to be concentrated in the hands of those in the private sector. This makes state and national politics more responsive than city politics to broad-based citizen input.

Admittedly, this conclusion contradicts several persuasive analyses of power in America. C. Wright Mills asserts, in his provocative study, that America is dominated by a power elite, a relatively small group of people "who are in position to make decisions having major consequences" (1956, 4). These people, continues Mills,

> are in command of the major hierarchies and organizations of modern society. They rule the big corporations. They run the machinery of the state and claim its prerogatives. They direct the military establishment. They occupy the strategic posts of the social structure in which are now . . . centered the power and the wealth.

Thomas Dye, in his discussion of power in America (1986), comes to a similar conclusion: Of the 7,314 elite positions he identifies in the United States, only 284 (3.9 percent) fall within the public sector. And William Domhoff (1983) concludes that the members of the upper class have a high degree of cohesion with respect to education, social and business ties, and outlook on social and political questions.

It is true, of course, that a small portion of our society owns a disproportionate share of its wealth. And it is also true that the business community occupies a privileged position in this and every other market society, for it is the transactions of the market that drive the economy (Lindblom 1977). But to say that the business community has a position of privilege is not to say that it masters and dominates the larger society. The wealth of America may be generated by market transactions, but those transactions are both facilitated by governmental policies and subject to governmental regulation at both the national and the state levels.[11]

This regulation is largely lacking at the local level, however, giving individuals from the private sector substantial political power. The city, in effect, is an aggregate of small economic units, ranging from corporate headquarters and manufacturing plants, to small shops and businesses, to individual households. Taken by themselves, decisions made by any of these units may be of only marginal importance to the city's economy. In the aggregate, however, they may affect the city in profound ways.

The importance of individual economic decisions is easy to understand in the case of a corporate decision to move its headquarters or a manufacturing plant into or out of a city, upon which hundreds of jobs and millions of dollars of municipal tax revenues may ride. But how can a local clothier's decision to close his or her store affect the city in anything resembling a profound manner? And even more so, how can a family's decision to buy or sell a house affect the city's well-being?

The answer lies partly in the psychological realm, but that makes its implications no less real. *[The theory of commodification of land and buildings]* When a downtown merchant packs up his or her wares and moves to another location, two things happen. First, an unattractive (and psychologically troubling) void is left in the downtown: Dark, or even worse, boarded-up windows decorated with "for lease" signs provide a stark contrast to an otherwise bright and busy area. Second, shoppers who would have visited downtown to purchase goods from the now-vacant store take their business

_____

11. At the national level, virtually all major industries are subject to considerable regulation and government control, even in an era of deregulation. As one example, the defense establishment is largely dependent on governmental contracts for its survival; and, in turn, governmental appropriations are dependent on those who hold public positions (i.e., the president, Congress). The banking industry provides a second example. Although banks can influence the national economy through their investment decisions, the Federal Reserve Board largely controls these decisions through its regulation of monetary flows. And we find a third example in the construction industry, where tax deductions for homeowners are used as a tool to stimulate building and buying. In short, the private sector is just as dependent on government as government is on it, and a kind of equilibrium exists between the two sectors of society. This provides at least indirect accountability to the public in most political decisions (defined broadly) made at the national and state levels.

elsewhere. This can have an important spillover effect on nearby businesses, which counted on purchases by the now-absent shoppers. (Most downtown businesses count on a "spree" style of shopping, expecting shoppers who come into the shopping area for one purpose to also visit other stores and perhaps purchase something that catches their eye.) A strong downtown shopping area can survive a vacant building, and another business may soon locate there. But if other businesses are barely surviving financially, even a small decline in sales may force them to move also, leading to further decline. Commercial analysts believe that the commercial viability of the downtown area degenerates rapidly as the vacancy rate approaches 35 percent.[12] It is no wonder business owners become nervous when one of their neighbors closes its doors and boards its windows, and that they feel relieved when a new business moves in.

Business and industry are not usually dependent on local government for their financial well-being; hence, they are free to pack up and move to another city, where they expect bigger sales, or lower taxes, or workers willing to work for lower wages. In fact, other cities are only too eager to invite new businesses to town, and they often offer tax incentives. But rather than making the business or industry dependent on city government, these incentives merely demonstrate governmental dependence on the private sector. This dependence gives the business or industry substantial leverage in working with city government, and governmental officials are very attentive to the suggestions of business owners concerning such issues as parking areas, street maintenance, police or fire protection, and garbage collection. And this connection to City Hall in turn gives the private business owner considerable political power.

This dependence is perhaps most pronounced in the case of the local land developer, an individual (or company) who develops property for residential or commercial use. This is the person who builds housing subdivisions and apartment complexes, shopping centers, and malls. He or she supports the local economy during construction by purchasing building materials and employing laborers. He or she also entices retailers to occupy the newly constructed stores. In short, the land developer invests capital into the community, and through this investment, he or she expects (and usually receives) access to city hall to discuss perceived problems in the city.

Even the individual household plays an important role in this local economic ecology. An empty house in a neighborhood reduces property values for other houses in the neighborhood ever so slightly; a number of vacant houses in a neighborhood reduces them dramatically. The individual homeowner's decision to buy or sell therefore has implications beyond his or her immediate pocketbook. While this impact is likely to be minimal in newer neighborhoods (someone is likely to buy and occupy the vacant house

---

12. This estimate is an abstraction of the estimates of several downtown-commercial-area consultants.

before *too* long), it is much more important in older and inner-city neighborhoods. An individual willing to move into and renovate an inner-city residence may literally be able to change the course of history in the neighborhood (after all, the herding instinct of humans is quite strong; after someone has demonstrated the economic viability of such a move, others may follow; see the discussion of gentrification in chapter 18). These early inner-city homesteaders are likely to become well-known at city hall, and they often receive incentives for their bold actions. This, too, represents a kind of power that simply is not found at the national or state political levels.

One other factor affects the distribution of power within local politics: the "nonpolitical" form of many urban governmental units. Specifically, two characteristics of urban reform contribute to the concentration of power in the private sector. The first is the nonpartisan nature of reformed governments; the second is *at-large representation*.

At the national and state levels, considerable political power rests in the hands of the Democratic and Republican party organizations. While not formally within the public sector, these organizations can be viewed as "quasi-public," in that they are ultimately accountable to the same voters who elect and unseat public officials. At the local level, however, reformed governments tend to be divorced from the local political party organizations, leaving a power void. *[The theory of urban reform]* This void often has been filled by private business interests.

At the national and state levels, every voter has his or her representative in Congress; and the voter is encouraged to believe that the representative has his or her interests in mind during each legislative vote. This system generates a clear sense of allegiance, and with it, a substantial amount of power in the legislative office. But in local reformed governments, city council members are often elected at-large, representing the city as a whole (and its interests) rather than particular groups of people. Allegiances are much less tangible in this situation, and the power of the at-large council is more ambiguous. This, in turn, gives considerable power to both the city administrator and to local business interests (which again fill the void).

Financial Security

A final comparison between politics at the urban level and politics at the state and national levels involves the relative financial standing of various governmental units. Government at the national level tends to be rather well-to-do, even in these times of fiscal cutback. This results at least partially from its ability to incur deficits to finance its day-to-day operations, a luxury from which its poorer cousins at the local level are legally prohibited. In addition, federal revenues represent the incomes of the wealthiest people across the country, from cities as well as rural areas, from businesses as well as individuals. State income suffers somewhat, but not much, in comparison. Some states are more wealthy than others; but even in the poorest states, a number of wealthy individuals and corporations reside. At the poorest end of the spectrum lie the big cities, whose inhabitants are typically among the poorest and whose financial responsibilities are typically the greatest.

In recent years, the federal government has made massive cuts in domestic expenditures, most of which previously had gone, in one form or other, to the cities (see chapter 15). States have stepped in to fill some of the void, but much of it remains unfilled. As a result, competition for existing tax dollars has grown fierce, even more so than at the other levels of government. At least for the present, the politics of compromise in urban politics seems to be giving way to the game of political hardball, where "winner takes all." As the resource pie continues to shrink, its smaller and smaller pieces will become less and less acceptable, and urban interest groups will become more willing to risk receiving nothing in order to chance the possibility of receiving a sizable chunk of that pie. In short, rancorous politics is likely to increase at the expense of widely distributive politics, where everyone is a winner.

Urban Politics and Democratic Norms: A Theory of Political Style

We began this chapter with an extended definition of politics which, in turn, opened the door to two related topics: the connection between democratic norms and the practice of politics, and the connection between urban life and democratic norms. Both topics, in turn, converge on a third topic—the ways in which the style of urban politics differs from the style of politics at other levels of government.

Urban life alters the way in which democratic norms constrain the practice of politics. And this alteration helps account for the ways in which the style of urban politics differs from the style of politics at other levels of American government. It is a style marked by business domination and the policy dominance of professional administrators, both of which constrict the norms of majority and minority rights. It is a style marked by low participation, both formal and informal. It is a style often marked by acrimonious conflict. And it is a style influenced by declining resources, which, in turn, may further constrict the norm of widespread benefit through participation. To explore still further the style of contemporary urban politics, we turn now to its institutional context: the forms of city government and the formal participants in the urban political process.

South Chicago. James Iska. Photograph. 1984.

Forms of Municipal Government _ 7
and Formal Participants
in the Urban Political Process

The excitement of politics got into my veins. . . I knew I had to say "no," but seldom could bring myself to say it.
James Walker[1]
Quoted in *Beau James,* by Gene Fowler

This chapter considers the formal participants in the urban political process. These include members of the city's elected governing body, the professional bureaucracy it employs, and the volunteer boards and commissions it appoints. These also include other elected officials, for instance the city clerk and municipal judge. We will attend carefully to several aspects of these positions: the personal characteristics of the individuals likely to hold them, their motives for seeking and maintaining the positions, their motives for actions taken in their positions, and the potential for conflict inherent in the positions. But before examining these features of formal political participation (and participants) in the city, we must distinguish among different urban governmental structures, for these, too, impinge on the politics that is practiced in the city.

---

1. James Walker was known as the "whoopee mayor" of New York City in the 1920s. His inability to say "no" seemingly extended to taking bribes.

An Inventory of Urban Governmental Structures

As suggested in chapter 5, the history of the large city in America is marred by corruption. Corruption occurred primarily under the mayor-council format, particularly where the powers of the mayor were weak. The weak-mayor format left a power vacuum, with no single member of the governing body sufficiently strong to counteract the corrupting force of the political machine, where true power was concentrated. In an attempt to conquer corruption in urban government, reformers proposed three structural modifications to urban government. First, they proposed strengthening the power of the mayor within the mayor-council format. Second, they sometimes proposed combining the political and administrative functions of government into a commission. And most dramatically (and as their preferred solution), they proposed placing administrative responsibility in the hands of a city manager, leading to a council-manager structure. In what follows, we consider the features of the original weak-mayor format as well as those of each of the three modifications, their prevalence in American cities today, the functions they serve for various types of cities, and their strengths and weaknesses.

Weak-Mayor Plan

Under the weak-mayor plan, the electorate typically elects council members, who in turn select one among themselves to be mayor for (typically) a one-year term. In some cities, all council seats are up for election every two or four years. More commonly, members serve four-year terms, with terms staggered so that roughly half of the seats are up for election every two years. But as varied as the election procedures may be, all cities governed under this plan have one thing in common: The mayor has no formal powers beyond those of other members of the council. He or she is responsible for presiding over council meetings, is often quoted in the newspaper as a community spokesperson, and performs numerous civic duties (e.g., ribbon cuttings) spared other members of the council. But these ceremonial powers do not extend to city governance, where the mayor is merely first among equals. His or her vote counts the same as that of each other council member, and the mayor cannot veto legislation, set the agenda for council meetings, or hire and fire city staff.

In the weak-mayor plan, the council is responsible for formulating and passing legislation that guides the city. In addition, the council hires department heads (e.g., parks and recreation director, community development director, fire chief and so on), who serve at its pleasure. This plan also provides citizens the opportunity to elect a number of other administrative officials; which positions are elected and which are appointed by the council vary greatly from city to city. Table 7.1 provides a rough breakdown of the most commonly elected positions under the weak-mayor plan.

When administrators are elected rather than appointed by the council, the council's power is considerably weakened. Elected administrators are free to pursue their own agendas without fear of interference from the council, and the position of the council as the central (and technically, the only) policy-making body in the city is thus diluted. No one is clearly in charge. However, even in weak-mayor cities the percentage of administrative positions that are elected has been declining over time. In 1936, 70 percent of these cities with over 5,000 residents elected at least one administrative officer; by 1966, only 48 percent did so. During the same period, the number of cities electing police chiefs declined by over 50 percent (Adrian and Press 1977).

The weak-mayor plan is typically found in small cities, where it is consistent with a general skepticism of both politicians and of government itself. By spreading power, this arrangement keeps any one officeholder from becoming "too big for his or her britches." It is also consistent with the small-town ethos of civic responsibility, for the weak-mayor plan demands that public office be spread around the citizens of the community. Indeed, it is not uncommon for a small town to have had more than thirty different mayors, and more than one hundred and fifty total elected officials, during the past half century.

The weak-mayor plan has much to offer the small city. Politics becomes synonymous with civic responsibility, and the town is governed by friends and neighbors, each pitching in to do his or her share. The concept of the professional politician, or even the professional municipal administrator, is anathema to many small towns and small townspeople, who would prefer to keep control of the city's administration in the hands of aldermanic committees. But

Table 7.1 Major Elective Administrative Positions in Cities Over 5,000

Position	Percentage of Cities	Number of Cities
Treasurer	29	883
Clerk	24	713
Assessor	13	384
Auditor	10	304
Attorney	8	235
Controller	4	114
Police Chief	4	125
Public Works Director	1	45

SOURCE: Adrian and Press (1977), adapted from *The Municipal Yearbook* (1966).

NOTE: These findings are obviously dated; given the general trend away from the long ballot, they are no doubt inflated. But to counter this bias, these percentages are based on all mayor-council cities, not just those with weak mayors. Were the appropriate adjustment made to delete strong-mayor cities, the percentages reported in table 7.1 would, in all probability, be underestimates.

as urban problems have become common to the small cities, amateur politics and amateur politicians may no longer be practical. For example, municipal liability for traffic accidents caused by malfunctioning traffic signals or alleged police brutality may demand a city attorney trained in municipal law rather than one who can appeal to the most voters. Increasing crime may require professionally trained police administrators. And the demands of economic development may require a politically minded mayor, one who is able to mobilize the community (or at least its economic sector), even if that means that he or she gains additional power in the process.

Even though the weak-mayor plan is most common in small cities, it can also be found in several middle-sized cities, particularly in the South. This may be cultural, for Southerners are traditionally more conservative than their Northern counterparts, a conservatism made manifest in suspicion of big (and powerful) government.

Strong-Mayor Plan

The increasing complexity of the city during the last quarter of the nineteenth century, coupled with the municipal corruption that seemed to flourish under the weak-mayor plan, brought calls for reform in the structure of municipal government, particularly in the large cities. During this period, four inventions helped add physical miles to the diameter of large cities (e.g., Kingsbury 1895)[2]: the modern bicycle (1885), the trolley (1873), the telephone (1876), and the automobile (1885).[3] With the advent of these conveniences, people no longer needed to live within walking distance of employment and friends; rather they could communicate and be transported over substantial distances with little effort. Many opted for the good life in the hinterlands, not far from the center of town by today's standards, but away from the hustle and bustle and pollution of the central city by turn-of-the-century standards (Jackson 1985, Warner 1972). But with urban expansion came the need for better administrative coordination, something the weak-mayor form of government was unable to provide.

Other developments during this same period further demonstrated the complexity of the urban environment and brought demands for even more administrative coordination. For example, the steam fire engine received widespread use in the Chicago fire of 1871, and for the first time the municipal fire department served a functional rather than a symbolic purpose. Now cities could actually expect to win their battles with fires rather than just fight to limit damage. But with this advance also came a change from a volunteer fire

2. Kingsbury's reference is reported in Banfield (1974).
3. See chapter 4 for a more thorough discussion of the growth of cities.

100

department to a professional fire department in many cities and an attendant need for increased administrative coordination. The advent of the automobile and the police call box made possible a truly mobile police force, but it also brought the need for better administrative coordination.

In general, technological changes brought with them increased complexity, and increased complexity brought the need for stronger administrative offices capable of providing better coordination. The easiest (and least radical) way to achieve this end was to strengthen the position of mayor, providing him or her with control over the urban bureaucracy and a position of leadership on the city council. Unlike a weak mayor, a strong mayor is always elected separately from the rest of the council, providing an unambiguous delineation of power and authority. The strong mayor not only runs council meetings, he or she typically sets the agenda for these meetings and usually has the power to veto legislation passed by the council.[4] Also unlike the weak-mayor plan, administrative positions are almost never elective under the strong mayor plan. Rather, the mayor has the authority to appoint department heads (who, in turn, are responsible for hiring staff); and he or she has the authority to fire them as well, often without even having to show cause. The strong mayor typically has a full-time position, even in smaller cities, and is paid a higher salary than other members of the council. (Council positions, in all but the largest of cities, are typically part-time or unpaid positions.)

Under the strong-mayor plan, the mayor emerges as the clear administrative and policy leader for the city. Although he or she is expected to perform a number of ceremonial duties, these are mixed with other responsibilities that carry with them a great deal of power. Since the mayor is able to appoint municipal department heads, he or she can build a team of administrators who share a common conception of municipal purpose and who are, therefore, able to work together. This results in a greater potential for coordinated services than is possible under the weak-mayor plan, where high-level administrators are either appointed by committee (i.e., the council) or elected by the voters. Under the strong-mayor plan, the mayor is the focal point of municipal government, and he or she can command credit for successful policies, and is subject to blame for unsuccessful policies. The strong-mayor plan also places the mayor in a position of extreme pressure in dealing with various interests in the city. The mayor's veto power leads various citizen groups and economic interests to make constant demands on him or her. As a result, the strong mayor makes many friends as well as enemies, and it is only the astute mayor who can manage to hold office for several terms.

Although a number of cities are considered to have strong-mayor plans, almost none has adopted the model in toto. The plan is found most often

4. Like the weak-mayor plan, there exist many variations on the strong-mayor format; this discussion portrays a "typical" city, even though no existing city may have every one of these features.

Table 7.2   Form of Municipal Government as a Function of City Size

	Type of Governmental Structure							
	Mayor-Council		City-Manager		Commission		Town Meeting	
Population	N	%	N	%	N	%	N	%
Under 2,500	131	32	220	54	3	1	50	12
2,501–5,000	1,532	70	466	21	39	2	164	7
5,001–10,000	1,000	57	579	33	33	2	136	8
10,001–25,000	735	46	673	42	54	3	125	8
25,001–50,000	236	36	365	56	30	5	21	3
50,001–100,000	106	35	179	60	9	3	5	2
100,001–250,000	40	34	72	61	6	5	0	
250,001–500,000	16	46	17	49	2	6	0	
500,001 and over	19	79	5	21	0		0	

SOURCE: Adapted from *The Municipal Yearbook*, 1988.

in larger cities, including Baltimore, Boston, Cleveland, New York, Pittsburgh, and St. Louis. But some large cities with a strong mayor plan have greatly restricted the power of the mayor. Perhaps the most interesting case is Chicago. Until his death, Richard J. Daley was arguably the most powerful mayor this half-century has witnessed. Yet, Daley's power derived not from the office of mayor but rather from his position as the head of the Cook County Democratic organization (the "Chicago Machine"). The actual limits to the power of mayor in Chicago have become clear since Daley's death, with subsequent mayors having little success in pursuing their political agendas. The weakness of the mayor's office became particularly apparent in the administration of Harold Washington, Chicago's first black mayor. In the 1983 Democratic mayoral primary, Washington ran against the incumbent mayor, Jane Byrne,[5] and the machine candidate, Richard M. Daley, the former mayor's son, beating both; he subsequently defeated Republican Bernard Epton in the general election. But Washington was consistently outvoted in the city council by a coalition of machine and Republican aldermen during the first years of his term, and his policy initiatives were largely ineffective. Not until 1986, following court-ordered redistricting, did Washington's supporters achieve a majority on the Chicago City Council.[6]

No statistics differentiate between weak and strong mayors, and it is difficult to determine exactly how widespread each plan is. But whatever the breakdown, the mayor-council plan is clearly the most popular governmental structure for both small and very large cities, as shown in table 7.2. Nearly three-quarters of all cities in the 2,500–5,000 range employ this format. And

5. In 1979, Byrne had run against and beaten machine candidate Michael Bilandic during the Democratic primary.

6. Actually, the 1986 election gave Mayor Washington a 25-25 tie on the council, which he could break with his vote.

although its popularity drops substantially as city size increases, it again becomes popular with very large cities: Over three-quarters of those cities with over half a million people employ the mayor-council format, and each of the six largest cities in the United States has adopted it. In general, the weak-mayor plan is probably most popular in the smaller cities, and the strong-mayor format is most popular in the larger cities. But as noted previously, the weakness of the mayor's office in such large cities as Chicago demonstrate the inadequacy of this generalization.

The mayor-council plan is most common in the major industrial states of the Midwest and East. Fifty-six percent of all mayor-council cities with more than 10,000 people (these are the only cities for which *The Municipal Yearbook,* the primary source of such information, reports data) are located in just eight states: Illinois, Indiana, Michigan, New Jersey, New York, Ohio, Pennsylvania, and Wisconsin. Even granting that these states have more than their share of cities in this population range (they account for 37 percent of all cities in the United States with more than 10,000 people), we must conclude that industrialization leads to this governmental format. In part, this can be explained by the greater heterogeneity to be found in cities in these states. Industrialization leads naturally to a more pronounced class structure, and in turn to a greater potential for conflict in the city. The mayor-council plan, more than any other, recognizes the importance of this conflict and literally builds it into the system. This plan produces more elected officials than any of the others (even strong-mayor systems typically have larger councils than do council-manager or commission plans), and council members are more likely to be elected from geographically defined wards rather than at-large. These features tend to promote interest-group activity and encourage citizen participation. More important, citizens have a greater sense that they have a say in city government.

Council-Manager Plan

The institutionalization of a city manager, even more than the strengthening of the mayor's office, was viewed by reformers as the way to simultaneously root out municipal corruption and coordinate municipal administration. In 1899, for example, Haven Mason, editor of *California Municipalities,* noted that every city that receives or expends $50,000 annually should have a salaried business manager (Adrian and Press 1977). These municipal managers, he noted, should be versed in engineering, street construction, sewers, building construction, water and lighting systems, personnel, accounting, municipal law, fire protection, and library management. Other reformers made similar pleas, and in the first decade of the twentieth century, two cities—Staunton, Virginia and Sumter, South Carolina—each hired a general manager for their city. In 1911, Richard Childs, a reformer who was later to become president of the National Municipal League, drew up a model city charter for council-manager government (later adopted by a number of cities). The popularity of the council-manager plan grew rapidly, with forty-six other cities (the largest of which was Dayton, Ohio) adopting it by 1915. Today, nearly half of all cities between 10,000 and 500,000 people have adopted the plan (see table 7.2).

The fundamental assumption of the council-manager plan holds that there is no Democratic or Republican way to pave a road or fight a fire, and that politics should therefore be removed from urban administration.[7] To this end, the city council hires a professional manager to oversee all the administrative responsibilities of the city, and the manager serves at the council's pleasure (i.e., the majority of the council can vote to fire the manager at any time, with or without cause). Although the manager serves at the pleasure of the council, the council typically refrains from meddling in the administrative affairs of the city, thus removing one source of politics from urban administration. In addition, since the manager is not required to seek electoral approval for his or her actions, a second source of politics is removed. Once appointed, the manager has complete authority to hire and fire department heads, who report only to him or her. This provides the manager with the opportunity to select a management team that reflects his or her philosophy of urban administration, thus increasing the opportunity for coordination. The manager is typically paid a professional salary, quite high by public-sector standards but considerably lower than that he or she might expect to receive for comparable responsibility in the private sector.[8]

Under the council-manager plan, the council is elected by the voters, usually in the same manner as that specified for the weak-mayor plan. Here, however, council members typically do not represent geographic wards but are elected at large, usually in nonpartisan elections; in fact, both government-by-management and at-large elections are outgrowths of the urban reform movement (see chapter 5). Mayors are typically selected by the council from among its members, usually for one-year terms. (In some cities, however, the mayor may be directly elected by the voters.) The office of mayor in the council-manager plan is, like the weak mayor, largely a ceremonial position, with no formal powers. Council members typically serve on a part-time basis and receive nominal salaries.

Under the council-manager plan, the responsibilities of the council and manager are clearly delineated, although as noted later, this delineation is clearer in principle than in practice. The council has responsibility for

---

7. For a critical dissent, see Herson (1957).

8. A 1980 comparison of city managers and industrial managers with comparable responsibilities shows industrial managers to earn, on average, 29 percent higher salaries than city managers (Lubin 1981).

formulating general urban policy. For example, council members develop taxing and spending policies, deciding where new revenue is to come from and priorities for spending it. They decide whether money for capital improvements will be spent to fix sidewalks and repair bridges, or whether to allocate money for new sewage treatment plants, fire engines, and additional police officers. And they decide how to generate funds to pay for these expenditures. Will neighborhood residents be charged, in the form of special assessments, for improving the sidewalks and roads in their neighborhoods, or will this cost be borne by all residents? Will the city seek to borrow money, through general obligation bonds? Will the sales tax be raised? Will fees be instituted for various services, for instance, using parks for organized softball leagues?

A second example involves zoning. The council typically decides where industries shall be allowed to locate, and whether duplexes (or apartments), grocery stores, and laundromats will be allowed in residential neighborhoods. A third example involves regulation and the development of ordinances. Council members often must decide what kinds of signs and billboards will be allowed within the city limits. They must determine speed limits for various roads in the city. And in some controversial decisions, city councils have banned the sale of drug-related paraphernalia and have attempted to outlaw abortions.

In contrast to these rather weighty responsibilities, the city manager's responsibilities seem light. He or she is responsible for preparing an annual budget and submitting it to the council, carrying out the policies that the council has formulated (e.g., ticketing speeders and building parks), and managing the urban bureaucracy, including making personnel decisions and resolving personnel conflicts. And the city manager may be asked to provide counsel and advice to members of the city council.

But herein lies the rub. Since council members typically serve on a part-time basis, they usually lack the expertise and the time to properly evaluate policy options. More often than not, they *do* turn to the city manager for counsel and advice, affording the manager many more responsibilities (and much more power) than his or her contract would suggest. Thus, the council may ask the manager to determine whether a new sewage treatment plant is warranted, the costs and benefits of constructing a new road, the viability of a new park, or the likely impact of an additional sales tax or a restrictive billboard ordinance. In short, the policy-administration distinction becomes blurred.

Table 7.2 shows the council-manager plan to be extremely popular among cities in the 10,000-500,000 population range and not particularly popular either in smaller cities or in the largest cities. This trend stems from the assumptions underlying the plan. The city manager plan is based, in essence, on the assumption that principles of scientific management can be applied to the problems of cities more efficiently than politics can. Take the paving of a road, for example. A city manager, who is able to divorce politics from administration, is able to choose a paving company based strictly on the merits of its bid, thus maximizing the quality of the job and minimizing its cost. A mayor, forced to make the same decision, has an additional set of factors to consider (i.e., those affecting his or her reelection), and efficiency must be tempered with the politics of not offending various bidders. Or take the decision to purchase new police cars. The manager again will consider cost and performance in choosing a local dealership from which to purchase the vehicles, whereas the mayor must also consider the political clout of the various dealerships. The conclusion seems inevitable: City government will be more cost efficient under a council-manager plan than under a mayor-council plan.

But is it really? Two factors cast doubt on this conclusion, or at least suggest that political costs are measured in more than money. First, politics is a way of life in small-town America. Constituents know their elected representatives on a first-name basis, and most interaction is very informal. By and large, elected officials know little about local government, and this keeps government from becoming too powerful (cf., Vidich and Bensman 1958). A professional manager potentially represents a threat to this ideal, making the municipal bureaucracy less accessible to the city's residents. The importance of this access for small-towners is suggested by Connery (1972, 140).

> [Small-town bureaucracy] is not a faceless bureaucracy, beyond the reach of the average man. The tax collector, visiting nurse, fire marshall, dog warden, probate judge, assessors, registrars of voters, park and recreation commissioners, justices of the peace . . ., members of the Board of Education, and others— they are all friends and neighbors. Like the teachers of our children, and the doctors and preachers and everyone else of importance, they are people we see on the street, meet in the stores, sit with in church.

Small-towners also tend to believe in the principle of accountability, that those in positions of trust are responsible for their actions, and any violation of the trust placed in them will be met with defeat in the next election (or, perhaps, with recall before the next election). A professional manager is not subject to this same accountability. Further, norms in small towns stress the importance of informal relationships, and successful politicians are "just one of the boys (or girls)." In contrast, city managers are often graduates of professional degree programs, and cities must typically hire outsiders to fill city management positions. Both of these factors militate against small-town residents accepting the city manager and against their using cost efficiency as a primary principle for evaluating their government.

In large cities, too, cost efficiency may not be the single most important factor in successful government (but for a different set of reasons). For example, the decision about which construction company to hire for paving roads may not be the most important one to make. A prior decision must take into account the relative merits of paving roads or providing other services, for example, day care for the children of working single mothers or shelter for the homeless. In cities with homogeneous populations, these policy issues are less important, for residents typically have similar priorities, and city management is the most effective way (because it is efficient) to implement priorities. But where urban residents are not homogeneous, stressing efficiency circumvents the need to examine priorities carefully, and, as suggested earlier, the middle class benefits to the detriment of the underclass. Large cities, particularly those in the industrialized states, therefore, tend to shun professional management in favor of a system that encourages politics, conflicts, and the sorting out of priorities.

But what of the findings, reported in table 7.2, that nearly 50 percent of American cities in the middle population ranges have turned to the council-manager plan? This seems to suggest its enormous popularity and its apparent success. But even these figures mislead. While forty-nine of the fifty states have at least one city in this population range using the council-manager plan, most of the cities employing this plan are concentrated in nine Western and Sunbelt states.[9] Outside these nine states, the popularity of the council-manager plan drops tremendously.

Commission Plan

The commission plan was another alternative to the strong-mayor format championed by municipal reformers. Its advent was more accidental than planned. In the wake of the hurricane in 1900 that destroyed large portions of Galveston, Texas, the state legislature suspended local government in the city, substituting a temporary government of five businessmen, the Galveston Commission. The commission's actions proved successful in the short run, and the city received a new charter in 1903 making the arrangement permanent (Adrian and Press 1977).

Under the commission charter, each commissioner is elected by the public but serves the dual role of legislator and administrator. Usually commissions consist of five members, although some small cities may elect only three commissioners. Each commission position carries with it administrative

9. More than 80 percent of the cities over 10,000 in each of the following states use council-manager plans: Arizona, California, Colorado, Florida, North Carolina, Oklahoma, Oregon, Texas, and Virginia. Together, these states account for 52 percent of the cities over 10,000 using the council-manager plan (*The Municipal Yearbook,* 1988).

responsibilities for one sector of municipal government. For example, a commissioner of public safety is responsible for administration of the police and fire departments, and a commissioner of public works typically is responsible for administration of street construction and repair, water treatment, sewage disposal, and so forth. In spite of the clear differentiation among administrative responsibilities, the commission's legislative responsibilities are typically undifferentiated. While one of the commissioners is designated to chair commission meetings, his or her formal powers are similar to those of a weak mayor. Thus, the entire commission formulates policy, but individual commissioners implement policy.

At first glance, this governmental structure should be among the most effective, for it provides a great deal of democratic accountability. In the weak-mayor plan, voters have direct control over a number of administrative positions. If an elected administrator betrays the public trust, the public is able to throw the rascal out of office in the next election. The strong-mayor plan makes accountability more difficult, for the mayor is in charge of all administration, and the public may be willing to overlook some areas of poor administration for other areas of good administration. For example, citizens may be willing to trade off poor park administration for well-maintained roads. Under the council-manager plan, the administrator is further removed from the public, and administrative accountability is all but lost to the voters. But under the commission plan, administrative responsibility is once again differentiated, and administrators are directly accountable to the public. The electorate can, for example, vote "nay" on the city's police department while giving the parks department a vote of confidence.

However, as Ralph Waldo Emerson said, every credit has its debit, and with the increased accountability of the commission plan comes increased difficulty in coordination. If the division between policy and administration were valid, the commission plan might work without a hitch. But as noted in the previous discussion of the council-manager plan, this division is not realistic. And under the commission plan, the breakdown of the division of labor sometimes has unfortunate consequences. The commission as a body develops policy, which is to be faithfully administered by the individual commissioners. But since administrators themselves have such a great impact on policy development, both through their expertise and through their discretionary implementation prerogatives, the commission format often finds individual commissioners pursuing policies that are at odds with the will of the commission as a whole. This situation sometimes leads to a great deal of political infighting among commissioners, who may develop very rancorous relationships with one another. More often, however, it leads to mutual accommodation, where the various commissioners acknowledge one another's administrative prerogatives and simply agree to maintain absolute power within each one's particular niche of municipal government. The result is a jealously guarded territoriality, with all pretense of overall administrative coordination abandoned.

Although initially championed by urban reformers, the commission plan fell from favor in a relatively short time. Following the Galveston experiment, Houston adopted the commission plan in 1905, Des Moines in 1907; by 1910 it had spread to 108 cities, and to over 500 cities by 1917. At this point, however, a reversal began to take place, and today it is the least popular of the major municipal governance plans, with fewer than 5 percent of cities employing it. Two factors may account for this decline. First, the initial success of the commission plan may well have been due more to the particular commissioners than to the nature of the plan. In Galveston, the commissioners were selected by the state legislature, reducing the impact of local politics on the plan's success. Further, those particular commissioners were apparently quite zealous in their efforts, and the situation itself was extraordinary. Other early converts to the commission plan may also have been attempting to respond to extraordinary circumstances. But after fifteen years of use, the commission plan began to show its defects, and it lost its appeal for many would-be converts. Perhaps more important, the decade between 1910 and 1920 witnessed the advent of the council-manager plan, which held even more appeal for municipal reformers.

Today, the commission plan is much more prevalent in middle-sized and larger cities than in smaller cities. Further, more than half the middle-sized and larger cities (i.e., over 10,000 people) with commission plans are located in just three states: Pennsylvania, New Jersey, and Illinois. All three are industrialized, with heterogeneous populations, suggesting that the commission plan may work best in cities with greater class conflict—by giving voice and substance to that conflict.

Town Meeting Plan

The most intriguing of the various municipal government arrangements is the town meeting, and its modern counterpart, the representative town meeting. These two formats are the exclusive domain of villages, towns, and a handful of small and middle-sized cities in New England. The format can be traced directly back to the town meetings of the New England colonies, and before that, to the field meetings of farmers in medieval Germany (Adams 1882). At least once a year (with as many additional meetings as may be necessary), the entire voting population of the town gathers to vote on whatever policy issues may be pressing. In addition, the town elects a board of selectmen to carry out the enacted policies. The meetings may be supplemented by various study groups and finance committees, whose task it is to recommend policy actions in general and town budgets in particular.

This format becomes unwieldy as the population of a town grows, and in larger towns the town meeting has been replaced by the representative town meeting. In this format, as many as a hundred (or more) representatives are elected to attend and vote at the town meeting(s); while everyone may still attend, voting is limited to the representatives.

In the early colonial days, attendance at town meetings was mandatory. Today, it is not, and the colonists would, no doubt, be shocked to discover the relatively light turnout (Zimmerman 1984). In small towns (under 2,500), turnout is by modern standards rather strong, averaging over 20 percent. But in larger towns (5,000–10,000), turnout drops to under 10 percent, with small cities (15,000–20,000) showing an even further decline to under 5 percent. Thus it may be that direct democracy has been replaced by "special interest" democracy, with town meetings dominated by a relatively small core of individuals with a particular interest in the current agenda. The *National Civic Review* (1965, 522) notes that the open town meeting "still lingers on as an instrument of control by small groups of self-seekers and without participation by 90 percent of eligible voters." And the Committee for Economic Development (1966, 30) argues that the open town meeting "met the needs of simpler times, but it was not designed to handle the complex modern problems confronting rapidly growing areas."

Appearances may be deceiving, however. James Bryce (1889, 591), who condemned cities as the one conspicuous failure of democracy, had a special place in his heart for the town meeting. He observed that it has been "not only the source but the school of democracy." Observers note that the quality of debate is usually good, and sometimes excellent, at the meetings (Zimmerman 1984). This debate is likely to bring conflict out into the open, where it can be constructive (e.g., Coser 1956) rather than suppress it, where it may well turn rancorous (e.g., Coleman 1957). Debate in town meetings also tends to limit the speed with which policy change occurs, as does the entire format of government by town meeting: With only periodic meetings, nothing can be accomplished very quickly. But this very deliberateness seems to fit the New England character. And if the Committee for Economic Development criticizes the format, that is probably all right with many small-town New Englanders too, for they are unwilling to see their villages and towns undergo major change (cf., Connery 1972).

Norm Versus Form: A Comparison of Adherence to Democratic Norms

At this point, a comparison of the major structural formats of urban government is in order. Our point of reference is the previous chapter's discussion of democratic norms, and we will focus on the governing style of each of the major forms of urban government and the extent to which each is likely to fulfill democratic norms and expectations.

Majority Rule

In discussing majority rule, we are concerned with the *distance* between the *citizen* and *public policy decisions*. In general, when this distance is small, as in the case of direct democracy, the *potential* for majority rule is maximized. On the other hand, when the citizen is separated from policy decisions by one or more buffers, which may or may not be accountable to the public, the potential for majority rule suffers. In this discussion, we consider the potential for majority rule rather than majority rule itself. Until cities achieve 100 percent voter registration and turnout, majority rule is merely an ideal rather than a reality. But with increasing citizen participation comes the opportunity for the majority of citizens to decide public policy issues.

The town meeting format (and its offspring, the representative town meeting format) offers the greatest potential for majority rule: Every adult has the opportunity to vote on community issues at the annual town meeting, giving citizens direct control over public policy. Next in order is the weak-mayor plan, particularly in those situations where a number of bureaucratic positions are up for election. In both the town meeting plan and the weak-mayor plan, political power tends to be diffused among a number of elected officials, and in this situation, there exists a greater potential for the public, particularly an activist public, to contribute to the political agenda. The commission plan follows next in descending order: Although power is diffused among elected officials, their administrative resources provide them with considerable insulation against public demands. Next comes the strong-mayor plan, where power is concentrated in the hands of the mayor. While this does not rule out the possibility of citizen input, it minimizes the impact of citizens because they have to work through individual council members. As the number of conduits for citizen inputs decreases, the impact of the citizenry on policy issues also decreases. Even so, the strong mayor is an elected official, which gives this format the nod over the council-manager format. Under the latter plan, power is not only concentrated, but concentrated in the hands of a nonelected official, and the public is twice removed from policy decisions.

But the distance between the public and policy decisions is not the only criterion by which we should evaluate majority rule. In addition, the conflict between public and private sources of power differs under each of the formats, with somewhat different implications for the norm of majority rule. When public power is diffused—as in the case of the town-meeting or the weak-mayor format—a power vacuum may invite private interest, including business owners, land developers, or neighborhood leaders, to take policy initiatives. While it provides the opportunity for citizens to become involved in the policy process, this kind of private power is typically less responsive to citizen input than is publicly-held power, and the opportunity for majority rule is accordingly diminished. Power is somewhat more concentrated in the strong-mayor and commission formats, allowing less opportunity for private interests to gain power in the city. This linear trend breaks down in the case of the council-manager plan, however. Although power is concentrated in the hands of the city manager, the strong business orientation of the plan lends considerable power to various business interests in the community. They, in effect, typically have the ear of the manager, and thus they have considerable say in the resolution of public policy issues. So, in this case, public access to policy decisions is twice buffered, and the potential for majority rule is severely constrained.

Protection of Minority Rights

We might initially expect that the concentration of power would prove the greatest threat to the protection of minority rights, and in many cases this is so. As Lord Acton said, power corrupts, and absolute power corrupts absolutely. Yet, a number of studies in this country show that the exact opposite effect is likely to occur: When power is concentrated in the hands of a political leader (or a set of political leaders), minority rights are more likely to be protected than when power is diffused and lies in the hands of the masses. For example, Thomas Dye and Harmon Zeigler (1975) note this *irony of democracy* in the following paradox. Political elites, as carriers of the political culture, tend to better represent the democratic norm of tolerance than do the masses. Thus, governance-by-the-elite is more likely to lead to tolerance in government and the protection of minority rights than government-by-the-masses; but in opting for the former over the latter, the norm of majority rule is, by definition, abridged. In contrast, majority rule is likely to sacrifice minority rights. By way of illustration, Lawrence Herson and Richard Hofstetter (1975) show that people with the greatest political tolerance tend to have higher incomes, to be better educated, professional, and politically active—exactly those who are most likely to hold municipal office.

This leads us to expect, then, that minority rights may be least well protected in the town-meeting and weak-mayor formats (since popular participation is more prevalent), and better protected in the strong-mayor and commission formats (since power is concentrated in the hands of the elite). But this is no simple (nor simply sketched) expectation. Much depends on the definition given to minority rights and on the specific minority being protected. If the minority in question is racial or ethnic, it will likely be best protected in strong mayor governments (especially when combined with council election by wards) and in commission governments. These offer minority voters direct electoral access to their urban governors. If the minority is defined as the economic underclass, it may be served least well by the council-manager format, for the strong emphasis on efficiency leads to policies that tend to favor the upper and middle classes and discriminate against the underclass. If, however, the minority is more transient (e.g., those who espouse an unpopular cause), different forces come into play. More than a century and a half ago, Alexis de Tocqueville expressed his fear that Americans are too much given to the tyranny of public opinion. Our desire to conform leads us to become intolerant of dissent and minority opinion. This seems especially dangerous in public meetings. Even though dissenters may have a legal right to speak their minds, they may find it difficult to speak up when the speech affronts the general sentiments of the community.

Participation

The earlier discussion of the town-meeting format suggests that it may not be particularly conducive to political participation, with attendance at meetings typically falling under 10 percent. Other studies suggest that reformed municipal governments, in their various incarnations (e.g., council-manager format, at-large elections, nonpartisan elections) have significantly lower voter turnout in municipal elections than their unreformed counterparts (Alford and Lee 1968).[10] These two findings are in fact consistent, for New England town meetings are traditionally nonpartisan. We should conclude, then, that mayor-council cities have the greatest potential for participation, followed by cities with commission formats (which typically are nonpartisan and always at-large), town meeting formats, and council-manager formats.

But, in addition to electoral participation, we must also consider other forms of political participation, including participation in neighborhood councils, local schools, protest groups, and so forth. And in considering this participation, we must also distinguish between *reactive* and *proactive* participation: The former involves participation in response to some perceived need or threat (e.g., a protest in response to a city council decision to locate a low-cost public housing unit in *my* neighborhood, or to zone *my* neighborhood for duplexes and apartment buildings), whereas the latter represents continuing participation intended to better living conditions in the community (e.g., a neighborhood association sponsoring neighborhood cleanups, or the League of Women Voters sponsoring a public forum about recycling). In general, reactive participation may be dysfunctional (not likely to serve the public good), leading to what Theodore Lowi (1969a) terms hyperpluralism, Douglas Yates (1977) terms street-fighting pluralism, and the popular press terms single-issue politics. Whatever its label, reactive participation leads to fragmented policies in which the con-

10. For further discussion of the Alford and Lee findings, see chapter 8.

text of issues is not sufficiently addressed. Issues are treated in isolation, without regard to how they impinge on other issues and with little concern for their long-term consequences.

In contrast, Bolland (1985b) shows that general political participation, particularly when it is accompanied by some sense of responsibility, leads to a better understanding of the interrelationships among various community issues. This sense of responsibility is typically associated with proactive participation, often born out of a sense of civic responsibility. Proactive participation is thus likely to lead to integrated and coordinated public policies and fewer contradictions in public programs.

But are the various governmental formats likely to differ in their degree of proactive versus reactive participation? Logic suggests that they are, although the evidence is only indirect. Strong political parties tend to take positions on most political issues (contrary to the views of the reformers, they believe that there *is* a Democratic and a Republican way to pave a street). Further, local parties provide both an ongoing organization and a number of offices—ranging from county chairman to precinct committeeman or committeewoman—for interested and loyal party members. Finally, parties have a political agenda that may supersede their reaction to specific events. These three factors, taken together, suggest that partisan governments provide a core of political participants who follow politics across issues, helping to ensure an appreciation for the contextual quality of urban politics. In a strong partisan system, this can militate against the tendency for special interests to form around specific issues. But in nonpartisan systems, this tendency toward single-issue politics is unchecked, and political activism tends to be overly responsive to events. We arrive, therefore, at a speculative conclusion that mirrors our conclusion about electoral participation: Proactive participation is most likely under the mayor-council format, while reactive participation is most likely under the town-meeting, commission, and council-manager formats.

Peaceful Management of Conflict

As noted earlier, mayor-council formats are most common in heterogeneous, industrialized areas whereas council-manager formats are more common in the homogeneous suburbs. This provides an initial indication of the conflictual orientation of the various formats. The mayor-council format provides the greatest opportunity for input from diverse community groups and interests, and this diversity of demands creates the opportunity for open conflict about policy priorities. Particularly in cities with strong mayors, the mayor can often perform a cathartic function, drawing out concerns and policy demands from different groups within the city. In the council-manager format, in contrast, policy priorities are assumed a priori to be the efficient

114

provision of municipal services (e.g., police and fire protection, garbage collection, street maintenance, traffic control).[11]

Thus, the conflictual orientation of the various municipal formats ties into the characteristics of the populations they serve: Heterogeneity leads to an overtly political format which in turn invites conflict, while homogeneity leads to a managerial format which in turn discourages conflict. But what happens when a mayor-council format is adopted in a homogeneous city, or when a council-manager format is adopted in a heterogeneous city? In the former case, conflict emerges around the edges of public policy issues (e.g., how many days to collect garbage each week, or priorities for snow removal routes), but by the very nature of the issues, the conflict is unlikely to become rancorous. In contrast, conflict over policy priorities in the latter case is suppressed, but not eliminated. Such conflict may fester until it reaches crisis proportions, at which time it may erupt as a breakdown in public confidence. In this situation, suppressed rancor may be unleashed, and it will take the city some time to recover. The conflictual orientation of the other municipal formats is less clear, although it seems likely that conflict may be encouraged by town meetings and commissions. As suggested above, however, this may help defuse truly rancorous conflict that might otherwise fester in the community.

Widespread Distribution of Benefits

In their classic study, Robert Lineberry and Edmund Fowler (1967) report a higher correlation between a city's demographic characteristics and its expenditure patterns in unreformed cities than in reformed cities. They argue that this demonstrates a greater responsiveness to citizen inputs in unreformed cities, from which we should conclude that participants are more likely to be rewarded for their participation in unreformed cities. This may be due to the greater electoral accountability on the part of policymakers in unreformed cities: By making sure that nobody goes home emptyhanded, elected officials are investing in their own political future. It may be that the norms of efficiency and political evenhandedness stressed in reformed cities precludes politically motivated gifts to political participants. Or it may be that in big cities, which tend to favor unreformed governmental structures, the sheer number of interest groups may create a climate of compromise that facilitates the disbursement of benefits to all participants. The truth probably embodies some combination of all three explanations.

---

11. Even the buildings in which various cities conduct their business suggest their conflictual orientation. City hall in mayor-council cities is typically an older structure built in a Greek or Roman architectural style; It conjures memories of argument and conflict. In contrast, city hall in many reformed cities is a newer building, constructed in the style of a modern office building or public school; one gets the feeling that voices should be hushed, conflict should be muffled, and disagreement quietly negotiated.

The commission format is more similar to the mayor–council format than to the council–manager format in its responsiveness to citizen input. Not only is the governing body highly political, but administration is also politicized (administrators, as commission members, are after all elected), and citizen demands are likely to be felt by both elected officials and administrators. In the town meeting format, participants are not likely to receive tangible rewards for their participation. But, on the other hand, the rewards for being able to vote directly on policy issues are psychological, and those who attend town meetings must surely leave with a sense of accomplishment and civic pride.

Formal Participants and Their Political Roles

We turn now to an examination of the formal political participants in the urban arena: members of the governing body, the mayor, the city manager, members of the municipal bureaucracy, municipal judges, and appointees to municipal boards and commissions.

The Governing Body

Who are the people who run for positions on a city council?[12] For the most part, the pay for council members is low: 1984 salaries for part-time council members averaged less than $3,500 across the United States (*Municipal Yearbook* 1985). Council members therefore are not people who are in politics to get rich. In fact, salaries are kept at a nominal level to discourage those interested primarily in gaining wealth from running for office. Rather, prestige and honor become the primary motivators for those seeking city council positions (e.g., Adrian and Press 1977), although other, less lofty motives are also present. For example, one successful candidate (of the authors' acquaintance) used his position as a way to meet people while drinking at local bars. Another ran for office to achieve a favorable zoning decision for his business interests. And still others use their positions to gain favors for their friends and neighbors in the community. In general, however, most people serve on a city council out of a sense of civic responsibility, and their primary reward comes in the form of honor and prestige.

The nature of this reward has important implications for the kind of person who is likely to seek municipal office. Because of the modest financial remuneration and the time required to do a good job (more about this later), only those in positions of some financial independence, or at least considerable occupational flexibility, are able to seek public office at the local level.

12. Whereas seats on the city council are typically part-time positions that do not pay well, seats on the city commission are full-time, well-paid positions, and commissioners resemble strong mayors more than they do city council members.

116

This includes, for example, attorneys, who have both sufficient income so that they can spend time away from the office and flexibility so that they are not penalized for doing so. Much the same can be said for a physician, a banker, a developer, or indeed, anyone who owns his or her own business. But note, however, that it may effectively preclude school teachers, nurses, secretaries, many salespersons, and others who either cannot financially afford to take time off from their jobs or who do not have flexibility in their work schedules to take time off. This conclusion is consistent with several studies of city council members. Charles Adrian and Charles Press (1977) report that most council members are moderately successful businessmen who are financially prosperous and relatively well educated. Particularly in smaller cities, these persons tend to be members of the community elite. A study of communities in Los Angeles County (Huckshorn and Young 1960) shows the typical council member to be forty-nine years old and male (only 6.7 percent were females).

The nature of the city council position is further demonstrated by council members' attitudes about public service. A study of Kansas cities shows that two-thirds of city council members had never held other positions in government or in their political party and that they disliked campaigning (Stauber and Kline 1965). For them, apparently, the reward was in the public service itself rather than in the associated politics. In addition, a study of San Francisco Bay area communities shows that most (71 percent) council members had no further political aspirations, and that the majority (62 percent) would give up their seats if their regular jobs demanded that they do so. They view public service as a civic responsibility, not as a means to further (and grander) political position. And for them, civic responsibility takes a back seat to their primary responsibilities to their careers (Prewitt and Nowlin 1969).

For the majority of council members who serve out of a sense of civic responsibility, the job can be very frustrating and tiring; perhaps this is why relatively few council members serve multiple terms. Consider the practical problems facing a city council member. Typically, he or she may be asked to run for the council position by members of a civic organization, a political party, a neighborhood association, or some other politically involved group (using the broad definition of *politics* developed in chapter 6). But after the initial flattery comes the hard work of campaigning, in which otherwise private people must bare their lives to the community. And with this inevitably come cheap shots taken by other candidates or interests, accusing the candidate of being unqualified, of representing special interests, of empire building. For the candidate who becomes politically involved at someone else's invitation and sees a council seat as a way of fulfilling civic responsibility, such accusations can be quite hurtful.

Now, assume that the candidate is lucky enough to be elected. What awaits him or her? Some cities have a half-day orientation for new council members, in which they are shown the ropes of public office. Others have a two-hour orientation, and some have no orientation at all. Yet, new council members are expected to attend their first council meeting and participate in a responsible manner. They are expected, for example, to understand the workings of the urban bureaucracy, to know where to seek information, to understand community issues and their broad implications, to understand the community itself, and to know where public opinion falls on various issues. These would be Herculean tasks for even the most seasoned council members, and they are beyond the grasp of most newly elected members.

But, city councils are in the business of making decisions, and members are required to vote on issues whether or not they understand the full complexity of the issues. And when these decisions turn out to be incorrect, or when a council decision runs contrary to some community interest, criticism results. Adrian and Press (1977) conclude that one of the most difficult aspects of service on a city council is adjusting to criticism. Again, imagine a small business owner who is encouraged to seek a council position and does so out of a sense of civic responsibility. When he or she is then openly criticized in the press for incompetence, or for naiveté, or even for voting incorrectly on an issue, he or she must begin to question whether election was worth the effort. That, coupled with the evening calls about barking dogs or garbage collection, and ten (or more) hours each week devoted to city business, leads many city council members to call it quits after their first term in office.

One of the most dramatic changes in the political landscape during the past two decades is the electoral success of minorities seeking city council positions. In 1970, 623 blacks held elective municipal offices; by 1985, this number had increased to 2,898 (Williams 1987). At least part of this increase is due to increased voter registration among blacks in the wake of the 1965 Voting Rights Act (for more on minority voting patterns and electoral coalitions, see chapter 8). But it is also due to intervention by the courts, pursuant to the Voting Rights Act, requiring that blacks be provided equal representation on city councils. In a number of cities, the courts found that blacks occupied far fewer council seats than their voting strength should command. To remedy this situation, they implemented two different solutions. First, in a number of cities where council members were elected by district, the courts ordered redistricting. Second, in other cities where council members were elected at-large, the courts ordered a change to election-by-district (see Renner 1988).[13]

In their discussion of political equality, Rufus Browning, Dale Rogers Marshall, and David Tabb (1984) argue that minority election to council positions is an important component of *political incorporation* (i.e., becoming an effective

---

13. This represents one of the clearest challenges to the ideals of the reform movement, and it implicitly holds that by taking politics out of municipal government, the reformers may have infringed on the rights of the minority. Or, put differently, the courts seem to have taken the position that politics may provide the best avenue for minorities to achieve equal status in our society.

part of the political process), which is, in turn, a necessary and sufficient condition for equality. According to the figures cited above, blacks (and other minorities) have come a long way toward the ideal of incorporation. Another component of incorporation is the election of minority mayors; it, too, is an area where much has been achieved over the past two decades. These changes are elaborated in the next section. But first, we turn to a general discussion of the mayor's role in the urban system.

The Mayor

In weak-mayor and most council-manager cities, the mayor is just another council member who serves on a part-time basis with few extra powers or perquisites. But in strong-mayor cities, the mayor has considerable power. This section discusses the role of strong mayor.

Because the position of mayor is more powerful than that of council member, it tends to attract a different type of person. First, the strong-mayor position is typically full time, and with a full-time position goes a much higher salary. Even in small cities, mayors receive a quite respectable salary, and in large cities their salaries rival the pay found at most levels of political office. For instance, the mayor's annual salary in the five American cities with over one million people averages about $70,000 (*Municipal Yearbook,* 1985).

Second, a full-time mayoral position literally requires its holder to give up his or her regular employment, and it is very easy for the mayor to consider becoming a "professional" politician. The strong mayor may thus seek subsequent terms as mayor once his or her current term has expired. And some mayors will use their records and name recognition to seek higher office, for instance, a position in the state senate or house of representatives, the governorship, or even federal office. In two recent cases, incumbent mayors unsuccessfully tried to parlay their positions into governorships (Tom Bradley of Los Angeles and Ed Koch of New York). Other big-city mayors have been more successful in their quest for higher office (e.g., Hubert Humphrey of Minneapolis, Pete Wilson of San Diego, who became a U.S. senator from California, and Richard Lugar of Indianapolis, who became a U.S. senator from Indiana). In this regard, Cleveland serves as a textbook example, with six mayors moving to positions of national political prominence during this century alone (Adrian and Press 1977). The actual success of mayors in seeking higher office is not the important point, however—in fact, *most mayors do not go onto higher office.*[14] But nonetheless, the perception remains that this

14. The mayor's office was once a springboard to higher office, but for today's big-city mayors the office is mostly a dead-end political job. The reason? Reputations slide as the mayor finds himself or herself unable to satisfy all the demands made upon the office, as the city finds itself overmatched and overcome by the problems that confront it, and as hyperpluralism holds sway (see chapter 8).

is a possible launching point for a political career, and no doubt a number of people have sought the mayorship with exactly this in mind.

Third, the very fact that the strong-mayorship is a full-time position means that it attracts a different kind of person than does a part-time city council position. Because of its greater pay, its greater prestige, and its potential for political advancement, the competition for the mayorship is fiercer than that for council seats. As a result, mayors tend to be somewhat older than their council counterparts, somewhat more successful professionally, and somewhat more visible in the community. They also tend to be self-employed, either as small business owners or as professionals with practices they can return to at some later time (e.g., lawyers, physicians). People in middle-level management positions would take a great risk were they to resign to become mayor, for their jobs may not be waiting for them when their term expires. In general, while civic responsibility is perhaps the primary motivation underlying the seeking of a part-time council position, it is not alone sufficient for seeking the mayorship.

Perhaps the biggest difference between the strong mayor and city council positions is the greater power incumbent in the former. The strong mayor, with power to appoint upper-level administrators, has greater access to information and bureaucratic support than do members of the governing body. By the same token, the mayor is the most visible person in the city. As Adrian and Press (1977) note, the mayor is expected to crown beauty queens, greet conventions, introduce presidents, dedicate parks, lay cornerstones, open baseball seasons, lead parades, launch charity drives, and cut ribbons. The mayor thus becomes the symbol for the entire city. And while these activities lack political substance (and often become tiresome for the mayor), they do afford the mayor with almost instant name recognition among the citizenry. In turn, this visibility provides him or her with easy access to the news media and, consequently, with a greater ability to publicize his or her own political agenda for the city than is afforded to council members. Yet, the power of the office does not guarantee that individual mayors will be uniformly powerful in setting urban policy. Differences in mayoral power typically stem from two sources: the mayor's resources and his or her mayoral style.

Mayoral resources. Jeffrey Pressman (1972) identifies a number of resources necessary for mayoral effectiveness. He notes, for example, that the mayor's office must have sufficient financial and staff resources for the mayor to plan for rather than merely react to unexpected situations (recall the previous comparison between proactive and reactive participation). Along the same lines, the mayor's office must be a full-time position, freeing the mayor from other occupational responsibilities. Pressman also notes that the city, and particularly the mayor's office, must have jurisdiction over various social programs in the city (e.g., housing, job training). Even a mayor with considerable financial

120

and staff resources will have little effective power if the city's low-cost housing program is under control of the court or if federal job-training money is available only with a variety of strings attached. In addition, an effective mayor must have access to a friendly local media willing to give front-page or prime-time coverage to his or her political agenda. Finally, Pressman notes that mayoral initiatives must be undertaken in an atmosphere of political support to be successful. Specifically, he observes that the mayor must be able to mobilize political organizations (e.g., his or her political party) if he or she expects policy initiatives to get off the ground.

This conclusion is perhaps Pressman's most important, and it has two significant implications. First, it suggests the importance of *political networks* through which ideas and information flow and ultimately through which power is transmitted. (See chapter 9, "Interpersonal Power.") These networks are necessary to mobilize support around public policy proposals, and in accordance with Pressman's suggestion, the mayor must be at the center of the city's political network to mobilize sufficient support to ensure success. Second, Pressman implies that political parties are important in these networks and that a mayor who is also a party leader is more likely to be successful than one who is not. Mayors in nonpartisan cities are unlikely to hold important party positions, and by implication, they are less likely to be successful than their counterparts in partisan cities. And mayors who run as mavericks, without party support, are likely to enjoy a miserable tenure in office. Note, again, the difficulties of Mayor Washington in Chicago.

Mayoral style. John Kotter and Paul Lawrence (1974) expand this view of political networks in their discussion of mayoral style. They note that mayors set the political agenda in their cities, but that in order to call proposals off the agenda and turn them into public policies, they must mobilize their political resources by building, maintaining, and using political networks. Richard Lee, the former mayor of New Haven, was a master at mobilizing political networks. Robert Dahl (1961, 204) describes him in the following terms:

> The mayor was not at the peak of a pyramid but rather at the center of intersecting circles. He rarely commanded. He negotiated, cajoled, exhorted, beguiled, charmed, praised, appealed, reasoned, promised, insisted, demanded, even threatened, but he most needed support and acquiescence from other leaders who simply could not be commanded. Because the mayor could not command, he had to bargain.

A mayor's willingness to work within existing networks or attempt to expand these networks reflects his or her mayoral style. At one extreme, Kotter and Lawrence identify the *ceremonial mayor,* who tends to focus on personal appeals to existing networks in the city. He or she feels comfortable in the role of ribbon cutter and parade leader and feels little need to initiate long-term policies or programs. When problems arise in the city, the ceremonial mayor reacts (or more frequently, instructs the urban bureaucracy to react). Existing political networks are thus probably sufficient for the ceremonial mayor's purposes. To the extent that existing networks reflect the ideas and priorities of those who built them, the ceremonial mayor is likely to follow the agenda of his or her predecessors. At the other extreme lies the *entrepreneurial mayor,* who has a distinct set of policy goals for the city and attempts to expand existing networks in order to maximize the potential for bringing these goals to fruition. This mayor, like Mayor Lee of New Haven, brings people together in an attempt to get them to share ideas. If they initially seem unwilling to do so, he or she cajoles them, or charms them, or threatens them into cooperating. In the case of New Haven, Mayor Lee effectively operated through a network of interests, including members of the urban bureaucracy, federal agencies, the city council, the business community, the Democratic party, and Yale University, to create support for one of the largest and most successful urban renewal projects during the 1950s (see chapter 11). By building political networks and paying constant attention to their maintenance, the entrepreneurial mayor is likely to be successful in his or her policy initiatives.

Some observers, however, have concluded that the days of the entre-preneurial mayor may have come and gone. Yates (1977) argues, for example, that declining resources have created greater fragmentation among urban interests, requiring the mayor more often to play the role of broker rather than entrepreneur. In such a role, he or she serves as a bridge between competing community interests that have no desire to communicate directly and work with one another. And while the mayor may still be at the center of the political network, his or her role as a bridge is very different from that of a hub. Consider the two hypothetical networks depicted in figure 7.1. In the structurally-integrated network, where the mayor serves as hub, ideas can move between network members with great ease. No member is far removed from any other member; and since the links in the network reflect lines of open communication through which ideas are exchanged, consensus is likely to develop rapidly. In contrast, the structurally fragmented network reflects a situation where the mayor plays the role of broker, or bridge, among different interests in the community. In this situation, no interest has a direct link with another, and all exchange of ideas must go through the mayor. Each interest is at least twice removed from the others, and the possibility for consensus is noticeably weakened. In addition, the mayor is placed in a very precarious situation. He or she must retain absolute neutrality among the various interests or risk becoming disconnected from those coalitions receiving nonpreferential treat-ment. Were this to occur, the community would become completely fragmented, with virtually no possibility for comprehensive, long-term

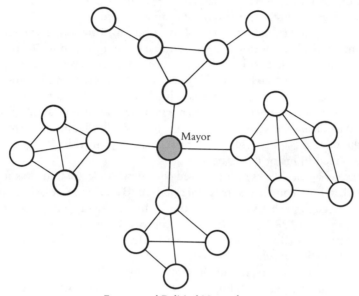

Fragmented Political Network

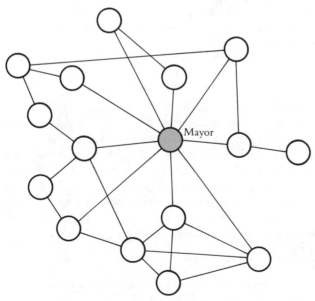

Integrated Political Network

FIGURE 7.1: The Role of the Mayor in Two Community Political Networks

planning and policy development. When complete fragmentation does occur, the role of the mayor reverts to one of *caretaker,* simply performing necessary urban services until the next administration is elected.

Declining urban budgets also may contribute to changing mayoral style. When the mayor has control over discretionary funds, which he or she can dole out as rewards, network-building efforts are likely to be more effective than in the absence of such funds. Cajoling people with diverse interests to sit down together and exchange ideas is likely to be much more successful when they can be tangibly rewarded than when they can be only symbolically rewarded. A business owner, for example, is more likely to support the mayor when the reward is a new sidewalk or parking lot than when it is a plaque being installed in his or her honor.

In recent years blacks have achieved considerable electoral success at the local level, in both council and mayoral elections. By 1985, 286 black mayors had been elected, in sharp contrast to the 48 black mayors who held office in 1970 (Williams 1987). Most (55.7 percent) black mayoral successes came in small (usually Southern) towns of under 5,000. However, blacks have also held the mayorship in twenty-seven cities with over 50,000 people, including five of the six largest cities: David Dinkins in New York, Harold Washington (and his interim replacement, Eugene Sawyer) in Chicago, Thomas Bradley in Los Angeles, W. Wilson Goode in Philadelphia, and Coleman Young in Detroit.[15] As noted earlier, this represents a component of political incorporation (Browning, et al. 1984), one potentially capable of creating political equality among the races. We will explore the impact of incorporation more fully in the next chapter.

The City Manager

A tough row to hoe. As noted in table 7.2, well over two thousand cities in the United States employ city managers, making this a sizeable professional fraternity. Several universities (e.g., the University of Kansas) have graduate programs designed explicitly to train city managers. City managers have created a professional organization—the International City Management Association (ICMA)—and meet annually under its auspices. They also have adopted a code of ethics. City management has become institutionalized into the American urban system. And in contrast to mayors and council members, city managers are professionally organized, with goals and an agenda orches-

15. Blacks have been elected as mayor of a number of other major cities, including Marion Barry in Washington, D.C., Richard Hatcher in Gary, Kenneth Gibson in Newark, Andrew Young in Atlanta, Ernest Morial in New Orleans, Richard Arrington in Birmingham, and Carl Stokes in Cleveland. For discussions of black mayors, see Preston (1987), Nelson (1987), Perry and Stokes (1987), Rich (1987) Ransom (1987), and Eisinger (1984).

trated largely through ICMA. Strong ties among managers are formed during school days, and some universities maintain an active alumni association of their city management trainees. The typical manager's career may take him or her to half-a-dozen (or more) cities, first as an intern, then as an analyst, then as an assistant city manager, and finally as a manager. During these experiences, more strong connections develop. So the annual meeting of ICMA represents an opportunity for old friends to get together. More than most professional organizations, ICMA serves as a strong support group for its members.

To understand city management, we must first understand the motives for embarking on a city manager career. The typical city manager has an undergraduate degree in the social sciences, and many now have graduate degrees either in public or business administration. This contrasts with a previous era, when most managers had an engineering background. Thus, most city managers are social scientists who believe that the best way to solve a problem is to work with the people involved, rather than engineers who approach problem solving from a more rigorous, technical perspective. Most city managers get their first taste of urban politics as undergraduates, perhaps as summer interns or through a course in urban politics or urban sociology. And this experience makes them aware of the challenges of urban government, so that most of those entering graduate programs to receive formal training in urban administration do so with a commitment to the importance of the public sector in contemporary urban America. For them, city management is not so much an occupation as a calling.

For most city managers, however, idealism is combined with a certain degree of naiveté, and they soon discover that their calling moves them along a rather bumpy road. Adrian and Press (1977) found, for example, that the average tenure for city managers was three years in Florida, six years in Illinois. In a more recent study, Green and Reed (1988) report that two-thirds of all city managers have been in their current positions for five years or less. While many city managers have a short tenure due to upward mobility (e.g., moving to a larger city), many others are fired by the city council. Thus, over a thirty-year career, many city managers may be fired several times. It takes a special type of person to be willing to jump back into the saddle after falling off (or being booted off) the horse once, let alone repeatedly.[16] It should become clear, now, what kind of support the ICMA provides for its members. It provides emotional support for people who have been fired. It provides them with job leads. And it lobbies for severance pay for

16. This uncertainty no doubt contributes to a considerable level of occupational stress among city managers. For a further discussion of the problem, see Green and Reed (1988).

city manager positions, so that in the case of termination, the manager may be provided with up to six months of salary.

Sources of Uncertainty. Why is the city manager's path so rough and fraught with uncertainty? Four major factors lead to job insecurity. First, the training and experience most managers receive are not commensurate with the demands of their positions. Second, the city manager serves at the pleasure of the governing body, and he or she is often forced to take the blame for its failures. Third, the city manager is often forced to take sides on policy issues, and he or she can get caught in the middle of policy conflicts. Finally, the city manager has a view of his or her responsibilities that differs from that of the governing body, often leading to friction and an eventual parting of the ways.

First, consider the responsibilities of a city manager. The National Municipal League's *Model City Charter* (1964) specifies the following duties:

1. Oversee the enforcement of all municipal ordinances.
2. Appoint, supervise, evaluate, and fire municipal department heads.
3. Prepare and submit the municipal budget.
4. Keep the city council advised on financial matters.
5. Keep the city council and public informed about matters concerning the city's operation.
6. Prepare and submit reports and memoranda to the city council as requested.
7. Make recommendations to the city council on matters that are deemed desirable.
8. Perform such duties as the city council assigns.

When we consider that even small cities have sizeable operating budgets and a large number of employees, we can understand the types of demands placed on the city manager. Consider, for example, a city like Upper Arlington, Ohio, with 11,000 residents. The city manager is responsible for administering an annual budget of nearly $10 million and supervising (directly or indirectly) over two hundred employees. Obviously, as a city's population increases, its manager has increasingly greater responsibility. As city size moves beyond 50,000, the typical city manager oversees a $30 million budget and is responsible for nearly four hundred municipal employees. And in the truly large cities—Phoenix, Miami, Kansas City, Rochester, Dallas—the city manager must oversee an annual budget in excess of $200 million, and he or she is responsible for over two thousand employees.

The responsibilities of a city manager are no fewer or less important than those of a chief executive officer of one of America's second-level corporations. Yet, city managers tend to have less experience than most CEOs. The typical city manager is in his or her early forties, although some are still in their mid-twenties. In addition, most city managers are hired from outside, so they have no experience with the city, its problems, and its politics. Finally, their lack of experience is not compensated for by their professional education. Many graduate programs in public administration are, in effect, only one year long, and they frequently employ a curriculum lacking in analytic rigor. The typical graduate of these programs emerges well-steeped in professional orientation but has few of the analytic skills required to be a successful city manager. To make matters worse, the salaries of city managers are well below those of their counterparts in the business world. Even in the largest cities, managers' salaries average only $87,000 (the manager's salary in Dallas is $95,000), and in the smaller cities they are substantially lower. The mean salary in cities between 50,000 and 100,000 is $56,000, and this drops to only $24,000 in cities with fewer than 2,500 people. The disparity between managerial salaries in the private and public sectors (see note 8) means that many of the more gifted city managers eventually will opt for the private sector. A case in point is Robert Kipp, the very successful city manager of Kansas City who resigned that position in 1983 to become president of the Crown Center Redevelopment Corporation. In short, then, people with fewer than fifteen years' experience in management and often with no experience in the local community are asked to administer sizeable annual budgets, supervise a small army of personnel, and offer sound counsel to the city council, all for comparatively little financial compensation. Our surprise should not be at a high rate of failure, but that so many city managers do so well.

A second factor that accounts for the high rate of turnover among city managers is their ready availability for blame in policy failures. This is not to suggest that the personalities of city managers are somehow aberrant, but rather that their governmental role itself invites criticism. A careful examination of the list of a city manager's responsibilities reveals that considerable formal power is invested in the office. He or she, after all, is responsible for implementing all of the council's decisions, for preparing the budget, for keeping the council abreast of community affairs, for advising the council on policy matters. With this responsibility, it is impossible for the manager to remain neutral on policy issues, and he or she is often asked to express preferences and policy recommendations to the council. Edward Banfield and James Q. Wilson (1963) observe that this expression of preference is very useful for the council. If a proposed policy is adopted and proves successful, the council can take the credit; after all, it had the ultimate responsibility for approving the measure. But what if the policy is controversial? Banfield and Wilson (quoting Kammerer 1961) suggest that if the boat must be rocked, council members want the public to think that the city manager's hand is at the tiller. And if the policy proves unsuccessful, council members can blame failure on bad advice and faulty information from the manager. In this situation, even if the manager is blameless, he or she may be sacrificed if the council is to maintain its public facade of innocence.

A third factor is the conflict that inevitably arises among proponents of the different sides of policy debate. Again, consider the responsibility of the city manager's position and how it forces him or her to take policy positions. No immediate problems arise so long as council members are in substantial agreement with one another. But when the council is divided, the manager's position becomes precarious. If the factions on the council are equally strong, an active—and according to Banfield and Wilson (1963), a smart—manager will play them off against each other. Such a strategy is not without perils, however, and sooner or later the manager likely will be accused of manipulation and come under fire. As an alternative strategy, the manager may remain inactive, simply performing his or her responsibilities without interjecting personal policy preferences into the process. But such a strategy is untenable in the long run, for each faction is likely to invoke the adage, "If you're not with me, you're against me."

When the council is divided but the balance of power lies with a stable majority, the smart manager obviously will side with the majority. As one city manager explained to the authors, he needs only to be able to count a majority of council votes supporting him to retain his job. In the short run, the manager who finds himself or herself in this position is likely to emerge as a strong leader in the community, able to pursue policy initiatives with the blessing of the council (or at least the blessing of its majority). But by openly playing to the majority faction, in terms both of policy preferences and willingness to dig out requested information, the manager alienates the minority faction. And given even a slight change in council composition, the manager may find his or her position in jeopardy. In other words, conflict is antithetical to happy management. This may help explain why most cities that have opted for the council-manager plan are homogeneous and have relatively few openly conflictual issues.

The fourth factor that accounts for the high turnover rate among city managers is the philosophical difference in orientation between the manager and council members. Despite the requirement that managers take policy positions in their reports and make recommendations to the council, most council members view city managers strictly as administrators. This view creates an obvious paradox in the demands the council places on the manager: It wants the manager to have a policy orientation—that is, play a political rather than strictly an administrative role—only when it asks him or her to, and it views any policy orientation outside those specific requests as inappropriate. But most managers understand that this shifting of roles at the whim of the council is impossible, and in 1952 ICMA dropped its repudiation of politics from the City Manager Code of Ethics. And as Robert Huntley and Robert Macdonald (1975) note, most managers claim a prerogative as policy leaders. In a survey of managers, they found that 90 percent claimed to set their local political agenda, 75 percent claimed to play a leading role in policy development, and 60 percent claimed to initiate new policies. These figures seem amazingly high for a profession whose formal responsibilities are merely supportive

128

of the council, and council members sometimes respond negatively when they see how powerful the manager has become. The result, when this occurs, is usually less happy for the manager than it is for the council.

The Municipal Bureaucracy

The municipal bureaucracy in the United States employs more than 4 million people, ranging from administrators to garbage collectors. Each year, members of the municipal bureaucracy make numerous decisions, ranging from the crucial to the mundane. For example, a city manager's decision not to fire striking firefighters, or the police chief's decision to crack down on speeding motorists, may have immediate and profound implications for the lives of community residents. At the other end of the spectrum, the decision by an individual police officer to cite a motorist for a faulty turn signal, or by a garbage collector not to empty a trash container that is marginally too heavy, may seem to be of little consequence in the larger urban picture. Yet, as Bryan Jones (1983) argues, it is the individually unimportant decisions that are collectively crucial to the urban lifestyle, exactly because of the discretion municipal bureaucrats exercise in making day-to-day decisions.

A bureaucracy, says Max Weber (1946), is any modern, rational form of organization possessing the traits of hierarchy, specialization, and impersonality. In the urban setting, bureaucracy's primary purpose is to provide services for the city's citizens, including police protection, fire protection, garbage pickup, street maintenance, animal control, clean drinking water and sewage disposal, public transportation, library services, and well-maintained parks.

Hierarchy. The first manifestation of Weber's bureaucratic principle is the hierarchy through which these services are provided. At the top of the hierarchy sits the city manager, the mayor, members of the city commission, or whoever serves as the city's chief administrative officer(s). He or she typically has the privilege of appointing department heads, each responsible for the provision of a different service, who serve at his or her pleasure. Seldom are these administrators protected by civil service guidelines: They typically can be fired without cause, and often are as a new administration takes office. Under the department heads come those people who actually provide the services, described so aptly by Michael Lipsky (1980) as street-level bureaucrats. They, too, may be differentiated by rank; for example, a city's police department has an elaborate chain of command, from the precinct captain to the beat cop. But each of these positions is usually governed by civil-service law, with recruitment, selection, promotion, and salary based on objectively measured job qualifications. Further, once a street-level bureaucrat has served for a probationary period, he or she may not be fired except for cause. This protection gives substantial power to urban bureaucrats, and they are well-

129

represented by the American Federation of State, County, and Municipal Employees (AFSCME) to ensure that their civil service rights are not abrogated.

Specialization. The second manifestation of Weber's principle of bureaucracy is the specialization—and with it, the division of labor—found among municipal employees. As urban service delivery systems have expanded to provide more services, and as technological advances have provided more effective and efficient provision of services, the generalist has given way to the specialist. Take for instance the municipal firefighter. At one time, during the days of the bucket brigades and all-volunteer fire departments, literally anyone in the community with the willingness and the physical ability to be helpful could be a firefighter. But today, modern firefighting equipment is very expensive and sophisticated, and strategies for fighting fires have also become quite technical and sophisticated. Very few untrained people today could even drive a pumper, let alone figure out how to read the various gauges and engage the various pumps. Firefighters have become specialists, and in turn, experts in their field. Even garbage collection has become specialized, with several different types of trucks that may be used in different types of situations. Again, with specialization comes expertise.

The expertise that comes with specialization is important in the urban political process, for it makes the city council dependent on its administrative branch. Given the experience and expertise of the municipal bureaucracy, the city council often defers to the judgment of administrators, and it typically lends street-level bureaucrats a great deal of discretion in dealing with the day-to-day problems they encounter. *[The theory of urban administration]*

Impersonality. The third manifestation of Weber's bureaucratic principle is impersonality, elaborated by Jones (1983) as the norm of neutral competence. This principal holds that a bureaucratic structure should not have its own agenda, or, put metaphorically, its own axe to grind; rather, it should grind the axe of the legislative body to which it is responsible. Thus, by taking politics out of administration, the bureaucracy becomes impersonal. In principle, any individual bureaucrat could be substituted for any other without changing the level of effectiveness or efficiency with which urban services are performed and without shifting the government's policy goals. This principle is Weber's undoing, however, for it does not hold true for the modern municipal bureaucracy.

In fact, most bureaucrats do have their own axes to grind. At the lower levels of the bureaucratic hierarchy, important goals are continuing employment, better pay, and improved benefits. The importance of these goals is clear from the work stoppages that have become prevalent, if not commonplace, among municipal employees. With few exceptions, public sector strikes are illegal, reflecting a belief among lawmakers that the common good of citizens

130

(e.g., garbage collection, police and fire protection) outweighs the rights of city employees. And until the 1960s, this view was generally supported by professional organizations representing many public sector employees (e.g., the National Education Association and the American Nursing Association). But during the 1960s, these attitudes begin to change, and public sector employees (and their unions) became more militant. For example, 1968 alone witnessed more public sector strikes than had occurred between 1958 and 1965 (White 1972). In one of the most publicized public-sector strikes during this period, the New York City Transit Workers Union, led by Mike Quill, went out on strike in 1966, literally bringing traffic flow in the nation's largest city to a standstill (see Yates, 1977, for a trenchant description of these events). Sixteen union officials were sent to jail for defying a court order to return to work, and the strike ended only after the city agreed to a 15 percent pay raise for its transit workers. Most other cities have also experienced public-sector strikes, which by 1985 were occurring at a rate of over four hundred per year. They continue to result in jail sentences and fines, and in some cases, striking employees have been fired. Yet, at the local level, public-sector strikes continue and even increase in frequency.

At the upper levels of the hierarchy, important goals of bureaucrats are usually a larger budget and increased authority over programmatic decisions. Thus, bureaucrats are program advocates, and the continuation and expansion of their programs sometimes becomes as important as the effective or efficient provision of public services. This concern for *turf,* coupled with the power vested in the municipal bureaucracy (through civil service law and through expertise), has led Lowi (1969b, 87) to characterize it as the *new urban machine:*

> They [municipal bureaucrats] are relatively irresponsible structures of power. That is, each agency shapes important public policies, yet the leadership of each is relatively self-perpetuating and not readily subject to the controls of any higher authority.

This, however, seems overly harsh, and a more benign view of the municipal bureaucracy is possible. While its motive for self-perpetuation and power is no doubt important, this represents a human motive as much as a bureaucratic motive. Indeed, our earlier definition of politics includes a power component, thus taking the urban bureaucracy out of the purely administrative realm and placing it squarely in the political realm. We will defer discussion of the implications of this interconnection until later (chapter 17), when service delivery in the city is discussed more explicitly. But for now, it is sufficient to consider the municipal bureaucracy as a not-so-impersonal force of employees with human needs and motives, who are given (and as humans, take advantage of) the opportunity to interpret policies and make discretionary decisions as they see fit.

Other Formal Participants

Clerks. One of the least understood but most important positions in America's urban system is that of city clerk. Most cities have clerks (by formal responsibility if not by name), but their positions are particularly important in small, mayor–council cities. As is shown in table 7.1, nearly one-quarter of these cities elect a clerk. The clerk's formal responsibilities entail secretarial service to the city council. But in most small cities, the informal responsibilities (and power) of the clerk go well beyond those of office manager (Adrian and Press 1977). Particularly in cities without a full-time administrator, the clerk takes on the role of policy advisor to the governing body. The clerk typically has considerable longevity (in spite of the electoral status of the position in many communities, the job responsibilities are seemingly so innocuous that, once elected, the clerk tends to be reelected indefinitely), providing him or her with a great deal of experience (and expertise) in city affairs. As new council members are elected, they often learn the ropes of city government and municipal policy from the clerk, who often (either unwittingly or intentionally) provides the council member with his or her own interpretation of the municipal mission. *[The theory of ideology]* Even experienced council members may treat the clerk as a trusted confidant, seeking advice on difficult policy decisions. But, as Adrian and Press (1977, 204) note,

> because the consequences of any action this advice may generate will be attributed to others—the council members, the mayor. . .—clerks go on their bland way toward retirement, calmly riding above the storms of controversy that confront their colleagues.

Judges. Another position that is important in the American urban system is that of judge. This position is sometimes elective, sometimes appointive, but almost always the selection process is noncontroversial, for municipal and county judges have relatively little judicial power. They are, in large part, bound by precedent at the higher levels of the judicial system, and their rulings are subject to reversal. On the other hand, they have no power of reversal themselves. On occasion, a local judge will come under fire for a decision, particularly in cases involving perceived insensitivity toward the victims of accused sexual offenders (e.g., *The Progressive,* Nov. 1985, p. 16). However, for the most part decisions are not controversial; but through these decisions, the judge may gain considerable power in the community.

Specifically, local judges become the center of what is often a fragmented and disorganized network of human service providers in the community. They have legal responsibility (and authority) to refer a guilty person to the community mental health center for counseling or to the local alcohol or drug abuse agency for treatment. They can refer abused spouses to a variety of social programs, and they have the power to do the same for abused children. They can assign those convicted of misdemeanors to perform community service, often through the auspices of social service agencies. In short, they have considerable contact with the human service sector of the community, and because of their authority, legitimacy, and high status, they often become de facto leaders and spokespersons for those services. Given the poverty, crime, and need for human services in most large and middle-sized cities, this provides judges with considerable power in the urban policy arena.

Board Members. The final formal position we will discuss is membership on one of the city's many independent boards or commissions. Following the Civil War, many cities instituted a variety of independent boards and commissions to serve as the governing bodies for specific municipal departments. For example, many cities adopted a police commission, a library commission, a school board, a hospital board, and so forth. But as it became clear that coordination among various municipal agencies and departments was necessary to provide comprehensive services in a complex environment, the governing function of these boards and commissions gradually gave way to an advisory function (and in many cases, they were disbanded completely). Today, most cities have a host of advisory boards, many provided with the power to make recommendations to the city council or administration. But only the school board, and in some cases, the library board and the hospital board, generally retain the characteristics of a true governing body. Today, most other boards and commissions have little formal power to make binding policy decisions. For example, most cities have a planning commission, charged with the responsibility for developing the city's long-range plan. In principle, this plan has legal status, but it can be (and routinely is) ignored or reinterpreted by the city council. In addition, the council's power to appoint members to the planning commission for short terms means that an inconvenient plan can be rewritten. Cities also appoint citizens to a civil service board, a housing authority board, a parking board, an appeals board, and even a garbage and trash management board. In fact, current estimates hold that, nationwide, more than a million citizens participate on advisory boards, commissions, and councils *in education alone* (Davies 1980), and Adrian and Press (1977) hypothesize that millions of hours are spent each year by unpaid citizens serving as board members. Yet, the actual power of these citizens is doubtful. One evaluation of boards in Pennsylvania (reported by Adrian and Press 1977, 280-81) shows similar sentiment. Excerpts are summarized below:

1. Boards insulate the legislative body and executive from types of political pressure. Since the members are (usually) nonelective, they can more easily do things that are thought necessary and desirable but which, in the short run at least, might be politically unpopular.

133

2. They take politics out of important areas of government.
3. They provide, especially at the local level, a great amount of staff work which, if paid for, would be very expensive. They, in other words, serve to socialize some of the cost of government.
4. Members often feel that they are not consulted frequently enough, that their advice is too frequently ignored, and that they are not informed of the disposition made of their recommendations.
5. For issues requiring decisive action and, outside of the work done by boards of adjustment, civil service commissions, and planning commissions, the professional administrative staff works more efficiently than boards can.

In short, advisory boards and commissions serve a number of useful functions, but not the one(s) which they were originally designed to serve. We have already observed the relative powerlessness of the city's governing body relative to its professional bureaucracy; a similar conclusion must be applied to most advisory boards. They simply do not have the experience or the expertise to compete with that of professional administrators, or even that of city council members. As a result, recommendations are often based on cues picked up from administrators or council members, or are tied to information that administrators provide for them. This difficulty is exacerbated by the charge of most advisory boards: They are asked to represent the entire community. And, in fact, many boards and commissions take great pride in their representativeness. But almost by definition, the greater the level of representativeness of the board, the more diverse its beliefs about the city, its problems, and its goals, and the greater the level of conflict and controversy on the board. If board members cannot even agree among themselves, they feel reluctant to push the administration to adopt their recommendations (Bolland and Redfield 1988).

But, as noted above, boards and commissions do serve several useful functions. They deflect political pressure from elected and appointed officials. They provide useful staff work in researching community problems. They are able to coordinate community resources, often serving as directors of fundraising or volunteer drives. They provide effective links between citizens and their government, often serving as useful conduits for information. And finally, they provide a mechanism for defusing potential controversy in the community. By appointing a vocal opponent to governmental policy to an advisory capacity on one of the city's boards or commissions the mayor or council may coopt the opponent onto the government team.

But, if advisory boards and commissions are without power in most cities, why do millions of citizens continue to participate on them? And what are alternative outlets for citizen participation? We consider these questions in the next chapter.

134

Handball. Ben Shahn. 1939. Tempera on paper over composition board. 22¾″ × 31¼″. The Museum of Modern Art, New York. Abby Aldrich Rockefeller Fund.

Informal Citizen Participation in Local Politics 8

The real illness of the American city today, and especially of the deprived groups within it, is voicelessness. . . . The Negro revolt is not aimed at winning friends but at winning freedom, not inter-personal warmth but institutional justice

Harvey Cox
The Secular City

The previous chapter discussed two ways citizens can participate in local politics: by running for public office and by appointment to one of the city's boards or commissions. In each case, participation is largely an individual activity, reflecting the motives and interests of the individual officeholder or board member. This chapter considers two additional forms of individual participation: voting and citizen-initiated contacts (i.e., the behavior of individual citizens as they contact city government about problems or services). In addition, it looks at participation through groups, including political parties, civic organizations, business associations, neighborhood associations, and organized (and unorganized) protest movements. Finally, it considers how urban leaders emerge through a combination of individual and group activities. This, in turn, leads to a discussion of urban political power in the next chapter.

Who Participates and Why?

Before discussing outlets for citizen participation, we first explore, in a general way, the extent of this participation. Sidney Verba and Norman Nie (1972)

define participation as any act aimed at influencing the government, either by influencing the choice of personnel or by affecting the choices made by those personnel. Using this definition, they found that approximately 78 percent of American citizens participate politically.[1] The largest segment (21 percent) participates by voting only, while smaller segments combine voting with other, more active forms of participation. Only 11 percent can be classified as complete activists. These data give both an optimistic and a pessimistic picture of political participation in America. From an optimistic perspective, it is comforting to note that democracy seems to be alive and well, with more than three-fourths of the adult population engaging in some form of political activity. But from a more pessimistic perspective, only slightly more than one in five adults devote more energy to the political process than an occasional pull on the lever of a voting machine. And only one in ten adults is anything like a well-rounded political participant.

Why do people participate in politics? At the national level, most political participation is of an expressive nature, reflecting largely philosophical or moral issues: gun control, the environment, defense spending, nuclear disarmament. At the local level, participation reflects more personal concerns that touch the lives of people on an everyday basis. For example, local issues involve dangerous intersections, zoning decisions, distasteful billboards, and baseball diamonds. People get involved in national politics largely to make statements expressing their values. But people get involved in local politics because they have problems they want to solve or complaints they wish to air. *[The theory of urban political style]*

Several studies of urban political participation shed light on who gets involved. Robert Lineberry and Ira Sharkansky (1978), for example, report that fewer than 15 percent of surveyed respondents claim to be active members of groups or organizations working to solve an urban problem. Even within this small set, a noticeable class bias exaggerates the process and outcomes of participation. At the upper end of the socioeconomic spectrum, over 25 percent claim activity in local groups or organizations, while at the lower end of the spectrum, this figure declines to approximately 6 percent. As a result, the problems of the upper and middle classes may be addressed because of their participation, while the problems of the underclass[2] may be largely

1. Verba and Nie's estimates are based on survey questions asking: "Have you ever. . .?" These questions therefore elicit estimates of participation during a lifetime, rather than just at the current time. For some modes of participation, such as voting, we should expect these to converge (e.g., people who vote once may be likely to vote throughout their lifetimes). For other forms of participation, such as organizing a protest group, we should not necessarily expect convergence, and estimates should not be taken to indicate current levels of participation.

2. The language of American politics often stumbles over words denoting social and economic class. Such words invariably carry emotional baggage. *Middle* and *upper class* are acceptable terms, and descriptive symmetry might suggest the use of a threefold class division—with *lower* as the bottom tier.

ignored. In another study, Elaine Sharp (1982) reports that only 11 percent of the poor in Wichita, Kansas, had ever contacted a municipal official, compared with 21 percent of middle–class citizens and 40 percent of upper–class citizens. Again, this trend suggests that officials are more aware of middle– and upper–class problems than of the needs of the underclass.

These findings are strangely paradoxical, for we should expect those people with greatest need to be most active. Yet, we find exactly the opposite: Those with the least economic need are most likely to participate, while those with the greatest need are least likely to do so. This paradox is at least partially explained, however, when we take into account both the means for participation among the underclass and the systemic bias of urban government against effective underclass participation. First, consider means: Most middle- and upper–class urban residents have direct (or at least indirect) access to municipal government. They may have a friend or neighbor on the city council or who is a city engineer. This provides them with an immediate contact; and even if the contact is somewhat removed from the municipal leadership, the citizen can approach the mayor or the city manager with the introduction, "Carol Taylor [or whoever] suggested that I talk with you." Even without this direct contact, most middle- and upper–class residents may know a prominent business owner, lawyer, or other professional in town who can provide much the same introduction. In contrast, the poorer citizen (who is less well connected) must make his or her own introductions, a difficult task at best and particularly difficult for a person not used to moving among the powerful at city hall.

As an alternative, members of the underclass may go directly to the complaint bureau that many cities have established; but this is often bureaucracy at its worst, and the citizen seldom receives much immediate satisfaction from such visits. Imagine a municipal employee whose sole responsibility day after day is listening to the complaints of citizens about the way the city conducts its business. The first week might prove exciting as he or she hears about all of the city's "dirty laundry." But even for a person committed to improving the plight of the poor, the job soon becomes tedious and frustrating, and since the city employee is, in the complainant's eyes, at least partly responsible for its problems, he or she is likely to take the brunt of the complaints as personal attacks. Over time, the employee may begin acting defensively, asserting his or her authority when given the opportunity. (The employee sitting at the complaint desk is, after all, a street-level bureaucrat.) While this strategy may make the job more bearable for the employee, it makes the encounter

_____

But there is no escaping what Charles Stephenson (1963. 32) calls "persuasive definition." Lower class is easily associated with the idea of low class, and worse, it is regarded by many as a term with racist connotations and an ethnic slur. Thus, we use the terms *underclass* and *poorer class*.

with government singularly unsatisfactory for the citizen, and he or she is likely to think twice about complaining next time.

Second, political information is more readily available to the middle and upper classes than to the underclass. Citizens often become informed about their municipal government through participation in such organizations as Rotary, Kiwanis, and the League of Women Voters. These organizations are typically bastions of the middle and upper classes, seldom frequented by the underclass. The upper and middle classes also tend to read local newspapers more frequently, giving their members greater knowledge about the city and its government. While this is a subtle bias, its effects may be large; for as Francis Bacon noted nearly four hundred years ago, knowledge is power.

The paradox of participation breaks down, however, when we examine the relationship between need and participation, controlling for skill. Verba and Nie (1972) report, for example, that urban blacks participate in municipal affairs more frequently than whites with comparable social backgrounds. In addition, "ethnics" participate more frequently than their nonethnic counterparts (e.g., Nelson 1979). And finally, participation tends to be higher in heterogeneous, working-class cities than in homogeneous, white-collar cities (e.g., Alford and Lee 1968). In each case, participation is likely to reflect greater need. Or put more directly, people are more likely to complain when there is more to complain about. But just as important, people are more likely to participate when participation is easy, or at least when roadblocks to participation (cultural, social, or bureaucratic) are not encountered.

During the past two decades, the federal government has made great efforts to remove these roadblocks, often with indifferent success. President Johnson, as part of his Great Society program, set a goal of "maximum feasible participation" by the nation's poor. Since 1960, local citizen participation has become a condition for a number of grant-in-aid programs to cities. While only 5 of these programs required citizen participation mechanisms prior to 1960, 155 had such requirements by 1978 (ACIR 1980).[3] An instructive example of this type of mandated participation occurs in the Community Development Block Grant, enacted in 1974 to provide cities with funds for urban renewal, basic water and sewer facilities, and historical preservation. The act required applicants to provide satisfactory assurances that they (a) provide citizens with adequate information on the availability of funds and the range of activities that may be undertaken, (b) hold public hearings, and (c) afford citizens an adequate opportunity to participate in the development of the application. Even so, the early days of this program witnessed considerable

---

3. ACIR is an acronym for the Advisory Commission on Intergovernmental Relations, created by Congress in 1959 to monitor the operation of the American federal system and to recommend improvements.

140

dissatisfaction with the lack of involvement by lower-income groups (ACIR 1980). The 1977 reenactment strengthened the citizen participation require-ments, mandating applicants to submit a written citizen participation plan. Many cities met this requirement by encouraging and facilitating the develop-ment of neighborhood organizations in low-income areas of the city. In many cases, they paid the operating expenses for these organizations, and residents of more than one urban neighborhood have enjoyed a picnic dinner at city expense.[4] But for all this, it is still unclear whether participation by the underclass can be successful, and systematic instances of successful participa-tion are difficult to document. We will explore this phenomenon in greater depth later in this chapter.

Individual Modes of Participation

Beyond seeking municipal office or volunteering for service on a municipal advisory board, individuals can attempt to influence political outcomes in two ways—through voting and by initiating contacts with city hall.

Voting

As he signed the Voting Rights Act of 1965, President Lyndon Baines Johnson boldly proclaimed that the right to vote is "the most powerful instrument ever devised by man for breaking down injustice. . . ." Taken at face value, this suggests that voting serves a practical function, keeping politics and politi-cians honest and representative. More important, it suggests that the desire to achieve some desired outcome motivates the decision to vote. For instance, a citizen who is disenchanted with the way he or she is represented by an elected official can vote to replace the representative with someone who will better represent the voter's interests. And from the other side of the ballot box, the elected official who realizes that the citizen has this power is likely to modify his or her behavior accordingly.

This rational view of electoral behavior (and, in fact, of democratic theory) has been challenged in a number of quarters. One of the most tren-chant criticisms holds that citizens may simply have insufficient knowledge, information, or understanding to vote their self interest. A rational vote requires the voter to understand not only the differences between candidates, but also how those differences affect him or her. In many instances, party affiliation serves as a convenient heuristic for assessing candidates, but this has been effectively eliminated in many cities by the use of nonpartisan elec-tions. Other criticisms of the rational model of democratic participation are equally important, and they are discussed below.

---

4. For a more complete discussion of this and other federal programs, see chapters 14 and 15.

Table 8.1   A November 8, 1988, Ballot Proposition in Alabama

Proposed Statewide Amendment Number Four (4)

To propose and provide for the submission of an amendment to the Constitution of
1901, as amended; providing that no law whose purpose of effect is to provide for a new
or increased expenditure of municipal funds held or disbursed by the municipal governing
body shall become effective as to any municipality of this state until the first day of the
fiscal year next following the passage of such law unless such law is approved by a resolution duly adopted by and spread upon the minutes of the municipal governing body of
the municipality affected thereby, or such law (or other law) provides the municipal
governing bodies with new or additional revenues sufficient to fund such new or
increased expenditures; providing for an election thereon and prescribing an effective date
for the proposed amendment.

Yes

No

Ballot propositions. Particularly in the case of referenda and initiatives—
which are often worded in language that is convoluted or otherwise difficult
to understand—the voter may not know what he or she is voting for or
against. David Magleby (1984) reports that the wording of ballot propositions
in California and Oregon is readable at the eighteenth grade level (i.e., two
years post-baccalaureate), well past the educational achievement of the vast
majority of voters in those states.[5] As a case in point, consider the
proposition listed in table 8.1. Even after careful reading, the exact purpose
of this amendment to the Alabama constitution, which *seems* to have important
implications for municipal governance, is likely to be unclear.

The typical voter entering a voting booth (which for many people is
itself intimidating) and encountering this proposition for the first time would
likely be confused by such convoluted wording, leading him or her either
to vote in an irrational (that is, uninformed) manner or simply to exercise his
or her right not to vote on the issue.

Complicated wording of ballot propositions yields a middle- and upper-
class bias to urban politics, particularly in cities without strong political parties.
Members of the under-educated and poorly informed underclass typically find
the party label more helpful in voting their self-interest than do members of the
middle and upper classes. By the same token, the underclass may be influenced
on ballot propositions by leaders of the local party. But in the absence of cues
from trusted political leaders (e.g., the party), underclass voters must interpret

5. By way of comparison, Magleby finds that *Time* and *Newsweek* are readable at approximately the
twelfth-grade level, and *Reader's Digest* at the tenth-grade level.

ballot propositions by themselves, attempting to determine which choice is in their best interest. For many underclass voters, this may be an impossible task, given the grammatical complexity of most ballot propositions. The result may be either nonparticipation or irrational participation in the voting booth. The better educated upper and middle classes are better able to comprehend ballot propositions and make a rational determination of self-interest.

Nonparticipation among the urban poor clearly lends a middle- and upper-class bias to urban elections; but so, too, does irrational participation, since irrational participants, voting in an uninformed manner, are likely to cancel out one another's votes.[6]

Misplaced faith in the power of elected officials. Another criticism of the rational model of electoral behavior concerns the assumption that elected officials determine policies. Certainly, at all levels of government obstacles emerge to the faithful fulfillment of campaign promises. For example, a revenue shortfall may prevent a promised road from being constructed or a sidewalk from being repaired. Or a lawsuit may prevent an old building from being razed to make way for a new parking facility. Another impediment to the fulfillment of campaign promises is the relative impotence of the city council in cities that have adopted the council-manager form of government. As noted before, the power of the council is greatly diffused by its lack of information and expertise, and it relies on the city manager to set the agenda and make recommendations. Because of the council's relative impotence, the link between the voter and policy outcomes is weak, even though the link between the voter and the elected official may be strong. *[The theory of grass-roots democracy]* (Again, there exists an upper- and middle-class bias, for upper- and middle-class interests are generally best served through government by administration.)

Another factor militating against the ability of elected officials to determine policies in the urban place is their inability to control private investment decisions. For example, a developer may choose to build a shopping mall just outside the city limits, where the city council is powerless. This decision will potentially draw businesses and shoppers from the downtown area. By the same token, a builder may decide to construct a new housing subdivision that will severely tax the city's existing water and sewer systems. So long as the builder meets local zoning requirements and building codes, the council is largely powerless to stop the construction project. Or a small manufacturing business may simply decide to move to a new city, enticed by attractive tax deferments that are offered there. If the council lacks sufficient funds to match

---

6. For these and similar reasons, many critics of our society view the election process as a significant instance of American class bias, and in the words of Sennett and Cobb (1972), another example of the "hidden injuries of class" in America.

143

this incentive, it is powerless to stop the move and the loss of local jobs that will result. *[The theory of commodification of land and buildings]*

In each case, policy is removed from the hands of the city council and twice removed from the hands of the voters. The impact on the upper and middle classes is softened, for capital investment decisions are typically in their best interests: new homes emerge, urban decay is excised, better roads are constructed, and so forth. But for the underclass, the lack of effective representation is more critical. As a case in point, William Keech (1968) found that in Durham, North Carolina, the vote is more important for (and effective in) achieving legal justice than social justice. That is, the vote (or the threat of the vote) broke down governmental barriers to equal rights and services, but it did little to break down social discrimination. Keech (1968, 105) concludes that "the really striking gains of Durham's Negro minority have come through resources other than the vote."

Symbolism versus utilitarianism. One possible conclusion is that the vote, particularly at the local level, serves a symbolic function much more than a utilitarian one. That is, people may vote because they are good citizens (and can take a certain pride in their behavior) rather than because they feel that their vote will make a difference in policy outcomes. This contrasts sharply with the view, considered earlier, that people are motivated to participate in local politics because they feel they can be effective.

Fortunately, a major study by Robert Alford and Eugene Lee (1968) of voting patterns in 282 cities sheds light on this matter. They examined voter turnout in these cities for municipal elections that were not concurrent with national or state elections, thus providing a useful estimate of electoral participation in local affairs. Their findings, summarized in table 8.2, show that

Table 8.2 Mean Percentage of Registrants Voting in Municipal Elections

	Cities with partisan elections			Cities with nonpartisan elections			All cities		
	Non-Manager	Manager	All	Non-Manager	Manager	All	Non-Manager	Manager	All
Ethnicity									
High	65	45	58	58	42	49	60	42	51
Low	62	49	58	48	40	41	53	40	44
Mobility									
High	60	40	50	52	39	41	54	39	42
Low	65	58	64	56	44	50	59	46	54
All cities	64	47	58	55	40	44	57	41	47

SOURCE: Adapted from Alford and Lee (1968).

voter turnout is highest in cities with nonmanager formats (57 percent vs. 41 percent turnout), partisan elections (58 percent vs. 44 percent), high ethnicity (51 percent vs. 44 percent), and low mobility (54 percent vs. 42 percent).

As previously noted, turnout is likely to be higher in partisan than in nonpartisan cities, for two reasons: (a) the cost of casting an informed vote is much lower in the former than the latter type of election; and (b) cities with partisan elections are likely to experience higher levels of socio-political conflict. But what explains the differences among other types of cities?

Participation is lower in cities with managers than in nonmanager cities. One possible explanation is that in these cities, people realize that the city council is without much power, and they simply assert their self-interest by staying home on election day. (This explanation would support the utilitarian explanation of voting: People choose not to vote because they realize it would be ineffectual.) But this explanation may attribute too much sophistication (and cynicism) to the voter (or in this case, the nonvoter). A better explanation recognizes that manager cities tend to be more homogeneous than nonmanager cities, and that elections in manager cities consequently tend to be free from conflict. Why vote, the citizen may conclude, if the candidates are not very different from one another? His or her self-interest is likely to be realized whichever candidate is elected, and therefore voting serves no utilitarian purpose. (This explanation also supports the utilitarian view of voting behavior.) A third explanation yields a different interpretation, however. Homogeneous cities tend to have small ethnic populations, while heterogeneous cities tend to have larger ethnic populations. Many ethnic groups, particularly those consisting of recent (i.e., first or second generation) European and Asian immigrants, tend to be more attuned to procedural democracy than their "WASPish" counterparts[7]; this perhaps reflects a sense of pride in their new country and their citizenship, or perhaps it represents a feeling of debt and gratitude. (Whatever its source, this commitment to electoral participation reflects a symbolic rather than a utilitarian motive.)

In addition, turnout is higher in cities with low mobility than in cities with high mobility. Again, this is probably artifactual, reflecting the distinction between homogeneous, high-mobility suburbs and heterogeneous, low-mobility central cities. But two other explanations are also important. First, greater geographical stability probably leads people to a greater pride in and commitment to their geographical region. For example, long-time residents of Cleveland are more likely to defend it than are new arrivals. This commitment may, in turn, manifest itself in a greater propensity to take part in its political processes, for example, by voting. (The decision to vote born out of pride is motivated largely by symbolic considerations.) Second, long-term

_____

7. This does not hold for Hispanic residents, who vote less often than either whites or blacks.

residents have developed friendships, they may have good jobs, and more generally, they have a familiarity with their surroundings. In short, they have a stake in their long-term future in the area, and they are more likely to be attuned to local politics and how those politics will affect them. In contrast, highly mobile individuals expect to move before any political decisions will affect them directly. Thus, less-mobile individuals participate in local politics to a greater extent than their more-mobile counterparts.

Citizen-Initiated Contacts

During their adult lives, most Americans probably will have at least one run-in with city hall. It may take any of a number of forms. For example, a person may complain that trash is not picked up regularly. Or a road may be filled with potholes, or the sidewalk may be crumbling. He or she may be concerned about inadequate police protection or may object to a city ordinance requiring fire alarms to be placed in all rental property. The person may insist that heavy (and excessively fast) traffic flow on a nearby street demands a traffic control signal, feel disgruntled that there are not enough baseball diamonds, or that there are too many baseball diamonds and not enough jogging trails, or may complain that a neighbor's dog barks through the night, or that its master parties loudly through the night. The list of possible complaints is almost endless.

"You can't fight city hall" is one of the most common political adages, and if followed, would lead people with these concerns to (a) complain to their friends and neighbors (but not to their elected officials or to the municipal bureaucracy); (b) vote against incumbent council members in the next municipal election; or (c) move to another neighborhood or city. Yet, every year millions of Americans disobey the conventional political wisdom and take their complaints directly to city hall. These citizen-initiated contacts are a unique form of political participation, for they are typically carried out by individuals (as opposed to groups) and they are motivated strictly by self-interest.

The fact that citizen-initiated contacts are individual expressions is important, for it makes them an unexpected form of participation. Another political adage (perhaps second in importance only to the supposed futility of fighting city hall) concerns strength in numbers and suggests that participation for most people is more palatable, less traumatic, and generally accomplished more easily when they act as part of a group rather than as individuals. Psychologists tell us, for example, that people become more bold in groups (Wallach, et al. 1962). In contrast, citizen-initiated contacts are strictly the acts of individuals, and we may surmise that only special circumstances (i.e., a situation perceived as intolerable) would move a person to this kind of bold activity. For example, a citizen who yesterday ruined his muffler by

146

driving through a pothole may today find his way to city hall to complain about the deplorable condition of the city streets. Or a business executive who fluffs an important presentation at work, brought on by a sleepless night of howling dogs and blaring music in her neighborhood, may take her case to city hall. But for most of us, the inconvenience of taking time to go downtown or even to find the right telephone number, and the intimidation of facing the vast urban bureaucracy alone, leads us to a more pragmatic approach: We simply trust government to fix the problem itself (or perhaps we wait for someone else to complain).

Thus, it makes little sense to say that some neighborhoods with high levels of need will be the source of most complaints to the city. Inhabitants of these neighborhoods, who may be primarily of the underclass, have fewer political skills than do their middle- and upper-class counterparts, and they are more likely to be intimidated by city hall. In addition, the expectations in many of these neighborhoods are likely to be lower. Uncollected garbage or barking dogs may be commonplace and therefore go largely unnoticed in underclass neighborhoods, whereas in middle- and upper-class neighborhoods, such events are unexpected and often draw immediate complaints.

A second conclusion holds that citizen-initiated contacts are motivated by self-interest. People contact city hall about potholes in the roads because it affects them directly, not because of a concern for the city's other motorists. People complain about the lack of softball diamonds in municipal parks because they want to play ball, not because of a commitment to increasing the cardiovascular capacity of the city's inhabitants. They complain about slovenly and haphazard garbage collection because they find garbage in *their* front yards, not because a passing motorist might find the situation aesthetically unpleasing.

And how does city hall respond to these complaints (if it responds at all)? Usually it does not reformulate its policies, but rather responds on a case-by-case basis. For example, the citizen who complains about potholes in front of her house may find a work crew filling those potholes the next morning, but ignoring similar ones a block away. Or a garbage truck, on a special run, may collect the missed garbage; but the city's garbage-collection policy remains intact. Given the motivations underlying citizen-initiated contacts and given the nonsystematic responses these contacts are likely to elicit, should we construe this activity as political?

In a word, *yes.* While the city is unlikely to modify its policies in response to a single complaint, it may, over time, modify policies in response to a series of related complaints. For example, the cost of sending out work crews to fix individual potholes in front of complainants' houses may be prohibitively high, and for only a little more money, the city may be able to systematically fill potholes all across town. Or the cost of sending a garbage truck on a special run to pick up spilled garbage, when aggregated over a number of complaints, may lead the city to reconsider its policy of leaving spilled garbage where it lies. In short, these private, self-interested complaints, taken together, may have important policy implications. But paradoxically, any complaint, considered alone, is likely to have little or no effect on policy, may or may not even ameliorate an immediate problem, and is accomplished at a psychological cost to the complainant.

Thus, we should expect that relatively few people take this route of political participation. Although a number of studies of citizen-initiated contacting behavior have been conducted, we are still somewhat unclear about the exact magnitude of the phenomenon. Estimates of contact with municipal government range from a low of 20 percent (Verba and Nie 1972) to a high of 58 percent (Katz, et al. 1975; see Coulter, 1988, for a review). But in some of these studies, *all* forms of contact are recorded, including (a) reporting a crime; (b) obtaining a building permit; (c) receiving job training; and d) visiting public health clinics. Such behaviors fall outside the purview of politics (as discussed in chapter 6), and they should not be confused with more overtly political activities, such as those described earlier in this chapter. Thus, when we examine actual *complaints* (as opposed to all forms of contact), we get a somewhat different picture. In Houston, for example, a central complaint agency set up to receive and address citizen concerns receives only between thirty-five and fifty complaints a day (Mladenka 1977). This represents under 20,000 complaints a year in a city with over 1.5 million inhabitants, or a complaint rate of only 1 percent (or, put in terms of households, approximately 3 percent). The central complaint agency is not the only avenue for citizen complaints, however, and others may go to individual departments and agencies. But even assuming that complaints to the central agency represents only the tip of the iceberg, it would be hard to imagine a complaint rate of over 10 percent. Since a person who has contacted city hall once may do so a second time (and a third, fourth, or fifth time), this generous estimate drops considerably. Of course, data from one city does not allow us to generalize to citizen participation across the country. But even by the most generous estimates, citizen-initiated contacts with city hall, in which complaints are aired and solutions requested, must be far below those reported in many studies of citizen participation in America. In short, only a small fraction of urban dwellers take it upon themselves to participate as *individuals* in the political process.

Group Modes of Participation

Largely because of psychological, social, and political barriers to individual participation, groups have become the modus operandi of American politics. At the national level (and with the exception of political parties), these groups form largely around specific issues: the National Rifle Association, the

National Organization of Women, the nuclear freeze movement, and so forth (e.g., Cigler and Loomis 1986). At the local level, however, groups tend to have a multi-purpose orientation. For example, the local chamber of commerce gets involved in most every economic issue (which, in the end, is virtually every issue), and neighborhood organizations often participate in a wide variety of social issues that affect them. One important distinction we can draw between individual participation and group participation at the local level is that the former tends to be motivated by self-interest (and to some extent by a sense of civic responsibility), whereas the latter often is motivated by concern for the group.

One of the most important elements of human nature is the need to affiliate with others. Humans (as Aristotle observed long ago) are social animals, which leads us to become involved in many different kinds of relationships. For example, marriage (and the family) has survived as a human institution exactly because of our need for companionship. And each of us maintains a complex network of friendships that, when studied, meanders through the urban terrain (Wellman 1979, Fischer, et al. 1977). We join bridge clubs, softball teams, bowling leagues, and sewing circles for exactly the same reason. And in the more political sphere, we join civic groups, neighborhood associations, and interest groups.

This is not to say that these political groups fill exactly the same human need as social groups. Participation in political groups actually serves two purposes: It is motivated by self-interest, and through it participants attempt to achieve those political and policy outcomes they believe to be important; and it is motivated by participants' needs to affiliate and to maintain contact with others. The mixture of these motives often leads political groups in directions different from those their individual members might take. For example, an emergent leader within a neighborhood association may have strong feelings about historic preservation within the community and get the association involved in efforts to save an historic train depot slated for demolition. Many members of the association may not care about the building; in fact, they may think it ugly and worthy of demolition. Yet, they go along with the association, for the value derived from membership in the group more than compensates for taking a political stance that mildly violates their self-interest. The same could be said for membership in such civic groups as the Rotary, Kiwanis, or the League of Women Voters. The various projects that these groups engage in probably reflects the interests of group leaders. Yet, members willingly go along, for the social benefits derived from membership in the group outweigh the costs of taking an insincere issue position. Note that in both of these cases, group leaders speak with the authority of the group, even though the group members, left to their own devices, may not individually participate in the issue at all.

With this as a precautionary note, we begin an inventory of political

groups active at the local level. In each case, we will consider motives for joining the group, political strategies employed by the group, political and policy
positions held by the group, and various impediments the group must overcome to be successful in its political mission.

Political Parties

Logic suggests that the power and the importance of the political party should
be greatest at the local level of government. First, local party organizations
are the building blocks of the national party. Congress, after all, represents
local constituents (see O'Neill 1987), and even presidential candidates must
put together coalitions of local leaders. Second, local parties are largely free
from the ideological divisions of national parties. For example, Democrats
in New York have a very different agenda from those in Alabama, who in
turn differ from those in Nevada. Yet, they all go by the same name. In contrast, these differences are minimized within a region and particularly within
an individual city. Thus, voters can give loyalty to the local party without
the need to check the ideological credentials of individual candidates. Third,
the party should be best able to reward its faithful supporters at the local level,
for (a) it is closer to its members there than at any other level of government,
and it should be better able to trade votes for services, and (b) most governmental jobs are filled at the municipal level.

However logical this may seem, parties are far from the center of political
action at the local level. As noted earlier, much of this decline is due to urban
reform, wherein politics (and hence the role of political parties) was removed
from municipal government. For example, the advent of government-by-
management concentrated great power in the hands of administrators who
could act independently of elected officials. Thus, the symbiotic link between
the party and its members, even if it still existed, could not guarantee desired
policy outcomes. More important was the decline of patronage through the
introduction of civil service requirements into municipal hiring decisions.
More important still was the advent of the nonpartisan election, which is by
far the most pervasive component of the reform package (e.g., city management, at-large elections). Among the largest cities in this country, only Pittsburgh, Jacksonville, Cleveland, Baltimore, New York, New Orleans,
Philadelphia, St. Louis, and Indianapolis have fully partisan elections (Judd
1984). In contrast, Phoenix, Columbus, Dallas, Detroit, San Antonio, San
Diego, Seattle, Los Angeles, Milwaukee, San Francisco, Memphis, Houston,
Denver, and Boston have nonpartisan elections. In Chicago, the mayor is
elected on a partisan ballot, while council members run without party labels.
In small and middle-sized cities, partisan elections are quite rare.

In general, then, parties have been left with a much diminished role in
local politics. As noted earlier, this results in a decline in electoral participation,

particularly among the underclass. And as Lineberry and Sharkansky (1978, 125-26) suggest, this probably increases the representation of middle class interests. "The voice of certain groups—e.g., business people, Republicans, upper-income voters, people who read newspapers regularly—is a bit louder." Thus, the urban reformers were more successful perhaps than even they had any reason to expect (see chapter 5), not necessarily in their stated purpose (removing the political machine from the urban landscape), but in a largely unstated purpose (recreating urban politics as a middle- and upper-class enterprise).

Business and Economic Groups

Perhaps the most pervasive groups in urban politics are those based on economic interests; these include the local chamber of commerce, the local board of realtors, local "good government" groups, and ad hoc business groups formed to promote economic development. These often have overlapping memberships, although their aims are different and their leadership styles vary considerably.

Chamber of commerce. The most visible economic group is the local chamber of commerce. In most cities of over 25,000, the local chamber of commerce typically employs an executive officer and (particularly in larger cities) a variety of staff assistants. These persons assume responsibility for maintaining a healthy economic climate within the city, and they do so in a number of ways. First, the executive officer actively solicits new businesses and industries into the city. He or she accomplishes this task in a number of ways: writing brochures, making phone calls, providing guided tours for potential newcomers, and traveling extensively—knocking on doors and extolling the virtues of his or her community wherever anyone will listen. Second, and more important for our purposes, the executive director meets regularly with the city manager and/or the city council, lobbying for policies promoting local growth. For example, he or she may lobby for the expenditure of city funds to expand the local airport or to provide additional downtown parking, promote the aggressive use of industrial revenue bonds to attract new businesses and industries to the community, or argue for the development of a new industrial park with city-subsidized water and sewer lines. Third, the chamber of commerce staff serves as a kind of local support group for business and industry, providing advice, counseling, and just plain encouragement for those who need or want it.

But beyond its staff, what kind of organization is the local chamber of commerce? Membership is open to anyone in the community, both individuals and businesses (for a modest membership fee, typically between $100 and $300 per year). Members annually elect a president, usually from the community's business or industrial sector. The chamber of commerce also elects from its membership a board of directors designated to provide direction to its economic development efforts. It typically organizes several mixers each year, providing opportunities for members to see one another and exchange ideas in an informal atmosphere. In addition, it sponsors a variety of programs, ranging from "issue breakfasts" (known locally as "issues and eggs") and candidate forums to leadership development courses.

As is the case with many such organizations, the chamber of commerce is largely a staff organization, reflecting the efforts and concerns of its executive director. And as is the case with the city council, the board of directors usually has neither the expertise nor the information to challenge the judgments of the executive director, who becomes the de facto policymaker for the organization. (But unlike the city council, the membership of the chamber is quite homogeneous, and seldom is there ideological conflict between the executive director and the board of directors.) Further, most members have neither the time nor the inclination to attend meetings regularly or to serve on committees.

The membership roster of the local chamber of commerce is typically large, reflecting what appears to be an impressive level of participation, from virtually the entire business community. This kind of participation is what we may term "checkbook participation," however, reflecting members' willingness to pay their dues and let someone else get involved. They support the principles of the chamber; they like to show support for economic growth and development by proudly displaying a chamber of commerce decal in their window; and they are very pleased to have an established organization behind them should they have a run-in with city hall. They accomplish this through dues, however, rather than through active involvement.

In the end, the mission of the chamber of commerce may be too amorphous to generate active participation among more than a small percentage of its members. It has become established in most communities, and it is the very essence of respectability. But although this gives chamber members easy access to city hall to discuss economic development, it also leaves the chamber without many acute issues that mean the difference between success or failure for its members. It addresses the gamut of economic development issues (espousing pro-growth and low-tax policies), and thereby appeals to the widest possible membership. But, at the same time, it necessarily fails to concentrate on the individual issues about which individual members get excited (e.g., downtown development versus shopping centers). This void is filled by a number of other economic groups that often lack the broad base of support enjoyed by the chamber, but which may, as a consequence, enjoy greater short-term success.

Board of realtors. One such group is the board of realtors, a group of local business persons involved in the development and sale of local real estate.

Members of this group have a single purpose, the promotion of their businesses, and they go about it by lobbying the city council and administration on policy issues that bear on real estate. Unlike the chamber of commerce, the board of realtors is a more narrowly focused group that does not spread itself too thin by pursuing a wide range of interests. In the same way, the very nature of the group encourages participation by its members. This, coupled with the importance of land development and promotion for the city's economic well-being, means that when the board of realtors speaks, people in positions of importance listen.

Downtown merchants' association. Another group that fills the void left by the chamber of commerce is the downtown merchants' association, a group of local business owners who organize to promote downtown economic development over that in outlying areas. Since the chamber of commerce represents all business interests in the entire community, it cannot take sides on the issue of downtown versus suburban development; but the downtown merchants' association can and does. It lobbies city hall for free downtown parking, for cleaner streets and sidewalks, for industrial revenue bonds to attract new retail businesses into the downtown area, and for renovation to make the downtown area more attractive. And in many cases, its efforts are successful. In an effort to revitalize downtown areas, many cities spend large amounts of money to plant flowers and trees in sidewalk planters and newly constructed medians, to install better street lighting, to build parking garages, and so forth.

Good-government groups. A third type of economically oriented group that has become particularly active in city politics over the past quarter century actively promotes what it terms "good government." Although good-government groups were initially associated with urban reform, their mission has changed in the years since the reform movement peaked. In San Antonio, for example, the Good Government League ran its own slate of candidates in each local election. It was phenomenally successful, electing seventy-nine of eighty-one candidates it nominated over a recent twenty-year period (Lineberry and Sharkansky 1978).[8] Similar groups have formed in other cities (e.g., Tucson, Dallas, San Jose). In each case, the group is composed of a coalition of business and other pro-growth interests whose purpose is to promote pro-growth policies in the city. Often, this is accomplished through local elections, where pro-growth candidates are supported and anti-

8. Ironically, the Good Government League has been criticized for working closely with a small and select group of Chicano business leaders to nominate a token slate of Chicano candidates for the city council, virtually guaranteeing that the council would be dominated by a white majority (Muñoz and Henry 1986).

153

growth candidates are opposed. In some cases, the symbolic name reflects group members' attempts to mask their own self-interest beneath altruistic rhetoric. In other cases, the name no doubt reflects members' genuine beliefs that growth is vitally necessary for the city, and that good government understands this necessity and acts on it.

Ad hoc economic groups. A clear example of the emergence and activity of a good government group occurred in Lawrence, Kansas, in 1982. At that time, the city manager in Lawrence had held his position for a decade and had demonstrated his friendship for local business and his support for aggressive growth policies in the community. But in 1981, two new anti-growth candidates were elected to the city council, giving anti-growth forces an absolute majority on the council. Most knowledgeable observers assumed it was only a matter of time before the city manager would be dismissed. Events reached a head one Friday in February, when one of the anti-growth council members wrote a letter to the city manager urging his resignation, with a council vote to dismiss him as the only possible alternative. Almost immediately (literally, over the weekend) a coalition of pro-growth individuals, primarily representing business interests, emerged under the name of the Lawrence Committee. It challenged the right of a council member to urge the resignation of the city manager, charged the member with malfeasance (among other things), and organized a strenuous recall campaign financed with contributions from a number of local businesses. In the end, the council member survived the recall election; but in a vote during the recall campaign, the city council opted not only to retain the city manager but also to give him a raise. In the next municipal election, anti-growth candidates were notable by their absence.

This example suggests that even when business interests are not formally allied in a community, clear lines of communication typically exist and can be activated at a moment's notice. These lines of communication are often activated, in fact, as various economic opportunities emerge and ad hoc economic development groups form, usually as an alternative to the local chamber of commerce. As was noted earlier, the local chamber is a multi-purpose and multi-audience group that serves a variety of interests, but it is often inadequate for the needs of individual businesses. It tends to be rather cautious in its initiatives, lest it offend any of its members; but this inertia may prove frustrating to those who want to quickly take advantage of new opportunities.

For example, a group may emerge around rumors that General Motors is considering the community as a site for a new automobile assembly plant. Or it may emerge to promote development of an industrial park on a parcel of land that has just become available. Or, as in San Jose, it may emerge to promote the community as a manufacturing center (Trounstine and Christensen 1982). In this case, David Packard, chairman of the board at

Hewlitt Packard, Inc., and Robert Wilson, chairman of the board of Memorex, formed the Santa Clara County Manufacturing Group during the late 1970s. Its purpose was to bring together the county's largest manufacturing and banking firms into an umbrella organization that would become the voice for industry in the Silicon Valley. By 1980, the Manufacturing Group had largely accomplished this goal; it membership consisted of sixty-five companies, including Lockheed Missiles, General Electric, Owens-Corning Fiberglass, IBM, GTE-Sylvania, Bank of America, Ford Aerospace, American Microsystems, and National Semiconductor. The Manufacturing Group works with both city and county government in an effort to promote efficiency and cut costs, and it has become involved in a number of issues, including transportation, housing, employment, and taxation. Within a year of its formation, the Manufacturing Group had outstripped the San Jose Chamber of Commerce as a center of community power, and it promises to be the dominant source of influence in the area during the coming decades.

Civic and Social Groups

In almost every community, a number of civic groups and social clubs exists. Traditionally, these have been segregated by gender (although traditional gender barriers seem to be breaking down). On the male side, such organizations as the Kiwanis, Lions, and Rotary clubs and the Jaycees (a kind of junior chamber of commerce with a service orientation) are active. These groups have regular meetings during which members share lunch and listen to a speaker discuss an interesting political or social problem in the community. These organizations often take on civic projects, usually contributing money to some worthwhile cause (for instance buying eyeglasses for school children who could not otherwise afford them). While some of the money for these contributions comes from membership dues, most of it is raised through various projects, for instance selling Christmas trees during the holiday season.

On the female side, organizations such as the League of Women Voters,[9] the Junior League, the Jaycee Janes, and the Soroptomists are active in most communities. Like their male counterparts, members of these organizations break bread at regular meetings, listen to speakers discuss vital issues for the community, and target specific service functions. For example, the League of Women Voters sponsors debates among political candidates, and members of the Junior League do volunteer work in libraries, hospitals, and social service agencies. One difference between the two sets of organizations is that while

9. The League of Women Voters is sometimes classified as a good-government group, and its effort to bring informed debate to political issues certainly represents an effort to improve government. But its mission is very different from that of other good-goverment groups operating today (see the previous section), and it makes more sense to classify the league with other *civic groups* instead.

the male organizations typically donate their money to community projects, women's organizations typically donate their time. A second difference is that while many male organizations (e.g., Rotary, Kiwanis, Lions) discourage female participation,[10] many women's organizations encourage male participation (e.g., the League of Women Voters).

People join these service organizations for a variety of reasons. One of the most important is social: They are able to dine with their friends on a regular basis and keep in touch in a way that busy schedules might not otherwise permit. When two businessmen meet by chance and agree to get together for lunch sometime, sometime rarely comes. But by joining Rotary, they regularly reserve lunchtime on Wednesdays to see each other (and other friends with whom they would like to keep in touch). A second reason for participation is to fulfill a sense of civic obligation. By joining the Junior League, a woman is returning to the community something of what it has given her, and it makes her feel good about both herself and about the community. A third reason for participation is political self-interest. By attending meetings, members have a chance to "network," to touch base with others who may be (or who may become) allies on policy issues. In one city the authors studied, managers from four industrial plants drove together to and from the Rotary meeting each Wednesday. During this time together (and whatever time they could manage together at the meeting itself), they discussed community issues relating to business and economic development. A fourth reason for joining is simply the visibility offered by membership in the organization. Administrators in a number of social and cultural service organizations (e.g., the Y.M.C.A., Boy Scouts, the Historic Preservation Society) attend because it gives them a chance to see and be seen by other important people in the community. By the same token, many banks, real estate firms, and other community businesses require senior-level employees to join at least one civic organization on the grounds that it simultaneously provides visibility for the business and demonstrates its civic commitment.

Most people with the first two motives are likely to participate only sporadically. While collegiality and civic responsibility may draw many people to join an organization, they can be easily overwhelmed by more practical considerations.[11] For example, a bank vice president anticipating a lot of work during the next week may opt not to attend a League of Women Voters meeting; for her, work and professional advancement are more important than

10. Until recently, Rotary International stipulated in its bylaws that women were barred from membership. However, a U.S. Supreme Court decision (*Board of Directors of Rotary International et al. v. Rotary Club of Duarte et al.,* 1987) overturned that stipulation, ruling that individual chapters could allow female membership. However, the organization remains overwhelmingly male.

11. For a thoughtful inquiry into the meaning of civic obligation in American life, see Bellah et al. (1985).

civic obligation. For another person, spending the weekend before Christmas with his family is more important than civic responsibility, and he will choose not to sell Christmas trees with fellow Rotarians. So although many civic organizations enjoy large memberships, relatively few of these members are regular and active participants in the organization. In addition, people who are most active are probably those who view their participation in self-interested terms: They use the organization for networking purposes, or they believe that the civic activities of the organization make an important policy contribution in the community.

Labor and Professional Organizations

In most American cities, a substantial proportion of working adults belong to some professional or vocational organization. For most blue-collar workers, this is a labor union, perhaps the United Auto Workers or the Teamsters' Union. For white-collar workers, it might be the American Medical Association, the American Bar Association, or the American Federation of Teachers. Yet as indicators of participation in local politics, high membership rates are deceiving for two reasons. First, most members of both labor unions and professional associations tend to be joiners but not participators. In the case of labor unions, membership is an occupational requirement in most states. In the case of professional organizations, membership is expected, and most people succumb to peer pressure and join. But in neither case is membership equivalent to participation in any but a nominal sense, and most members do little more than vote (for officers, to strike, and so forth).[12]

Second, most labor unions and professional organizations tend not to get involved in local issues. The American Medical Association has an active lobby in Washington, for instance, and a keen interest in a variety of health-related federal policies. It is also quite active in state capitols, lobbying for tort reform in the area of medical malpractice. But most health policy at the local level is merely a reflection of that developed at the federal or state level, and the AMA has few local concerns. While the American Bar Association does get involved in nominating candidates for local judicial positions, its major activity is also concentrated at the state and federal level. Finally, labor unions become involved in local politics through their decisions to strike or not strike. But while strikes by public employee unions (e.g., the American Federation of State, County, and Municipal Employees; the American Federation of Teachers) are designed to disrupt the flow of urban life, most private-sector strikes affect only the industry involved, the strikers, and their families.

12. Often, membership in professional organizations provides economic and professional benefits for members, for example, group rates for professional liability insurance and access to law libraries. See Olson (1968) for a general discussion of the benefits of participation in groups.

Beyond job actions, however, most union political activity focuses at the state and national levels, where labor policy is decided. For example, minimum-wage legislation is passed or rejected by the U.S. Congress or state legislatures, as are occupational safety requirements. Labor unions, with an active interest in these and related matters, tend to lobby in Washington, D.C., and they maintain political action committees to support the campaigns of federal and state office seekers. But since little occupationally relevant legislation is passed at the local level, such effort would be largely wasted there. The one exception to this occurs for craft unions, whose members may have a great stake in local building codes and regulations.

Even when labor unions attempt to get involved in local politics, they are rarely successful. The membership of many unions is racially and ethnically diverse. And while this diversity has little impact on the union's support for national programs (minimum wage, occupational safety, comprehensive health insurance), it often creates disagreement about local policies. For example, many union members are critical of proposals to increase local taxes for such programs as subsidized day care, mass transit, or public health clinics, even though these programs may benefit the working class. As another example, middle-class housing in many cities remains, for the most part, racially segregated, and many white union members resent local ordinances designed to integrate neighborhoods. Yet, among the union's black membership, these ordinances are of great importance. Finally, most unions are quite divided on the use of ethnic, gender, or racial quotas. These cleavages, if allowed to surface, could tear apart the union; hence, most unions prefer simply not to get involved in local issues.

Neighborhood Organizations and Homeowner Associations

One of the favorite scenes of movie and television screenwriters shows an elderly man or woman, often the recent victim of a crime, looking out onto a dirty, rundown section of town and saying something like, "The old neighborhood just isn't the same anymore." This, no doubt, is an accurate observation. But, in fact, *American society is changing,* and it is merely taking its neighborhoods along for the ride.

Neighborhoods defined. Before considering exactly how neighborhoods are changing and the political ramifications of these changes, we must consider what constitutes a neighborhood. In an exceptionally thorough exposition, Anthony Downs (1981) elucidates several factors that may be used to define a neighborhood. At a broad level, he suggests that *the immediate neighborhood* is the small cluster of houses right around one's own. This is perhaps what most of us think of as a neighborhood, but it is too narrow for a discussion of urban politics. There are simply too many such neighborhoods, each with too little political clout. Downs suggests that the *homogeneous neighborhood* is the area up to where the market value of housing noticeably changes or where the mix of housing types or values changes. This, in fact, is the definition that many cities invoke in identifying neighborhoods, particularly ones that are planned around future housing developments. A parcel of land is given some attractive name (Prairie Meadows, Ridgeland, Seminole Hills) and zoned for certain types of houses (e.g., a minimum of 2,000 square feet, a minimum of one-third acre, only single-family dwellings). Further, builders tend to construct houses in these new neighborhoods that conform roughly to a single architectural style (modern, split-level). And when a sufficient number of houses have been constructed and families have moved in, a neighborhood exists. These neighborhoods tend to be relatively small, seldom with over five hundred houses, and often with fewer than one hundred houses.

This style of neighborhood development is relatively new. Older neighborhoods tended to develop on some other basis. Downs suggests several possibilities. One is a common space as a focal point for personal interaction, perhaps a public park. A second is a common relationship with some nearby institution, perhaps an elementary school, a church, or a police station. A third is common membership in an ethnic group. In most large cities, Italian, Greek, Polish, Jewish, black, and Hispanic neighborhoods are common. A fourth is a common relationship to a physical barrier or a set of physical barriers. For instance, neighborhoods are often bounded by busy streets that children are not allowed to cross, thus encouraging intra-neighborhood rather than inter-neighborhood interaction.

Changing neighborhood character. This comparison between old and new definitions of neighborhoods suggests an important change in American society: the decline of social interaction as the basis of urban life. Several neighborhood-level trends suggest this shift. First, newer neighborhoods are constructed out of developers' plans and market considerations, whereas older neighborhoods emerged largely around social interaction. A second trend is demographic: The average person is older today (and even older tomorrow) than at any other time in recent memory. An elderly population is past its child-bearing years; hence, there are (and will be) fewer children to play with one another, and in so doing, to help knit the bonds of neighborhood interaction. Moreover, an elderly population is less physically active than its younger counterpart. As a result, neighborhoods where the elderly are concentrated experience an absolute decline in the potential for social interaction. A third trend, discussed in chapter 6, involves an increasing number of working mothers with little time to interact with neighbors. And with working mothers comes the need for child care, usually in a preschool outside the immediate neighborhood. Thus, children are more likely to develop friendships that take

159

them outside the neighborhood to play. A fourth trend, also discussed in chapter 6, is increasing crime and fear of crime. The fear of crime may lead people to stay home and engage in indoor rather than outdoor recreation. A fifth trend is the aging process, in this instance not of people but of buildings. The infrastructure of most cities is simply getting older, and with age comes deterioration. In most inner cities, habitable apartment buildings are less habitable than they once were, and in cities like New York, habitable buildings are interspersed with burned-out structures. Sidewalks, too, are decaying. In general, the neighborhood as an inviting place for interaction has seen better days. Finally, Americans have become more mobile, and greater mobility leads to a greater sense of transience. Many neighborhood dwellers, particularly in newer neighborhoods, simply do not have a commitment to the neighborhood as a place where they expect to spend their lives. And even in older neighborhoods, many younger people discover that they can buy old, often run-down houses for bargain prices, live in them for a couple of years, renovate them, and sell their property for a handsome profit. This *gentrification* of older neighborhoods no doubt improves their physical appearance, but usually at a substantial cost to neighborhood stability.

Types of neighborhood participation. So the screenwriters are right: The old neighborhood just isn't the same. And the opportunities for social inter-action—and as an outgrowth of social interaction, political participation—are fewer than they were twenty-five years ago. Many neighborhoods have responded by promoting various clubs, organizations, and institutions within their boundaries, most with dual (but related) purposes of promoting social interaction and neighborhood pride. In many situations, neighborhood associations have formed as umbrella organizations, designed to promote the overall interest of the neighborhood. These neighborhood associations, as well as a variety of the organizations that have emerged within neighborhoods, became an important vehicle for citizen participa-tion during the 1970s and 1980s, and they seem to support the conclusion that American society has become more participatory over the years. But in considering neighborhood participation, the validity of this conclusion deserves careful inspection.

Several writers have discussed the kinds of organizations that are typi-cally found within neighborhoods. Downs (1981) suggests that they include extended families, government service agencies (e.g., elementary schools), religious and social organizations (a Catholic Parish, a Salvation Army cen-ter), and political organizations (e.g., the Democratic precinct office). Douglas Yates (1977) notes that many sections in the Lower East Side of Manhattan had two to three community organizations on the same block, and in twenty-square-block area, he counted more than two hundred different community organizations. His partial list of these organizations includes:

church associations

neighborhood chambers of commerce

service clubs (Rotary, Kiwanis, Lions)

parent-teacher associations

racial organizations (NAACP, CORE)

ethnic associations

senior citizen centers

community action agencies

neighborhood health councils

tenant councils

food coops

drug prevention groups

street patrols

neighborhood associations

In addition, many neighborhoods publish neighborhood newspapers. Some, for example the *Village Voice* from New York's Greenwich Village, have developed national reputations. Most however, serve a local audience. In Minneapolis, for example, thirty-seven neighborhood newspapers were published in 1977, up from twenty-three only three years earlier (Boyte 1980). The largest single goal of these papers is to inform the neighborhood about itself and promote a sense of neighborhood identity and pride. Only of secondary concern are information about available social services and communication with outside interests.

These organizations no doubt facilitate social interaction within the neighborhood, but whether they have created an absolute increase in the level of social participation is open to question. In past decades, for example, many parents participated in local education through such activities as attendance at PTA meetings, and school newsletters served the function of today's neighborhood newspapers. Today, some observers feel that parental participation in the schools is lower than during past decades (e.g., Henderson 1988), due to a number of factors: the demographics of the aging process (fewer people have school-aged children); the logistics of two-income families (working parents have a hard time coming home from work at 5:30, cooking dinner, and finding the energy to attend a PTA meeting at 7:00); the breakdown of the family (participation is highest among families with both natural parents; Dornbush and Ritter 1988); and the demise of the neighborhood school in many cities (due to school busing). In many locations, an elected council of parents meets with educators in place of more general PTA participation. By the same token, the trends cited earlier have reduced the potential for social interaction in the neighborhood. In general, the proliferation of neighborhood groups and organizations has been useful in fighting the trend toward isolation that has occurred for many families, but it is unlikely that they have increased political participation beyond levels achieved during the middle years of this century.

Goals of neighborhood associations. At a higher level of aggregation, many neighborhoods have created neighborhood associations to promote the interests of the entire neighborhood. The viability of these associations ultimately rests on the assumption that the neighborhood is a homogeneous entity with a single interest. Or put differently, a neighborhood association is most likely to be successful in its mission if it represents a set of homogeneous neighbors. Downs (1981) describes the mission of a neighborhood association as follows:

1. enable children and adults to develop social and other skills through interaction with neighbors;
2. pressure government and private agencies to improve services to the neighborhood and neighborhood residents;
3. provide services to neighborhood residents;
4. create a local base for political support;
5. increase participation among local residents.

To these goals can be added:

6. increase neighborhood pride and identification;
7. increase (or at least maintain) the value of real estate within the neighborhood.

Obviously, many of these goals cannot be achieved if the neighborhood consists of heterogeneous groups. For example, one way in which real estate value is maintained is through the exclusion of (a) multi-family dwellings, and (b) houses that cost below the prevailing market value. But if a geographic neighborhood (but obviously not a social neighborhood) simultaneously consists of wealthy families living in expensive houses and poor families living in multiple-family units, a zoning decision that benefits one must necessarily hurt the other. So, too, a neighborhood that consists of both blacks and Hispanics may have difficulty creating a single base for political action. In any event, those seeking to create politically effective neighborhood associations must carefully attend to drawing geographic boundaries, with an eye to maximizing (where possible) homogeneity.

Once formed, how does a neighborhood association attempt to achieve its goals? First, most neighborhoods hold annual or semiannual picnics, during which they elect officers and hold their business meetings. In addition, the neighborhood may sponsor a Little League baseball team or an adult softball team. Both facilitate interaction among neighbors. Second, neighborhood associations pressure both public and private agencies for better services. For example, black neighborhoods may pressure retail or manufacturing firms in the city to hire more minorities or banks to provide more residential loans (more on this in chapter 17). In addition, many neighborhood associations work with local government to identify neighborhood problems and develop budget priorities for addressing these problems. For example, advisory councils from eighty-six Birmingham, Alabama, neighborhoods worked with city hall to develop service and program priorities; in Dayton, neighborhood priority boards ranked city problems for the purpose of fund allocation; and in Atlanta, the Division of Neighborhood Planning divided the city into neighborhood groups to set neighborhood priorities (Stone , et al. 1979). Even where neighborhood participation has not been institutionalized into the city planning process, neighborhoods may become involved through less conventional protest activities. Poor neighborhoods, with the feeling of nothing left to lose, have been known to disrupt business at city hall until their concerns have been heard. In a later section of this chapter, we will further consider such protest activities as another form of political participation.

Third, neighborhood associations often sponsor or even provide services of their own. Perhaps the most common is Neighborhood Watch, a program sponsored by police departments in which neighbors (a) meet with a representative of the police department to learn how to deter crime and (b) commit themselves to actively watch for unusual occurrences that might signal a crime in their area. Some neighborhoods have also sponsored nonprofit daycare programs for the children of working parents (sometimes subsidized with federal, state, or local funds). And some neighborhood associations, for example the Woodlawn Organization in the South Side of Chicago, have contracted with cities to provide such services as managing a public housing project and conducting vocational education programs (Boyte 1980).

Fourth, neighborhood associations have often become bases for local political mobilization. This occurs most notably for minorities, with the neighborhood association becoming a catalyst for black or Hispanic participation in local politics. Consider, for example, Chicago's Woodlawn Organization, created by Saul Alinsky and Father John Egan in the 1950s. It was largely responsible for mobilizing blacks during the early years of the Civil Rights Movement, and it served as a model for other black neighborhoods across the country (Boyte 1980). Alinsky's principles, set forth in his book *Reveille for Radicals* (1946), are worth noting briefly. First, advises Alinsky, people must be organized for power. They must be motivated by perceived self-interest around concrete issues; and given this motivation, they can work together as a body wielding more power than any individual might possess. Second, the organization must be built around indigenous leadership. In the Woodlawn neighborhood, for example, Alinsky worked toward organizing himself out of a position by training local people to take over his leadership functions. He worked toward developing and strengthening local networks of churches, clubs, small businesses, unions, and other institutions that could develop and act on self-interest. Third, Alinsky believed in organizing to win. He was the ultimate pragmatist, believing that for society's have-nots, the end justified any means that might be employed (Alinsky 1971).

Even in middle-class neighborhoods, neighborhood associations often serve a political mobilization function. A case in point is the 1966 conflict in New York's Greenwich Village over New York University's decision to construct a new six-story library on a site adjoining Washington Square Park (Yates 1977). This library, the university argued, was necessary for continued academic excellence. Further, university administrators pointed out with pride, it had contracted with a renowned architect to design a structure that would represent an important architectural contribution to the city. It would, they hinted, even provide the park with a symmetry and elegance of design comparable to the Place Vendome in Paris. But neighborhood residents were not convinced by the proposed architectural elegance. Instead, they were concerned about how the proposed building would impede the flow of sunlight to the park and the increase in pedestrian traffic that inevitably would follow. Neighborhood groups effectively mobilized and coordinated citizen participation. And although city hall finally overruled the neighborhood protest and allowed construction of the library, the neighborhood had become a potent political force in the dispute.

Fifth, neighborhood associations often sponsor activities designed to promote neighborhood identification and pride. Many neighborhoods, for example, display luminaria (lighted candles) along their streets during Christmas season. Another favorite neighborhood activity is the annual cleanup, where residents volunteer to spend a Saturday picking up litter along the streets. In addition, most neighborhood associations put out a short newsletter to inform residents of neighborhood news (the date of the annual cleanup, recent births, available babysitters).

Sixth, many neighborhood associations, particularly in middle- and upper-class neighborhoods, view their primary purpose as the protection of property values. *[The theory of lifestyle and territory]* In some areas, in fact, this emphasis is reflected in the name the association has taken, for example the Prairie Meadows Homeowners' Association or the East Lawrence Improvement Association. One way in which property values are protected is through zoning laws prohibiting multi-family dwellings, prohibiting nonstationary residences (i.e., trailers), or requiring minimum floor space in a house. Whenever a developer even suggests constructing duplexes (or even worse, apartments) in a neighborhood of single-family dwellings, neighborhood association representatives are in the front row at the next city council meeting arguing against any change in zoning. Or if the city proposes a subsidized low-income housing unit for a neighborhood, the association is sure to protest. In general, the neighborhood association looks out for the interests of its members; and for most members, their houses represent their largest single investment, and therefore their primary interest.

The effectiveness of neighborhood associations: An assessment. Do neighborhood associations really increase political participation? Certainly, in the case of minority mobilization they have. Mayoral victories for such minority candidates as Tom Bradley in Los Angeles (1973) and Harold Washington in Chicago (1983) would not have been possible without substantial grass-roots mobilization in black neighborhoods. But on other levels, the answer is less clear. Annual membership dues for neighborhood associations are modest, typically a dollar, and seldom more than five dollars. This pays for duplicating the newsletter, providing supplies for luminaria, and preparing supporting materials for city council meetings. It also guarantees almost full membership. After all, who can't afford a buck a year? But while large membership lists are impressive to the city council as well as to those who study political participation, they may be misleading. In the final analysis, most neighborhood associations are staff organizations. They have a president, and when volunteers can be found, a vice-president, a secretary, and a treasurer. But in most cases, they have very few active members (often only these four officers). In one neighborhood association the authors studied, the president had held that position for four years. She was not power hungry; she just could not find anyone else willing to fill the position. She was faced with the situation of either continuing as its leader or dissolving the association. When she called meetings, she was able to hold them in her living room (and a small living room at that). People simply were not interested in participating, unless their self-interest was affected directly.[13] This type of limited participation may be more common than not. And those who argue, based on such evidence as the proliferation of neighborhood groups and associations, that political participation in American cities is increasing, are missing an important distinction between membership in organizations and active participation in the political arena.

Ad Hoc Groups

In the best tradition of American politics, a variety of groups spring up in urban areas to address many different kinds of social problems. A recent example is Mothers Against Drunk Driving (MADD), a national group founded by a mother whose child was killed by a drunk driver. Since its inception, local affiliates have formed in many cities throughout the country. Groups have also formed in many cities to protest a variety of other problems, including litter, racial or gender discrimination, poor traffic control, lack of low-cost housing, and so forth.

One of the most innovative of these groups emerged recently in Montgomery, Alabama, bearing the unlikely name of "The Friendly Supper Club" (Phillips 1986). Racial tensions in Montgomery have always run high, and

13. Even in this neighborhood, self-interest was narrowly defined. During the time of our study, a neighborhod boy had been tragically struck and killed by a car on his way to school; yet, the president of the neighborhood association had difficulty mobilizing residents to demand that the city install a traffic signal.

they were brought to a head in 1983 when a violent confrontation in a black household left a white police officer severely wounded. The blacks involved in the incident, who maintained that they were severely beaten by the police officer, were brought to trial. When the case ended in a mistrial, it left Montgomery embittered and racially polarized. Shortly thereafter, an anonymous man, using the pseudonym Jack Smith, wrote letters to a number of black and white civic leaders inviting them to dine together the following week in a local cafeteria. The invitation noted

> Outright segregation has disappeared, but there is still very little interaction beyond the most superficial level. Few blacks that I know visit socially with whites, or whites with blacks, in the way that builds understanding between friends. Because we don't know one another, crises tend to swiftly open old wounds. (Phillips 1986, 10)

As a result of this letter, approximately thirty-five people, including leaders of Montgomery's black and white communities, met for dinner. These individuals committed themselves to monthly dinners, and today as many as three hundred people participate in these meals.

While these ad hoc groups may be fairly common in American cities, they do not represent large-scale participation. For example, three hundred participants in a city the size of Montgomery (with an approximate population of 200,000) is a small drop in a large bucket. Much more important is the *number* of such groups that have emerged over the past decade, rather than the absolute level of participation they generate.

Participation Through Protest

A number of studies point to the importance of economic position in the community as a basis for effective group participation. Thomas Dye (1969a, 249) notes that

> civic associations are the predominant style of organized interest group activity at the local level, that businessmen, reform groups, taxpayer associations, merchants, service clubs, developers all organize themselves into civic associations for action at the local level.

In a complementary finding, Betty Zisk (1973) reports the results of a survey of San Francisco Bay area city council members asking them to identify the most influential pressure groups. The results came out much as Dye indicates they might:

166

1. Economic groups, including the chamber of commerce, taxpayer groups, and neighborhood groups, were identified as influential by 43 percent of the respondents.
2. Civic groups, including Parent-Teacher Associations, the League of Women Voters, churches, and service clubs, were identified as influential by 31 percent of the respondents.
3. Special interest groups, including conservation associations, builders, and senior citizens groups, were identified as influential by 23 percent of the respondents.
4. Semi-official bodies, including the planning commission and other advisory boards, were identified as influential by only 2 percent of the respondents.

Others have concluded that power in such communities as Seattle (Miller 1958), Atlanta (Hunter 1953), Ypsilanti (Schulze 1961), and San Jose (Trounstine and Christensen 1982) resides in the hands of local business owners.

Taken together, these findings suggest that homeowners (through their neighborhood associations) and business owners (both through their chamber of commerce and ad hoc initiatives) are likely to benefit from their civic and community participation. By the same token, such traditionally middle-class organizations as service clubs and the League of Women Voters may also see their participatory efforts come to fruition as policy outcomes. But missing from the ranks of the influential are the underclass and underclass advocates. For example, urban housing authorities, which oversee public housing and represent underclass interests, fall into the set of "semi-official bodies" that Zisk reports are largely powerless. The same can be said for most social service agencies, traditional spokespersons for the underclass (Bolland and Selby 1988). This leaves the underclass with but two participatory options: electoral mobilization and protest.

Electoral Mobilization

This strategy is risky and not at all guaranteed to be successful. Two difficulties underlie underclass electoral mobilization. First, the underclass is not itself homogeneous, and as a result it often experiences severe cleavages in both strategy and tactics. In contrast to the upper class, which is racially (and to some extent, ethnically) homogeneous, the underclass comprises a number of racially, ethnically, and demographically distinct subgroups. Most cities, for example, have an underclass black community, an underclass Hispanic community, and an underclass white community. Further, each of these communities can be divided into elderly and nonelderly populations, which find themselves in the underclass for quite different reasons. The elderly, for example, may have belonged to the middle class at one time, but due to meager retirement benefits, they now find themselves in difficult economic straits. In contrast, younger people find themselves in difficult economic straits because of lack of jobs, poor education, racial barriers to advancement, and (often) mismanagement of their finances. The underclass white community can be subdivided along ethnic lines, with different ethnic groups having different traditions and approaches to solving problems. In short, then, there is no single underclass community and no single underclass voting block within most cities.

The divisions within the underclass make it very difficult for a candidate to mobilize the poor for an electoral victory. For example, Harold Washington won the mayoral election in Chicago in 1983 only because his Hispanic support increased from 13 percent in the primary to 75 percent in the general election (Muñoz and Henry 1986; also see Preston 1987). But such a "rainbow coalition" is more the exception than the rule. In New York City, for example, an attempt to select a consensus minority challenger to Mayor Koch in the 1985 mayoral election failed because when no strong black candidate agreed to run, blacks in Harlem refused to support the candidacy of Hispanic leader Herman Badillo (Mollenkopf 1986).

Second, even if a rainbow coalition can be mobilized, it is not clear that election translates directly into policy outcomes. Many minority mayoral candidates find it expedient, either during their campaign or after their election, to invite business leaders into their coalition. This makes practical sense, for business leaders have the resources both to allow the candidate to wage a successful campaign and to run the government effectively.

Tom Bradley in Los Angeles. In Los Angeles, Tom Bradley courted the business community to fulfill his political agenda (Sonenshein 1986), as did Wilson Goode in Philadelphia and Henry Cisneros in San Antonio (Muñoz and Henry 1986). This strategy is likely to pay impressive dividends in times of economic prosperity. For example, after his election in 1973, Mayor Bradley was able to use a mix of federal and private dollars to substantially redevelop the downtown area. At the same time, he was able to obtain federal money to begin a wide variety of new social service programs, most located in poor and minority communities (Sonenshein 1986). But while it is easy to put together a coalition of business and underclass interests in times of prosperity, it is considerably more difficult to do so in times of economic retrenchment.

Wilson Goode in Philadelphia. Wilson Goode made a considerable effort to be responsible to both sets of interests following his electoral victory in Philadelphia in 1983. He was elected with overwhelming support from black voters, coupled with support from white liberals and some of the city's labor unions. During his first hundred days in office, he reaffirmed his commitment to a classic liberal agenda: His early initiatives included summer jobs for youth, housing and mental health programs for the homeless, and an adult literacy program (Muñoz and Henry 1986). But he went about his administration in a manner that most business people could relate to and appreciate. He appointed biracial boards to recommend people for his administration, for example, and almost invariably followed their suggestions. But before long, the bloom was off the rose. In a law-and-order gesture, Goode ordered local police to assault the local headquarters of MOVE, a radical black protest group. As a result, an entire residential block in a poor, minority neighborhood burned to the ground, and eleven people (including five children) were killed (see Ransom 1987, for a discussion of Goode's election and term in office). While this action may have displayed a symbolic insensitivity to the concerns of the poor, a more practical display occurred in the 1985 city council election. During the Democratic primary, Goode supported Angel Ortiz, an Hispanic, who finished seventh in a field of fifty-seven candidates seeking five seats. When one of the five Democratic nominees died during the general election campaign, Goode declined to fill the opening with Ortiz, choosing instead Francis Rafferty, a defeated incumbent (Muñoz and Henry 1986). And in 1986, Goode alienated organized labor in Philadelphia (which had supported him during his election) by breaking a strike by the city's sanitation workers. More recently he has threatened to privatize garbage collection.[14]

Electoral mobilization and political incorporation. The previous chapter briefly discussed the concept of political incorporation, introduced by Rufus Browning, Dale Rogers Marshall, and David Tabb (1984). They argue that incorporation—which they suggest is both a necessary and sufficient condition for political equality among minorities—exists within a city when:

1. minorities obtain seats on the city council;
2. a minority candidate is elected to the office of mayor; and
3. minority officeholders become part of the city's dominant coalition.

On the evidence presented here and in the previous chapter, we should conclude that the first two components of political incorporation have been achieved in many cities. But the third is problematic, largely precluded by an intriguing paradox. As noted above, the dominant coalition within most American cities resides in the business community, stressing growth policies and economic development. This contrasts sharply with the needs of the underclass within the community and the priorities of those representing underclass interests: social equality and social services (Browning, et al. 1984;

14. As another example, Henry Cisneros, elected mayor of San Antonio in 1981 with substantial business support, does not promote either his Chicano identity or the specific interests of the Chicano community. Rather, he has focused his attention largely on non-Chicano issues (Muñoz and Henry 1986).

Bolland and Selby 1988). Minorities elected to municipal office are almost always faced with a dilemma. As elected officials, they require the support of the business community (and its resources) to govern effectively, and they are typically offered the opportunity to participate in its dominant coalition. But their participation carries with it a cost: minority officeholders participate only by accepting the pro-growth agenda of the business community in place of that espoused by their natural constituents. Thus, virtually all black mayors in major cities have been accused of turning their backs on the needs of the underclass in favor of the needs of local businesses. But if black elected officials turn down the invitation to participate in the dominant coalition, they run the substantial risk of an ineffectual administration at the hands of business opposition.

Violent Protest

In the absence of either electoral mobilization or group activity as an avenue to effective participation, many of the urban poor, particularly blacks, have taken a more violent route. When we think of urban political violence, we tend to think of the race riots of the 1960s, beginning in Watts on an August day in 1965.

> On August 11, 1965, a Los Angeles police officer named Lee Minikus, acting on a tip from a truck driver, pursued and stopped a young man named Marquette Frye for speeding, driving without a licence, and driving while intoxicated. By the time Minikus and his partner had arrested Marquette Frye an angry crowd had gathered, and before the night was over, the Watts district of Los Angeles was engulfed in a series of street riots. (Ross and Stedman 1985, 96)

In 1966, similar riots erupted in Cleveland and Chicago, and by the end of the decade, urban racial rioting had spread across the entire country, affecting over one hundred fifty cities, including Newark, Milwaukee, Detroit, Houston, Cincinnati, Phoenix, Atlanta, New Haven, Tampa, and Grand Rapids. During these riots, at least two hundred twenty people were killed, more than eight thousand were injured, and over fifty thousand were arrested (Downes 1970).

Yet, the 1960s were neither the beginning nor the end of violent protest in the city. Between 1917 and 1963, seventy-six major racial disorders occurred in urban America, beginning with riots in East St. Louis in 1917 and Chicago in 1919 (Fogelson 1971). And during the 1980s, urban racial violence returned, with riots in Miami in 1980 and 1982 and in Baton Rouge in 1988. These recurrences, though not nearly so severe as the racial violence of the 1960s, suggest that this is a problem we may not yet have put behind us. It is not surprising, then, to note Ted Robert Gurr's (1989) finding that between 1966 and 1970, the United States ranked twenty-third out of eighty-seven countries in civil conflict.

Violence as participation? But does violence constitute real political participation, or is it the action of hoodlums and hooligans who shoot, loot, and burn for strictly nonpolitical motives? Banfield (1974), taking a quizzical perspective in a book chapter entitled "Rioting Mainly for Fun and Profit," views the riots as unrelated to race, attributing them instead largely to an underclass need for stimulation and excitement. Others also have taken a cynical view, attributing the riots to a relatively small (1-2 percent) "riff-raff" of unemployed, unattached youths, people with criminal records, and migrant rural Southerners who were disenchanted with life in the big city (see Fogelson and Hill, 1968, for a discussion of these theories). Yet, neither explanation holds up to close scrutiny. First, the most common triggering event in the riots concerned the police, a symbol of oppression in most ghettos. For example, in Watts a black man was arrested; in Harlem in 1964, an off-duty white police officer shot and killed a fifteen-year-old black youth; and in Miami in 1980, an all-white jury acquitted four white police officer accused of killing a black man. In each case, the event demonstrated the impotence of the black community in using legitimate political channels and triggered a violent political response.

Second, most of the participating rioters were politically aware of this impotence and resented it. When blacks were later asked to attribute cause to the riots, they almost universally identified societal causes, such as unemployment and racial discrimination. This is not to suggest that all rioters were politically motivated, however. No doubt, some *were* participating mainly for fun and profit. Yet, this seems to be a less important and less credible explanation for the bulk of participation than one that focuses on political motives.

Third, who actually did participate in the riots? Was it riff-raff or was it a broad cross-section of the ghetto population? Here, again, the cynics seem to be contradicted by the evidence. According to a study by Fogelson and Hill (1968), commissioned by the National Advisory Commission on Civil Disorders (Kerner Commission), the typical rioter :

1. was slightly better educated than other ghetto dwellers;
2. was likely to have been born in the area where the riot occurred;
3. was employed, although at a job requiring little education;
4. had an income approximately equal to that of other ghetto dwellers; and
5. was no more likely than anyone else in the area to possess a police record.

Further, the Kerner Commission found that in Watts, 15 percent of ghetto residents were active participants in the riot and that between 34 percent and 50 percent of the residents were sympathetic. Similar figures emerged for other cities.

These findings address a second important question: Does violent participation represent a means for mass participation in American politics?

Certainly, within those cities where riots occurred, participation was remarkably high, perhaps higher than voter turnout among the ghetto population. But since the 1960s, participation through violence has declined, as has participation in general. As Banfield suggests, political violence may be transient, a time-bound phenomenon like rock groups: popular one decade, virtually gone and almost unremembered the next. Perhaps as a form of expression, violence simply went out of style (and like most things that go out of style, it returns sporadically for short visits). Or perhaps it accomplished its purpose. It drew attention to the plight of inner-city blacks, generated a commission to study both racial tensions and political violence, and created some changes in social programs and opportunities for blacks.

But probably the most common explanation for the decline of racial violence is the lack of positive outcomes and the plethora of negative outcomes it generated. Few cities responded positively to the riots. Instead, cities that had experienced riots significantly increased police expenditures (Welch 1975). And a number of cities showed a tremendous white backlash; for example, in 1971 former police chief Frank Rizzo ran successfully for mayor in Philadelphia on a blatantly anti-black, law-and-order platform. With so much to lose and so little evidence of tangible gain, violent protest has understandably ebbed. In contrast to 1968, when nearly 20 percent of blacks believed that they should be ready to use violence to gain rights (Campbell and Schuman 1968), today relatively few believe that violence is an effective strategy.

Nonviolent Protest

Although violent protest makes newspaper headlines, nonviolent protest is much more common. In a study of 120 protest incidents in forty-three cities, Peter Eisinger (1973) found all but 6 percent to be peaceful. This is not to say, however, that nonviolent protest is not disruptive. In fact, Eisinger (p.14) defines protest as "a device by which groups of people manipulate fear of disorder and violence while at the same time they protect themselves from paying the potentially extreme costs of acknowledging such a strategy." The very fact that a protest group has violence as an option but chooses to restrain itself potentially provides its members with leverage in dealing with municipal government. As we noted before, the public is not tolerant of violence as a political tool, and survey findings show that citizens believe more rather than less force should be used to squash violent protest (Converse et al. 1969).

This public pressure may cause governments to be unresponsive to protestors' demands. On the other hand, when protestors are more cautious in their strategies, they may avoid triggering widespread public reaction, and governments may be better able to fashion a positive response to protest demands (Schumaker 1978).

The restrained potential for violence has been the hallmark of the Civil

Rights Movement in the United States, particularly under the leadership of the Reverend Martin Luther King. Again, it should be stressed, that movement was designed to be disruptive but nonviolent, for instance by conducting sit-ins and openly challenging statutes. And always underlying the movement was the idea of confrontation. Contention and disputation can be a useful way of forcing problems on the attention of those in positions to solve them. For it is nonviolent, direct action, said King (1964), that can create a crisis and foster so great a tension "that a community which has constantly refused to negotiate is forced to confront the issue."

Mobilizing the urban poor. A similar strategy, developed largely by Saul Alinsky, has been employed by those attempting to mobilize the urban poor. For Alinksy, the ghetto is a political structure, created and maintained by existing power arrangements between the haves and the have nots in American society. It can be changed, he argues, only by mobilizing an effective counterforce to these arrangements. And since the ghetto poor do not have access to the traditional resources of power (wealth and interest group representation), they must rely on the resources they do possess—the ability to disrupt society through their protest. As a pragmatist, Alinsky believed that no action was too severe to achieve the revolutionary ends he proposed; but as a pragmatist, he also realized that violence was often counterproductive, and that simple disruption, with the threat of violence thrown in, was usually more productive. In an elaboration of his means-ends calculus, Alinsky (1971) proposed eleven "ethical rules."

1. One's concern with the ethics of means and ends varies inversely with the degree of one's personal vested interest in the issue.
2. The judgment of the ethics of means is dependent upon the political positions of those sitting in judgment.
3. In war, the end justifies almost any means.
4. Judgment about the ethics of any means must be made in the context of the times in which the action is taken.
5. Concern with ethics increases with the number of means available, and vice versa.
6. The less important the desired end, the more one can afford to engage in an ethical evaluation of means.
7. Success or failure is a mighty determinant of ethics.
8. The morality of a means depends on whether it is being employed at a time of imminent victory or imminent defeat.
9. Any means which is effective is automatically judged by the opposition to be unethical.
10. You do what you can with what you have and clothe it in moral garments.

- 11. Phrase goals in general terms, like "Liberty, Equality, Fraternity" or "The Common Welfare."

Taken together, these rules imply that those in positions of power improperly sit in ethical judgment of those without power and of the means they employ to gain a voice. Further, the more successful the underclass is in improving its lot, the more judgmental the ruling class becomes. Finally, the symbolism employed by both sides is mere rhetoric, adopted to mask the tactics that are actually being employed. Alinsky argues, in essence, that the struggle for power is tantamount to war; as such, one's ethical judgments of tactics employed by the enemy are little more than self-serving justifications for the tactics employed by oneself.

Alinsky and his colleagues developed a number of tactics for advancing the cause of the poor, several of which make very good press and demonstrate the potential for nonviolent disruption.

> He once proposed feeding a hundred kids a baked bean dinner before sending them off to a Rochester Symphony concert. Another time he threatened to use demonstrators in a literal sit-in to tie up the toilets at O'Hare Airport in Chicago. When a department store was recalcitrant about hiring blacks and a boycott proved ineffective, Alinsky proposed the opposite—a buy-in. His plan called for busing in three thousand blacks who would inundate sales clerks with questions about the price and quality of goods, make endless exchanges and returns, order a large number of items C.O.D., and then refuse to accept delivery. (Stone, et al. 1979, 107-8)

On a less theatrical level, Alinsky and his colleagues organized a variety of rent strikes and secondary boycotts.

These (and other) actions resulted in a number of initial successes during the 1960s. For example, the department store buy-in netted 186 new jobs for minorities, virtually overnight (Alinsky 1971). But the early successes were difficult to build on. One reason has already been discussed. The urban poor are not a unified group, but rather a collection of very different people with different racial and ethnic allegiances and different problems and concerns. In most cities, once the initial enthusiasm of this loose coalition began to fade, the natural divisiveness of the groups composing the coalition began to assert itself, and agreement on an agenda became increasingly difficult to obtain. In addition, the easy problems were targeted early and were solved; but after the easy problems (like getting local merchants to hire minorities) were solved, much more resilient problems remained. Further, grassroots organizations, like the Woodlawn Organization in Chicago, became vested in the system after achieving initial success. As Alinsky implies, those with nothing have nothing to lose by trying to gain a foothold in the political system, and they risk nothing by using radical tactics. But once a foothold has been gained, the tactics must change for fear of losing the foothold. Thus, many once-radical organizations have begun to work within the system, and their threat of violence is greatly diminished.

But what happens when a protest group becomes part of the system? In general, it becomes a staff organization run by paid professionals. And although members still pay their dues, checkbook participation is more common than not. The excitement and possible large gains of bucking the system are replaced by a slow and steady pace. Although slow and steady wins the race, it is not exciting, and participation suffers. Thus, violence and disruption are the same as other forms of participation: The opportunities exist, but relatively few people choose to use them.

Political Participation in American Cities: An Assessment

Many scholars believe participation in America to be increasing. The previous discussion brings us to a somewhat different conclusion, however: Participation in urban politics is actually declining. This decline creates the opportunity for urban government and politics by administration (both governmental and ad hoc), but not for government according to the democratic precept of wide and effective political participation. *[The theory of grass-roots democracy]*

We should, however, temper this conclusion by acknowledging the greater *opportunity* for participation, particularly in the urban arena, particularly over the past decade. Even as late as the mid 1970s, many cities still held their council meetings at 2:00 P.M. on a weekday, making it almost impossible for most citizens (other than business owners and professionals) to attend. Now things have changed, and meetings are held in the evenings, maximizing the opportunity for attendance. In many communities, city council meetings are also televised. In addition, the number of political groups active at the community level has proliferated during the past decade, with groups becoming more narrowly focused in their goals. We have seen this with the increase in neighborhood groups, support groups, ethnic and racial groups, and business groups. And with the proliferation of groups comes the opportunity for participation.

But, as noted previously, the opportunity for participation in no way guarantees participation. Granted, more people attend city council meetings; but still, the number of people who show up for any given meeting is limited, perhaps no greater than fifty or one hundred in most cities. So, too, the opportunities for participation in neighborhood politics has increased, but typically only a handful of people actually get involved. In contrast, the more general trends in American society create a countervailing force that is actually driving participation down in most cities.

175

Towards an Explanation of the Ungovernable City[15]

A long but straightforward chain of logic leads us to the conclusion that decreased participation is contributing to the *ungovernable city*. It begins with the basic tenet of politics, forwarded by Madison two centuries ago in *Federalist 10*: Increased political participation serves to protect the rights of the minority.[16] For Madison, as well as other observers of the American political system, participation by a large number of people leads to self-interested competition, and through competition to compromise, wherein diverse attitudes and values are reduced to a common denominator. Thus, a person deciding alone can act quickly and decisively, having to consider only those consequences of the action that will affect him or her; two people acting together can act half as quickly and half as decisively; they must consider more consequences than a single individual; and a collective can only inch along, considering every possible angle of a decision and thus making few decisions that vary from the status quo. (This is one basis for what has been termed incremental decision making.) A group that cannot act decisively, that considers all possible consequences of a decision, and that tends to reaffirm the status quo is unlikely to engage a new policy that may intentionally or unintentionally abridge the rights of a segment of society.

But how does this affect the governability of a city? In fact, increased participation would seem to make a city more ungovernable by limiting its ability to act decisively. This is the argument made by Theodore Lowi (1969a) for national politics and by Yates (1977) for politics at the local level; they label the difficulties engendered by increased participation *hyperpluralism* and *street-fighting pluralism,* respectively. But both authors note that it is not the individual participants in national or urban politics that make it ungovernable; rather, it is the proliferation of groups and group demands that causes government to react rather than lead. Yates went so far as to liken the urban political arena to a penny arcade where municipal officials are forced to play a political game similar to that found in a shooting gallery. Targets, in the form of group demands, constantly pop up unexpectedly and disappear from sight almost as unexpectedly as new demands emerge. But where do these group demands originate? Ultimately, with the group's active membership. And this takes us to the third link in the chain of reasoning.

A political group with a large, active membership is as indecisive as a political body in developing and articulating its demands, and once developed, the demands are likely to be relatively weak. In contrast, a group with

15. In a sardonic entry, political commentator William Safire (1978) defined *ungovernable city* as "what pessimists consider every major American city to be."

16. Madison says: "...take in a greater variety of...interests; you make it less probable that a majority...will have a common motive to invade the rights of other citizens...and to act in unison" (Madison 1971, 83).

176

few active members can act much more decisively, articulating much stronger demands. This is the difference between many local chambers of commerce and ad hoc economic development groups. As was pointed out in the discussion of San Jose, the larger, more diverse group must develop policy demands that satisfy all of its members, whereas the smaller group has fewer diverse members to satisfy. In Yates' terminology, the targets created by groups with large, active memberships will pop up more slowly and more predictably than will targets created by groups with a small active membership. But in the current era of proliferating groups and declining participation, city decisionmakers face the worst of both worlds: more targets that pop up faster and less predictably than ever. Thus, the number of targets is not the major problem; rather, the problem lies in the speed and decisiveness with which those targets emerge. This speed and decisiveness contributes greatly to reaction rather than proaction, and it leads, in large part, to what has been termed an ungovernable city.

One last link completes the logical chain. As a larger number of groups articulate their demands with increasing speed and decisiveness, they must necessarily compete with one another for governmental attention and resources. This competition leads to the potential for intergroup conflict that, if left unchecked, can threaten the social life of the city. Again, we can lay the cause for escalating conflict, when it does occur, directly at the feet of declining participation. A logical extension of Madison's argument holds that as political participation increases, people find themselves on both sides of cross-cutting cleavages. Edward Banfield and James Q. Wilson (1963, 46) summarize the logic of cross-cutting cleavages as follows:

> If cleavages run across each other . . . , they may serve to moderate conflict and to prevent "irreconcilable differences," because those who are enemies with respect to cleavage *a* are close allies with respect to cleavage *b* and indifferent (and therefore in a position to moderate) with respect to cleavage *c*.

Members of two neighborhood associations may thus find themselves embattled with respect to the allocation of funds for sidewalk repair, but they may find themselves allied on historical preservation. Limited participation may mask this potential alliance, which may be discovered by residents in the two neighborhoods only with their regular attendance at historical preservation meetings. And while it is perhaps easy to hate a "composite person" who lives ten blocks away and whom you never see, it is difficult to hate that person when you meet her in the flesh and actually work with her on a project of interest to you both. Thus, cross-cutting cleavages repress the escalation of conflict (as suggested by Coleman's conflict model; see chapter 6). But cross-cutting cleavages can occur only in a participatory society. If, as suggested, urban society is becoming less participatory, then it is also becoming potentially more conflictual and hence less governable.

Perhaps the ultimate but heretofore unstated question posed by this discussion concerns the distribution of power in American cities. After all, people are drawn to political participation when they expect to achieve desired outcomes. How does participation affect power, and how does power affect participation? These are questions we consider in the next chapter.

State Street. John Kimmich. Photograph.

180

Power in the City ___ 9

Power is always gradually stealing away from the many to the few, because the few are more vigilant and consistent.
Samuel Johnson
The Adventurer

The search for power—who has it, how they got it, and how they use it—is an enduring theme that haunts the literatures of biography, fiction, drama, history, psychology, sociology, and, of course, politics. Politics, some would say, is nothing more than power struggling to find a home. Thus, a discussion of power in the city can bring to temporary closure the ideas discussed in the previous chapters.

One of the earliest systematic studies of political power in America was conducted by Robert and Helen Lynd (1929) in Middletown, a pseudonym for Muncie, Indiana. Since then, researchers have studied political power in numerous cities, including Atlanta (Hunter 1953), Chicago (Banfield 1961), New York (Sayre and Kaufman 1960), Baltimore (Bachrach and Baratz 1970), Seattle (Miller 1958), San Jose (Trounstine and Christensen 1982), and New Haven (Dahl 1961). In these studies, the focus on power at the urban level is synecdochic, for most of the conclusions are directed at American society in general rather than the city itself. This larger purpose is justified on several counts. First, since most Americans live in cities, what better location to study the use of power in the political process? Second, researchers make the simplifying (although not necessarily accurate; see chapter 6) assumption that city politics provides a microcosm for American politics, and that findings from cities provide an adequate depiction of the overall American society. Third, cities provide a convenient laboratory in which studies of power can be conducted. It is no accident that many power studies have been conducted in university towns, including Ypsilanti, Michigan (Schulze 1961), Baton Rouge, Louisiana (Pellegrin and Coates 1956), Oberlin, Ohio (Wildavsky 1964), Lawrence, Kansas (Bolland 1984; Schumaker 1990), and New Haven, Connecticut (Dahl 1961).

The Early Studies: A Picture of Social Stratification

Middletown (a.k.a. Muncie)

The earliest studies showed power to be concentrated in the hands of a small number of economically advantaged individuals and families. In Middletown, the Lynds (1929) found the community to be dominated by the business class.[1] Eight years later, in a follow-up study (Lynd and Lynd 1937), they found that this dominance had narrowed to an inner group of business interests dominated by a single family, whom the Lynds called the X family.

> *(BALL FAMILY)*
> *BALL STATE*
> Middletown has . . . at present what amounts to a reigning royal family. The power of this family has become so great as to differentiate the city today somewhat from cities with a more diffuse type of control. If, however, one views the Middletown pattern as simply concentrating and personalizing the type of control which control of capital gives to the business group in our culture, the Middletown situation may be viewed as epitomizing the American business-class control system. It may even foreshadow a pattern which may become increasingly prevalent in the future as the American propertied class strives to preserve its controls. The business class in Middletown runs the city. (Lynd and Lynd 1937, 77)

A widely cited quotation, taken from a local Middletown man in 1935, shows how the X family had come to dominate all facets of community life in Middletown.

> If I'm out of work, I go to the X plant; if I need money, I go to the X bank, and if they don't like me, I don't get it; my children go to the X college; when I get sick I go to the X hospital; I buy a building lot or house in the X subdivision; my wife goes downtown to buy clothes at the X department store; if my dog stays away he is put in the X pound; I buy X milk; I drink X beer, vote for X political parties, and get help from X charities; my boy goes to the X Y.M.C.A. and my girl to their Y.W.C.A.; I listen to the word of God in X-subsidized churches; if I'm a Mason I go to X Masonic Temple; I read the news

---

1. For a summary of this and other studies of community power, see Nelson Polsby's (1980) excellent review.

from the X morning newspaper; and if I'm rich enough, I travel via the X airport. (Lynd and Lynd 1937, 74)

We must remember that this follow-up study was conducted during the Great Depression, when wealth (and presumably power) was starkly maldistributed. But even so, it says something revealing when a man-on-the-street, whose political knowledge and understanding is typically quite low, believes that a single family so dominates the life of his community.

The Lynds found that the business elite in Middletown ruled largely in its own interest, noting that "the control system operates at many points to identify public welfare with business-class welfare" (1937, 99). Further, they note that the "inner business group of bankers and businessmen often were using relief expenditures to pull certain of their business chestnuts out of the fire" (1937, 117). Finally, the Lynds note (1937, 329), this elite dominance created an uneasy relationship between local businessmen and city hall.

> The professional politician in a city like Middletown occupies in reality a position somewhat apart. He is not ordinarily a person accepted in the inner councils of the business class, and yet he must work with it in order "to get anywhere." And, on the other hand, the business class have . . . little respect for local politics and politicians, viewing them as a necessary evil which business supports and controls only enough to ensure cooperation in necessary matters.

Morris, Philadelphia, Baton Rouge, and Ypsilanti

During the next two decades, a number of other researchers reached much the same conclusion. In two independent studies of Morris, Illinois, conducted at different times (but published in the same year) by Lloyd Warner (1949) and August Hollingshead (1949), each uncovered a dominant upper class that appeared to exert considerable political pressure within the community. Hollingshead (1949, 72) cites one informant who described the community as "an aristocracy of wealth, nothing else." And like the Lynds, Hollingshead found that politicians in the community were subservient to the interests of upper-class families.

> Large tax bills accompany extensive ownership: consequently these . . . families have a direct interest in keeping assessments and tax rates low. They accomplish this effectively, within the community and county, through the control of the two major political party organizations on the township and county levels. (Hollingshead 1949, 86)

In another study, Digby Baltzell (1958, 35) found a business elite in Philadelphia that exercised "power over other men in making the decisions which shape the ends of a predominantly business-oriented social structure."

183

Along the same lines, Roland Pellegrin and Charles Coates (1956) found elite dominance in Baton Rouge. And they found the familiar pattern of relationships between the ruling class and elected politicians. Their informants

> described local government officials as relatively powerless figures who do not have the backing of influential groups but secured their positions through the support of working-class voters. Indeed, these officials were more often than not targets of ridicule for those who evaluated their positions in the power structure. (Pellegrin and Coates 1956, 414)

This did not mean that elected officials were without power; indeed, they sometimes managed to sponsor civic projects that were successful in spite of elite opposition. Nonetheless, the business-oriented climate proved dominant within the city.

In a variation on this theme, Robert Schulze (1961) found a bifurcated power structure in Ypsilanti, Michigan. On the one side, he found a set of economic elites who monopolized potential for determinative action. But on the other side was a new power elite, consisting of middle-class business and professional men, who monopolized the overt direction of political and civic life in the community. At first glance, it might appear that these different groups of elites would have fundamentally different political interests. After all, one represents the monied upper class, while the other represents the less affluent middle class. But the latter is firmly steeped in the business ethos—business owners through their livelihood and professionals through their education and training. Therefore, while the goals of the two groups may diverge at times, they are more similar than divergent.

Regional City (a.k.a. Atlanta)

Finally, in one of the most widely discussed studies of power, Floyd Hunter (1953) reaches a similar set of conclusions about Regional City (his pseudonym for Atlanta). Regional City (says Hunter) was dominated by an upper-class cadre of businessmen who interacted socially and determined policy informally and behind the scenes. "The test for admission to this circle of decision-makers is almost wholly a man's position in the business community. . . ." (Hunter 1953, 79). Further, Hunter found that this group of prominent businessmen appeared to be stable, enjoying its position of power for nearly two decades. The most powerful person among this group of business elites was a man pseudonymously named Mr. Homer, the owner of a manufacturing plant in Atlanta. To attest to his importance, Hunter reports a full-sized portrait of Homer in the Mayor's office. Like authors of the other studies, Hunter found elected officials in Atlanta to be relatively unimportant, and he terms them the *understructure of power.*

184

Conclusions about Stratification

These researchers reach a number of general conclusions about power and politics in the communities they studied, creating the basis for an emergent *stratification theory* of power. This theory holds that society is marked by distinct and separate social "layers": upper, middle, and lower. Each layer (or stratum) is united by a common set of interests and a common set of beliefs. In some variants of the theory, these beliefs are determined by social standing, but in most variants (e.g., Weber 1947), wealth (or lack of wealth) determines social class and political behavior. The theory holds, moreover, that each stratum works to promote its own interests, often at the expense of the other strata. Thus, stratification theory contains more than a hint of the Marxian postulate that politics is the struggle among economic classes.

Polsby (1980) summarizes the conclusions of stratification theory as follows:

1. The upper class rules in community life.
2. Political and civic leaders are subordinate to the upper class.
3. A single "power elite" rules in the community.
4. The upper-class power elite rules in its own interests.
5. Social conflict takes place between the upper and under classes.

In reviewing these conclusions, Polsby argues that they represent a distorted view of American society. Others, however, disagree (e.g., Domhoff 1978). In view of this disagreement, it seems worthwhile to consider the implications of stratification theory in more detail.

An Assessment of Stratification Theory

Upper-class dominance? The central conclusion of stratification theory is that an upper-class rules community politics. But the validity of this conclusion depends on the meaning we attach to the concept of *rule*. If we view *rule* as total dominance, the conclusion is subject to numerous counter-examples (see Polsby 1980). But if we take a less stringent view, the conclusion receives general support. We need only look back to our initial discussion of the informal rules of democracy to see a built-in upper-class *bias* in urban politics. For example, the unwritten norm that conflict should be managed peacefully means that the urban boat will usually not be rocked or at least not rocked violently. This norm ensures the protection of upper class values, for by limiting change, it maintains the current distribution of economic resources within the city. And we need not look far to discover that the distribution of resources favors the upper class. The lack of a coherent urban policy at the national level allows—or perhaps encourages—a kind of laissez faire distributional policy at the urban level, which favors those who can best fend for themselves (i.e., the upper and middle classes).

As a society, we are perhaps unique in our orientation to the business and economically privileged classes. As historians now agree, the American Revolution was in considerable measure economically motivated, and the American Constitution puts private property under national protection (Herson 1984). The American dream is one of wealth, and the American myth is that, with a little luck, anyone can attain that wealth. In fact, we are the only industrialized nation where the inability to achieve wealth is viewed as a character flaw (e.g., Merton 1957, Coser 1965). In the city, this outlook manifests itself as a belief in the privileged place of private property. *[The theory of the commodification of land and buildings]* Virtually everyone, including the poor and the propertyless, subscribes to this dream, and policies that protect the privileges of wealth are widely supported. These beliefs inevitably place considerable power in the hands of the upper class. But, to return to the original point, inordinate power is not the same as absolute rule, and the first conclusion of stratification theory has been the subject of considerable debate.

Political subordination? A second conclusion of stratification theory is less obvious, but its implications are no less important. It asserts that political and civic leaders are subordinate to the upper class. But again, the idea of subordination requires explication. When we search for overt and obvious instances of subordination, we are typically disappointed. We rarely find political and civic leaders to be without some independence of mind or action. As a consequence, critics of stratification theory view this second conclusion as invalid, arguing that politicians do not behave as mere subordinates, taking orders from the city's economic dominants faithfully and without hesitation.

But if we are willing to accept a more subtle form of subordination, stratification theory may be less susceptible to challenge. First we must ask, Why might political and civic leaders be subordinate to the upper class? One obvious answer lies in campaign contributions.[2] While perhaps a factor in the development of urban policy, this is not the most important factor contributing to upper-class dominance. More important is the market economy of the city. As was noted in earlier chapters, the city is literally built on capital investment decisions. If local investors make it known, however subtly, that they will find it difficult to invest capital in local projects in an unfavorable busi-

---

2. The costs of running for office today require local politicians to go, hat in hand, wherever money may be found, and this often entails trips to local business establishments. And, it might be argued, $25 here, $150 there, and the odd $1,000 contribution create a substantial indebtedness to the preferences of a candidate's supporters. Or conversely, local businesses typically support with contributions those candidates who are most likely to vote for pro-business, pro-growth policies. In turn, these contributions increase the probability that those candidates will win.

ness climate, the message usually comes across loud and clear at city hall. These investors are experts in monetary affairs, with expertise built up over a lifetime of successful fiscal transactions. Successful politicians are largely pragmatists, and they know where to turn for useful advice on local economic policy. The business class is willing to offer its advice on such matters. Finally, many city managers are trained either in public administration or business programs, both of which stress the importance of businesslike principles in running government. City managers therefore find discussion with business owners and managers quite comfortable, and they are likely to take advice when it is offered. In none of these situations is the public sector strictly subservient to the private sector; but in each case, the concerns of the upper economic class receive the attention of city hall.

A single power elite? The third conclusion holds that a single power elite rules the community. If this is taken literally, it asserts too much. Common sense and everyday observation suggest that the rich can and do squabble among themselves. For example, those with "old money" often have a different outlook from those with "new money," and these different outlooks lead to different political purposes and policy preferences. Preservation of the status quo versus economic development is one such animator of upper-class quarreling. But among the economic dominants, those whose wealth is mostly earned tend to be of one mind about the need for aggressive growth policies in the city. And all sectors of the upper and middle classes tend to be of one mind about the need to protect the rights of private property. When threatened on either of these points, the upper and middle classes tend to unify and are capable of dominating the agenda. The previous chapter, for example, discussed the city council member in Lawrence, Kansas, who openly questioned the city's pro-growth policies and the city manager's role in those policies. Almost overnight, a coalition of business interests emerged to mount a recall campaign against this council member. And although the council member eventually survived the recall election, he subsequently voted to retain the city manager. In the next municipal election, no candidate even raised the issue of economic growth.

Issues such as economic development and growth are, *in reality,* nonissues. They are not seriously debated within the political arena.[3] Bachrach and Baratz (1962) characterize the ability to keep such nonissues off the agenda as the silent face of power, contrasting it with the more vocal and visible form of power we typically see when we consider urban politics. So long as these nonissues are not raised, upper- and middle-class interests appear to be either in disarray or uninvolved in local politics. Under these

3. But see chapter 18 for exceptions.

circumstances, political and civic leaders are given great latitude in their implementation of economic policies. But let some determined politician raise one of the forbidden issues, and economic dominants rise rapidly to the fight.

A class that rules in its own interests? The fourth conclusion holds that the upper class rules in its own interests. This would initially seem to be contradicted by the large number of social programs that the upper class largely supports with its tax dollars. If it ruled strictly in its own self-interest, why would it support public programs and facilities it does not use, such as public education, day-care centers, inner-city playgrounds, public transit, and public health clinics? Yet, even these altruistic projects may serve the upper-class self-interest, broadly defined. So long as members of the underclass believe that they are sharing in the American dream, they will continue to subscribe to the value of private property. But if they believe that this dream is beyond their grasp—that even with hard work and a little luck they cannot escape their poverty—they may abandon their commitment to private property.[4] This, in turn, may become the one true threat to the continued power of the upper class. So, the amenities become a form of social control of the underclass.[5] (Frances Fox Piven and Richard Cloward, 1971, put this argument with sledgehammer force: Social welfare programs control the poor by buying them off—from violence and ultimately from revolution.) This is a small price, maintain stratification theorists, for the upper class to pay to maintain its dominant position in society.

Class conflict? The fifth conclusion holds that the upper and the under classes are in conflict. This conclusion is the most difficult to assess, for much depends on the meaning attached to conflict. If we take conflict to mean the clash of lifestyle and outlook, then Banfield (1974) has argued that the underclass in American cities is in constant conflict with the middle and upper classes.[6] The assertion is more difficult to assess if our inquiry turns to physical conflict. Crimes of violence are common in the big cities (though not exclusive to them). But are they caused by poverty and privation, or do their antecedents lie elsewhere? Crimes against property are subject to similar arguments over interpretation. So are the race riots of the 1960s. Were these

---

4. Stratification theorists might conclude that the race riots of the 1960s were property riots, aimed at the destruction of the wealth that eluded the rioters. For other interpretations, see chapters 8 and 18.

5. As one example, the public education system instills middle- and upper-class values in its students, who learn about democracy and its informal norms. For greater detail, see Schumpeter's (1947) discussion of the role that expectations of success play in keeping the capitalist ethos alive.

6. Banfield argues that while members of the middle and upper classes strive for tranquility and order in their lives and plan for the future, members of the underclass prefer the excitement that comes with disorder and disarray, demanding instant gratification and living for today. For excellent and sympathetic discussions of the underclass lifestyle, see Liebow (1967), Sheehan (1977), and Kozol (1985).

violent eruptions triggered by discrimination inflicted by whites upon blacks, or were they an assault upon property, wrapped inside resentment against the dominant white ruling class? Lack of incontrovertible answers to these questions, coupled with a distinct lack of ongoing and clear-cut class violence in American society, would seem to suggest that the stratification theorists claim too much.

But for all its inconclusiveness (not to mention difficulties of definition), the general absence of overt, continuous, and widespread class conflict does not necessarily disprove stratification theory. This *null finding* may well testify to the superb job of social control the middle and upper classes have achieved. The underclass may, in fact, have been coopted into believing that what is good for the middle class is good for the country, that middle-class values are indeed its own![7]

This discussion of stratification theory sets the stage for another set of studies of power that attempted to dispel this dour view of American society.

The Pluralist Response

Hunter's study of power in Atlanta was published in the midst of Joseph McCarthy's Senate hearings on communism and an America much obsessed with anticommunism. Over the next several years, the Cold War would escalate to new heights. Yet, here in the very midst of academia were scholars (mostly sociologists) who argued openly that democracy in America was a sham (see Wildavsky, 1979a, for a discussion that places these studies within a broader political context). Thus, it is understandable that another group of scholars, whose field was political science, would examine the state of American democracy from a different perspective and that they perhaps would come to a different conclusion.

These researchers found flaws in the methods employed by the stratification theorists, and they argued that these flaws invalidate findings of social stratification in the United States. The early researchers employed a straightforward and simple methodology: they asked key informants within a community to name the powerful people. For example, Hunter asked his informants in Regional City to name the "biggest man in town." This approach became known as the *reputational method* for studying power.

---

7. These thoughts take us into the realm of "false consciousness," an idea discussed by Plato, Rousseau, Marx, and Mannheim. Karl Mannheim (1936) argues that in modern societies, the economic underclass develops its values not out of self-interest, but rather borrows them from the economically dominant classes. This idea came again to the forefront of political discussion in the 1960s (e.g., Marcuse 1964).

A Critique of the Reputational Methodology

Critiques of the reputational methodology abound (e.g., see Polsby, 1980, for a review), and we will consider them in only a very cursory manner. First, the method assumes that power is visible to all observers. But, in reality, do powerful people operate in an open and visible fashion, or do they more often work behind the scenes? Perhaps people who are truly powerful prefer to operate covertly, where they are not subject to the same constraints and scrutiny as those who have visible positions of power. Further, we might suspect that people who are truly powerful have no need for public recognition. Rather, it may be only those people who desire power but who have no *real* power who feel the need to be seen, to advertise their power. Hunter and others, of course, recognize this problem by discounting the power of the most visible people in the community, the politicians. But they assume that their informants were privy to behind-the-scenes goings on, a leap of inference that is not easily justified. It may well be that the more powerful a person is, the fewer the number of people able to detect his or her influence.

A second difficulty concerns the wording of the questions used to elicit the names of powerful people. Polsby (1960) equates asking, "Who is the big man in town," to asking the respondent if he still beats his wife, in that any response will provide the researcher with a misleading picture of power in the community. The very wording of the question assumes that there is a "big man" in town, and the respondent would have to refuse to answer the question in order to suggest the absence of such a person. In short, the reputational method is almost guaranteed to find a power structure.

A third difficulty was that the methodology guaranteed that the uncovered power structure would consist of economic elites. At any given time, a community may experience a number of problems dealing with such diverse issues as containing health care costs, improving public education, downtown development, reducing unemployment, attacking drug abuse, and reducing crime. Within any of these issue areas, different kinds of people are active and influential. For example, in the area of health care, physicians and hospital administrators are likely to initiate policy proposals. But what is the common denominator *across all issues*? In one word, money. And while people who control the community's economic assets may have only a minor role in educational or health care policies, they are the *only* people who have *some* influence across *all* issues. Thus, when a researcher asks an informant to name the biggest man in town, without regard to specific issues, the names of economic elites are typically forthcoming.

Decisional Studies: A Contravening Methodology

Robert Dahl and his colleagues address these methodological problems, shifting their methodological emphasis from *reputation to action* by studying actual decisions taken within specific issue areas. The prototypical decisional study was conducted in New Haven (Dahl 1961), with research focusing on "significant" decisions concerning education, urban renewal, and political nominations within the community.

For each decision, Dahl identified the persons or groups responsible for initiating or blocking proposals, and he calculated indices of success and failure for the various participants in each issue. Of fifty people who were identified as influential in New Haven, only three (including the mayor) were influential in all three issue areas. Even within issue areas, power tended to be distributed across a number of people. More than half of the influentials were able to exert influence on only a single decision. Thus, Dahl found support for one of the basic principles of *pluralist democracy*: Power is diffused, not concentrated in the hands of a few. It is fluid and mobile, dependent largely on a person's interest and motivation for participating in the resolution of an issue coupled with the resources (expertise, experience, and perhaps money) he or she can bring to bear on that issue. Further, Dahl argues that democratic processes were practiced in New Haven: most adult residents were legally entitled to vote, and elections were free from violence and fraud, contested by two political parties which offered rival slates of candidates. Dahl was not willing to say that this guaranteed equal power to all citizens. He did argue, however, that "New Haven is a republic of unequal citizens—but for all that a republic" (Dahl 1961, 220). A number of other researchers using the decisional approach have reached the same conclusion (Banfield 1961, Martin et al. 1961, Wildavsky 1964, Sayre and Kaufman 1960, Schumaker et al. 1986). There is only one, seemingly unavoidable conclusion to this massive body of research: Democracy is alive and well in America.

A Pluralist America?

But just as reputational methodology is subject to criticism, so is decisional methodology (e.g., Dye 1969b). We will briefly consider three of these criticisms here. First, critics argue, by examining each individual *decision* as if it were unique, researchers are unduly impressed by the situational aspects of the decision. The history of the issue, dating back to previous decisions in which ground rules may have been established, is ignored in favor of current factors that ostensibly (but perhaps not in fact) influence the decision. Some of these precedents may be major. For example the assumption that growth is good for cities likely served as a precedent for all urban renewal decisions in New Haven, but Dahl ignored the economic interests responsible for this underlying policy assumption in his study. Other, less pervasive, but nonetheless important links among decisions may also be ignored. For example, the decision by the city to encourage and fund neighborhood political groups may have long-term consequences for the amount and style of political participation in the community. By ignoring these prior decisions, the decisional approach yields a biased view of power.

A related criticism concerns the decisional approach's potential for disaggregating a powerful community body, treating the participation of each of its *members* as unique and unrelated. In his reanalysis of power in New Haven, William Domhoff (1978) found Yale University to be a significant force in community politics and one largely ignored by Dahl. For example, Domhoff found that Prescott Bush, Connecticut's senior senator and an important force in New Haven's redevelopment program, was a Yale alumnus and trustee, and that other trustees were important figures at both the national and the local level; that Yale had guaranteed a loan to a redevelopment project at a critical time; that Mayor Richard Lee had come to political office fresh from an executive position at Yale; that Yale provided important connections between the mayor and prospective retail stores that later moved to New Haven; that a principal redevelopment administrator was related to one of the Yale deans; and that Yale alumni worked in law firms favored by local business owners.[8] By treating each of these people as unrelated individuals, Dahl found power in New Haven to be dispersed. By observing their common Yale connection, Domhoff found power in New Haven to be concentrated at Yale University.

Second, "significant" decisions (such as those studied in New Haven) are usually steeped in conflict. And conflict, by its very nature, draws a wide range of participants into the decision process (Schattschneider 1960). This gives the appearance of widely distributed power. In contrast, participation in the resolution of less important issues (or of nonissues) engenders participation on a much smaller scale, limited largely to those people with a high stake in the outcome. And more often than not, high-stakes players—those with the most to gain and the most to lose—are part of the business community. Thus, we might again conclude that most decisions are guided by an economic elite.

Third, conflictual decisions raise the potential for compromise, and the decisional approach may identify as powerful someone who happened to be at the right place at the right time with a compromise proposal. A person may suggest a successful compromise that nobody likes, but because of its very innocuousness, is the only solution acceptable to all participants. The decisional approach, however, would incorrectly attribute power to him or her.

---

8. For additional discussion of redevelopment in New Haven, see chapter 11.

So, What's the Real Story?

In a telling study, John Walton (1966) compared the findings of community power studies conducted by political scientists and by sociologists, finding that sociologists tend to uncover concentrated power while political scientists more often than not find dispersed power. Walton (1966, 688) concluded:

> The disciplinary background of the investigator tends to determine the method of investigation he will adopt, which, in turn, tends to determine the image of the power structure that results from the investigation.

If we assume that sociologists generally employ a reputational methodology in their studies and that political scientists generally employ a decisional methodology in theirs, we indeed find general confirmation for our previous point: The way the question is posed influences the answer. But we also find that the relationship is not *determinate,* that is, it is not perfect. In some cases a reputational methodology uncovers dispersed power, just as a decisional methodology can find concentrated power. But the contentiousness of the debate between those who argue that power in America is stratified and those who argue that power in America is pluralistic largely obscures this subtle but important point. In looking to condemn the sociological findings, political scientists failed to realize that some in their own ranks, using their own methodology, also found power to be stratified. And those on the other side committed a similar judgmental error.

Some Preliminary Conclusions about Power in American Communities

Unfortunately, the name-calling detracted from a much more interesting discussion that began to materialize in both political science and sociology, centering around *why* some studies found concentrated power and others found dispersed power. The most plausible explanation is intercity differences (see Herson, 1961, for an early discussion). We will consider how different urban characteristics affect the distribution of power shortly. But initially, let us draw some general conclusions about the distribution of power in American communities.

First, it is quite likely that power in American cities is neither as concentrated as the Lynds found in Muncie nor as dispersed as Dahl found in New Haven. The Lynds' studies were, after all, conducted just before and during the Great Depression, when resources were, in fact, inequitably distributed. And, like the Cheshire Cat's grin in Alice's Wonderland, reputations of power may linger far longer than an individual's actual power (Bolland and Herson 1989). This possibility suggests that the respondents in Hunter's study may have been describing the structure of power in Atlanta at some point in the

193

indeterminate past (perhaps during the Depression) rather than as it was in the early 1950s. At any rate, American society may not be as stratified as it once was. And given the tendency of the reputational method to overestimate stratification, the estimates of the early studies were likely biased.

Yet, it is equally likely that the conclusions of many political scientists who find for a pluralistic society are overstated. In studies of a number of communities, the present authors have discovered that informants resonate to the basic idea of a power structure. These informants recognize that power is not equally distributed through the city's population, but rather resides in a handful (or several handfuls) of community influentials, and that these influentials, through their private investment decisions, largely determine policy development in the city.

We must conclude, then, that reality lies somewhere between pluralism and stratification. And, in fact, it differs in different cities, depending on a number of demographic and political characteristics of the city. For example, James Madison, writing two hundred years ago in the *Federalist Papers,* concluded that power tends to be diffused through participation. Thus, in communities with an activist population, concentrated power tends to be difficult to achieve.

Political participation and political power. Lawrence, Kansas, is a good example of an activist city. In a study of power there, Schumaker (1990) found more than six hundred people (out of a permanent population of only 35,000) active in various community issues, and Bolland (1984) found the concentration of power to be significantly lower than in other comparably sized cities. Whenever an issue was contested, a coalition was able to emerge to either block or delay action. For example, the merits of a downtown shopping mall have been debated in Lawrence for over a decade, and three different developers of record have been named; but so far, not so much as a shovelful of earth has been turned toward its construction. In the same way, at least one residential development has been blocked by citizen protest. As one influential figure noted, "every time I try to take a shortcut in getting something done, someone is there to stop me, and I have to backtrack." In Lawrence, community activism prevents decisive action, and influentials have largely stopped trying to assert their power. The message is clear: Citizens there value the ethos of political participation and shared power much more than the potential economic benefit to be gained through quick and decisive decisions, and they refuse to muzzle the activist minority that emerges on individual issues.

By way of comparison, consider Olathe, Kansas, a suburb of Kansas City with 40,000 people, located only thirty miles from Lawrence. A study (Bolland 1984) showed power in Olathe to be concentrated in the hands of four people, two with considerable wealth and two with important administrative positions in public agencies. Political participation in Olathe is notable by its absence: In contrast to the more than six hundred participants found in Lawrence, only about two hundred participants were identified in Olathe (Bolland 1984). Also notable in Olathe is the speed with which changes are accomplished. In less than the time that it took to *contemplate* a mall in Lawrence, the housing stock in Olathe doubled, with little protest. Further, this construction was spearheaded largely by the two economic elites identified in the study, and they made considerable profit from their investments. In addition, a new high school and hospital were planned and built with speed that would have been impossible in Lawrence.

We should recognize that it is possible for a small minority to delay action (even in a nonactivist city like Olathe) largely through litigation (actual or threatened). For example, for years uncompleted freeway exit ramps, originally intended to route traffic to proposed bypasses, adorned many cities. But, in many cases, construction was suspended by the actions of citizens concerned that the road would disrupt their neighborhoods. In some cases, construction was stopped in midstream through litigation, with the courts finding in favor of the neighborhood. In other cases, construction was stopped by threatened litigation: The city recognized that the legal process would potentially delay construction by a decade and cost the taxpayers considerable money, with the ultimate outcome in question.

As another example, referenda are sometimes used to delay the expenditure of public funds for construction projects. A case in point is the construction of the Kingdome, Seattle's domed stadium, approved by voters in 1968. Within six months, a site had been selected, and construction was ready to begin—only to be delayed by local businessman Frank Ruano, who had obtained sufficient signatures objecting to the site to place the issue on the ballot. In 1970, voters rejected the initial site, and the stadium planners returned to the drawing board, recommending a second site by the end of the year. But again, Ruano objected, and again he obtained sufficient signatures to place a site selection referendum on the ballot. However, in 1982, a county judge ruled that this action was inappropriate, and ground was finally broken in November 1982. But through this legal maneuvering, Ruano had managed to delay construction by over four years. And in the process, construction costs increased from the originally projected $40 million to $67 million.[9] (See Sears, 1976, for a complete chronicle of the Kingdome's development.)

Determinants of Participation Reconsidered

What makes a community politically active? Several partial explanations, derived from the discussion of participation in chapter 6, come to mind. Zoning policies

---

9. Lester Thurow (1980) argues that this strategy of delay is one of the ultimate weapons in American politics.

and architectural styles may have a lot to do with political participation. For the most part, newer areas of town are subject to Euclidean zoning norms (named after the city in Ohio rather than the Greek mathematician), wherein residential areas are strictly residential and commercial areas are strictly commercial. This zoning pattern creates more homogeneous neighborhoods with higher property values, but it precludes the potential for neighborhood businesses (e.g., grocery stores, laundries). Thus, the Mom and Pop store, which in days gone by largely provided neighbors with convenient shopping and the opportunity for social encounters, has disappeared from the new urban landscape. In newer neighborhoods, residents now drive instead of walk to the store to buy their groceries, and the possibility of the social encounter (or for that matter, any encounter other than a fender bender) is largely reduced. In addition, recent architectural styles favor the back patio rather than the front porch, so that now even were people to walk through their neighborhood, they would have few people with whom to converse.

One of the most important bases of grassroots political activism is neighborhood contact, already reduced by social trends such as crime and increased television viewing. When social contact is further reduced by zoning and architectural constraints, an almost insurmountable burden is placed on community activists, and community activism is restricted still further. Consider some of the factors that limit or facilitate political participation.

Zoning policies. As an example, zoning regulations in Lawrence are relatively inclusive, with 34 percent of all housing units located in areas zoned for multiple (including commercial) use. In contrast, Olathe has relatively exclusive zoning, with less than 1 percent of its housing units located in areas zoned for multiple uses. Also by way of comparison, Lawrence has nearly three times more houses with front porches than Olathe. And as was earlier noted, participation is considerably higher in Lawrence than in Olathe.

Nonpolitical participation. Opportunities for nonpolitical participation may, in turn, enhance the likelihood for political activism. A college town like Lawrence provides a large number of activities and events that residents can participate in or attend. Virtually every day the university offers sports events, concerts, recitals, films, forums, and/or debates that are open to the public, and a surprisingly large segment of the population takes advantage of those opportunities. In contrast, most small towns offer little by way of such cultural opportunities.

Participation in these sports and cultural events accustoms people to the idea of going out during the evening rather than staying home. Thus participation in evening meetings of neighborhood associations or activist groups may seem routine. Further, participation in cultural activities provides an opportunity for additional social contacts with others likely to be one's allies (or even one's opponents) on political issues, increasing the strength of interpersonal ties (in an insightful turn of phrase, Edward Laumann (1973) referred to these ties as the *bonds of pluralism*).

Community commitment. Commitment to the community enhances the opportunity for political participation. As noted earlier, we are becoming a more transient society, with more and more people expecting to live in their current house (or their current city) only until they become wealthy enough to move to a better location. Given this outlook, people are unlikely to form strong attachments with their neighbors or to their neighborhood, for they realize that these bonds will be temporary. By the same token, they are unlikely to participate politically, for they expect to be gone by the time that desired change is implemented. Another type of community commitment comes from business and industry. Capital investment decisions are more likely to benefit the community when businesses and industries are locally owned than when they are owned in absentia. After all, decisionmakers in the former situation are part of the city, and civic responsibility is an important motive potentially underlying their decisions. In contrast, the decisions of absentee owners are motivated by profit considerations, and they are potentially less beneficial to the community. Local owners of business and industry may be powerful political participants in the community; again in contrast, managers or franchisers of absentee-owned industries or businesses are less likely to participate in community affairs, for their loyalty moves in corporate rather than community directions. With the advent of the grocery chain, the fast-food franchise, and the shopping mall (where virtually all stores are absentee-owned and locally franchised), it is difficult to find a community where local ownership is the norm rather than the exception.

City size and heterogeneity. Participation is likely to be higher in smaller cities than in larger cities or in suburbs, due to what may be termed an energy factor. In today's labor force, where nearly as many women work as men, couples run out of energy by the time they get home from work, cook dinner, and do the dishes. In a small city, where the time to commute home from work is minutes, there is still time to recover before an evening meeting or concert. But in a large city or a suburb, where the time to commute home from work may exceed an hour, the logistics of political activity in the evening become difficult.

Heterogeneity also facilitates participation. In a perfectly homogeneous city (if one could be found) political participation would be nonrational. Since all residents should have similar concerns and goals, one spokesperson could speak for everyone, alleviating the need for political participation by others. But as a city becomes more heterogeneous, political concerns tend to diverge, and political participation becomes a necessary ingredient of survival.

197

Form of government. Finally, certain kinds of political structures are more likely to facilitate political participation than others. As noted in chapter 8, nonpartisan and at-large elections reduce the likelihood of citizen participation. And council-manager governments reduce the role of the city council in policy development, which in turn may limit the attractiveness of (and the competition for) those positions. Further, the elected mayor is an important political force who can potentially generate political activity around a community issue. But in cities with council-manager governments, the mayorship is a ceremonial position largely without this kind of influence.[10]

Some Final Conclusions about Power in American Communities

The foregoing comparisons lead to several final remarks about the distribution of power in American communities. In communities with exclusive zoning policies and modern-style, porchless homes, power is likely to be more concentrated than in cities with inclusive zoning and older-style homes. We might further note an obvious relationship between these factors and the city's age. Euclidean zoning is a fairly recent development (dating back no earlier than 1926; see chapter 17 for a further discussion of zoning), and 1950 is an approximate turning point for residential architecture, away from the front porch and toward the back patio. Not surprisingly, studies have shown that older cities have higher levels of participation (e.g., Alford and Lee 1968) and less concentrated power (e.g., Gilbert 1968) than their newer counterparts.

Beyond these, four other conclusions emerge. First, increased opportunities for social contact may lead to increased political participation, and in turn, to more diffused power. Second, absentee ownership of businesses and industries leads to more concentrated power. Third, power is more concentrated in reformed cities than in unreformed cities. And fourth, central cities may have generally less-concentrated power than suburbs.

This last observation is more ambiguous than the others, and several factors may account for it. Given their size and cultural diversity, central cities tend to have more *types* of politically relevant organizations than suburbs, including more industries, unions, and state and federal agencies. The social problems of central cities are typically greater than those of suburbs, leading to a wider participation in the former than the latter. In addition, suburban

---

10. These various factors help explain the differential participation rates and concentration of power in Lawrence and Olathe. For example, Lawrence is an ethnically and racially heterogeneous college town, while Olathe's population is ethnically and racially homogeneous. Lawrence's nonstudent population is more stable, while Olathe's is more transient. Business in Lawrence tends to be locally owned, while that in Olathe tends to be absentee-owned. Only in form of government are Lawrence and Olathe similar. Both use the council-manager plan. See Bolland (1984) for a more detailed comparison of these cities.

workers typically commute further to work than their urban counterparts, and they have less time and energy for political participation.

Community Power: Toward an Alternative Theory

Previously discussed theories viewed power in *systemic* terms as the ability to affect the *political system* in some manner and achieve some desired political outcome. For example, stratification theorists hold that power resides in the hands of an economic elite because urban policies are generally biased in their favor (see Stone, 1980, for a discussion). And pluralists hold that power resides in the hands of diverse groups and individuals within the city, with specific decisions reflecting diverse preferences of political participants. But neither formulation acknowledges that power is a multifaceted concept consisting of several distinct components. First, some people (e.g., city council members, school board members, the mayor) have power because they are able to vote directly on policy proposals. Second, some people (e.g., the city manager, individual police officers, the school district superintendent) have power because they exercise discretion in the implementation of policies once they are enacted. Third, some people (e.g., lawyers, protestors) have power because they are able to stall policies once they have been enacted, either through litigation or through disruptive protest. Fourth, some people (e.g., business owners, homeowners) have power because of their private or corporate investment decisions. And fifth, some people have power because they are able to influence others and mobilize support around policy proposals. The dynamics of these different components of power are quite different. If they are lumped together into a single phenomenon called *power,* the results are bound to be misleading. As an alternative, we will develop a multifaceted definition of power that breaks the concept into three different components.

The first component, which might be described as *direct power,*[11] is the ability to affect policy outcomes *directly* through one's actions. This is the easiest type of power to conceptualize and describe, and it is what most of us imagine when we think of power. Direct power in urban politics lies in the hands of formally designated policymakers and their agents (members of the urban bureaucracy).

A second component of power, which we might term *indirect power,* is the ability of private citizens to affect outcomes through their decisions and actions. For example, citizens, through their vote, elect policymakers. For another example, the land developer who decides to place a large housing development on the city's west side may affect the city's growth patterns for

---

11. While these components of power inevitably blur around the edges, each is sufficiently recognizable that we can proceed as if they were truly distinct.

years to come, which in turn affects the city's decisions concerning the location of new schools and zoning policies. By the same token, the chief executive officer of a major manufacturing corporation who decides to renovate a local plant rather than move it to another location affects the city's employment patterns (and through them, its tax base and service delivery policies). And for a third example, the attorney who files suit to stop construction of a highway, or a protest group that threatens to stage sit-ins at city hall, may delay the implementation of an enacted policy indefinitely. While these people are unable to affect the city's policies directly (after all, they have no formal authority over the enactment or implementation of those policies), they are able to affect policy outcomes indirectly.

A third component of power, which we might term *interpersonal power*, is the ability of any citizen (either private or holding a governmental position) or group to affect urban outcomes by mobilizing support around one or another policy proposal. This may take place during the enactment of policy legislation, for instance a local business owner may be able to lobby a council member to support her position on a specific piece of legislation. Or it may occur during the agenda-setting phase of the policy process, as local problems are identified and possible solutions are discussed and debated within the community.[12] This type of power is least studied (and least understood), and in the following section we will consider it in some detail.

Interpersonal Power

When people talk politics, they seldom attempt to coerce one another.[13] Rather, they attempt to convince each other of the relative merits of their ideas, suggesting that if a political problem is viewed from their perspective, the solution will become clear. Thus, *ideas* are the coin of the political realm, and the exchange of ideas is the essence of interpersonal power.[14] (Herson, 1984, recognizes the importance of this formulation with the title of his book on the history of American political thought: *The Politics of Ideas*.) Thus, the power

---

12. With this distinction between policy enactment and agenda setting, we anticipate the discussion of the policy process in chapter 11.

13. While it is true that politicians have been known to take bribes in exchange for legislative votes, and that voters have also been known to take bribes for their support of political candidates at the polls, we should view this type of coercion as an anomaly, not often likely to affect the process of urban politics. By the same token, some politicians may be coerced through blackmail, but again this occurs infrequently enough that we should ignore it in our discussion of interpersonal influence.

14. Victor Hugo seemingly took much the same approach to understanding politics when he observed, "Greater than the tread of mighty armies is an idea whose time has come." But the present argument diverges from Hugo by taking a more anthropocentric approach. It holds that great ideas do not just emerge, they are generated and spread by people. The great idea that no one hears is not great. But on the other hand, even the mediocre idea that is spread effectively through the body politic will have important consequences.

to lobby a council member reflects the ability to exchange ideas about a particular issue. And in these same terms, the power to set the agenda[15]—that is, to mobilize support for and generate consensus around policy priorities and long-range policy goals—is *the ability to spread ideas.*[16]

Hence, interpersonal power is based on interpersonal relationships. An individual, *A,* has power over another person, *B,* to the extent that *B* solicits and listens to *A*'s ideas. But in order for this power relationship between *A* and *B* to materialize, *B* must have some motive for listening to *A*. *B* may believe that *A* has good ideas, because his or her ideas have been good in the past. *B* may believe that *A* has access to important information or that he or she possesses expertise on a particular subject. *B* may find *A* to be charismatic or may be impressed by his or her willingness to commit substantial time to community projects.

To the extent that ideas are transmitted from person to person and permeate the community's political agenda, they become ideas "whose time have come," likely to affect political thinking and policy development in the community. In considering the ability of political participants to influence one another—and thus to influence the agenda—we must take stock of the resources they possess and see how these resources work to facilitate the flow of their ideas through the community. In the following section, we consider various types of political participants, exploring the ways their resources enhance their interpersonal power.

Who's Powerful and Who's Not: An Inventory of Urban Political Participants and Their Resources

Formal Political Participants

The governing body. The most obvious participants in the urban political process are members of the governing body (either commissioners or council members). These individuals exercise *direct* power, for their votes are the ultimate determinants of many urban policies, ranging from taxing and spending to land use and zoning. But, as was suggested earlier, most council

15. As chapters 13 and 14 suggest, the ability to set the urban agenda lies to a large extent outside the city's boundaries, in county, state, and national governments. But, for now, discussion concentrates on forces indigenous to the city.

16. "I have a dream," exclaimed the Reverend Martin Luther King in his 1963 speech commemorating the centennial of the Emancipation Proclamation. Rev. King's dream is an example of our *idea,* and much of King's power lay in his ability to communicate that idea to others. His and others' ability to mobilize support around the dream of an equal society was, in large part, the impetus of the modern Civil Rights Movement in America. But while the dream no doubt had been dreamt by many others before, it had failed to trigger anything approaching the activity it generated during the late 1950s and the 1960s. This suggests the importance of great people over great ideas.

members have neither a firm grasp of nor a strong desire to learn the complexities of urban economics or service delivery. They are therefore largely dependent on those people who possess this expertise, mostly urban administrators and bureaucrats inside government and successful business managers outside government. So, although members of the governing body may make formal and binding decisions (and thus exert direct power), they must often rely on the advice of others when it comes to setting the agenda and enacting policy legislation. In other words, they are subject to the interpersonal power of others. Some council members are able, in turn, to exert interpersonal power as they lobby one another during policy enactment and mobilize support during the agenda-setting phase of the policy process. After all, they run for office with varying political orientations. *[The theory of ideology]* And once in office, they may be expected to act on those orientations. But in many cities, the long-term consequences of the urban reform movement, in its attempt to remove politics from government, have reduced the probability that persons with platforms and agendas for change will be elected to the city council. The mathematics and logic are straightforward: In an at-large election, those elected tend to be candidates whose political preferences (and political orientations) are acceptable to the greatest possible cross-section of the electorate, which is to say, candidates without strident views or extreme preferences.[17] Thus, lobbying and agenda-setting activities of council members in reformed cities will be largely in support of the status quo.

For those council members who seek to set the community's agenda, one resource is very much theirs to use: They have the legitimacy of office. They are, after all, elected by the citizenry, and thus they are the legitimate spokespersons for that citizenry. As elected spokespersons, they are in an advantaged position to spread their ideas through the community. But even so, anecdotal evidence from a number of community studies (e.g., Lynd and Lynd 1929, Hollingshead 1949, Hunter 1953) suggests that other, high-status people in the community (business leaders) view municipal elections as merely popularity contests and, accordingly, have little interest in listening to what elected officials have to say. Bolland's (1984) findings from Olathe and from Lawrence suggest that each council member had a small but loyal following who listened attentively every time he or she spoke; but beyond these small audiences, few people were motivated to attend to their ideas.

Further detracting from legitimacy as a resource of council members is an often present public cynicism concerning the honesty of public officials. "The finest city council that money can buy," is one of the hoary jokes of urban politics. To

17. Unlike partisan primary elections, where party activists (whose views tend toward extremes of liberalism or conservatism) influence the slate of candidates considered in the general election, nonpartisan elections are characterized by a moderating influence, and extremist candidates tend to be weeded out early.

the extent that the public thinks it true, this perceived truth further limits the ability of council members to spread ideas and build consensus for those ideas.[18]

What about more personal resources, for instance, charisma, creativity, and the contribution of time to community projects? In many instances, individuals who possess these resources have little interest in running for council seats. Others will listen to their ideas whether they hold public office or not, and most often they are more effective working outside the public limelight. By running for office, much of their power may actually be diluted by the excess publicity to which politicians are subjected.

The mayor. In contrast to members of the city council, the occupant of the mayor's office may possess many of the resources necessary to exercise both direct power and interpersonal power. In strong-mayor governments, the mayor usually presides over council meetings and usually casts the deciding vote in cases of a voting tie. The strong mayor is also the city's chief administrator, a position that gives him or her access to bureaucracy's information and (as a result) considerable expertise in day-to-day governmental operations. These resources give the mayor considerable direct power.

Just as important, as chief executive of the city, the mayor usually has free access to the media and to various groups and committees within the city. This access (enhanced by the fact that he or she is the elect of all the people) is a resource providing the mayor with considerable interpersonal power, for it means that when the mayor talks, people (including council members) listen. And as they listen, the mayor is able to spread his or her ideas and policy priorities through the community.[19]

Administrators. Another set of persons with both direct power and interpersonal power is the city's chief administrators: the city manager in council-manager cities, the school district superintendent, the administrator of the city's public hospital, and others who oversee a large public budget. Like the mayor in mayor-council governments, local administrators have access to—in fact, are responsible for collecting—information in urban bureaucracies. They are in a position to tell the city council, the school board, or the hospital board which issues demand action and which do not, and how those demand-

---

18. Ironically, urban reform seems to have had little affect on this cynicism. Even today, most citizens believe that corruption occurs in urban government, and there is some evidence that municipal corruption may be widespread. For discussions of this problem, see Gardiner and Lyman (1978) and Gardiner and Olson (1974).

19. Even in weak-mayor systems, the mayor is likely to have greater interpersonal power than other council members. Research in Olathe and Lawrence shows, for example, that the mayor (although operating in a weak-mayor system) was more central in the policy network than any other member of the council.

ing action should be addressed. In one telling set of studies of urban school boards, Harmon Zeigler and his colleagues (Zeigler and Tucker 1981, Zeigler and Jennings 1974, Tucker and Zeigler 1980) found that board members deferred to the superintendent's recommendations in the vast majority of all decisions. We should expect similar findings for hospital board members and city council members. Thus, administrators have considerable interpersonal power in dealing with their governing bodies.

Also like strong mayors, administrators develop considerable expertise in a short period of time, and others in the community are interested in hearing ideas developed through this expertise. Further, they usually have advanced professional degrees, giving them the benefit of a theoretical as well as a practical understanding of the city and its problems. Finally, the mere fact that they exercise so much administrative authority provides them with a wide audience for their ideas. Given that their preferences are likely to influence policy decisions, others in the community are anxious to understand these preferences, so as to anticipate their consequences. The studies of both Lawrence and Olathe support these conclusions: In both cities, the city manager was at the center of the policy network[20]; and in Olathe, the school district superintendent also maintained a central position. Philip Trounstine and Terry Christensen (1982) found similar results in their study of power in San Jose.

In addition to interpersonal power, urban administrators are able to exercise considerable direct power. As was previously noted, city managers have the power to hire and fire municipal staff, and hospital and school district members have the power to hire personnel in their organizations. Thus, the behavior of individual police officers, school teachers, nurse supervisors, and other employees will at least partially reflect the orientations and preferences of these administrators. Urban administrators, in addition, frequently provide policy directives to their staff, to be implemented by the various street-level bureaucrats within the community. Again, these policy directives reflect the preferences and orientations of the administrators issuing them. Finally, administrators implement the policies developed by their elected superiors. But since these policies are often ambiguous, the administrator is afforded great latitude to instill his or her own preferences into policy decisions.

Street-level bureaucrats. Another set of urban political participants with direct power consists of employees within the city's governmental bureau-

20. A policy network consists of the web of interpersonal relationships through which political participants share ideas and information relevent to the city's policies. In this way, we add a layer of meaning to the concept of interpersonal power: Those who are located at the center of the community's policy network have the greatest interpersonal power. For further discussion of the concept of networks in urban politics, see the work of Laumann and his colleagues (e.g., Laumann and Pappi 1976, Laumann, et al. 1977, Galaskiewicz 1979).

cracies (e.g., police officers, street maintenance personnel, schoolteachers, nurses, physicians). As has been noted throughout, these individuals have considerable direct power, reflected in their ability to use discretion in implementing policies handed down from above. For example, the police officer exercises considerable discretion in deciding when to stop speeding motorists and when to issue traffic citations.

Just as important, street-level bureaucrats become experts in a narrow range of urban policy, providing them with a basis for interpersonal power. For example, a patrol officer may be the city's greatest expert on crime, and perhaps even life, in the area he or she patrols. And a first-grade teacher is one of the city's great experts on the behavior problems of first graders. This expertise provides street-level bureaucrats with an ability to influence others, at least within the narrow area of their expertise. However, since this area of expertise tends to be narrow, their overall impact on the urban agenda, and the range of their lobbying efforts, is likely to be small.

Members of community advisory boards and commissions. Still another set of formal political participants with the potential for interpersonal power consists of members of the community's advisory boards and commissions. This power is, however, in most cases, quite limited. In some cities, advisory boards may be elected to office. Much more frequently, they are appointed. Overall, advisory board members are hampered by the same constraints that keep members of the city council from exercising interpersonal power, but even more so. They work without compensation, so the effort they put into their positions is strictly dependent on their sense of civic responsibility. But unlike members of the city council, they have little opportunity to parlay that effort into interpersonal power. As was noted earlier, members of the city council have public recognition: They are quoted in the newspaper, they are seen at public events, and so forth. A member of the parks and recreation board, in comparison, enjoys relative anonymity, with his or her efforts known only to friends and relatives.[21]

Members of advisory boards are also without much direct power. Like the city council, they are dependent on municipal administrators to provide them with information and to set the agendas for their meetings. Advisory committees typically vote to *recommend* policy decisions, whereas the city coun-

---

21. Of course, members of advisory committees *are* often important in setting the urban agenda or in lobbying council members before important votes, but not because of their positions on the advisory committees. For example, an important developer may be appointed to the parks and recreation board, or the president of the chamber of commerce may be appointed to the mental health board. But in these cases, the appointment derives from his or her power rather than vice versa.

cil and the school board actually vote to *enact* various policies. Thus, advisory board members are once removed from positions of direct power.[22]

Informal Participants

As we move from formal urban participants to informal participants, we leave direct power behind, for the ability to enact and implement legislation is the exclusive domain of formally designated policymakers and their agents. But at the same time, a discussion of informal participants yields new applications of indirect power and interpersonal power. Among informal participants in the city's governance, two groups—voters and protestors—play important roles, although they are relatively powerless in setting the urban agenda. In contrast, neighborhood groups and business associations are notable for their indirect and interpersonal power—and through that power for their overall influence on urban politics.

Voters. In principle, voters are the ultimate holders of indirect power in the city, for it is they who elect the officials who enact public policy. Voting, however, is not an ongoing political act. In most cities, municipal elections occur only once every two years. Except in instances where policy is created through referenda and bond elections, voters do not exercise direct power. Between elections, city officials pay formalistic attention to what the electorate thinks (e.g., by answering telephone calls from concerned citizens; stopping for offhand advice during social meetings[23]), but there is little evidence that officials actively seek out voters' advice or that they attend to that advice once given. For one thing, most elected officials devote most of their time and energy attending to specific complaints (trash collection, police response, and so forth). For another, typical voters simply do not possess the resources (beyond the vote) that would give them interpersonal power, and few people

22. Another set of formal political participants consists of municipal judges, who have a paradoxical potential for interpersonal power. They, along with the chief of police and the county sheriff, are the community's greatest experts on crime and punishment. Further, many of their cases directly or indirectly involve social services. For example, claims of mental illness, as well as of alcohol or drug dependency, must be considered in sentencing decisions; as another example, the court must decide whether minors are to be remanded to a social service agency in the case of domestic disputes. This provides judges with great expertise in the link between crime and social services in the community. Judges hold high-status positions in the community, and their presumed impartiality gives them great credibility. No one expects them to have an axe to grind. In short, people are willing to listen to what judges have to say. Paradoxically, however, most judges do not have much to say on community issues, for they view political activity as anathema to their judicial roles; for them, involvement in community issues would destroy the impartiality that allows them to be effective judges. In other words, judges have interpersonal power only until they attempt to use it, at which point it may disappear.

23. Former Mayor Edward Koch of New York, for example, was famous for asking citizens on the street, "How am I doing?"

beyond friends and relatives seek their advice or ideas on political matters (Huckfeldt and Sprague 1987).[24]

Within the electorate, of course, individual voters are not as powerful as voting blocks. But even voting blocks often find themselves without much interpersonal power once the election has been decided. For example, Hispanics and Jews provided the crucial votes in Tom Bradley's victory in the 1973 Los Angeles mayoral election, yet, these groups have often felt slighted by the actions and policy decisions of his administration (Sonenshein 1986). And as was noted earlier, the policy actions of Mayor Wilson Goode in Philadelphia have often been aimed more at local white business owners than at the predominantly black coalition that elected him.[25]

Protestors. In principle, protestors have indirect power. On the one hand, stubborn and rancorous protest, not to mention violence, can potentially be used to delay the implementation (perhaps indefinitely) of policy legislation. But just as often, it hardens the resolve of council members or administrators already committed to a policy.[26] Most often, rancorous or violent protest results in symbolic gains for the protesting group. For example, the race riots of the 1960s netted the establishment of the Kerner Commission to study the racial situation in American cities, but they resulted in very few policy changes.[27] Just as important, rancorous or violent protest alienates those to whom it is directed, and protestors often relinquish any interpersonal power they might otherwise have claimed.

24. That the electorate generally plays a passive role in the policy process gives rise to a good deal of discussion among democratic theorists. Of course, the principle of representative government begins with the proposition that elected officials are surrogates for the electorate. But as surrogates, are they to give the people what they want or what the representatives believe will best serve the public interest? Each answer has its philosophic defenders. For John Stuart Mill (1926) and others, full citizen participation in all aspects of government helps promote citizen virtue, intelligence, and morality. But given low voter turnout, coupled with citizens' limited grasp of complex issues (Converse 1964), it may not be surprising that another group of democratic theorists argues that a healthy democracy does not require direct voter involvement in policy formation. It is enough (say these theorists) for voters to choose those who do make policy (Lipset 1960, Schumpeter 1947). But in rebuttal, see Bachrach (1967).

25. In some cases, events rather than personalities conspire to limit the success of voting blocks in translating preferences into policies. For example, in 1973 Janet Gray Hays ran for (and was elected) mayor of San Jose. She ran an essentially no-growth campaign, employing the slogan "Let's make San Jose better before we make it bigger." Yet, during her tenure in office, San Jose was the fastest growing city in the United States (Trounstine and Christensen 1982).

26. Examples of rancorous protests that successfully halted policy actions are difficult to identify. On the other hand, numerous examples of unsuccessful protests come to mind, including the Clamshell Alliance's attempt to stop EPA approval of the Seabrook Nuclear Reactor in New Hampshire and the American Agricultural Movement's tractorcade in Washington, D.C., not to mention the race riots of the 1960s. This is consistent with Schumaker's (1975. 521) conclusion that "the effect of militancy may be overestimated by some scholars."

27. Many politicians are wary of acceding to political demands attached to violent protest for fear that they will be portrayed as weak by their opponents during the next election.

On the other hand, nonviolent protestors may have considerable indirect power through their ability to bring issues to the top of the political agenda, particularly if the public believes their grievance to be genuine and their demands legitimate. The nonviolent civil rights protests of the 1950s and the early 1960s are a case in point. By bringing intolerable conditions to the attention of the nation, Martin Luther King (along with others) was able to create a climate for changing civil rights policy within the United States (Branch, 1988). In addition, nonviolent protestors do not burn bridges behind them. Their actions, while forceful, do not disrupt avenues of interpersonal communication and power.

Neighborhood groups and economic interests. Although we could consider a large number of other informal participants in the urban political process, we will concentrate on two more: neighborhood groups and economic interests. In the final analysis, these may be the most important sources of indirect and interpersonal power in the city.

In order to understand this power, let us reconsider one of the themes of this book, that the city is at heart an economic entity. Although the city has many functions in today's society, its primary functions center around the creation of jobs and the provision of services. Both, in the end, are economic functions. Jobs obviously provide a livelihood for the city's inhabitants, and they provide the capital necessary for the city to collect taxes. Services are the primary source of urban expenditures (both through capital outlays, such as police cars and playground equipment, and through the salaries of those who provide the services). Thus, the city is necessarily an economic enterprise, with the success of municipal government coupled to the local business climate. This gives the business community considerable indirect power. When the climate is healthy, new businesses and industries move to town, providing more jobs and more taxes to provide better services. And in turn, businesses and industries are more likely to move to cities that provide good services and good neighborhoods for their employees. Thus, we observe a three-way relationship between business, neighborhoods, and municipal services that serves to define the city's economic climate and its growth potential.

The three-way relationship in action. With this in mind, then, let us consider how local business and industrial leaders affect policy decisions, and in doing so, offer a final canvass of both indirect and interpersonal power. Through their capital investment decisions (in the case of owners) and recommendations (in the case of managers), business owners and managers directly affect the lives of a number of urban residents (i.e., their employees) and the city's coffers (i.e., the recipient of their tax dollars).[28] It therefore behooves the city's decision-makers to listen when business leaders talk about the needs and goals of the community. This dialogue may focus on specific issues, for example the construction of a downtown parking garage or a convention center, or it may be more amorphous, relating to broader issues such as crime, education, and the quality of urban services. But whatever the issue, business leaders generally have open access to the mayor, city council members, and/or the city manager. This, in turn, provides them with considerable interpersonal power.

But it should be noted that this access is not strictly, or even at all, coercive. In other words, it is not necessarily the threat of closing down manufacturing plants or retail businesses that makes decisionmakers want to listen to the ideas of economic leaders. Just as important is the fact that these individuals are economically successful and, over the years, have built up credibility as community boosters. Recall that the city management movement grew out of a desire to run cities as businesses and that most city managers are trained in a business tradition. Further, note that most city council members are themselves part of the business community, as bankers or lawyers or insurance salespersons. They respect people with demonstrated success in financial management. Finally, most successful business owners have put considerable time and money into their businesses. For them, what's good for the community is good for business, and vice versa. Over the years they have developed into local boosters, often serving as honorary chair of the United Way campaign or chair of the local delegation to the community's sister city in Japan. They are well known. And perhaps most important, they are trusted. All of these factors make them among the most valued political friends and advisors of many formal decisionmakers, who frequently turn to them for ideas and advice.

With homeowners, we face a somewhat different explanation for power. Individual homeowners have very little power, either indirect or interpersonal, but as a group they are able to exercise considerable indirect power over a rather narrow range of issues. For example, a group of homeowners is often able to block the placement of a low-income housing unit, a group home for mentally retarded adults, or a new fire station in their neighborhood. In principle, they have no more direct access to council members, who make the final decision on these issues, than do any other groups of voters. But in reality, theirs is an implicit threat to move if an intolerable situation arises—to "vote with their feet" (Hirschman 1970). And if a sufficient number of neighborhood residents exercise this option, neighborhood instability may follow.

Do all neighborhoods have equal power? As a rule, no. Underclass neighborhoods typically consist of rental units, often characterized by high transience. They are also often seen as problem areas, requiring more than their share of the city's services (e.g., fire and police protection, emergency medical

28. Through tax dollars, which affect the quality and availability of municipal services, business owners and managers in turn have an impact on a still larger segment of the urban community. And as was noted earlier, the quality of services affects both neighborhood development and the business climate, which creates a recursive impact.

services, and so forth). The city council is not easily swayed by the threat to move from these neighborhoods. But in middle- and upper-class neighborhoods, two factors make the council take note. First, residents of these neighborhoods are professionally (and therefore residentially) mobile, and moving to a new job in an adjacent city would present them with little hardship. In other words, their threats to move are not to be taken lightly. Second, the neighborhoods themselves are more stable, so an outflux of residents would be quite noticeable and potentially quite disruptive to the community's economic climate.

Idiosyncratic Factors Affecting the Distribution of Power

Finally, we should note that every city is different, and the distribution of power (of whatever type) in each city has its own idiosyncracies. In university towns, for example, the university president and members of his or her staff inevitably exercise indirect power by contributing university resources to solving local problems. In Lawrence, Kansas, for example, the University of Kansas joined the city in designing and developing a high-tech industrial park, while in Tuscaloosa, Alabama, the University of Alabama contributed its technical expertise to improve efficiency in the local Rochester Products (a subsidiary of General Motors) plant. But in turn, this commitment allows university administrators access to other, important people in the community, providing them with interpersonal power. In addition, most cities have at least one dominant church, and the pastor of that church may be a vocal participant in social and moral issues within the community. Pastors in predominantly black neighborhoods command considerable respect among their parishioners, and they are usually quite important in mobilizing the black community around political and social issues. And many cities have at least one charismatic leader who may hold no formal political or economic position in the community, but nonetheless is able to command the attention of people due to his or her "presence."

Implications for Public Policy

Based on this discussion of power, several general conclusions can be suggested about the role of power and the powerful in the development of urban policy. First, there exists an *economic bias* in this process, with policies generally favoring economic interests within the city. City officials in Detroit are, no doubt, convinced that what is good for General Motors (and Ford and Chrysler) is good for Detroit, and, where possible, public policies are supportive of (or at least not detrimental to) the auto industry.[29] Other cities

29. See the discussion of Poletown, a Detroit neighborhood in chapter 10.

share a similar orientation toward their dominant industries. If we introduce a somewhat artificial distinction between economic and social issues within a community, this distinction will suggest that economic issues take highest priority, with social issues finishing a poor second.

Second, a *class bias* exists in the development of public policy, even though it is often subtle and may even go unrecognized by those in positions of authority. Successful people, people of accomplishment, are the ones who command the attention of others. By definition (and popular perception), members of the underclass are not successful, and they therefore fail to command attention. Once people attain positions of importance in the community, they also tend to listen to the ideas of others with similar experiences and backgrounds, further reducing the voice of the underclass.

Third, urban public policy reflects technical considerations more than social considerations. Considerable power resides in the hands of municipal bureaucrats, who gain expertise in the day-to-day management and operation of their agencies. This experience often may lead to choices based on factual and technical considerations rather than on social considerations (see the discussion of technical versus social policy in the following chapter). For example, the city manager, in projecting the path of a new street, may be likely to consider the cost of condemning property, the terrain through which it must pass, and its capacity to move vehicles efficiently rather than the social disruption that it may cause for a neighborhood. The former is easily quantifiable in dollars and cents, while the latter is not.

Fourth, the more people involved in the policy development process, the slower and less definitive it is. Like the camel in the old joke (a camel is a horse designed by a committee), public policies designed by a large collective tend to be lumpy and ungainly, while those designed by a small group of like-minded people tend to be sleek and decisive. Both types of policy carry costs as well as benefits. In general, however, the more participants, the more diffused power is in the community. And without someone (or a small set of people) to serve as an issue entrepreneur, few dramatic changes will occur.

Fifth, when policymakers listen to the ideas of a large number of people, policies are more likely to address public problems successfully than when policymakers limit the number of people to whom they listen. If a decisionmaker consults only those in his or her inner circle, he or she will seldom be exposed to alternative views of the world. This is self-limiting and leads to a type of insularity that Irving Janis (1982) described as *groupthink,* wherein advisors tell a decisionmaker only what they believe he or she wants to hear. Many of the foreign policy catastrophes of this century can be blamed on groupthink, and, arguably, many urban policy failures have similar origins.

Finally, poor public policy results when competing interests in the community distrust the motives of one another. This, essentially, is the situation characterized by Yates (1977) as street-fighting pluralism, and he blames it for what he sees as our ungovernable cities. But an alternative formulation suggests that the ungovernable city derives from the breakdown of democratic norms in the urban political style. Adherence to these norms creates an atmosphere of trust and fair play, while deviance from them engenders suspicion and uncertainty. Mistrust engenders rancor, and rancor breaks down communication. In turn, uncertainty grows for political participants. Their ability to anticipate the course of community issues deteriorates, and their style of participation becomes defensive and reactive. With defensive reaction, groups become internally more cohesive (i.e., members become more supportive of one another) but more externally combative (Bolland 1985a). And the agenda-setting process fragments still further as competing groups refuse to cooperate with one another.

But despite these difficulties, cities continue to make policy and provide services to their residents. The following chapters consider more thoroughly the urban policy process and the policies it generates.

Part Four

Urban Politics and Policy: Context and Constraints

Bronx Apartment Houses. Peter Busa. 1937. Lithograph. Lent by the WPA. 640.1943. © 1989 The
Art Institute of Chicago, All Rights Reserved.

The Styles and Stages ————— 10
of Urban Policy[1]

> Nothing is harder than to make people think about what they're going to *do*.
> André Malraux
> *Man's Fate*

Dreams and Reality: "World Enough and Time"

In the prescriptive-democratic theory of philosophers' musings, public policy is a completely rational enterprise. Goals are plainly stated. Means to ends are carefully considered. And goals are always achieved effectively and efficiently—which is to say, actions produce their intended effect with the least expenditure of time, money, and other things of value. What is more, those who construct this rational policy always keep in the forefront of their minds a well-considered vision of the public interest. Consider, for example, the following fanciful dialogue among rational policymakers.

First Policymaker: What is the problem? Exactly what are we trying to achieve?

---

1. This chapter and the one to follow link with all ten theories of urban politics outlined in chapter 3, but especially the theories of commodification, influence, lifestyle and territory, and street-level bureaucracy. These chapters draw on a number of general studies of public policy, including Jones (1983), Lindblom (1980), Lindblom and Cohen (1979), Rein (1976), Eyestone (1978), Rivlin (1971), Brewer and deLeon (1983), Ripley and Franklin (1987), Cobb and Elder (1983), Kingdon (1984), and Olson (1968).

Second Policymaker:	What has been tried in other places? And how has it worked?
Third Policymaker:	Which among these many possible solutions is most likely to solve the problem that confronts us? Would an alternative solution work just as well—but cost us less in terms of money, time, and effort?
Fourth Policymaker:	Well then, are we all agreed? We try our preferred solution for a limited time? And if it doesn't do what we hope it will do, we try something else?

In the real world, this scenario is rarely, if ever, enacted. Anyone who attends a meeting of a city council (or county commission, or state legislature, or Congress) quickly learns that the give and take of policy discussion bears little resemblance to the rational style and courtly utterances of a Platonic dialogue. In the real world, policymakers operate within constraints that limit totally rational problem solving. First, they are constrained by resources—time, knowledge, and money. Second, they are constrained by selective perceptions and the screening out of information that contradicts the policymakers' dominant ideologies. *[The theory of ideology]* And third, they are constrained by the piecemeal responsibilities and scattered jurisdictions of local government (e.g., Ripley and Franklin 1987, Herson 1986). *[The theory of grass-roots democracy]*

Constraints Imposed by Limited Knowledge

In creating rational policy, no resource is more important than knowledge. Those who aspire to rational policy need to be able to choose from alternative courses of action. Moreover, they need to know how and why things happen—which is to say, they need well-validated descriptive theories. And perhaps most important, they need to know the likely costs and benefits of an intended course of action (Rivlin 1971, Rein 1976).

Technical Decisions and Technical Policy

Generally speaking, urban policy is of two broad types: technical and social. Technical policies involve material things, most especially the brick, steel, and concrete components of the city. Thus, technical policies deal with such matters as street construction, water and sewer lines, and the purchase of cars, trucks, and other supplies. On one level, technical policies invite an easy rationality, for they make use of scientific and engineering knowledge. (What paving materials stand up best under heavy loads? What are the comparative costs of asphalt and concrete? What kinds of pumps can deliver how much water and under what pressure?)

But on another level, scientific and accurate information can carry the policymaker only a limited distance. Technical policies are not made in a vacuum. It is easy to ascertain the costs of building a road, but putting the road in one part of the city may mean not putting the road somewhere else. To buy a new fire truck may leave less money to hire more firefighters. Thus, technical policies can be rational in their own, limited sphere, but an awareness of their broader implications constrains and diminishes the policymaker's capacity for what can be called an overall rationality (Lindblom 1965).

Technical policy exemplified: Freeway construction. Not only must the decision-maker weigh the consequences of one technical policy against all the others that might go unattended, but the decisionmaker must also confront the fact that any technical policy spills into other domains (Marris and Rein 1973). Who, for example, could have foreseen the unanticipated consequences of the great highway building projects of recent decades? Highways were built primarily to link distant cities and to ease traffic congestion within cities, but their unanticipated consequences have been awesome—and some would say, devastating. The new freeways contributed to the flight to the suburbs of an affluent and mostly white middle class, leaving the central cities with an increasingly poor, black, and Hispanic population. Freeways cut through old established neighborhoods, dislocating the mostly poor and elderly who lived there. And in cutting through old neighborhoods and tearing down houses that were in the way, freeways also depleted the stock of low-rent housing available to the poor. Freeways also destroyed many small, family-run businesses. They frequently isolated what was left of older neighborhoods. In these and other ways they broke the social and economic bonds that had once served to create a sense of community.

Equally important for what might be called the economic good-health of the cities, freeways also helped close down the central city's business area as a lively shopping place. They accomplished an unanticipated deterioration of downtown by making commercial property on the city's rim easily accessible by car. Shopping malls sprang up on what had once been farmland. Compared to downtown land prices, mall developers got cheap land and often put cheaply constructed store spaces on them. Merchants were attracted by rents lower than those downtown, and customers were lured by unlimited free parking and the visual pleasure of modern shops built in a consistent architectural style. Shopping malls became urban gathering places. To go there was more than a shopping trip; it was to see and be seen, an important social occasion. (For the young, a Saturday at the shopping mall had become a replacement for yesteryear's Saturday movie matinee.) Meanwhile, in many cities, downtown shopping went into steep decline. Stores and cinemas were boarded up and abandoned by their owners to avoid high property taxes. In many cities, the once-bustling downtown has been transformed into a parking-lot desert, its sidewalks menacingly empty, its stores gone away.

Thus, freeway building may have started as technical policy. Whether intended or not, it solved one problem, and created a host of others.

217

Social Policies: A Problematic Context

As the term is intended to suggest, social policies deal with the human dimensions of urban life, with the effects of population density, and with the problems that are part of urban living. Crime, poverty, traffic congestion, urban blight, and urban sprawl are prime examples of urban social problems. Policies intended to solve or lessen such problems are prime examples of social policies.

Social problems are the most difficult problems to confront the policymaker. Given their importance, social problems challenge the policymaker to achieve the highest possible rationality. But by their nature, social problems stubbornly evade and defy easy resolution (Rivlin 1971).

Most of the city's important social problems are in the city, but not created by the city. They are visible in the city, but like icebergs, their mass lies elsewhere, in the larger society. Urban policymakers can and do attempt to pound at the icebergs' tips, but they realize that if the larger mass is to be moved or made smaller, only the national government may be equal to the task (Ripley and Franklin 1987, Cleaveland, 1973). Urban policymakers may try to solve the city's social problems, but their efforts are marked by a gnawing sense that as far as effectiveness goes, most city policy can do no more than touch the iceberg's tip.

Social policies often suffer a fatal flaw: In all too many cases, our stock of empirical (that is, descriptive) theories is deficient. We are far from certain that we know the causes of the problem we are attempting to solve. Moreover, what we see as a cause of the problem may not be the "cause" at all, but the consequence of the viewers' beliefs and values (see Berger and Luckman 1967, on the social construction of reality). *[The theory of ideology]* Take, for example, poverty (or for that matter, crime, the high school drop-out rate, or the widespread use of illegal drugs). Is poverty (or crime, or the school drop-out rate, or taking illegal drugs) the result of a personal failing, something approaching a lack of determination to get ahead in life? Or is poverty (or any other social problem) a consequence of our economic system? Or is it perhaps a failure of our society to take proper care of its poor and its maladjusted?[2] (See the aptly titled *The Dilemmas of Social Reform,* by Marris and Rein, 1973.[3])

Our stock of empirical theories is deficient in a second important sense. Careful observation may help us to see what changes, if any, came after a new

2. As an example, three causal interpretations of alcoholism abound in our society: the moral interpretation (i.e., alcoholism as a character flaw), the medical interpretation (i.e., alcoholism as a disease), and the social interpretation (i.e., alcoholism as a result of the demands placed on an individual by a drinking society). For a discussion of these perspectives, see Watts (1982).

3. James Q. Wilson (1975) offers a spirited critique of policymakers who attempt to fight urban crime on the basis of the search for its root causes. The search for root causes, he argues, is perforce an exercise in futility. Better, he says, to concentrate policy energies on dealing with criminal behavior and on lessening opportunities for such behavior.

policy was put in place; but given the tangled skein of all that constitutes human nature and human motives, we are far from certain that any specific policy resulted in (caused) the changes that followed. For example, if student performance on college entry tests improves over time, shall we assume that the improvement was caused by different teaching methods, or by such other factors as a change in the motivation or social class of those seeking college admission? (See Rivlin 1971.)[4]

If we are unsure about what it was in past policies that "really worked;" if we are unsure about the "real" causes of a problem; and if we are also prone to ideological quarrels over the "best" steps we can take to meet the problem—most likely, our policy steps will be halting, reluctant, and small. (There is an old saying in politics: The bigger the problem, the smaller will be the steps to resolve it.)

Given our society's success at solving technical problems ("We put a man on the moon, didn't we?"), it is understandable that we are reluctant to concede that our most important social problems may be unsolvable. ("Well, then, why can't we stop drug addiction? Why can't we solve the problems of the homeless?)[5] But social problems contain too many imponderables to admit any easy solution—or perhaps any solution at all! And that being the case, those who make social policies labor under few illusions that they are going to solve those problems. They know that they will do well if only they can cope with (and perhaps, alleviate) social problems by tackling them one small step at a time.

Incremental vs. Reconstructive Public Policy

To create public policy in small steps is, of course, an attempt to make social and political change also in small steps. This style of small-step policy and change is not confined to cities. It is a style in general use at all levels of American government (Herson 1984). *[The theory of social learning]*

Incremental policy. This incremental style of policy making (to give it its social-scientific label) is, in fact, common to all democratic societies. The reasons for its widespread use are several. First, incremental policy is relatively

---

4. It is not surprising that the problem of discovering and tracing social causation has vexed social scientists for a very long time (e.g., MacIver 1942). In fact, as Thomas Haskell (1977) so brilliantly demonstrates, the establishment of modern social science disciplines came about because the academic community had grown impatient and mistrustful of amateur scholars asserting that they had discovered the "true" causes of social change and the links between social behaviors and root causes. Most contemporary social scientists are (as are lawyers) content to work at discovering "proximate" rather than root causes. For a joining of the physicist's and social scientist's concerns over causality, see Norwood Hanson (1958).

5. For an insightful exploration of the moon-ghetto metaphor, see Nelson (1974).

nonthreatening to the status quo (proposed changes are small). Second, the monetary costs of incremental changes are also relatively small. Third, incremental changes are less likely to unroll a long chain of unanticipated consequences—or, if they do (and if they are unwelcome), policymakers can then attempt corrective action.

Incremental policies abound on the local level, the most obvious example being the city's annual budget. Policymakers invariably decide on what is to be spent (and where the money is to come from) by building on the city's present budget—adding a program here and there, putting additional money into selected programs, taking funds from others (Wildavsky 1979b).

Of course, it would be an almost impossible task for the city council to start afresh every budget year, with no established plans or commitments. Every city has standing programs and obligations (fire protection, police, parks, and so forth). To begin at the beginning every year, with every expenditure and every program to be (potentially) terminated would be unthinkable—a time-consuming and wearying process. It would lead budget makers into a swamp of indecision and delay (not to mention interest group anxiety over threatened programs). Thus, budget makers tinker with last year's budget and then proceed by means of incremental changes.

Reconstructive policy. Reconstructive policy stands in sharp contrast to incremental policy. As its name is intended to suggest, reconstructive policy seeks to alter and reconstruct the status quo. Reconstructive policy usually seeks to alter and remedy a fairly wide range of social, political, or economic affairs. It is often the goal (or consequence) of reformers and reform movements, and though urban policymakers do not attempt to reconstruct the economics of city life, other types of reconstructing policies do get tried. *[The theory of social learning]* As the earlier discussion of the Progressive era (chapter 5) indicates, what is presently in place as the urban reform package is a noteworthy example of reconstructive urban policy.[6]

Symbolic vs. Substantive Policy

Both incremental and reconstructive policies attempt genuine change. Their intent is substantial and thus substantive; they are intended to deal effectively

---

6. In general, reconstructive policy is the province of the national government. Such policy usually occurs in a time of crisis (war, economic depression, and the like). As will be noted in chapter 14, many of the national government's policies of the 1960s were reconstructive in intent (the War on Poverty, the Civil Rights acts) and directly affected the cities. Another explanation for the fact that cities do not attempt reconstructive policy intended to alter the economic status quo is consistent with the theory of influence and is persuasively advanced by Bachrach and Baratz (1962). The city's economic elites, they argue, usually have sufficient influence to prevent such policies from rising high on the urban political agenda.

with a problem or an issue. Symbolic policy, in contrast, deals only with the surface of an issue (Edelman 1964). Symbolic policies are cosmetic in that they seek to cover or disguise the problem; they do not assault, obliterate, or remedy the problem. It is often the case that urban policymakers, when puzzled about what to do, or hesitant about incurring the costs of substantive policy, will escape into symbolic policies. Thus, as a familiar form of symbolic decision (and symbolic policy), city councils often appoint a committee of inquiry to study and make recommendations for future council consideration of an important problem or issue (e.g., violence in the schools, a rising rate of building abandonment, the decline of downtown shopping). Or, as another form of symbolic policy, urban administrators may make a visible display of what the public is intended to see as "action." Thus, if the crime rate is perceived as rising, or if murders go unsolved, those making law-enforcement policy may conduct street-sweeps of suspicious persons or increase the frequency of police patrols in a high-crime area.

Symbolic policy offers the symbols of change. It affords the policymakers (and sometimes a clamoring public) the sense that something is being done. By its nature, symbolic policy is low in cost.[7] It is therefore a form of coping with difficult and perhaps unsolvable problems without great expenditure. Moreover, it buys time. And meanwhile, perhaps, public attention will flag. The heat will be off the policymakers. And perhaps—just perhaps—the problem will go away all by itself.

Limitations of Time

Though symbolic policy will sometimes buy time for policymakers, it must also be recognized that time itself is an important constraint on policymakers' ability to achieve effective and rational policy. In most cities, the council's agenda is crammed to overflowing. There are taxes to be levied, a budget to be passed, complaints and petitions to be heard, contracts to be approved, and ordinances to be considered. The bigger the city, the fuller the agenda. And with only rare exceptions, councils do not employ an administrative or a research staff to help with their work. Thus, to be a council member is usually to have too much to do and too little time to do it.

But to conclude that the constraints of time do nothing more than limit the amount of information (or careful canvass of alternatives) available to council members is only to state the obvious. Other, more subtle constraints are also at work. First, as was noted in chapter 7, council members in most cities serve on a part-time basis, deriving their principal incomes elsewhere. They

---

7. It may have high *opportunity costs,* however. That is, the opportunity to develop a substantive policy that may prove useful in ameliorating a problem is lost when a symbolic policy is implemented.

tend to hold jobs that permit (or are enhanced by) council service. In most cities, council members are lawyers, real-estate brokers, insurance agents, employees of banks and public utility companies. Occasionally, they are union officials. Thus, they carry into the council a view of the public interest that is biased by their occupation and social standing. *[The theory of ideology]*

A second consequence for policy follows from the first. With too much to do and too little time to do it, city councils tend to get information (concerning costs, the experience of other cities, and so forth) either from the city administrators or from data furnished by persons and groups interested in a particular policy or an item of legislation. Thus, councils may often frame policy around the testimony and viewpoints of organized groups: the chamber of commerce, real-estate developers and the like—all of whom have a direct and obvious interest in policy formation and policy outcomes.[8]

A third consequence that follows from time constraints has to do with the style of urban public policy. Again, our reference point is prescriptive democratic theory. In an ideal democracy, public policy ought to be far seeing and carefully arranged with respect to thoughtfully considered priorities. Policy ought not be a hasty response to a single, immediate problem, but a considered response to a host of connected problems. In short, policy ought to be *proactive* rather than *reactive*.

But in the real world, most urban policy is reactive—a specific reaction to a specific problem. Douglas Yates (1977) calls this style of policy "crisis hopping," putting out fires already lit and burning, using resources of government to take care of present problems, but paying little attention to those that may lie ahead. And while this may not always and in every case make for nonrational policy, it surely leads (through the connection between time and reactivity) in a direction away from policy at its most rational best.

The Politics of Policy-Making: Four Types of Policy

The previous classification of urban policies has led us to distinguish between technical and social policies, between substantive and symbolic policies, and between incremental and reconstructive policies. But however informative these distinctions, it must be confessed that in real-world practice, they are not always sharp and clear. For example, symbolic policies, however cosmetic their intent, sometimes have substantive outcomes. Thus, beefed-up police patrols and periodic street-sweeps may bring new ideas about how best to use police personnel—which, in turn, may bring a reassessment of the most efficient use of motorized equipment (a technical policy).

Nevertheless, distinctions and classifications provide useful details. They

8. This extends the previous chapter's discussion of the indirect and interpersonal power of these groups.

help convey the realities of city government-in-action. And they also introduce us to the politics of policy-making: what the stakes may be, who wins and who loses, who the players are, and what strategies are most likely to be used by those seeking to influence policy outcomes.

To introduce the politics of policy-making, four other types of policy will be sketched; but once again, it is easier to assert a set of policy types in the abstract than to find them neatly separated in real-world use.

Regulatory Policy

Regulatory policy involves the direct and open attempt to control citizens' and business firms' behavior. Most typically, regulatory policy deals with matters of health, safety, and morals—in short, with matters that fall under the state's police powers (see chapter 13). Familiar forms of regulatory policy are ordinances that deal with crime, prostitution, the quarantine of those with communicable disease, the regulation of barbershops, taxicabs, restaurants, and automobile traffic. Regulatory policy also establishes standards for building construction and maintenance and extends to zoning—restricting certain kinds of businesses and buildings to designated areas of the city.[9]

As might be expected, every regulatory policy falls more heavily on some persons (and groups) than on others. Regulatory policy makes a difference in the way persons or groups are treated—some being restricted in what they do, others being let alone. Thus, as it is being framed and as it is being enforced, regulatory policy almost always produces conflict and bargaining: protests, arguments, petitions from those who stand to win most and from those who stand to lose most. Such actions, of course, are the essence of ordinary, everyday politics; it is for this reason that regulatory policy is usually perceived by policymakers (and the general public) as being part of the ordinary process of government and a necessary activity on behalf of the public good. As a consequence, quarrels over regulatory policy are fairly subdued, often being resolved in the courts. They usually entail argument over the wisdom or usefulness of the policy, not diehard, acrimonious protest from those who will be adversely affected.

Distributive Policy

As the term may suggest, distributive policies are those that parcel out the services and resources of government among and between the citizenry. Garbage collecting, street paving, police and fire protection are among the commonest forms of distributive policy. Distributive policies can be broken down

9. The implications of zoning policies are considered more fully in chapter 17.

into two sub-types: those (e.g., street paving, police and fire protection) intended to be evenhanded and to distribute benefits equally among the citizenry; and those that single out groups and geographic areas for benefits and assistance (e.g., neighborhood parks, shelters for the homeless, high-intensity street lights, public swimming pools).

Distributive policies sometimes invite more intense political conflict than regulatory policies; the reason lies in the fact that no matter what the intent, distributive policies can never operate according to a principle that everyone agrees is fully just and fair and equal. For example, in the abstract, most would agree that benefits for the poor are morally and politically justified, but disagreement often follows when questions are raised as to whether benefits to the poor should take priority over, say, needed street lights or beautifying downtown to attract new business and thus provide more jobs for the city's poor.[10]

More difficult still is deciding how to weigh the special needs of areas and neighborhoods against equal treatment for all areas and neighborhoods. Consider, for example, street paving, fire and police protection, and garbage pickup. No matter how policymakers may attempt an even-handed distribution of services, the distribution will be open to challenge. Again, consider fire protection: City policy may call for one fire station for every three square miles.[11] Under this standard, fire protection could be said to be equally distributed. But by another standard, it is not. Neighborhoods with newer housing and fewer persons per living unit will have fewer fires than areas of older housing, higher population densities, and lower per capita income. Perhaps, then, the decision rule ought to be one that allocates personnel and equipment according to the number of fires likely to occur in an area. If that is the decision rule (and in many cities it is), those with property in less-protected areas are likely to complain that, as a consequence of the rule, their fire insurance rates are too high.

In essence, distributive policies are arranged according to decision rules built around ideas concerning equality and equity (of which more later), and it is argument over what constitutes equal benefits that fuels the politics of distributive policy. Argument over equality and equity also helps blur the distinction between distributive and redistributive policies.

Redistributive Policy

These are the most conflict-laden policies. They seek to redistribute the resources of government (and in the long run, of society) from one social and

---

10. An even greater debate, epitomized by such tax revolt measures as Proposition 13 in California and Proposition 2½ in Massachusetts, concerns how these services are to be paid for. See chapter 16 for further discussion.

11. More specifically, policy may call for no area of the city to be further than 1.5 road miles from the nearest fire station.

economic class to another. Usually, this redistribution runs from those better off to those least well off. The income tax is the basic vehicle of redistributive policy. (In some cities, this takes the form of a tax on wages.) Under its terms, those whose incomes are highest usually contribute most to government. This arrangement comports with what has become a basic precept of our society: Equity and social justice—"a fair share for everyone"—require that each member of society be brought up to some minimum standard with respect to those things necessary to maintain a reasonably decent and healthy life.

This precept is at the center of ideological dispute (and thus, of politics) in America today. Some would ask, What is fair about fair shares? Is it fair to take money from those who have earned it to help those who have not? Others would ask, Is it the case that those who have earned money have been able to do so because the government (which after all, represents *all* the people) has maintained and protected the economic system that makes possible the accumulation of wealth? But even if such points and counterpoints are not readily resolved, most in our society accept the concepts of equity and social justice but continue to disagree on their real-world application—just how much by way of government benefits and services does it take to achieve fair shares?

In our political system, most redistributive policies lie with the national government (Ripley and Franklin 1987). But while wealthy towns and suburbs engage in virtually no redistribution at all, central cities with sizeable numbers of poor do what their politics and resources permit: city funding in support of hospital emergency care, shelters for the homeless, counseling for drug users and the mentally disturbed, the rehabilitation of run-down, low-income housing. (For details concerning redistributive policy in New York, see C. Morris 1980.) Most such redistributive benefits are undertaken as part of larger federal- and state-supported welfare programs, with city funds being used to supplement those programs. Even so, the politics of city redistributive policies assume a familiar ring. How much is our city's fair share? Should our money be used for other purposes?

Development Policies

Development policies aim to ensure the economic growth and prosperity of the city (P. Peterson 1981). Familiar examples of development policies are proposals to build a sports arena or convention center, to bring new industry to the city, and to revive the central business district. *[The theory of commodification of land and buildings]*

Development policies often require levying additional taxes (or issuing bonds to be repaid with tax revenues over the next decade) to build the proposed sports arena and convention center and to rebuild downtown. Bringing new business to the city often requires the lure of tax abatements (relinquishing a tax ordinarily collected). Development policies are advanced as being good for

225

the entire city. ("It will bring new jobs to our town. It will be something we can all be proud of.") But oftentimes, as is the case with most policy proposals, argument erupts over who will derive most benefit, who will pay a disproportionate share of new taxes, and who will lose most in city services if the arena is built or the tax abatement is used to bring new industrial development.[12] Development policies have a considerable allure, but they also entail social costs. In 1980, for example, the city of Detroit, suffering from high unemployment, attempted to keep General Motors from locating a proposed new plant elsewhere. To make it possible to build the new factory inside the city, Detroit offered to use its powers of eminent domain[13] to clear a large tract of land and turn it over to General Motors.

Under the terms of the city's proposal, eleven hundred homes in an old neighborhood called Poletown (a sobriquet connoting the area's ethnic inhabitants) were to be razed to make way for General Motors' project. The new factory would be built on the Poletown site, and it was estimated that six thousand new jobs for auto workers would be created. But choosing Poletown was an excruciating policy decision. Should the city destroy an old neighborhood with its distinctive way of life, its shops, its parish church, its houses that represented a lifetime of pride and ownership, in order to bring new jobs to the city? Or should it risk the almost certain outcome that an industry that had been a mainstay of Detroit's employment for three-fourths of a century would relocate elsewhere?

In the end, despite mass demonstrations by the people of Poletown and their angry and emotional appeals to save their way of life *[The theory of lifestyle and territory]*, the argument of the greatest good for the greatest number prevailed. Poletown was torn down. But for those who once lived there, the psychological scars remain. (For details of the Poletown saga, see the *New York Times,* March 15, 1981 and April 30, 1981.)

As the story of Poletown suggests, development policy aims at the common good, but achieving the common good may have its price. To explore this tension more fully, it will be useful to look at other examples of development policy. Doing so will further sketch the politics of making policy and lead to an outline of the several stages of policy-making.

12. These tax abatement programs were massive in many areas of the country. For example, the New York State Commerce Department's Job Incentive Board granted hundreds of millions of dollars in ten-year tax credits between 1975 and 1980, with beneficiaries including the Long Island newspaper *Newsday* ($16.2 million), Lehman Brothers ($3.4 million), Morgan Stanley ($5.6 million), Proctor & Gamble ($14 million), Hooker Chemical Company ($40 million), Alien & Company ($1.3 million), and WKBW-TV ($1.7 million). For a discussion of the New York (and other) tax abatement program and for a critical assessment of the use of tax abatements, see Tabb (1984).

13. Eminent domain is "a government's right to take private property for the public's use," on payment of fair compensation (Shafritz 1988).

Olympus (New York). Gerald Geerlings. 1929. Etching. Gift of the Chicago Society of Etchers. 1969.351. © 1989 The Art Institute of Chicago, All Rights Reserved.

228

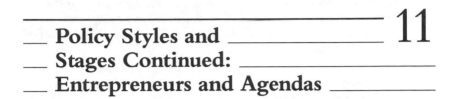

Policy Styles and Stages Continued: Entrepreneurs and Agendas   11

Let the great world spin forever down the ringing Grooves of Change.
Alfred Lord Tennyson
Locksley Hall

Policy Entrepreneurs

Most policy, but especially development policy, springs from the energy and commitment of policy entrepreneurs—the handful of persons who become fixed on a proposal and dedicate themselves to pushing it, step by step, stage by stage, to its final accomplishment. Policy entrepreneurs are found everywhere in city government: on the council, in the administrative bureaucracy (fire chiefs and police chiefs, for example), and in the office of the city's chief executive. Most policy entrepreneurs concern themselves with small-scale matters, dealing with such things as the arrest powers of the police, enforcing building codes, scattering miniparks around the city, and so forth. But when it comes to development policies, persons outside the government in what is usually called the private—meaning business—sector (see chapter 6) often play a crucial role. Inside the government, it is usually the mayor or the city manager who plays the role of development-policy entrepreneur.

Mayors and Managers

Mayors and managers are newsworthy. They command public attention. They draw on the knowledge and expert advice of the city's bureaucracy. Mayors make use of the political influence that derives from their role in party politics (in partisan cities) and their expertise (in all cities with strong mayors). What is more, mayors can also claim a special sort of policy legitimacy. As the sole occupant of one branch of government (unlike the multiple members of the city council) and as the elect of all the voters, mayors can claim to know best what the voters want, and they can further claim to speak on behalf of all the people of the city.

In big cities especially, mayors have been successful in creating what is called an executive-centered coalition. These coalitions of business leaders and politicians have been responsible for a number of large-scale projects: freeway building, housing complexes, and revitalization of the downtown business district (Banfield 1974, Salisbury 1964). Many such coalitions owe their success to getting massive federal grants—a success that in turn owes much to the mayor's political influence with his or her state's congressional delegation and to the importance of city voters in presidential elections.

Land Developers and Business Leaders

But policy entrepreneurs do not come exclusively from the ranks of public officials. In most cities—and particularly when it comes to development policy—the most effective entrepreneurs are often business leaders. As has been the case for more than two centuries, real estate developers continue to change the face of cities. [The theory of commodification of land and buildings] Office construction is the present form of this change, with tall buildings rising all across the country. And in many places, developers are building "urban complexes"—office and apartment buildings, shops and theatres, all sited together—in an attempt to bring back shoppers, residents, and visitors, and in so doing to give vitality to the old downtown.[1]

Pittsburgh's Golden Triangle, Boston's Faneuil Hall shopping area and tourist attraction, and Detroit's Renaissance Center are all examples of the accomplishments of the business (private sector) entrepreneur. Working with elected officials, these private sector, policy entrepreneurs provide money and leadership for massive urban development.

---

1. For a critical view of the role of business persons in city development, as well as a critical view of the entire principle of the commodification of land and buildings, see Molotch (1976) and Ambrose and Colenutt (1975). And for a discussion of successful downtown redevelopment projects, see, for example, Black et al. (1983).

Policy Entrepreneurs and Development Policy: A Tale of Several Cities

Richard C. Lee and New Haven

Richard C. Lee is the archetype of the entrepreneurial mayor who builds and then leads an executive-centered coalition. First elected mayor of New Haven in 1953, he was reelected for eight consecutive terms, choosing not to run again in 1969. During his sixteen years in office, Lee became one of the best-known, most written about mayors in the United States. He was elected president of the U.S. Council of Mayors, and all over the country was much in demand as a public speaker and adviser to cities. No fewer than eight books (e.g., Wolfinger 1974, Powledge 1970) have been written about his mayoralty; his city's public information office once issued an eighteen-page bibliography citing 242 magazine articles—all extolling his accomplishments in turning a small city (population around 150,000) into what was widely heralded as a model city, a model of achievement for other cities to emulate.

Under Lee's entrepreneurship, New Haven accomplished massive slum clearance and large-scale urban renewal. One project (the Oak Street project) cleared and then rebuilt forty-four acres of dilapidated, run-down housing. An enthusiastic writer (Jeanne Lowe, *Harper's,* Nov. 1957) declared Oak Street to be a symbol of New Haven's "pride and hope,"

> the first integrated step in a grand design which will gear the city to the automobile age, rebuild its rotten commercial core, shore up slipping neighborhoods, and draw the disenchanted back from the suburbs.

Oak Street, said another writer, was also a symbol of the successful participation of business in redevelopment, for Lee had persuaded the telephone company to build "a $15-million headquarters in the project area" (Powledge 1970, 37).

The Church Street project was even more massive. It razed four blocks of the central business district and eventually brought to New Haven

> a new department store . . . a 19-story hotel; the Chapel Mall, a two level collection of small retail stores; . . . a 14-story office building . . . [and] a 320-foot-tall building to house the international headquarters of the Knights of Columbus. (Powledge 1970, 37)

And still other projects followed. Most of the money for what was accomplished came from the federal government. Lee was one of the first mayors to realize the potential for massive change that lay in federal urban-renewal funds. More important, his was one of the first cities to prepare a comprehensive plan to support an application for federal money. (As is often the case, federal agencies, when they are charged by Congress with disbursing money, work willingly with those who are first in line for that money.)

The federal government responded to New Haven with massive support, and toward the end of the 1960s, it was estimated that federal urban-renewal allocations to New Haven

> were equivalent to $790 for each man, woman, and child. By contrast, Newark, New Jersey . . . was getting $286 per capita; Boston had $268 and New York had $42. (Powledge 1970, 19)

A large part of New Haven's success in getting federal funds was owed to Mayor Lee's creating a Citizens' Action Committee (CAC), which satisfied Congress' requirement that urban renewal involve broad citizen representation (Wolfinger 1974). The CAC served not only to legitimate Lee's program, it constituted a powerful coalition, nearly one hundred strong, which included business persons (concerned with retail sales and traffic congestion downtown), union leaders (who foresaw job opportunities in new construction), and political liberals (concerned about New Haven's slums and the plight of the poor who lived there).

Members of the CAC, said Mayor Lee, flex the "biggest set of muscles in New Haven . . ."

> because they control wealth, . . . industries, banks . . . , because they represent the intellectual portions of the community. They're muscular because of their financial power and because of the accumulation of prestige they have built up over the years. . . . (Dahl 1961, 136)

Mayor Lee's remarks are consistent with the theory of urban influence developed in chapter 9, but in the case of New Haven, the theory stands at the edge of controversy. Arguments over the power of the CAC and its accomplishments have never been laid to rest. Robert Dahl (1961), in his important study of political power in New Haven, views the CAC as indicative of democratic pluralism: widespread citizen participation in political decisions, operating within a widely shared set of democratic values.[2] Other observers, however, have been more critical. Some see the CAC as the pawn of the business community, whose members were only too happy to have the CAC provide the superficial trappings of democratic pluralism—all the while protecting the special economic interests of New Haven business. Others, using a different perspective, have seen the CAC as a collection of "yes-people," flattered to

2. Because Dahl's study of New Haven (1961) is central to political science's examination of power in America, it has generated an enormous amount of scholarly comment, both pro and con. That comment was canvassed in chapter 9; chapters 6, 7, and 8 put Dahl's New Haven study in its fuller context.

232

be on the committee, but only a rubber stamp for Lee's ideas. And still others argue that Lee proposed to the CAC only those things he knew would reflect the committee's business-oriented goals.[3]

But whatever the motives of the CAC's participants and whatever the CAC may reveal about a theory of urban influence and of democratic pluralism, it was the effective pivot of Lee's highly successful urban coalition. At the height of its effectiveness, the CAC had become what one writer calls "the parallel government" of New Haven (Powledge 1970, 34). It was outside the formal government but inside every important development decision, and it was completely part of the business community.

Mayor Lee's successes are apparent and impressive. New Haven is physically transformed. A shabby downtown is now new and architecturally distinguished. A new road leads from the interstate highway directly downtown, and acres of slums are now replaced by modern housing.

But success in reshaping a city physically does not readily translate into solutions for its social and economic problems. As previously said, policy achievement often has its unanticipated consequences. The poor in New Haven mostly stayed poor. White flight to the suburbs continued, and New Haven's unemployment rate rose and fell with national trends. When urban rioting flashed across the country in the 1960s, New Haven was not spared (its major riot took place in 1967). And the New Haven riot produced considerable discomfort for those in Mayor Lee's coalition. New Haven, after all, was supposed to be a model city. What had gone wrong?

With the wisdom of hindsight, it is now argued that the CAC could not have represented the community (nor given outreach to pluralistic participation) as had once been touted. The CAC included no blacks. Perhaps, then, what had been accomplished was done over the objections and resentment of an important segment of the city. Almost seven thousand families and individuals had been dislocated because of urban renewal. Nearly all were poor, and very large numbers of them were black. Sizeable numbers had not been relocated in equally good or equally affordable housing. And as to the much-vaunted beautiful new New Haven (said not a few critics), perhaps those shining symbols of urban affluence served only to remind the poor of their powerlessness and their alienation from the progress that Mayor Lee had once proclaimed.

Henry Ford and Detroit's Renaissance

When Henry Ford created the first mass-produced automobile, he changed America forever—and most of the rest of the world as well. What had once

---

3. These views are consistent with the arguments advanced in chapters 6-9, that considerable power in American communities resides in the hands of the business community.

been a plaything for the rich soon became a social and economic necessity for everyone else. Henry Ford (it is often said) put America on wheels, and the social, political, and economic consequences have never stopped spinning.

Crime and criminality changed as cops and crooks took to wheels. Mortality patterns and medical practice changed as death on the highway vied with natural pathologies to become the nation's leading killer. Employment patterns changed as workers were freed of the streetcar in going to office and factory. Patterns of courtship and sexuality changed as young people used the automobile to escape the chaperoning presence of an older generation. Routines of agriculture and factory production changed as industries found it possible to spread their workspaces horizontally across a now-accessible countryside and as farmers found it possible to ship produce to distant markets without dependence on the railroad.

Thus, the impact of the automobile is on our society everywhere, but nowhere greater than on our cities. The automobile not only created air pollution and the snarl of commuting traffic, it also altered the physical form of cities as more and bigger roads were built. The automobile undercut ridership on public transportation, and in city after city, public transportation disappeared—leaving the poor and the elderly isolated in their neighborhoods, unable to go in search of distant jobs (or to get to those jobs), unable to visit faraway friends, or even to seek medical assistance. The automobile made possible the leapfrogging of city residents into distant suburbs, and cars and trucks together made it possible for entire industries to depart the older cities in search of cheaper land and higher profits.

Henry Ford's masterpieces of mass production were made first in Detroit. Other car makers also set up in Detroit, and for half a century (from about 1905 to the 1950s) Detroit prided itself on being the motor capital of the world. But after World War II, "Motown" fell on hard times. Car makers shifted production elsewhere, and the American car industry was devastated by foreign competition. By the 1960s, Detroit was a city in trouble. Its downtown had nearly as many vacant lots as stores. Its middle class had gone suburban. Urban blight was spreading. Poverty and unemployment were widespread. Large patches of the city had been burned down in the urban riots of the 1960s. Racial strife was marked by sporadic violence—in police shoot-outs such as the Algiers Motel incident (Hersey 1968)—and in the resistance of white enclaves to black incursion. What is more, Detroit had achieved the dubious distinction of murder capital of the world—its population being reduced by more than one homicide a day.

Added to a pervasive sense of Detroit as a city in deep trouble was the undeniable fact that the office-building boom, going on in other cities, had thus far failed to take hold in Detroit. Headquarters for the automobile industry had long ago moved out of downtown, and (said one observer) "the city's skyline is remarkably unchanged from the 1930s" (*New York Times*, July 3, 1983).

In the 1960s, Henry Ford II (grandson of the first Henry),

> then confident about the future of the auto industry, decided that only a gargan-
> tuan building project could revive the urban core. So he set out in 1971 to build
> what became a $357 million office and retail complex named, hopefully, the
> Renaissance Center. Ford's . . . [company's] $300 million total outlay . . . may
> represent the largest civic investment ever made by a private corporation. (*New
> York Times*, July 3, 1983)

The RenCen (as it is called) is handsome urban architecture: four glass-
sheathed, octagonal thirty-story office towers standing on elevated ground, facing
the lake, surmounted by a seventy three-story hotel. But, sad to say, the RenCen
has not fulfilled the hopes of its planners. It has failed to spur significant building
in the rest of downtown. And to make matters worse, as a financial investment,
the RenCen is shaky. Through much of its life, many of its shops have stood
empty, and office space has been rented at prices far below investment costs.

It may be that a single, grandiose project discourages rather than
encourages other projects. Or it may be that too much industry has moved
from Detroit to sustain a large-scale office tower with tenants that are
necessarily purveyors of services to commerce and industry. It may also be
that the fault of the RenCen is in its design. It sits, fortresslike, on high ground;
best approached by cars that enter its interior garage, it does not beckon the
downtown walker or contribute to foot traffic in the downtown core. Or it
may simply be that Henry Ford chose to promote the wrong kind of project.
Policy entrepreneurs, when they work on a grand scale, always envision an
alternative future. Sometimes, though, the vision may be faulty.

James Rouse and the City as Festival

James Rouse has been a different kind of urban visionary. Like Henry Ford,
he sees cities being revitalized by private investment, and like most other
private-sector entrepreneurs, he expects city officials to work within the
outlines of his master plan—shifting streets, passing special ordinances, and
making way for new construction by exercising the city's power of eminent
domain. In other words, Rouse, too, has operated through an executive-
centered coalition, but it is a coalition dominated by the private sector.

In size and money, the Rouse corporations are massive. To date, they
have financed more than $3-billion-worth of real estate through their cor-
porate banks. They have financed and built more than thirty-five regional retail
centers and manage more than a dozen others in the United States and Canada
(*Time*, Aug. 24, 1981).

Outside the business community, Rouse's considerable fame comes from his distinctive—and distinctively successful—projects in city redevelopment. Wherever possible, he renovates old buildings rather than tear them down. He gives old buildings new life by giving them new use, retaining their distinctive eighteenth- and nineteenth-century styles. And he takes advantage of each redevelopment site's historical resonances by revitalizing waterfronts, warehouse districts, and old-towns.

Jane Jacobs (an eminent architectural critic and urban historian) has argued that cities derive their vitality from thronging people—strolling, shopping, and watching each other (Jacobs 1961)—and Rouse makes human dynamics the mainspring of his restorations: Baltimore's Inner Harbor, Santa Monica's Santa Monica Place, Philadelphia's Market Street East, New York's South Street Market, and Boston's Quincy Market.

Baltimore's Inner Harbor development exemplifies Rouse's projects. Some thirty years ago, the 3.2 acre site was part of a "250-acre wasteland of rotting wharves, warehouses, and railroad yards, the worst of Baltimore's then decrepit downtown" (*Time,* Aug. 24, 1981). Today, Inner Harbor is a vibrant shopping area and tourist attraction, vying with Disneyland in the number of visitors it attracts each year. A tall, angular, modern building houses one of Inner Harbor's major attractions, an aquarium. But mostly, people come to Inner Harbor to move in and out of its two retail pavilions "to eat, drink, shop, stroll, play and just lounge around in the evocative maritime atmosphere" (*New York Times,* May 26, 1985). The jobs and profits for retailers, hotels, and restaurants have brought a new prosperity to Baltimore (not to mention the value added to its tax rolls). In the years since its opening in 1980, Harbor Place (says one writer) has become the anchor "of a genuine waterfront renaissance that Baltimoreans believe has transformed the look and the life of their once tired city" (*New York Times,* May 26, 1985).

But major change is rarely accomplished without critical sallies or without unanticipated consequences. *[Theory of commodification of land and buildings]* Critics argue that places like Inner Harbor take money and attention away from a city's other problems—slums, for example—in less picturesque parts of the city. Others complain that building an economy based on frivolity is a sorry substitute for attending to such pressing problems as a rising crime rate or the quality of city schools. But success always has many friends, and all across the country, cities send delegations to Rouse's corporate planners, hoping that their city may be next on his entrepreneurial agenda (*New York Times,* Aug. 28, 1977).

Stages of the Policy Process

Public policy is not created all at once and in final form. It is built in stages, and there is a pattern to these stages. Generally speaking, there are three stages:

first, an initiating or *agenda-setting* stage; second, a *policy-formulation* stage; and third, an implementation stage. Each of these stages flows one into the other; but often the process comes to a halt at one or another stage, leaving the process unfinished, the policy never carried through.

Of the three stages, implementation is perhaps the most complicated, for implementation in the city is characterized by a considerable dispersion of policy authority. In implementation, policy authority rests in many hands. It is dispersed and highly pluralistic, so much so that cities are sometimes described as governments that do not govern—they merely administer.[4] But to understand this assertion, a closer look at the stages of policy-making is now in order.

Agenda Setting

An agenda is a statement of priorities, a list of things to be accomplished.[5] In the agenda-setting stage, the critical act is an obvious one: getting policymakers to pay attention to one of the many matters that vie for attention—getting them to put the problem on their agenda. How that happens is sometimes a matter of chance, but a number of factors contribute to a common pattern. For one, the problem must be (or must be thought to be) one that can be dealt with by government action. (Nothing that cannot be dealt with is likely to make its way on to the policymakers' agenda.) For another, policymakers must be able to perceive that the problem does, in fact, exist and that it is important enough to deserve government's attention. Third, problems that make their way onto the policymakers' agenda are those that can be transformed into an issue—a proposal around which contending groups or persons can rally and take sides. (In other words, the problem must generate politics, animating policymakers and an attentive public to think and worry about who gets what, when, and how.) And last, but hardly least, the problem that does make its way on to the policy agenda is more often than not a problem that is of special concern to a person or group of persons who

4. See the discussion of hyperpluralism in chapter 8. Theodore Lowi (1969b) uses the phrase, "functional feudalities" to describe the administration of large cities; each department (and sometimes divisions within it) resisting control by elected officials and maintaining its independence from all other administrative units—insulated and protected by employees' civil service status and the support of the interest groups that it serves. (See also Lowi 1964b.)

5. Every government agency has its own long-standing agenda, shaped by its history and its overall mission. Within cities, for example, the public works department is almost always committed to improving traffic flow, and to that purpose, the department will have on file (and in the plans and dreams of its administrators) an overall, general agenda—widening the major arteries, building ring roads around the city, limiting the number of on-street parking places, and so forth. And, as a rule, every city agency's standing agenda is in competition (for funds and authorization) with the standing agenda of every other agency. Thus, the standing agenda does not become an effective agenda until (a) its several components are arranged according to a set of priorities, and (b) one or more of its priorities can capture the attention of policymakers and policy entrepreneurs outside the agency.

assume the role of policy entrepreneur (C. Jones 1983, Cobb and Elder 1983, Crenson 1971). This last point is particularly important, for it ties back to the previous discussion of agenda-setting as the exercise of interpersonal power in the city. And it suggests that the policy entrepreneur must have access to at least some of the resources associated with interpersonal power (e.g., charisma, information, standing in the business community, public office, and so forth).

Policy Formulation

Many issues get on the policymakers' agenda, but most are not of sufficient importance to go to the very top of that agenda. If an issue *does* get to the top, sooner or later it is likely to receive further attention. When it does, the critical and necessary act is twofold: identifying the goals to be reached and deciding which course of action is most likely to achieve those goals. Here, of course, policymakers encounter their fullest opportunity for policy rationality. And here is where all the impediments to rationality have opportunity to flourish.

Vague or imprecise goals must now be made narrower and more precise. Alternative courses of action can now be considered. Information must be assembled so that costs and benefits can be weighed. Interest groups must be given opportunity to be heard, and opposing demands must be reconciled. Eventually, a course of action is decided on, and policy can now be "actualized" and legitimated by means of an ordinance or an administrative ruling.

Agenda Setting and Policy Formulation as Interacting Processes

The agenda-setting and policy formulation stages often take place almost at the same time, each interacting with the other. In this interaction, both policy entrepreneurs and interest groups play important roles. Newspaper reporting also plays a part—particularly the newspaper expose that makes for lurid reading. (Consider the attention commanded by the headline: "Crime, Drugs, Prostitution in Our City!") Sometimes a disastrous or lamentable event will define the problem and move it high on the policymakers' agenda—a devastating flood, the murder of a prominent citizen, a nursing-home fire, or the collapse of a building under construction.

"The idea whose time has come:" The war on poverty as a case in point. Large-scale projects, of the sort that deserve the label reconstructive policy, are moved through the policy stages by forces and factors that defy easy analysis. Philosophers have long puzzled over such forces, wondering why, at certain times and in certain places—great social and political changes burst forth. *Zeitgeist,* the spirit of the times, is the term sometimes affixed to these elusive

238

forces—in Victor Hugo's memorable words, "more powerful than the tread of armies is the idea whose time has come."

It is sometimes the gift of the policy entrepreneur to catch the spirit of the times. And occasionally it will be the work of scholars that serves as catalyst to agenda setting and policy formulation. To illustrate these forces, consider the arrival, in the 1960s, of the national government's War on Poverty.

Widespread poverty is among the oldest of social problems. But from the period that ran roughly from the end of World War II to the 1960s, poverty in the United States lay largely outside public attention. Then, in the 1960 presidential primary campaign in West Virginia, John F. Kennedy made poverty a campaign issue, influenced largely by what he saw around him in the coal fields. Within two years, concern for the issue of poverty was reinforced by a much discussed book, political scientist Michael Harrington's *The Other America* (1962).

Harrington and the presidential candidacy of Kennedy helped make poverty a matter of public concern, but the road from public concern to an item on the policy agenda is never straight. A matter of public concern must first be made actionable before it can move high on the policy agenda. Someone must have an idea regarding what to do. A proposal for action must come forward, and the proposal must be such that it can take on the qualities of a political issue, with interest groups and opinion leaders taking sides on that issue. Thus, in the case of poverty moving from public concern to political issue, the work of another scholar was to play a critical role.

Oscar Lewis (1959, 1965), an anthropologist, had studied poor families in Mexico, Puerto Rico, and the Hispanic settlements of New York City. From his studies of families in poverty, Lewis derived the idea of a *culture of poverty*: Families in poverty have characteristic ways of thinking about the world and of their lives in that world. *[The theory of ideology]* What Lewis saw in families living in a culture of poverty was their sense of being ruled by fate, of being unable to take charge of their own lives, and of being unable to change their lives for the better.

From Lewis' work, other scholars (with assistance from the Ford Foundation) took the short but logical step of calling attention to the cycle of poverty—the process by which poverty enters the lives and thoughtways of a family and gets carried down through subsequent generations. It was only a short step further for the ideas of the culture and cycle of poverty to make their way onto the joint agendas of Congress and President Lyndon Johnson by means of an actionable program: The War on Poverty.

The War on Poverty was an umbrella term for a series of policies all united by the idea that government could break the culture and cycle of poverty by providing poor families with job training, with nutritional and educational programs for their children (school lunches, Operation Head Start), and with opportunity to develop self-esteem and a sense of personal efficacy—

239

this last to be accomplished by giving the poor a voice in urban agencies established to administer War on Poverty funds.

Recounting the further history of the War on Poverty will wait for chapters 14 and 15. For the present, perhaps all that needs to be said is that in its agenda-setting and formulation stages, the War on Poverty brought the national government full tilt into urban politics, and, in its search for new and experimental policy, seemed to embody the "spirit of the '60s."

Policy Implementation

The policy implementation stage generally has two components. The first is fairly obvious: a policy has been enacted, but provision must be made to carry it into effect. Money must be appropriated, and often new personnel will have to be hired.

The second component is less obvious, but more important. It involves the procedures and arrangements under which the policy is put into effect. As a general rule, it usually falls to administrators to decide on the specific details of such procedures and arrangements. Funds must be acquired, legislation must be interpreted, staff must be trained, and services must be delivered "in order to put flesh on the [policy] bones" (Ripley and Franklin 1987, 2). In these and complementary ways, administrators create a supplementary (implementing) set of policies. And they do so largely removed from public view. It is here, in the implementation stage, that policy becomes fleshed out, and it is here that policy-making becomes dispersed and pluralistic. Three aspects of this process can now be illustrated.

Administrators as policymakers. Few, if any, policy decisions are self-enforcing. For example, the city council may decide to invoke a teen-age curfew. The resulting ordinance might specify the age of those subject to the curfew, the hours of the curfew, and punishment for its violation. But it is usually the chief of police, in consultation with division heads, who decides how many police are to be assigned to enforce the curfew, what kinds of patrols are to be mounted, whether warnings or arrests are to be emphasized, whether undercover officers are to be used, and, most important, for how long a time curfew enforcement is to receive special attention. (Is curfew enforcement to be symbolic or substantive?)

Obviously, if the police chief decides merely to include curfew enforcement in the long list of laws the police are presently enforcing, the results will be very different from those that would follow a decision to give special attention to the curfew. Supposing that the chief of police (or head of the juvenile crime unit) decides to enforce the curfew to the fullest possible extent, in which areas of the city does he or she concentrate police effort? If drive-ins and pizza-parlors are singled out for special attention, owners of those businesses will

240

complain of police harassment. Alternatively, if the chief decides that areas of high juvenile crime get special attention, then other parts of the city may complain of neglect. And if enforcement is even-handed across the city, middle- and upper-class parents are likely to complain (and even go to court) over what they perceive as police harassment. In the end, the chief will use his or her best judgment and make what seems a useful and practical decision. And the "real" policy will be the policy made in the implementation stage.

Subgovernments as policymakers. In the example given, more than likely it will not be the administrators alone who create policy through implementation. It will be policy arrived at by what is often called subgovernment—an informal coalition of administrators, one or two specially concerned council members (perhaps those who introduced the legislation and steered it through), the mayor's administrative assistant, and a small number of concerned and affected citizens and interest groups (unions, the chamber of commerce, downtown and neighborhood business and civic associations, and so forth).[6]

As an illustration of the role of subgovernment in implementation, the city council may decide that more street lights are needed; to fund its street-lighting ordinance, the council will no doubt appropriate money for that purpose. But what kinds of lights are to be installed? And where are they to be located?

Within the department of public services (whose head is usually appointed by the mayor or city manager) there is likely to be a street-lights division. In putting into effect the street-lighting ordinance, the head of the public service department will most likely turn implementation over to the chief of the street-lights division, who, in turn, will consult with some of the division's engineers. And they, in turn, are likely to seek further consultation and advice—outside input.

Perhaps an informal committee will then be constituted, consisting of a core group from the street-lights division, one or two members of city council (most likely chairpersons of relevant council committees), and representatives of business and civic associations. Here, then, is subgovernment in action, for it will fall to the informal committee to argue, discuss, and decide: Should the new program put greatest emphasis on lighting as a deterrent to crime? Or should it use street lights to improve traffic safety? If traffic safety is to be emphasized, then the new lights ought to go to the main traffic arteries, but if a deterrent to crime is to be emphasized, then new lights ought to go to high-crime areas. Perhaps, then, high-intensity, broad coverage, vandal-resistant lights are in order.

---

6. Subgovernments are "clusters of individuals that effectively make most of the routine decisions in a given substantive area of policy" (Ripley and Franklin 1987, 8; see also deHaven-Smith and Van Horn 1984).

But in this scenario, those who live in higher-income residential areas are not likely to be pleased with the emerging decision. Their homes need protection: but, please, not by using high-intensity lights—they will be out of keeping with neighborhood esthetics. *[The theory of lifestyle and territory]* And lower-income areas will also have their pleas and concerns. (Most likely, more lights, but no new taxes to keep the street-light program going.) In the end, the informal committee (which is to say, the subgovernment) will come to its decision, doing what it thinks best for the entire city—but no doubt greatly influenced by the values and interests of its own members. *[The theories of ideology and influence]* And its decision will be another instance of government-by-subgovernment and policy through subgovernment implementation.

Street-level bureaucrats as policymakers. Policy implementation in cities has a special quality that is captured by the previous reference to a theory of urban administration and street level bureaucracy (Lipsky 1980). The term *street-level bureaucracy* refers to the fact that much of city policy is carried into the lives of city residents by officials who interact with city dwellers directly, personally, and often on a one-to-one basis.

Federal and state policies, in contrast, are enforced more impersonally. Taxes are paid by mail, and it falls to those who owe taxes to take the initiative in paying them. Violators of the law are usually not arrested in handcuffs, but summoned to appear in court or before an administrative agency. Enforcement of city policies is different. The city's police are on the street. Firefighters, sanitation workers, and health inspectors appear at houses and places of work.

In such circumstances, implementation is dispersed and pluralistic, often a matter of personal judgment and personality. True, street-level bureaucrats must operate within the policy framework established at central headquarters (and through the work of a relevant subgovernment). But central headquarters cannot follow street-level bureaucrats on their daily rounds, supervising their moment-by-moment activities.

Thus, sanitation department rules may require that trash be set curbside, in containers or securely tied in bundles. But it is the trash collector who decides whether or not to haul away a curbside stack of discarded auto tires and whether or not the container left on the lawn is more or less equivalent to being at curbside. Department policy usually instructs the police "to keep the peace," meaning maintain order and prevent violence and crime. But it falls to the officer on the beat to decide whether keeping the peace requires dispersing a group of streetside idlers (the "corner gang"), whether a suspicious looking person is to be confronted, and whether a sidewalk poet declaiming his lines is a breach of the peace (Wilson 1972, 1975, Muir 1977). Far more important, every police department in the country has rules concerning the permissible use of deadly force, but as every watcher of television drama knows, written rules do not always decide whether a situation is truly life-threatening, or what the police should do if it is.

Thus, street-level bureaucrats implement policy in a personal and personally judgmental way. Street-level bureaucrats bring government directly to the people, and the consequences are important. By its nature, street-level bureaucracy is labor intensive. It is therefore costly, consuming a significant portion of the city's budget. By being labor intensive, street-level bureaucracy is also labor extensive, requiring a high ratio of public employees to city population. As the number of city employees increases with city size, they become an important interest group. They try to influence budget allocations and legislation. And in cities where they are unionized (in most cities of any size), the wage and work demands of employees' unions become part of city politics and a factor in the constantly rising costs of city government.[7]

Street-level bureaucrats are a recurring source of government corruption. In former machine cities, where traditions of plunder are well established, street-level bureaucrats help maintain that tradition. It is, after all, relatively easy for the police to look the other way when prostitutes solicit, gamblers gamble, and drug dealers deal. And it is just as easy for the health inspector, fire inspector, and building inspector to demand a bribe—or else!—threatening to close down a business or force the owner to suffer the costs of constant reinspection.

Street-level bureaucrats have stirred the cauldron of racial and ethnic unrest and the disaffection of minorities and the poor who perceive (often correctly, but sometimes wrongly) that they are being treated harshly or are being singled out for close surveillance by those who are supposed to protect and serve them. (More on this in chapter 17.) Where such grievances are long standing, a triggering incident (what sociologists call an *occasioning factor*) has several times resulted in race rioting and mob violence. Such was the case in the urban riots of the 1960s.

Thus, the implementation stage—as do all the stages of policymaking—brings to mind two often-quoted adages:

---

7. Unions of city employees use their bargaining powers to raise members' salaries, often to offset the effects of inflation. New York is no doubt the extreme case. The city has turned over physical control of its schools to the nine hundred-plus janitors who are members of the custodians' union. They control access to the schools, "and sometimes refuse to admit students and teachers... Just for deigning to open the doors before 8 am or after 3, each custodian can legally extract thousands of dollars for 'opening fees.' Since every school has a breakfast program beginning at 7:30, the city must pay an extra $2.1 million to the custodians just for this program, although no extra custodial work is generally required... To make matters worse, no principal has the power to order a custodian to change a light bulb or fix a broken window because ... it's not in the contract. In fact senior custodians pulling in $62,000 a year earn more than some of the principals" (Howard Kurtz, *New Republic,* April 11, 1988, p. 23).

Multitudes, Multitudes
In the Valley of Decision
  (*Book of Joel*, 3: 11)

For forms of Government, let fools contest
Whate'r is best administered is best.
  (Alexander Pope, *Essay on Man*)

It will be useful to keep these adages in mind as we turn to politics and policy in the metropolitan area in the next chapter.

Part Five

The Larger Web:
Cities, States, and the Nation

Night Shadows. Edward Hopper. 1921. Etching. Gift of the Print and Drawing Club. 1944.156.
© 1989 The Art Institute of Chicago, All Rights Reserved.

Politics and Policy in the Metropolitan Area — 12

Extend the sphere and you take in a greater variety of parties and interests; you will make it less probable that a majority of the whole will have a common motive to invade the rights of other citizens.

James Madison
Federalist 10

Most Americans are imprinted on the idea that local government is preferred government. *[The theory of grass-roots democracy]* Dividing the country into small units of government (says conventional wisdom) will enable each unit to protect its own definition of the public interest. Not to permit the citizens of an entire state (or the entire nation) to constitute a sole and single voting majority will thus safeguard the interests of those who, though a majority in their own unit, might be a threatened minority in a vastly enlarged unit of government.[1]

This line of reasoning helped give rise to our federal system and the Constitution's provisions for separation of powers and checks and balances. And it is this reasoning that helps give rise to the multiple units of government that constitute the metropolitan area. However rational it might be to consolidate these units into one, overall government, the idea of localism stands as a first line of defense against metropolitan consolidation. And lacking this

---

1. As is the case with most political theorizing, this reasoning has its critics. Electoral participation in local politics is usually low. Thus (say the critics), the safeguards afforded the local majority are often vitiated by a low voting turnout. More to the point, (they continue), limited electoral participation delivers disproportionate influence to those most motivated to vote—usually the middle class and members of interest groups.

consolidation, the metropolitan area stands sharply stratified and divided—racially, socially, economically. Blacks, Hispanics, and other minorities are concentrated as an economic underclass in central cities, while whites of the middle and working classes dominate the suburbs, generally segmented there by income and, occasionally, by religious and ethnic allegiances.

Metropolitics and Metropolicies

Seen from an airplane, a metropolitan area is all of a piece: a sprawling spread of buildings, a network of roads, a swarm of motor vehicles, and (it may be presumed) a mass of people. Seen through the windows of an automobile, the metropolitan area appears in greater detail: a central business district, areas of industry close to the business district, sectors of older houses and apartment buildings, often mingled with factories and warehouses, and then, gradually, as the car moves across town, more affluent neighborhoods. On one side of a street may be houses inside the territory of the central city; across the street may be houses that lie in an adjacent suburb. The demarcation is not always clear. Further on, green spaces and countryside will appear, then another cluster of houses or a shopping mall, or perhaps a small town, complete with its own business district.

The distance between the central city's business district and that "last" cluster of houses may be considerable. For example, in the Columbus, Ohio, metropolitan area, the motorist would have to travel as much as fifteen miles from the city's center before coming to open country. In other, larger metropolitan areas, this distance is considerably greater. And even then, another town may lie just ahead—all part of the urban-suburban sprawl.

In crossing the metropolitan area the traveler is hard put to discover where one town or city ends and another begins. If it were not for signs and notices, the jurisdictions of the separate governments would be invisible to the eye. Even more invisible, for often there are no marking signs, are the other governments that criss-cross the metropolitan area—townships, counties, and special purpose governments. Each has its own officials, its own authority to make policy, to tax, and to spend. Thus, for the resident of the metropolitan area (and for the student), obvious questions arise: How did this patchwork of governments come about? What do the governments do? Do they coordinate their efforts? If so, how? And, perhaps most important, which social classes and which groups are most helped and which are most hurt by this configuration? We begin with some fairly obvious observations.

Cities and Their Suburbs

As a rule, the central city came first. Suburbs came later as the railroad (and later the automobile) made it possible for upper- and middle-income wage

248

earners to commute to work. Hence, it was usually the affluent who went first to the suburbs. Generally speaking, the impulse behind the move was status differentiation—homes on large lots and a countrified lifestyle were emblems of superior social status. Philadelphia's Main Line suburbs came into being this way (on the main line of the Pennsylvania Railroad). So did the North Shore suburbs of Chicago (set along the North Shore Line).[2]

As the automobile became more affordable, the impulse to achieve suburban status was no longer limited by the proximity of railroad lines. New suburbs filled in the land between railroad lines; and, at the same time, what had once been small towns outside the commuting reach of the central city became (in the 1920s) dormitory suburbs for a commuting middle class.

In the decades after World War II, the great out-migration from central cities was in flood tide. It was a time of the exploding metropolis. New technologies (interurban trucking and heavy, motorized material handling) made possible the building of suburban factories and the settling nearby of industrial employees (Banfield 1970, ch. 2). For an increasingly affluent working class, the motive of status differentiation was now overlaid with the values and aspirations that are part of owning a single-family home. Where, in Europe, the affluent have traditionally remained as apartment dwellers inside the central city (the closer in, the greater one's status), affluent Americans seek to escape the city and apartment living. We share with the British a tradition that countryside living in single-family houses is the rightful badge of the socially and economically successful.

By the 1950s another great migration had begun—the migration of poor Southern blacks to Northern cities. Small-scale (and sharecropping) farming was on the decline; labor-intensive agriculture was being superceded by cotton-picking machinery and other capital-intensive equipment. Thus, the motives of status differentiation and single-family home ownership were layered onto a rising desire of urban whites (regardless of social and economic status) to flee the increasingly black central city.

By the 1960s, suburbia was no longer the province of an upper- and middle-class. Suburbs were now of many kinds: upper-and-middle class, working class, and here and there, a predominantly black suburb. Some suburbs are home to the truly affluent, while others are home to those who live in poverty. Some suburbs cluster around a nearby factory; some are completely dormitory suburbs—wage earners drive elsewhere for employment. And some suburbs carry on the tradition of the small towns they once were—cities in miniature, with neighborhoods and small-town business districts.

Thus far, we have explained the metropolitan patchwork by invoking

2. This discussion draws chiefly from works by Warner (1972), Glaab and Brown, (1976, especially chs. 13 and 15), Jackson (1985), Kantor (1988), Miller (1973, part 3), Wilson (1970), Owen (1956), Mowbray (1969), and the editors of *Fortune* (1958).

a number of converging theories: grass-roots democracy, status differentiation, land development through a market economy, and a cultural tradition that drives Americans to prefer home ownership to apartment living.[3] To round out this explanation, one more factor must be noted. Suburban sprawl has also been propelled by a policy of the national government: tax policy that permits a tax rebate (or write-off) for interest paid on a home loan. In effect, this policy has amounted to a governmental subsidy for the middle class, permitting it to offset (with lower taxes) a significant portion of the costs of home ownership. Without this subsidy-through-taxes, far fewer Americans would now be living in single-family houses.

Metropolitan Governments: Layers and Divisions

Central cities and their suburbs are not the only governments within the metropolitan area. Layered over and around cities and suburbs are other units of government: *counties* and *special districts*. Both have significant consequences for the cities, towns, and villages within the metropolitan region.

Counties

Counties share with cities, towns, and villages a common legal status. They are all *general purpose* governments, empowered to enforce and implement the overall policies and laws of state government. Thus, they are empowered to deal with matters within the state's police powers: health, safety, welfare, morals, and public convenience.[4] Both counties and cities are responsible for enforcing state laws within their jurisdiction, but cities are also empowered to implement state laws through legislation (ordinances) that deal with problems that are primarily urban—problems that arise when people live in close physical proximity.

Typically, county government is in the hands of an elected, multiple-member, policy-making board called the county commission. It is also the usual case that heads of county offices (sheriff, recorder, tax collector, real estate assessor, prosecuting attorney, judges, engineer) are directly elected (and thus, independent) officials, creating what is, in effect, a dispersed and pluralistic style of county governance (Bollens 1969).

The county covers a relatively large territory. Cities sit inside a county (sometimes within two counties), and the metropolitan areas spread across one or more counties. (The New York metropolitan area spills into New Jersey and across several of its counties as well.) County government is only

---

3. For a comparative perspective on land development and the market economy, see Cox (1978), Ambrose and Colenutt (1975), and Castells (1977).

4. Two states, Connecticut and Rhode Island, have no counties. Alaska and Louisiana have administrative units comparable to the county, called boroughs and parishes, respectively.

peripheral to our concerns, except to note that every city must accommodate itself to the authority of the county or counties that contain it. Often, state statutes spell out the details of this accommodation. But state laws are implemented through legal contracts, memoranda of agreement between county and city officials. Thus, the sheriff's department (and county engineer) usually does not operate within city limits. The city, however, will depend on the county treasurer to collect and disburse the city's share of county taxes. City and county health officials cooperate in enforcing quarantines, while the city's health department usually will take responsibility for testing the purity of city water and inspecting restaurants and food stores within the city limits. And it is often the case that small villages, instead of operating a village police force, will contract to pay the county sheriff for village police protection.

But the line of demarcation between city and county responsibilities is constantly shifting. As cities grow in size, they lessen their dependence on the county. And more important, as counties become urbanized, the unincorporated areas of the county are given county services of the kind that once belonged exclusively to city government. Many counties, for example, now operate fire departments, libraries, and refuse-collection services (see the discussion of megacounties in chapter 18).

Special-Purpose Government

Special-purpose governments are the fastest growing units of American government. Their number today stands well over twenty-six thousand, and it continues to increase.[5] Sometimes called ad hoc government, special purpose governments are created to accomplish special rather than general-government purposes. Table 12.1 provides a guide to the functions of different types of special-purpose governments operating in the United States today. School districts are the most common variety of special-purpose governments. Their jurisdiction has mostly to do with building and maintaining school buildings, hiring teachers, and planning and implementing instruction.[6]

What special-purpose governments lack in scope, they make up for in

5. By way of comparison, there were only about nine thousand special-purpose governments during the decade of the 1940s. See McFeeley (1978) and McManus (1981).
6. This discussion of school districts formalizes what has been treated informally to this point: the relationship between cities and school districts. In some cities, education is the responsibility of the municipal government. But most often, primary and secondary education are under the auspices of a special-purpose government, the local school district, which is totally autonomous from the general-purpose municipal government. Yet, the style of politics that is practiced within a school district is much like that practiced within the municipality. Municipal issues impinge on school district issues, and vice versa. For instance, the school district, in attempting to control drugs in the schools, may seek the assistance of the municipal police force. And the same people involved in local municipal issues (e.g., crime, streets, and recreation) are also likely to be involved in school issues. Much the same can be said for the host of other special-purpose governments that reside within the urban area.

sheer numbers. They are everywhere on the governmental map. Several may exist inside the boundaries of a single city (e.g., park districts, transportation authorities, and water districts). Some cross city and county boundaries, bringing central cities and distant suburbs into their special domain (water districts, sewage disposal districts, and mosquito control districts are the commonest form of boundary-

Table 12.1 A Catalogue of Special-purpose Governments

Content	Purpose	Examples	Jurisdiction
Natural Resources	Conserve and develop parks, wildlife areas, nature preserves Control animals and insects	Park board Forest preserve Water conservancy district Mosquito control authority	Usually extends across metro area but can operate as special district inside one city
Public Utilities	Administer water supply: impound, transport, purify Administer sewage system: purify and dispose Administer electric system: generate and sell	Water reservoir authority Sanitary district Public power authority	Metro wide Some may be of primary service to single city Most operate plants and facilities outside city limits
Transportation	Build and maintain toll roads, airports, bus depots	Turnpike commission Airport board Transportation authority	Metro wide
Building	Build and maintain sports arena, convention center, low-rent housing	Housing authority Local building authority Civic improvement board	Usually within a single city
Amenities	Administer zoos, recreation centers, libraries, racetracks Regulate betting, racetrack operations	Zoo board Library board Racing commission	City specific, but sometimes county wide Often operates outside city that funds and controls it
Education	Operate primary, secondary, and special schools Operate state and city universities	Board of education Board of trustees	Usually city specific, but can be county wide or state wide

crossing ad hoc government). And some even cross state lines, bringing their special authority to bear on otherwise separate jurisdictions.

As a rule, special-purpose governments are created (some would say imposed) by the state legislature. The reasoning behind their creation is three-fold. First, and most obvious, ad hoc governments are created to overcome the problems that follow from multiple jurisdictions existing side by side in the same geographic area. After all, most problems do not stop at government boundaries. And many are too complex to be managed by one local government. For example, if control of mosquitoes is to be accomplished, insecticide must be sprayed area-wide. And if water resources are to be conserved, water management must extend across an entire watershed. There is, of course, an irony (and more than a little counterlogic) in this reasoning: The legislature creates more governments to deal with the problem of too many governments!

Special districts are also created as a residue of what was earlier described as the urban reform package, an attempt to "take politics out of government." Of course, no such thing is possible, nor in a democracy would we want it so. But school districts as special-purpose governments, for example, were often created in an attempt to free the schools from the depredations of political machines. Education, it was usually said, is too important to be a plaything of politicians. For another example, forest and park districts have been established in hopes that their managing boards would consist of conservationist-minded citizens and horticultural specialists instead of the usual run-of-the-mill politicians.

A third reason behind creating special governments has to do with money. Cities and counties are limited by their state constitutions (as well as statutes) in the amount of money that can be raised through taxes or borrowed by issuing bonds to be paid back later with tax revenue. But special governments can tax and borrow independently.[7] Think now of the problems that can be solved and the temptations that arise in special purpose governments. City and county governments can be cut free of the costs of maintaining parks and schools and the like. Cities and counties may have reached the limits of their indebtedness. (State constitutions and statutes usually limit local bonds to a percentage of property values in each local government.) But a special district can issue its own bonds and thus make available to the local area an additional source of government money. Equally important, interest groups can gain the opportunity to promote new and controversial projects such as a sports arena, a convention center, and even publicly financed housing projects for the poor.

---

7. Ironically, special-purpose governments have been responsible for most of the recent governmental fiscal defaults. See chapter 15.

The Port Authority of New York and New Jersey,
or, What's Wrong with Special-Purpose Government

Some special-purpose governments have so much power that they dominate the social and economic life of an entire region. The Port Authority of New York and New Jersey exemplifies this domination. Created in 1921 through a compact between the two states, its governing board (a "businessman's board," appointed mostly from the ranks of corporation executives) is appointed jointly by the two state governors. Once appointed, its members are almost beyond removal and are thoroughly insulated from popular control.

The Authority's purpose is to develop commercial and transportation resources in the two-state area. It was given no taxing powers, but quickly developed its own highly lucrative revenue sources, initially by issuing bonds, later by charging for its services.

> By 1931 it was operating four toll bridges and the Holland Tunnel. The next year it opened a freight terminal. In 1944 it opened a grain terminal, and in 1948 it took over its first airport. During the 1950s, it acquired the rest of New York's major airports. During the 1960s it entered the real estate business and constructed the 110-story twin towers of the New York World Trade Center. By the start of the 1980s, the Port Authority's assets had grown to nearly $5 billion, and its various enterprises brought in about $3/4 billion in annual revenue. Port Authority facilities include six interstate bridges and tunnels, two bus terminals, the World Trade Center, and one railroad system. (Harrigan 1985, 267)

But however successful as a profit making enterprise, the Port Authority has long had its bitter critics. For half a century it has promoted automobile transportation instead of mass transit, leading, critics charge, to a worsening of New York's traffic congestion as the Authority's bridges and tunnels became giant conduits through which commuter traffic pours into the city. (In Manhattan, many times each day, congestion is so bad that it is quicker to walk a mile than to ride.)

Worse still, say the critics, these same bridges and tunnels also serve as "population pumps," with devastating consequences not only for New York but for every place within fifty (and even a hundred) miles of the city. Easy road access to the suburbs has quickened outward migration from the city, leaving the city's population increasingly poor, black, and Hispanic. In the process, outward migration has also destroyed the open countryside, leaving in its wake an ugly urban sprawl. And the spaghetti-like strands of freeways in and around New York have sliced open and destroyed once lively and liveable neighborhoods.

The Port Authority has also been accused of working with and perpetuating local political machines, mainly by way of the jobs, influence, and money that are part of its construction projects, land purchases, bond-issues, and bank loans. But the most trenchant criticism turns on familiar questions: Whose definition of the public interest prevails here? A definition arrived at by the Authority's nonelected governing board? Or that which might have been arrived at if the Authority were run by elected officials? Would the Authority's sprawl-creating projects have been carried through by elected officials? And would elected officials have been more sparing when it came to tearing down houses and razing neighborhoods to serve the needs of the automobile commuter?

Appraising the Metropolitan Patchwork

Metropolitan areas have great variety and also a common pattern: The larger the central city, the greater the number of separate governments within its metropolitan area. Metropolitan New York City, for example, contains more than fifteen hundred separate governments. Metropolitan Chicago has over eleven hundred governments, Pittsburgh has over seven hundred, and Philadelphia over nine hundred.

What, then, are the consequences of numerous governments layered over each other and stacked side by side? Frankly, much depends on the values that the appraiser brings to the subject. [The theory of ideology]

Simplicity versus Organized Complexity

For those who prize symmetry and simplicity, the metro area is an affront. It follows no simple organization. It is not easily charted in schema or diagram (e.g., Wood 1964, Bollens and Schmandt 1982, ch. 4). And its everywhere present, multiple member governing boards and commissions contradict our tradition of separation of powers. Critics find even greater fault in the complex layering of governments in the metropolitan area that (when combined with multiple officials to be elected) confounds several cherished notions concerning democratic responsibility.

A Theory of Democratic Responsibility

> In framing a government which is to be administered by men over men, the great difficulty is this: you must first enable the government to control the governed; and in the next place, oblige it to control itself.
> James Madison
> *Federalist* 51

Democratic theory has no objection to policy authority resting in many hands. For an important group of theorists (*pluralists,* as they are usually styled), shared and distributed power better assures majority preferences than too narrow a concentration of policy authority. In parallel fashion democratic theory also makes room for the argument that local government is better able to protect the local interests of local residents than a large, centralized government. *[The Theory of grass-roots democracy]* On these grounds, a strong case can be made for the multiplicity of governing units that make up the metropolitan area.

But in prescriptive theory, almost every argument has its counterargument. When governing authority lies in many hands, it may also be obscured from public eyes. It is difficult for the electorate to know which official has responsibility for doing what. And hence, the electorate may be diminished in its ability to control its rulers.

By obscuring the locus of power and responsibility, the metropolitan patchwork may invite and encourage political corruption. (If we don't know who is responsible for doing what, how can we vote against the wrongdoers?) As a matter of historical record, county governments—with their multitude of elected officials and multiple member governing boards—have had a long tradition of political corruption. And, so too, have special-purpose governments. To exemplify, we turn to another of the numerous ad hoc governments that honeycomb the New York metropolitan area and scrutinize one of its most influential officials.

Robert Moses of New York. Robert Caro (1974) presents a massive indictment of New York's Triborough Bridge and Tunnel Authority. Its long history of corruption, he concludes, springs from three sources. First, it has been run by nonelected officials, not therefore subject to the public scrutiny that ordinarily takes place at election time. Its massive building projects and the revenues generated by those projects enabled its long-time head, the late Robert Moses, to build a personal political machine out of the willing cooperation of labor unions, revenue-bond brokers, lending banks, and elected officials. And in building and using his political power, Moses was further assisted by the Triborough Authority's public relations office, which constantly touted the engineering accomplishments of the Authority.

Robert Moses held no elected office, but as Caro puts it, he was "a political boss with a difference."

> He was not the stereotype with which Americans were familiar. His constituency was not public but some of the most powerful men in the city and state, and he kept these men in line by doling out to them . . . the sugar plums of public relations retainers, insurance commissions and legal fees. . . . Robert Moses was America's greatest builder. He was the shaper of the greatest city in the New World. . . . To build his highways, Moses threw out of their homes 250,000 persons. He tore the heart out of a score of neighborhoods. . . . By building his highways, Moses flooded the city with cars. By systematically starving the subways and the suburban commuter railroads, he swelled that

flood to city-destroying dimensions. By making sure that the vast suburbs, rural and empty when he came to power, were filled on a sprawling, low-density development pattern relying primarily on roads instead of mass transportation, he insured that the flood would continue for generations. . . . For highways, Moses dispossessed 250,000 persons. For his other projects . . . he . . . dispossessed close to half a million. . . . He evicted tens of thousands of poor, nonwhite persons for urban renewal projects, and the housing he built to replace the housing he tore down was . . . not housing for the poor, but for the rich. The dispossessed had no place to go but into the already over-crowded slums. (Caro 1974, 19ff)

This portrait of the power of single official may be overdrawn; but it is an accurate portrayal of the power that can lie with a single, special pur-pose government. And as portrait, it sharpens our appreciation of democratic theory's insistence that one of the surest safeguards against arrogant or unwise government is to insist upon popular election of its officials.

Prescriptive Theories of Social Justice and Social Equity

Nothing more easily invites argument than an attempt to define social justice and social equity. Both terms are grounded in prescriptive theories of equality, ethics, and fair dealing. Social justice carries in its definition the idea of equal treatment, and social equity carries in its definition the idea of fair shares. Both terms are thus grounded in ideas about social and ethical responsibility: Should the individual person assume primary responsibility for what happens in his or her life, or does some large part of that responsibility rest with society?

As our earlier discussion may suggest, theories of social justice and equity link to redistributive policy: What do the rich owe the poor, and what are society's obligations to its least well-off and least autonomous members (infants, the elderly, the ill)?

Around such questions Liberals and Conservatives draw the battle lines of argument.[8] As Conservatives see it, social justice and equity are to be

---

8. It would mislead to suggest that liberal and conservative ideologies are limited only to ques-tions of social justice and equity. Other questions include:

1. government's use of its power to promote and protect citizen morality and virtuous conduct and preserve society's traditional values. Conservatives generally favor vigorous government action, while Liberals seek to give the individual as much life-space freedom as possible.

2. the extent to which government should steer the economy (and intervene in market transac-tions) in order to alleviate economic distress and prevent underemployment, inflation, and falling industrial productivity. Conservatives tend to be wary of such interventions in the market; Liberals tend to favor them, most fully when they work to assist the least well-off.

3. the proper locus of policy-making authority: Should such authority be given back to the states or kept at the national level? Here, the arguments conflate with (1) and (2) above. Conservatives often speak of getting government (especially the national government) "off our backs and out of our pockets," and they generally argue for handing power back to the states. Liberals argue

judged primarily in terms of equality of opportunity. Each person shall be free to make of life what he or she is able to—without undue government interference. Each person shall be permitted to compete for life's rewards as he or she defines those rewards—again, without undue government interference.

As Liberals see it, the moral quality of any society is in direct proportion to its concern for its least well-off and least autonomous members. Poverty and other social problems, they reason, are as much a consequence of our society's social and economic arrangements as of personal failings. Accordingly, responsibility for social outcomes must lie with society as well as with the individual. Thus, social justice and equity are to be judged in terms of equality of outcomes. Government shall take responsibility for ensuring that every person receives something that approaches an equal— or at least minimum—share of life's needs and rewards (including income, housing, education, and health care).[9] Equally important, government shall do all it can to spare minorities and the poor the burdens of segregation— whether it be in jobs, education, or place of residence—for segregation not only leaves psychological scars, it also hinders equality of outcome by denying those who are segregated full access to jobs, housing, and social services (see chapter 17).

Social Justice and Equity in the Metropolitan Area

These seemingly abstract considerations operate with great vigor in any appraisal of metropolitan governance.[10] Consider the following facts. Metropolitan regions tend to be highly segregated. Their central cities contain a disproportionate share of the metropolitan area's poor and minorities. Central cities are home to most of the region's major social problems: violent crime, drug abuse, school dropouts, not to mention the homeless. But central cities are revenue poor and have great difficulty in responding to their social problems. Per capita, they are less able than most suburbs to spend for such basic services as fire and police protection, and they are even less able to spend for such urban amenities as parks and recreation.

---

that only the national government has the resources, authority, and compassion sufficient to effect redistributive policies—and thus assure, for everyone, a degree of equal outcomes.

The literature that explains, defends, and argues the liberal and conservative positions noted here is vast. References and further discussion may be found in Herson (1984).

9. On these matters, one of the most influential liberal spokespersons of our generation is John Rawls (1971); conservative views are represented by the journal The *Public Interest* and in the writings of its editors (e.g., Kristol 1978).

10. See, for example, Smith (1979, vii), who examines American cities from the points of view of writers who see the cities as a "repressive social institution" and urban problems as consequence of our society's "economic and social inequality."

In contrast, many suburbs are revenue rich. They are able to provide a high quality of education for their children as well as a high standard of urban services and amenities. And even where not revenue rich, most suburbs are white and given over to the several strata of the middle class—"white collar" and "blue collar." Thus, all through suburbia, housing as well as urban services reflect the socioeconomic status of their residents. What is more, suburbs use their governmental powers to keep their social, economic, and racial distance from the central city—and from all would-be settlers of a different social or economic class. They use that power to maintain zones of exclusivity, often passing ordinances that limit house construction to single-family homes, often to be set on large lots. Some suburbs require that builders, not the city, pay the costs of installing gas, water, and sewer lines, and that developers pave the streets in new housing developments. All such requirements drive up housing costs and serve to price out of the market those families with incomes below the suburb's norm. And many suburbs also forbid the location of businesses and industries of a type that might be expected to employ low-skill, low-wage earners. *[The theory of lifestyle and territory]*

It is not the suburbs alone that contribute to the social, economic, and racial separation within the metropolitan region. By concentrating welfare assistance facilities such as medical services in central cities—especially in the inner core of central cities—state and county governments also serve to anchor the poor there. (For further discussion, see chapter 17.)

Consider now how life in the metropolitan area might change if all territorial boundaries were swept away and suburbs merged with the central city.[11] Central cities would have their tax and revenue bases enhanced and might then attempt redistributive policies aimed at improving the lives of the poor. The quality of urban services—including education—would be equal all through the metropolitan area. Low-rent apartment buildings could be sited all through the area, and minorities and the poor would no longer be confined to the central city. The location of factories and shopping malls might be made a matter for area-wide planning, and urban sprawl might be better controlled through more orderly land development. And with a single government operating throughout the area, there might be less need for constantly multiplying special purpose governments.

Of course, the changes we sketch are not likely to happen anywhere soon. Our society's preference for localized government probably has too strong a hold on our culture to permit this sort of reconstructing policy. What is more, obliterating suburbia would also challenge the values that are part of our society's commitment to a market economy. Not only do many of us believe that lifestyle and territory ought to go together, many of us also believe

11. This scenario is suggested by the analysis in Lowi (1969a, ch. 7). On "opening up the suburbs," see Downs (1973).

firmly in the idea of market equity: Each of us ought to be free to buy whatever lifestyle we can afford—providing, of course, that it is not illegal or immoral.

Thus, suburbia tends to pit market equity against social equity, with market equity thus far the winner. In fact, the metropolitan area has been likened to an arrangement of lifestyle markets. Those who offer this analogy suggest that each separate governmental jurisdiction functions as a marketplace, with those living there likened to consumers who have purchased the lifestyle that goes with that territory. To merge jurisdictions, it is argued, would deprive lifestyle consumers of their freedom of choice. The argument is strengthened by the further assertion that the metropolitan area is a series of competitive market economies, with each governmental unit attempting to improve its position relative to all other units in the area. In this view, each unit is seen as the producer of a package of values that is purchased by those who live there. Each unit, therefore, if it is to retain its residents (and attract new settlers), has an incentive to produce its values competitively, offering services, amenities, and tax rates in such fashion as to generate the optimal degree of consumer satisfaction. In this view, the metropolitan area ought not be viewed as a patchwork at all. Rather, it is to be judged as a governmental arrangement that maximizes opportunities for satisfying the preferences that go hand in glove with freedom of choice, lifestyle, and territory (Tiebout 1956, Ostrom et al., 1961).

The Metropolitan Area as a System

Whether the metropolitan area is seen favorably as a competitive market or unfavorably as a patchwork that thwarts the spread of social equity—and preserves the racial, social, and economic status quo—very much depends on the observer's point of view and (of course) the observer's angle of ideological vision. But not to be overlooked is the fact that from still another point of view, the area works well as an integrated economic system, with goods, services, shoppers, and commuters moving freely across the area. It also works well as an integrated communications system, with electric lines, telephone lines, and roadways also moving freely throughout the area (Williams 1971, 86-93). Thus, jurisdictional boundaries get attacked and defended when access to lifestyles is the issue. But short of that, the metropolitan area works well in terms of two of its more important systems, economics and communications. Seen in this way, the present organization of the metropolitan area has its many defenders who often invoke the practical adage "If it ain't broke, don't fix it."

The Metropolitan Area as a Bargaining Arena

Because the dozens and even hundreds of governments in the metropolitan area are each independent policymakers, each is more or less free to create its own policies more or less independently of all the other governments. Sometimes, however, cooperation is preferred. One or more governments may think it useful and economical to buy services (e.g., police and fire protection, sanitation service) from another government. And governments may also choose to share the costs of providing a needed service (a water purification plant, for another example).

In such arrangements, and even though each unit of government is a more or less free agent and free bargainer, many find cooperation to their mutual advantage. Matthew Holden (1964), in fact, likens the intergovernmental arrangements in the metropolitan area to intergovernmental relations in international politics. Independent bargainers pursue their own definitions of self-interest through diplomacy, alliances, and occasionally harmful conflict (also see Dye 1962). Of course, the analogy is imperfect. Real wars do not break out, and unlike national behavior in the international arena, cities are answerable to a higher authority, their state and the national government. But even as an imperfect analogy, it points, as we now shall see, to the possibility of cooperative steps toward greater degrees of metropolitan integration.

Steps Toward Metropolitan Integration

> The great and chief end of men . . . putting themselves under government, is the preservation of their property.
>
> John Locke
> *Treatises*

> Whatever arguments may have arisen in the past over the existence of a . . . privileged aristocracy, it is clear to me that today no argument can stand that supports unequal opportunity or any intrinsic disqualification for sharing in the whole of life.
>
> Margaret Mead
> *Blackberry Winter*

For more than a half century, metropolitan integration has been the goal of many policy entrepreneurs. To date, five fairly distinct reform arrangements have been used to advance metropolitan-area integration: annexation, service delivery contracts, city-county consolidation, two-tier government, and planning coordination. In attempting—or even suggesting—these arrangements, policymakers are strongly influenced by economics and lifestyle differences.

Annexation

With annexation, a city takes over an area that lies on its border. In most states, annexation requires the approval of a majority of voters in the area to be annexed. Where voters perceive few lifestyle differences between themselves and those living in the annexing city, annexation is easiest. Conversely, it is most difficult to accomplish where there are obvious lifestyle differences between the annexing city and the place to be annexed. *[The theory of lifestyle and territory]* Occasionally, two towns have merged; but because a town's charter of incorporation is protected by legal safeguards, the most common type of annexation involves an area on the city's rim that is unincorporated and relatively unpeopled.

A number of annexing cities have adopted carrot and stick strategies: inducements to come under the annexing city's umbrella and disincentives for staying out. One such strategy is to withhold city water and sewage services to any area that refuses annexation. And where the refusal crimps pending plans for real estate development, the strategy is sometimes effective. (A partially rural, partially urbanized area can make do with wells and cesspools; but state health laws usually require a centralized water and sewage system for any urbanized area reaching a prescribed population density.)

Carrot and stick strategies are not always effective, however. Those living in the area proposed for annexation may like things as they are: a rural or near-rural environment without city taxes and without city laws, especially zoning and building codes, constricting their cherished lifestyle.[12] Of considerable importance in recent years has been the preference of those outside the central city to stay outside and thus escape incorporation in the central city's school district and whatever school busing (to achieve racial integration) the federal courts may have imposed on it.

Thomas Dye (1964) enlightens us on these matters. He studied annexation and population growth in 212 Standard Metropolitan Statistical Areas (SMSAs)[13] for the years 1950 to 1960. Thirty-five cities in this study had populations that surpassed 50,000 for the first time in the 1960 census. On average, these cities had annexed 22.3 percent of their population during the 1950s. In contrast, the forty-nine cities that had achieved 50,000 people by 1890 had annexed only 4.2 percent of their populations during the 1950s. In other words, the older the central city, the less its reliance on annexation as a tool of metropolitan growth.

We can infer from these data that the older the central city, the more it is likely that its suburbs will also be old, and an old suburb is likely to be venerated by those who live there. More important, lifestyles in those suburbs have been fixed over time. So too have the social relationships and social adjustments that are part of that lifestyle. As Dye (1964, 305) says,

12. Donald Connery (1972, 155), quoting an anonymous New Englander, nicely sums up the frustration of many small-towners forced to deal with increasing regulation, "Every time you want to do something in this town there's some damned ordinance that says you can't."

13. In June 1983, the Bureau of the Census gave up its SMSA designation in favor of the MSA—Metropolitan Statistical Area.

The longer these adjustments have been in existence, the greater the discom-fiture, expense, and fear of unanticipated consequences associated with change.

Other explanations are also embedded in Dye's data. In the older central cities of the Northeast, status differential between central cities and suburbs is greater than between central cities and suburbs in the newer metropolitan areas of the Southwest and West. And the greater the status differential, the greater the resistance of those of higher social status to being annexed to the central city. Equally, where race and ethnic differences are most clearly marked, these differences also become motives to resist annexation.

Service Delivery Contracts

Everywhere in the metropolitan area, governments sell services to other governments. But the one arrangement that commands greatest attention has as its prototype the arrangement between Los Angeles County and the nearly one hundred incorporated places within the county. The county maintains an inventory of about sixty services for sale, and any town, village, or city in the county can buy these services. The inventory includes: administration of local elections, health inspection, jail facilities, prosecution for violations of local ordinances, tax assessment and collection, ambulance service, fire protection, and helicopter police patrols. This arrangement is known as the Lakewood Plan (named after the first city to use the services of Los Angeles County; see Kuyper 1970).

Counties elsewhere offer parallels to the Lakewood Plan. And their experience helps policymakers to understand a question that has long puzzled those who propose metropolitan integration: Will further steps toward integration promote *economies of scale?*

In everyday language, economies of scale are the savings that result from activities comparable to mass production in industry (Thompson 1968, ch. 7, Bish 1971, Hirsch 1976, Reich 1983). Whether it is making automobiles or collecting garbage, the unit costs of production tend to go down as output increases and as the same product is continuously produced in a long production run. After the factory is built or the garbage truck paid for (these are sometimes called "sunk costs"), the expenses of building the factory or truck can be charged off against each subsequent unit of production—the greater the number of units, the less the cost of investment for each unit. But at some point, economies of scale stop. This occurs in part because the costs of labor and other materials remain relatively fixed and in part because no piece of equipment can go on forever without wearing out or needing repair.

Thus, cities can save money by contracting for services that involve a substantial investment in equipment to be used in long production runs; but it is not clear that contracting for services that are primarily labor intensive

263

will result in economies of scale. For example, police protection and health and building inspection require that they be carried out by people more than by machinery, and the people who perform these services make small-scale individual (often on-the-spot) decisions, not long production runs. *[The theory of urban administration]*

There are also many urban services for which economies of scale are less important to policymakers than citizen satisfaction. And citizen satisfaction is often tied to local control, for it is local control that can bring urban services into conformity with local lifestyles (e.g., the respectful behavior of small-city police, the fire department ready to rescue cats from trees). In this vein, Elinor Ostrom (1973) reports that citizen satisfaction with the work of police departments is inversely correlated with the size of the department. Thus, a small and relatively costly to operate police department may be preferred to a larger department whose contracted services might result in an economy of scale (also see Wilson 1972). *[The theories of grass-roots democracy and lifestyle and territory]*

City-County Consolidation

As the term implies, city-county consolidation involves merging these two levels of government. A single government merges all chartered local governments in the county (central city and suburbs) with the government of the county. Thus, the county commission is replaced by a county council; all city councils are abolished; city police departments merge with the sheriff's department to become the county police; and mayors are abolished county-wide and replaced with a county manager or administrator.

As a reform proposal, city-county consolidation has been around for nearly two hundred years. In the nineteenth century, it was carried through in New Orleans (1805), Boston (1822), Philadelphia (1822), New York (1898), and Honolulu (1907). Then the consolidation movement came to a halt. As is often the case, reformers' energies moved to a different cause: In the Progressive period the cause became the urban reform package.

But following the Second World War, proposals for city-county consolidation again caught the attention of policy entrepreneurs. This was the time of the exploding metropolis, the time of the great out-migration from the central cities, and thus the time of spreading suburbia. From the 1950s until the mid 1970s, sixty-eight proposals for city-county consolidation were put before metropolitan-area voters, but only seventeen were approved (for discussions of city-county consolidation, see Jackson 1985, ch. 8; Bollens and Schmandt 1982, ch. 11; Greer 1962). And of these, only three involved more than 250,000 people: in Tennessee, Nashville-Davidson County (1962); in Florida, Jacksonville-Duvall County (1967); and in Indiana, Indianapolis-Marion County (1969).

These three cases are instructive. In the Indianapolis consolidation, local reformers, long frustrated in their attempts to strengthen the mayor's office, persuaded the state legislature to pass a consolidation statute that required no approval from metropolitan-area voters. The state legislature (traditionally dominated by rural Republicans) saw in metropolitan consolidation an opportunity to dilute the voting strength of Democrats concentrated in Indianapolis. *Unigov* (as the consolidation proposal was named) was thus partially an attempt to improve government in metropolitan Indianapolis and partially an attempt to settle old political scores. Unigov was imposed by the legislature, and the imposition thus avoided Unigov's almost certain rejection by suburban voters—had they been permitted to vote. As was said by suburbanites, they had not migrated into the suburbs to be thrown back into association with the government and politics, lifestyles and ethnicity of Indianapolis (Wilburn 1973).

Nashville, Tennessee, has had a long history of political corruption and machine politics (Key 1950, ch. 4). By the 1950s, partly as a result of desire to escape the machine, most of Nashville's population growth was in its suburbs. But the suburbs were revenue poor, and an estimated 100,000 suburbanites were using backyard wells for drinking water and septic tanks for waste disposal, at least 25 percent of which were faulty. Contaminated drinking water from septic tank leakage was a threat to public health. Police and fire departments were understaffed and underequipped. More and more, suburban residents were turning to private police and fire protection. For suburbanites here, the incentives for city-county consolidation outweighed the disincentives. The vote for consolidation was carried in 1962 (Hawkins 1966).

In Jacksonville, Florida, the consolidation proposal was propelled by a series of crises and exposés. The city's school system was far enough below standard to have been threatened with loss of accreditation. Sewage was polluting the river. And indictments had been recently returned against eight city officials for offenses that ranged from grand larceny to bribery and perjury. (In short, machine-style politics was alive and well in Jacksonville.) Thus, for Jacksonville voters, the proposal for consolidation was moved by a strong incentive: the opportunity to sweep away an unsatisfactory city government and begin again under a new, consolidated government (Carver 1973, Rabinowitz 1969).

Two-Tier Government

To understand the logic of two-tier government, two previously stated ideas must be kept in mind. First, integration in the metropolitan area is resisted where lifestyle differences are marked. Second, the metro area works well as an integrated economic and communication system. Well, then, why not take advantage of what is easiest to accomplish and avoid debate and argument over what is resisted? Such is the logic behind the two-tier government now at work in Dade County, Florida.

Dade County established two-tier government in 1957. At the time, twenty-six municipalities were anchored across the county, and traffic between them was snarled and slow. Each city insisted on its own speed limits and its own traffic pattern. Urban services in the unincorporated areas were often minimal, if not primitive. And the quality of services in each city was a direct function of that city's wealth. The biggest city, Miami, provided water and sewer services to nearby cities, but lifestyle differences underscored by race, ethnicity, and per-capita income made other forms of intercity cooperation almost nonexistent.[14]

As a way of addressing Dade County's metropolitan problems, the Florida state legislature asked the county's voters to approve a new county charter. Under terms of the charter (approved by the voters in 1957), both county and all city governments in the county were reorganized. The reorganized county government was given responsibility for county-wide (mostly service) functions and problems, including mass transit, water pollution, public health, and some police and fire services. All other functions— particularly those wrapped around lifestyle maintenance—remained with the cities: education, police, local zoning, and land use. The elected county commission retained its traditional legislative powers, but provision was made for an appointed county manager whose authority included power to appoint a number of county officials who previously had been elected. And each city retained its own form of government mostly intact (Sofen 1963, Lotz 1973).

The new governmental organization did not, of course, eliminate friction between Dade County cities, nor did it solve the problems of problem cities. Miami, in particular, is a city with problems. It has a history of police corruption and, more recently, of police violence against blacks.[15] Miami, in addition, has become celebrated as the "Cuban capital" of the United States, with refugees from Castro's Cuba now prospering and assuming roles of leadership in the city—and, unusual for urban politics, making anticommunist foreign policy an important concern of local politics. In addition (as watchers of a recently popular television series know), Miami is notorious as a major drug distributing center in the United States. Understandably, nearby cities have resisted being drawn into too close cooperation with Miami, but overall (most observers conclude) the quality of county-wide services has improved under two-tier government. Even so, and even though the logic of two-tier

_____

14. The lifestyle differences between Miami and its exclusive and wealthy neighbor, Palm Beach, produce almost daily friction. Until a 1985 court decision enjoined Palm Beach, its ordinances required all those coming into the city for employment to carry identification cards. In that case, lawyers for Palm Beach argued that registration of outsiders was a means of protecting the lives and property of the city's residents, Palm Beach being an island of affluence in an ocean of surrounding poverty.

15. Sparked by police killing of a young black businessman, protest turned to riot in the Libertyville area of Miami in 1983 (Newsweek, Jan. 10, 1983).

266

government is attractive, Dade County remains as its only example in the United States.

Councils of Government

If we cast our thoughts back to the analogy of the metropolitan area as a group of free bargainers akin to nation states, one logical device for achieving mutual cooperation and assistance lies in creating an agency (something on the order of a "United Nations") to promote that cooperation and assistance: a *council of governments* (COG) that plans solutions to metro-area problems. The first such council was probably created in the Detroit area in 1954, but their numbers did not greatly increase until the 1960s. By early 1970, three hundred COGs were in existence, brought into being by a push from the national government.

The national government did not so much impose COGs as offer incentives for their creation. What happened was this: As the number of federal grants to cities began to multiply in the 1960s, congressional concern also grew that cities were about to engage in intense competition for those grants (with losers demanding remedial action from their congressional delegations). Moreover, concern also grew over the prospect that federal grant money would produce duplication of effort. (After all, how many airports might a metropolitan area need?) Thus, the Housing and Urban Development Act of 1965 made councils of government eligible to receive planning and research money for a broad range of activities, including data collection, land-use planning, and economic and resource development. In other words, it would cost metro-area cities nothing to cooperate in setting up COGs, and the result promised to be beneficial to all who cooperated in doing so. Then, in 1966, Congress stipulated that all new grants to cities in a metropolitan area must be approved by a metro-wide authority (Wikstrom 1985, Scarborough 1982). And in 1969, the Office of Management and Budget (OMB) further extended the review process (now termed A-95, after the OMB memorandum detailing its use).

How successful have COGs been in coordinating metro planning? One view has it that since COG members are appointed by their cities, they function primarily as agents of those cities, and that the COG serves merely to rubber stamp each city's proposals—each government taking its turn in obtaining whatever is being bargained for. (In short, COGs are exercises in logrolling, to use the familiar political term.) But another view has it that the COG serves as a forum that promotes intergovernmental planning and cooperation. (This view is bolstered by psychological studies of small-group behavior and by studies of committees at every level of government showing that interaction between bargainers leads them to share ideas and values and, in turn, to cooperate. See Homans 1950, 127; Fenno 1973).

"To Thine Own Self Be True": Counter Logic and Counter Trends

As this discussion thus far has indicated, steps and arrangements to promote metro-area integration are accomplished most easily where "system access" (e.g., road-building, and waste disposal) is the issue, whereas no arrangements are easy where lifestyle access is the issue. Where lifestyle is visibly and directly threatened, counter trends are sometimes set in motion. In some instances, they move the metropolitan area toward smaller, more localized governance. Other times they involve a desperate determination to keep lifestyle from being altered by newcomers' incursions.

Old Settlers versus New

One manner in which suburbs differ is in the degree to which their populations split between old settlers and new. The old settlers are often more than merely long-time residents. Frequently, they are children and grand-children of those who settled the city when it was a nonsuburb, a town far outside the ambit of the central city. As old settlers, they watch with growing unease the rising tide of new arrivals. Characteristically, the old settlers resist attempts by more recently arrived settlers to change the town's package of urban services in the direction of added amenities (parks, social centers, counseling centers, and the like), and they also resist services that result in higher taxes.

Resistance may well turn rancorous as newcomers attempt to introduce into the schools what old settlers see as big-city values (recall the discussion of rancorous conflict in chapter 6). Where the town historically has served as a commercial center for nearby farms (with a grain elevator, feed and hardware store, tractor sales, and so forth), the old settlers carry traditions of a rural life. They are thus understandably resentful of proposals to change the schools—for example, by emphasizing a college-preparatory curriculum at the expense of vocational training, or by altering the schools' dress code. And nerves may be rubbed raw as new settlers attempt to bring what old settlers regard as big-city values to books in the school libraries.[16] Overall, such issues, like tax issues, may be no more than emblematic: a rallying point for those who seek to stem the tide of metropolitan-area integration. (The larger social context for this rallying point is conveyed by the title of Vidich and Bensman's 1958 book, *Small Town in Mass Society.*)

16. For example, Clarence Stone and his coauthors (Stone et al. 1979, 91) report that when the old settlers of the Long Island suburb of Island Trees, New York, moved the school board to ban such books as Vonnegut's *Slaughterhouse Five,* Morris' *The Naked Ape,* and Cleaver's *Soul on Ice,* the new settlers responded with an attempt to take over the school board by means of a hard-fought election, and some went to court to seek an injunction against book banning.

Another Dimension of Equity: Race and Ethnicity in Central Cities

The previous discussion of equity and social justice highlighted the distinction between social justice and market equity and the implications of this distinction for separate governments for central cities and suburbs. There, we noted that the ideal of social justice might have to be achieved at the expense of market equity and that metropolitan integration might be demanded as the suitable instrument for achieving area-wide equity.

But in politics, as in life generally, few arguments stand without exceptions or without taking into account changing times and conditions. As central cities have become increasingly black and Hispanic (and as the Voting Rights Act of 1965 changed voting patterns across the country), more and more black and Hispanic mayors have come to office, and increasing numbers of minorities have taken seats in city councils and become heads of central-city administrative departments (see chapters 7 and 8). There is a new convergence of black (and Hispanic) political power in central cities, and those who hold that power (as well as whites who approve of this new convergence) are now reluctant to see the dominance of black and Hispanic voters in the central city diluted by proposals to wipe out or expand the central cities' boundaries. They fear that an expanded (metropolitan-wide) voting unit would return the city's blacks (and Hispanics and other ethnic groups) to a voting minority in a government that extends over the entire metropolitan region. Some also fear that dispersion into the suburbs of blacks, Hispanics, and the poor might also subject them to patterns of non-protection and general indifference at the hands of the police and other suburban service providers. For it is generally the pattern in urban America that in everyday dealings with the public, service providers reflect the outlook of the community's dominant social and political classes. Thus, with a logic that mirrors that used by the early urban reformers, many who now resist metropolitan integration argue that election by small constituencies best assures that elected officials will be sensitive to the concerns and demands of those who live in those constituencies. *[The theory of grass-roots democracy]*

Small Is Beautiful

Over and beyond the concern for black city officials, the push to metro governance is also cross pressured by a set of ideas that came to prominence during the decade of the 1960s. At that time, and as black unrest gave rise to urban rioting, liberals both black and white began to argue an alternative future for American democracy. That future was to be a return to the idea of small-scale government[17]: localized units of government that might be expected to bet-

---

17. *Small Is Beautiful* (Schumaker 1973) was not only the title of an influential book—it was a call for a return to small-scale enterprises in social, economic, and political affairs. See also Sale (1980).

ter reflect the needs and aspirations of the small community. (Or, as Aristotle once said, he who wears the shoe knows where it pinches!) Acting under such slogans as, "Small is beautiful," "Community control," "Power to the people," and "Participatory democracy," several cities attempted to decentralize their governments (Altschuler 1970, Kotler 1969, Mansbridge 1980). Some created neighborhood commissions whose elected members were to advise the city council on such neighborhood matters as traffic, zoning, and business signs. Other cities created mini-city halls, placing administrative units of city departments in neighborhoods to better respond to citizen complaints (Nordlinger 1972). And some cities took steps toward even greater decentralization by giving measures of autonomy to neighborhood councils and school system sub-districts.[18]

If there is a lesson to be learned from these examples of counter logic and counter trends, it is an obvious one. While metropolitan integration that promotes system access (roads, communication, and the like) will no doubt continue, lifestyle integration will remain a difficult and emotion-filled enterprise. But to gain some further purchase on these lessons, it will be useful now to turn to the legal and political relationships between cities and their states, the units of government which in very large measure control what cities may and may not do.

18. Neighborhood participation was also encouraged by provisions of the Model Cities and Demonstration Act of 1965 (part of the anti-poverty program), which mandated neighborhood councils having a voice in administering federal poverty programs. See chapters 8 and 15.

Narrow Street. Armin Landeck. 1949. Drypoint and engraving. Gift of the Chicago Hospital Council. 1980.375. © 1989 The Art Institute of Chicago, All Rights Reserved.

272

Cities and Their States ——————— 13

Governments, like clocks, go from the motion men give them. . . .
William Penn
Pennsylvania's Frame of Government

States and Cities: A Complex Relationship

The complex relationship between cities and their states is framed by three broad principles of American political life. First is the principle that operates everywhere and at all levels of American government, that policy making-authority must be scattered and dispersed. Behind this dispersal lies a political tradition grounded in fear of concentrating power too narrowly. As Madison said in *Federalist* 47,

> The accumulation of all powers, legislative, executive, and judiciary in the same hands . . . may justly be pronounced the very definition of tyranny. (1961,301)

In previous chapters, we surveyed this dispersal of policy authority in cities, noting the use there of separation of powers; the role of administrators in agenda setting, policy framing, and policy implementation; and the important role played by persons in the private sector in framing and implementing policies—especially development policies.

The second broad principle that frames city-state relationships has also been previously noted. Cities are creatures and agents of their state government. As such, they are required to enforce and implement state laws and

273

policies; and all that cities do must be justified legally as stemming from a grant of authority from the state.

The third broad principle is that cities do not have exclusive jurisdiction over their own territory. Each city shares and competes for governing authority with its county and with numerous special-purpose governments.

The upshot of all this is that city governments do not govern merely by carrying out or implementing state policy. Instead, they govern through a complex process that involves pressure-group politics, rural-urban rivalries, and the often difficult business of negotiating, bargaining, and adjudicating with their state government and with the counties and special-purpose governments that surround them. To explicate this process, we look again at the legal principles that bind cities to their states.

Legal Principles of City-State Relationships

When the American Revolution turned colonies into states, the evolving American legal system carried forward the logic and law of the colony. States were deemed to be the effective units of government, and every city within a state was held to be subordinate to that state. As creatures and agents of the state, cities were required by state courts to enforce state laws within the city's domain, and to do nothing to contravene state laws.

As general legal principles, these requirements might seem obvious and straightforward. But few things at law are either obvious or straightforward. Does a city need specific authorization from the state legislature for its every ordinance? Or may a city enact ordinances so long as they do not expressly contravene state law? For example, if state law does not expressly forbid a certain practice (say, a tax on business), can the city enact that tax? For another example, if the state has in place a tax on business, can a city levy an additional tax—or does the state tax preempt all city business taxes?

Alexis de Tocqueville, the great commentator on American democracy, remarked that, in the United States, sooner or later all questions of policy end up before the courts. The courts settle policy cases by applying such general rules as *principal* (the state) and *agent* (the city). But as Supreme Court Justice Oliver Wendell Holmes once noted, general rules do not decide concrete cases. Thus, over the decades, case by case, and state by state, courts have built up an enormous body of case law that decides what cities may and may not do— all within the abstract principle of agency and the related principle that cities are creatures (and agents) of the state.

Dillon's Rule

Something approaching a nationwide doctrine was achieved in the post-Civil War period when a state judge, John Dillon of Iowa, published his treatise,

Commentaries on the Law of Municipal Corporations (1872). In that treatise, Dillon enunciated his now famous rule[1]:

> It is a general undisputed proposition of law that a municipal corporation possesses and can exercise the following powers, and not others: first, those granted in express words; second, those necessarily or fairly implied in or incident to the powers expressly granted; third, those essential to the . . . purposes of the [municipal] corporation—not simply convenient, but indispensable. Any fair, reasonable, substantial doubt concerning the existence of power is [to be] resolved against the corporation and the power denied. (Dillon 1911, 448)

In 1923, the U.S. Supreme Court gave approval (and standing in Federal Law) to Dillon's Rule:

> The city is a political subdivision of the state, created as a convenient agency . . . for the state. . . . The state, therefore, may at its pleasure, modify or withdraw all such powers [as it gave to the city] . . . and [even] destroy [the city]. . . . In these respects, the state is supreme. (*Trenton v. New Jersey*, 262 US 182)

Dillon's Rule still stands, more or less, as the law in every state, but legal doctrine is also bound up in practical considerations. States have rarely abolished cities, and rarely have they attempted to take over the day-to-day administration of cities. State legislatures, however, have frequently interposed in financial matters, in granting franchises, and in creating special-purpose governments. Over the years since Dillon, however, the rigidity of his rule has been softened (Grumm and Murphy 1974). A brief historical sketch will outline this softening and note its connection to the changing nature of urban-rural conflict.

A Bold and Meddlesome Hand

> The New York legislature . . . passed more laws for New York [City] . . . in the three years from 1867 to 1870 than Parliament passed for all of the cities in the United Kingdom from 1835 to 1885; in the year 1870, thirty-nine state laws were passed for the city of Brooklyn alone. Jersey City's charter was amended by state action ninety-one times between 1837 and 1875. (Glaab and Brown 1976, 163)

In the nineteenth and early twentieth centuries, it was the practice of state legislatures to play a bold hand with their cities. Sometimes that hand was

---

1. See Buckwalter (1982) for a further discussion of Dillon's Rule.

played in helpful and benign ways—helping cities to solve problems that lay beyond their territorial limits. For example, in 1905, the New York Legislature created a special district, the City of New York Board of Water Supply, which enabled the board to acquire a chain of water reservoirs and an aqueduct system reaching to the Catskill mountains and the Delaware River, thus ensuring a water supply for New York. And following the devastating hurricane of 1900 in Galveston, Texas (one-sixth of its population drowned; one-third of the city's property destroyed), the Texas legislature abolished Galveston's government and set in its place a commission of five businessmen to manage the city's government and take charge of its physical reconstruction. At other times, state legislatures have intervened in city government out of concern for the corruption of big-city politics. For example, the legislature of Missouri long ago gave the governor power to appoint the commissioner of police for St. Louis.

At still other times, it was corruption in the state legislature itself that produced state intervention in city governance. Such was especially the case where fortunes were to be made in granting franchises to operate streetcar lines. For example, in Illinois (in 1895) Charles Yerkes, the streetcar baron of Chicago, bribed members of the legislature to grant him a ninety-nine-year monopoly over Chicago's streetcars, and offered the governor a half-million dollars to sign the "eternal monopoly" into law. When the governor rejected the bribe and vetoed the bill, Yerkes returned to the legislature, this time bribing members to enact a new law that returned franchise-granting powers to the Chicago City Council—whose members Yerkes had correctly surmised were not beyond his powers of cash persuasion (Andrews 1946).

Rural-Urban Conflict

But over the years, more than either money or helpfulness has played a part in legislative interference with cities. An important part of that interference has sprung from the cultural rivalry between rural and urban America. All through the nineteenth and the first half of this century, state legislatures everywhere were dominated by representatives from rural areas. And almost until the present, those from rural areas tended to see cities (especially big cities) as the vortex of foreign and evil ways. Thus, there was present in the legislature—sometimes as undertone and sometimes overt—a rural-urban lifestyle conflict. And even in those states where city populations had become a majority in the state (New York, Illinois, Pennsylvania), rural representatives held power in the legislature by refusing to reapportion and redistrict their state according to population.[2]

---

2. A celebrated case, *Colegrove v. Green* (328 US 549, 1946) had the U.S. Supreme Court upholding the Illinois legislature's refusal to redistrict, saying that redistricting was a political matter, in which (given the principle of separation of powers) the courts ought not intervene. At the time of the

Lifestyle conflict between rural and urban America has had many dimensions. In recent decades, the conflict has taken on overtones of race: blacks,
black–Hispanics, and Asians in central cities versus rural and suburban whites
elsewhere. A half-century ago, the conflict turned on modes of livelihood
(agriculture versus commerce and industry), on religion, on the recency of
immigrant status, and on the ethnic identity of that immigrant status. As earlier
chapters point out, all four dimensions of the conflict were interwoven in the
nineteenth century, when cities were home to vast numbers of European
immigrants. It was then that livelihood differences were exacerbated by
religious and ethnic differences (native-born Protestants residing predominantly in the countryside, more recently arrived Catholics and Jews residing
predominantly in the city).

But religious differences between rural and urban America have been
more subtle and more profound than can be indicated by distinguishing merely
among Protestants, Catholics and Jews. John Buenker (1973, 167) sees the
religious dimension of rural–urban conflict as a cultural struggle sometimes
involving "almost incompatible world views." Cities have been home to what
is sometimes called the *ritualistic tradition* in religion. For Roman Catholics,

> the commandments of God and the Church serve . . . as guides to moral con-
> duct. . . . The key . . . in the use of all fleshy pleasure . . . [is] moderation,
> and defect . . . condemned . . . [as much] as excess. . . . [Q]uestions of
> morality . . . [are thus] left to the individual conscience, with the Church as
> the only guide.

Jews, notes Buenker, closely resemble "the ritualists in their attitudes and practices." Man had it within him to descend to great evil, "but he was not
inherently bad" (Buenker 1973, 169).

Contrast, then, these views with an outlook prevalent in rural America.
Traditionally, the countryside has been home to pietistic religions. Rejecting
a prescribed ritual, pietists tend to stress the requirement of personal conver-
sion (as opposed to membership at birth) and the individual is

> much more on his own against evil in the world and hence much more anx-
> ious to eradicate all potential barriers to his own and his neighbor's salva-
> tion. . . . [T]he only way he . . . [can] do that is to purge the world of evil.
> (Buenker 1973, 167)

---

suit, the Illinois legislature had not reapportioned its house of representatives for fifty years. The
Chicago area had a preponderant majority of the state's population but only a minority of seats of seats in
the Illinois House. But in 1962, this practice of malapportionment came to an end. The Supreme Court
reversed the Colegrove case and mandated that the 14th Amendment required that state legislatures
adhere to the principles of equal representation and one person, one vote (*Baker v. Carr,* 369 US 186).

With these ideas in mind, it becomes perhaps easier to understand the preoccupation of earlier, rurally-dominated state legislatures with perceived misconduct and sinfulness in big cities and to understand one aspect of the origins of legislative interference in city government.

Home Rule

Politics (as the old saying goes) breeds strange bedfellows. Consider, in the early decades of this century, the alliance between urban Progressives and rural state legislators. Both wanted to clean up the mess of city politics. And both perceived the immigrants to have a hand in that mess. Progressives wanted to bring worthwhile citizens into city politics—a goal generally approved by legislative moralists. But to make the efforts of what Lord Bryce had called "the better class" effective and rewarding, Progressives also proposed that cities be given a greater measure of control over their own affairs.

As Frank Goodnow, one of the early leaders of the Home Rule Movement, put it,

 the fact that a city is an organization for the satisfaction of local needs makes it necessary that its actions be determined by local considerations. To this end, it must have large local powers. (Quoted in Glaab and Brown 1975, 175; also see Goodnow 1895.)

The home rule proponents had an early success in a revision of the Missouri constitution in 1875 and still more success during the high tide of Progressivism. Since then, about half the states have given home rule to their cities. Today about two-thirds of all cities with a population of 200,000 or more are beneficiaries of some form of home rule. Each state, of course, has its own version of home rule. The National Municipal League (in an effort to standardize these fifty versions) offers a model and definition for home rule that is proposed for incorporation in every state constitution:

A . . . city may exercise any legislative power or perform any function which is not denied to it by its charter, is not denied to . . . cities generally, or to . . . cities of its class, and is within such limitations as the legislature may establish by general law.[3]

But despite its name, home rule is not *complete* home rule. Cities are never to be free from state control. (Otherwise, they would be separate state governments—e.g., "The State of the City of New York.") No city may pass

---

3. The National Municipal League, *The Model State Constitution*, Sec. 8.02. See also Bender (1983).

278

laws that contravene state law or general state policy. Essentially, what home rule accomplishes is a softening of Dillon's Rule in some or all the following ways.

1. When they achieve some specified population size, cities may vote to choose among alternate forms of city government (for example, a city manager form instead of mayor-council form).
2. In choosing an alternate form of government, cities are to receive from the state a prepackaged charter (a home rule charter) whose provisions usually include concentration rather than dispersal of executive authority (the mayor or manager being given power to appoint and remove heads of major service-delivery departments). The package charter also usually provides for a small rather than a large city council—usually elected at large.
3. By declaring itself to be a home rule state, the state constitution (and legislative statutes) serves notice to courts and judges that doubtful cases concerning the extent of a city's authority are to be resolved in the city's favor (in effect stating that the severity of Dillon's Rule is no longer to be in force).

But when all home rule reforms are said and done, doubtful situations will continue to arise and to find their way to the courts. As Duane Lockard (1963, 124) notes, home rule charters are an attempt to distinguish the general powers of the state from matters that are of purely local concern, but such distinctions are never fast and firm. Sooner or later, they will require the intervention of the courts.

> What does a court do when it faces a dispute about local control of traffic on a state highway which runs through the middle of a city? Is that a local matter because the street is in the city, or a state matter because it concerns a state highway? Are the working hours and conditions of local employees a matter of 'municipal affairs' or does the state's power over labor and public employment supersede the powers of the city?

And so, home rule or no, cities remain in the state and of the state. How then is their relationship with the state carried forward? How do cities deal with their states?

Cities and States: Mandates, Politics, and Bargaining

Cities deal with their states—and states with their cities—through complex arrangements that move along multiple pathways, including cooperation, bargaining, mandates, incentives, and disincentives. The circumstances under which these activities take place are considerably different than they were thirty or forty years ago. Some degree of rural-urban conflict continues in the state legislature, but it has been moderated considerably by at least three sets of social forces. First, television, the two-car family, and fast roads have made urban life much more accessible to those living in rural areas. The city is no longer a place to be experienced vicariously, through books and sermons from the pulpit. Second, urban dwellers today are less concentrated in big cities than they were fifty or seventy-five years ago. Most urban dwellers today live in the suburbs, and suburbs are perceived by rural legislators as having lifestyles congenial to their own and, accordingly, deserving of respectful legislative treatment. And third, state legislatures are no longer as dominated by rural representatives as they once were. (The U.S. Supreme Court has mandated periodic redistricting of state legislatures to conform to the one person, one vote principle.[4]) Accordingly, cities and states now deal with each other along the lines described below.

Mandates

As state governments attempt to wrestle with the issues and problems of contemporary life, they often resort to mandates (orders to cities that they carry out designated tasks and perform specified functions). For example, a state legislature may require all cities of a certain size (say 100,000 or more) to add emergency medical services to fire department duties—along with equipment for such services. Or, for another example, the legislature may require all cities to carry personal injury insurance to cover accidents on city playgrounds. Or, for still another example, the legislature (responding to what it perceives to be a decline in patriotism) may mandate that all schools offer instruction in the American system of government. Sometimes, the legislature will appropriate funds to assist cities in meeting the mandate. Frequently, it does not—leaving it to each city to provide the necessary funding.[5]

Court decisions are another form of mandate. And given the blurred boundaries between state and local matters, every city (it is often said) is either preparing to defend some ordinance in court, or is in the process of doing so, or has just finished doing so.

The City as Lobbyist: Legislative Policy Formation

Urban representatives elected to the state legislature are constantly at work lobbying for—or lobbying to defeat—proposed state laws. This is especially

---

4. *Baker v. Carr* (see note 2). Periodic redistricting to reflect population shifts means that sparsely populated rural areas will have fewer legislators than densely populated urban and suburban areas.

5. Some states have attempted to restrict the legislature's ability to pass legislation that requires municipal expenditures. The Alabama state constitution, for example, was amended in 1988 to require that municipalities be given at least one year to plan for these added expenditures.

true when one or more cities are considering a local policy that is new or that departs from established precedent. For example, many cities now levy some form of tax on income, on theater admissions, and/or on restaurant dining. But will a proposed tax on hotel rooms stand up in court when challenged by hotel owners? One way of assuring the legality of the new tax is to get the legislature to add hotel-bed taxes to the list of taxes it permits cities to levy.

Given the fact that city administrative personnel usually have ties to professional associations and to their counterpart administrators in other cities, it is quite usual for them to join in a statewide organization: the state's mayors' association, the state association of city health workers, the state police chiefs' association, the state association of city police, the state association of city treasurers and accountants, and so on. Thus, as bills affecting their areas of administrative and professional competence move through the legislature, it is also quite usual for spokespersons for a relevant professional association to appear before the legislature seeking to mold and shape the proposed legislation (in other words, to work as lobbyists on the cities' behalf).[6]

The City as Lobbyist: Policy Implementation

More and more, state legislatures pass laws that set forth general policy goals, leaving it to administrators to implement the law through the development of local standards and procedures. Thus, city officials engage in constant interaction with state administrators charged with the task of transforming policy goals into policy action. In doing so, city officials work to bring state policy into accord with city goals. For example, city street engineers negotiate with state highway officials in establishing routes for new roads. City water officials work with state environmental protection agents to establish water-purification procedures. Quite often city officials negotiate and bargain with state officials over the standards that will be used to establish the quality of city water. City health officials confer with state officials on the vaccines to be used in school inoculation programs. And city officials frequently lobby state officials to get them to change implementation rules and procedures.

Variations on this theme of city-state relations are extensive. But the main point is this: Cities are creatures of their state, but not passive or supine creatures. They follow state laws and policy directives, but they do so only after they have had full play in attempting to shape those laws and directives. City administrators and elected officials constitute an informal interest group (or groups) that works at influencing the state legislature. City administrators bargain and negotiate with state officials in the implementation of state laws.

6. In effect, these spokespersons become part of the state's subgovernment (Hamm 1986).

Urban representatives are in the legislature. They form coalitions there, and they lobby their fellow representatives to pass legislation that will benefit the cities. City officials are charged with enforcing state laws. They do so, and in the process often bend and interpret those laws to suit city purposes. And city voters have an important voice in the outcome of state elections. Their votes help decide who will be elected to state offices—governor, treasurer, judges of the state supreme court, and so on. Thus, the web of urban politics is not confined merely to politics in the city. It is politics that extends into the operation of state government as well.

An Even Larger Web

City voters also have a powerful say in the outcome of national elections. As we turn next to consider the relationship between cities and the national government, it will be useful to keep in mind the fact that cities are well represented in Congress. Some 261 members of the House of Representatives (60 percent) come from predominantly (i.e., two-thirds) urban districts, and 86 senators come from states where the urban population is in the majority. As the nation has grown more urbanized, the President comes to depend more and more for his election on voters from the cities. And lest he need reminding of this fact, no fewer than four of his cabinet members direct departments with important urban concerns: Housing and Urban Development, Education, Transportation, Health and Human Services.

We turn now to exploring the extended web: city-national government interactions.

View from the Tugboat "Desplaines" on the Calumet River. Ron Gordon. Photograph. 1987.

Cities and the _____ 14
National Government _____

Nationwide thinking, nationwide planning, and nationwide action are the three great essentials to prevent nationwide crises for future generations to struggle through.

Franklin D. Roosevelt
Speech, New York, April 25, 1936

I am going to build the kind of nation that President Roosevelt hoped for, President Truman worked for, and President Kennedy died for.

Lyndon B. Johnson
Speech, December 1964

Cities and the Nation

For the student of politics, few subjects are more intriguing than the ways in which a political system changes or the ways in which political practice diverges from formal constitutional pronouncements.

The United States Constitution is the organizing framework of our system of government. It sets forth and defines the authority of the national government. By reference and implication, it also defines the authority of the states. This division of authority between central government and constituent states is the essence of federalism—an arrangement whereby two independent governments occupy the same territory. Better said, federalism is an arrangement whereby the central government and constituent states are each assigned a specified set of powers and authority (Riker 1964, Leach 1970).

In the American federal system, the states came first. Their union was provided for in the Constitution ("We the People of the United States. . . ."). In the Constitution, the national government is given powers that have mainly to do with commerce, trade, and national defense. By implication (and the words of the Tenth Amendment) the states retain the power to do everything else—to regulate matters pertaining to health, welfare, morals, public safety,

285

and public convenience. In short, the states retain the power to regulate matters pertaining to the affairs of everyday life: marriage, the family, crime and criminality, business transactions and employment, ownership of property, public education, and proper moral conduct.

In the Constitution, no mention is made of cities. The Constitution ignores them. Presumably, as subdivisions and agents of their state, they are part of their state's constitutionally assigned governmental authority. Strictly and formally speaking, they are not connected to the national government. And from the adoption of the Constitution in 1789 to about half a century ago, the national government had almost no direct dealings with cities. Then, in the 1930s, an explosion of relationships took place. Without formal amendments to the Constitution, the old pattern of federalism was shunted aside to make way for a new federalism that blurred the distinction between national powers and states' powers. Under this new federalism, the national government would henceforth take responsibility for solving all the major problems confronting our society—including the problems of American cities.

Most great governmental changes are powered by the engine of crisis, both real and perceived. And the crisis that hoisted the new federalism into place was the Great Depression which had begun in October 1929. The faltering economy, with its strangled productivity, widespread poverty, and millions of unemployed could not be dealt with by state governments. Their resources were not adequate. More important, the United States was an integrated economic system—only the national government would have the resources and the geographic jurisdiction to deal with the entirety of the nation's economic system. By congressional action and Supreme Court consent, a new style of federalism displaced the old dual federalism.

Under this new federalism, the national government would take responsibility for managing the economy. It would use its taxing and spending powers to stimulate industrial productivity, regulate conditions of employment, and give welfare and other aid to the poor (Herson 1984, ch. 12). The upshot of the new federalism was that, henceforth, the national government and its policies would be a visible presence in the policies and politics of American cities.

The New Federalism

The new federalism has been a constantly changing concept. The idea of the *new* has a powerful hold on the American political imagination, and every president since Franklin Roosevelt has proclaimed his version of a new federalism. As a rule, Democratic presidents have urged an increased measure of national government policy initiatives, while Republican presidents have urged that the national government give power and policy-making responsibility back to the states. But mostly, each of these versions of a new

286

federalism differs only in degree from what was begun in the New Deal. The national government has become the initiating center of public policy programs. (For a delineation of the new federalism under President Nixon, see Reagan 1972; for its meaning under President Reagan, see Benton 1985.)

Under the new federalism, none of the national government's programs has been self-accomplishing or self-enforcing. All require administrative implementation. They thus bring a large corps of federal administrators (portrayed in table 14.1) into direct contact with state and local officials. As a consequence, the new federalism is marked by a high degree of interaction among administrative personnel at all levels of government: national, state, county, and city. The pattern of their interaction is comparable to that between city and state administrators—cooperating, bargaining, compromising, and ultimately deciding on the rules and procedures that transform policy into the specifics of governmental action. (In short, it is an interaction that is realized through subgovernment and in the policy implementation acts of that subgovernment.) To understand this interaction we note some of its components.

Table 14.1 Number of Federal Employees in Selected Departments and Agencies (in thousands)

	1932	1940	1950	1960	1970	1980	1985
Total	568	1,119	1,961	2,398	2,921	2,875	3,021
Selected Departments							
Agriculture	26.4	81.9	84.4	98.6	116.0	129.1	117.7
Commerce	17.8	25.3	60.8	49.3	57.7	48.6	35.1
Education	—	—	—	—	—	7.4	4.9
Health and Human Services	—	—	—	61.6	108.0	155.7	140.2
Housing and Urban Development	—	—	—	11.1	15.2	17.2	12.3
Justice	9.0	17.8	26.4	30.9	39.3	56.3	64.4
Labor	5.5	3.7	6.1	7.1	11.0	23.5	18.3
Transportation	—	—	—	38.3	66.0	72.4	62.2
Selected Agencies							
Environmental Protection Agency	—	—	—	—	—	14.7	14.0
Small Business Administration	—	—	—	2.2	4.3	5.8	4.9
Veterans' Administration	34.1	41.1	188.4	172.3	168.7	228.3	240.4
Civil Rights Commission	—	—	—	.1	.2	.3	.2
Equal Employment Opportunity Commission	—	—	—	—	.8	3.5	3.0
Federal Deposit Insurance Corporation	—	1.8	.3	1.2	2.5	3.5	8.7
Federal Home Loan Bank Board	—	—	—	1.0	1.3	1.5	.8
Federal Trade Commission	.4	.6	.5	.8	1.3	1.8	1.1
General Services Administration	—	—	11.7	28.2	37.9	37.7	23.1
National Endowment for the Arts	—	—	—	—	—	.4	.3
National Transportation Safety Board	—	—	—	—	—	.4	.3

SOURCE: U.S. Department of Commerce, *Statistical Abstract.*

Fiscal interdependence. None of the new federalism's programs is self-supporting. Each requires a considerable outlay of money. One consequence is the rise of government spending at every level of government (see chapters 15 and 16). Another consequence is the very great dependence of cities and states on federal money. Cities and states continue to raise their own revenues, but a large percentage of the (total) money they spend comes from the national government.

The principal vehicle by which federal funds have been given to cities and states is the grant-in-aid (also called the categorical grant).[1] With this device, policy is created by national legislation and money is appropriated ("granted") to implement the policy. The usual arrangement for a grant-in-aid is that the national government contributes the greater portion of funds, with states and/or cities contributing some matching percentage of the money —say, 80 percent to 90 percent coming from the federal government, with cities or states contributing the rest.

Policy interdependence. In grant-in-aid programs, Congress not only specifies the purpose for which receiving governments are to spend the money ("a grant in aid of . . ."), but it often specifies the conditions that are to be part of the grant. (In politics, as in country dances, he who pays the fiddler gets to call the tune.) In this way, the national government not only promotes a specific policy, but it can also implement vast and sweeping social programs. To illustrate, Congress has used the grant-in-aid to enable cities to build low-income housing. In accepting such grants, cities are required to enforce a federal regulation that stipulates that all building construction using federal money shall pay prevailing union wages; that no person or corporation or governmental agency receiving federal money may discriminate in its hiring practices; that every federally supported housing project must use a specified tenant-income formula in admitting occupants to the project; and that the project must be located (sited) in such fashion as to contribute to citywide racial integration.[2]

The grant-in-aid thus works to draw cities and states into the federal web in both a direct and indirect way—direct in the sense of enlisting city and state into serving designated categories of federal programs (road construction, welfare assistance, low-income housing, airport improvements, and hundreds of others) and indirect in the sense that still other and broader social

---

1. As an instrument of intergovernmental fiscal transfer, the use of the grant-in-aid declined under Presidents Nixon and Reagan, replaced by other arrangements to be noted in the following chapter. For a fuller discussion of the grant-in-aid, see chapter 15.

2. As will be noted in chapter 17, some cities have found these requirements so restrictive that they have opted to do without federally funded housing projects. Other cities have spent considerable time and effort—usually to no avail—attempting to contravene these requirements.

programs can be wrapped around the categorical grant (Sundquist 1969, Berkeley and Fox 1978, Hale and Palley 1981; for liberal and conservative perspectives on these grants, see Wright 1968 and Kantor 1988). For example, were a city to receive a grant-in-aid to purchase new equipment for its police department, any business firm attempting to sell that equipment to the city would be required to demonstrate that it is in conformity with the federal government's affirmative action policy, vigorously pursuing a policy of hiring and promoting women, blacks and members of other designated minority groups.

Policy spillovers. Just as cities are drawn into the federal web by grants, they are pulled there even more forcefully by national programs that deal with national defense and the management of the nation's economy. In its attempts to maintain a sound economy, the national government makes use of two techniques and strategies: fiscal and monetary controls. Fiscal controls involve taxing and spending for what are sometimes called counter-cyclical purposes: taxing and spending to counter (and reverse) economic cycles. In times of declining productivity and underemployment, the national government has increased its purchases of goods and services, for example, those connected with national defense,[3] and it has appropriated money for major construction projects, including highways, airports, river and flood control, and public housing. Every city has been affected by counter-cyclical spending projects. The greatest of these has been the interstate highway system, (launched in the 1950s, it is often said to be the greatest public works project since the Egyptian pyramids), whose urban throughways and ring roads have completely changed land-use and development patterns in every metropolitan area in the nation.[4]

The national government (through its Federal Reserve Board) exercises monetary controls by expanding and contracting the nation's money supply and raising and lowering the interest rates banks charge for lending money. The prevailing interest rate affects the ability of cities to borrow money by issuing bonds, and it also has a decisive effect on the home and commercial building industry—building new homes, refurbishing old houses, and building factories and office towers. In this way, the national government's control over the money supply and interest rates powerfully affects the physical structure of cities. The growth and decline of a city's central business district, its network of factories, the spread of its suburban ring, and its overall physical form are all directly and intimately affected by the national government's changes in monetary policy.

3. Cities such as Houston, Seattle, Huntsville, and St. Louis that are heavily dependent on the space, defense, and aircraft industries are very directly affected by federal spending: A cutback in defense orders brings a local but acute economic depression.
4. To date, 42,000 miles of inter-city and around-the-city freeways have been built, at a cost of $86 billion and with 90 percent of the funding coming from the federal government.

But for overall effect on cities, nothing compares with a single provision of the national tax code: permitting homeowners and real estate financiers a tax deduction for interest paid on borrowed money. This tax provision is of enormous importance to the middle class. (Some would say it creates and defines the American middle class.) With it, the middle class has been assisted in buying single-family homes, and in so doing, has spread residential neighborhoods to the borders of the city and, leapfrogging the city, has created the urbanized metropolitan area. Needless to say, this same tax provision has also fueled the engines of shopping mall construction, the building of suburban business parks, and the building of office towers in the CBD (central business district). It is only a slight exaggeration to say that in the past half century, every building in the city and around the city has been the beneficiary of federal tax policy.[5]

The New Deal and the New Urban Politics

In the economic turmoil of the 1930s, voters behaved as they have always behaved in bad times. They voted the party in power out of office. From the Civil War onward (with an occasional interregnum)[6] the Republican party dominated both Congress and the presidency. But in the election of 1932, Franklin Roosevelt and a Democratic Congress were swept into office by an electoral landslide.[7] And ever since that election, all candidates for the presidency have campaigned as did Roosevelt on promises to guard the national economy and set to rights all the major problems that beset the country. What is more, every president since has been mindful of the great political coalition that first swept Roosevelt and the Democrats into office. That coalition constituted what was in effect a transformed Democratic party. Traditional Southern Democrats aligned with big-city voters of the North (Catholics, Jews,

5. In addition to tax benefits for money paid as interest on loans, federal tax policy affects urban development in other important ways. For example, interest paid on money borrowed by cities and states (i.e., interest on state and municipal bonds) is free of federal income tax. As another example, commercial real estate is permitted a tax write-down (i.e., for tax purposes and federal tax payment, the value of the property can be depreciated over a considerable number of years). As may be anticipated, the financial benefits extended by U.S. tax policies to homeowners, real estate developers, and bond buyers is part of the larger argument concerning fair shares and social equity. Is the middle class deserving of what is, in effect, financial assitance, while those who cannot afford to buy a house receive nothing? Are municipal bonds a tax haven for the rich, while money in the bank accounts of the less well-off remains a source for taxation? Does tax depreciation for commercial property encourage needless office-tower building and the proliferation of endless suburban shopping malls—all the while leaving central cities to cope with their consequences?

6. From 1876 to 1896, Democrats controlled the House of Representatives more frequently than did Republicans.

7. A forerunner of that landslide was the election of 1930. The House of Representatives, reflecting the newfound importance of the urban vote in national affairs, was dominated by a Democratic majority.

blacks, blue-collar workers, and union members, along with "ethnics"—children and grandchildren of those immigrants who, in an earlier time, had come from southern and eastern Europe).

The election of 1932 thus signaled the importance to national elections of the urban vote. Given the workings of the Electoral College (with a majority of each state's voters awarding that state's entire Electoral College vote to the majority candidate—winner take all), the urban voter is crucial to a presidential candidate's capturing a majority in the Electoral College. Accordingly, every presidential candidate in the past half century has been mindful of the need to court the urban voter and address the nation's urban problems. Those who become presidents thus stand ready to put urban problems fairly high on their policy agenda. In doing so, they set in motion the wheels of urban policy-making in Congress. And equally important, they animate the hundreds of interest groups and thousands of lobbyists who seek to advance their own definitions of urban needs and their own visions of urban public interest.

Interest Groups and Presentday Federalism

Thus, presentday federalism has still another set of important consequences for the cities: it proliferates the number of interest groups that seek to benefit from federal urban programs. These interest groups are the city-based lobbies seeking tax benefits for their members, trying to head off legislation harmful to their members, working to get those who implement federal policy to shape that policy so as to benefit their members.

Many interest groups that are vigorously active today were founded long before the 1930s ushered in an explosion of federal programs. But as that decade got underway, every interest group with hopes of influencing national legislation in any significant way expanded its Washington staff and considered moving its headquarters there to be near the source of money and power.

Several interest groups deserve special mention for their roles in influencing the course of national urban programs over the past half century: the National Municipal League, the International City Managers Association, the United States Chamber of Commerce, the National Association of Real Estate Boards, the Outdoor Contractors Association, the American Federation of Labor-Congress of Industrial Organizations, the Mortgage Bankers Association, the United States Savings and Loan League.

These groups—and hundreds like them—also deserve special mention for their roles as spokespersons for the ideologies that dominate our political system and our political thinking. For instance, interest groups that represent realtors, bankers, builders, and business persons are powerful voices in support of the free market and an unregulated economy. Traditionally, they have resisted public housing for low-income families. On the other side of the policy coin, such housing projects are usually supported by central-city officials and economic liberals (union spokespersons, for example, and leaders of associations for welfare rights).

But to better understand presentday federalism and the connection between cities and the national government as well as the connection between federal programs and interest groups, another backward glance is in order, a brief canvass of a half century of federal urban programs. In the more than half century since Franklin Roosevelt first took office, the national government has enacted several hundred programs that affect the nation's cities. Among those with greatest impact are programs (and policies) dealing with jobs, home mortgages, low-rent housing, slum clearance, highway construction, the amelioration of poverty, and grants for the support of city services. Because important federal programs are extensive in scope and costs, they may begin under one president but not reach their apogee until the administration of another. Nevertheless, some sense of chronology is useful, and for this reason federal urban programs will be outlined by presidential tenure.

Roosevelt and the New Deal [8]

Jobs and Mortgages

In 1932, with the country battered by business failures, President Roosevelt and a cooperative Congress inaugurated the programs that were to constitute the New Deal. Their purpose was to get the economy moving upward and to lessen joblessness and its resulting poverty. The programs that had the greatest effect on cities were not city programs as such, but programs to help those who lived in cities. Officials of two newly created government agencies, the Works Progress Administration (WPA) and the Public Works Administration (PWA),[9] worked hand-in-glove with city and state officials to plan and build streets, bridges, sewers, and parks, along with such urban amenities as bus-stop shelters, public drinking fountains, and recreational facilities. Their primary purpose was to give jobs to the unemployed; but the consequences were to leave in policymakers' memory the idea that the government can serve as employer of last resort and that the employed poor—who are given "workfare not welfare"—can be put to work improving the quality of urban life. (This memory was to come to life again in

8. Histories of Roosevelt and his New Deal are extensive. Of general importance to the present discussion are Schlesinger (1959), Leuchtenburg (1963), and Goldman (1956). Of more specific relevance are Mollenkopf (1983, ch. 2), Jackson (1985, chs. 11 and 12), Warner (1972, part 3), and Gelfand (1975).

9. It was the New Deal that popularized the practice of naming government agencies using initials and acronyms.

the Comprehensive Employment and Training Act of 1973—CETA; and the idea of "workfare not welfare" moves in waves through periodic considerations of welfare policy reform.)

A second of the national government's indirect aids to cities was the National Housing Act of 1934. The act created the Federal Housing Administration (FHA) and the Federal Savings and Loan Insurance Corporation (FSLIC). Both were designed to bring life to the then-moribund house building industry and to stop the tide of bank foreclosures on family homes. Neither act was intended to bring government into competition with the mortgage banking industry. Instead, private mortgage banking was to be assisted by the government, and through that assistance, the homeowner and buyer were to benefit. Then, as now, the issue of government intrusion into the marketplace was the occasion for heated ideological debate. And then, as now, the usual resolution was to have government assist the private sector, not supplant it.

The FSLIC offered government insurance for savings accounts, and was thus intended to coax private savings out from under the mattress and into savings and loan associations; those corporations would then use this money to make home mortgages. In addition, the FHA served as insurer for mortgage lenders. The rationale for the FHA was simple. With government insurance against loss, lenders would have incentive to make loans available, would require a smaller down payment, and would charge less interest. Borrowers would thus have an incentive to buy new homes, refinance existing mortgages, and restore and repair old homes. And jobs in the building industry would expand, more persons would be able to afford homes, older homes would be renovated, and cities would be spared the stain of spreading slums.

Much of the FHA program worked as planned, and the FHA and FSLIC programs remain today the backbone of the mortgage and home-building industries.[10] But as with most government programs, the law of unanticipated consequences also took its toll. FHA mortgages have done relatively little to improve inner-city housing, and the net effect of FHA has been to support and intensify the segregation of urban blacks and the poor. The poor, after all, do not buy homes. They are apartment dwellers, and FHA lenders have consistently shown preference for single-family homes over apartment buildings. What is more, FHA administrators have tended to share the ideological orientations of those with whom they work most closely, the banking and real estate industries. Until quite recently, that orientation was not

---

10. For example, in 1981, over 4 million homeowner mortgages were insured by the FHA, accounting for $88 billion. Many families who in pre-FHA days might never have been able to afford home ownership have acquired homes of their own. FHA's mortgage practices have also created industry-wide standards. Thus, today's mortgages often run thirty and thirty-five years (compared with the ten-year mortgage common in the 1920s).

one to champion racial integration. Thus, FHA mortgage money was an important factor in the racially white suburban explosion of the 1950s, as upwardly mobile white families used that money to make house dreams come true (Warner 1972, ch. 8). An FHA underwriting manual, issued to banks in 1938, offered these guidelines for making loans:

> If a neighborhood is to retain stability, it is necessary that properties shall continue to be occupied by the same social and racial classes. A change in social or racial occupancy generally contributes to instability and a decline in [property] values. (Quoted in Judd 1988, 281)

In addition to its sometime role in promoting racial segregation, in several cities the FHA seems also to have played a role in perpetuating machine-style politics. Robert Green (1977, 181) reports:

> Bribes from business profits were sometimes passed from sellers to FHA appraisers. Inner-city buyers were particularly inexperienced and, as usual, limited in their choice of housing. Bribed appraisers overpriced housing and ignored structural faults, thus allowing substandard housing to receive FHA blessing for the 100-percent mortgage insurance provided under the program. Often the financial statements were forged by middlemen, making it possible for those who did not qualify for mortgage insurance to receive it.

Further, Green argues, the FHA program was structured so that defaults were in the best interest of the banks, and foreclosures became commonplace. In Chicago, for example, FHA-insured houses had a foreclosure rate three times higher than houses with conventional mortgages. And in parts of Detroit, the foreclosure rate for FHA-insured houses ran 30 percent (Conyers 1976, Green 1977). By the mid-1970s, mortgage-banking companies were charging the government $20 million each month to maintain vacant houses (National Training and Information Center 1976). Foreclosures, in turn, fueled urban blight. By 1975, HUD owned 105,000 vacant homes (in Chicago's Roseland community, for example, 8 percent of all homes had been abandoned; see Green 1977). During the Carter presidency, a moratorium was placed on foreclosures, and requirements have been modified in an attempt to curb these abuses.

Housing for the Poor

If there is a dominant American view on housing for the poor it is probably captured by the phrase "filter down." In this view, housing for the poor is best provided by the private sector of the economy. The poor take the housing they can afford, and as persons rise on the economic scale, they move from less desirable to more desirable housing—making available what they have vacated to those on lower rungs of the economic ladder (in short, allowing better housing to filter down to the poor).

Filter-down housing has been the traditional arrangement in American cities; and the principle underlying filter-down housing has been largely responsible for the historic movement of new-home construction outward from the city center. For economic Liberals, filter-down is not a satisfactory policy position. *[The theory of ideology]* [11] Dilapidated housing (Liberals argue) should not be all that is available for the poor. A concern for equality of outcomes requires that the government help provide good housing for the economic underclass.

Economic Conservatives take a different view. Government works best (they argue) when it does not compete with private industry. If the poor are to be assisted to better housing, government ought to stimulate the overall economy so that more jobs become available to the poor. Over time, Conservatives continue, the poor will move up the economic ladder and buy housing suitable to their improved economic status.

The New Deal helped turn liberal sentiments into policy, and a Housing Division was established within the Public Works Administration to build low-cost, low-rent housing for the poor. As might be anticipated, spokespersons for the building, banking, and real estate industries objected strenuously, and though the PWA built relatively few low-income apartment buildings, precedent was established for later housing programs (Jackson 1985, ch. 12). Equally important, the PWA housing ventures set into place many of the implementation practices now common in state-city-federal programs. For example, state governments created local housing authorities (special-purpose governments that could accept federal grants for purposes of building low-rent housing), and these local housing authorities were authorized to operate under principles of state sovereignty for purposes of acquiring building sites. (Thus clothed with state sovereignty, the local housing authority could use the state's powers of eminent domain to condemn existing buildings and force their sale to the housing authority so as to provide building sites for new construction.)

The 1937 Public Housing Act was a further development of national housing policy. As is often the case in matters of heated ideological conflict, Congress let one side win, but the loser did not lose completely. The purposes of the act were defined in its title:

> An Act to provide public assistance to the states and the political subdivisions thereof for the elimination of unsafe and unsanitary housing conditions, for the eradication of slums, for the provision of decent, safe, and sanitary dwellings for families of low income, and for the reduction of unemployment and the *stimulation of business activity.* (Quoted in Judd 1988, 261, italics added)

11. The debate over filter-down housing is another manifestation of the larger debate over market equity versus social equity (see chapter 12).

The act established the United States Housing Authority (USHA). The USHA was empowered to make long-term loans (as it turned out, sixty-year, low-interest loans totaling upwards of $800 million) to local authorities for the construction of low-rent housing. States and localities, in turn, were to become partners in the projects by contributing operating and maintenance costs (over time, the federal government used its own funds for these costs), with local officials—operating under federal guidelines—setting rents and standards for tenancy.

All in all, the USHA and its successor agencies have constructed nearly 4.5 million low-rent housing units. How shall this effort be judged? Much depends on one's angle of vision, and on the ideology which focuses that vision. Judged by their numbers, national housing ventures, with state and local cooperation, would be pronounced a considerable success. But low-rent housing projects are not judged by numbers alone. They are also judged according to one's vision of the good society and government's responsibility for that good society.

With lofty rhetoric, the 1949 Housing Act spoke of "a decent home and a suitable living environment for every American family." No government program has ever even remotely approached that goal. And a significant portion of the low-rent housing that has been built has been plagued by serious problems: tenant destructiveness, inept and incompetent management, general disrepair, and tenant crime—drug-dealing, burglary, and personal assaults, with the poor victimizing the poor. For liberal critics of public housing, such problems are understandable and foretold. Listen, for example, to Sam Bass Warner, Jr. (1972, 239):

> Since the goal of . . . a "decent home and a suitable living environment for every American family" has never been popularly accepted as a right of citizenship either by the victimized poor or the fearful affluent, a terrible incubus of philanthropy has plagued public housing and steadily brings on it cycles of sickness. With public housing perceived as a burden and an expression of charity rather than a right of citizenship . . . both local and federal governments have consistently scrimped, saved, and limited the program.

One consequence of this scrimping and saving, continues Warner, is the problems that beset public housing:

> As residents of ill-designed and ill-managed facilities, tenants have often felt little responsibility and resented the public stigma of institutionalized charity.

It is a stigma reinforced by the geographic siting (often amounting to isolation) of public housing. The costs of site acquisition, when combined with the resistance of middle-class neighborhoods to the "intrusion" of public housing, almost always means that public housing has been set inside former slum territory. And almost always, in an effort to minimize site costs, low-rent housing is massive—high-rise apartment buildings, squarely set on "concrete lawns." One very serious consequence of the practice of replacing old slums with new housing is still another unanticipated consequence of public housing programs: the number of housing units available to the poor has been reduced. Overall, more housing units have been destroyed than built (Anderson 1964).

These, of course, are important issues and criticisms, and they became dramatically visible in 1972 when one of the largest public housing projects, Pruitt-Igoe in St. Louis, was dynamited by housing authority order. Thirty-three eleven-story buildings (containing 2,700 apartments) crumbled into smoke and dust—as television cameras whirred—and what had been built only twenty years earlier as the showcase of American public housing was pronounced by a conservative commentator as a "graveyard of good intentions" (Glazer 1967).[12]

Overall, the slash of conservative criticism of public housing has a familiar ideological edge. Say many Conservatives:

> Buildings don't make slums. People do. To take slum dwellers and put them in new buildings is only to set in motion—all over again—the process that starts slums. Instead of building public housing for the poor, let the filter-down process work. The poor will be better assisted by rent subsidies. And they can use those subsidies in the private market. Landlords will have incentive to keep their buildings in repair. Destructive tenants can be removed. And the poor—instead of suffering the stigma of living in public housing—might take better care of where they live.[13]

Liberals are far from persuaded. They point to public housing projects that are well maintained. They note that tenants in many housing projects behave with regard for their fellow tenants. Say many Liberals:

> If Pruitt-Igoe was a disaster, the fault came from two sources: The local housing authority was poorly administered, and the size of Pruitt-Igoe was too big. It was lacking in human scale. It was so vast that *anomie* and non-caring became commonplace. Its corridors were so long and empty that they couldn't be looked after by the tenants. They became hiding places for muggers. And the buildings were so tall that mothers were afraid to let children play down at street level where

---

12. On the lessons of Pruitt-Igoe, see Rainwater (1967) and Meehan (1975).

13. Milton Friedman, one of our most distinguished (and conservative) economists, argues for a system of rent vouchers to replace public housing. Qualified poor are to be given publicly-paid-for rent vouchers which they may then use as rent payment (full or partial, depending on their needs, desires, and abilities) in privately owned housing. With rent vouchers, the poor will escape the stigma and isolation of public housing, landlords will make a profit and thus be encouraged to maintain their buildings, and in the long run (it is asserted), the costs to taxpayers will be far less than is the case with public housing (Friedman and Friedman 1981).

they couldn't be seen from upstairs. There was nothing to do but let the kids play in the corridors. No wonder the halls were a mess![14]

The Truman Presidency (1945–1952)

New government programs are rarely new. They usually depend for inspiration and legitimacy on programs previously established. New programs build on the old by layering new purposes on old programs and by altering their scope. And if the old program is one that engendered fierce ideological debate, the new program will usually carry the scars of those old debates. Such was the case with urban renewal (Greer 1965).[15]

The 1949 Housing Act was an amalgam of three purposes: low-rent housing for low-income families; slum clearance; and support for the private real estate market. The first two purposes were more or less compatible. The third was not. Taken together, the three were to produce a highly volatile politics.

Under the 1949 Act, the Housing and Home Finance Agency (HHFA) was empowered to offer grants-in-aid to local public agencies (many of which were specifically created by state legislatures to permit their cities to participate in the program) for purposes of site acquisition and clearance. The Housing Act required that construction on the acquired sites be accomplished by private enterprise. Sites were to be in slum areas, and to induce private developers to take part in the program, local agencies were empowered to use federal money to write down acquisition costs by buying sites at fair market value and selling them below cost to private developers.

Under these arrangements, urban renewal stirred up strenuous and often acrimonious politics. In city after city, old neighborhoods resented and resisted being designated as slums. Neighborhood groups pressured the city council to look elsewhere for slum clearance. Chicago's experience was typical. All through the 1950s, its politics was dominated by issues of urban renewal (Meyerson and Banfield 1955). In the abstract, urban renewal might be splendid, but in practice it was an election death knell for any city council member who failed to resist efforts to put it in his or her ward.

Even more daunting for Chicago's elected officials than the prospect of razing a neighborhood was the certainty that a slum-cleared area would be a devastated area for years to come. New construction would not (could not) begin anytime soon. Ten years from start to finish was a realistic timetable. Daunting, too, was the fact that those moved out of areas slated for renewal were the city's

14. The literature on creating a sense of urban community is extensive. With a sense of community, public areas are watched over and protected by those who live nearby. Jane Jacobs (e.g., 1961) is perhaps the most influential writer on the subject. In related areas, Oscar Newman (1972) has written on public housing designed to engender a sense of community and tenant caring, and Kirkpatrick Sale (1980) and Lewis Mumford (especially 1961, chs. 5 and 6) have written on the human scale in cities.

15. Chapters 15–17 reconsider several federal programs such as urban renewal, filling in some of the details merely sketched here. But the perspective in these later chapters changes explicitly to one of urban finance and service delivery, examining how federal funding sources complement local funding sources as cities attempt to pay for the services they provide their citizens.

poorest residents. And quite likely, they were black as well. Those displaced were not going to be welcome in white neighborhoods. And threats were in the air that force would be used to keep displaced blacks away (Kaplan 1963, Henig 1985, ch. 6).

Still another issue roiled the waters of a proposed urban renewal project: What would replace the old slum area? In most cities (and Chicago was typical), run-down areas border the central business district (CBD). To the business groups that dominated the CBD (department stores, hotels, restaurants, office buildings, theaters) and to business-oriented interest groups (e.g., the chamber of commerce, the board of realtors, and newspapers), the answer was obvious: Rebuild and revitalize the CBD (Sanders 1980, Mayer 1978, chs. 5-7).

Their arguments were difficult to assail. Chicago depended on the CBD—the famed Loop—for its economic good health and for its sense of civic identity. Moreover, if the city was to stop losing its middle class to the suburbs, it would need to upgrade close-in neighborhoods and attract the middle class back toward the CBD (Sanders 1980, Mayer 1978, chs. 5-7).

The issues and arguments of urban renewal in Chicago were typical of what went on in other cities. However, their resolution in Chicago was much more decisive—thanks to the power of Chicago's political machine. Urban renewal would concentrate first on downtown renewal, and if it extended into residential neighborhoods, it would be mostly confined to black neighborhoods. (That, of course, is what we encountered in the earlier discussion of New Haven's urban renewal.)

Nationwide, and in about a decade (from 1950 to 1960), urban renewal tore down about 126,000 housing units, most of which were substandard. Using this measure, supporters give high marks to urban renewal. But fewer than 30,000 housing units replaced those torn down, and of these, relatively few were low-income, public-housing units. As is often the case with government policy that combines antithetical purposes, urban renewal has had paradoxical outcomes. Initiated with liberal intentions to further social equity, urban renewal ended by becoming what economist Martin Anderson (1964) has called "the federal bulldozer." It decreased the stock of housing available to the nation's poor; it sent black families from poor housing into poorer and even more overcrowded housing; it expanded the nation's reliance on filter-down housing; it rebuilt the CBD; and—paradox on paradox—it enriched the private real estate industry.

The Johnson Presidency (1963–1968)

Lyndon Johnson's presidency coincided with a time of turbulent, mass-action politics: student takeovers of college campuses, demonstrations against the Vietnam War; protests and marches against hunger in America; and marches, sit-ins, sit-downs, and lie-ins to overturn racial segregation in the South and racial insults in the North. The Johnson presidency also provided leadership for two far-reaching packages of legislation—the civil rights acts of 1964 and 1965 and a variety of legislative actions widely known as the Great Society Program. Both had profound effects on the cities.[16]

Cause and effect in policy-making can be traced only with uncertainty. Policy proposals do not rise high on the legislative agenda until public attention turns them into issues. And issues do not get translated into policy until they can command a significant measure of public support. Thus, the marches and protests of the early 1960s no doubt helped set the stage for the civil rights acts of 1964 and 1965 and the Great Society Program.

Especially important for the civil rights acts was the role played by television in arousing the conscience of the nation against racial discrimination. Beginning with television coverage of the bus boycott by blacks in Montgomery, Alabama, in 1955-56, viewers nationwide came into visual contact with racial segregation in the South. And what began as more or less detached curiosity turned into public dismay and mounting anger as the camera eye caught scenes of peaceful civil rights marchers knocked to the ground by fire hoses and attacked by police using clubs, cattle prods, and dogs.

What was being protested was an iron-bound discrimination in the South: laws that required blacks to ride at the back of trains and buses, use separate toilets and drinking fountains and confine themselves to separate waiting rooms in public places, stay out of all-white restaurants, marry only blacks, and enroll only at all-black schools and colleges. Equally important was a network of laws and customs (backed by threats of violence) that excluded blacks from voting. In the North, as an aroused national conscience was becoming increasingly aware, segregation was based primarily on social practice, not law. But custom was almost as effective as law in creating all-black neighborhoods, and all-black primary and secondary schools. (See chapter 17 for a discussion of the impact of residential segregation patterns in the North.)

The Civil Rights Acts of 1964 and 1965

> The vote is the most powerful instrument ever devised by man for breaking down injustice and destroying the terrible walls which imprison men because they are different from other men.
> Lyndon Johnson
> Address on voting rights, August 6, 1965

The Civil Rights Act of 1964 and the Voting Rights Act of 1965 were the most comprehensive attempts by the national government in a hundred years (since

16. Even after two decades, the Great Society Program continues to stir controversy. Critics hold that it promised much and delivered too little, and that public disillusionment with "liberal social engineering" brough forth the Reagan era's conservatism (e.g., Murray 1984). But many others disagree (e.g., Levitan and Taggart 1976, Schwartz 1983).

the post Civil War's Reconstruction era) to make good on the promises of the Fourteenth and Fifteenth Amendments to the Constitution. Among their many provisions, they guaranteed blacks equal access to public accommodations and equality of employment opportunities. They required all state officials to administer registration and voting laws in a nondiscriminatory manner (banning discriminatory literacy laws as a condition of voting), and they authorized the U.S. district courts to suspend, where necessary, local registrars from office and to appoint federal examiners to supervise the election process.

Old practices and reigning social outlooks die hard, and the transition from a color-biased society to a color-blind society is far from complete. Nor have the great changes of the past twenty-five years come easily. (Constant litigation, as we shall presently see, has been part of this transition.) Among the important consequences of the civil rights acts of 1964 and 1965 has been the coming to political office of black city officials all across the country and the belief of black and other minorities that in city politics, as elsewhere, participation is a key to social and political change (e.g., see Stanley, 1987, for a discussion of black electoral mobilization in the South). But electoral equality does not necessarily translate into social equality. Or put differently, the dominant market emphasis of our political tradition couples with the power of the business entrepreneur to make it likely that, left to their own initiatives, cities will develop agendas and policies promoting economic development in the private sector over social development for the poor (Bolland and Selby 1988). Aware of these realities, the federal government pushed forward the programs of the Great Society.

The Great Society

Ever since Franklin Roosevelt, presidential speechwriters have strained to create the *magic phrase* that captures popular imagination, commands voter support, and remains fixed in public memory. Lyndon Johnson's speechwriters hoped that they had discovered the magic phrase when the president declaimed in a New York speech on May 28, 1964:

> So I ask you tonight to join me and march along the road to the future, the road that leads to the Great Society.

As Johnson and his advisors saw it, the Great Society would go the New Deal one deal better. It would be guided by the polestar of liberal aspiration, equality of outcomes. And guided by that aspiration, from 1963 to 1967, Congress legislated over a hundred new programs, including food stamps, Medicaid, regional and local health facilities, elementary and secondary school assistance, and Appalachian regional development. At the center of the Great Society were two programs directly concerned with cities: the War on Poverty and the Model Cities Program. For the first time in the long development of national policy, city problems were proclaimed a matter of national public policy. (Previous programs had addressed city problems, but only indirectly. They aimed at helping those who lived in cities, not cities per se.) And even more of a departure from the past, the War on Poverty and the Model Cities Program did what no national legislation had ever done before. They gave the poor a direct voice in government programs intended to afford them a better life.

The War on Poverty. The War on Poverty was launched with the Economic Opportunity Act (EOA) of 1964. Floated with appropriate rhetoric ("For the first time in our history it is possible to conquer poverty. . . .") the EOA was committed to a theory of social causation that saw poverty as *structural* rather than personal. This theory holds that the causes of poverty do not lie with the person (as a result of such factors as lack of ambition or bad luck); rather, it asserts, the poor are victims of the society that has created the circumstances of poverty—bad housing, poor education, prejudicial hiring practices, poor health care, and so on. Structural conditions help foster a culture of poverty wherein poverty gets passed from one family generation to the next (e.g., Ryan 1976, Piven and Cloward 1971).

Thus, the War on Poverty was fought not only by giving material benefits to the poor (e.g., food stamps, school lunches), it was also fought by attempting to pull the poor out of their culture of poverty. The Head Start Program provided pre-kindergarten schooling for poor children so they would be better prepared for first grade. The Upward Bound Program encouraged poor children to set their sights on college by means of special counseling and by visits to and study on college campuses. The Adult Workshops Program taught job applicants the importance of good work habits, and similar programs created job workshops to teach employable skills. Volunteers of the Vista Program (a domestic counterpart to the Peace Corps) went to the inner city to assist the poor toward managing their daily lives better; and lawyers in the Legal Services Program set up storefront offices to help the poor thread their way through government bureaucracies, claim legitimate welfare benefits, and (in many instances) protect themselves from predatory landlords and police harassment.

In what turned out to be two of the most controversial aspects of the War on Poverty, state and city governments were bypassed in favor of direct links between federal agencies and the urban poor, and the poor were given a direct voice in managing poverty programs through the Community Action Program (CAP).

The Community Action Program required the establishment of Local Community Action Agencies that would make decisions dealing with coordination of

the delivery of services in their [local] neighborhoods, make decisions regarding the specific mix and style of programs undertaken, and provide the poor with a greater sense of involvement and commitment. (Henig 1985, 103)

Providing the poor with a sense of involvement and commitment was in keeping with a theory of structural poverty and its concern to break the poor free of their culture of poverty. (To take charge of one's own life, to acquire a sense of one's own efficacy is, after all, the embodiment of the self-reliant person, able to rise above structural constraints.) And to this purpose, the law creating CAP had mandated "maximum feasible participation" by all those benefiting from the program—which was translated by the program's implementers into a requirement that representatives of the poor serve as voting members of Local Community Action Agencies—LCAAs (Moynihan 1969a).

Just who found their way onto the governing boards of LCAAs is still a matter of controversy. The method used for putting "people's representatives" onto the LCAAs varied widely. Elections were a common method, but even more common was low voter turnout. Most observers conclude that those who served on the LCAA's were not typical of the urban poor, but were "poverty entrepreneurs" who used entry into the LCAA as foothold for entry into other enterprises (e.g., the permanent bureaucracy, politics, and business—especially the business of operating job workshops paid for by the War on Poverty). On these terms, CAP may not have given most of the urban poor a sense of control over their lives, but it did provide opportunity for many to rise up the social and economic ladder.

As to bypassing state and local governments, Dennis Judd (1988, 316) reckons that

> of all community action funds spent by OEO by 1968 only 25 percent were given to public agencies at all, the remainder going to private organizations, including universities, churches, civil rights groups, settlement houses, family service agencies, United Funds, or newly established nonprofit groups.

Understandably, city officials and city politicians were upset by the presence of and funding for LCAAs. Not only did they bypass the city's fiscal structure, they were creating a new group of politically important persons, operating outside the ordinary arrangements of city politics.

A number of critics viewed CAP (in fact, the whole War on Poverty) as an attempt by the Johnson administration and Democrats in Congress to strengthen voter support for the Democratic party by binding blacks and the urban poor to the party more tightly than ever before. Other critics voiced concern that the tenor and style of the War on Poverty enhanced a Marxist sense of class struggle in our country by imparting to the poor a conviction that their condition was chiefly a consequence of the structure of society—a structure created and controlled by the political and economic upper class.[17]

17. An accessible polemic setting out the thesis of the American class struggle is Cohen and Rogers (1983).

This criticism was fueled by a workbook for local policy implementers issued by the Office of Economic Opportunity. This workbook noted the concept of class struggle, and it spoke to an idea then favored by advocates of reconstructive change: Useful change is facilitated by deliberately invoking conflict, and it is more speedily accomplished through confrontation with government authorities and institutions that protect the status quo.[18] Still other critics voiced concern that CAP had created a government outside the government, one that worked at cross-purposes with mayors and councils and undercut their authority.

In light of all such criticisms and concerns, a 1965 resolution by the United States Council of Mayors is understandable.

> Whereas, no responsible mayor can accept the implications of the Office of Opportunity Workbook that the goals of this program can be achieved by creating tensions between the poor and existing agencies and by fostering class struggle. . . . Now THEREFORE BE IT RESOLVED that the Administration [of President Johnson] be urged that. . . any policy. . . be fiscally responsible to local officials. (Quoted in Judd 1988, 318)

Shortly thereafter, Congress legislated to rein in OEO's poverty warriors and blunt their lances. Henceforth, all OEO agencies would be required to work with elected city officials and their administrative departments.

Model cities. Mindful of the whirl of uncoordinated activities that marked the work of LCAAs, a President's Task Force on Urban Problems (appointed in 1965) recommended a concerted effort on selected areas within a few, selected cities. The objectives were:

> to completely eliminate blight in the designated area, and to replace it with attractive, economical shelter . . . [thus changing] the total environment of the area affected, with ample provisions of public facilities, schools, hospitals, parks, playgrounds, and community centers. (Haar 1975, 296)

In this way, the selected areas would serve as path-breaking experiments, demonstrations for future urban programs.

These were ambitious goals, and the Demonstration (Model) Cities Act of 1966 contained the following words:

> The Congress hereby finds and declares that improving the quality of urban life is the most critical domestic problem facing the United States. (Public Law 89-754, 89th Congress)

---

18. See Horton (1966) and Saxton and Kaufmann (1971) on conflict theory.

But between the ambitions of the president's task force and the realities of congressional politics, several important changes were made in the Model Cities Program. First, and as might be anticipated, few members of Congress were willing to support a program that omitted important cities in their districts. Thus, the legislation was extended to invite the participation of every city in the United States. (By late 1967, sixty-three cities had been awarded Model Cities planning grants.) Second, and mindful of the tension between city officials and LCAAs, Model Cities implementers (located in the recently created Department of Housing and Urban Affairs) made it a point to require that every city's demonstration agency be closely connected to the decision-making power of elected city officials.

The funding for the Model Cities program was generous. The federal government would contribute 80 percent of each city's matching contribution to all other federal grants being used in the demonstration area. And cities would have considerable discretion in using federal "demonstration dollars." Thus, a city might use federal money in place of its required contribution to a grant-in-aid, or it might underwrite projects not federally funded, but needed by the city—such as improving refuse collection or playground equipment.

Given this funding arrangement, and given, too, Model Cities' provision for control by elected officials, two results were likely—if not inevitable. First, participation by residents of targeted areas was far less than under the Poverty War's Community Action Program. And second, city officials were understandably given to spending Model Cities money less on services for the poor and more for such established city services as schools, police, sewage, and sanitation.

Congress had appropriated $1 billion for the first three years of Model Cities. This was a great deal of money, but not an enormous sum considering that it was to be spread over sixty-three cities. (By way of comparative perspective, it is estimated that in a single year, 1968, $2 billion was spent on a single "federal program," the Vietnam War.)

Overall, Model Cities promised much but delivered relatively little. Urban services were assisted, and targeted areas were improved. But slums remained slums, and the quality of life in the inner cities was not much altered. After the rhetoric of the War on Poverty—and with the foundering of the Vietnam War—a mood of cynicism swept the nation. And given the investment of money and emotion in the War on Poverty and the Model Cities Program, the mood of the country seemed to be reflected in a slogan that was to become a rallying point for economic conservatives during the next two decades: "You can't solve problems by throwing money at them."[19]

19. However, Levitan and Taggart (1976, 1981) have argued quite persuasively that the War on Poverty and the Model Cities Program accomplished far more than they are usually given credit for.

The Nixon and Reagan Presidencies (1969–1974, 1981–1988)

All in all, the Great Society period was a time of rising federal aid to cities. Compared with federal programs for nonurban areas, federal assistance to cities

 led to increases in the level of assistance. . .at a rate five times greater than increases in funds for non-urban areas. . . . The Great Society marked the time when urban areas first received from the federal government a level of assistance approximately proportional to their population. (Brown, et al. 1984, 15)

But the change in public mood signaled by the election of Richard Nixon ushered in a new approach to federal spending on cities. Ever since Franklin Roosevelt, a mainstay of the major conservative tradition has been mistrust of national power and a yearning for the old federalism, in which power and policy initiatives lie with the states. Some of this yearning is rooted in fears of an overly powerful national government. Some is rooted in a conservative tradition that dislikes social experiments. (State governments, historically, have not been much given to social experiments.) And still another source of this yearning is rooted in economic self-interest, tied to the fact that, also historically, states have been less willing than the national government to interfere with private-sector economics.

But whichever tradition of conservatism most animated them, both President Nixon and President Reagan (as did President Eisenhower before them) spoke of turning back the rising tide of government, "getting the national government off our backs and out of our pocketbooks." It is in this context that we can understand the Nixon program for an altered federalism, to be accomplished through a program of revenue sharing.

Revenue Sharing and Block Grants

The Nixon version of federalism (he, too, called it a *new* federalism) was built on the idea of "sorting out" the functions of government. The national government, said the president, ought to do what it does best: raise money and distribute it to state and local governments to do what they do best—solve state and local problems. Thus, federal revenues were to be shared with state and local governments and given directly to general-purpose governments— not the special-purpose agencies and authorities that had proliferated under the Johnson presidency.

General revenue sharing began with the State and Local Fiscal Assistance Act of 1972, with Congress appropriating about $30 billion over five years to about 39,000 units of general-purpose local government (Brown, et al. 1984, 27). The act gave mayors and councils a good deal of discretion in spending the money they received. And for the first time, "all subnational

general-purpose governments were made part of the federal aid system."
(Brown, et al. 1984, 27).

Two other revenue-sharing acts followed. Both were *block grants,* a concept that took revenue sharing a further step. The Housing and Community Development Act (1974) was a watershed in the development of federal grant programs directly aiding the cities" (Brown, et al. 1984, 27).

The act consolidated into a single block seven ongoing grant-in-aid programs, including Urban Renewal, Model Cities, water and sewer facilities, open spaces, rehabilitation loans, and public facilities loans. Unlike previous grants-in-aid, the new block grants required no matching funds from the receiving cities, and to qualify for block grants, city officials had only to demonstrate to the Department of Housing and Urban Development that plans for using the funds were consistent with the city's needs.

The Comprehensive Employment and Training Act of 1973 (CETA) ran administratively parallel to the Housing and Community Development Act. CETA funds could be also be used with considerable discretion by local elected officials. In its purposes, CETA now replaced the Great Society programs that provided job counseling and training and on-the-job work experience. Equally important, CETA programs were to be administered by elected local officials (Franklin and Ripley 1984).

With Community Development and CETA grants firmly in the hands of elected city officials, traditional city politics came to the fore. Federal funds were spent more for traditional city services than on services for the poor (not because elected officials were indifferent to the needs of the poor, but usually because nearly every city is constantly short of money for basic city services). And in many cities, the CETA program was turned from job training into public-works employment. For instance, cities used the better-educated CETA trainees as substitute help in city departments, and they used younger, less-educated trainees for general maintenance and clean-up work.

In a study of the uses of Community Development funds, Brown et al. (1984) found that the framework of a city's government and the traditions of its politics were the determining factors in the use of this money. For example, in Boston, Detroit, New York, and Chicago, it was the politically potent mayor (and his upper-level administrators) who was chief decision maker. In Detroit, the funds were used by the mayor to build political support among neighborhood groups by favoring them with neighborhood improvements. And in Los Angeles, city council members used the funds to build personal political coalitions.

The Reagan presidency brought no major innovations to federal-city relationships. President Reagan's economic policies used tax cuts and monetary controls as instruments of economic management. These, along with increased national defense spending and a zooming government deficit, have made less federal support available for cities. Thus, cities have been learning—often painfully—to make do with less federal money. But this does not mean that cities have slipped the bonds of involvement with the national government. Even with a falling off of federal funds, cities are more than ever bound to national policy through forty years of Supreme Court decisions.

The Supreme Court's Urban Policies

The United States Supreme Court has been a major actor in creating policies that directly affect the cities. Most such policies are those involving racial and ethnic discrimination, and they come mainly from the Court's interpretation of the Fourteenth Amendment, which reads in part:

> No State shall make or enforce any law which shall abridge the privileges and immunities of Citizens of the United States; nor shall any State deprive any Person of life, liberty, or property without due process of law; nor deny to any Person within its jurisdiction the equal protection of the laws.

Cities, as agents of their states, thus come under the provisions of the Fourteenth Amendment.

Supreme Court rulings have affected cities directly and indirectly in a number of different areas: law enforcement protocols and the rights of the accused, zoning and residential segregation, protocols for the targeting and delivery of municipal services, school desegregation, and affirmative action in hiring practices. This chapter sketches several of these rulings and their broad implications for urban public policy. Details must wait for chapter 17, however, which discusses race, poverty, and the delivery of municipal services.

Housing Patterns and Residential Segregation

Since the early years of the century, the courts have permitted cities to practice land-use planning through the enactment of zoning ordinances. Using these ordinances, cities have been able to designate certain areas as "industrial," others as "commercial," and still others as "residential." Within these broad divisions, cities are permitted to designate subdivisions, for example, "light-industrial" versus "heavy industrial" and "single-family residential" versus "multi-family residential." One obvious purpose of zoning is the control of traffic flow. Another is planning for expansion. But perhaps the most important single purpose is the preservation of property values for homeowners. [The theory of life style and territory] (Imagine how the value of housing in a residential neighborhood would plummet if a steel mill or a prison were to locate across the street.)

308

But with this latter purpose comes the possibility that minority rights will be abridged. For example, a city might invoke any number of rules and provisos in its zoning code, permitting only large, single-family dwellings on large lots in one area of town, modest-sized single-family dwellings in another, and small houses and apartments in others. The result maximizes the preservation of housing values; but it also leads to class (and often racial) segregation. In some cases, in fact, zoning ordinances have been little more than thinly veiled racism.

The Black Jack case is instructive. In 1970, the Federal Home Administration (FHA) approved a federally subsidized housing project to be located in Black Jack, Missouri, an unincorporated area of three thousand people (93 percent of whom were white) located near St. Louis. Sponsored by the Inter-Religious Center for Urban Development, the project was to contain 108 two-story racially integrated townhouses in an area that had been previously zoned for multifamily units.

Residents of Black Jack were angered by the proposal. Some spoke openly of their fears of bringing another Pruitt-Igoe to their neighborhood; others confessed even more openly of their fear of black intrusion. The residents petitioned the county commissioners for legal incorporation of Black Jack. The incorporation was granted and (as might be anticipated) the newly formed city council of the new town of Black Jack enacted a zoning ordinance that would keep new multiunit dwellings out of the city. As might be further anticipated, the zoning ordinance was challenged in the courts by the Inter-Religious Center and a number of outside groups pledged to the principle of racial integration. Thus, the Black Jack case was transformed from an issue of local politics to one of national importance.

In 1974, the U.S. Court of Appeals ruled against the city in favor of the plaintiffs,[20] and the Supreme Court denied petitions for appeals.[21] But meanwhile, the time allotted for funding the proposed project had run out. Thus, Black Jack had its victory after all.[22] (On the Black Jack case, see Danielson 1976 and Kirby et al. 1982.)

Similar cases—involving both zoning and other exclusionary practices—have risen in federal courts all across the country. In cases where it could be demonstrated that zoning was clearly an exercise in racial discrimination, the courts struck down local ordinances. But in other cases, the courts

20. *United States v. City of Black Jack, Missouri* (508 F2d 1179).

21. 442 US 1042, 1975; 443 US 884, 1975. In a related decision, the court awarded the developer $450,000 in damages (Park View Heights Corp. v. City of Black Jack, 467 F2d 1208, 1972).

22. Winners and losers in this case had an old principle of politics reaffirmed: Take every case to court. Sometimes the court will be on your side; sometimes not. If you lose, appeal to a higher court. And if enough time goes by, your opponents may run out of energy, or money, or both.

determined that while zoning which excluded multiple-family, low-rent housing might have the indirect effect of excluding minorities and the poor, that effect was only incidental to the legitimate function of zoning as an exercise of a city's powers to zone for aesthetic and property-value uniformity.

School Desegregation

Although the Fourteenth Amendment was ratified in 1868, for three quarters of a century the Supreme Court gave it only the most timid reading, preferring to let social practice and state discriminatory laws stand.[23] Then, after World War II (fought, after all, in democracy's cause) the Court began interpreting the amendment more vigorously. Several decisions struck down blatantly discriminatory housing practices. But no plain reading has had greater impact on cities than the Court's new approach to state-mandated school segregation. The bombshell case was the now-famous *Brown v. The Board of Education of Topeka*.[24] In that case, the Supreme Court overturned what had been an undemocratic and unhappy fixture of American life, the legality of state laws that provided for separate education for blacks and whites. Such separation, said the Court, in its *Brown* ruling, "had hung the badge of inferiority on Negro children."

> To separate them from others of similar age and qualification, solely because of their race generates a feeling of inferiority that may affect their hearts and minds in a way unlikely ever to be undone.

Then, in a subsequent case (*Brown II*,[25] it is sometimes called) the Court turned over to federal district courts the job of implementing its decision, instructing them to get on with the job of desegregating the schools "with all deliberate speed."

Public anger in the South, where segregated schools were almost everywhere the law, went quickly beyond mere indignation and denunciation of the Court. In Georgia, for example, the legislature declared the Court's decision to be null and void and of no effect in the state. In other southern states, legislatures enacted school placement laws giving school boards the power to retain segregation by shuffling students among schools. And Louisiana made desegregation by school officials

---

23. The controlling case was *Plessy v. Ferguson* (163 US 537, 1896), which announced *separate but equal* as a constitutional principle.

24. 347 US 483 (1954).

25. *Brown v. Board of Education of Topeka* (349 US 294, 1955).

a crime, placed control of New Orleans' schools in a special legislative committee, and denied accreditation, free textbooks, and financial aid to desegregated schools. (Kelly and Harbison 1955, 952)

One by one, and case by case—sometimes school district by school district—the federal courts forced integration on the South. But until the 1970s, judicial interventions had been confined largely to the South. There, federal courts had intervened against state statutes and city ordinances used to maintain segregated schools. (It was intervention against statutory segregation.) Then, the issue of segregated schools moved north. In the 1970s, the Supreme Court began hearing northern school cases, and where it discovered a pattern of segregation that had been aided by past or present schoolboard actions— even though the primary source of segregation lay in neighborhood housing patterns—the Court moved to overturn segregation, this time using busing as its instrument of implementation. "Desegregation plans," said the Court, "cannot be limited to the walk-in school."[26]

School cases in the Northeast, Midwest, and West are different from those in the South. North of the old Mason-Dixon Line, statutory segregation was accomplished mainly through informal practices such as assigning only black teachers to schools in black neighborhoods and by discouraging pupil assignments across attendance boundaries—which almost always were drawn to coincide with patterns of racial and neighborhood settlement. In practice and logic, these informal procedures could be used only in large (multischool) school districts, meaning that (a) northern cases have involved only medium-to-large cities, and (b) the busing remedy has entailed transporting hundreds or even thousands of school children across the city. Thus, the hallmark of northern school integration has been federal judges' willingness to take over (quite literally) the management of newly integrated school systems. To create a workable and judicially acceptable integration plan, federal judges have placed entire school systems into what is tantamount to receivership. They have appointed special administrators (court-appointed masters) to draw up integration plans, and they have given those masters general supervision over the school district: allocating funds, supervising teacher placement, contracting for buses and drivers, and reviewing student achievement and discipline.

The consequences of northern school integration will be examined in chapter 17. But we can anticipate that examination by noting a conjoined concern of policymakers in northern cities. The demise of the walk-in school (they believe) may further erode the sense of neighborhood as community, and parents who object to having their children bused may move to suburban homes and suburban school districts.

26. *Swann v. Charlotte-Mecklenburg Board of Education* (402 US 1, 1971).

Affirmative Action

The intellectual roots of affirmative action lie ideologically in the idea of equality of outcomes. Blacks, Hispanics, Native Americans, and women are to have educational, career, and job opportunities in proportion to their numbers in the population, and they are to achieve those opportunities through affirmative government action. Affirmative action thus links to the idea of fair shares and, additionally, to the concept of inter-generational equity (i.e., government must take action to compensate the present generation of minorities and women for the discriminatory behavior of the white, male society of generations past).

The legal roots of affirmative action lie in the civil rights legislation of the 1960s, in the executive orders of Presidents Kennedy and Johnson, and in administrative implementation of those orders. Executive Order Number 10925, issued by President Kennedy, first uses the term affirmative action: Contractors receiving federal funds were to act affirmatively in recruiting personnel. And as Nathan Glazer (1975, 46) notes:

> Executive orders, just as laws, breed their attendant throng of regulations and guidelines, which the contractor in search of government business must attend to as carefully as . . . the executive order itself. By the time we reach guidelines, the President and his advisors are far away: the permanent or semipermanent officials engaged in the program of contract compliance are the chief formulators of guidelines.

As guidelines for affirmative action emerged from administrators' workbooks and reference manuals, the details of affirmative action fell into place. Records concerning race, gender, and ethnic background would be kept; and not only would contractors be required to demonstrate that they had made earnest efforts to recruit minority workers, their record books would have to provide evidence that minorities were properly represented in the company's ranks and that recruiting goals had been achieved.

Two further sets of events now worked to complicate affirmative action. First, guidelines were extended to include all institutions and agencies receiving federal funds, thus extending affirmative action to cities. Second, and as might be anticipated, affirmative action guidelines were challenged in the courts.

Court challenges have turned on two arguments. First (said the challengers), keeping records on race, gender, and ethnic background smacks of hiring by quotas and not merit. And second, giving special treatment and special job opportunities to members of a designated group is a plain denial of the Fourteenth Amendment and its requirement of equal protection of the laws.

Affirmative action cases are of great importance to cities, particularly as they concern police and fire departments. Women have brought suit on

312

grounds that civil service performance tests are gender biased. Blacks and other minorities have brought suit against civil service written examinations on grounds that they are biased against those who speak nonstandard English, and biased also against those whose reading and comprehension have been nurtured outside the dominant white culture.

Most often, it is not individual plaintiffs who bring these suits. Rather, plaintiffs are usually joined and assisted by such interest groups as women's rights organizations, Hispanic rights organizations, and the NAACP (National Association for the Advancement of Colored People). And on the other side, often joining the defending city are municipal unions such as the Fraternal Order of Police and the Firemen's Protective Association.[27]

The upshot of these many cases is that in city after city, federal courts have taken command of the city's administrative departments. Judges supervise civil service examinations to eradicate race and gender bias and (as in school cases) they often appoint special masters to create and administer court-approved civil service examinations. In addition, judges and their special masters often set recruiting and promotion policies. In typical cases, judges have ruled that a city may not hire or promote any additional white male police and fire personnel until a court-specified number of women and minority persons have been incorporated into police and fire department ranks.

A recent case typifies. In 1986, Cleveland's Local 93 of the International Association of Firefighters sued to overturn an affirmative action plan set in place by a federal court decision of 1983. The Firefighter's case asserted that the affirmative action plan denied equal treatment to whites and that it therefore constituted *reverse discrimination*. The affirmative action plan now being challenged had been brought originally by an organization of black and Hispanic firefighters (called the Vanguards) who had charged the city with past and present discrimination in hiring, assigning, and promoting firefighters, all in violation of the Civil Rights Act of 1964 and the Fourteenth Amendment. Under terms of the settlement supervised by a federal judge, the city had pledged to award 50 percent of all future promotions to minority firefighters.

The white-dominated firefighters' union appealed to the Supreme Court (*International Association of Firefighters v. City of Cleveland,* 478 U.S. 501, 1986). In its decision, the Court was careful not to define reverse discrimination, nor say precisely how it might figure into a reading of the Fourteenth Amendment. Instead, the Court (by a six-to-three vote) let the original decree stand undisturbed—saying in effect that judges are to have broad discretion

27. Recall the earlier discussion of the relatively minor role of unions in urban politics. Here is a case in point. By going to court against affirmative action, the union is fighting a battle which pits its minority members against its majority members. Such conflict will often show up later on the job; for example, race relations within many police forces are poor.

in finding ways to remedy past discrimination.[28] But affirmative action
cases—and the issue of reverse discrimination—are far from being settled.
Early in 1989, the Supreme Court (its composition changed by recent appointments) "rethought" its position on affirmative action as it applies to cities doing
business with private contractors. In a case involving Richmond, Virginia,
the Court (by a six-to-three decision) ruled that Richmond's ordinance

> similar to measures in effect in 36 states and nearly 200 local governments
> violated the constitutional rights of white contractors to equal protection of
> the law. (*City of Richmond v. J.A. Crosson Co.,* 102 L.Ed. 2nd 854, 1989)

The Richmond ordinance required that 30 percent of all city contracts be
reserved ("set aside") for minority-owned business firms. But, said the Court,
such "set-asides" were not in accordance with the Constitution unless it could
be proved that they were a remedy for specific (and specifically proven) acts
of prior discrimination. Though the population of Richmond is 50 percent
black, and though only two-thirds of one percent of the city's contracts had
been previously awarded to minority firms (during a five-year period running from the late 1970s to the early 1980s), these statistics (said the Court)
did not prove that specific acts of discrimination had occurred. Further, said
the Court,

> An amorphous claim that there has been past discrimination in a particular
> industry cannot justify the use of an unyielding racial quota. (*New York Times,*
> Jan. 24, 1989, p. 12)

Next Steps

In these past several chapters we have traversed a considerable intellectual
distance, moving from ideal public policy, to types and stages of urban policy,
and finally to the interlocking of city, state, and national policies. To learn more
of the ways that policies are carried into effect, we turn next to the delivery
of urban services and the means for financing them.

---

28. Whether affirmative action constitutes a remedy for past discrimination and thus a form of
compensatory justice *or* a form of reverse discrimination is a thorny legal and philosophic problem. For
discussions of this dilemma, see Greenwalt (1983) and Fullinwider (1980).

Part Six

Urban Finance and
Service Delivery

The Flat Iron. Alfred Stieglitz. 1903.
Photogravure. 32.9 cm × 16.7 cm. The
Alfred Stieglitz Collection. 1949.838.
© 1989 The Art Institute of Chicago, All
Rights Reserved.

316

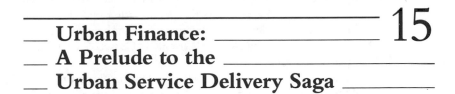

Urban Finance: 15
A Prelude to the
Urban Service Delivery Saga

Taxes are what we pay for civilized society.
  Oliver Wendell Holmes
  Compania v. Collector, 275 US 87 (1904)

Wars and economic depressions are powerful levers of social and political change. The Great Depression of the 1930s brought the national government full tilt into the welfare state and altered forever federalism's relationships among states, cities, and the national government. The Second World War was no less important as a fulcrum of social and political change. As a crusade against fascist dictatorships, it helped arouse the American conscience against the racism then endemic to our society. Almost immediately following war's end, President Truman ordered racial integration of the armed services. And that same year, 1948, the Supreme Court (*Shelley v. Kraemer,* 334 US 1) ended restrictive housing covenants—designed to preclude blacks and ethnic minorities—in the sale of real estate. Two years later, the Court forbade racial discrimination in admission to law schools and graduate schools (*Sweatt v. Painter,* 339 US 629, 1950; *McLaurin v. Oklahoma State Regents,* 339 US 637, 1950), and in 1954 it handed down its dramatic decision on school desegregation *(Brown v. Board of Education of Topeka).*

Each of these events had profound consequences for our cities, and the great chain of cause and effect continues to unroll. The war production effort, which provided job opportunities hitherto closed to blacks, combined with agricultural mechanization to create a great migration from the South to northern cities by the 1950s. At war's end, with cheap mortgage money now available to veterans, the great out-migration from central cities to suburbs also began. By the 1960s, northern cities had been transformed into enclaves of blacks and the poor, so that by decade's end the urban riots could be understood—at least retrospectively—as violence waiting to happen. (Or as the Spanish philosopher Ortega y Gasset once said of violence: It is reason exasperated.)

These events and their attendant social forces have brought profound changes to our cities, not merely in terms of their racial and social composition, nor only in terms of blacks' accession to council and mayoral positions, but also in terms of the city's role as *provider of urban services.* City government, as we have observed before, exists to make life liveable for city dwellers. And particularly since the Second World War, quality of life has become conflated with the provision of city services.[1] *[The theory of urban political style]*

We will examine this increased demand for urban services in the next chapter. But first, we must consider the fiscal foundations of urban services. Then, in chapter 17, we will trace the connection between urban services, race, and poverty in the city today.

Growth and Retrenchment

Over the past four decades, the growing demand for city services has carried a substantial price tag. Municipal general expenditures, most of which go toward the provision of public services, grew by 307 percent (in constant dollars)[2] in the twenty-five years between 1950 and 1975, and by over 500

---

1. Douglas Yates (1974) argues that the "save the cities" agenda that was prominent during the 1960s (and was reflected in such programs as Model Cities and the War on Poverty) has been replaced by an agenda that emphasizes service delivery as the central issue and problem of urban policy-making.

2. Because of inflation, the purchasing power of the dollar is not the same today as it was in 1945, or even what it was last year. In times of low inflation (e.g., 1950-1960), only a minor adjustment is necessary to compare dollars. But during periods of high inflation (e.g., 1970-1980) dollar figures are incomparable without a substantial adjustment. In all analyses in this chapter, dollars are converted to a 1967 base, when the consumer price index was arbitrarily set to 1.00 (i.e. $1.00 would purchase exactly a dollar's worth of goods and services). The price index for other years of the study are listed below.

1950	.721	(i.e., 72.1 cents would purchase a dollar's worth of goods and services)
1955	.802	
1960	.887	
1965	.945	
1967	1.000	
1970	1.163	
1975	1.612	
1980	2.468	
1985	3.222	

percent between 1945 and 1975.[3] While this is a large expansion of the public sector by any standards, its true enormity can be gauged best by comparison with the federal budget. We tend to think of the 1960s and the early 1970s as a time of enormous growth in the federal government.[4] During this decade, a number of new programs (many outlined in the previous chapter) greatly expanded the role of the federal government. Yet, the federal budget increased by only 240 percent between 1950 and 1975.

Common sense suggests that municipal budgets could not continue to expand indefinitely at this rate of growth. Expansion ground to a halt be-tween 1975 and 1980, with municipal budgets (and the services they fund) in the 1980s actually retreating from their 1975 levels.

Before considering the factors contributing to the dramatic growth and then retrenchment in the provision of municipal services, we must first under-stand the sources of urban revenue and how these have changed since 1945. Municipalities have several sources of revenue, and like persons selecting food in a cafeteria, they tend to mix and match these sources to meet their preferences and needs. The first, and most common, source of revenue is taxes. Another common source of revenue is fees charged for the use of urban services. A third source of revenue is intergovernmental aid handed down from both federal and state governments. A fourth source of revenue is municipally owned water, electric, or gas utilities and municipally owned transit systems. Finally, cities have a number of other minor sources of revenue, including fines and interest on municipal accounts. The following sections of this chapter discuss each of these sources of municipal revenue, suggesting how they have changed in response to social, economic, and political pressure since World War II.

Taxes

Municipal finance is greatly complicated by the place of the city in the intergovernmental system. While the city is home to most social problems, it faces the greatest restrictions in (a) generating revenue to address these problems and (b) formulating innovative solutions to them. Constraints on problem solving come in the form of strings attached to state and federal grants to cities, and they will be discussed later. Constraints on revenue generation result from state laws and constitutional provisions limiting the taxing power of municipalities.

---

3. Unattributed statistics in this chapter were obtained from the *Statistical Almanac of the United States* and *City Government Finances,* both published by the Bureau of the Census.

4. In fact, the growth in the federal budget between 1950 and 1975 nearly rivals that encountered during any twenty-five year period in the nation's long history. Only those twenty-five year periods ending during a war (e.g., 1839-1864, 1892-1917, 1919-1944) and those encompassing the New Deal (e.g., 1925-1950) showed greater federal growth.

As noted in previous chapters, the U.S. Constitution specifically acknowledges the needs of the nation, the states, and the people. But noticeably lacking is any mention of cities. In the minds of the Founding Fathers, municipalities fell under the aegis of the states. Municipal needs were to be met through state resources, and municipal prerogatives were to be limited to those allowed by state constitutional and statutory law. The broadest interpretation of these limitations has been provided by Judge John F. Dillon, who (in 1868) explicitly delineated the superordinate-subordinate relationship between the city and the state. His opinion, which became known as Dillon's Rule and which is discussed at length in chapter 13, effectively limits the tax revenues of municipalities to those statutorily or constitutionally allowed by the state. Most states allow cities to levy taxes on property, and cities traditionally have used the property tax as their major source of revenue. Only two states—Ohio and Pennsylvania—universally allow cities to levy income taxes, although other states allow income taxes on a city-by-city basis. And most of the forty-seven states that levy a sales tax also allow cities to levy a tax on sales. But in each case, the amount of tax that can be collected by municipalities is strictly limited by state law.

Property Tax

Rationale. The property tax has traditionally been the most important source of municipal revenue. In principle, this tax can be levied against either real property (e.g., land, buildings) or personal property (e.g., furniture, automobiles, stereo equipment). Logistical considerations make the latter very difficult, however, and most personal property (with the exception of automobiles) is exempt from taxation. The rationale underlying the property tax is straightforward: real property is *real* (i.e., true) wealth. Moreover, the ownership of real property is related to (a) ability to pay a fair share of the costs of government and (b) need for governmental services (e.g., the costs of maintaining courts and records for ensuring the safe acquisition and sale of real property, the cost to government of protecting that property). And for city government, a tax on land and buildings has an additional element of legitimacy. Since the value of urban real estate is influenced much more by population density (and the market factors that accompany density) than by improvements the owner may make, the community may legitimately tax that property in order to address the negative externalities of population density (e.g., crime, traffic congestion). For further discussion of the rationale underlying the property tax, see Hale (1985).

To this day, the property tax continues to be an important source of municipal income; but its original rationale has diminished. In an age of "paper wealth" (stocks, bonds, and bank accounts), real property is no longer a measure of either personal wealth or of ability to pay a fair share of the costs of government, and the property tax is generally viewed as *regressive.*[5]

Assessment procedures. For all the mystery that surrounds property tax, it is rather straightforward. A tax assessor gauges the value of real property, based on its fair market value, and multiplies it by the *assessment rate* (typically between 25 percent and 100 percent), to determine the assessed value of the property. The owner is billed the assessed value multiplied by the *nominal tax rate* (which is set by the city and its voters, but must fall within state limitations).[6] Thus, the owner of a house whose assessed value is $50,000, living in an area where the nominal property tax rate is 6 percent, would have an annual property tax bill of ($50,000 x .06) = $1,200. The assessment rate, multiplied by the nominal tax rate, yields an *effective tax rate.*

State law may limit the effective tax rate in any of three ways. First, it may set a maximum assessment level; for example, municipalities may be prohibited from assessing property at more than 60 percent of its fair-market value. Second, it may limit the nominal rate at which property may be taxed. For example, Pennsylvania limits the nominal tax rate to 7 percent, and Washington allows 4 percent. Or third, states may limit the effective tax rate. For example, Alabama sets the strictest limits, with a maximum of 1.25 percent written into the state constitution. Table 15.1 shows assessment rates, nominal tax rates, and effective tax rates for several large cities. Clearly, both assessment rates and property tax rates vary widely across cities, with the highest effective tax rates generally occurring in the Northeast and Midwest, and the lowest in the South and the Southwest. As is also clear, effective property tax rates have generally declined since 1975.

Problems with the property tax. The property tax has had an uneven history, and municipal reliance on it has been declining over the past fifty years.

---

5. A tax is progressive to the extent that people with greater assets (i.e., the rich) pay a larger *percentage* of their assets in taxes than those with fewer assets, and regressive to the extent that this does not occur. Property tax may be viewed as doubly regressive. First, it taxes expensive and inexpensive real property at the same rate (although some suggest that inexpensive property may be taxed at a higher rate than expensive property, exacerbating regressiveness; see chapter 17). Second, a larger portion of the disposable income available to the poor is tied up in real property than that available to the rich (although this trend may have begun to reverse during recent years; see note 17 in chapter 16). Much of contemporary debate over tax policy turns on considerations related to "fair shares." However, the rationality of the debate is muddied by the fact that the underlying concepts—regressive and progressive—are veneered with additional emotive meaning, with progressive conveying the sense of progress and regressive conveying an opposite meaning.

6. The logistics of assessing personal property are considerably more difficult. In the case of real property, what you see is what you get, and the assessor's task is straightforward. But to adequately assess personal property, the assessor would be required to actually inventory all the owner's belongings and assign a value to them. In the case of automobiles, this is relatively easy. But in the case of artwork, stereo and camera equipment, and jewelry, much of which could be conveniently "hidden" when the assessor comes calling, the task would be enormous.

At the turn of the century, nearly 75 percent of all municipal general revenue was generated through the property tax, and this heavy reliance continued for the next forty years. But in the 1940s, the need for alternative revenue-producing strategies became apparent, and by 1960 property taxes accounted for only 50 percent of all municipal general revenue. By 1980, this figure had further declined to less than 30 percent. Several factors have accounted for this increasing disaffection with the property tax. One was the taxpayer revolt of the late 1970s (to be discussed in the next chapter), which reduced caps (i.e., ceilings) on property assessments and tax rates. Another was the increased availability of state and federal funds during the 1960s and 1970s (to be discussed later in this chapter). But also of importance, other forms of taxation began to replace the property tax in municipal revenue generation schemes. Figure 15.1 shows the decline of the property tax and the growth of the sales tax in the years following World War II. For the most part, this shift reflects inherent weaknesses in the property tax, which we will consider now.

The first weakness is a built-in bias in assessment rates that favor older property. Property values are not assessed every year, or even every five years,

Table 15.1 1987 Assessment Rates and Property Tax Rates for Selected Cities

	1987			1975
	Assessment Rate	Nominal Tax Rate	Effective Tax Rate	Effective Tax Rate
Boston, MA	1.000	.0120	.0120	.0784
Detroit, MI	.499	.0820	.0409	.0371
Indianapolis, IN	.150	.1037	.0156	.0423
Milwaukee, WI	.967	.0360	.0348	.0359
Baltimore, MD	.432	.0621	.0268	.0276
Philadelphia, PA	.340	.0748	.0254	.0309
Atlanta, GA	.400	.0500	.0200	.0239
Chicago, IL	.160	.1035	.0166	.0171
Houston, TX	1.000	.0171	.0171	.0244
Memphis, TN	.250	.0709	.0177	.0194
New York, NY	.127	.0933	.0118	.0193
St, Louis, MO	.190	.0537	.0102	.0214
Jacksonville, FL	.981	.0200	.0196	.0167
Cleveland, OH	.350	.0595	.0208	.0197
Honolulu, HA	.890	.0066	.0059	.0082
Washington, DC	.911	.0122	.0111	.0180
New Orleans, LA	.100	.1262	.0126	.0096
Seattle, WA	.950	.0129	.0122	.0176
Denver, CO	.180	.0497	.0089	.0116
Los Angeles, CA	.612	.0105	.0064	.0294
Phoenix, AZ	.054	.1183	.0064	.0173

SOURCE: Government of the District of Columbia (1979, 1988).

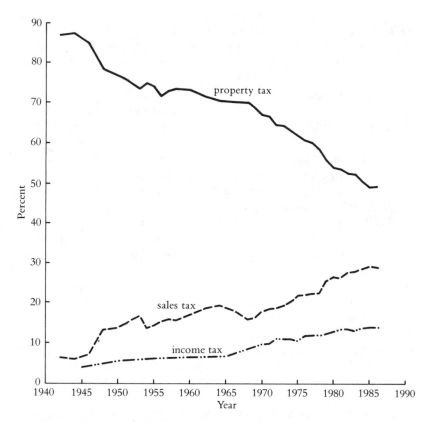

FIGURE 15.1: Percentage of Total Municipal Tax Revenue Produced by Property, Sales and Income Taxes

and as a result most assessed property values lag a number of years behind their true market values. In uninflationary times, this makes little difference. But runaway inflation during the 1970s resulted in substantial underassessment in older neighborhoods. In contrast, the value of new houses is assessed at the time of their construction, resulting in a higher assessed value in newer neighborhoods.

Second, a considerable amount of property, including that used by non-profit, charitable, and religious organizations, and by governmental units, is exempt from property taxes in most cities.[7] While the value of this property

7. The U.S. Supreme Court established this principle of exemption for governmental property in *McCulloch v. Maryland* (2 Wheaton 316, 1819). "The power to tax is the power to destroy," said Chief Justice John Marshall, meaning that if states and the national government were to be independent of one another, neither should be permitted to tax the property of the other.

initially may seem inconsequential, estimates place it as high as 41 percent of total urban property, with a value as high as $1.9 trillion. Observers estimate that as much as 54 percent of the property in Boston, 35 percent of the property in New York, and 50 percent of the property in Washington, D.C. is tax exempt (Meyer and Quigley 1977).

Third, it is unclear how property should be assessed, or more precisely, exactly what constitutes fair-market value. Is this the value that the property would bring if it were sold for its current use, for instance farming? Or is it the value that the land could bring if it were sold for a more lucrative purpose, for example a shopping mall? The discrepancies in these two valuation procedures can be enormous, and the standard chosen generally reflects the power of various lobbying groups. Realtors and land developers are powerful lobbies, and most undeveloped land thus tends to be underassessed.

Finally, the property tax is difficult to collect. Unlike the sales tax, which is collected at the point of retail payment, and the income tax, which is automatically deducted from paychecks, most people pay their property taxes only when they receive tax due (or tax overdue) notices in the mail.[8] Delinquency rates for property tax payment in major cities range between 2 percent and 15 percent (Lake 1979).[9] Most often, delinquent taxpayers are those owning unprofitable commercial property such as slum apartment buildings, and they often find it more profitable to abandon the property than to pay taxes on it. In such cases, the city usually takes possession of the property, but like the former owner, seldom finds it profitable (in fact, the cost of remodeling or razing the building is often greater than the sale value it will command).

Delinquent taxes also have a habit of backing up on residential developers, particularly in times of economic stagnation. Developers construct houses and housing subdivisions with the expectation of quick sales; when this happens, all tax liability transfers to the new property owners. But in a slow economy, when new houses often remain unsold for months at a time, developers are responsible for the taxes assessed on the unsold property (and as we observed above, these assessments on new houses are disproportionately high). When this unexpected expense is added to an already precarious cash-flow situation, many developers are unable to meet their tax obligations. Cities are left with two options: they can either seize the delinquent property, or they can defer tax payments on these properties until the economy improves. As was noted in chapter 6, cities tend to view developers' contributions to the community very favorably, believing that capital investments in the community are essential to its economic viability. City officials therefore are usually

8. This applies to owners of commercial property more than to owners of residential property, whose property tax payments are most often collected by the bank as part of their mortgage payments.
9. Quoted in B. Jones (1983).

unwilling to alienate developers by seizing their property. Scrupulous developers will pay their tax bills as soon as they are able; but a sizeable number of developers *always* seem to be living on the edge of bankruptcy, and they may carry a tax bill with the city for a number of years and never pay what is owed.

Sales Tax

Rationale. A second tax used by municipalities is the sales tax, collected as a percentage of goods (and in some locations, for instance New York City, services) sold within the city limits. As with the property tax, the tax on sales is assumed to tap one's ability to pay for services provided by the city; but it has the added benefit of tapping the resources of out-of-towners who come to the city to benefit from its retail, business, or cultural opportunities. Most states allow cities to supplement state sales tax with a municipal sales tax, although again they limit the rate of supplemental taxation. As indicated in figure 15.1, reliance on sales tax has increased since World War II, perhaps in response to growing discontent with the property tax and its faults. But the sales tax raises a different, although no less important, set of problems.

Problems with the sales tax. The first problem with the sales tax is its marked regressiveness. The philosophy underlying the sales tax assumes that purchasing power is commensurate with wealth. A wealthy family can afford more expensive clothes, meals, cars, and other goods and services than a poor family. But a family living at the edge of poverty must spend nearly 100 percent of its income on essential commodities, and therefore most of its income is subject to sales tax (except, of course, that spent on rent). In contrast, middle- and upper-income families often are able to put a substantial portion of their income into savings accounts, the stock market, or other investments, thus protecting much of their income from sales tax. Further, many of the services on which middle- and upper-income families spend their money (e.g., babysitting, gardening, legal advice, accounting services) are often not subject to sales tax. Some states attempt to reduce the regressiveness of the sales tax by excluding certain commodities from taxation, such as food and prescription drugs. But this has created considerable confusion. For example, Ohio taxes food purchased for consumption in a restaurant, but does not tax that same food if it is eaten off the premises. Thus, the consumer pays sales tax on his Big Mac if he eats it at McDonalds, but not if he eats it on the road.

Several states, in contrast, appear to have formulated their sales tax to make it starkly regressive. For example, the state sales tax in Alabama is 3.5 percent, and many municipalities supplement this with an additional 2 percent to 4 percent. But the state sales tax on new automobiles is only 2 percent, and new automobiles are exempt from local sales tax. This gives a

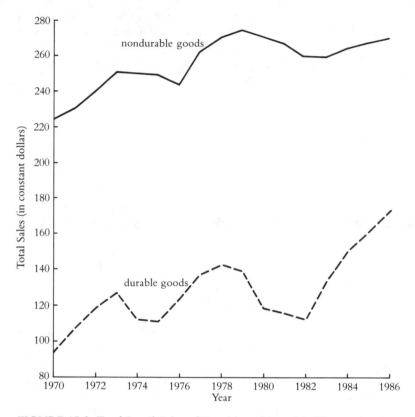

FIGURE 15.2: Total Retail Sales of Durable and Nondurable Goods

substantial tax break to people who can afford to buy expensive new cars (and today, all new cars are expensive). In contrast, used cars are subject to full state and local sales tax.

A second problem with the sales tax as a source of municipal revenue is its susceptibility to economic trends. Figure 15.2 indicates the variability of retail sales for durable and nondurable goods since 1970, measured in constant dollars. Since everyone must eat, even in economic recessions, the trend for nondurable items is relatively stable, and cities are guaranteed at least some revenue from the sales tax in good times and bad. But particularly in cities that do not tax food and prescription drugs (which account for nearly one-third of all nondurable goods purchased in the United States), sales-tax revenue depends largely on purchases of durable goods, prompted by extra cash on hand. A sizeable chunk of this revenue comes from "big-ticket" items, such as a new refrigerator, a home computer, a videocassette recorder, or an automobile. In good economic times, this type of purchase is common, and

326

the city's coffers may swell with sales tax revenues. But in bad economic times, such as 1974 and 1980 (see figure 15.2), these purchases are less common, and sales-tax revenues are insufficient to finance urban services. Any city counting on stable sales-tax receipts to finance services will inevitably feel the pinch in recession years.

Herein lies the paradox of the sales tax. If the city requires a stable source of revenue, then the sale of disposable goods must be taxed, and the sales tax becomes quite regressive. But if the city desires to reduce regressiveness by exempting the sale of certain disposable goods from taxation, it then runs the risk of unstable and unpredictable tax revenues.

Income Tax

Rationale. The third major source of tax revenue for municipalities is the income tax. In comparison with the sales tax and particularly the property tax, the municipal income tax is a little-used method of revenue generation (see figure 15.1). Even so, a number of large cities rely on the income tax as a means of financing municipal services; these include Washington, D.C., Baltimore, Detroit, Philadelphia, Pittsburgh, Kansas City, St. Louis, New York, Cincinnati, Cleveland, and Columbus. Large cities rely more on income tax than small cities do for two reasons. First, it provides a way of taxing people who work in the central city but live in the suburbs (small cities do not have suburbs). Second, the tax base for property tax is relatively lower in the central cities than in other areas, while the income-tax base may be higher. Table 15.2 indicates the strength of the relationship between city size and income tax. Cities that assess an income tax are not uniformly distributed across the country; rather, they tend to be concentrated in the Northeast and Midwest (particularly in Pennsylvania and Ohio).

Table 15.2   Municipal Income Tax Assessments by City Size, 1986

City Size	Percent of Tax Revenue Generated by Income Tax in 1986
1,000,000 or more	25.8%
500,000–999,999	17.9
300,000–499,999	10.7
200,000–299,999	9.7
100,000–199,999	3.4
50,000–99,999	4.2
49,999 or fewer	5.8

SOURCE: Adapted from U.S. Department of Commerce, Bureau of the Census, *City Government Finances in 1985-86.*

327

Table 15.3 Selected Corporate Outmigration from New York City, 1969–1985

To Sunbelt Cities		To Frostbelt Cities	
Shell Oil	Houston	Continental Oil	Stamford, CT
Atlantic Richfield	Los Angeles	General Electric	Fairfield, CT
American Petrofina	Dallas	American Can	Greenwich, CT
Harcourt Brace		AVCO	Greenwich, CT
Jovanovich	Orlando	Standard Brands	Stamford, CT
American Airlines	Dallas	Hooker Chemical	Stamford, CT
M.K. Kellogg	Houston	Ingersoll-Rand	Woodcliff Lk., NJ
Oxford Paper	Richmond	Bangor-Punta	Greenwich, CT
Warner Bros.	Los Angeles	Pepsico	Harrison, NY
MGM	Los Angeles	Uniroyal	Oxford, CT
		Union Camp	Wayne, NY

SOURCE: *Fortune*, 1968-1986; Quante (1976).

Problems with the income tax. Like the property tax and the sales tax, the municipal income tax is a flawed source of revenue. In principle, the income tax *can* be progressive, as it is at the federal level; that is, the tax rate can be scaled to income. But in practice, municipal income tax is typically assessed at a flat rate (e.g., 5 percent) across all income categories, thus making it regressive. Even so, however, it is not as regressive as the sales tax, which is assessed at a flat rate and applied disproportionately to wealthy versus poor individuals and families.

Second, like the sales tax, the income tax is sensitive to changes in the economic climate in general and to unemployment in particular. When urban unemployment rates hit 10 percent (and inner-city unemployment rates hit 20 percent), annual revenues from income tax are bound to suffer. In general, the impact of fluctuating urban unemployment is not great, since those most prone to unemployment are unskilled or semiskilled workers with low earning power. (Seldom are bank presidents or other high-salaried professionals the victims of unemployment.) Much more problematic, however, is the long-term industrial and corporate decline of many northeastern and midwestern cities that rely on the income tax. For example, when steel plants shut down in Pittsburgh and Cleveland, or when automobile plants cut back production in Detroit, those cities lose the income of many skilled, well-paid employees, as well as the tax on their income. And when New York City loses the corporate headquarters of American Airlines to Dallas, or Cleveland loses the corporate headquarters of Diamond Shamrock and Harris (both members of the Fortune 500) to Dallas and Melbourne, Florida, respectively, they also lose the incomes of a number of high-paid executives, corporate lawyers, and other professional support staff. New York has been the hardest hit of such cities, losing seventy-eight corporate offices and over 30,000 corporate jobs between 1967 and 1972 alone (Quante 1976). The most dramatic of these moves have been toward the South and Southwest; but as table 15.3 demonstrates New

York has also lost a number of corporate headquarters to the suburbs. Regardless of the circumstances of the migration, it is costly to cities that rely on an income tax.

Other Taxes

In addition to the three types of tax discussed above, cities collect a number of miscellaneous taxes. New York, for example, assesses a *corporate tax* for the privilege of doing business in the city. The present rate (approximately 9 percent) is levied on the entire net corporate income or the portion thereof allocated to New York City. But many corporate activities, including those involving major financial transactions, are nontaxable. Further, since both New York City and New York State corporate taxes are high, national companies try to keep their New York transactions (and hence their tax assessments) as low as possible. As a result, corporate taxes in New York City account for a relatively small proportion (approximately 10 percent) of the municipal tax revenue. New York City also charges a *commercial rental tax* (6 percent on all annual rent over $11,000), but this, too, accounts for relatively little (4.4 percent) municipal tax revenue. And like many other cities, New York City charges a tax on motor vehicle licenses, on the sale of alcoholic beverages, gasoline, tobacco products, and other selected items, and on the use of public utilities. But altogether, these selected sales taxes and other taxes total less than 10 percent of New York City's tax revenue (New York City Budget Office 1988). Across the country, the same trend holds, with miscellaneous taxes seldom totalling more than 15 percent to 20 percent of a city's total tax revenue. Figure 15.3 shows the breakdown of New York City's tax revenues for 1988.

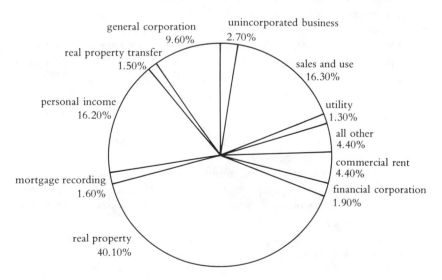

FIGURE 15.3: Sources of New York City's 1988 Tax Revenue

User Fees

Rationale and Level of Use

In addition to taxes, which are assessed more or less according to an individual's, family's, or company's ability to pay, fees are assessed for a number of services provided by the city more or less according to the amount an individual, family, or company uses them. Across all cities, fees and charges account for approximately 11 percent of all revenue, although on average, they account for only 8 percent of municipal revenue in the nation's largest cities (i.e., those over a million people). Table 15.4 provides a general breakdown and specific examples of the revenues generated by various types of services in large cities.

Cities obviously differ in the services and commodities they offer and for which they charge. Relatively few cities, for example, have municipal colleges, art galleries, stadiums, zoos, or municipal golf courses. Most do have parks and recreation departments, however, which may or may not charge for participation in municipal softball leagues or for tennis instruction. Greens fees for municipal golf courses vary widely from city to city, as do transit fares (in some cities, bus passengers ride free in downtown zones). By the same token, some cities allow free parking, while others charge for virtually every available parking space. Finally, some cities establish "benefit districts" in which residents pay special assessments for street, sidewalk, and sewer improvements in their district, while other cities distribute the costs of such improvements across the entire tax-paying populace.[10]

Ironically, even though large cities have considerably more opportunities to collect revenue for services rendered, they take less advantage of that opportunity than do smaller cities (more about that later). And even large cities vary considerably in their reliance on user fees as sources of revenue. One useful point of comparison is the ratio of revenue generated from specific fees and charges to that generated by general taxes, shown for large cities in table 15.5.

Problems with User Fees[11]

Some user fees are little more than highly regressive taxes in that they are assessed to all residents regardless of their ability to pay; these include fees for trash pickup, sewer hookup and monthly charges, and emergency 911 service. In other cases, user fees represent a means for regulating use of selective services, in that the city provides them on a pay-as-you-use basis; these include

10. Some consider benefit districts to be different from user fees (e.g., ACIR, 1985). They are combined here for the sake of parsimony.
11. A more complete discussion of both the benefits and problems of user fees is provided by ACIR (1985).

Table 15.4 Revenue from Municipal Charges and Fees in Cities over 300,000

General Area Specific fees and charges	Percent of Municipal Revenue
Education	.2%
School lunches	
Adult education tuition	
Municipal college tuition	
Charges for books	
Charges for gymnasium uniforms or equipment	
Highways	.6
Road tolls	
Bridge tolls	
Health and Hospital	1.2
Hospital charges, including per diem rates and service charges	
Ambulance charges	
Inoculation charges	
Sewerage	2.4
Sewer system fees	
Other Sanitation	.5
Trash collection fees	
Industrial waste charges	
Parks and Recreation	.5
Parking charges	
Concession rental	
Golf course greens fees	
Softball league enrollment fees	
Tennis class charges	
Day camp charges	
Admission charges to municipal swimming pools	
Admission charges to zoos, museums, etc.	
Housing/Community Development	.8
Rent from public housing	
Street-lighting installation charges	
Convention center charges	
Airport	1.6
Terminal rental	
Landing and departure fees	
Hangar rental fees	
Water Transport Terminal	.4
Parking Facilities	.3
Miscellaneous Commercial Activities	.1
Other	.7
Charges for false burglar alarms	
Fees for fingerprinting	
Leases on municipal stadiums	
Building inspections	
Licenses (e.g., liquor, taxicab, etc.)	
Emergency 911 service	
Special Assessments	.5
TOTAL	9.9

SOURCE: Adapted from U.S. Department of Commerce, Bureau of the Census, *City Government Finances in 1985–86;* Mushkin and Vehorn (1980).

services provided by the parks and recreation department, admission to municipal facilities (e.g., zoos, museums), parking in municipal parking lots, and health care provided by the municipal hospital. But by regulating services through user fees, many of the city's poor are effectively precluded from using important services.

Some cities would not be able to offer services if they did not charge for them. But other cities have found a way to avoid these fees, particularly in the area of recreational services. For example, Chicago and Newark charge no user fees for park and recreation activities, allowing all residents to participate in these activities regardless of their ability to pay. Fifteen other cities, indicated by ★ in table 15.5, use fees to fund less than 15 percent of their

Table 15.5 Ratio of Service-Generated Revenue to Tax-Generated Revenue for Cities Over 300,000 in 1977 and 1986

City	1986	1977	Form[a]	City	1986	1977	Form
Austin	1.148	.894	Mg	San Jose★	.410	.387	Mg
Long Beach#	1.141	.648	Mg	Toledo	.404	.593	Mg
Atlanta	1.081	.598	M	Seattle	.390	.482	M
Albuquerque	1.054	.544	M	Buffalo	.382	.209	M
El Paso	1.022	.498	M	Portland	.375	.386	Co
San Antonio★	.906	.396	Mg	Baton Rouge	.356	.194	M
Oklahoma City#	.900	.309	Mg	Nashville	.319	.292	M
Phoenix★	.814	.302	Mg	Kansas City	.316	.311	Mg
Denver	.652	.501	M	Tucson	.296	.288	Mg
Oakland★	.645	.456	Mg	Detroit★	.289	.317	M
San Diego#	.580	.524	Mg	Omaha#	.288	.231	M
Jacksonville★	.562	.836	M	Newark★	.288	.034	M
San Francisco	.560	.244	M	Dallas	.281	.210	Mg
Charlotte	.541	.289	Mg	Cleveland★	.271	.556	M
Minneapolis	.536	.336	M	Boston★	.249	.165	M
Indianapolis	.534	.418	M	St Louis	.249	.219	M
Milwaukee#	.520	.219	M	Miami#	.228	.115	M
New Orleans	.510	.454	M	Chicago★	.215	.152	M
Memphis#	.502	.481	M	Honolulu	.203	.233	M
Cincinnati#	.465	1.139	Mg	New York★	.185	.166	M
Fort Worth	.462	.408	Mg	Philadelphia★	.174	.148	M
Houston★	.439	.289	M	Baltimore★	.159	.229	M
Tulsa★	.432	.354	Co	Washington	.105	.089	M
Columbus★	.427	.423	M	Pittsburgh★	.048	.050	M
Los Angeles#	.427	.285	M				

a. Form of government: Mg = Council-Manager; M = Mayor-Council; Co = Commission
★ Less than 15 percent of expenditures for parks and recreation generated by user fees
More than 30 percent of expenditures for parks and recreation generated by user fees
SOURCE: Department of Commerce, Bureau of the Census, *City Government Finances in 1985–86; City Government Finances in 1976–77.*

total parks and recreation budget. On the other hand, eight cities use fees to fund more than 30 percent of their parks and recreation budget; they are indicated by # in table 15.5.

Many city services are provided for the public good, reflecting a philosophy that what benefits the city as a whole should be financed by the city as a whole, through general taxes. Such services as crime and fire protection, street and park maintenance, and trash collection obviously fall under this classification. But many argue that this conception of the public good should be expanded to include a number of other services, such as public transit, recreation programs, social service programs (e.g., day care), public health, and public housing. Even if these services are used disproportionately by the economically disadvantaged, they benefit the community in important ways. For example, recreation programs keep juveniles out of trouble. Public housing keeps families out of tenements. And public transit not only provides opportunities for people without cars to find jobs and commute to work, it also reduces traffic congestion. In other words, each of these services directly benefits its clientele. But it also provides indirect benefits to virtually all other segments of the community.

Most cities accept (although perhaps grudgingly) this view of the public good, and as noted previously, municipal funding for public services has increased steadily and dramatically since World War II. As table 15.5 shows, however, the large "frostbelt" cities, particularly those located in the Northeast, tend to embrace this philosophy more readily than their counterparts in the South and West. These northern cities tend to fund programs mostly through tax dollars rather than through user fees. Thirteen (65 percent) have fee-to-tax ratios of .35 or less. In contrast, large cities in the South and the West embrace the pay-as-you-use philosophy much more fully. Sixteen (55 percent) of these cities have fee-to-tax ratios of greater than .50, and only four (14 percent) have fee-to-tax ratios of .35 or less. Table 15.5 also shows that reformed cities have higher fee-to-tax ratios (.621) than unreformed cities (.413). This finding is similar to that reported in table 16.2, which shows that unreformed cities have achieved a much higher rate of public transit ridership than reformed cities. Both the reliance on user fees and encouragement of private means of transportation suggest that reformed cities treat municipal services as private goods, to be paid for by people who use them. In contrast, unreformed cities seem more willing to treat municipal services as public goods, to be paid for through general municipal revenue. This is consistent with the overriding philosophy of the reform movement, that cities are to be managed efficiently, like businesses. *[The theory of urban reform]*

Table 15.5 also suggests that many cities have turned to user fees to replace revenue lost to the municipal tax revolt of the late 1970s. Overall, the ratio of user fees to taxes increased between 1977 and 1983. This increase is particularly noticeable in California cities, where the fee-to-tax ratio increased

from .273 to .418 in the wake of Proposition 13, a ballot issue that capped
the property tax that municipalities in California could assess (see chapter 16).
But some cities (e.g., Austin, Jacksonville) charged dearly for services even
before the tax revolt.

Intergovernmental Revenue

Federal Aid

Another major source of municipal revenue is provided by other governmental
units, particularly the federal government. Expenditures for municipal services grew at a much faster rate than municipal tax receipts in the years between 1945 and 1975 (see chapter 16), suggesting alternative sources of
municipal revenue. Part of this additional revenue was generated by user fees
and by several other revenue-producing strategies to be discussed later. But
most of the increase was provided by federal funds. In general, since World War II—but
particularly since the advent of the Great Society programs during the
1960s—the federal government has recognized that cities are unable to solve
their problems without financial help, and as table 15.6 shows, that help
increased at a substantial rate during the 1960s and the 1970s.

Categorical grants-in-aid. During the 1950s and the 1960s, most of this
assistance came in the form of categorical grants-in-aid, tied to specific programs that the federal government initiated.[12] Very little discretion was
afforded to recipients of these grants, who were required to spend funds
according to a number of specific conditions placed on their receipt (e.g.,
expenditures were allowed only for certain uses). Further, record-keeping
requirements were quite strict, and tales of paper trails by the yard are legendary. One of the largest categorical grant-in-aid programs was the Housing
Act of 1949, which provided local governments with funds to purchase
blighted, inner-city property and sell it to private developers, who in turn
would raze decaying buildings and construct in their place low- and medium-
cost housing. A 1954 amendment to the Housing Act shifted the emphasis
from destruction and reconstruction to renovation, giving rise to the term
urban renewal. This amendment also allowed 10 percent of funds to be used
for nonresidential construction; by 1961 the allowance had been raised to 30
percent. For cities, these changes in the original law were a godsend, for
residential areas with relatively little property value (and hence little tax value)
could be replaced by more valuable office buildings, banks, restaurants, and
department stores at comparatively little local cost. (Typically, the city had

---

12. Federal aid programs are examined from a different perspective in chapter 14.

Table 15.6 Federal and State Aid to Cities, 1950–1986 (In millions of constant 1967 dollars)

| | Federal Aid to Cities | | |
	Total	Revenue Sharing	State Aid to Cities
1950	$ 128.9		$1,181.7
1955	251.9		1,541.1
1960	544.5		2,106.0
1965	635.8		2,904.8
1970	1,149.6		5,307.8
1971	1,534.2		6,101.4
1972	1,997.6		6,653.6
1973	3,283.2	1,206.6	7,283.2
1974	3,695.3	1,590.4	7,084.6
1975	3,625.3	1,369.7	8,097.4
1976	4,364.8	1,281.5	8.077.4
1977	4,912.9	1,311.3	7,843.5
1978	5,237.5	1,272.7	7,411.5
1979	4,984.8	1,150.4	7,116.8
1980	4,405.2	996.8	6,458.3
1981	4,142.1	907.9	6,240.1
1982	3,804.2	856.7	6,553.8
1983	3,574.4	827.1	6,611.6
1984	3,305.0	791.7	6,599.8
1985	3,194.3	760.4	7,170.4
1986	2,988.1	726.2	7,498.8

SOURCE: Department of Commerce, Bureau of the Census, *Statistical Abstract of the United States.*

to match 25 percent to 33 percent of the federal contribution with local funds.) But even as cities gained in revenues and refurbished business districts, they lost housing stock for the poor. Urban renewal, in effect, had become urban removal—of the poor. By some estimates, these urban renewal projects doubled tax revenue from the renovated areas (Lineberry and Sharkansky 1978). And while urban renewal money was not given merely for the asking, it was reasonably available to those cities with trained grant writers: Between its enactment and 1974, the Housing Act of 1949 provided $7 billion to over two thousand projects.

Although the best known, urban renewal was not the only federal program to provide cities with grants. During the Truman Presidency, between 1946 and 1952, 71 federal grant programs were authorized; and during the Eisenhower presidency, 61 new authorizations were added, for a total of 132 grant programs in 1960 (Walker 1981). Table 15.7 shows some of the major programs that directly or indirectly (through state government) provided aid to cities. One major, albeit indirect program, the Hospital Survey and Construction (Hill-Burton) Act of 1946, funded states to inventory their hospital facilities and needs and, where necessary, to construct public and private hospitals. Most of this money was channeled through cities, and by 1960, 4,400 construction projects had been approved at a cost approaching $1.2 billion (Bingham , et al. 1978).

Under the Kennedy and particularly the Johnson presidencies, between 1961 and 1968, categorical grant programs expanded at an even faster pace. During the Johnson years alone, 209 new grant programs were enacted, 70 of which provided direct disbursement of funds to cities (Walker 1981). These included the Economic Opportunity Act of 1964, which provided funding for such programs as Head Start and Community Action programs; the Elementary and Secondary Education Act of 1965, which provided grants to public schools to assist in the education of economically disadvantaged children; public housing legislation, passed in 1968, to provide housing subsidies; a 1965 amendment to the Social Security Act establishing the Medicaid Program, which was administered through state agencies to provide medical assistance to the indigent; and the Demonstration Cities and Metropolitan Development Act of 1966, which funded the Model Cities Program (see chapter 14). This latter program was designed to fund a limited number of demonstration projects, with awards to be made on the basis of

Table 15.7 Major Federal Grant-in-Aid Programs, 1945–1960

Date	Purpose
1946	Airport construction
1946	Scientific agricultural research
1946	Hospital construction
1946	Mental health
1947	Disaster relief
1947	Cancer control
1948	Heart disease
1949	Slum clearance
1950	Civil defense
1950	Aid to the permanently and totally disabled
1950	School construction in federally impacted areas
1950	School operation and maintenance in federally impacted areas
1954	School milk program
1954	Urban planning
1954	State and local preparedness planning
1956	Waste treatment facilities
1956	Water pollution control
1956	Library services
1956	Interstate highway system
1956	Defense educational activities
1958	Education for the mentally retarded
1960	Medical assistance for the aged

SOURCE: Walker (1981).

the quality of the applicant's proposed neighborhood revitalization plan. Once selected, model cities would be eligible to receive all existing federal grants on a priority basis. Further, to meet uncovered expenses in their revitalization efforts, these cities would be eligible to receive supplemental grants, so long as they matched 20 percent of the federal contribution with local money. In 1966, 63 applications were approved, and in 1967, another 87 were approved, bringing the total number of demonstration projects to 150. A total of nearly $300 million was authorized for these projects in 1970 alone. Yet, they were, for the most part, unsuccessful, and their lack of success points out several inherent flaws in categorical, project-based federal aid programs.

Problems with grants-in-aid. Two factors account for the failure of the Model Cities Program. First, although applications were to be evaluated on their merits, the final decisions were largely political (Harrigan 1985). Most of the sixty-three cities chosen to participate in the program in 1966 were large urban centers with representative urban problems, but several were conspicuously different. For example, Smithfield, Tennessee, home of the chairman of the House Appropriations subcommittee that oversaw the HUD budget, was chosen. Montana, home of Senate Majority Leader Mike Mansfield (and hardly an urbanized state), saw two of its cities selected; and Maine, home of Edmund Muskie, the bill's floor leader, contributed three more. Were these isolated instances, they would not count for much. But they reflected a general pattern in which the most needy cities did not necessarily get the most money in federal grants. For instance, Alabama, home of Senator Lister Hill, an original co-sponsor of the Hospital Survey and Construction Act, received a disproportional share of Hill-Burton grants. The funding of project-based, categorical grants is largely driven by a "pork-barrel" mentality, wherein a representative or a senator can parlay funded projects back home into votes in the next election.

In general, the number and variety of federal aid grant programs is so great that knowledge of what is available, skill in preparation of grant proposals, and the ability to lobby effectively for funds are often more important than need in receiving funds. For example, most federal grant applications tend to be complicated and cumbersome (as anyone who has filed a federal income tax return would expect), and they can easily intimidate those without experience in the art of grant preparation. Further, grant money tends to be awarded on a first-come, first-served basis, and cities had to get their grant applications in early before the pool of available resources was exhausted. This meant that cities needed to keep their ears to the political ground to learn of funding opportunities and prepare grant applications literally before the enabling legislation had been passed. New Haven, for example, was inordinately successful in receiving urban renewal grants (see the discussion in chapter 11). This success has been attributed not so much to need—surely

337

other cities had bigger and nastier slums than New Haven—as to the ability of Mayor Richard Lee to put together a team of grant writers and lobbyists who were skilled at pursuing federal dollars. And this same factor tends to favor professionally managed cities with strong planning departments.

A second deficiency demonstrated by the Model Cities Program was lack of federal coordination. One of the purposes of the program was to coordinate a number of federal programs channeling funds into urban neighborhood redevelopment. It attempted to accomplish this through its stipulation that model cities were to receive priority in getting related grants from other government agencies. But, for the most part, this intended cooperation never occurred, and various agencies continued to set their own priorities. It became clear that urban problems were not unidimensional, but rather multidimensional. Urban neighborhood decay, for example, was not simply a function of deteriorating buildings, but also of crime, poverty, lack of education, and a host of other social maladies that combined in complex ways to create the problem. And it became equally clear that the vast federal bureaucracy, with its various autonomous agencies and fiefdoms of power, was not capable of mounting a comprehensive and coordinated effort to address simultaneously the multiple components of the problem.

A third difficulty of categorical grants-in-aid, relevant to the Model Cities Program but also to most other programs, was their matching requirement. Urban Renewal, for example, provided cities with vast amounts of money to tear down or renovate their slum areas (although in some cases cities were allowed to count improvements for schools and parks as part of their match), and with such a carrot few cities could refuse the opportunity to apply for funds. But for each million it received in federal dollars, a city was required to put up between $250,000 and $333,000 of its own. Thus, municipal priorities were often shifted away from the development of parks or the construction of roads or libraries to the construction of office buildings and department stores.

Finally, the Model Cities Program, as well as other categorical grant programs, demonstrated the difficulties of excessive *conditionality* on intergovernmental funding. The federal bureaucracy tends to be insulated from local politics, and many of the conditions attached to categorical grants assumed that the application for federal dollars (a political activity) could be divorced from the administration of those funds (a bureaucratic activity). Yet, as noted in previous chapters, this politics-administration dichotomy breaks down at the local level, and politics tinges virtually all administrative decisions. Thus, the ability to spend grant money in a way that simultaneously addresses local problems and conforms to local political norms may be constrained by federal requirements, often leading to political squabbles and roadblocks that prevent funds from reaching targeted populations and areas at all. For example, in 1951, Toledo received federal urban renewal funds earmarked for the Chase Park project. Eleven years later, the *Toledo Blade* wrote,

> The Chase Park project may look simple on paper, but it's hard to recall a single undertaking in recent years that got bogged down in such a mass of confusions, frustrations, blunders, and boo-boos as has struck activities in Chase Park. (June 27, 1962, p. 20)[13]

Stinchcombe (1968) argues that the project failed largely because of political squabbles it raised.

As another example, Oakland began a $23-million federally funded economic development project in 1966, but within three years only $3 million had been spent and few project goals had been realized. Pressman and Wildavsky (1973) conclude that this failure was largely due to the inappropriate segregation of bureaucratic and political activities resulting from flaws in the grant administration process.

Block grants. Problems associated with grants-in-aid contributed to the emergence of alternative federal funding strategies in the late 1960s. One of these provided funds in the form of *block grants,* in which money was distributed to cities and states to meet broadly defined objectives rather than to fund specific projects. In principle, therefore, they were designed to maximize the discretion of recipient jurisdictions, thus overcoming one of the major criticisms of categorical grants. Further, they were allocated in accordance with statutory formulae, thus reducing the role of politics in the funding process and overcoming another criticism of categorical grants. Two major block grant programs were established under the Johnson administration. The Partnership for Health Act of 1966 consolidated seventeen separate categorical grant programs into the Partnership for Health block grant, whose purpose was to help localities develop comprehensive health plans. And the Omnibus Crime Control and Safe Streets Act, passed in 1968 in the wake of the urban riots, established a block grant to assist state and local governments in the development of innovative crime control programs.

Problems with block grants. The Safe Streets block grant is worth careful consideration (see Palley and Palley 1981 for a thorough discussion), for the obstacles it encountered are typical of those encountered by other block grant programs, and they demonstrate a major weakness of the block grant philosophy. The Safe Streets Act established the Law Enforcement Assistance Administration (LEAA), which was charged with three major responsibilities: (a) encourage states and localities to prepare and adopt comprehensive plans based on an evaluation of state and local needs; (b) authorize grants to states and localities to implement these plans; and (c) encourage research on innovative approaches to the prevention and reduction of crime. The block grant

---

13. Quoted in Stinchcombe (1968).

provided funds to all fifty states, in two different forms: planning grants and action grants. Planning grants provided 90 percent of the funds to establish and maintain state planning agencies, with a substantial pass-through provision to local governments (i.e., although awarded to the states, these funds were earmarked for localities). Action grants provided 75 percent of the funds necessary to implement the plans at the state level, with a 25 percent local match. This arrangement was designed to provide states with flexibility in establishing priorities, and localities with flexibility in developing programs to meet these priorities.

But the promise of the Safe Streets block grant was never fulfilled, for two related reasons. First, although eligibility requirements were established, LEAA was lax in providing guidelines for program development. As a result, action grants were often applied to marginally relevant programs. For example, California spent $75,000 to study learning problems of kindergarten children, and New York approved $216,000 to fund a youth employment service project; such actions led the General Accounting Office to conclude that as much as 30 percent of the funds allocated to California and New York had been spent on inappropriate projects. Second, planning requirements were often overlooked in the allocation of funds under the block grant, and state and local plans tended to be insufficiently thought out, poorly developed, and only loosely followed. As a result, much of the allocation to localities was spent on hardware (e.g., helicopters, automobiles, firearms and ammunition, computer information systems, communication control systems, police radio equipment, electronic surveillance equipment) without concern for either need or interagency coordination (Palley and Palley, 1981).

These excesses led to passage of the Crime Control Act of 1973, which revised the Safe Streets block grant substantially. First, it strengthened the planning requirement by mandating that localities with more than a quarter million people submit comprehensive plans with their applications for pass-through funds. This requirement was designed specifically to curb the uncoordinated purchase of hardware. Second, a number of specific project grants were incorporated into the block grant. For example, the federal government would provide 90 percent of the funding needed to implement programs to strengthen public protection, recruit and train personnel, provide public education for crime prevention and police-community relations, and develop neighborhood crime prevention councils. In addition, it would provide 50 percent of the funding necessary to construct correctional facilities, centers for drug addicts, and temporary courtroom facilities. Finally, increased reporting and review requirements were instituted. For example, applicants were required to certify compliance with twenty-seven federal statutes addressing such issues as animal welfare, historic site preservation, clean air, safe drinking water, solid waste disposal, and discrimination (Walker 1981). With these changes, the Safe Streets block grant largely reverted to a series of categorical grants over which the federal government retained substantial control. It is instructive to note that the Partnership in Health block grant underwent almost identical modifications, with Congress adding 18 separate categorical grant programs as supplements and extensions between 1970 and 1976 (Bingham et al. 1978).

In spite of their flaws, block grants became even more popular with the election of Richard Nixon to the presidency in 1968. Local discretion in the expenditure of federal funds was a cause dear to Republican leaders ("get the federal government off the back of the city"), and for that reason alone the new president could be expected to support block grants. But in addition, formula funding reduced the politics of the funding process, which was dominated by the majority Democratic party in both the Senate and the House of Representatives. Thus, block grants became a way of circumventing Democratic control of the federal aid program.

In 1971, President Nixon proposed consolidating a number of existing categorical grant programs into six major block grant programs in the areas of education, law enforcement, community development, urban development, manpower training, and transportation (Aronson and Hilley 1986). Although not completely successful, this proposal did lead to legislation establishing two major block grant programs. Title 1 of the Comprehensive Employment and Training Act (CETA) provided formula funding (based on recipient need) to localities, allowing them to provide work experience, job training, placement, and counseling to unemployed individuals. Between 1973, when CETA was passed, and its termination in 1983, $56 billion in CETA funds was spent, with over 1.1 million people participating in the program annually at its peak (Franklin and Ripley 1984). Initially, localities were given considerable discretion in the expenditure of this money, particularly in targeting funds to the areas of greatest need. Yet, as with the Safe Streets and the Partnership in Health block grants, members of Congress and the federal bureaucracy soon began to fear that money was not being spent in accordance with federal priorities, and restrictions were eventually applied (Aronson and Hilley 1986).

The second major block grant program initiated under the Nixon administration was funded through the Housing and Community Development Act of 1974. It consolidated seven categorical grant programs, including urban renewal, Model Cities, construction programs for water and sewer systems and neighborhood facilities, and land acquisition programs, into a single program designed to provide local recipients with great discretion in allocating money to the areas of greatest need (see Judd, 1984, for a thorough discussion of the Housing and Community Development Act). Under the new legislation, most of the block grant funds were to be distributed according to a formula based on population, poverty, and housing overcrowding. This formula, of course, favored the largest cities, and during the first year of the program 80 percent of funds were allocated to SMSAs. In this sense,

341

the program was successful. The block grant program provided cities of over 100,000 people with a small increase in funding (2 percent) over their HUD categorical grant allocations, while smaller cities registered a substantial net decline (18 percent) in funding. But rather than increasing local discretion in the expenditure of funds, federal oversight and regulation grew over the course of the program as instances of local abuse came to light.[14]

Revenue sharing. In spite of the apparent popularity of block grants, or perhaps because of the local abuses to which they were subjected, block grants never really replaced categorical grants as a mechanism for intergovernmental funding. In 1966, before the Partnership in Health block grant, categorical grants accounted for 98 percent of all federal assistance to states and cities.[15] This figure had declined to 72 percent by 1977 (Bingham, et al. 1978), but by 1980 it was back up to 80 percent (Walker 1981). Further, not all this erosion was due to the introduction of block grants. In 1972, Congress passed the State and Local Assistance Act, which provided $30.2 billion over a five-year period in unconditional, general-purpose grants to states (33 percent) and localities (67 percent). In 1976, the allocation was extended for an additional five years at the same level. These revenue-sharing funds were allocated according to a formula based on population, per-capita income, and tax effort. And because of their unconditionality, they were vigorously embraced by the Nixon Administration.

Cities benefited greatly from the flexibility provided by general revenue sharing funds. As noted in table 15.6, these unconditional grants provided 43 percent of all direct federal aid to cities in 1974, although this figure had declined to under 30 percent by 1975 and had stabilized at approximately 23 percent by 1980. Over its first decade, general revenue sharing funds accounted for between 3 percent and 4 percent of total municipal revenues. Most cities used this income for capital improvements, for example the construction of a new city hall or a new water treatment plant. Some, however, used the additional funds to reduce property taxes or delay tax increases.

14. In its first-year evaluation of the block-grant program, HUD reported that 71 percent of funds were allocated to priority areas. In the second year, however, evaluation procedures focused on actual recipients rather than geographic areas, and the figures were much more disturbing: Only 44 percent of funds had been allocated to directly benefit low- and moderate-income groups. This abuse was particularly notable in southern states, where the Southern Regional Council concluded that "local diversions from national purpose are not just occasional abuses, but rather form a pattern inherent in the implementation of the Act" (quoted in Judd 1984, 350).

15. Since these figures represent grants to both cities and states, they do not give an accurate picture of the relative importance of categorical grants and block grants to municipal finance. These estimates are not easily obtained, since a proportion of many federal grants awarded to states are passed through to cities.

Even here, in the least restrictive of federal aid programs, the federal government imposed a number of restrictions on the expenditure of revenue-sharing funds. For example, they could not be used to match federal categorical or block grants or to retire municipal debts. Further, localities were required to establish mechanisms for citizen participation, provide audits of expended funds, comply with prevailing wage scales for construction workers, and protect against discrimination in the recruitment of various population groups (Walker 1981).

Revenue sharing continued in conjunction with block grants and categorical grants through the Ford, Carter, and the first years of the Reagan presidencies, with few substantive changes. However, since revenue-sharing funds remained fixed at 1972 levels, their importance to cities declined with the ravages of inflation (each revenue-sharing dollar allocated in 1983 would purchase only 43 percent of what it would have bought a decade earlier). Further, beginning in about 1975, increases in federal funding for cities began to decelerate. After 1980, with the election of President Reagan, the deceleration turned into an absolute decline, and by 1986 (the program's last year) direct federal funding for cities was less than 70 percent of its 1980 level.

State Aid

In comparison with cities, states tend to be revenue rich, for most levy both a sales tax and an income tax; and by the late 1970s many states were accumulating budget surpluses (Pfiffner 1983). Thus, it is not surprising that as direct federal aid to cities began to decline, states felt pressure to fill the void. Overall, state aid to cities dwarfs federal aid, as suggested by table 15.7. Although state aid is very important for the city's survival, accounting for between 15 percent and 20 percent of all municipal revenue (and between 35 percent and 50 percent of local school district revenue) during the past two decades, it is qualitatively quite different from federal aid. One major source of state aid to municipalities is federal funds that are passed through states to the cities. This, in effect, is not really state money but rather federal money that the states happen to receive as an intermediary. They often, however, have discretion in deciding to which municipalities federal funds will be allocated. A second major source of state aid is tax-sharing funds, the majority of which go to fund public education (62 percent in 1984, down from 86 percent in 1902). By restricting the taxes municipalities may collect, and by exempting different types of income and property from taxation, the state often becomes the tax collector for the city. Tax sharing is simply a way of returning some of this "borrowed" revenue, although again the state can exercise discretion in the allocation of tax-sharing funds to municipalities.

343

Other Sources of Municipal Revenue

Utility Charges

Municipalities have at their disposal a number of other sources of revenue, most of which provide them with little flexibility in their provision of services. The most important of these is revenue generated from municipally owned utilities. In 1986, for example, municipalities took in $26 billion (21.3 percent of all municipal revenue) from the sale of water, gas, and electricity to municipal residents, and an additional $1.6 billion (1.3 percent of all revenue) from transit fares. While this may seem to be an important source of revenue, it is illusory: Cities expended $28.2 billion to provide water, gas, and electricity, and an additional $3.7 billion to provide public transportation for their residents. In other words, every penny of revenue generated by municipal utilities (and considerably more) was tied up in production costs.

While this conclusion may hold for the aggregate, however, it is not completely correct for individual cities. For example, fourteen of the nation's forty-two largest cities (i.e., over 300,000 people) with municipal water systems (San Francisco, Jacksonville, Atlanta, Chicago, New Orleans, Boston, Minneapolis, Newark, Buffalo, Cincinnati, Columbus, Philadelphia, El Paso, and Milwaukee) showed a 1986 profit from their water utilities, while another nineteen showed a substantial loss. If we view this revenue as a user fee, we might conclude that it is in all cases regressive (i.e., poor people spend a larger percentage of their income on water than richer people). Further, we would view it as particularly regressive in the former, profit-making cities, where people are charged more for water than is required to provide it. By the same token, we would view water bills as less regressive in the latter cities, where general revenue dollars are used to subsidize the cost of providing water to residents. However, this pattern largely runs contrary to some of our earlier conclusions. Boston, Buffalo, Chicago, and Newark all run their municipal water utilities on a money-making basis, yet they tend not to rely on user fees. In contrast, many of those cities that operate their water systems in the red (e.g., Austin, Denver, Ft. Worth, Nashville, Phoenix, San Antonio) are among the nation's leaders in the assessment of user fees.

An alternative interpretation that is more consistent with the findings reported earlier is based on patterns of water consumption within most cities. Although residential users account for the bulk of water consumption, industrial users also account for a considerable portion of this use; and on a per-capita basis, industrial consumption is much greater than residential consumption. Therefore, cities whose water systems show a profit are, in effect, levying an industrial tax, while those whose water systems operate at a loss are, in effect, subsidizing local industry.

The discussion of city politics in previous chapters should lead us to expect that reformed cities are more likely to take the latter approach than unreformed cities, and an analysis of the nation's forty-two largest cities with municipally owned water utilities supports this conclusion. In reformed cities, the mean revenue-to-expenditure ratio is .821, with only one of fourteen cities (7 percent) showing a profit on their water systems. In unreformed cities, this ratio is .966, with thirteen of twenty-eight cities (46 percent) showing a profit on their water systems. Obviously, subsidization is one way to attract industry to a community, and these findings suggest that reformed cities may be more aggressive in these efforts than unreformed cities.

Sale of Municipal Property

A minor source of revenue is the sale of municipally owned property (e.g., undeveloped land, office buildings, housing stock, municipal utilities). Overall, this accounts for only a small percentage of a city's total revenue, with a national average ranging between .17 percent and .51 percent since 1973. Yet during any given year, it can become an important source of a city's revenue. For instance, in 1986 both Denver and Tucson received 2.5 percent of their total revenue from property sales; and in 1984 Oakland received 13 percent of its total revenue from property sales.

Fines and Forfeitures

Another minor source of revenue is the collection of fines and forfeitures, which accounted for .91 percent of total 1986 revenue in large cities. Although perhaps not the most important source of fines, the traffic ticket is certainly the best known. Some cities are legendary for their speed traps, and traffic fines are rumored to be their major source of revenue. But this is a an unimportant source of income for larger cities. Some discrepancies among cities have been noted, however, in John Gardiner's (1968) study of traffic citations issued in cities with over 25,000 people. He found some police forces to be exceedingly vigilant in finding and citing speeders and other traffic wrongdoers, while others seemed content to look the other way in most traffic matters. Nearly 35 percent of cities ticketed fewer than one-in-ten motorists during the course of a year, while another 25 percent ticketed more than one-in-four. Gardiner cites several examples of inter-city differences. Police officers in Niagara Falls, New York, and Wichita Falls, Texas, both cities with approximately 100,000 people in 1960, issued 1,245 and 10,211 tickets respectively in 1964. Police in Springfield, Massachusetts, and Grand Rapids, Michigan (both with 1960 populations of 175,000), wrote 14,720 and 36,727 tickets respectively. But the most dramatic difference is between Boston and Dallas, both cities with approximate 1960 populations of 700,000. Police in Boston wrote 11,242 traffic tickets in 1964, while police in Dallas wrote 273,626.

Dallas typically leads large cities in income generated from fines and forfeitures, with its 1986 revenue from this source accounting for 2.7 percent of its total revenue.

Interest Payments

A final source of revenue for most cities is interest payments from banks and other financial institutions. Municipal expenditures tend to be spread over the course of a year, while much of its revenue (e.g., property tax, income tax) is received in lump sums. A smart city administrator will, therefore, place these funds in interest-bearing accounts until they are needed. Because of annual fluctuations in sales tax and income tax revenues, some cities will show surpluses at year's end, which will also generate interest if properly invested. For the nation's largest cities, interest earnings in 1986 accounted for 4.1 percent of total revenues, with southern and western cities showing the largest percentage (e.g., 20.7 percent for Tulsa, 15.6 percent for Jacksonville, 11.4 percent for Oakland) and the smallest percentage for cities north of the Mason-Dixon line (e.g., 0 percent for Toledo, 1.5 percent for Washington, D.C., 2.0 percent for New York, 2.4 percent for St. Louis and Baltimore). In general, interest earnings have a greater impact on the budgets of reformed cities (7.7 percent of total revenue) than on nonreformed cities (5.8 percent of total revenue).

Bonded Indebtedness

The federal government is the only government permitted to borrow money to pay general operating expenses. Thus, municipalities are forced to pay personnel costs, equipment costs, energy costs, and so forth out of their general revenue, or with surpluses from previous years.[16] In a lean year, they may be forced to lay off personnel and curtail services as money runs out. In fact, many school districts have been forced to close their doors early in the face of budget crises, for they are not permitted to borrow money to fund their normal operational expenses.

Were this principle applied to *all* municipal expenditures, the city would never have developed as a service delivery system, for the costs of capital construction and improvements are simply too large to be accommodated within a single year's budget. For example, school construction costs are now measured in the millions of dollars, and the cost of a municipal park, complete with playground equipment and baseball diamonds, may exceed $3 million. The cost of a new waste-water treatment plant may be $50 million.

16. Municipalities are allowed to obtain short-term loans to improve their cash flow, so long as these loans are backed by expected revenue (e.g., property tax receipts).

And a new municipal hospital costs between $100 million and $150 million to construct. Clearly, the cost of any of these projects would be well beyond the capacity of most cities (*total* general expenditures in cities with between 50,000 and 100,000 people averaged $58 million in 1986, and general expenditures of cities with fewer than 50,000 people averaged only $2.4 million).

However, cities *are* allowed to issue bonds, typically to finance large, capital construction and improvement projects. And more recently, cities have used their long-term borrowing capacity to issue industrial revenue bonds (IRBs), designed to provide incentives (e.g., tax abatements, low-interest loans) for new businesses and industries to move to (and existing businesses and industries to remain in) the city. IRBs accounted for only 4 percent of total long-term municipal bonds issued in 1975; by 1980, this had grown to 15 percent, as cities competed for business and industry during a period of economic uncertainty. In fact, these incentives have become so commonplace that local officials often have to offer them just to stay in the competition for business and industry. Alberta Sbragia (1983) provides a useful discussion of long-term municipal bonds, particularly the debate over their benefits to the public and private sectors.

In 1986, municipalities issued $41 billion in bonds, and municipal bonded indebtedness totaled over $164 billion. By 1986, twenty individual cities had each accrued a debt of $1 billion or more. These include Denver ($1.1 billion), San Diego ($1.4 billion), San Francisco ($1.8 billion), San Antonio ($2.7 billion), Washington ($2.7 billion), Chicago ($2.9 billion), Philadelphia ($3.1 billion), Los Angeles ($4.4 billion), and New York ($15.7 billion). Even some relatively small cities had acquired considerable debt by 1986: for example, Pamona, California, with a population of 116,000, owed nearly $600 million in bonds; Lafayette, Louisiana, with a population of 89,000, owed $487 million; and Owensboro, Kentucky, with a population of 56,000, owed $354 million. In 1985, the bond issues of cities, school districts, and other special purpose governments totaled over $59.5 billion. And when municipal debt is combined with school district debt, total local indebtedness approaches $357 billion (compared with a 1986 national debt of $1.8 trillion).

The most common form of municipal bond is the general obligation bond, which specifies that in the case of municipal bankruptcy, obligations to bondholders will be honored before any other obligations the city may have. States place strict limitations on the issuance of these bonds, specifying how much municipalities may borrow and under what conditions. These limitations are often circumvented, however, with the issuance of non-guaranteed bonds; these may be used to finance specific revenue-producing enterprises, such as low-interest loans to industries as an inducement for location in the community. Generally, capital improvement projects, and the bond issues to finance them, must be approved by the voters, while industrial revenue bonds need only the approval of the governing body.[17]

When bonds are issued, interest rates are determined largely by the city's bond rating, assessed by one of two financial services (Moody's Investor Service, Standard and Poor's Corporation) to establish the city's credit risk. These ratings, conducted for an annual fee of between $500 and $2,500, are based on a confidential formula that employs several factors apparently related to growth and tax base. This proves beneficial to cities located in the South and West, where bond ratings have improved relative to those in the North and Midwest (J. Peterson 1981).

In recent years, municipal bonds have been attractive investments for the middle and upper classes, for the interest they yield is tax free and they are virtually risk-free. This former point means that municipalities can pay interest somewhat below the prevailing market rate, resulting in a de-facto federal and state subsidy to municipalities. The tax-free status of municipal bonds has undergone some modification with the 1986 federal tax law, however, and we will have to wait to see how this will affect the municipal bond market. The latter point, concerning risk, may seem counterintuitive to some readers who remember New York City's near bankruptcy[18] and Cleveland's actual default in the 1970s. And between 1838 and 1969 there were six thousand recorded governmental defaults on bonds. But fewer than 33 percent of these involved municipalities, and most occurred during the Depression years of 1930-1939. Since 1945, 431 governmental units have defaulted on bond obligations. But the largest defaults are by four special-purpose governments: the West Virginia Turnpike Authority, the Calumet Skyway Toll Bridge, the Chesapeake Bay Bridge (ACIR 1973), and the Washington Public Power Supply System (Leigland and Lamb 1986).[19] Even Cleveland's default, based on a $14 million payment that it failed to make on December 15, 1978, was technical in nature, for the city had already arranged to repay the loan later, which it did on February 27, 1979.[20]

17. A more recent type of municipal bond is the revenue bond, which is backed by the expected revenue from a project being constructed or a service being provided (e.g., a municipal water plant). These bonds are not guaranteed, and they do not usually require voter approval. For a more complete discussion of bonds, see Sbragia (1983).

18. The New York City financial crisis is discussed in greater detail in chapter 16.

19. The West Virginia Turnpike Commission, Calumet Skyway Toll Bridge, and Chesapeake Bay Bridge and Tunnel Commission defaults accounted for approximately $333 million. In contrast, the Washington Public Power Supply System default accounted for $2.25 billion.

20. Alberta Sbragia (1983) convincingly argues that Cleveland's was a "political default," brought about by antagonism between then-Mayor Dennis Kucinich and Cleveland's business community, including local bankers who held Cleveland's short-term notes (see note 16). Members of the business community (including the bankers) had earlier spearheaded a recall campaign against the mayor, who in turn referred to them as "blood-sucking vampires." It is not surprising, therefore, that the banks refused to extend Cleveland's short-term credit until its cash flow stabilized. Sbragia (1983,

In most cases, the urban fiscal crisis has been brought on by a declining tax base coupled with growing demand for municipally provided services. But it has been exacerbated by a tax revolt promulgated by voters during the 1970s. The next chapter explores the factors that led to the growth in urban services between 1945 and 1975, and the factors that have led to their subsequent decline.

---

83) notes "the refusal by banks to extend further credit may thus reflect not only a judgment on the city's finances but also the state of relations between the city government and the business community."

Cafeteria. Rafael Sawyer. 1936. Lent by the WPA.748.1943. © 1989 The Art Institute of Chicago, All Rights Reserved.

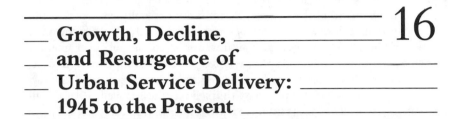

Growth, Decline, and Resurgence of Urban Service Delivery: 1945 to the Present **16**

"...it takes all the running you can do to stay in the same place. If you want to get somewhere else, you must run at least twice as fast...."
 Lewis Carroll,
 Through the Looking Glass

Four Roles of Urban Government

In discussing the relationship between urban government and politics, Oliver Williams (1961) identifies four different roles that urban government may play. In its first role, municipal government is an *instrument of community growth;* its purpose is to promote economic development through favorable public policies (e.g., the development of favorable zoning laws, support of industrial revenue bonds and other tax breaks). In its second role, municipal government is a *provider of life's amenities,* ensuring that community residents live the good life. It performs this role through its fiscal policies (e.g., funding parks, libraries, schools, and street maintenance) and its regulatory policies (e.g., zoning out undesirable industry and the poor). In its third role, municipal government is a *caretaker,* whose responsibility is to provide only minimal services to its inhabitants (e.g., garbage collection, police and fire protection, minimal levels of public education, minimal street maintenance). And in its fourth role, the city is primarily an *arbiter of conflict,* serving as a referee to ensure that the rights of various minorities are not violated.

Williams and Charles Adrian (1963), in a subsequent study, observe that virtually no city exercises any of these roles exclusively. Instead, certain groups and individuals within each city may prefer one role to the others; but seldom does one group have sufficient power to completely dictate the functions of urban governance. For example, the business community typically supports municipal government in its growth role; and as was noted in previous chapters, the power of the business community generally ensures that this is an important priority. *[The theory of urban influence and power]* On the other hand, middle-class homeowners typically support municipal government in its amenity-provider role; and again, as noted previously, the power of middle-class homeowners in most communities generally ensures that tax dollars are spent on amenities. Elderly people with fixed incomes, as well as fiscal conservatives, typically support municipal government in its caretaker role. For reasons outlined in previous chapters, both the elderly and fiscal conservatives often run into opposition from the much better organized and more powerful homeowner associations. But they are not without power, as the success of Proposition 13 in California and Proposition 2½ in Massachusetts attests. And the battles among proponents of the first three roles of municipal government, coupled with the great heterogeneity evident in most larger cities, guarantee the importance of municipal government in its arbiter role. In the end, city government wears many hats, representing these four (and perhaps other) roles. But while the roles remain constant and constantly in evidence, their exact mix varies from city to city.

Whatever the mix, however, urban government since World War II has *increasingly* become the deliverer of services to its citizens. In fact, the four roles coalesce around that common theme. For example, growth is often justified as a means for increasing the city's tax base, thus allowing it to provide better services for residents. And even fiscal conservatives see the need for and the desirability of city-operated police and fire forces, regular trash collection, and paved streets. Finally, with budgets for these services amounting to millions of dollars, even for small cities, the potential for conflict is great, centering on such issues as fair and equitable distribution of services, tax burden, and priorities for expenditures.

We can see exactly how important the city's service delivery function has become by comparing the post–World War II increase in municipal general expenditures (most of which are consumed by the delivery of services) with the increase in population during this period. If we take population as a roughly objective indicator of the need for given service levels, figure 16.1 shows that these levels (measured in uninflated dollars)[1] far outpace what would be required by population growth alone. (In figure 16.1 and subsequent figures, the vertical axis describes increases or decreases in expenditures and other trends from 1945 levels).

1. As in the previous chapter, all fiscal statistics in this chapter are calculated in constant 1967 dollars. See footnote 2 in chapter 15.

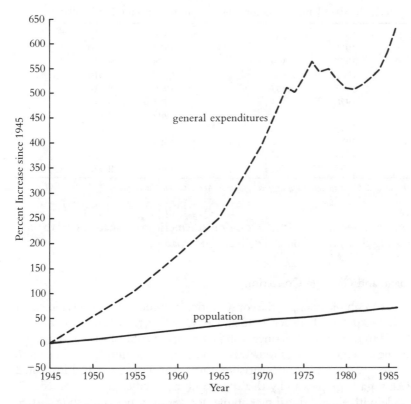

FIGURE 16.1: Increase in Population and Municipal General Expenditures, 1945–1986 (expenditures in constant dollars)

In the next sections, we will consider why service delivery so quickly outpaced population in the years between 1945 and 1978. We will also discover, however, that the growth of urban services dramatically levelled off about 1978, and only recently have begun to resurge.

Service Delivery as the *Raison d'Etre* of the American City: 1945–1978

Since World War II, a number of changes have occurred in urban society. Perhaps the most important, and the one that has triggered many of the others, is the greater affluence of the average American household. As shown in table 16.1, the standard of living in the United States improved dramatically during the middle years of this century. However, this growing affluence has had

Table 16.1 Median Family Income 1945–1986 (in constant 1967 dollars)

1945	$4,861	1976	$8,773
1950	4,603	1977	8,820
1955	5,509	1978	9,028
1960	6,336	1979	9,010
1965	7,362	1980	8,518
1970	8,484	1981	8,219
1971	8,479	1982	8,105
1972	8,872	1983	8,273
1973	9,054	1984	8,969
1974	8,735	1985	8,773
1975	8,751	1986	8,970

SOURCE: U.S. Department of Commerce, *Statistical Abstract of the United States.*

a number of important side effects for most Americans, which has led to their increasing dependence on the delivery of urban services.

Garbage and Garbage Collection

By way of a simple example, the consumption of nondurable goods increased by over 140 percent between 1945 and 1980, and in turn American families had need to dispose of ever-increasing amounts of rubbish and garbage; by 1975, the average family of four was generating 9.6 pounds of garbage *each day* (Savas 1976).[2] It is not surprising, then, that most cities had instituted biweekly garbage pickup by this time, and many cities supplemented this schedule with an additional pickup day for special types of trash (e.g., tree branches, washing machines, and other bulky items). In short, opportunity (affluence) increased demand, and demand increased service, but at a cost to consumers. In addition to increased demand, technological advancement has also made garbage collection more costly. In contrast to the modified dump-trucks that were used to collect trash immediately following World War II, all garbage trucks today have hydraulic trash compactors to increase their load. And garbage trucks come in different sizes and styles: hydraulic front-loaders, rear-loaders, and side-loaders, all designed to mechanically hoist dumpsters of various sizes and shapes. This technology makes garbage more convenient to store for the consumer, easier to load for the trash collector, but more costly for the taxpayer. In the years between 1945 and 1978, municipal budgets for trash collection (and other forms of sanitation) increased by 765 percent (see figure 16.2).[3]

2. When aggregated across urban inhabitants, this amounts to 410,000 *tons* of garbage produced by residents of American cities and towns *each day.*

3. This, and other unattributed statistics reported in this chapter, are adapted from two Bureau of the Census publications, *Statistical Abstract of the United States* and *City Government Finances.*

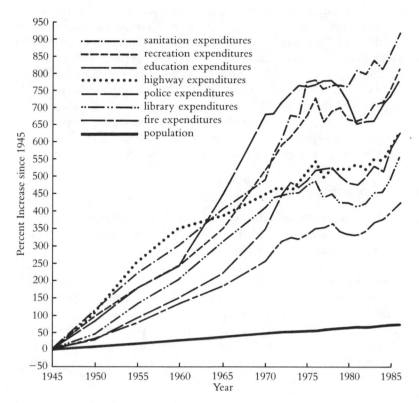

FIGURE 16.2: Increase in Expenditures for Selected Urban Services,
1945–1986 (expenditures in constant dollars)

Paradoxically, the more trash a city collects, the more difficulty it has
in disposing of it. In an effort to euphamize trash, cities have turned garbage
dumps into "landfills." But a garbage dump by any other name is still a garbage dump: It is unsightly, it stinks, it attracts rodents and insects, and it reduces
property value in the area. Several innovations have been attempted to solve
the garbage problem, some with more success than others. One of the more
creative is the use of incinerators to burn garbage.[4] These incinerators in turn

4. Another, much less successful innovation is the attempt to ship garbage away from the area
where it is collected. A case in point is the freighter *Pelicano*, which set sail from Philadelphia in
September, 1986, filled with 14,000 tons of incinerator ash. It spent more than two years at sea, looking in vain for a port to unload its cargo. Between 1986 and 1988, some three million tons of hazardous waste have been transported from the United States and Western Europe on ships like the *Pelicano*

produce energy, which can be sold to commercial customers. Today at least one hundred cities and counties have built trash incinerators, but at a considerable construction cost: For example, Batesville, Arkansas (with a population of seven thousand) spent $1.2 million; Broward County, Florida (with a population of over a million) spent $570 million; and New York City's Department of Sanitation has estimated a cost of $3 billion. While these plants may be profitable (Peekskill, New York, receives a $1 million annual credit from Con Edison, which purchases the electricity produced by the plant), operating expenses eat up much of this profit (Hershkowitz 1987). And many are concerned that the pollution produced by the incineration may be worse than the original garbage.[5]

Crime and Law Enforcement

A second (but not necessarily direct) consequence of the growing American affluence has been the growth of crime. With increasing disposable income, Americans have been able to purchase new luxuries that had never been available or affordable before.[6] For example, by 1960 nearly 90 percent of American homes had at least one television set. By the 1970s, many households had blenders, stereo record and tape players, and stereo cassette players in their cars. And during the 1980s, a growing number of homes have acquired food processors, microwave ovens, expensive camera equipment, videocassette recorders, and microcomputers. Each of these items makes our lives a bit easier or a bit more fun. But each is also easily stolen and easily "fenced" at a tidy profit for the burglar.[7] As figure 16.3 shows, crime has increased since 1945,

to countries in Africa and Eastern Europe (*Time*, Jan. 2, 1989). Others, far less scrupulous, have simply dumped their garbage at sea, creating a crisis along the Eastern Seaboard during the summer of 1988 as trash washed up on public beaches.

5. One of the inevitable emissions of garbage incinerators is dioxin, which is suspected of causing a wide range of illnesses, including cancer and birth defects. To date, no standards for dioxin emissions have been established in the United States. In addition to emissions, the ash produced by incineration is also toxic, containing dioxin and heavy metals, and its safe disposal continues to be an unresolved issue. See Allen Hershkowitz (1987) for a discussion of these and other issues related to garbage incineration.

6. James Burke (1978) argues that new technologies are often due more to social forces than to scientific advancement. Thus, the increase in leisure time following World War II, coupled with the increasing profitability to be found in new "gadgets" for modern living, may have contributed to the myriad new inventions of the post-war period.

7. When the coauthor's brother was seventeen, a cassette player was stolen from his car, and he angrily approached a number of friends for information concerning the thief. After much digging, he discovered the likely culprit to be a boy who lived just down the street. After being confronted, the thief unabashedly went into his garage and returned with the tape player, saying, "I'm sorry, I didn't know whose car it was. I don't steal from people in the neighborhood." Certainly, neighborhood ties are not always so important, and not all victims of crime are so fortunate as the brother. But the incident does suggest the importance of understanding that trends do no occur in isolation, and that in many cities, the increase in crime has been accompanied by a decrease in the strength of neighborhood relationships. Hence, the effect of each is even more severe.

reaching its period of fastest acceleration between 1960 and 1975; during these years, reported burglaries (per capita) increased at an annual rate of 8 percent (although during the following decade, they actually decreased by a small amount). This rise, coupled with rapidly growing violent crime (8 percent per capita annual increase between 1960 and 1975, with a levelling effect following 1975), has led many Americans to fear crime as the most important domestic problem facing this country.

Cities responded quickly during the years immediately following World War II by hiring more police officers (an annual increase of over 1 percent) and purchasing more sophisticated law enforcement equipment; the result was a steady increase amounting to a 527 percent rise in municipal expenditures for police protection between 1945 and 1978. Figure 16.3 shows that this increase keeps rough pace with the increase in crime during the same period, and it greatly outdistances the population increase during the same period. Between 1975 and 1980, however, municipal expenditures for police protec-

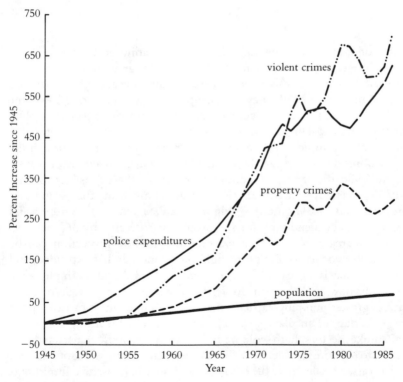

FIGURE 16.3: Increase in Crimes and Municipal Police Expenditures, 1945–1986 (expenditures in constant dollars)

tion remained nearly constant (an increase of less than 2 percent in constant dollars), only to rise again during the 1980s.

Examples of attempts to reduce urban crime abound, but each carries with it a substantial price tag. In one experiment (conducted in 1972-73), the police department in Kansas City, Missouri, increased police visibility in high-crime areas by increasing use of routine patrols (e.g., Davis and Knowles 1975). In a more recent example, the Washington, D.C. police department initiated its *Repeat Offender Program,* wherein resources are targeted toward the arrest of repeat offenders.[8] Evaluation of the Kansas City experiment shows concentrated patrols to have little impact on the reduction of crime, while preliminary results show the Washington, D.C. program to be more effective. But regardless of outcome, crime prevention is heavily dependent on costly human resources, which severely tax municipal budgets. No less important in the urban police arsenal of crime-fighting tools, and no less costly, is high-tech hardware, including sophisticated surveillance equipment, communication equipment, and computers.

Fires and Fire Protection

A third consequence of growing affluence is escalating property value. Between 1955 and 1986, the median size of a new house grew from 1,140 square feet to 1,660 square feet; this, plus more elegant interiors and other amenities, drove the median price of a new house up by 64 percent during this same period. Escalating property values have driven insurance companies to lobby for stricter municipal fire codes; and to keep insurance ratings low, many cities have invested in new and better fire-fighting equipment. Although the number of residential fires in the United States actually decreased between 1952 and 1986, the per capita economic losses from these fires increased by nearly 55 percent over the same period, just about mirroring the real increase in property values (see figure 16.4). Figure 16.2 shows that between 1945 and 1978, municipal expenditures for fire protection increased by 365 percent.

The increase in municipal expenditures for fire protection can be attributed to two factors. First, fire-fighting technology has expanded, and equipment today is more effective in controlling fires. As one example, some departments now use helicopters for rescue work. As another, modern equipment has greater pumping capacity than older equipment; it carries with it a greater variety of ancillary gear (e.g., self-contained breathing apparatus, foam, smoke ejectors, high-volume hoses); it carries more water; and it is designed to be more reliable. In 1945, most residential fires were fought with a head-on assault, which had the effect of washing most household furnishings

8. This program was the subject of a 1987 segment of *60 Minutes,* produced by CBS News.

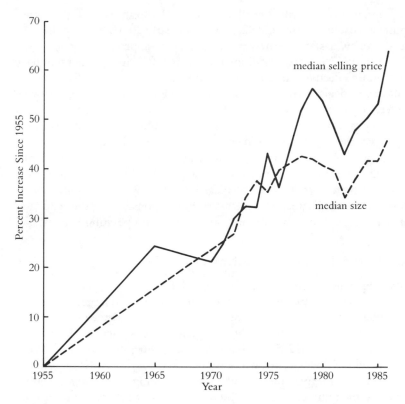

FIGURE 16.4 Median Size and Median Selling Price of Houses, 1955-1986 (selling prices in constant dollars)

out the back door, and water damage was often greater than that caused by the fire. With modern equipment, today's firefighters are able to find the heart of the fire and combat it effectively with a minimum of water damage. In addition, modern equipment is safer to drive, with more visible flashing lights to alert traffic. Finally, dispatching procedures have become more sophisticated over the past three decades. In the 1950s, these were rudimentary, relying on telephone or radio communication to alert firefighters of the location of a fire. Today, these procedures are computerized in many larger cities and are often tied into the city's emergency 911 network. Further, cities that have gone to computerized systems typically have the special needs of virtually every residence, office, or other structure in their jurisdiction cataloged in the computer; and firefighters know immediately about any hazardous material (or other potentially complicating factors) that they must contend with.

Improved equipment is costly, however. For example, a state-of-the-art pumper cost approximately $25,000 in the early 1950s ($30,000 in 1967 dollars). Today, a state-of-the-art pumper costs approximately $150,000 ($50,000 in 1967 dollars). Additionally, as fire-fighting procedures have become more effective, more municipalities have turned away from an all-volunteer fire department to a professional one (or a mixed professional-volunteer department; see Jacobs 1976). By 1980, only 35 percent of all municipalities had volunteer fire departments.[9] But even this misleads, for today all-volunteer departments tend to be concentrated in cities with under 5,000 people, and very few are found in cities with over 25,000 inhabitants; so only 13 percent of the population in the United States is served by all-volunteer departments (Bryan and Picard 1979).[10] While the shift toward professional fire departments is at least partly responsible for the reduction in fire damage, it also entails an obvious increase in operating expenses.[11]

Leisure Time and Recreational Activities

A fourth area where increasing affluence yields benefits for the typical American family is leisure time. With greater income (generated largely from two wage earners), fewer people find it necessary to work overtime or at a second job, and the average number of hours spent at work each week declined substantially between 1945 (43.4 hours) and 1986 (38.8 hours).[12] Many people spend their newfound leisure time in front of the television set. But others spend the time playing softball, golfing, jogging, or reading. As figure 16.5 shows, the number of golfers increased by over 500 percent between 1945 and 1986, and the number of adult softball teams increased by

9. Two major differences between volunteer and professional fire departments involve training and response time. Professional firefighters receive considerably more training than volunteer fire-fighters, allowing them to respond to a wider variety of situations. Professional firefighters can also respond to fires more quickly than volunteer firefighters, since they are located at the fire station. And since the speed of response is critical in controlling damage, this makes professional departments more effective. In 1979, for example, volunteer fire departments averaged $2.85 loss per $1,000 of valuation, compared to a loss of $1.05 for professional departments. Interestingly, those departments that used both paid and volunteer firefighters fared best, with a loss of $.78 per $1,000 of valuation (Bryan and Picard 1979).

10. Data showing how the composition of fire departments has changed over time is sketchy. However, John Hall of the National Fire Protection Association has been collecting these data since 1983. He finds that even for this short period, the number of volunteer firefighters fell by 8% while the number of career firefighters increased by 7% nationally.

11. A third factor in the growth of municipal expenditures for fire protection is the advent of the emergency medical services (EMS) component of many fire departments. EMS crews are trained in the provision of emergency health care, and they respond to local calls entailing all types of medical need, including heart attacks, burns, and trauma. Again, the human resources, training, and equipment required to provide EMS for the community is expensive, and it accounts for an important part of the real growth in fire department budgets since World War II.

12. These figures exclude families caught in the cycle of poverty, without any employment.

360

600 percent between 1950 and 1986. But with this leisure activity comes a substantial price tag. For example, the number of municipal softball diamonds increased by 42 percent between 1950 and 1965, and the number of municipally owned golf courses increased by nearly 500 percent between 1950 and 1986. Overall, municipal budgets for parks and recreation increased by 691 percent between 1945 and 1978; and municipal budgets for libraries increased by 451 percent during the same period. As with the increase in police expenditures, the increase in expenditures for parks and recreation is clearly in response to demand (e.g., golfers, tennis players, softball teams) rather than to the increase in population (see figure 16.5).

Transportation and Streets

A fifth consequence of growing affluence is the love affair between Americans and their cars. In 1950, only 59 percent of American families owned a car; by

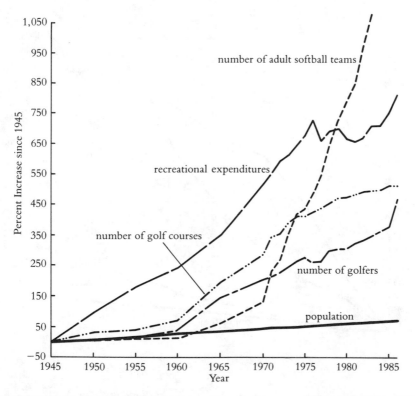

FIGURE 16.5: Increase in Recreational Expenditures and Demand, 1945–1986 (expenditures in constant dollars)

1974, 84 percent of families owned at least one car (with nearly half owning more than one car), and by 1986 this figure had reached 87.3 percent. Since the end of World War II, the number of miles logged by passenger cars in urban areas has increased dramatically, from 111 billion in 1945 to over a trillion in 1986 (see figure 16.6); during this same period, the number of passengers riding buses in urban areas actually decreased, from 9.89 billion in 1945 to 6.02 billion in 1986 (see figure 16.7). By 1974, 78 percent of all people commuting to work in urban areas drove (or rode as passengers in) private cars. The figures for 1980, broken down by individual MSAs with over a million inhabitants in table 16.2, show that only one city (New York) achieved a sizeable public transit ridership.

As a result, public funds increasingly have been allocated to the construction and maintenance of urban streets and highways during the middle years of the century. As figure 16.6 indicates, the amount of urban highway

FIGURE 16.6: Increase in Local Roads, Passenger Miles, and Highway Expenditures, 1945–1986 (expenditures in constant dollars)

Table 16.2   Principal Means of Transportation to Work—1980

Metropolian Area	Private Vehicle: Drive Alone	Private Vehicle: Car Pool	Public Transportation	Other
New York, NY	30.7%	11.6%	45.1%	12.6%
Chicago, IL	57.6	16.7	18.0	7.7
San Francisco/Oakland, CA	57.9	15.7	16.4	9.9
Boston, MA	56.0	17.0	15.7	11.3
Washington, DC	53.7	22.9	15.5	7.9
Philadelphia, PA	59.1	17.6	14.0	9.2
Nassau/Suffolk, NY	63.7	17.6	12.5	6.2
Pittsburgh, PA	60.7	19.4	11.5	8.4
New Orleans, LA	61.7	20.6	10.9	6.8
Newark, NJ	64.0	17.9	10.7	7.4
Cleveland, OH	67.9	16.0	10.6	5.5
Baltimore, MD	59.8	22.3	10.3	7.7
Seattle/Everett, WA	63.9	18.2	9.6	8.3
Minneapolis/St. Paul, MN	63.1	19.9	8.7	8.3
Portland, OR	65.3	18.0	8.4	8.2
Milwaukee, WI	65.0	19.0	7.7	8.3
Atlanta, GA	68.7	19.6	7.6	4.1
Los Angeles/Long Beach, CA**	68.7	16.8	7.0	7.5
Miami, FL*	67.4	19.6	6.6	6.4
Buffalo, NY	66.6	18.6	6.6	8.2
Cincinnati, OH*	68.8	18.8	6.5	5.8
Denver/Boulder, CO	65.4	20.2	6.1	8.3
St. Louis, MO	67.3	21.4	5.7	5.6
San Antonio, TX*	66.9	19.9	4.6	8.6
Columbus, OH	70.3	18.2	4.6	6.8
Kansas City, MO*	69.3	21.5	4.1	5.1
Detroit, MI	75.1	16.9	3.7	4.3
Sacramento, CA*	69.0	17.6	3.5	9.9
Dallas/Ft. Worth, TX*	71.2	20.6	3.4	4.8
San Diego, CA*	63.8	17.4	3.3	15.5
Indianapolis, IN	70.3	21.0	3.2	5.5
San Jose, CA*	72.5	16.6	3.1	7.9
Houston, TX	69.5	22.4	3.0	5.0
Anaheim/Santa Ana, CA*	74.8	16.1	2.1	7.0
Phoenix, AZ*	70.2	19.0	2.0	8.9
Ft. Lauderdale/Hollywood, FL*	73.7	18.1	2.0	6.2
Tampa/St. Petersburg, FL**	72.0	18.4	1.8	7.8
Riverside/San Bernadino, CA**	71.9	18.3	.9	8.9

* Cities with council-manager governments
**One of the two listed cities has a council-manager government
SOURCE: U.S. Department of Commerce, *Statistical Abstract of the United States.*

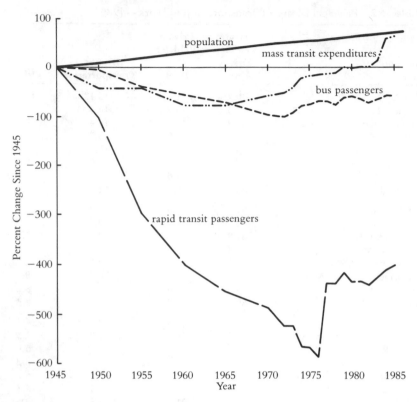

FIGURE 16.7: Change in Mass Transit Ridership and Expenditures, 1945–1986 (expenditures in constant dollars)

mileage under local control has doubled since 1945, and municipal expenditures for maintenance of these streets increased by 40 percent between 1950 and 1960 alone. Municipal expenditures for highways increased by 522 percent between 1945 and 1978.

One of the inevitable byproducts of this expansion in the use of the private automobile is the demand for more and better transit arteries in America's larger cities. As more people drive their cars to work, the task of negotiating rush-hour traffic becomes more difficult and time consuming. Nobody knows the exact rush-hour capacity of urban arterials, but anyone who has driven in rush-hour traffic in New York, Chicago, Los Angeles, or any other major city knows that we are approaching that capacity. And in New York, during recent public transit strikes, capacity was surpassed as automobile traffic ground to a virtual halt. Observers have even coined a name for the situation—*gridlock.*

Most major cities have developed public transit systems as a means of relieving some of the rush-hour pressure on their arterial system. Some cities, such as New York, Chicago, Boston, Washington, Cleveland, Philadelphia, San Francisco-Oakland, and Atlanta have invested millions of dollars in rapid rail systems. When the Bay Area Rapid Transit System (BART) opened in the early 1970s, it represented the first major mass transit system to be constructed in the United States in many years, and it was quite expensive: The original 1962 referendum allocated $800 million, but costs totalled over $1.5 billion by the time it was completed. The mass transit systems in Atlanta and Washington, constructed after BART, carried with them price tags of over $2 billion and $6 billion respectively. The efforts of other cities have been much more modest, mostly in the form of bus systems and trolley cars. Since 1952, municipal expenditures for public transit have totaled over $30 billion, with only slightly more than half of that recovered in the form of fares. And between 1945 and 1986, expenditures increased by 112 percent, while at the same time ridership showed a decline; for example, although BART was designed to accommodate 200,000 riders each day, actual ridership is tending toward 125,000, and Washington, D.C.'s METRO system is running at approximately one-third capacity. But it costs just as much to operate a subway system with a few as opposed to a lot of passengers, and cities seem to have concluded that public transit represents a "public good" for which they are willing to expend considerable money.

Education and Public Schools

In addition to affluence, other factors contribute to the city's increasing role as a deliverer of services to its residents. First, and perhaps most important, a pair of events occurred in the 1950s that, jointly, contributed greatly to the increasing budgets of most school districts. One of these events (or perhaps trends would be more accurate) was the coming of school age of the post-World War II "baby boomers." Between 1950 and 1960, the number of school-age children in the United States increased by over 40 percent (figure 16.8a), requiring a substantial increase in capital outlay for school maintenance, repair, and construction (95 percent), number of teachers (52 percent), and local taxes for education (88 percent). This expanding cohort of youngsters (in the years between 1945 and 1960) and young adults (in the years between 1960 and 1970) also had an inevitable impact on crime. Crime statistics show that over half of all arrests involved youths in the fourteen to twenty-four age range, even though they accounted for only about 15 percent (in 1945) and 20 percent (in 1975) of the population. It should be clear that this growth in the

365

pool of young adults substantially increased the number of people engaged in criminal activity, and coupled with the increasingly attractive targets of crime, led to the large increase in crime and police services between 1945 and 1978.

Not all increases in educational expenditures can be attributed to demographics, however; in 1957 an event shook the foundations of American education for a decade or more. In October of that year, the Soviet Union launched Sputnik I, the world's first man-made Earth satellite; a month later, the Soviets proved that this was not a technological fluke by launching Sputnik II, a satellite that carried a live dog. The United States clearly had been beaten, and beaten badly, in the space race, and our national pride was severely wounded. As a response, the federal government encouraged an expanded math and science curriculum in the public schools, and it encouraged special enrichment programs for gifted students. Local school districts enthusiastically

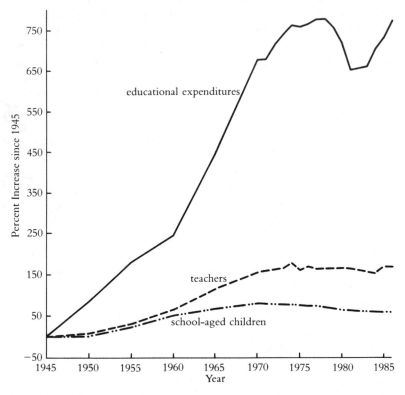

FIGURE 16.8a: Increase in School-Aged Children, Educational Expenditures, and Teachers, 1945–1986 (expenditures in constant dollars)

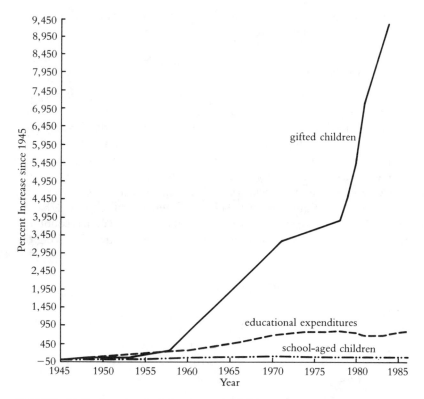

FIGURE 16.8b: Increase in School-Aged Children, Educational Expenditures, and Gifted Students, 1945–1986 (expenditures in constant dollars)

jumped on both bandwagons; figure 16.8b[13] shows that between 1958 and 1963, for example, the number of schoolchildren participating in "gifted" programs rose from 52,000 to 215,000, increased steadily over the next decade (to 481,000 in 1971), and grew at an even faster pace during the 1970s and 1980s (reaching 1.8 million by 1984). But the bandwagons turned out to be expensive. Although the federal government footed some of the bill (e.g., through the National Defense Act in 1958, Public Law 91-230 in 1969, and Public Law 93-380 in 1974), cities and states were responsible for the rest,[14]

13. The numbers of students participating in gifted programs are inexact, since definitions of these programs have changed somewhat over time. Even so, the increase is difficult to mistake.

14. In 1982, the federal government phased out its Office of Gifted and Talented, and virtually the entire cost of providing gifted education fell on states and localities (see Sisk 1987 for a review of the history of funding for gifted education). However, in 1988 Congress passed the Javits Gifted and Talented Students Education Act, providing $8 million in seed money for school districts and universities for programmatic development.

and this expansion of the curriculum accounted for at least some of the increase in local educational expenditures during the decade.

Services for the Needy

A second factor in the growth of urban services has been growing public sensitivity to the plight of the needy. For example, following World War II, the public became increasingly aware of and sensitive to the needs of exceptional children (e.g., those who are visually, aurally, or speech disabled, socially or emotionally maladjusted, learning disabled, mentally retarded). As these children were deemed educable, special education programs were developed and implemented in the public schools, with enrollments growing dramatically through the 1960s (figure 16.8c): 1947 enrollments totalled only 378,000, whereas 1970 enrollments totalled over three million. This trend has continued gradually to the present, but with one important difference. In 1975, Congress

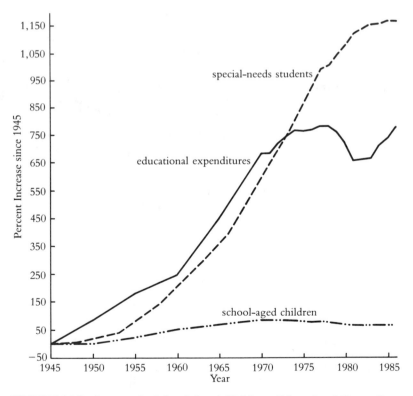

FIGURE 16.8c: Increase in School-Aged Children, Educational Expenditures, and Special-Needs Students, 1945–1986 (expenditures in constant dollars)

passed the Education for All Handicapped Children Act (Public Law 94-142), mandating that all children are entitled to a free and appropriate public education in the least restrictive environment (Levine and Wexler 1981). The intent of this law was to "mainstream" exceptional students out of special education classrooms and into regular education classrooms whenever appropriate, and it largely succeeded in this intent. The special education movement and the mainstreaming movement successfully expanded the scope of public education to 3 million new students, but at a considerable financial cost. In the case of special education, this included new teachers, new equipment, and new facilities, while in the case of mainstreaming, it included additional teacher training and more new facilities.

The plight of the mentally ill is another area where increased awareness has led to increased services. The needs of the mentally ill have been dramatized in recent years by a number of events, beginning with the development of psychotropic drugs in the 1950s. As a result of this breakthrough, state psychiatric hospitals gradually began a process of deinstitutionalization, through which patients were released into the community to receive therapy on an outpatient basis. In 1963, President Kennedy urged Congress to pass legislation funding community mental health centers, arguing that this would enable the mentally ill to be treated in their own communities. However, following passage of the Community Mental Health Centers Act in 1963, community mental health centers were slow to provide services to deinstitutionalized mental patients, focusing instead on new populations in need of acute services. By 1980 these centers were servicing over 3 million clients each year, only a portion of whom had previously been institutionalized (Goldman and Morrissey 1985). This trend was complicated, however, by several court decisions in 1973 that found the circumstances and the conditions of psychiatric institutionalization to be wanting. In the wake of these decisions, state psychiatric hospitals opened their doors for a mass exodus of mental patients into the community, with community mental health centers serving as their only source of clinical support (see Badger et al., 1981, for a further discussion of the impact of these decisions).

Yet, at exactly the time of this mass institutional exodus and the burgeoning demand for community mental health services, federal support for community mental health centers began to decline. In many locations, state tax dollars have picked up the slack; but in other cases, it has been the localities (through both public and private funding) that have paid for mental health services. In 1980, 9 percent of the total support came from local sources, 9 percent from the federal government, and 82 percent from state governments (National Institute of Mental Health 1985). In many communities, the municipal government also provides support for other social services, including homes for battered spouses, drug and alcohol counselling services, public health clinics, shelters for

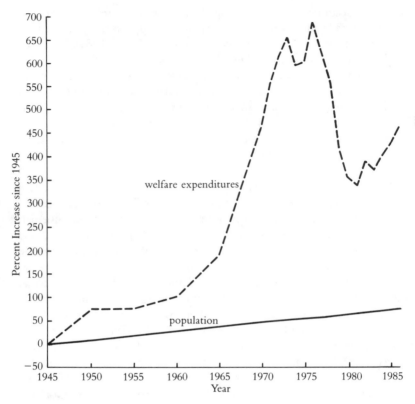

FIGURE 16.9: Increase in Population and Municipal Welfare Expenditures, 1945–1986 (expenditures in constant dollars)

the homeless,[15] and meals for the hungry. Even when these facilities and programs are not funded directly by the city, they often receive public contributions through local agencies such as the United Way. For example, in 1985, United Way contributions in the United States exceeded $2 billion. However, since 1960 total United Way contributions have increased very little, while demand has increased considerably. In the end, the survival of these programs depends largely on the willingness and the ability of municipal government to support them, and as we have seen, municipal government has often risen to the challenge. As figure 16.9 shows, between 1960 and 1978, public welfare

15. The dramatic increase in the number of homeless in the large cities is tied (albeit indirectly; see Goldman and Morrissey 1985) largely to the deinstitutionalization of mental patients, and thus it links to the previous discussion. While the exact number of homeless is impossible to know, estimates place the figure as high as 2 million. Many cities have designated shelters for the homeless, adding to the demands on municipal budgets.

expenditures by cities, for a number of social programs including those discussed above, rose by 446 percent.

The Theme Restated

Let us return now to the original argument and examine more closely its implications. We began by noting that the delivery of services has become the most important function of the city during the last half of this century. And we have seen that economic, demographic, social, and technological factors have all contributed to its growth. But as the demand for services has increased, so has their cost. First, cities are simply providing more services than ever before, to more people than ever before. Second, technological developments are pushing the price of services upward. But a third, and perhaps most important factor in the rising cost of urban service delivery is the increasing labor costs of providing services. The greater the demand that is placed on a commodity or a service, the more it typically costs. When demand was low for garbage collection, sanitation workers could be paid a low wage, and nobody was much affected if they walked out on strike. But as urban residents have come to depend on twice-weekly trash pickup, the social costs of uncollected garbage escalate, and cities are willing to pay sanitation workers more money to ensure that garbage is picked up efficiently. Much the same can be said of education and law enforcement. In periods of low crime, police could be underpaid with little consequence. But in periods of high crime, law enforcement officers can command higher salaries; between 1965 and 1975, for example, police salaries increased at an annual rate of approximately 7.5 percent, exceeding annual salary increases in the private sector (approximately 6 percent). Since urban services tend to be labor intensive, even small wage increases magnify the overall costs of services.

With increasing demand and increasing cost, municipal expenditures for services accelerated between 1945 and 1978, as indicated by figure 16.1. But after 1978, expenditures actually began to decline, as did the number and scope of services funded by the municipal budget. In the next section, we will explore this trend, seeing specific causes and considering specific responses.

The Decline of Urban Services: 1979-1982

New York on the Verge of Bankruptcy

In 1975, the expansion of municipal services came to a dramatic halt in New York City as the Big Apple teetered on the brink of bankruptcy. Although municipal bankruptcy had been commonplace during the Depression, it has been rare in the years since; this, coupled with the preeminent place of New York City in our urban hierarchy, demands that we pay New York's fiscal crisis more than passing attention, for it served notice to the rest of the nation that the era of unbridled expansion in the growth of urban services was at an end.

Following C. Levine et al. (1981), we will examine New York's fiscal crisis in its component stages.[16] Its earliest roots are found in the years between 1965 and 1970, when the city responded to growing racial unrest and rioting. During this period, expenditures for social programs for blacks increased greatly. Also during this period, the city made a commitment to higher education, greatly increasing funding to the New York University system and to municipal hospitals. These budgetary increases had little adverse effect, since the economy was expanding. But an expanding economy led to inflation during the last years of the decade, and New York's union leaders sought substantial pay increases. After the embarrassment of the Transit Workers' strike in 1966, Mayor John Lindsay saw union support as necessary both to his reelection and to his ability to govern effectively, and the city acceded to union demands for higher wages.

Had economic growth continued, New York City's fiscal crisis likely would never have occurred. But the economic slump of the early 1970s brought with it an erosion of private-sector jobs in the city, particularly high-paying manufacturing jobs. Further, federal grants to the city declined in the early 1970s. The city administration made some effort to respond by cutting eight thousand fire, sanitation, and education jobs; but increasing funding for higher education and hospitals more than compensated for these cutbacks. As a final resort, Mayor Lindsay took the politically expedient route of covering budgetary shortfalls with short-term loans (which carry higher interest rates than long-term loans); by 1974, 20 percent of New York City's total debt was in the form of high-interest, short-term bonds. This situation could perhaps have continued indefinitely, except that in 1974 the New York State Urban Development Corporation—created by the New York Assembly to sell bonds, and with the proceeds of the bond sales to make loans to New York cities—defaulted on payment of its debt, and creditors became concerned about New York City's ability to pay *its* debt. Several banks sold their New York City bonds, setting off a panic that effectively ended the city's ability to issue any further short-term bonds.

Thus, by the beginning of 1975, default seemed imminent, and the only way that it could be forestalled was to borrow money outside the bond market. The federal government in general, and particularly President Ford, seemed uninterested in bailing out New York. The *New York Daily News* summarized Washington's sentiment with its large-type headline on October 30, 1975: FORD TO CITY: DROP DEAD. As a last resort, New York State created the Municipal

16. For other perspectives on New York's fiscal crisis, see C. Morris (1980), Shefter (1980), and Sbragia (1983).

Assistance Corporation (MAC) to lend New York the money it needed to service its debt. But over time, even MAC had difficulty selling bonds, and it was forced to negotiate austerity measures with the city and its unions. These included:

1. a wage freeze, and deferral of a 6 percent cost of living increase for municipal employees;
2. a rollback to 1973 wages for management-level employees;
3. a promise from the city to avoid frills in future union negotiations;
4. increased user fees for municipal services;
5. a $22-million cut in the city's budget allocation to New York University;
6. consolidation or elimination of several municipal departments;
7. appointment of a management team to oversee the city's fiscal practices.

When the city's deficit was discovered to be four times larger than projected, however, another state agency—the Emergency Financial Control Board (EFCB)—was created to act as a receiver for the city. EFCB consisted of the mayor, the governor, the city and state comptrollers, and three additional gubernatorial appointees, so that effective control was placed in the hands of the state rather than the city. All municipal revenues were deposited directly into an EFCB account and disbursed according to a three-year plan developed by the city. Between 1975 and 1978, New York City cut 60,000 municipal jobs and established severe guidelines for labor negotiations. Although no one was happy with the arrangement, an uneasy peace had been established by 1978 among the city, the state, the federal government (which, in the end, did provide some short-term loans), the unions, and the banks. Today, New York City is on firmer financial footing, and its officials would prefer to forget how close to financial catastrophe it had come during the mid-1970s.

The factors that led to New York City's financial crisis are faced by all large cities, to a greater or lesser degree. By the same token, the austerity measures employed by New York are also used by other cities in combating fiscal stress. In the remainder of this section, we will take a closer look at the factors creating fiscal stress in American cities. And in the following section, we will consider in greater depth the steps cities have taken to regain fiscal solvency.

Taxpayer Revolt

Previously, this chapter outlined a trend of growing affluence in the United States, beginning immediately after World War II. The steepest part of this growth curve occurred between 1960 and 1973, when median family income increased by 43 percent. By 1973, the typical family had annually $2,700 (indexed to 1967 consumer prices) more at its disposal than it had in 1960. But between 1974 and 1982, another trend began to emerge in the United

States. The growth in affluence ground to a halt, and it actually began to reverse itself. Between 1973 and 1977, for instance, median family income fell by 3 percent, while municipal expenditures increased by 5 percent, and per-capita local taxes to pay for these municipal expenditures remained stable. Figure 16.10 shows median family income, local taxes, and municipal general expenditures. It is clear from the nearly coincident plot of income and taxes that the growing affluence of American families fueled the growth of municipal budgets. It is also clear that these budgets—and the taxes to pay for them—took on a life of their own, and particularly in the period between 1960 and 1973, deviated from trends in income. But by 1980, both municipal budgets and taxes had come into line with the stark reality of the American economy.

Several factors converged during the early and mid-1970s to bring taxes and expenditures back into line with income. First, taxpayers staged a revolt during this period, protesting any new or increased taxes and in some cases

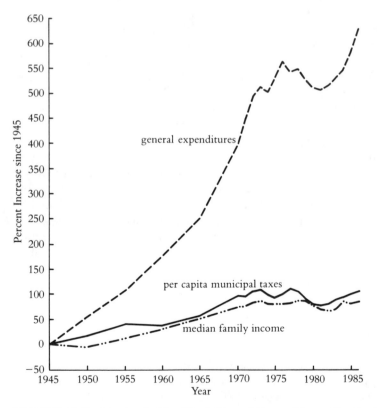

FIGURE 16.10: Increase in Municipal General Expenditures, Per Capita Municipal Taxes, and Median Family Income, 1945–1986 (expenditures, income, and taxes in constant dollars)

374

rolling back taxes to previous, lower levels. Although Proposition 13 in California and Proposition 2½ in Massachusetts are the best-known instances of this tax revolt, it has its origins in the early 1970s in cities and school districts across the country. In most states, school districts must regularly go to the voters for approval of any funding beyond a fixed millage necessary for such projects as new construction and the development of new programs. During the 1960s, the voters of most cities regularly said yes to such requests; approximately 70 percent of the school bond issues passed during that period and 70 percent of the requested funds were approved. By the early 1970s, however, fewer than 50 percent of the school bond issues put to the voters passed, with only about 40 percent of the requested funds approved. Although both passage rate and allocations improved slightly during the late 1970s, neither approaches the level it achieved during the 1960s. These trends are reported in table 16.3.

Municipal bond elections followed a similar pattern. Cities must seek voter approval to sell bonds necessary for most capital improvement projects, including the construction of municipal pools, parks, water treatment plants, and so forth. Long-term bonded indebtedness of American municipalities, also reported in table 16.3, increased substantially from 1950 through 1970, then slowed and gradually declined through the 1970s and the early 1980s. The implication is clear: Whereas the voters in urban America were willing to finance new municipal projects while their earning power was increasing, they became wary of such projects once their earning power leveled off.

These indications of taxpayer concern were, of course, formalized with the 1978 passage of Proposition 13 in California, which cut property taxes in the state by 60 percent (and strictly limited future property assessments). California voters overwhelmingly supported Proposition 13, concluding that government spending could be cut by as much as 25 percent without any deterioration in services (Sears and Citrin 1982). But several other factors also contributed to the success of those who sponsored Proposition 13 (most notably Howard Jarvis, a California businessman). First, they were able to enlist the support of conservative voters who resented the growth of governmental subsidies for the poor, with two-thirds of those who voted *yea* believing that welfare payments should be cut. In contrast, citizens generally opposed cutbacks in police, fire, education, public transportation, recreation, or mental health expenditures (Sears and Citrin 1982). Thus, supporters did not necessarily resent paying taxes, just those taxes earmarked for welfare and related programs.

Second, voters seldom have the opportunity to directly indicate their opposition to taxes, and when given that opportunity they are likely to take it. Opponents were not necessarily protesting local taxes; in fact, by 1978 resentment toward federal taxes equaled that toward local property taxes (Rose 1980). But since federal taxes cannot be directly challenged, many voters

Table 16.3 School District Bond Issue Success and Long-Term Municipal Bond Indebtedness

	School Districts		Municipalities
	Percent of Bond Issues Approved	Percent of Value Approved	Long-Term Bonded Indebtedness*
1950			$12,514
1951			12,375
1952			15,236
1953			16,121
1954			17,257
1955			19,080
1956			20,609
1957			21,569
1958		72.8	22,371
1959		79.6	23,999
1960		67.1	24,694
1961		75.9	26,001
1962	72.2	68.8	27,703
1963	72.4	69.6	28,176
1964	72.5	71.1	29,896
1965	74.7	79.4	30,984
1966	72.5	74.5	31,782
1967	66.6	69.2	32,185
1968	67.6	62.5	32,942
1969	56.8	43.6	33,036
1970	53.2	49.5	33,422
1971	46.7	41.4	34,740
1972	47.0	44.0	36,579
1973	56.6	50.6	37,029
1974	56.2	53.0	36,148
1975	46.3	46.0	34,609
1976	50.8	46.1	36,433
1977	55.5	54.0	36,875
1978			38,374
1979			34,477
1980			33,365
1981			32,254
1982			33,051
1983			36,757
1984			38,468
1985			42,145
1986			48,460

*millions of constant (1967) dollars
NOTE: The National Center for Educational Statistics compiled school district data for the years shown.
SOURCE: U.S. Department of Commerce, *Statistical Abstract of the United States.*

376

apparently took out their frustrations on the only available target: local property taxes.

Third, property taxes had really become quite a burden in the late 1970s, particularly in California. The value of residential property across the state grew at an annual rate of over 12 percent between 1973 and 1976, with annual growth rates in large cities (e.g., San Francisco, Los Angeles) approaching 20 percent during this period. With this increase came higher property tax assessments, which increased by as much as 30 percent a year in San Bernadino and Orange Counties during the same period.[17] Again, this occurred during a period when earning power was not increasing, and the additional taxes became unbearable for many people.

It is unclear (and perhaps unimportant) exactly how much each of these factors contributed to the passage of Proposition 13 in California. What is important is that the measure gave notice to governmental units across the country that unorganized instances of taxpayer revolt were becoming organized, and that municipalities and states must moderate their spending before the voters forced them to do so. Post-Proposition 13 sentiment across the country favored restrictions on property taxes, with two-thirds of those surveyed expressing sentiment for tax reform (Sears and Citrin 1982). About the same time as Proposition 13, voters in many other states considered similar propositions, which either strictly limited (or rolled back) property tax or limited municipal spending levels. In 1978, residents of Idaho (with an already low property tax burden) and Nevada passed Proposition 13-type measures, limiting increases in assessments to 2 percent per year. In the same year, voters in Arizona, Hawaii, Michigan, and Texas approved bills limiting spending (Lucier 1980). But in contrast, 1978 witnessed the defeat of tax relief propositions in Oregon and Colorado, and voters in Michigan defeated a companion bill to the one they approved. In 1979, property tax relief measures were passed in twenty-two states, income tax reductions in eighteen states, sales tax reductions in fifteen states, and spending limits in eight states (Poole 1980). And in 1980, residents of Massachusetts passed Proposition 2½, which limited property tax to 2.5 percent of assessed real estate value. As a result, by 1980 per capita taxes on urban residents had dropped to 85 percent of their 1973 levels (see figure 16.10).

Although the most publicized cause of decreasing municipal revenues and expenditures, the tax revolt was not the only (or even the most impor-

17. During this period the middle and upper classes were purchasing ever larger and more expensive homes, which helped boost the housing market so dramatically. Homes simultaneously became a status symbol and an investment. As the middle and upper classes invested more of their savings and earnings into houses, the regressivity of the property tax largely disappeared, and it became among the more progressive of local taxes. Ironically, the taxpayer revolt occurred not among those paying an unfair and regressive tax (as we might expect) but rather among those who were subjected to a fair and progressive tax.

tant) cause. Indeed, it simply came at a time when other trends were severely limiting the ability of municipal governments, particularly in large cities, to provide services, exacerbating the impact of those trends. The first of these trends is the economic slump that has intermittently plagued the United States since the early 1970s. The second is the movement to the suburbs, initiated after World War II but particularly important during the 1970s. And the third is the changing policy of the federal government toward sharing revenue with the cities, begun in 1981 with the inauguration of President Reagan.

Economic Stagnation

During the 1970s and the early 1980s, the economy performed in a generally sluggish manner, moving between recession and mild recovery but never toward full recovery. In this poor economic climate, unemployment ranged between 6 percent and 10 percent nationally, and considerably higher than that in the nation's inner cities. Thus, income tax receipts that might help the city directly (in those cities that assess an income tax) or indirectly (through state or federal grants) were significantly down. By the same token, unemployed people do not spend as much money on nondisposable goods, and municipal sales tax receipts also lagged. In such a sluggish economy, new business starts were down and business failures were up, again reducing the tax base. Finally, the 1970s witnessed an important industrial trend in the United States, with many manufacturers moving their base of operation overseas (where labor is cheaper); a complementary trend saw an increase in overseas imports of manufactured items (e.g., steel). For example, a 1984 survey showed that in the previous five years, 11.5 million workers had lost jobs because of plant closings or other economic cutbacks (Wicker, Aug. 18, 1987). The two trends converged to create a sharp reduction in high-paying manufacturing jobs in American cities (of those people who were victims of manufacturing displacement, most eventually found work, although at levels of pay considerably less than that they previously received; further, about 20 percent of the new jobs created since 1980 pay only minimum wage). In addition, this loss of high-paying jobs resulted in a reduction of taxable corporate profits and an additional strain on municipal coffers.

Economic stagnation and unemployment also lead to increased need for city services. People without jobs still need to eat, and the burden of providing food often falls on municipal agencies. Continuing unemployment leads to psychological depression and anxiety, and demands on the community mental health center are likely to increase. In addition, high rates of unemployment, particularly among youths, may contribute to greater crime within a city, and demands on municipal police departments may increase. But in each of these cases, fewer resources are available to meet these greater demands.

378

Table 16.4   Regional Growth Patterns, 1930–2000 (percent change)

	1930–1940	1940–1950	1950–1960	1960–1970	1970–1980	1980–1986	1990–2000 (proj.)
Northeast	4.5	9.7	13.2	9.8	.2	1.8	2.4
Midwest	4.0	10.8	16.1	9.6	4.0	.8	− .3
South	10.1	13.3	16.5	14.3	20.0	10.1	11.0
West	16.7	40.4	38.9	24.2	23.9	12.9	13.7

SOURCE: U.S. Department of Commerce, *Statistical Abstract of the United States.*

Population Shifts

Also during the 1970s, a long-term population shift toward the suburbs continued, with twice as many people moving from central cities to suburbs as from suburbs to central cities. In the early years, this shift largely reflected changing life-style preferences: Americans, tired of the bustle, crime, and poverty of city life, opted for a place in the country (or at least in the suburbs). The freeway construction program of the 1950s and the 1960s made this movement possible by substantially reducing the commuting time for people who opted to work in the city but live away from its problems. Thus, the continuing outmigration from the central city reflects another type of taxpayer revolt, with both citizens and corporations voting down higher taxes with their feet rather than at the ballot box. Like Howard Jarvis' coalition in California, these citizens and corporate heads are not opposed to services and taxes: They typically support strong fire and police departments, street repair, libraries, parks, and schools. They are, however, unwilling to pay the taxes required for services aimed at ameliorating (or at least controlling) the problems of the inner cities, for example, mass transit, subsidized health care, and public housing. Ironically, however, they are the very people who can best afford to pay for these services. By moving away from the central city, they escape both the problem and the need to pay for it. But they leave in their wake a much smaller tax base for the city.

Another important demographic shift has been away from the northeastern and midwestern frostbelt states and to the western and southern sunbelt states. As table 16.4 indicates, the population in the West has been growing at a faster rate than that in other parts of the country for the past half century. But while growth rates in the Northeast and the Midwest have declined precipitously since 1970, those in the West have remained constant and those in the South have accelerated. The impact of this migration is even more clear if we examine population shifts in major cities in each region, as reported in table 16.5. Most of this migration is *not* a movement of unemployed people looking for work: Only about 10 percent of inter-regional migration involves people living in poverty. Rather, it represents a shift in the location of professional and service jobs, with over one-third of all inter-regional migration involving people in the professional or managerial classes (Bureau of the Census 1984). And as tables 16.4 and 16.5 suggest, most of this movement has been out of the Northeast and into the South and West. For example, when American Airlines moved its corporate office from New York to Dallas, a number of professional-level employees also left. But this is just the tip of the trend, for corporate relocation may also trigger movement in banking and financial institutions, law firms, and a host of other service organizations (cf., Mollenkopf 1983). In other words, people and businesses that have been supporting municipal services in the Northeast and Midwest with their tax

Table 16.5 Growth Patterns of Selected Metropolitan Areas, 1960–1986 (percent change)

	1960–1970	1970–1980	1980–1986
Northeast			
New York	4.5	− 3.6	2.4
Philadelphia	11.1	− 1.2	2.7
Buffalo	3.2	− 7.9	− 4.9
Boston	7.9	.8	2.1
Pittsburgh	− .2	− 5.2	− 4.4
Midwest			
Chicago	12.1	2.0	2.2
Cleveland	8.1	− 5.5	− 2.4
St. Louis	12.4	− 2.1	2.6
Detroit	12.3	− .7	− 3.2
Kansas City	14.9	4.4	5.9
Mid-Atlantic			
Baltimore	14.8	5.3	3.6
Washington	38.8	6.9	9.6
South			
Atlanta	36.5	27.0	19.8
Houston	39.8	43.0	17.2
Miami	35.6	40.0	10.1
Dallas	36.8	24.6	24.7
West			
Los Angeles	16.6	15.2	13.7
Phoenix	46.1	55.4	25.9
Denver	32.6	30.7	14.2
San Francisco	17.4	12.9	9.5
San Diego	31.4	37.1	18.2
Seattle	28.7	13.9	9.2

SOURCE: U.S. Department of Commerce, *Statistical Abstract of the United States.*

dollars are moving to the South and West, leaving behind cities that have no fewer problems but many fewer resources to deal with them.

Federal Cutbacks

The previous chapters chronicled a shifting pattern of federal aid to American cities, beginning with categorical grants and moving through block grants and revenue sharing into the Reagan presidency. But the story was left largely unfinished, for yet another shift has occurred in the years since 1978: a shift toward *no aid*. Table 15.6 shows how dramatic the decline in federal aid to cities has been since 1978.

The Overall Effect

Any of these four factors—the tax-payer revolt, economic stagnation, the shifting population, and cutbacks in federal aid—would have slowed the growth of service delivery in the city. But taken together, they resulted in an absolute reduction in the total revenue available to cities. In response to this crisis, cities were forced to respond in either of two ways: cut back services or find alternative sources of revenue. Most cities adopted a combination of these two strategies, and beginning about 1979, urban government entered an era of cutback management.

Creative Finance in the City

The handwriting on the wall foretold of municipal fiscal stress during the early 1970s; yet it was largely ignored until the end of the decade. Why the delay? The most convincing explanation is wishful thinking (Levine, 1980, has termed this the tooth fairy syndrome). We should not find it surprising, then, that administrators and politicians also resisted the notion that the good days had come to an end, and that instead of continuing to expand services they would be forced to cut them back.

The handwriting on the wall became hard to ignore in 1975, when New York City teetered on the brink of bankruptcy. But it was ignored, with municipal officials elsewhere arguing that, after all, the Big Apple was different. To point out these differences, a number of cities (including Wichita, Sacramento, Indianapolis, St. Paul, and Dallas) formed the National Alliance for Financially Responsible Local Government (Lineberry and Sharkansky 1978). The same kind of rationalization occurred after Cleveland defaulted in 1978 ("after all, what can you expect from a city whose major waterway catches fire?"). Even after Proposition 13 passed in California in 1978, people attributed it to "kookie California politics" (Clark and Ferguson 1983). But within a short time, it was clear that virtually all cities faced the challenge of

381

cutting budgets without disrupting services. This challenge was met in various ways. These included cutting back services, coproduction and volunteerism, improving efficiency in service delivery, adopting user fees, and contracting out services to the private sector.

Cutting Back Services

The most obvious approach to saving money in the provision of municipal services is to cut them, and many cities adopted this strategy. In a detailed study of the cutback strategies of Oakland, Cincinnati, and Baltimore, for example, Charles Levine and his colleagues (1981) found extensive curtailment of services. In Oakland, Proposition 13 left the city with a 4.6 percent decrease in operating capital. It attempted to meet this crisis by reducing library and museum hours, street sweeping details, street maintenance, and weed abatement, and by eliminating a city hall switchboard, some fire alarm boxes, and the film program at the public library. When further cuts were required the following year, the city closed a fire station and four branch libraries, reduced criminal investigation operations in the police department, and reduced park maintenance and after-school recreation programs in the recreation department. While these cuts reduced operational expenses, they also resulted in the loss of 170 municipal jobs. In Cincinnati, 893 full-time municipal positions were cut from the payroll in 1977 in the face of declining revenues. And in Baltimore, a decade-long economic crisis during the 1970s resulted in the reduction of 435 positions in the police department, nearly 100 firefighters, and 1,200 school district personnel; in addition, the library system suffered a 20 percent cut in professional staff and a 35 percent cut in maintenance personnel.

While reduction in services is an obvious solution, it carries with it two important political costs. First, each of the reduced services has a clientele that is likely to object to curtailments. For example, closing a branch library is likely to anger residents in the neighborhoods affected, as is closing a fire station. In most cases, cities opt to reduce low-visibility services with low demand (e.g., the library film program). But low demand is not the same as no demand, and even a small number of vehemently vocal citizens can be an embarrassment to the municipal administration. Second, municipal employees (and their unions) are unlikely to accept layoffs silently, or if they do, they extract a high price. For example, between 1974 and 1977 Detroit, Cleveland, and New York City all reduced their municipal work forces, but in the bargain, unions were able to extract higher wages for remaining employees (Clark and Ferguson 1983). If unions are able to achieve neither job security nor higher wages through negotiations, they may strike, resulting in political embarrassment for the city administration and potentially crippling its ability to govern effectively. Given these consequences, it is not surprising that cities have searched for alternative ways to save money in the provision of services.

Coproduction and Volunteerism

How can cities cut back services without actually reducing services citizens receive? While in an absolute sense this can be accomplished only with mirrors, many cities have adopted a reasonable approximation in the form of *coproduction,* an arrangement wherein the city and its citizens work together to provide services. For example, garbage collection in most cities is coproduced, with residents carrying their trash out to the curb, where it is picked up by municipal garbage trucks. So, too, police protection in many cities is coproduced, through programs such as the neighborhood crime watch.

A related concept is volunteerism, through which cities use unpaid volunteers to provide services that would otherwise be provided by municipal employees. The most obvious use of volunteerism is in fire departments. Ninety-one percent of American cities use volunteer firefighters either exclusively or to supplement paid firefighters; for example, in New York State only sixty-two cities use all paid firefighters, while more than eighteen hundred use volunteers (Poole 1980).

Many cities have also initiated volunteer security patrols. For instance, the 120-member East Midwood patrol provides an all-night patrol service for a twenty-five-block area in Brooklyn; it asks residents in this area to donate a $10 annual fee to cover expenses. Similar units provide service to approximately 25 percent of the neighborhoods in New York City. Other cities, such as Boston, Baltimore, St. Louis, Chicago, San Jose, Norfolk, Newark, Detroit, Washington, New Orleans, and Los Angeles, also make use of volunteer citizen patrols (Poole, 1980).

A third area where volunteers are used broadly is public education. Many schools actively recruit parents to chaperon field trips (and in the upper grades, school dances), to help out in the classroom, and to grade papers and examinations.

Problems with coproduction and volunteerism. An obvious problem raised by the volunteerism and coproduction movements is the quality of services provided. As citizens rather than municipal employees, volunteers are largely unaccountable for their actions. The volunteer firefighter who does not respond to a fire alarm cannot be fired; nor can an unconscientious educational volunteer. Perhaps the greatest threat lies in the area of security patrols, however. Law enforcement officers receive considerable training, designed to (a) minimize the likelihood that they will be injured while performing their jobs; (b) minimize the threat to bystanders; and (c) preserve the rights of those they apprehend. While the purpose of security patrols is to observe and report crimes (and therefore never to get involved directly), they may nonetheless unavoidably be caught up in a crime. Yet, without the proper training, they may well pose a threat to themselves and to others.

383

Improving Efficiency

If asked, most people within the United States would probably say that their governments operate inefficiently; further, they would state that if governmental waste were stripped away, their taxes could be cut without sacrificing any crucial governmental functions. This logic contributed to the taxpayer revolts in California and other states, and to the federal tax cuts during the Reagan administration. Also at the federal level, it contributed to the formation of the Grace Commission. This commission consisted of people from the private sector, headed by businessman Peter Grace, who developed 23,000 pages of suggestions that it projected would save the federal government over $420 billion.[18] Several states and even some cities have adopted similar strategies.

Cities have used five such strategies to improve efficiency in the delivery of municipal services. First, many cities have initiated practices designed to use municipal personnel more efficiently (Poole 1980). For example, firefighters in many cities spend most of their working hours waiting for a fire alarm. Some cities have attempted to make more efficient use of this "down" time. While not actively fighting fires, firefighters in these cities give presentations on fire safety to community organizations, work with citizens to fireproof their homes, issue bicycle licenses, conduct municipal inspections, and repair city water meters. Police departments have also adopted management innovations during the past several years. For example, a number of cities (e.g., Scottsdale, Miami) have hired young adults to serve as community service officers (CSOs); these CSOs act as traffic control officers at accident locations, refer citizens to appropriate municipal agencies, write reports, perform first aid, and carry out crime prevention programs at about half the cost of sworn officers.

Second, cities have attempted to trim expenses through more efficient equipment acquisition strategies (Poole 1980). For example, some municipal fire departments (e.g., Syracuse, Des Moines) moved away from large pumpers to smaller mini-pumpers, which can be handled by two-person crews and cost only 20 percent as much as the larger pumper. In addition, many cities are purchasing compact or mid-sized police patrol cars rather than full-sized models.

Third, cities have begun using more aggressive maintenance procedures to sustain the life of their equipment. For example, the city manager in Olathe, Kansas, discovered that the park maintenance equipment experienced an inordinate number of flat tires, and crews were left idle while the tires were repaired. As a solution, he ordered that tires be filled with sand; this made for a less comfortable ride for park department employees, but it considerably reduced the down time for this equipment. In a similar vein, many cities have reduced

18. Private commissions have a considerable precedent in the federal government. For example, former president Herbert Hoover headed one such commission during the presidency of Harry Truman.

Table 16.6 Percentage of Urban General Expenditures Allocated to Salaries for Selected Departments, 1984

Department	Percent of Expenditures for Salaries
Fire	80
Police	78
Education	75
Health and Hospital	48
All Expenditures	87*

*Includes administrative salaries; without administration, this figure is approximately 78 percent.
SOURCE: U.S. Department of Commerce, *Statistical Abstract of the United States*, 1988.

the maintenance interval for their police patrol cars. While this creates a minor inconvenience every few weeks while the oil is changed and the engine is tuned, it reduces expensive repairs.

Fourth, most cities have purchased a mini-computer (or in some cases, a small mainframe computer) to serve a number of accounting functions, including budgeting, billing, and word processing. Some cities have computerized their traffic signals to achieve optimal traffic flow. Others use computers for law enforcement functions, for example, tracking suspected criminals and preparing court calendars.

Fifth, administrators in various cities have sought out inefficient work practices among municipal employees. In Pittsburgh, for example, Mayor Pete Flaherty took this task upon himself, arriving unannounced at worksites throughout the city in search of inefficiency. In San Diego, Mayor Pete Wilson hired a management consulting firm which conducted detailed time and motion studies to identify inefficiency. Changes growing out of these investigations resulted in approximately a 10 percent reduction in expenditures in each city (Clark and Ferguson 1983).[19]

What price efficiency? If we stop to consider exactly how much money can be saved by making urban government more efficient, however, we are bound to be disappointed. First, the major function of municipal government is the provision of services; and as table 16.6 suggests, these services are labor

19. These results must be interpreted cautiously. An early study conducted in 1927 at the Western Electric Company in Hawthorne, Illinois, showed that by changing the lights to a higher wattage, productivity among workers increased. However, this increase was short-lived. Then, in a followup study, wattage was decreased below the original level, and productivity once again increased (but again for a short period). In other words, almost any change in working conditions results in a short-term gain in productivity and efficiency. This is known as the *Hawthorne effect* (Roethlisberger and Dickson 1939). In the Pittsburgh and San Diego examples, a 10 percent reduction in the cost of producing services is impressive *only* to the extent that it represents a long-term effect.

intensive. For example, 80 percent of all municipal fire-fighting expenditures and 78 percent of all municipal law-enforcement expenditures are earmarked for employee salaries. Across all categories of the municipal budget, salaries account for approximately 87 percent of general expenditures. The *only* way to cut this large segment of expenditures without also cutting services would be to reduce the number of administrators in each municipal department; for obvious reasons, this is a path that urban administrators are reluctant to pursue.

Second, the growth of technology is extracting a substantial toll from municipal governments. State-of-the-art fire-fighting equipment is costly, but most citizens would not want their city to settle for second-rate fire protection. State-of-the-art crime detection equipment is also expensive; and anyone who has purchased a new car recently knows that keeping the city's fleet of police cars up-to-date (even with compact models) is an expensive proposition. Municipal hospitals must purchase modern diagnostic and treatment equipment, none of which is inexpensive. Citizens demanding efficiency in the purchase of equipment ultimately face the tradeoff between expense and quality. Most, faced with the possibility that they may someday depend on that equipment, tend to opt for the more expensive but higher quality line.

Third, municipal governments now provide more services for more people than ever before, and many of these services are redistributive in nature. For example, many municipal budgets include funding for direct welfare payments to the needy.[20] Some include funding for health and social programs. For those who disagree with municipal fiscal policies, these are among the most criticized services. But criticism has little to do with improved efficiency, and, in turn, improving efficiency would have little impact on the cost of providing these services.

In the end, the introduction of efficient practices into the delivery of urban services will result in *little* long-term savings for taxpayers. While the exact savings is impossible to predict, it is unlikely to exceed even 5 percent of municipal general expenditures, with 1 percent to 2 percent a more realistic guess. This, of course, is not to be scoffed at.

But the true benefit of efficiency in the delivery of urban services lies in the domain of public confidence. Citizens are more likely to support taxes if they believe that their tax dollars are being spent efficiently. And many of the management practices described above are public relations bonanzas. For example, computers epitomize efficiency, and it is no accident that the pur-

20. Different municipalities carry different responsibilities for funding various social and welfare programs. In some cases, the city bears no responsibility, with all funding provided by the federal government, the state, and/or the county. In other cases, however, the city's contribution is large. This helps explain why the fiscal crisis hit some cities harder than others. In the 1970s, for example, the state of New York mandated that New York City assume 25 percent of the cost of providing welfare and Medicaid to its residents, and the burgeoning cost of these programs occurred at a time when the city's financial resources were already stretched thin (see Stone et al., 1986).

chase of new computer equipment is accompanied by a front-page story in the local newspaper, complete with picture. By the same token, when the mayor goes on the road to root out inefficiency, publicity abounds. And by bringing in a management consulting team from the private sector, the city serves notice that it is serious about saving taxpayers' dollars. Finally, compact police cars are visible to motorists every day, and they serve as a constant reminder that the city is doing what it can to provide services for less money.

The end result, then, is that some money is saved (after all, even 1 percent of the general expenditures in Austin, Texas, amounts to $4.7 million, for example; and in New York City, a 1-percent savings amounts to over $200 million); but more important, the municipal administration is afforded some relief from the public pressure it faces on taxing and spending issues, and it is more likely to be successful next time it places a bond issue on the ballot.

User Fees

The previous chapter discussed user fees as a source of municipal revenue. Here, we will consider how cities have applied the concept to their delivery of services, paying particular attention to the consequences of user fees—particularly for the city's economically disadvantaged.

User fees are most commonly found in the area of municipal parks or recreation, where they might include parking and entrance fees, rental fees for equipment, and sales of souvenirs, food, and beverages. For example, a number of museums throughout the country aggressively pursue merchandizing strategies, not just in museum gift shops but also through mail orders. The New York Metropolitan Museum of Art took in $12.5 million in retail sales in 1977, and the Museum of Modern Art took in $1.5 million (Poole 1980). In addition, many art museums rent self-guiding cassette tours for a nominal fee, and many zoos rent devices that patrons can use to listen to recorded descriptions of exhibits. And in one of the most imaginative revenue-generating ventures to date, Cincinnati built a fountain in the Yeatman's Cove Municipal Park. Although water flows continually through the fountain, a quarter buys a spectacular three-minute display (Poole 1980).

Problems with user fees. One of the dangers in the aggressive use of fees as a means of generating municipal revenue is that people who cannot afford the fees are unable to use the service. For example, when Oakland, California, removed admission charges to two municipal swimming pools serving low-income neighborhoods, attendance increased by 29 percent and 67 percent respectively (Poole 1980). Presumably, if fees were introduced on free services, the number of economically disadvantaged people who use a service would decline dramatically.

The Washington-based Heritage Conservation and Recreation Service

387

suggested several strategies to reduce the impact of user fees on low-income groups. These include fee waivers or sliding fee structures, fees subsidized by local businesses or service clubs, and volunteer work in lieu of fees. A number of cities have used these suggestions (or developed their own arrangements) to reduce the economic hardship of user fees (see Poole 1980). For example, many museums waive admission at least one day a month (and some as frequently as one day each week). Second, many cities (e.g., Dallas, Santa Barbara) charge increased rates for nonresidents to use recreational facilities; although this does not directly affect user rates for low-income groups within the city, it indirectly affects these rates by reducing the total amount of revenue that must be produced from local sources. Third, some places (e.g., Sacramento) actively encourage local businesses to provide "recreational scholarships" for low-income children, while others (e.g., Fairfax County, Virginia) identify needy children and provide them with free passes to sports areas.

While these strategies no doubt improve access for low-income individuals to municipal recreational facilities, their symbolic benefits may be greater than their real benefits. In other words, municipal administrators may feel very magnanimous about opening museum doors without charge on the third Thursday of every month; but this strategy may (a) lead to overcrowding and detract from enjoyment on those free days and (b) preclude people who must work at low-paying (and often inflexible) jobs during the week. Further, the city that encourages local businesses to provide recreational scholarships to economically disadvantaged youth may be providing a symbolic more than a real benefit to its low-income residents, especially when the number of disadvantaged far exceeds the number of available scholarships.

Nationally, user fees accounted for approximately 15 percent of municipal general revenues in 1986, representing a flow of over $18 billion into municipal coffers. The very size of these figures almost ensures that at least some of the people who cannot afford services are being systematically excluded from those services. Yet, unlike the introduction of efficiency measures into municipal service delivery, user fees have become an important and integral part of municipal finance, one that most cities could ill afford to give up.

Privatization and Contracting-Out for Services

Probably the most dramatic innovation adopted by cities attempting to reduce their budgets is the *privatization of services*. Cities opting for this alternative may discontinue the service (e.g., garbage collection) altogether, allowing market forces to dictate the private companies that will offer the service and the price they will charge. Alternatively, cities may contract with a private company to provide the service, awarding the contract on the basis of bids submitted by interested parties in the private sector. In either case, the city gets out of the service delivery business, and the private sector quite likely is able to provide the service more efficiently and at a lower cost. By contracting-out, the city still maintains ultimate responsibility for the service, while under privatization it relinquishes the responsibility altogether.

Garbage collection is one service that many cities have turned over to the private sector. For example, Boston, Oklahoma City, Omaha, Dallas, Almagorda, New Mexico, and Utica, New York, all contract for garbage collection services, at a substantial fiscal savings. In a comprehensive study of privatized garbage collection, Stevens (1977) found that 36 percent of all urban dwellers in the United States are served by private trash collection firms, with some rather sobering results. In cities with more than 50,000 people, she found that costs of garbage collection by municipal agencies to be 68 percent higher than those of private firms. Several factors account for these savings: Private firms have lower absenteeism rates, use smaller crews, bigger trucks, and longer routes, and offer better labor incentives than municipal sanitation departments. An extreme example of the cost differential between public and private garbage collection occurs in a 1975 comparison between New York and San Francisco: The annual charge for municipal garbage collection in New York City was $297 per household, while the annual cost of private garbage collection in San Francisco was $40 per household (Poole 1980).

Fire protection is another area where privatization has become common. For example, in 1980 the Rural/Metro Fire Department, Inc. served thirty locations in five Arizona counties. Its fee structure of approximately $25 to $50 per year for most houses proved attractive, and it listed over 50,000 subscribers (mostly homeowners) on its books. Rural/Metro responded to fires in the homes or businesses of nonsubscribers, but the cost was dear: The fee levied for this response was fourteen times the annual subscription fee, *plus* $50/hour per fire vehicle and $10/hour for each command vehicle used, *plus* $15/hour per firefighter responding to the fire (Poole 1980). Similar arrangements have been offered by private fire departments in Georgia, Oregon, Montana, and Tennessee. In addition to strict privatization of firefighting services, some municipal governments contract with private fire companies to provide fire protection for their residents. For example, Scottsdale, Arizona contracts with Rural/Metro, at a cost approximately 25 percent below providing its own service (Poole 1980).

A third area where private companies offer subscriptions is emergency ambulance service. For example, in 1980 the Acadia Ambulance Service served 480,000 rural residents in nine Louisiana parishes. Seventy-five thousand families in the area subscribed at a rate of $15 per year, with nonsubscribers charged directly for any services they require. Similar subscription services are available in Oklahoma City and Eugene, Oregon (Poole 1980).

A fourth area where private companies offer services is law enforcement. For example, Lexington, Kentucky, and St. Petersburg, Florida, both contract with private firms to patrol high-crime areas. Additionally, exclusive residential areas in many cities employ their own private security force. Estimates suggest that private security firms employ between 500,000 and a million uniformed guards, compared with only a half-a-million police officers employed by municipal governments (Poole 1980).

Hidden costs of privatization and contracting-out. Across the board, privatization and contracting out for services may substantially decrease municipal expenditures. But those in favor of these strategies often lose sight of several hidden costs. First, private subscription services may not be affordable for people living near or below the poverty line. And given the increased costs of service for nonsubscribers, a nonsubscriber may perhaps not seek emergency ambulance service when it may save his or her life; or the non-subscribing homeowner with a small fire may attempt to control it himself or herself, thus risking greater damage to the entire neighborhood; or he or she may attempt to defeat burglaries with deadly boobytraps.

Second, private companies will provide services only so long as they are profitable. But once the profit has gone, the company has no legal obligation to continue the service, perhaps leaving the city and its residents in the lurch. Just as important, deregulation of private service providers may well result in differential fee structures for different neighborhoods: Those that generate the most demand will pay higher subscription rates than those with lower demand. Particularly in such areas as police and fire protection, those high-demand neighborhoods are likely to be low-income areas where residents are least able to pay subscription fees. The result may well be two levels of service: exemplary service for those who can pay for it and poor (or no) service for those who cannot.

The Resurgence of Urban Service Delivery: 1983 to the Present

Figures 16.1 and 16.2, and table 16.3, suggest that the urban service delivery saga does not end on a negative note. Since 1982, municipal expenditures have once again been on the rise (figure 16.1), and cities seem once again willing to borrow the money they need to finance capital projects (table 16.3). Thus, the days of cutback management may be behind us, and cities may be—once again—foresquare in the service delivery business. But rather than embracing this news too quickly—after all, it is too early to tell whether the years between 1983 and 1986 represent a trend, or whether they represent random fluctuation in a continuing decline—it will be useful to consider why the reversal may have occurred and the prospects for a continued resurgence.

One explanation involves need. Richard Hill (1984, 309) describes an urban infrastructure literally falling apart.

390

Two out of five of the nation's bridges must be replaced or repaired, at an estimated cost of $41 billion. $31 billion must be invested in sewer systems and waste water treatment plants over the next five years to meet pollution control standards. Cities must spend $110 billion over the next two decades to maintain their water systems.

Hill goes on to catalog what several older cities must do if they are to meet their needs:

- New York City will have to spend $40 billion to repair 6,000 miles of streets, 6,200 miles of sewers, 775 bridges, and a 1.5-billion-gallon-per-day water system;
- Chicago will have to spend $3.3 billion to repair or replace deteriorating streets, bridges, sewers, and transit lines;
- Dallas will have to spend over $700 million to repair a deteriorating water and sewer system.

Faced with these stark realities, many cities no doubt realize that increased expenditures are inevitable, particularly those involving capital improvements, and this realization helps fuel the growth in bonded indebtedness reflected in table 16.3.

Another explanation has similar origins. Faced with the need to cut back services, many cities laid off street-level bureaucrats, closed public facilities, or reduced service delivery schedules. To an electorate that had come to depend on these services, cutbacks pinched, and demands may have grown for services to be restored to their pre-1978 level (and beyond).

A third explanation holds that various strategies for financing municipal government during the 1979-1982 fiscal crisis were more successful than expected, bringing in sufficient municipal revenue to allow the expansion of services. For example, user fees and the sale of municipal property provided cities with over 15 percent of their general revenue in 1986, up from 11 percent in 1976. As cities developed additional revenue enhancements during the cutback years, they may have discovered that they had sufficient funds to provide more services without higher taxes.

A fourth explanation is tied to the economy. During the cutback years, the economy was sluggish, interest rates were high, and inflation was rampant. As a result, tax revenues were down, and cities were understandably reluctant to borrow money at prevailing interest rates. But since 1983, the economy has expanded, and both interest rates and inflation are down. And with economic recovery, tax receipts are up (see figure 16.10): Between 1982 and 1986, annual per capita taxes on urban residents have gone from $90.90 to $103.35, nearly equal to the 1977 high-water mark of $105.07. In times of economic well-being, with increased tax revenues and increased voter optimism in the future, politicians may be more willing to expand the scope of service delivery.

Whichever of these explanations holds—and it is likely that all have some merit—the delivery of urban services in the future is likely to follow an erratic path. The decaying infrastructure is not likely to improve at any time soon, and cities will continue to face the need for repairing, rebuilding, and modernizing their facilities. Yet, cities are unlikely to fund those projects without outside assistance: Recent history shows that taxpayers are unwilling to write the city a blank check. In an age-old dilemma faced by virtually all governments, citizens demand services, but they are unwilling to pay for those that do not benefit them personally. So we are likely to witness a growing demand, but a reluctance to pay for what is demanded. In addition, if the delivery of services continues to be tied to economic performance, city services are likely to rise and fall according to national trends completely beyond local control. So if there is one certainty, it is that urban service delivery will be less certain than in the past, when the growth of services continued virtually unabated for three decades (1945-1978), unimpeded by economic fluctuations, voter sentiment, or need.

Night on the "El" Train. Edward Hopper. 1920. Etching. Gift of the Print and Drawing Club. 1944.154. © 1989 The Art Institute of Chicago, All Rights Reserved.

Poverty, Race, and the Delivery of Urban Services

For the middle class, the police protect property, give directions, and help old
ladies. For the urban poor, the police are those who arrest you.
  Michael Harrington
  The Other America

Politics, as noted all through these pages, is the struggle for power, and an
important aspect of power is the ability to set the political agenda, and through
the agenda, to achieve one's desired ends. Policy is thus the embodiment of
both politics and power. But politics and power are not limited to the single
individual acting on his or her own behalf and seeking outcomes that are only
personally rewarding. Politics and power are also group endeavors whose outcomes affect whole populations and large classes of people within those
populations. These are the ideas that have guided our discussion thus far; and
nowhere are these ideas more applicable than in an examination of city service delivery—particularly as these services have become bound up with the
lives of the urban poor and social minorities.

But to prepare for the analysis that follows, it will be useful to extract
from previous chapters other, equally important themes and theories. Seven
such themes and theories provide the foundation for our exploration of
poverty, race, and the delivery of urban services.

1. Most of the major problems of the city are in the city, but not of the
   city (their roots, however defined, are in the larger society and not in
   the city per se).

2. Major social problems are not readily or easily solved. Social policy (in contrast to technical policy) usually carries unanticipated consequences. More important, most social problems have multiple causes, and attempted solutions usually involve heavy costs, both fiscal and social.
3. What is observed by social critics may be less a matter of "fact" than a matter of interpretation, with interpretation (in its turn) a consequence of deeply held personal values and beliefs.
4. American society is dominated by a long-standing commitment to a market economy. This translates into a commitment to the privileged place of private property, the ideal that each of us is entitled to whatever share of life's goods and services we can pay for, and the belief that each of us bears responsibility for the successes and failures in our lives.
5. American society holds an equally strong commitment to the view that a reasonable share of life's goods and services ought to be the birthright of all. This commitment combines with that cited in 4 above to produce tension between social equity and market equity.
6. Concepts of lifestyle and territory create a metropolitan patchwork. This metropolitan patchwork, coupled with considerations of social and market equity, lead us to consider the (a) equity (or lack of it) in the disparity between central-city and suburban expenditures for urban services, and (b) strategies the affluent use to wall out the poor.
7. Public policy at the urban level is largely implemented by street-level bureaucrats. As a result, policy may be distorted, particularly in its application to the poor and minorities, by uneven implementation practices.

With these considerations in mind, we turn now to an exploration of the connection between poverty, race, and the delivery of urban services.

The Demographics of Poverty

Popular Misconceptions of Poverty[1]

Two popular views of poverty in America are that (1) the vast majority of the nation's poor reside in cities, and (2) most of the nation's poor are black or Hispanic. Neither statement holds up to scrutiny. In 1986, for example, nearly 5 million white families (22.9 million people) survived on incomes below the

---

1. The poverty statistics reported in this sction are taken from two Bureau of the Census publications: *Poverty in the United States 1985* and *The Statistical Abstract of the United States.*

Table 17.1a   The Demographics of Poverty in America—1985

| | Metropolitan Areas | | Nonmetropolitan | |
	Central City	Suburbs	Areas	Total
Families living in poverty	3,012	2,029	2,182	7,223
Percent white	54.2	81.7	78.2	69.0
Percent black	41.7	15.7	18.7	27.5
Percent Hispanic[a]	23.5	12.3	5.4	14.9
Percent of all families living in poverty				
White	11.5	6.0	12.7	9.1
Black	30.3	19.2	36.6	28.7
Hispanic[a]	30.3	16.5	32.7	25.5

a. Hispanics may be of any race. Percentages therefore do not sum to 100.
SOURCE: Adapted from U.S. Bureau of the Census (1985).

poverty level,[2] compared with approximately 2 million black families (nearly 9 million people) and just over 1 million Hispanic families (approximately 5 million people).[3] Further, while about 70 percent of the poor *do* reside in metropolitan areas (42.5 percent in central cities, 27.5 percent in the suburbs), 30 percent live outside these areas. However, when these two misconceptions are joined, they produce a different conclusion: *Urban* poverty and race are related. For example, 61 percent of poor blacks and 64 percent of poor Hispanics live in central cities, compared with 35 percent of poor whites. Further, whereas 27 percent of the nation's poor are black, 38 percent of the nation's poor, central-city dwellers are black. Similarly, 7.6 percent of the nation's poor are Hispanic, but 24 percent of the poor in the central cities are Hispanic. Still, even in central cities, the vast majority of people live above the poverty line.[4] Tables 17.1a,b summarize these and other demographic characteristics of the poor.

2. The definition of poverty is complicated, depending on family size and age of family members. In 1985, the cutoff levels for annual monetary income were as follows:

1 person			
under 65	$5,593	4 people	$10,989
65 or older	5,156	5 people	13,007
2 people		6 people	14,696
householder under 65	7,231	7 people	16,656
householder 65 or older	6,503	8 people	18,512
3 people	8,573	9 or more people	22,083

3. It is the case, however, that a larger *percentage* of blacks and Hispanics than whites live in poverty: In 1985, 9.1 percent of white families had incomes below the poverty line, compared with 28.7 percent of black and 25.5 percent of Hispanic families.
4. 89 percent of white families, 69 percent of black families, and 69 percent of Hispanic families living in inner cities have incomes above the poverty line.

Other misconceptions also stand in the way of an understanding of poverty in America. The largest single age group living in poverty is children under six (23 percent of all children under six live in poverty), followed closely by older children aged six to seventeen (19 percent) and young adults aged eighteen to twenty-four (17 percent). The elderly, many of whom live on fixed pensions, constitute a fourth major poverty category (13 percent). Most families living in poverty are small. Fifty-six percent consist of three or fewer

Table 17.1b The Demographics of Poverty in America—1985

		Poverty			
	Nonpoverty	All	White	Black	Hispanic[a]
Mean family size	3.17	3.56	3.44	3.78	3.81
Percent of heads of households with a high school degree	77.3	49.2	49.4	48.1	45.9
Percent of families headed by a female	16.1	48.1	39.1	73.2	48.5
Age distribution of persons living in poverty (percent)					
under 15	20.0	33.6	30.9	39.8	42.3
15-17	4.5	5.7	5.2	6.8	7.5
18-24	11.1	13.5	13.9	13.0	13.8
25-44	32.8	23.9	24.6	21.4	24.5
45-64	19.9	12.8	13.6	11.1	7.8
65 and older	11.7	10.5	11.8	8.0	4.2
Percent of all persons living in poverty		14.0	11.4	31.3	29.0
under 15		21.5	16.8	44.9	40.4
15-17		17.1	13.2	37.1	39.2
18-24		16.5	14.0	31.2	28.0
25-45		10.8	8.8	32.4	22.6
45-64		9.5	8.0	22.2	16.8
65 and older		12.6	11.0	31.5	23.9
Percent of heads of households not working during the previous year	19.2	48.9	44.6	59.4	49.4
Reasons for not working					
ill or disabled	18.4	23.9	23.7	25.6	21.3
keeping house	10.0	40.3	38.2	44.9	42.8
attending school	1.2	3.8	3.5	2.9	
unable to find work	1.7	14.5	12.9	16.5	35.9
retired	67.9	15.2	18.1	9.0	
other	0.8	2.3	2.9	1.2	

a. Hispanics may be of any race.
SOURCE: Adapted from U.S. Bureau of the Census (1985).

members, with a mean size of 3.56. Fewer than half the families living in poverty are headed by mothers, although among blacks this figure reaches 73 percent. Approximately 50 percent of the heads of families living in poverty are high-school graduates (and 16 percent have completed at least one year of college); this figure is somewhat lower than the 77 percent high-school graduation rate for non-poverty families, although not as low as popular wisdom would lead us to expect.

Of those families living in poverty in 1983, 51 percent were partially supported by the earnings of a family member who worked at least part time. Often this was the head of the household: Fifty percent worked at least part time, and 20 percent worked full time for forty or more weeks during the year. Holding down a job and caring for children is obviously most difficult for single parents, most of whom are women. The statistics support this conclusion. In two-parent poverty-level families (with children present), 74 percent were supported by wages brought in by at least one parent; in contrast, the householder worked at least part time in 62 percent of those poverty-level families (with children) headed by a single male householder, and in 40 percent of those poverty-level families (with children) headed by a single female.[5] Among those heads of households who do not work, 24 percent are ill or disabled, 40 percent are caring for children and keeping house, 14 percent are unable to find work, and 15 percent are retired. Thus, the assertion that those living in poverty are doing so by choice does not hold up.

Nor does the popular misconception of the welfare recipient living the good life at the taxpayer's expense. The largest public assistance program is AFDC (Aid to Families with Dependent Children), which disperses nearly $13 billion dollars a year to the poor. Yet, in most cases, the monthly checks that a typical family receives are meager. In some states, average monthly AFDC payments have been generous, at least comparatively: $532 in California (in 1986), $507 in Minnesota, $496 in Wisconsin, $474 in Michigan, $466 in Connecticut, $431 in Washington. In other states, however, they are pitifully low: $116 in Mississippi, $171 in Texas, $114 in Alabama, $143 in Tennessee, $186 in South Carolina, and $178 in Arkansas. But in no case does this income, even coupled with other programs such as food stamps and Medicaid, allow a person to escape entirely from poverty. For example, in 1986 the median monthly rent in San Francisco was approximately $480, which took a healthy bite even out of California's comparatively large AFDC payment. And in cities like Dallas (with a 1985 median monthly rent of approximately $376), the rent for decent housing by itself more than consumed monthly AFDC payments.

5. The percentage of poverty-level families headed by workers employed on a full-time basis are obviously lower: 31 percent for two-parent households, 22 percent for households headed by males, and 7 percent for households headed by females.

The Plight of the Poor

Housing. For the most part, the poor do not live in decent housing. One rough and ready measure of housing inadequacy is related to overcrowding. On average, the majority of housing units within the United States are not grossly overcrowded, although most of us wish for more space from time to time. For example, the 1980 census shows that only 4.5 percent of all living units housed an average of more than one person per room. However, this figure is subject to substantial variation. Using this one-person-to-a-room criterion as a rough definition of overcrowding, 8.2 percent of the families in New York City live in overcrowded conditions, compared with 13 percent in Los Angeles, 12.4 percent in El Paso, 12.3 percent in Newark, and 19.9 percent in Miami. Other cities have lesser degrees of overcrowding: For example, only 4.2 percent of families in Philadelphia live in overcrowded conditions, 2.8 percent in Seattle, 2.1 percent in Buffalo, and 2 percent in Minneapolis.

More troubling is the lack of indoor plumbing for 1.6 million families in the United States. As might be expected, this is not a randomly distributed phenomenon: While only 1.7 percent of housing units occupied by whites are without plumbing, 3.8 percent of those occupied by Hispanics and 5.5 percent of those occupied by blacks are without plumbing. In another comparison, only 2 percent of those families occupying uncrowded housing units (i.e., one or fewer people per room) are without plumbing, compared with 4 percent of those families occupying overcrowded housing units (i.e., 1.01-1.5 persons per room) and 12 percent of those families occupying severely overcrowded units (i.e., more than 1.5 people per room). Many families go without heat during the winter; while this may pose little discomfort in many parts of the country, it can be life-threatening in others. Finally, and even worse, many go without homes altogether. The problem of the homeless has received considerable attention recently, and estimates place between half-a-million and 2 million people in this category.[6]

Health. The lack of sufficient—or for the homeless, any—shelter is not the only health hazard faced by the poor. Robert Green (1977, 247) describes the reality of poverty this way:

> Poverty is protecting your baby from rodents, eating Argo laundry starch straight from the box, knowing chronic tuberculosis, accepting the neighborhood psychotic ("He's just crazy"), waiting and more waiting for health care in the clinic, tolerating painful tooth decay, feeling the clutches of death come early, filling out interminable forms, being denied medical treat-

6. *Time* (Oct. 24, 1988) reports that on any given night, "an estimated 735,000 people are homeless. As many as two million may be without shelter for one night or more during the year."

ment unless a magic insurance card or money is apparent, living in life-threatening housing, learning the virtues and limitations of home remedies, being jobless and without health insurance (or being unable to afford the deductible), feeling the lack of respect from professionals, praying that your children will somehow survive and face a better world.

A number of statistics attest to his conclusions. For example, blacks lose 15 percent more days to disabilities each year than whites, and those with low incomes lose over 200 percent more days than those with higher incomes.[7] As another example, blacks and whites see physicians at approximately equal rates, but whites visit dentists 60 percent more frequently than blacks. Even in the case of physician contact, different patterns emerge for blacks and whites, and for wealthy and poor. For whites, 71 percent of all contacts with physicians are through office visits, with another 13 percent through phone consultation. For blacks, less than 60 percent of all contact is through office visits, and only 5 percent through phone consultation. Instead, 27 percent of all contact is in emergency rooms (compared to only 11 percent for whites), where individuals are treated either for accidents or for acute emergencies that might have been prevented through regular visits to physicians' offices. The pattern is even more pronounced for the poor (and particularly for poor blacks), for whom 34 percent of all contact with physicians is in emergency settings.

Living and dying in poverty. These discrepancies are epitomized by morbidity and mortality rates. One study found anemia rates among the poor to be over two times higher than among those living outside of poverty (Department of Health, Education, and Welfare 1977). Another found a disproportionate level of heart disease, mental and nervous conditions, arthritis and rheumatism, high blood pressure, orthopedic impairments, and visual impairments among the poor (Department of Health, Education, and Welfare 1971).[8] A third study shows that while 60–65 percent of middle- and upper-class people with cancer survive, only about 30 percent of poor people with the same cancer survive (Associated Press, September 24, 1989). A fourth study shows that the poor suffer from mental retardation and mental illness at rates

---

7. This comparison between blacks and whites is not intended to emphasize a racial difference. Rather, it simply acknowledges that a larger percentage of blacks than whites live in poverty, particularly in urban areas. Thus, we should conclude that any differences are due to class rather than to race per se. Race serves as a proxy for class for two reasons: First, statistics are much more readily available by race than by class or income, making some comparisons possible and others easier. Second, income often confounds the comparison. For example, in comparing days lost to disability for different income classes, we face two problems. When days are lost to disability, income suffers, leading to the alternative conclusion that disability causes loss of income rather than that lack of income causes disability; and those employed in low-income jobs may face greater risk of disability than those in high-income jobs.

8. This and the previous study were quoted by Palley and Palley (1981).

considerably higher than those found for the nonpoor (Fried 1975); for example, admission rates to state and county mental institutions for schizophrenia run four times higher for nonwhites than for whites, and admission rates for organic brain syndrome run nearly two-and-one-half times as high (Department of Health and Human Services 1986). Mortality rates, particularly those related to childbirth, tell a similar story (Department of Health and Human Services 1986). The infant mortality rate for whites is 9.7 per 1,000, while that for blacks is 19.2. Maternal deaths for white women are 5.9 per 100,000, compared to 16.3 for non-whites. Much of the blame for these divergent statistics can be laid on the availability of care for whites versus that for blacks and the poor (Green 1977). While whites receive prenatal care at the offices of private physicians, inner-city blacks receive such care at overcrowded public clinics or not at all.

In general, life expectancy for blacks (71.3 years) is lower than for whites (75.2 years). Even more disturbing is the way in which those living in poverty die prematurely. For example, accidental death, homicide, and suicide rates for those living in poverty are between 50 percent and 100 percent higher than for those living above the poverty level (Palley and Palley 1981). One finding that should give pause to city dwellers shows a 2 percent likelihood that any baby born in the nation's twenty-six largest cities (i.e., those with populations in excess of 500,000) will be murdered (Green 1977); and among black males, the murder rate is 5.9 times higher than among white males. As most know, crime in the United States tends to be committed by the poor (39 percent of prison inmates were unemployed at the time of their arrest; 61 percent had not completed high school). But perhaps more surprisingly, the poor are also the most frequent victims of crime. For example, the poorest of households (i.e., annual income under $3,000) are burglarized at an annual rate of 12.1 percent, compared to a rate of under 7 percent for higher-income households (i.e., $15,000 + annual income). In Detroit, 80 percent of all perpetrators *as well as victims* of homicide and assault are black (Wells 1975).[9] In short, crime in large cities tends to be by the poor against the poor.

The Ramifications of National Urban Policy Reconsidered

We now have had the experience of a half century of federal policies and programs that attempt to address the problems of poverty and discrimination in the city (see chapters 14 and 15). All in all, these programs have done much to improve the lives of the poor and those who suffer the consequences of racial and ethnic discrimination. But these programs are not without their failures. Persistent and widespread problems do not easily give way to solutions. Their causes are manifold and deeply woven into the fabric of society.

---

9. This compares with a 63 percent black population in Detroit.

Accordingly, we can gain some better sense of the intractability of urban problems—along with some better sense of their ramifying roots—by extending the discussion of the previous chapters, looking again at two aspects of inequality in the city—education and housing. This second look may also assist in understanding how and why policies that seek major social change can never be undertaken without considerable social and political costs, and why policies seeking major social changes are never without disputation over fundamental values and beliefs.

Bias in the Classroom

The legally sanctioned segregation of pupils by race and ethnicity is now ended (as noted in chapter 14). But just as important, the reluctance of the courts to require metropolitan-wide school integration makes it likely that schools in the central city will be increasingly populated by minority students, for those who can afford to purchase houses in the suburbs take themselves—and their school-aged children—out from the central cities.

But even in those areas where schools in the central city remain integrated due to within-district busing or integrated residential patterns, is it likely that blacks and other minorities—and more generally, the poor—receive an education equal to that of whites? In general, no.

One explanation for this inequality begins with an uncontrovertible fact: The poor are relatively undereducated. As noted earlier in this chapter, those who head poor households have received fewer years of schooling than those heading non-poor households. This, in turn, affects their earning power and their ability to escape from poverty. But even more to the point is the differential dropout rate for the underclass and for the middle and upper classes. For example, 22 percent of all high school sophomores from lower socioeconomic strata drop out of school, compared with 12 percent of those from the middle socioeconomic strata and 7 percent of those from the upper strata (National Center for Education Statistics 1985). Further, once they have dropped out, students of higher socioeconomic status (SES) are two-and-one-half times more likely than lower SES students to reenter school or attain a General Education Degree. Even within SES groupings, minorities are more likely to drop out and less likely to return to school once they have dropped out (Kolstad and Owings 1986). The children of underclass households are less likely to receive a diploma (and attain the earning power that a diploma commands) than children of middle- and upper-class households.

Tracking. A further explanation holds that public policy is inequitably distributed among underclass and economically advantaged students. For example, many schools still use a tracking system, emphasizing college-preparatory courses for better students and a basic or vocational curriculum

403

for less-able students. While the policy itself may be without social or racial bias, its implementation is often biased in favor of upper- and middle-class white students. The bias centers around the difficulty in determining a student's ability. While a number of intelligence tests have been developed, critics charge that these are culturally biased (in both content and administration), discriminating against black, Hispanic, and other minority students (e.g., Persell 1977). Further, these paper-and-pencil tests often measure achievement rather than ability and creativity, again biasing them in favor of students who have had richer cultural experiences and against those with relatively deprived childhoods (see Gould, 1981, for a general discussion of bias in intelligence tests).

In the absence of valid measures of student academic potential, teachers often rely on other cues, including stereotyping, to identify those students who would benefit most from a college-preparatory curriculum (Lipsky 1980). Unfortunately, these cues may have a racial and class bias. In one study, Eleanor Leacock (quoted in Green 1977) shows teachers to have more negative attitudes toward black children than white children (43 percent vs. 17 percent), and to favor middle-class over lower-class children (40 percent vs. 20 percent). As a result, students from low-income homes in general and blacks and Hispanics in particular are tracked disproportionately into the basic-skill and vocational curricula, with middle- and upper-class students in general and whites in particular guided into a college-preparatory curriculum (Rosenbaum 1976, Goodlad 1984).

At first glance, this tracking bias would seem to be a rectifiable error: Even after being incorrectly categorized, students can demonstrate their ability, be reevaluated, and reclassified into more advanced academic tracks. While this is possible in principle, and has no doubt happened on many occasions, it is easier in principle than in practice. The underlying impediment to high student achievement in the face of negative teacher expectations is that teacher expectations, themselves, act as barriers to achievement. Teachers spend more time with, demand higher quality work from, and offer more encouragement to those students they expect to succeed, and in the process hinder the progress of students they expect to fail (Rosenthal and Jacobson 1968; see Dusek, 1975, for a review).[10] And teacher bias toward underclass students, however

---

10. In their seminal study, which they published as *Pygmalion in the Classroom,* Robert Rosenthal and Lenore Jacobson (1968) examine the impact of teacher expectations on second-grade students in San Francisco. They identified two groups of second-grade students, ostensibly based on their first-grade achievement test scores, but in reality based on random assignment. Thus, while one group of students was identified as "academic spurters" and the other group as "ordinary students," the two groups were, in reality, no different in academic ability or achievement. Rosenthal and Jacobson shared these classifications with second-grade teachers. At the end of the school year, student achievement levels were again measured, and the "academic spurters" outperformed the "ordinary students." Since at the beginning of the year these two groups were identical in academic ability, the only explanation for the change was differential teacher behavior toward the two groups of students.

subtle, may keep minority and poor students from advancing as rapidly as white middle- and upper-class students. Just as important, a student who is tracked into a basic skills or a vocational curriculum may grow to doubt his or her ability, and academic performance may suffer. So, for whatever reason, tracking negatively affects the achievement of students placed in the lower ability groups (e.g., Alexander, et al. 1978).

Other policies. Differential treatment of the poor and minorities is also manifest in the implementation of disciplinary policies within schools and school districts. For example, in 1977 the NAACP argued in a suit against the New York City Board of Education that black and Hispanic problem children are routinely assigned to problem schools, while white children with similar behavior problems are routinely helped in their own schools (Lipsky 1980; see Green, 1977, for other examples).

The point of this discussion is not that nothing can be done to scrub the educational process clean of class, racial, and ethnic discrimination. Rather, the discussion is intended to secure a basic idea: The causes of major social problems are manifold and that they are deeply woven into the fabric of our society. It is a point to be encountered again as we turn to issues and problems of residential segregation in urban America.

The Politics and Policies of Residential Segregation[11]

Unlike legally sanctioned segregation in the classroom, legally sanctioned residential segregation has not ended. Until the middle years of this century, cities employed heavy-handed approaches to keeping minorities and the poor segregated. In the late-nineteenth and early-twentieth centuries, for example, a number of municipalities (e.g., San Francisco, Baltimore, Atlanta, and Louisville) enacted ordinances mandating racial or ethnic segregation. These were uniformly overturned by the courts by 1920 (Rice 1968, Johnston 1984). As an alternative, cities, neighborhoods, and land developers fashioned a number of strategies for maintaining residential segregation. The most effective of these was the *restrictive covenant*, a formal and binding component of the

---

11. One commonly invoked explanation for residential segregation in the United States is that blacks prefer to live in segregated areas (e.g., Coleman 1979). However, several studies (summarized by Darden 1983) cast doubt on this conclusion. For example, McGehee and Watson (1977) report that 77 percent of blacks in a Detroit survey indicate a preference for integrated housing. Darden (1983) explains the continuing popularity of the segregation-by-choice hypothesis by suggesting that it provides a rationale for maintaining the status quo and delaying or preventing residential integration. Further, he suggests that its advocates, in drawing parallels to the white European immigrant groups who clustered together to enjoy a common linguistic, cultural, or religious tradition, fail to understand that blacks are drawn together not by choice but as an involuntary adaptation to white discrimination; and once together, they do not share a common culture so much as a common set of grievances.

deed of sale prohibiting the owner of land from engaging in certain specified activities or behaviors associated with the property.[12] Some covenants prohibited the owner from selling property to members of specific racial or ethnic groups, for example blacks and Jews. Such restrictions were widespread in many major cities (Vose 1959). This practice was allowed to stand until 1948, when the United States Supreme Court, in *Shelley v. Kraemer*,[13] ruled it unconstitutional. By that time, however, housing patterns had largely been established in American cities, and once established they were difficult to break down.[14]

One result of the *Shelley* ruling was that cities—particularly suburbs—invoked other, more subtle practices and ordinances to achieve comparable restrictive purposes, resulting in de facto segregation. As previously noted, de facto segregation is legally assisted through zoning ordinances aimed at preserving property values and land use assignment (e.g., zoning that prohibits multiple-family dwellings or factory location; zoning that requires large lots, property setbacks, or otherwise places a neighborhood or city beyond the purchase price of low-income families). Such zoning, where the intent is not clearly racial exclusion, is generally permitted by the courts, for they are usually reluctant to interfere with that basic American value—private property.

Real Estate Practices

Although de facto segregation is attributable largely to exclusionary zoning, it also derives from the informal practices of the real estate and mortgage banking industries. Real estate owners and agents are forbidden by law to refuse to sell or rent housing because of race, religion, or national origin. That practice was ruled unconstitutional by the U.S. Supreme Court in 1968[15] and outlawed by the Fair Housing Act of 1968.[16] Yet, the practice continues

12. Clarence Stone (in a note to the authors) suggests that in addition to restrictive covenants, racial and ethnic segregation was maintained through the development of roads and parks to create physical barriers between neighborhoods or to remove small concentrations of minorities in otherwise white areas, and through selective law enforcement.

13. 334 US 1.

14. Other types of covenants were invented in an effort to keep blacks and ethnics out of neighborhoods. One provides neighbors (and in some cases the land developer) with first right of purchase if a lot in the neighborhood is placed on the market. Another ties residence to membership in a particular social group or club (for example, membership in a country club may be required of all residents in a neighborhood bordering a golf course). In the first case, blacks and ethnics may be effectively prohibited from purchasing land through neighbors' right of first refusal. In the second, they may be prohibited residence through exclusionary membership policies of the social group or club.

15. *Jones v. Alfred Mayer Co.,* 392 US 409.

16. The Fair Housing Act made it unlawful to "refuse to sell or rent after the making of a bona fide offer, or to refuse to negotiate for the sale or rental of, or otherwise make unavailable or deny, a dwelling to any person because of race, color, religion, or national origin." However, the law offered an

informally and in most instances seemingly beyond the reach of the law.[17] For example, a telephone solicitor for a Wheaton, Maryland, real estate developer in 1969 (after passage of the Fair Housing Act) reported that if she contacted someone who she suspected was black, company policy dictated that she not follow up on that contact. Further, she reported, while solicitors were given a bonus when they arranged interviews between a salesperson and a prospective client, this bonus was not provided if the client turned out to be black (Arkes 1981).

As another example, Diana Pearce (1976) found considerable evidence of "racial steering" in Detroit. In a 1975 study, she sent demographically identical white and black couples seeking housing to a number of real estate firms. Whereas agents showed homes to 75 percent of the white couples, only 25 percent of the black couples received the same treatment. Further, when they were shown homes, the black and the white couples were taken to different areas. In a more recent national study, Pearce (1983) found similar evidence of unequal treatment and steering.

In addition, William Tisdale (1983) outlines several procedures that real estate agents and apartment managers use to keep minority applicants away from rental housing. These include:

1. Requiring larger application fees (e.g., an entire month's rent and the security deposit) of minority applicants than of white applicants.
2. Requiring more stringent application criteria (e.g., higher income, longer time on the job, more references) of minority applicants than of white applicants.
3. Requiring that a prospective tenant be recommended by a present tenant.
4. Advertising available rental units only in publications with limited circulation (predominantly among non-minority readers), by word of mouth, or on bulletin boards of all-white churches or clubs.
5. Using a telephone answering machine to screen out applicants (i.e., calls from people suspected of being black are not returned).

---

important loophole by distinguishing between a strictly private act of discrimination (i.e., individuals selling private residences) and one relying on public resources *of any kind* (e.g., individuals selling residences through the use of real estate firms, the media, agents, mail, or posted notices). Under the law, the former acts are exempted, while the latter are prohibited. Note the similarity between this private-public distinction and the one used to define politics in chapter 6. One implication is that nonpolitical acts of discrimination are tolerated, while political acts of discrimination are not. For a useful discussion of the 1968 Fair Housing Act, see Arkes (1981).

17. Filing a lawsuit can be expensive, and proving intent to discriminate is difficult.

Banking Practices

A complementary practice employed by banks is "redlining," or withholding loans for reasons other than the applicant's financial standing.[18] Christine Klepper (1983) reports that lending institutions are much more likely to issue home loans to applicants buying houses in predominantly white areas of Chicago than to those in largely black areas: Whereas 69 percent of the loan applications in census tracts with 0 percent to 5 percent black residents were approved, only 5 percent were approved in census tracts containing more than 20 percent black residents (and only 2 percent were approved in census tracts containing more than 50 percent black residents). While several factors may account for this finding, she concludes that redlining and discrimination are critical. Nationwide statistics show that blacks are turned down for home loans twice as often as whites, and that high-income blacks are rejected at about the same rate as low-income whites (*Atlanta Constitution*, Jan. 22, 1989, p. 1). The Community Reinvestment Act, passed by Congress in 1977 to allow low-income families in low-income neighborhoods to obtain mortgages, has done little to alleviate these discriminatory practices, and when mortgage money has gone to targeted neighborhoods, it seldom goes to the poorest or the most disadvantaged in those neighborhoods (*American Banker*, Dec. 29, 1988, p. 5).

Zoning

The legal line that separates zoning for racial exclusivity and zoning to foster rational land use and protect property values is very fine indeed. Beginning in 1926, when it ruled in *Village of Euclid v. Ambler Realty Co.*,[19] the U.S. Supreme Court has consistently upheld the right of municipalities to regulate the use of their land and resources to ensure the public welfare. In the following years, most urban governments have taken advantage of this right, for example by restricting certain neighborhoods to single-family residences. In addition, many zoning ordinances specify minimum lot sizes, setbacks, side yards, and floor areas for specified neighborhoods; others restrict trailer parks.[20] Although these ordinances limit the access of the poor to many neighborhoods (or even to entire cities), the courts justify limitations in three ways:

18. The term "redlining" derives from the practice of marking out an area on a map in red, thereby designating it as a high-risk investment area.

19. 272 US 365.

20. The courts have generally upheld these ordinances (e.g., *Village of Belle Terre v. Boraas*, 416 US 1, 1974; *Vickers v. Township Committee of Gloucester Township*, 371 US 233, 1962; *James v. Valtierra* and *Shaffer v. Valtierra*, 402 US 137, 1971; *Warth v. Seldin*, 442 US 490, 1975). See Johnston (1984) for a discussion.

1. zoning protects neighborhoods from unwanted externalities (e.g., noise, litter)[21];
2. the poor can equally well live elsewhere[22];
3. a law that disadvantages a particular group (e.g., the poor) does not necessarily deny equal protection.[23]

This latter argument was used again by the Supreme Court in *Arlington Heights v. Metropolitan Housing Development Corp.*[24] Residents in Arlington Heights, a Chicago suburb, objected to the construction of a federally funded, high-density housing project on land designated for single-family residences. The city denied the Metropolitan Housing Development Corporation's request for a zoning variance, citing the availability of land already zoned for apartments. The court upheld the city's decision, ruling that although it precluded predominantly black public housing recipients from locating in the area designated for single family residences, this differential impact is insufficient evidence of intent. Rather, the court argued, "proof of a racially discriminatory motive, purpose, or intent is required to find a violation of the Fourteenth Amendment" (Mandelker 1977, 1236).[25] Municipalities, therefore, may zone as a way of ensuring economic homogeneity without violating the equal protection clause of the Fourteenth Amendment, even though race and income are highly correlated.[26]

A recent decision by the New Jersey Supreme Court raises questions about the long-term acceptability of zoning to keep out the poor. In 1975,

21. In the *Belle Terre* case (see note 20), residents kept students attending a nearby college from locating in their community through a single-family zoning ordinance. In upholding this ordinance, the court wrote:

> The regimes of boarding houses, fraternity houses, and the like present urban problems. More people occupy a given space; more cars rather continuously pass by; more cars are parked; noise travels with crowds. . . . [The right to zone] is not confined to elimination of filth, stench, and unhealthy places. It is ample to lay out zones where family values, youth values, and the blessings of quiet seclusion and clean air make the area a sanctuary for people. (P. 804)

22. *Ybarra v. City of Los Altos* (503 F2d 250, 1974).

23. In the *Valtierra* case (see note 20), the court explicitly noted that discrimination on the basis of wealth is not a constitutional violation since, it concluded, discrimination by wealth does not necessarily mean discrimination by race.

24. 429 US 252, 1977.

25. One such case was *United States v. City of Black Jack, Missouri.* The details of this case are discussed in chapter 14.

26. However, the courts have taken a less permissive view of boundary gerrymandering, often overruling laws that they viewed as capricious, or that otherwise violated due process. For example, in the mid 1950s, 80 percent of the residents of Tuskeegee, Alabama (population 6,700) were black and unregistered to vote. The predominantly white electorate voted to change the boundaries of the town from a square to a twenty-eight-sided figure, thus placing 80 percent of the black population outside the city limits. The U.S. Supreme Court overturned this boundary change (*Gomillion v. Lightfoot*, 364 US 339, 1960) as an abridgment of black residents' Fourteenth and Fifteenth Amendment rights. See R.J. Johnston (1984) for an excellent review of this and other decisions.

the court had ruled in *Southern Burlington NAACP v. Township of Mt. Laurel* [27] that the New Jersey Constitution, in providing its citizens the right to acquire, possess, and protect property, precluded municipalities from excluding the poor to keep property taxes low. The decision established:

> That every developing municipality has an obligation to provide the opportunity for the satisfaction of its fair share of the regional need for housing of persons of low and moderate income. This "opportunity" must be provided through non-exclusionary (or "inclusionary") land-use controls and other "necessary and advisable" actions. (Bisgaier 1977, 140) [28]

In other words, it established a precedent for protecting the poor, as well as minorities, from unequal treatment (at least in New Jersey). By the 1980s, however, the court was dismayed to discover that municipalities were doing little to change their exclusionary zoning policies. However, the enforcement mechanism it provided—litigation—was unlikely to be effective, for three reasons (Bisgaier 1983):

1. there were few private litigants and no public litigants willing to undertake litigation;
2. litigation was costly and tended to drag on endlessly, and there was no guarantee of success in the lower courts;
3. recalcitrant municipalities had little fear of the consequences of losing suits, since they were in existence before the *Mt. Laurel* decision.

To remedy this situation, the New Jersey Supreme Court issued a second decision on Mt. Laurel (*Southern Burlington NAACP v. Township of Mt. Laurel.* [29] In *Mt. Laurel II,* the court changed the enforcement mechanism to a so-called builder's remedy: Builders who successfully litigate cases are granted approval, within certain limitations, of their development proposals. This created an enormous incentive for builders to challenge vulnerable municipalities, creating overnight a large class of potential plaintiffs (Bisgaier 1983). Although the final implications are not yet clear, it seems likely that this ruling will create an incentive for municipalities to modify their reliance on exclusionary zoning. And just as important, the courts in other states (e.g., New York; see Bellman 1983) have considered similar actions. Yet, given the conflicting standards set down by the United States Supreme Court in its

27. 67 NJ 151.
28. Quoted in Johnston 1984.
29. 92 NJ 158, 1983. Since the court based its *Mt. Laurel* decision on the New Jersey Constitution rather than the Fourteenth Amendment of the United States Constitution, it is unlikely to be overturned in federal courts.

Arlington Heights decision and the New Jersey Supreme Court in its *Mt. Laurel* decisions, nationwide change in exclusionary zoning laws seem unlikely in the near future.

Siting Decisions

Low-cost housing. Zoning ordinances are not the only means for enforcing residential segregation. Also important are municipal decisions concerning the location of low-income housing units within the city. In St. Louis, for example, public housing has been constructed in dilapidated and rundown areas, often surrounded by abandoned buildings (see the discussion of Pruitt-Igoe in chapter 14; also see Meehan 1975). More generally, low-cost housing sites have not been selected to allow residents access to transportation, shopping, work, or efficient services. Rather (say many critics), they have been selected to keep the residents out of sight (Hartman 1975).[30] For example, in the late 1960s, approximately 96 percent of Cleveland's black population lived east of the Cuyahoga River. In an effort to break down residential segregation, the Cuyahoga Metropolitan Housing Authority proposed to construct public housing in West Cleveland, and it gained the necessary permits from the city council. However, in the 1971 municipal election, several council candidates proposed to revoke these permits in any area where the majority of residents opposed the project, and upon their election fulfilled their campaign commitment. The district court, however, overturned these revocations,[31] arguing that the city had not demonstrated good cause (Johnston 1984).

Urban administrators, politicians, and residents often justify these siting policies on the basis of fiscal considerations. After all, they argue, the cost of land is considerably lower in dilapidated areas of the central city, and to maintain low rent and an adequate number of units, the city must concentrate housing units in these areas. But the inadequacy of this explanation is pointed up by the fact that most of the cost is borne by the federal government and that some cities (e.g., New York) even forfeited federal funds rather than integrate low-income housing units into middle- and upper-class neighborhoods.[32]

30. In contrast, public housing for the elderly has been better located, more attractive, and more livable (Hartman 1975). This again suggests a class bias in urban public policy: The plight of the younger and middle-aged poor is of their own making (assumes the policy), and they should be held accountable, while the plight of the elderly poor is due to the aging process, which they cannot control.

31. *Banks v. Perk,* 341 FSupp. 1175, 1972.

32. Palley and Palley (1981) report that during the late 1960s, the Department of Housing and Urban Development developed policies that encouraged cities to scatter low-income housing units throughout middle-income neighborhoods rather than concentrating them in poor neighborhoods. By the early 1970s, and in response to a specific HUD directive, New York City planned to locate 840 low-income housing units in Forest Hills, a white, middle-income section of Queens. However, this proposal generated considerable protest among Forest Hills residents, and the city scaled back its

Health and service facilities. A final means a city may use to promote residential segregation (or to exclude the underclass completely) involves siting policies for health and human service facilities. Many urban politicians and administrators have argued that it is more efficient to concentrate low-income families in one area because this allows them to take advantage of nonmobile municipal services housed nearby (e.g., sheltered workshops, community mental health centers, neighborhood health clinics, legal aid centers, drug treatment centers, day care facilities). A similar logic has been used to argue for the concentration of nonmobile municipal services around the poor (see Wolch 1982, for a review). This circular logic creates a self-fulfilling prophecy, typically leading to segregated residential patterns: Those dependent on community-based health and human services are concentrated in one part of town, while the middle and upper classes are located in another. But as above, the public argument often masks a more important underlying logic: Residents of middle- and upper-class neighborhoods usually do not want to associate with service-dependent individuals, many of whom are recently deinstitutionalized mental patients, ex-convicts, former drug addicts or alcoholics, or juvenile wards of the courts (e.g., Rabkin 1974), and many residents fear a reduction in property values were the poor (or the service delivery facilities they use) to locate in their neighborhood.[33] Similar arguments are advanced to keep health and human service facilities out of communities altogether.[34]

The Extent of Residential Segregation in American Cities

Just how successful have cities been at maintaining residential segregation? According to most statistics, very successful. In 1980, for example, central city populations in the United States averaged 21.4 percent black, compared to suburbs with an average of 6 percent black population. A study of residential segregation within major U.S. metropolitan areas (summarized in table 17.2) shows that between 1960 and 1970, little integration occurred (and in many cities, 1970 showed greater levels of segregation than 1960). By 1980,

---

proposal to 432 units, 180 of which were designated for the elderly (who were more acceptable to community residents; see note 30). As a result, the city was required to contribute a substantial portion of the construction costs of these housing units. Mario Cuomo (later to become governor of New York), who negotiated the compromise between city officials and community representatives, has set down a complete description of the project and its controversies (Cuomo 1974).

33. In fact, few of these concerns about property values are warranted. Numerous studies have failed to discover any significant effects of facility siting on either market activity or property values (see Wolch 1982 for a review).

34. People object not just to human service facilities in their neighborhoods, but to virtually all public facilities. Christopher Smith (1980) found that out of twenty-eight such facilities, urban residents wanted none located on their block, only one—a park—on the next block, and only two—an elementary school and a public library—within their neighborhood.

Table 17.2 Racial Segregation Indices for 38 Selected Metropolian Areas, 1960–1980

Metropolian Area	Dissimilarity Index[a]		
	1960	1970	1980
New York	.744	.738	.728
Los Angeles-Long Beach	.892	.885	.764
Chicago	.912	.912	.863
Philadelphia	.771	.780	.770
Detroit	.871	.889	.871
San Francisco-Oakland	.794	.773	.682
Washington	.777	.811	.693
Dallas	.812	.869	.762
Houston	.805	.784	.719
Boston	.808	.793	.758
Nassau-Suffolk (NY)	—	—	.754
St. Louis	.859	.865	.815
Pittsburgh	.744	.745	.728
Baltimore	.824	.810	.741
Minneapolis	.833	.799	—
Atlanta	.771	.817	.768
Newark	.728	.788	.786
Anaheim-Santa Ana	—	.723	.404
Cleveland	.896	.902	.875
San Diego	.795	.762	.586
Miami	.895	.857	.771
Denver	.846	.847	.678
Seattle	.833	.781	.656
Tampa-St. Petersburg	.836	.845	.773
Riverside-San Bernadino (CA)	—	—	.495
Phoenix	.811	.754	.565
Milwaukee	.904	.895	.834
Cincinnati	.832	.818	.779
Kansas City	.874	.833	.784
San Jose	.656	.511	.403
Buffalo	.868	.857	.796
Portland	.813	.802	.680
New Orleans	.650	.742	.704
Indianapolis	.787	.838	.786
Columbus	.761	.809	.727
San Antonio	.768	.740	.545
Ft. Lauderdale-Hollywood	—	.949	.833
Sacramento	.721	.661	.525
Median	.8115	.8095	.754

a. The measure or racial segregation used here is the Racial Dissimilarity Index. It is calculated for geographical units (e.g., census tracts), and it specifies the percentage of blacks (or whites) that would have to move from their geographical location in order to achieve an equal distribution of that race across all sub-areas of the city. Thus, it ranges from 0.0 (indicating perfect integration) to 1.0 (indicating complete segregation).
SOURCE: Clark (1986).

substantial movement toward integration had begun to occur in every city; but even with this advance, many areas merely reattained their 1960 level of integration. Even by 1980, no metropolitan area even *approached* complete integration, and a number (e.g., Chicago, St. Louis, Detroit, Milwaukee, Ft. Lauderdale-Hollywood) remained substantially segregated (Clark 1986).

Chicago remains one of the most residentially segregated cities in the country, particularly with the movement of the white upper and middle classes out of the city and into the suburbs. Fred Wirt and his colleagues (Wirt et al. 1972), for example, compared the 1970 racial composition of 147 Chicago suburbs (with over 2,500 people). They reported 19 (13 percent) of these to be exclusively white, and another 97 (66 percent) to contain fewer than 1 percent blacks; in only 10 suburbs did they find greater than 11 percent blacks, and 4 of these were predominantly black (i.e., over 60 percent). By 1980, these figures had not changed appreciably. Seventy-six percent of the suburbs contained 2 percent or fewer blacks, compared with Chicago's central city black population of 40 percent. Also by 1980, 28 Chicago suburbs had black populations greater than 11 percent, and 6 of these were *predominantly* black.[35] A 1976 study of the Chicago metropolitan area found that 83 percent of suburban blacks were concentrated in just 15 of the city's 237 suburbs (Danielson 1976). In 1978, similar, albeit less distinct, patterns existed in most other metropolitan areas (Dimond 1978), leading to the conclusion that racial segregation across suburbs was extensive (Farley 1976).

Although residential segregation by income is not nearly so pronounced (Dimond 1978), wealthy suburbs in most metropolitan areas have nonetheless successfully prevented the poor from moving in. For example, mean family income among Bostonians in 1970 was $9,409, compared with $13,500 for those living in Boston's suburbs. More striking was the distribution of low-income families in the area: Nineteen percent of those families living in Boston had an annual income under $3,000, compared with only 5 percent of those families living in Boston's suburbs (ACIR 1973).[36] Similar trends hold

---

35. These figures were adapted from the Bureau of the Census *Current Population Reports,* 1980.

36. A geographical analysis of the distribution of income in Boston and its suburbs (reported by Dimond 1978) is even more revealing.

	Median Family Income	Percent of Families Below Poverty Level
Boston	$ 9,133	11.7
Inner-Tier Suburbs		
Cambridge	9,815	8.6
Chelsea	9,739	8.4
Lynn	9,739	8.4
Malden	10,204	6.4
Medford	11,145	4.4
Somerville	9,594	7.5

for virtually all other cities in the Northeast and Midwest. Only in the sunbelt (e.g., Houston, Atlanta, Los Angeles) does the trend break down; and even here, suburban pockets of wealth exceed the general wealth of the central city.

Inter-City Disparities in the Delivery of Urban Services

We can now begin to explore whether or not the underclass experiences a systematic bias in the delivery of municipal services. In considering this bias, we start with the potential impact of residential segregation on the delivery of services.

We need not look far to find the first vestiges of bias in the differential taxation and expenditure rates among cities within the metropolitan patchwork. Table 17.3 shows that, by several different criteria, suburban residents fare better than their central city neighbors in the delivery of services. First, per-capita income is higher in the suburbs, by an average of over $1,017. But this varies greatly by region. In the South and the West, for example, the differences average $330 and $485 respectively, and in cities like Dallas, Los Angeles, San Diego, and Seattle, per-capita income is actually higher in the central city than in the suburbs. On the other hand, differences in per-capita income between the central city and suburbs in the East and the Midwest average $2,156 and $1,368 respectively.

We should not find these discrepancies surprising, given the earlier discussion of the demography of poverty. But they do have two important implications for the delivery of services. First, the lower average income in the central city is an indicator of greater need for services.[37] For example, the greater prevalence of crime and fires in the central city suggests a greater need

	Median Family Income	Percent of Families Below Poverty Level
Middle-Tier Suburbs		
Arlington	12,247	4.1
Watertown	11,400	5.3
Belmont	13,559	2.7
Concord	16,463	2.4
Revere	10,325	6.6
Wellesley	19,401	2.0
Outer-Tier Suburbs		
Burlington	13,236	3.2
Sudbury	17,798	2.9
Marshfield	11,742	4.4
Pembroke	10,998	3.5

In general, the further from the central city, the more affluent the suburbs become.

37. If every person in the central city earned $7,000, poverty would be virtually nonexistent. But as a mean, this aggregates a considerable number of people who earn six-figure and seven-figure incomes with those who earn very little.

for public safety services, and the greater population density suggests a greater need for parks and recreation services. The greater prevalence of poverty suggests a greater need for health and human services, for day care facilities, and for public housing. And lower levels of educational achievement in the central cities, coupled with higher drop-out rates, suggests a greater need for compensatory and alternative educational services. Further, a number of central cities partially support municipal colleges and technical schools that serve the entire metropolitan area. In addition, central cities are typically older than their suburbs, and hence their physical infrastructure (e.g., roads, bridges, sewers) is showing its age and demands costly repair. Finally, as the hub of the metropolitan area, the central city often provides a repertoire of municipally supported cultural attractions (e.g., civic operas and symphonies; zoos; museums; repertory theaters) that service the entire metropolitan area. Taken together, these factors place a substantially higher demand on the budget of the central city than on its suburban neighbors.[38] Table 17.3 supports this conclusion. On average, central cities spend over $1,000 per capita on noneducational services, compared with under $600 in the suburbs. Of the cities reported, suburban noneducational expenditures per capita exceed those in the central city only in San Diego (where they are virtually equal).

Educational Expenditures

Ironically, educational expenditures follow a different pattern. Although we should expect the greater need within central cities to result in higher educational expenditures, the opposite holds. On average, suburbs spend $471 per capita for educational services, compared with $420 in central cities. Although this discrepancy is modest (and is even reversed for some MSAs), it becomes large when coupled with the differing needs of the suburbs and central cities. An examination of educational statistics from the Detroit metropolitan area (Dimond 1978), is a case in point. Table 17.4 shows that Detroit's students have a different socioeconomic status than their suburban counterparts, and this in turn reflects different levels of need (e.g., lower achievement test scores, higher dropout rates). Yet, the level of support, reflected in per-pupil expenditures in general—and teacher-student ratios in particular—is higher in the suburbs.

The lower per-capita income in the central cities also means that fewer tax dollars are generated to pay for needed services. As a result, residents of central cities must tax themselves at a higher rate simply to provide the same service levels, let alone the greater service levels required to meet their special

---

38. Neenan (1972) reports that during the late 1960s, Detroit residents subsidized their suburban neighbors to the extent of $80 per capita per year, with 6.5 percent of the entire city budget used to provide services to suburban "free riders."

Table 17.3 Measures of Central City—Suburban Fiscal Disparities for 37 Metropolitan Areas

Metropolitan Area	1980 Per Capita Income		1980 Tax Burden		1981 Per Capita Expenditures Educational		Noneducational		1981 Per Capita Educational Aid[a]	
	CC[b]	OCC[c]	CC	OCC	CC	OCC	CC	OCC	CC	OCC
Washington, DC	$8,960	$10,469	.198	.057	$461	$503	$2,523	$ 581	$ 97	$172
Baltimore	5,877	8,422	.075	.053	394	452	1,136	458	277	189
Boston	6,555	8,385	.134	.084	482	481	962	563	296	138
Newark	4,525	9,112	.101	.066	595	502	1,340	727	226	93
Paterson, NJ	6,163	9,937	.056	.065	417	484	745	530	241	274
Buffalo	5,929	7,537	.084	.082	466	542	1,177	907	322	313
New York	7,311	9,252	.144	.106	392	752	1,597	1,060	241	274
Rochester	6,492	9,361	.103	.064	576	619	1,293	706	336	309
Philadelphia	6,067	8,383	.107	.048	361	505	1,031	474	259	209
Pittsburgh	6,845	8,335	.085	.038	376	465	918	597	191	213
Providence	6,857	7,086	.071	.057	392	377	442	340	152	146
Chicago	6,945	8,831	.074	.075	405	473	925	546	329	166
Indianapolis	7,259	8,913	.053	.030	449	357	689	319	264	229
Detroit	6,222	9,068	.082	.066	536	551	1,204	665	347	223
Minneapolis	7,883	9,321	.058	.039	408	527	1,255	754	433	322
Kansas City	7,251	8,604	.087	.046	360	446	824	584	224	279
St. Louis	5,880	7,906	.097	.049	385	420	877	405	258	203
Cincinnati	6,889	7,894	.082	.041	326	418	1,007	345	168	231
Cleveland	5,770	8,700	.105	.063	529	448	1,033	732	287	203
Columbus	6,823	7,806	.058	.051	369	480	833	419	212	215
Dayton	5,776	8,077	.091	.043	517	462	920	478	292	255
Milwaukee	7,104	9,411	.056	.049	486	528	958	743	317	230
Miami	6,084	9,472	.097	.043	378	378	1,065	787	285	285
Tampa	6,610	8,052	.053	.028	356	347	832	429	272	261
Atlanta	6,539	8,778	.112	.040	483	404	1,438	484	212	198
Louisville	6,281	7,610	.071	.033	279	371	830	320	177	236
New Orleans	6,463	6,888	.064	.048	316	338	713	507	232	206
Dallas	8,644	8,570	.060	.042	333	412	689	492	202	255
Houston	8,868	9,158	.059	.069	306	595	709	520	167	285
San Antonio	5,734	7,433	.042	.033	364	344	542	248	327	278
Phoenix	7,552	7,982	.047	.037	461	409	788	673	306	286
Los Angeles	8,421	8,222	.053	.041	458	452	1,012	812	441	454
San Bernadino	7,069	7,170	.054	.045	623	428	1,059	831	589	380
San Diego	8,016	7,623	.045	.044	398	482	811	831	315	415
San Francisco	8,406	10,264	.067	.043	350	436	1,429	947	392	378
Denver	8,555	9,460	.059	.055	421	551	930	526	167	263
Portland	8,092	8,461	.081	.055	449	560	1,160	494	194	267
Seattle	9,127	8,838	.048	.034	359	542	941	521	267	389

a. Aid from both federal and state sources.
b. Central city.
c. Outside central city.
SOURCE: ACIR (1984).

417

Table 17.4 Indicators of Educational Need and Effort in Detroit
and Its Suburbs

	Detroit	Suburban (median)
Socioeconomic Status of Students[a]	.020	.790
Student Achievement[a]	.257	.580
Dropout Rate	.137	.041
Pupils per Teacher	26	22
Per-Pupil Expenditure	$1,271	$1,302

a. Percentile of Michigan school districts with lower scores on this indicator.
SOURCE: Dimond (1978).

needs. Table 17.3 also shows differential tax burdens for selected cities across the country. Nationally, central cities tax their residents at an average rate of 6.8 percent of income, compared with 4.8 percent of income in the suburbs. But regional differences belie these averages. In the East, for example, central city residents bear a 10.5 percent tax rate, compared to 6.5 percent for suburban residents. This discrepancy is particularly noticeable for cities like Washington, Philadelphia, and Boston. In contrast, residents of central cities in the West bear a 5.4 percent tax rate, compared with 4.1 percent for suburban residents. And in several cities (e.g., Denver, San Diego, San Bernadino), the discrepancy is virtually nonexistent.

To restate the argument, residents of central cities must tax themselves at a higher rate than suburban residents simply to generate the same revenue level and at a *substantially higher rate* to generate sufficient revenue to address their special needs. Yet, given the discrepancy in income, even a comparable tax burden would be regressive, and the higher tax burden in the central city is severely regressive. This creates a paradox that is partially responsible for the white (and affluent) flight to the suburbs. The higher the tax burden within the central cities, the more likely the more mobile middle and upper classes are to vote with their feet, packing up and moving to the suburbs; but the more the tax base erodes through such flight, the greater the tax burden becomes on those who remain.

Attempts to equalize educational spending patterns in central cities and suburbs has met with mixed success. Although the role of the federal government and the states in funding local education has increased since 1960,[39] the principal criterion in allocation decisions has not always been need; in fact, during the 1970s, suburban school districts actually received *more* aid per capita than did central city school districts. Not until 1981 did per-capita aid to the

39. The federal share of local education budgets grew from 4.4 percent in 1960 to nearly 10 percent in 1980, while the state share grew from 35.2 percent to 46.8 percent during this same period.

central cities and the suburbs equalize ($261 per capita to central cities, $257 per capita to suburbs). The issue of equalization has been contested in the courts, with mixed results. One case grew out of the disparity between the Edgewood School District, located in San Antonio's inner city, and the Alamo Heights School District, located in one of its suburban areas. In 1971, Edgewood spent $356 per pupil ($26 from local taxes, $222 from state funds, and $108 from federal funds), compared with $594 per pupil in Alamo Heights ($333 from local taxes, $225 from state funds, and $36 from federal funds), even though Edgewood citizens were taxed at a much higher rate than their Alamo Heights counterparts. This disparity became the basis for a suit claiming that the Texas school system discriminates against the poor. However, the U.S. Supreme Court ruled that Texas policy did not violate the equal protection clause of the Fourteenth Amendment.[40] Further, it found that since the state was actually providing more funds (both absolutely and relatively) to Edgewood than to Alamo Heights, the contention of discrimination was invalid. In other words, the court found that states must not provide fewer funds to poor school districts than to wealthy districts, but neither must they compensate for district wealth by providing more funds to the poorer districts (Johnston 1984). However, the California Supreme Court ruled that financing local education with local property taxes was inherently inequitable, and that the state must develop a more equitable funding scheme.[41]

Put differently, equalization through state aid means different things in different states, and accordingly, wide variation exists in the distribution of state educational funds to suburbs and central cities across metropolitan areas (see table 17.3). In most of the northeastern and midwestern metropolitan areas, aid to central cities exceeds that to suburbs, sometimes by a considerable amount (e.g., Boston, where the former exceeds the latter by 214 percent). In the South and the West, however, the trend is reversed, with aid to the suburbs often exceeding that to the central cities (e.g., Houston, where aid to the suburbs exceeds central city aid by 170 percent). Although this regional variation can be explained at least partially by differences in central city need (i.e., central cities in the South and West are wealthier in comparison to their suburbs than those in the Northeast and Midwest), part of the explanation may also be attributed to regional differences in the perceived role of the central city in the metropolitan area. In the Northeast and Midwest, for example, central cities are held in high esteem as the cultural, professional, financial, and commercial center of the metropolis, with the suburbs serving largely as "bedroom communities." Money invested in the central city, for education as well as other services, represents a commitment to the quality of life

40. *San Antonio Independent School District v. Rodriguez* (411 US 1, 1973).
41. *Serrano v. Priest* (557 P2d 929, 1977).

for the entire metropolis. In the South and West, however, suburbs have largely taken over the professional and commercial functions of the metropolis, thus reducing the commitment to preserving the central city for its own sake.

Intra-City Disparities in the Delivery of Services

The Shaw Decision

In 1971, the U.S. Fifth Circuit Court decided *Hawkins v. Town of Shaw*,[42] concluding that Shaw, Mississippi, was engaged in a racially motivated denial of equal rights in its provision of street, water, and sewer services to its residents. The statistics clearly demonstrate the disparity in service provision to whites and blacks (Merget and Wolff 1976). For example,

- 56 percent of the roads in black neighborhoods were unpaved, compared with 3 percent of the roads in white neighborhoods;
- 19 percent of black homes were not served by sanitary sewer lines, compared with 1 percent of white homes;
- 51 percent of white homes were located on roads served by storm sewers, compared with no black homes;
- 98 percent of the homes located on unpaved roads were occupied by blacks;
- most fire hydrants and traffic signals were located in white residential areas.

The *Shaw* decision was touted as a landmark case,[43] serving notice to municipal governments that the delivery of sharply different quantities or qualities of services to black and white neighborhoods would not be tolerated under the equal protection clause of the Fourteenth Amendment. However, it largely failed to live up to expectations (Lineberry 1984).

Tests of the Underclass Hypothesis

Lineberry (1984, 189) attributes this failure, in part, to the inherent lack of precedent in the *Shaw* case. The blatant inequality in Shaw was "more reminis-

---

42. 437 F.2d 1286.
43. Several other cases, decided during the same time period, set similar precedents for the equal distribution of urban services (e.g., *Hadnott v. City of Pratville,* 309 FSupp 967, 1970; *Farmworkers of Florida Housing Project Inc. v. City of Delray Beach,* 493 F2d 799, 1974). However, some cities decided to discontinue the services rather than provide them on an equitable basis. For example, in 1962 Jackson, Mississippi, operated five swimming pools, four designated for whites and one for blacks. Rather than comply with a desegregation order, however, it chose to close four of the pools and revert the lease of the other to the YMCA, which operated it for whites only. The U.S. Supreme Court, in *Palmer v. Thompson* (403 US 217, 1971), upheld the constitutionality of that action. See Johnston (1984) for a discussion of these and related cases.

cent of the Jim Crow era than representative of the intricate, subtle, and difficult-to-measure patterns of service delivery in a large, complex, urban system." In an effort to test the "underclass hypothesis,"[44] Lineberry (1977) explored these intricate, subtle, and difficult-to-measure patterns in the fire and library services offered by San Antonio. While he found clear variation in the quality and quantity of services received by various neighborhoods across the city, he found no consistent bias against any group or area across services. Lineberry terms this variation "unpatterned inequality." Further, he found that low-income and minority neighborhoods actually receive *better* fire and library services than higher-income and white neighborhoods. And while he urges caution in the interpretation of these results, he also suggests that they cast doubt on the generality of the conditions the court discovered in Shaw.

Like Lineberry, other researchers have studied the allocation of urban services among neighborhoods, with similar findings. Researchers studying the distribution of services relating to libraries (e.g., Martin 1969, Levy, et al. 1974, Mladenka and Hill 1977), parks (e.g., Mladenka and Hill 1977), education (e.g., Baron 1971, Levy, et al. 1974), police (e.g., Block 1974, Coulter 1980), streets (Boots, et al. 1972), housing inspection (e.g., Nivola 1978), and fire (Coulter 1978) have found overwhelmingly that (a) resources are distributed in a manner that does not discriminate against poor and black neighborhoods; (b) variation in resources allocated to neighborhoods are inevitable, but tend to be unpatterned; and (c) these variations are just as likely (or more likely) to favor poor neighborhoods as rich neighborhoods. Urban administrators, it would seem, bend over backward to guarantee that the allocation of services within the city does not discriminate against low-income neighborhoods.[45]

The Underclass Hypothesis Reconsidered

With this accumulation of evidence, it might seem reasonable to lay the underclass hypothesis to rest and to conclude that Shaw, Mississippi was, indeed, an anomaly. Yet, several factors keep the underclass hypothesis alive. First, even in situations where allocation decisions are based on non-discriminatory factors, the decisions may have unexpected consequences that bias the delivery of services in an inequitable direction. For example, Frank Levy and his colleagues (1974) found allocation decisions for streets and libraries in Oakland that, on the surface, seem equitable. They found highway

44. This hypothesis states that neighborhoods that are poorer, or have large shares of minority residents, or are politically unorganized receive less in services for their tax dollars than advantaged neighborhoods.

45. Several researchers, however, show results that contradict those reported above (e.g., Bolotin and Cingranelli 1983, Koehler and Wrightson 1987).

funds to be allocated according to patterns of traffic volume, traffic flow, and accident rates, and library resources to be allocated according to circulation rates and other professional norms. But while these criteria may be legitimate guidelines, they may also affect the distribution of resources in unintended ways. The criteria for allocating highway funds, coupled with legal requirements for the use of gasoline tax revenue, results in the allocation of funds primarily to freeways and cross-town arterials. These allocation guidelines primarily benefit upper- and middle-class residents of the city's outlying neighborhoods and suburbs. And while the criteria for allocating library resources primarily benefit the central library (which, in turn, benefits poor central-area neighborhoods as well as upper- and middle-class professionals employed in the downtown area), they also disproportionately benefit branch libraries located in more affluent neighborhoods.

This pattern of allocations raises an important equity question. Seldom should we expect to find a case where the delivery of services discriminates so clearly as in Shaw, Mississippi, and therefore we should not be surprised that the *Shaw* precedent has not controlled other cases.[46] Yet, what would on the surface seem to be rational and equitable criteria for allocating resources may create subtle but important biases in the delivery of services. For example, would a municipal decision to concentrate books in branch libraries serving the better-educated (and more affluent) parts of town constitute discrimination? Or would a decision to locate the newest fire equipment in a station serving the most valuable houses (which would represent the greatest actuarial loss were they to burn) violate the equal protection clause of the Fourteenth Amendment? Or would a decision to locate golf courses on the outskirts of the city, where land values (and the cost of construction) are considerably lower, be inappropriate? Certainly, a strong case could be made for an affirmative answer to all three questions.

In addition, conclusions about service equity may reflect the research methods and assumptions as much as the reality of the situation. For instance, evidence suggests that property in poorer neighborhoods tends to be assessed at a higher proportion of its market value than property in more affluent neighborhoods (e.g., Peterson et al. 1973, Feiock 1986).[47] Richard Feiock

46. Historically, however, it is easy to find cases of blatant discrimination. For example, Lineberry (1984), quoting Kraus (1973), sites the case of Austin, Texas. In 1927, the city hired a private planning firm to develop systematic plans for the extension of public service facilities (e.g., sewers, streets, water mains, parks, street lighting). In this plan, the firm concluded that racial segregation could not be legally maintained through zoning ordinances, but it proposed to maintain pockets of racial segregation that had developed during the nineteenth century by locating facilities and conveniences for blacks within particular districts of Austin. This would serve as an incentive to draw the black population to those areas.

47. A variety of explanations have been advanced for this phenomenon. For example, Peterson (1973) argues that it may represent a deliberate attempt to keep from pushing wealthy families out of the city. And Paul (1975) argues that it is an inevitable byproduct of urban inefficiency and corruption.

(1986) shows that when this factor is ignored, the distribution of services among neighborhoods in Erie, Pennsylvania, resembles that uncovered in other studies (i.e., unpatterned variation). But when service delivery is assessed against an equity standard tempered by tax burden, the distribution of these services is regressive, favoring affluent neighborhoods.

A similar problem is demonstrated by Bryan Jones' (1980) study of services in Detroit: While he found little class bias in the *allocation of service resources* across neighborhoods, he found that *outcomes* of services tend to favor more affluent and white outlying neighborhoods over inner-city black neighborhoods. For instance, predominantly black, inner-city neighborhoods experience less satisfactory services related to environmental enforcement (e.g., control of litter, weeds, rodents, and so forth), garbage collection, and building inspection and code enforcement than more affluent neighborhoods on the city's periphery. Yet, in no case is this discrepancy due to an inequitable distribution of resources among these neighborhoods; in fact, the inner-city neighborhoods often received greater per-capita allocations than the outlying neighborhoods. Rather, discrepancies result from two other causes. First, inner-city neighborhoods have different and more complex needs than outer neighborhoods. For example, agencies enforcing building codes are less likely to obtain compliance with their citations in inner-city neighborhoods because absentee landlords, who own much of the housing, are more difficult to locate and more willing to abandon their buildings rather than pay for costly repairs.

Second, service providers often engage in discriminatory practices. For example, more uncollected garbage accumulates in inner-city neighborhoods than in outlying neighborhoods. The most likely explanation is that the supervision of garbage collection crews in black neighborhoods is more lax than in white neighborhoods. Thus, by asking different questions of his data, Jones draws different conclusions than his counterparts studying other cities. We will consider the importance of discriminatory practices in the actual delivery of services in the pages that follow. But first, we turn to the question of need.

Distribution of Services on the Basis of Need

Richard Rich (1982) argues that the locational service-delivery question (i.e., *where* are services to be allocated?) should be preceded by a more important question: *Which* services are to be provided? By concentrating on the former rather than the latter question, researchers may bias their conclusions about equity, much in the way that Jones demonstrates in his study of Detroit. Rich argues that most urban expenditures are tied to distributional policies, directed at services that yield roughly equal benefits across all social classes, including public safety, education, roads, parks, and garbage collection. Yet, such expenditures, he concludes, serve to perpetuate the current distribution of wealth in the community. Only through redistributional policies, aimed at concentrating services in those areas where they are most needed, can the current distribution of wealth and opportunity—the cycle of poverty—be disrupted.[48]

If we examine the distribution of services according to this need-based standard of equity, we come to conclusions different from those reached by researchers employing an equal-distribution standard of equity. In a study of the distribution of four services (police protection, parks and recreation, public education, and garbage collection) relative to need in fifteen major cities, Doh Shin (1982) found strong evidence of inequity. His results show that in all fifteen cities, all-white and mostly white neighborhoods receive the most favorable police protection relative to need, while all-black and mostly black neighborhoods fare least well. He obtained similar results for other services. In a complementary finding, Terrence Jones (1982) shows that in St. Louis, transition neighborhoods whose populations are rapidly changing from white to black receive the least favorable services, while those that remain white (or that change slowly) receive the most favorable services.

Inequity in Health Services

Using the standard of need as a criterion for level of service, we need not look far to find other examples of inequity in the delivery of urban services. One example falls in the area of health services. Health care expenditures that most benefit the underclass involve the direct provision of health education and health services to inner-city residents. Such services can be provided only by qualified health professionals through clinics and hospitals, yet the availability of these resources to inner-city residents is largely inadequate. For example, in Chicago during the 1970s, three out of four black emergencies were treated by only one of Chicago's eighty hospitals. During this same period, black neighborhoods in Chicago had only 10 percent of the physicians they needed, and most of those physicians lacked the credentials to admit patients to hospitals (De Vise 1973). And across the country, municipal and private hospitals serving inner-city areas increasingly have been closed, partly dismantled, or consolidated due to bankruptcy, unprofitability, and outmoded facilities. Between 1975 and 1977 alone, more than two hundred such hospitals closed their doors to patients (Palley and Palley 1981).

Increasingly, the role of the private sector physician has been replaced by the public clinic in most inner cities. Although these clinics date back to the early days of the twentieth century (e.g., New York's Henry Street Settlement House, Chicago's Hull House), the modern impetus has its roots in the 1969 Healthright Program, sponsored by the U.S. Office of Equal Opportunity. By 1979, the program was partially funding 864 community health

---

48. This represents yet another manifestation of the different ideological perspectives that largely shape urban policy.

centers in medically underserved areas, and providing services to three million people (Palley and Palley 1981). Even so, this constituted only a partial chunk of the 19 million uninsured people living below the poverty level.[49] But as demand has increased and federal funding has been reduced, cities have largely failed to fill the financial void, and today community health centers are unable to provide services to all who need them.

Inequity in Educational Services

Much the same situation exists in the area of education. Given differential drop-out rates between inner-city and economically advantaged students, as well as differential performance on achievement tests, an equal allocation of resources may be insufficient to create equitable outcomes. Rather, equality may best be achieved through compensatory programs (e.g., Head Start). The Head Start program, initiated under the War on Poverty program (see chapter 14), is designed to help overcome the handicaps of economic disadvantage by providing preschool children from low-income families with a comprehensive program designed to meet their educational, social, health, nutritional, and psychological needs. By most accounts, the program has achieved some success in meeting these goals (e.g., Smith 1975). It currently provides services to 400,000 children. Most school districts are delighted to accept federal money for this program, but their commitment to supplement these federal funds with local funds has been limited. In fact, Levy et al. (1974) found that Oakland achieved distributional equity in the delivery of educational services *only when federal compensatory funds for poor neighborhoods were counted.* In other words, compensatory funds took the place of local funds, largely defeating their goal of equalizing outcomes.

Compensatory policies represent only one approach to reducing inequalities, however. Another approach, procedural in nature, is desegregation of the schools. Beginning in 1954, with *Brown v. Board of Education of Topeka*[50] and four companion cases, the courts have consistently held *de jure* segregation of the schools to be unconstitutional.[51] The language of the *Brown* decisions (*Brown and Brown II;* see chapter 14) was vague, however, calling only for a prompt and deliberate start to desegregation. This encouraged some school districts, particularly in the South, to resist integration through a

---

49. In all, 37 million people in the United States are without medical insurance (Sigelbaum 1988).
50. 347 US 483.
51. *De jure* segregation is segregation by law; for example when blacks and white are statutorily required to attend different schools. At the time of the *Brown* decision, cities in twenty-one states (plus the District of Columbia) were allowed (or required) to maintain separate schools for whites and blacks. Just as important, but more subtle, is *de facto* segregation, where blacks and whites attend different schools due to segregated housing patterns. The courts would not address this issue for nearly another twenty years.

number of different ploys. Most blatant was Arkansas Governor Orville Faubus' decision to close the schools in Little Rock rather than integrate them; this was overturned by the Supreme Court.[52] Other states employed more subtle, although ultimately no more effective, means to delay or circumvent the integration order (Lord 1977)[53]: Mississippi, for instance, passed legislation claiming that *Brown* did not apply there; Virginia disbanded its public education system, replacing it with grants to whites attending private schools; and a number of districts operated "freedom of choice" programs allowing students to choose which school to attend. All of these efforts to maintain segregated school districts were overturned in the courts (see Johnston 1984, for citations). In short, the courts had ruled that students have the right to attend the school nearest their residence.

By 1969, the Supreme Court had replaced its "all deliberate speed" criterion *(Brown)* with one requiring "immediate operation of unitary school systems."[54] While that decision seemingly laid to rest the question of *de jure* segregation, it left the question of *de facto* segregation unanswered (and unaddressed). From that point forward, however, the focus of the courts changed to *de facto* segregation: What should be done when segregated housing patterns create segregated school districts? In two 1971 decisions, the Supreme Court concluded that busing was the answer, specifying that students in all-black or all-white catchment areas should be bused to other schools to achieve racial balance.[55] During the next decade, the Supreme Court affirmed these precedents[56] by ordering district-wide busing in a number of cities, including Denver,[57] Dayton,[58] and Columbus, Ohio.[59]

However, the Supreme Court has been unwilling to take a next step, requiring metropolitan-wide busing to rectify racial disparity *among* metropolitan school districts. In a test case, the U.S. Supreme Court over-

---

52. *Faubus v. Aaron* (361 US 197, 1959).

53. Quoted in Johnston (1984).

54. *Alexander v. Holmes Board of Education* (369 US 19).

55. Due to residential segregation, nine elementary schools in Mobile County were all black. In *Davis v. Board of School Commissioners of Mobile County* (402 US 33, 1971) the U.S. Supreme Court ruled unanimously that in such situations busing must be used to break down segregation. In the Charlotte-Mecklenburg School District (which provided educational services for residents in the city of Charlotte and Mecklenburg County), the situation was more complicated, since most blacks resided in the city rather than the county. Nonetheless, the U.S. Supreme Court ruled in *Swann v. Charlotte-Mecklenburg Board of Education* (402 US 1, 1971) that the district must provide free transportation to any student who voluntarily moved away from an all-black or all-white school, and that non-contiguous catchment areas should be grouped as a means for creating racial balance.

56. However, in refusing to hear an appeal of *Bell v. School, City of Gary, Indiana* (342 F2d 209, 1963), the Supreme Court established that if school boundaries are established without consideration of race, desegregation is not required. The district court noted that the Constitution does not require integration, it forbids segregation.

57. *Keys v. School District No. 1* (413 US 89, 1973).

58. *Dayton Board of Education v. Brinkman* (443 US 526, 1979).

59. *Columbus Board of Education v. Penick* (443 US 449, 1979).

426

ruled lower court decisions requiring busing among the Detroit School District and fifty-three suburban school districts serving the Detroit metropolitan area.[60]

These court decisions have been based on considerations of equal treatment. But in the policy debate that accompanied the quest for desegregation, several other considerations arose, including the implications of busing (and more generally, of equal opportunity) for educational achievement, local political conflict engendered by busing, and white flight to the suburbs to escape integrated schools. Thus, we again discover that urban issues and policies cannot be considered in isolation, but rather that they are tied both to multiple and complex causes and to unintended and unanticipated consequences.

The importance of desegregation became increasingly important with the publication of research by James Coleman and his colleagues (1966) showing that the quality of the school a child attended had little impact on his or her educational achievement; rather, achievement was most affected by (1) the parents' educational background, (2) the family's standard of living, and (3) the percentage of black students in the school. Although originally questioned on methodological grounds (Cain and Watts 1972, Armor 1972), this latter finding has been replicated since busing began: Achievement (particularly for young children) improves for black students who are bused without adversely affecting achievement of white children (Stephan 1978, Cook 1984). And some studies even show an improvement of racial attitudes as a result of busing, although others (reviewed by Stephan 1978) are equivocal; none, however, shows a deterioration of racial attitudes.

Yet, no issue since fluoridation has generated as much local conflict as school busing. The integration of Boston's public schools was an exceptionally difficult and bitter case. It brought into play a long festering resentment of the predominantly Irish residents of South Boston against those whom they viewed as the old Protestant establishment. "Southies," as they call themselves, did not give in easily to the orders of the court. At several critical moments, they physically massed themselves against school buses to keep them from rolling, and the integration issue spilled into a subsequent mayoral election, with some candidates pledging themselves to stop integration. In the end, of course, the buses did roll, and integrated schools are now the norm in Boston.[61] (For an insightful account of the Boston school case and its effects on the lives of several families, see Lukas 1985.)

---

60. *Milliken v. Bradley* (418 US 717, 1974). However, the Supreme Court did allow a metropolitan-wide solution to segregation in Willmington Delaware, by refusing to overturn a lower court decision (*Evans v. Buchanany*, 379 FSupp 1218, 1974).

61. For Southies, this same resentment against forced integration later found another target: defiance of the U.S. Department of Housing and Urban Development's order that the Boston Housing Authority admit black families to its 18,000 apartments. As of spring 1988, a review by HUD found that the Boston Housing Authority had "systematically excluded" blacks from units in South Boston (*Time*, April 4, 1988).

427

In a number of other cities, candidates for mayor, city council, and school board have also run on an antibusing platform. But in no instance has local protest against busing been successful, for ultimately it is the courts that decide when constitutional protection of equal opportunity is violated. Actions by individual citizens, taken independently but having a great aggregate impact, have proved the greatest local threat to school integration, however. One such action involves enrolling students in private or parochial schools, most of which are not integrated and serve primarily whites. Since 1954, approximately 16 percent of students in central cities have enrolled in such schools (in northeastern cities, this figure is nearly 23 percent); while this is not a large figure, it noticeably constrains the overall effectiveness of integration efforts.

A much more important shift is the migration of white families to the suburbs. James Coleman and Sara Kelly (1976, 252) conclude that there is "sizeable acceleration of the general loss of whites from the central [city] school districts when substantial desegregation occurs within that system." This led Coleman to reverse his earlier support for school desegregation. Others disagree with this conclusion (Farley 1975, Rossell 1976), arguing that flight to the suburbs was occasioned by a host of other social and political factors. But regardless of the immediate cause, white migration to the suburbs, coupled with the Supreme Court's rejection of metropolitan-wide busing as a solution to school segregation, has largely defeated the utilitarian benefits of school desegregation. Harvard Sitkoff (1981) summarizes the success of twenty-five years of school desegregation efforts with the following statistics: As of 1980, two-thirds of black students in the United States attended schools that were at least 90 percent black, and by 1980, more black students attended segregated schools than at the time of *Brown*. This trend is epitomized in New York City, where the white school population fell from 68 percent in 1957 to 29 percent in 1977 (with projections of 15 percent by 1989; see Harrigan 1989, 295ff). And Diane Ravitch (1974) found minority students to outnumber whites in twenty-one of the twenty-nine largest cities. Schools, as she puts it, have not simply desegregated. They have re-segregated.

Other Examples of Inequity

Other examples of inequity—relative to need—are readily identified, although we will consider them here in a cursory manner. The high crime rate and the high incidence of fires in inner-city neighborhoods, for instance, should suggest that the equal allocation of resources throughout the city is inadequate; to achieve equitable outcomes, *substantially* higher allocations of public safety resources may be required for the inner city. The lack of yards for most families living in the inner city suggests that more playgrounds would, at best, merely equalize the recreational opportunity for inner-city youths. And while enormous funds are spent to build and repair streets, equity in transportation can be achieved only by improving the city's public transit capability—since the poor have fewer cars than the middle class.

It is unlikely that cities will reverse these trends in the near future, for services that exclusively (or even disproportionately) benefit the poor are politically unpopular. After all, it was popular sentiment against public assistance programs that fueled support for Proposition 13 in California and similar tax revolts across the country (see chapter 16). In short, services that provide equal benefits to all (even if the benefits they provide are "more equal" in poorer neighborhoods) are popular with the middle and upper classes, while those aimed at redistributing wealth generate controversy.

With the notable exception of education, the courts have been concerned more with equity in the distribution of services than with equity in the achievement of outcomes. For example, in *Beal v. Lindsay,*[62] blacks and Puerto Ricans argued that parks in the Bronx were not maintained at a level commensurate with parks in predominantly white neighborhoods. While city officials did not dispute this point, they countered that the discrepancy was due to vandalism rather than neglect. The court sided with the city, finding that the city had met its obligations by providing equal levels of services, even though equal outcomes were not attained (Johnston 1984).

Equal and Unequal Treatment in the Provision of Services

Bureaucratic Discretion Reconsidered

Previous chapters have discussed the importance of implementation in the policy process. Like other policies, those creating urban sevices tend to be drawn with broad strokes, with detail to be filled in later by municipal administrators who determine procedures for implementing the policy and by employees who actually carry out those procedures.

Trash collection. A municipal statute enacted by the city council may specify that municipal sanitation workers are to collect trash from all residences and businesses located within the city limits. Administrators, however, are left with the task of developing routes and schedules, determining the number of pickups per week, outlining procedures for dealing with unexpected circumstances (e.g., snow, cold weather) and for servicing complaints and establishing rules governing the behavior of individual trash collectors (e.g., what to do when garbage cans are overflowing or too heavy, or with old washing machines left by the curb, or when a growling dog threatens the trash collector). But it is ultimately the trash collector who must implement these

---

62. 468 F.2d 287, 1972.

rules, and he or she is typically afforded some discretion in this process. For example, the trash collector must decide whether or not to lift a marginally heavy garbage can, or to pick up a newspaper that has fallen out of a container, or to ignore a growling dog. And it is these individual decisions by street-level bureaucrats and their supervisors that may constitute a source of potential bias in the delivery of urban services. Even trash collectors without any class bias may be more likely to pick up stray trash in affluent neighborhoods (where the elegant houses and yards make any stray trash seem out of place) than in poor neighborhoods (where the houses or apartments may be in need of repair, the lawns—where they exist—are often weedy and overgrown, and stray trash is not incongruous). Alternatively, their supervisors may enforce such rules in affluent neighborhoods but not in poor neighborhoods. Either behavior, in the aggregate, constitutes a class bias.

Law enforcement. The situation for police officers is even more complex. An individual officer is forced to make hundreds of decisions every day, ranging from the mundane (e.g., whether to cite a motorist going 32 mph in a 25 mph zone for speeding, or simply issue a warning) to the critical (e.g., whether to shoot a suspect who may be reaching for a gun, or who may be reaching for identification). While departmental guidelines suggest appropriate behaviors for the officer under these and most other circumstances, the officer is typically offered considerable discretion in implementing these guidelines. Even in the case of the speeding motorist, the officer may take into consideration a number of factors in his or her decision to issue a citation or a warning: the weather conditions, traffic flow, evidence of alcohol consumption, and the demeanor of the driver. In deciding whether to pull the trigger in a life-threatening situation, the number of factors is much greater, and the officer must process and integrate all the available information in a very short time.

As a result, police officers tend to isolate a small number of specific cues (i.e., pieces of information) that they use to evaluate each type of situation they are likely to encounter, and they use these cues to form a decision (Lipsky 1980, Swanson and Bolland 1983). This reduces the complexity and stress of their jobs. Imagine if they had to treat each traffic citation as a completely unique event and evaluate a half dozen factors in their decision calculus. And cue-taking may save lives in dangerous situations, for decisions based on one or two cues may be made more quickly and consistently than those based on twenty cues or more.

Stereotyping and Bias

However, the tendency to stereotype is often inherent in these behavioral routines. For example, an officer's willingness to let a deferential motorist off with a warning, while citing an argumentative and verbally abusive motorist

430

may represent a belief that the former is a better, more governable citizen than the latter, one less likely to cause other types of trouble. Thus, the officer may believe that a verbally abusive motorist is likely to have committed other offenses for which he or she was not caught, and issuing a citation becomes a way of compensating for these other offenses. In more serious situations, the officer may view verbal abuse as an indicator of threat, and he or she may feel justified in taking more forceful action than might otherwise be warranted.

This tendency to stereotype creates a potential class bias in the delivery of police services, however, for observers have suggested that members of the underclass may be less deferential in their dealings with police officers than are members of the upper and middle classes (e.g., Charles 1986); this is consistent with Oscar Lewis' (1965) observation that the poor are more likely to engage in actions that provide immediate gratification (e.g., arguing with a police officer), without regard for the longer-term consequences of these actions. Yet, this is perhaps the most important single cue in most police officers' decisions. Swanson and Bolland (1984) found that 69 percent of officers they studied relied primarily or exclusively on the deference of motorists suspected of drinking in deciding what action to take. Even in domestic disturbances, where a number of cues (e.g., level of conflict, wife's condition, the presence of children, the husband's sobriety) may be critical in assessing the danger of the situation, 42 percent of officers ignored these objective indicators of threat and concentrated instead on the husband's deference toward them.

Another cue that officers may use in determining their response, particularly in dangerous situations, is the suspect's race. After all, the police may reason, blacks commit considerably more crimes per capita than whites, so a black suspect is more likely to be guilty than a white suspect (Ryan 1976). As a result, officers expect encounters with blacks to be more dangerous than those with whites, and their actions are likely to be more severe (e.g., arrest, physical restraint). Again, this constitutes a bias in the delivery of services, and it is reflected in the strained relationship between police departments and black residents of the community. For example, 54 percent of Denver's white residents gave police officers high ratings in a 1966 survey, compared with 22 percent of blacks and 31 percent of Hispanics (Bayley and Mendelsohn 1969). Arthur Niederhoffer and Alexander Smith (1974, 36) catalogue a list of common complaints blacks make about police, including the following:

- Police are brutal, hostile, unconcerned, callous, and racist.
- Police do not respond promptly to emergency calls.
- Police violate constitutional and civil rights with impunity.
- Police humiliate the men in the community by field interrogation and "stop and frisk" procedures.
- There are no legitimate grievance mechanisms when citizens desire to lodge a complaint against police.

The attitudes and beliefs of service providers may bias the delivery of many other municipal services as well. Service providers in virtually all areas of government subscribe (to a greater or lesser extent) to the prevailing orientation toward the poor in the United States: Poor people are responsible for their poverty (Lipsky 1980). Thus, the poor generally tend to be subject to neglect and disrespect. In the public schools, for instance, upper- and middle-class students gain greatest teacher attention, in part because they are better students, but also in part because teachers expect them to benefit most from this attention. By the same token, the courts invoke different sentencing criteria for the middle and upper classes than for the underclass. As one example, Robert Emerson (1969) found that juvenile court judges determine sentencing severity largely on the basis of the apparent worthiness of the client. As another, Green (1977) reports that the average sentences for blacks convicted of murder or kidnapping (and out on appeal) was 66.1 months, compared with 5.8 months for whites. The unstated assumption is that whites will benefit more from rehabilitation and early release programs than will blacks.

Another implementation practice that represents a class bias is "creaming," or selecting recipients who are least in need of the service. For example, the Upward Bound program, a compensatory education program designed to enrich the educational experiences of disadvantaged high school students, has been criticized for taking too many students who are *already* likely to attend college. And employment counselors often send those people who are most employable out for job interviews, neglecting those people who are most difficult to place (Lipsky 1980). In both situations, better-off clients are most likely to benefit from the service, and they provide the greatest psychological reward for the service provider. Yet, by their very nature, compensatory programs are designed to help those people in greatest need of service rather than those who would benefit most from it.

We leave this discussion with a familiar refrain, suggesting that the problems of implementation are yet another manifestation of the complexity of social problems and the difficulties facing those who fashion solutions to them.

Poverty and Urban Policies

Poverty abounds in explanations. Perhaps the most enduring is the idea that poverty is an inescapable component of the human condition, part of the natural order of life. ("Ye have the poor always with you," said Jesus.) No less enduring is the idea that poverty is the result of some personal failing (lack of ambition, not enough hard work) and the idea that poverty is bad luck or bad timing.

Many liberals assert a different explanation, arguing that poverty is inherent in the structure of market societies, a concomitant of capitalism's cycles of boom and bust, its recurring periods of underemployment, and its com-

432

modification of labor—with wages and jobs determined by supply and demand. Another explanation (consistent with, but not dependent on, this structural perspective) sees poverty as the consequence of attitudes and adaptations passed down through generations—the consequence of a culture of poverty. And still other explanations see poverty among minorities as a consequence of discrimination and educational underachievement.

Given this abundance of competing and conflicting explanations, it is not surprising that policies seeking to ameliorate poverty are halting and unsure. If policymakers are uncertain about poverty's true causes, or unsure about whether poverty can ever be truly extirpated, their policies will reflect that uncertainty.[63] At the national level, poverty policies have been mostly redistributive and ameliorative, aimed at lifting the burdens of the poor by means of welfare payments. (The War on Poverty operated with a different logic, aimed at lifting the poor out of poverty by breaking the cycle of poverty. But here, too, the policymakers avoided having to fix on the "ultimate and true" cause of poverty; for them, it was sufficient merely to interrupt its cycle of perpetuation.)

For urban policymakers, poverty policy is also ameliorative, but with a difference. First, they confront problems of scale. No city has the monetary resources to equal or outdo federal programs, and no city wishes to risk a wholesale outmigration of its middle class by attempting widespread redistributive policies. (By the same token, most urban policymakers have learned the lesson of Proposition 13, and few are willing to risk their political futures by even proposing such redistributive policies.) To the extent that the middle and upper classes have a disproportionate share of urban power, it is understandable that they put fullest emphasis on distributive rather than redistributive policies. Thus, they are most willing to fund programs from which they benefit directly, including public safety, education, parks, transportation, and libraries. But it is also the case that they are willing to use such programs to redress the inequalities of race and poverty by concentrating benefits in the inner city.

Second, urban policymakers face the genuine problem of finding formulae that will distribute urban services in equal measure to all sectors of the population, while taking into account considerations of social equity. Given present political realities, the resources committed to alleviating the problems

---

63. An example of the kind of policy paradox that results from this uncertainty is found in urban housing projects for the poor. These projects were no doubt created out of the sense that society owes all of its citizens a home. But when this commitment is tempered by a view of poverty as a personal failing, it gives rise to slipshod construction, cheap materials, and out-of-the-way locations. After all, if the facilities will be trashed by their inhabitants, the policymakers may argue, it makes no sense to invest substantial resources in their construction or maintenance. Within a matter of years, many housing projects have become uninhabitable. But rather than taking this as evidence of incorrigible inhabitants, we could also view it as evidence of a self-fulfilling prophecy.

of poverty remain relatively fixed, and the delivery of social services within the city has become a zero-sum game: what one group gains in service benefits another must necessarily lose. And since the underclass consists of a complex patchwork of blacks, whites, and recently arrived immigrants (e.g., Vietnamese) living in different neighborhoods and with different needs and priorities, even a policy that meets most standards of equity must necessarily favor some interests over others.

Third, urban policymakers face the equally genuine problem of distributing urban services with an even hand through an administrative system of street-level bureaucracy. While it is one thing to generate government policy sensitive to the needs of the underclass, it may be an entirely different matter to overcome a lifetime of learning and experience on the part of those implementing the policy.

Fourth, urban policymakers must attend to issues and assertions of discrimination. As central cities have become increasingly black and Hispanic, urban policymakers have become increasingly sensitive to using the resources of city government to reduce (and eliminate) racial and ethnic discrimination—even as suburban policymakers, under federal scrutiny and perhaps moved by public conscience, struggle to find ways of using their zoning powers to maintain lifestyle homogeneity without giving way to racist exclusivity.

Thus, for the foreseeable future, poverty and its attendant problems will continue to dominate the politics and policies of both central cities and suburbs. Such changes as may take place in the ways that urban governments deal with poverty will most likely come as a consequence of two factors: demographic trends and changes in national government policies. For an exploration of both, we turn now to our final topic: the future of cities and cities of the future.

Looking to the Future:
An Epilogue

Chicago. Bob Thall. Photograph. © 1981.

436

The Shape of Things to Come ___ 18

We end this book as we began it, invoking themes set out in the first chapter.

- Every city is a web—of government and politics, of social relationships, of economic enterprises.
- The essential purpose of a city's government is to make urban life practical and possible—with lives lived among strangers reasonably safe, comfortable, and free from violence.
- Cities tend to be judged according to their government's ability to accomplish this essential purpose.
- Cities—especially big cities—are the creators and repositories of many of our cultural and artistic achievements.
- As units of government, as networks of social roles and economic enterprises, and as carriers of our culture, cities are shaped by what has gone before, which is to say that the urban web is anchored to history.

With these ideas in mind, let us look again at cities in the near past and in the present, asking one of the oldest questions of urban politics: What are present-day cities doing to improve the lives of those who live there? And from that question and from the vantage point of the near past and the present, perhaps we may catch a glimpse of city futures; for if the past shapes the present, then perhaps the present may foretell what is to come.

The Urban Crisis

Two decades ago, the most commonly used metaphor to describe American cities was that of crisis—crisis defined as a moment of decisive change. Soon, matters would become disastrously worse, or they would become decisively improved. And to give fuller meaning to the crisis that was said to invest our cities, the second most used set of metaphors were those borrowed from the languages of medicine and war: Our cities were described as "sick" (Gordon 1966); confronting "death" (Jacobs 1961); "under siege" (Boesel and Rossi 1971); and "in revolt" (Feagin and Hahn 1973).

The Urban Riots in Retrospect

As for cities in revolt, the metaphor was apt. For about five years (from 1964 to 1969) large-scale rioting had erupted in virtually every major city in the nation: New York City; Jersey City, Elizabeth, and Patterson, New Jersey; Detroit; Washington, D.C.; Los Angeles; and the list goes on. Between 1964 and 1968, 257 cities had exploded in riot violence (Downes 1970); and in one year alone (1967) over a half-million persons were arrested for rioting, over eight thousand were injured during riots, and more than two hundred were killed (Feagin and Hahn 1973).

Almost all the rioting took place in predominantly black urban areas. For many who undertook to analyze and explain the riots, their cause and meaning was clear. Blacks were angry and frustrated over their relative poverty in a nation of affluence, their thwarted attempts to climb the ladders of economic opportunity, and their lack of full access to the political equality promised in our Constitution. This anger and frustration had, in turn, been transformed into riot and violence (see note 1). A presidential commission (called, after its chairman, the Kerner Commission) created in 1967 to study the causes of the riots agreed. The causes of the riots, it concluded, were embedded in the social and economic structure of our society. And things were going from bad to worse. Our nation, said the Kerner Commission,

> is rapidly moving toward two increasingly separate Americas. . . a white society located principally in the suburbs. . . and in the peripheral parts of large central cities; and a Negro society largely concentrated within large central cities. (National Advisory Commission on Civil Disorders 1967, Introduction)

In a stinging rebuke to the nation, the commission went on to conclude:

> Segregation and poverty have created in the racial ghetto a destructive environ-
> ment. . . . White institutions created it, white institutions maintain it, and white
> society condones it.[1]

The Riots as Portent of Things to Come?

With the causes of urban rioting thus seen as woven into the social and
economic fabric of our society, it was perhaps inescapable that many would
also see the urban riots as prelude to what was still to come: a society forever
teetering on the brink of civil insurrection (Bienen 1968) and cities as the seed
of its disorder (Shefter 1984). And it is true that urban riots—as a consequence
of black anger and frustration—have occasionally reappeared in the years since
the late 1960s. In 1980 and 1982, the Liberty area of Miami exploded in riots:
in the first instance, as protest against the acquittal of white police officers
on charges that they had beaten to death a young black businessman, and in
the second instance, as protest against an Hispanic police officer's killing a
black teenager (*Newsweek*, Jan. 10, 1983). And in 1988, violence erupted in
Baton Rouge and again in Miami, both times in response to a racial incident.
But it is also true that riots have broken out in circumstances having what
would seem to be only the most tenuous connection to the plight of the inner
city. In 1977, a power failure plunged New York into darkness, and thousands
went on a rampage of plunder. An estimated two thousand businesses were
looted, with property losses reckoned at several hundred million dollars; four
hundred police were injured while attempting to arrest almost four thousand
rioters; and half a hundred firefighters were injured in efforts to control over
a thousand set fires (*Newsweek*, July 26, 1977).

But by and large, and at least for the present, the "days of rage" seem
mostly to be ended. Yet, conditions in the inner cities are appreciably no better than in the 1960s. (And some might argue that they are worse.) Suburbs
continue to stand as emblems of white affluence; and poverty in the inner cities
remains pervasive. If America consisted of two nations in 1967, one black and
one white, and if white institutions were the source of black privation, then

---

1. Not all, of course, agreed with this diagnosis. Much depended on the observer's life experiences and angle of ideological vision (e.g., Silver 1968, Platt 1971). Thus, the conservative members of
the President's Commission (mostly businesspersons and public officials) tended to see the riots as a
breakdown of law and order and as acts of criminality. In contrast, its liberal members (mostly staff
analysts, drawn from the ranks of academic social scientists) saw the causes of the riots in more complex terms: as frustration turned into aggression; as the consequence of social and structural (i.e.,
institutional) failures of our society. And some even took the view that violence is always "politically
defined." Ours, they suggested, has always been a violent society, and the kind of acts that get classified as violent "vary according to who provides the definition and who has superior resources for
enforcing his definitions" (Skolnick 1969, 4). Perhaps the most memorable dissent from the view of
the riots as a consequence of black frustration over the social and economic failures of our society was
provided by Edward Banfield's (1974) essay "Rioting Mainly for Fun and Profit."

little has changed since the 1960s. But despite all this, cities no longer seem to teeter on the edge of civil insurrection; or if they do, they have not for a long time tumbled over that edge.

Thus, if little has changed in the cities, how are we to explain the current style of urban politics? Given the woeful predictions of the 1960s, we must either conclude that urban racial violence has subsided, or that it is gathering metaphoric and sociological strength before a new explosion. And what about the "crisis" of the cities—and the expectation that matters must either worsen appreciably or improve considerably? Four answers seem possible.

- The crisis has simply disappeared.
- The crisis was more an invention of urban critics than an accurate description of the condition of the cities.[2]
- The span of public attention is short lived, and what was one generation's sense of crisis is another's sense of the everyday.
- Urban policymakers, sensing that many of the problems of the city are intractable, have shifted their attention elsewhere.

The last two answers seem most plausible, but whichever answer is most fully correct, the urban crisis seems to have drifted away from political consciousness. But even if the sense of an urban crisis has drifted from public concern, memories of the 1960s remain. They, and the social forces that produced the sixties' sense of an urban crisis, are now part of present-day urban trends and outlooks. And it is these that are now at work, helping to shape the urban future, especially in such areas as the plight of the urban poor, the growth of megacounties, shifts in population, and small-town America.

Small Towns and Small-Towners

The small town in many ways remains much as it has over the past three decades (and more): a place where residents embrace traditional values, carefully guarding against the encroachment of perceived "city problems." Historically, many small towns have been farming communities, where commercial businesses largely support farmers and their families. And it has not been unusual for several generations of small-town families to live in close proximity to one another, with farms and businesses being passed down from parent to child.

But in other important ways, the small town in American life has changed dramatically during the past decades. With the decline of the family farm, the small-town economic base has changed, and many small towns are

---

2. On the political rhetoric of the 1960s (its imagery and its style), see DeMott (1970) and Dickstein (1977).

forced to find alternative sources of jobs for their residents. In some cases, residents are forced to drive many miles to find work in larger cities. In other cases, industries and manufacturing businesses move to town—carrying with them exactly the kinds of negative externalities that small-towners have always guarded against: growth, pollution, crime, and a breakdown of the trust that has grown out of generations of personal interaction among residents. Nor is the small town as immune as it once was to larger societal changes. With the growth of the interstate highway system, small towns are no longer as isolated as they once were, and the old saying that "you can't get there from here" may no longer apply. So, too, the problems of pollution have spread nationwide; for example, many New England villages, without any industry of their own, are affected by acid rain created by emissions from industrial plants in Ohio, Michigan, Indiana, and Illinois.

In short, the small town can no longer live in stubborn isolation, and although small-towners still cling to their traditional values, they are forced to accommodate those values to a world changing around them.

Non-Cities and Megacounties

In successive editions of Peter Hall's (1966,1984) book on the world's great (i.e., largest) cities lies an arresting fact: in 1950, seven of those cities were in the United States; but by the year 2000, according to current predictions (Lockwood and Leinberger 1988), only two (New York and Los Angeles) will be in the United States.

Where, then, have all the great American cities gone? Part of the answer lies in the fact that urbanization is expanding all around the world, and that particularly in developing countries cities continue their historic role as population pumps—pulling impoverished rural folk into the cities in search of a new and better life. Mexico City, for example, is estimated to have a population of 10 million (with another 5 million packed into the city's adjacent area); Rio de Janeiro has about 9 million people; and Cairo has about 6 million people (with a metropolitan area population of about 10 million).

The other (and for our purposes, more important) part of the answer lies in two trends previously explored: the increasing suburbanization of the United States, and the increasing population density of unincorporated areas—located within counties rather than cities per se—that are part of the metropolitan area. Those who live in these densely populated, unincorporated areas (shall we call them *exurbanites?*) bring into the county an urban outlook and a demand for urban services—which many county governments now provide. And along with density of a residential population, these urbanized counties have also become the site of office-complexes, light industries and industrial parks, along with shopping malls and such other attributes of urban and suburban life as restaurants and cinemas. These high-density, deeply settled places in the countryside have every attribute of sprawling suburbs except one: by fierce determination of their residents, they remain unincorporated and are legally non-cities.

The Imperatives of Megacounty Growth

The social and economic forces behind the rise of megacounties are more than familiar, for they are (in Edward Banfield's phrase) the imperatives of metropolitan growth (Banfield 1970, ch. 2). They are characterized by:

- large land tracts, available fairly cheaply, providing opportunity for land-developers' profits;
- the relative absence of land-use restrictions (in other words, zoning laws) in the countryside, again providing opportunities for land-developers' profits;
- the middle-class desire for status differential, along with the opportunity to escape central-city problems;
- the interstate highways and ring roads which help ease the difficulties of long-distance commuting;
- the aesthetics of office buildings and factories set in wooded preserves and park-like surroundings;
- the greater efficiency and flexibility of production lines that can be arranged on the large floor spaces of new, horizontally dispersed factories;
- the location of numerous accounting, advertising, inventory control, and upper-management departments which—due to the arrival of computer technology—need no longer be located in close physical proximity to manufacturing sites.

Thus, almost everywhere in the United States, the urbanized county has become the newest and most intensive form of metropolitan area development. *Megacounties* is the term commonly used to describe them. For example, in the Chicago metropolitan region, DuPage County is thick with office buildings and several huge shopping malls. And Fairfax County, Virginia, is not only residential home to Washington, D.C., exurbanites, it is also a place of imposing corporate wealth.

> Tysons Corner, an unincorporated area of Fairfax County, thirteen miles from Washington, was once a sleepy crossroads with little more than a gas station; today it contains more office space than either Baltimore or downtown Miami. (*Time,* June 15, 1987, p. 13)

The pattern repeats in other metropolitan areas. "The Corporate Woods office complex in Overland Park, Kansas, boasts 275 businesses and 5000 jobs; built on 300 acres, it has room for more" (*Time,* June 15, 1987, p. 13). Along with urbanization have come still more residents (wishing to live near places of work and cut down on commuting time) as well as construction jobs and service jobs.

Megacounty Problems and the No-Growth Movement

If there are reasons to be concerned about the rise of the megacounty, they are familiar. Megacounties are the new form of urban sprawl—gobbling up huge chunks of the countryside, lacking any pattern or plan for orderly growth, creating their own forms of traffic snarl, and suffering rising air pollution, overcrowded schools, and inadequate water and sewage facilities.

Nearby suburbs, fearful for their own futures, have responded by attempting to enact no-growth zoning legislation designed to limit population densities. Thus, suburban voters in the megacounties that are part of the Los Angeles and San Francisco metropolitan regions have recently used the state's ballot initiative laws to enact a series of no-growth laws:

> "We are being packed in like sardines," complains . . . a San Fernando Valley no-growth activist. . . . [In counter argument], critics say that the growth-control measures will mean even higher housing costs for California, where the average home price tops $152,000. They also say that the anti-growth sentiment is a sign of racism and elitism. . . . "But," says another no-growth advocate, "It's like the lifeboat that says 65 (capacity). . . . The 66th guy steps in. They all drown." (Associated Press, June 9, 1988)

Megacounties and Central Cities

The residents of the urbanized megacounties are mostly white and relatively affluent; and their move to the megacounty contributes to the "two Americas" of our previous discussion, one black, poor, and central-city dwelling, the other white, affluent, and at home on the city's rim. Job opportunities in the megacounty continue to expand, but those jobs are mostly beyond the reach of the central city's poor. There is, after all, little public transportation out to the megacounty, and the inner-city poor often lack automobiles.

The metropolitan region of Atlanta, Georgia, typifies these trends and concerns:

> Suburban Gwinnett County has been the nation's fastest growing large county for three years running. Neighboring Cobb County is a perennial top 10. At the same time, the population of Atlanta proper is shrinking—down 13 percent since 1970 to 430,000. . . . Blacks make up 70 percent of the population [of Atlanta] including a sizable [college educated] middle class. . . . But for the greater number of blacks, who have little education and low skills, there is little opportunity. The areas of the city where blacks are in the majority saw

just a 4.7 percent rise in jobs between 1970 and 1985, compared with a 71 percent rise in the greater Atlanta areas that are more than 90 percent white. (*Wall Street Journal,* Feb. 2, 1988)

With high-paying executive jobs and high-valued property now moving to exurbia, the central city is deprived of property and income-tax revenues. Moreover, when corporate headquarters move to exurbia, the central city is deprived of those business leaders who, in the past, were important to the executive-centered coalitions that helped push forward major central-city development projects. Again, Atlanta typifies:

Atlanta was built by natives whose business and civic interests were indistinguishable. But today's business corps is largely corporate gypsies, operating largely outside city limits. . . . That means that for all its present glory, Atlanta lacks its old visionary leadership. The city that built a ballpark in a year in the '60s can't drum up private sector support for a new domed stadium. (*Wall Street Journal,* Feb. 2, 1988)

Population Shifts and Demographic Trends

The scholarly literature of a decade ago was studded with concern for the rapidly growing sunbelt cities and their possible effects on the older cities of the Northeast (e.g., C. Morris 1980, R. Morris 1980). For some analysts, the flow of population out from the old snowbelt cities of the Northeast into the South and West suggested the likelihood of a serious depopulation of our oldest cities, perhaps to leave them—like the silver-mining towns of Colorado—ghost towns, awaiting some future tourist boom to bring them back to life. And those preoccupied with changes in the South and West (the sunbelt) were given to wondering whether the newly prosperous sunbelt cities were someday to suffer the decline of the old, northeast cities, and whether or not ways could be devised to stem that decline (Perry and Watkins 1977, Sale 1975).

In the 1980s, these preoccupations seem overextended. The older cities of the Northeast, it is true, have failed to find replacements for the heavy industries (steel, automobiles) that have been closed down by foreign competition. But, at the same time, the prosperity of cities such as Houston, Dallas, and Phoenix has been pushed upward and pulled downward by the same national economic trends that affect most other cities (and it has been pulled severely downward with the fortunes of the oil industry); and the sometime office-building boom of Houston, Dallas, and other Southwest cities has come onto hard economic times.

Sunbelt Futures

Nonetheless, the shift of population into the sunbelt continues. It is presently estimated that half of the national population growth expected by the year 2000 will take place in forty metropolitan areas—and most of these will be in the South and West. Eleven are in California, six in Florida, five in Texas, and two each in Arizona and North Carolina. By the year 2000, the Los Angeles metropolitan area is expected to have added more than a million persons to its population (bringing its total to 16.4 million), and between a half-million and a million persons are expected to be added to each of the following metropolitan areas: Houston, Riverside-San Bernadino (California), Atlanta, Phoenix, Dallas, Anaheim-Santa Ana (California), San Diego, and Washington, D.C. (NPA Data Service, quoted in the Associated Press, June 29, 1988). Small wonder, then, that no-growth policies are under active consideration in these areas! By comparison,

> the United States as a whole is expected to add 23,616,000 people between 1986 . . . and 2000. That means that the 40 [metropolitan] areas would account for 49.57 percent of the nation's growth. (NPA Data Service, quoted in the Associated Press, June 29, 1988).

Racial and Ethnic Changes

Even as the South and West experience considerable population growth, another population shift of equal or greater import is afoot. The racial and ethnic composition of the United States has been changing, and—as a consequence—the racial composition of large, central cities is being altered considerably. The Bureau of the Census currently predicts that in the year 2010, "the population of the United States will be 10 percent Asian, 17 percent black, 28 percent Hispanic, and 46 percent white" (*New York Times*, July 20, 1988).

Central Cities and Housing Segregation

As whites become a minority in the United States, they quite likely will continue to move outward from the central cities, leaving these areas more and more to the oncoming American majority of Asians, Hispanics, and blacks. It is also likely that the federal courts will be more and more involved with lawsuits seeking to "open up" the metropolitan area—which is to say, to make it less segregated and economically segmented.

In the summer of 1988, the issue of urban zoning received renewed legal and public attention as a federal court threatened the city of Yonkers, New York, with massive fines (and jail sentences for its city council) for having failed

445

to pass a zoning ordinance that would permit the siting of low cost apartment housing in single-family, all-white residential areas (*New York Times,* Aug. 4, 1988). A majority of the Yonkers' city council asserted that their refusal to obey the court lay in their determination to protect residential property values and not (as the court and plaintiffs asserted) in an attempt to maintain racial exclusivity. But in the swirl of publicity that surrounded the Yonkers' case, public attention was once again fixed on a central fact of central cities, the racial segregation of their housing.

As was reported in table 17.2, residential segregation in most metropolitan areas remains high. For example, it runs at a rate of over 80 percent in the Chicago, Detroit, St. Louis, Milwaukee, and Ft. Lauderdale metropolitan areas, and over 70 percent in most other major metro areas. (Notable exceptions to this generalization include several California cities, where fewer than half of the residents live in segregated areas: Anaheim, Riverside, and San Jose.)[3]

Sunbelt Cities and Ethnic Changes

For sunbelt cities, present trends in racial and ethnic composition are expected to continue. Los Angeles (it is predicted) will become America's first "third-world city."

> . . . its ethnic composition is [even now] becoming less Anglo and more Latin and Asian. The Anglo population will drop from 60 percent to approximately 40 percent in 2010. . . . The non-Hispanic black population will rise from 9 percent to 10 percent, increasing by 800,000. The Asian population will grow from 6.2 percent to 9.3 percent, increasing by almost one million. The Hispanic population will rise from 24 percent to 40 percent, increasing by more than four million. (Lockwood and Leinberger 1988, 41)

If the only meaning we give to *third-world city* is that non-Hispanic whites will be Los Angeles' new minority, then the prediction is no more than an extrapolation from present trends. But the prediction carries other meanings as well, for most third-world cities are marked by crushing poverty, illiteracy, disease, disastrous unemployment, and an economic system that gives scant comfort and hope to the local inhabitants—an economic system in which the local population provides industrial manpower while profits and a rising standard of living are exported elsewhere. Is it possible, ask many who strive to uncover the future, that third-world parallels lie in store not only for Los Angeles, but for most of the other central cities? Given the problems that now beset many of our central cities, they ask, is a third-world future already here?

---

3. These statistics are taken from Clark (1986).

For those who raise these questions, the answers may lie not only in such trends as may be revealed by census and other data, but also in the angles of ideological vision from which question-askers view their data.

The Future of Central Cities: Ideologies and Interpretations

Most everyone agrees that the problems of many central cities are massive. Even to present them in barebones outline is to yield to the temptation of being discouraged about the future: homeless people living and sleeping on the streets; high rates of unemployment; housing segregation and housing decay; white flight; juvenile street gangs; drug dealing and drug wars; school drop-outs; the obsolescence and breakdown of the city's physical plant (water pipes, bridges, sewage systems, and the like), which has been in place often for over a century in the older cities of the Northeast; and for many central cities a declining tax base, which limits the ability of central cities to adequately address this long list of problems.

"Who Shall Decide When Doctors Disagree?"

Given the enormity of the problems confronting many central cities—especially the older, industrial cities—it should not be surprising to discover wide and deep disagreement over what, if anything, *should* be done; and there is equally wide and deep disagreement over what, if anything, *can* be done. In general, these disagreements are organized around the fault lines of ideology and the perceptions of reality framed by those fault lines.

   Economic conservatives generally take the view that central-city problems are closely linked to the evolution of market societies. Capital flows to places of greatest profitability (they argue), and while dislocations (such as joblessness, housing decay, and technological unemployment) are among the social costs of a market economy, the long-term benefits to the entire society are great. It is an historic truth, they say, that market societies are the freest and most prosperous of all societies. As needed, government ought to assist those individual persons who suffer the consequences of economic dislocations, but it should not engage in massive programs to save the cities.[4]

   In a related vein, Banfield (1970, 1974) argues that conditions in central cities have more to do with perception than reality:

---

4. See, for example, Friedman and Friedman (1981) and Wanniski (1978). For the argument that government's role is to assist the private entrepreneur, see Gilder (1981). And for extension of the proposition that democratic societies historically have evolved inside market societies, see Lindblom (1977) and Friedman and Friedman (1981).

For something like two-thirds of all city dwellers, the urban problems that touch them directly have to do with comfort, convenience, amenity, and business advantage . . . these are "important" problems, but not "serious ones." . . . [Thus,] although things have been getting better absolutely, they have been getting worse relative to what we think they should be. (Banfield 1970, 6, 19)

Liberals, in contrast, advocate federal intervention not only to assist the cities, but also to assist those who live there. It is time, they say, for a return to the compassion that lay behind the Great Society programs; equally, it is time to try again for extensive national programs designed to solve central-city problems. And if massive national programs are not to be invoked, they conclude, then let federal government embark on a series of city-assisting, small-scale interventions.

Framing both sets of arguments is another observation that deals both with changing economic conditions and with perceptions of reality—in this case, the collective perception of the entire society. Cities, writes George Sternlieb (1971), no longer perform their historic functions. Formerly, with their deep pools of immigrant labor, they provided the work force that ran the American industrial system. But now, the need for strong backs and the fifteen-hour day

has been reduced to almost nothing by the transportation revolution, which has the effect of homogenizing time and distance. Much of our labor-intensive work is now imported from abroad. Welfare legislation, minimum wages, maximum working hours, and the like have minimized the economic functions of the conglomerations of poor-but-willing people in our cities.

The city, says Sternlieb, has become a *sandbox,* a place where our society has parked those who are no longer productive, so that the rest of society "can get on with the serious things of life" (p.17).

If our cities have indeed become sandboxes, then perhaps nothing can be done for the cities—except to make the unproductive poor who live there as comfortable as our resources and generosity will permit. And even more important, if society perceives the city as sandbox, then perhaps nothing *will* be done—except again to make the city's unproductive poor as comfortable as our resources and generosity will permit. Is this a realistic perception? Or a counsel of despair? Both perhaps, or neither? It is not so much that only time will tell, but that the idea of the city as sandbox—as a self-fulfilling perception—may get in the way of present and future plans to help the cities.

448

Battling Urban Decay

Private Initiatives With and Without Public Assistance

Cities have never lacked private-sector initiatives in either their development or revitalization. It has always been a matter of the extent of those initiatives and whether or not they are likely to be of sufficient scale to help revitalize present-day cities. Previous chapters (11, 14) noted the role of the private sector entrepreneur in transforming shabby central business districts. And they also noted their limited success in bringing new life to areas that lie beyond the central business district.

Most of the entrepreneurial projects earlier noted were fairly large scale. (Perhaps it is characteristic of our society that we most notice and admire those who work on a grand scale, and who—in the words of a long-ago Chicago developer—"make no little plans.") But cities also offer ample opportunity for the small-scale entrepreneur; and in recent years, piecemeal private initiatives have made a considerable impact on many cities. (For an optimistic canvass of recent attempts at urban revitalization, see Gratz 1989.)

Gentrification is the word commonly used to describe the process whereby single householders and small-business firms buy up and transform an entire city area. German Village and Victorian Village in Columbus, Ohio, the Lincoln Park area of Chicago, Queens Village in Philadelphia, Capitol Hill and Adams Morgan in Washington, D.C., are all examples of gentrification (Gale 1984, McGrath 1982). As the term itself suggests, gentrification not only restores to former glory the physical character of a residential neighborhood, it also brings to the area a gentry (i.e., middle) class. And perhaps more important, success in restoring one part of the city tends to encourage comparable restorations in other parts of the city.

Most gentrification projects have won the praise of city officials and civic leaders. Some are hailed as the best and surest road to city revival. But hard facts and spillover consequences also travel that same road. The pull of suburban life remains strong among the American middle class, and relatively few in that class give evidence of a desire to return to the central city. More important and more sobering is the fact that gentrification increases property values and sends rents soaring. As a result, gentrification displaces the poor who once lived in the area, forcing them back into what is likely to be an already overcrowded market for low-rent housing.

Urban restoration is the commercial counterpart of gentrification, in which old business buildings are bought and restored through private enterprise. All forms of urban revitalization receive some form of government assistance (at the very least, an income-tax benefit for interest paid on borrowed money). But urban restoration projects also receive additional forms of government assistance. For example, in 1966 Congress enacted a law establishing the

National Register of Historic Buildings. Buildings designated for inclusion in the register are protected from the wrecker's ball; more important, those who restore them are eligible to receive a restoration grant. In this way (and often with further assistance from local and state government), several cities now proudly display restored areas of Victorian and Romanesque architecture: Pioneer Square in Seattle; the former Tivoli Brewery (a Hollywood-Bavarian fantasy of shops, offices, restaurants, and cinemas) in Denver; the Old Post Office building (a multi-storied atrium, banked by restaurants and boutiques) in Washington, D.C.; the Lit Brothers Department Store Block in Philadelphia; the Ohio Theatre (a 1920s Moorish fantasy) in Columbus; and an area of small art-deco hotels in the south Miami Beach area (to name only a few such restorations).

Urban restoration projects do much to bring a sense of life and vitality back to central cities. They bring shoppers and strollers to the central business district, add jobs to the work force, and enhance the city's tax base. Perhaps most important of all, they give visual and sensual pleasure to those who appreciate the bustle of urban life and its kaleidoscopic variety. But there is also criticism of these urban restoration projects which bears an old and familiar ring. They divert money to the benefit of the privileged classes that might be better spent on overcoming the problems of the urban underclass.

Urban Homesteading

Successful public policies remain locked in memory long after they cease to be. During the Civil War, in an attempt to open the West for settlement, Congress passed the Rural Homestead Act of 1862. Under the act, settlers could stake out 160 acres of homestead. If a settler family built a house on those acres, lived there, and cultivated the land for at least five years, then on payment of a modest fee the land would belong to the family. ("A five year bet with Uncle Sam" was the refrain of a song of that time.)

Rural homesteading was a considerable success, and many Plains states families today trace their farmstead back to the Homestead Act. Recalling that success, policymakers in the 1970s, as they confronted the problem of urban decay, transferred the idea of homesteading to the central city. Baltimore and Philadelphia were among the first to try the idea of urban homesteading, and as the idea gathered wider support, Congress in 1974 authorized a national homesteading program. Under the terms of the Housing and Community Development Act, cities were invited to "designate a target neighborhood that was not severely blighted, but which contained HUD-owned one-to-four family properties" (Marshall 1985, 6).

Each city would receive from HUD money sufficient to buy a number of these properties (each valued at less than $15,000), which the city, in turn, would hand over to urban homesteaders. Homesteaders were required to live in these homes for at least three years, repair and restore them (usually with the assistance of low-interest federal loans), and at the completion of restoration and occupancy, would come into ownership of their refurbished property.

Overall, and nationwide, only a few thousand houses have been homesteaded. Some critics explain this meager success by arguing that the homesteading experience was a nightmare of government rules, regulations, and red tape. Others argue that home ownership is essentially a middle-class attribute, and those who have this attribute do not want to live in areas targeted for homesteading, while those who live (and are willing to live) in those areas are usually lacking in middle-class attributes.[5]

Enterprise Zones

Following Ronald Reagan's election to the presidency in 1980, many conservative policy planners began advocating enterprise zones (i.e., designated inner-city areas in which private enterprise would be given tax benefits and other forms of government assistance). The idea was to attract business enterprises to those areas, thus providing jobs for those who lived there. The idea behind enterprise zones is straightforward. No matter what other measures may be tried (say enterprise-zone advocates), in the end the quality of urban life will rise or fall in accordance with the success or failure of private enterprise; for it is business enterprise, not government, that provides the surest, most efficient instrument for lifting the poor out of poverty.[6]

About twenty states have enacted enterprise-zone legislation; and while many in those states have claimed success for their enterprise zones, their overall impact on the economy of inner cities has thus far been minuscule.

---

5. Few ideas invoke more argument than defining the psychological attributes and personality structure of the middle class. Karl Marx spoke of the outlook of the bourgeois class, and to be one of its members still carries a derisive overtone. Even so, there is a good deal of agreement that to be middle class in America (whatever one's income) is to have a sense of thrift, a self-discipline that puts the future ahead of the present (and its demands for immediate gratification), and an ability to plan for that future. More than one hundred fifty years ago, Tocqueville (1945) saw these attributes as the essence of the American character, and it worries many contemporary scholars—as well as ideologists—that these attributes may be disappearing from American life. (See, for example, Riesman 1950, Gilder 1981; and for a recent inquiry into the conflict between private desires and the public good, see Bella, et al. 1985). Even so, a fierce intellectual debate followed Banfield's (1970) assertion that the urban poor differed from the rest of American society precisely on grounds that they were outside the middle-class value structure.

6. Critics of these programs argue that economic opportunities for the underclass may be largely meaningless without social opportunities provided by improved health care, housing, and education. While these improvements may be obtained through economic opportunities, they come slowly if the poor must rely solely on their earnings; and in the meantime, substandard health or housing may threaten continuing employment. Finally (argue the critics), without job skills, the urban poor are likely to receive only minimum wage, which may be insufficient to pull them from the cycle of poverty.

451

Business Firms in the Inner City

But with or without enterprise zones, several large corporations have established a presence in the inner city. Their purpose is essentially philanthropic and civic-minded (though they do benefit from federal tax programs that offer tax benefits to businesses hiring new entrants into the job market and the hard-core unemployed). In most cases, "urban-blight enterprises" are moved forward by the same rationale as the urban-enterprise zones: Business, not government, is to be the effective lever of urban transformation. For example, Control Data Corporation has built factories and hired inner-city workers in a number of cities: Minneapolis, St. Paul, San Antonio, Toledo, Baltimore, and Washington, D.C. (*Ebony,* June 1982).

As is the case with urban restoration, enterprise zones, and other private initiatives, the "corporation in the ghetto" has had many individual successes, but no overall success. Perhaps those who expect massive changes in the inner cities expect too much. Or perhaps the problems of setting up a manufacturing plant in an inner city are so great that big companies become intimidated and are too easily discouraged.

Looking to the Future: Urban Economic Trends

Those who scan the economic skies looking for a revival of heavy industry in America must surely be doomed to disappointment. Steelmaking, automobile making, and most of their related industries have fled to the havens of cheaper labor abroad. And textiles, electronics, and a host of other industries that once made American production a source of domestic pride and foreign envy have also gone abroad (Bluestone and Harrison 1982, Reich 1983). In cities of the Midwest, Northeast, and along the Atlantic coast, those were the industries that were major employers for skilled and semi-skilled workers. And those, too, were the industries that had once been magnets for city-bound immigrants from rural America and from abroad.

Now those industries are mostly shut down, their jobs gone and not likely ever to return. And the once thriving textile, steelmaking, and automobile cities are riddled with unemployment and tagged with the title "rustbelt" cities. What, then, is going to take the place of employment in textiles and heavy industry? Service jobs, say most economic forecasters. To bear this out, 80 percent of the jobs created since 1980 have been in the service sector. And of the 700,000 jobs created in 1987, 94 percent were in the service sector—and more than half paid less than $7,000 a year (Report, University of Michigan Business School, cited by Tom Hundley in the *Chicago Tribune,* June 20, 1988). Along the same lines, Peter Drucker (a noted writer on economic trends) predicts that, by the year 2000, the number of people holding jobs in manufacturing will have dropped from 20 percent to 10 percent of the national work force (Lockwood and Leinberger 1988).

But service jobs pay far less than manufacturing jobs, and the transition to a service economy is especially disruptive for those moving from skilled industrial jobs into the service sector. To make matters worse—at least for rustbelt cities—a significant portion of the manufacturing jobs that will be available in the year 2000 are forecasted to be in the sunbelt.

What, then, of future service jobs for most central-city workers? Who will provide them? And what will they be like? Perhaps part of an answer is to be found in a recent report on Cleveland, Ohio:

> In a blue-collar neighborhood where there once were small factories and tool shops, a giant, pink granite pyramid rises above the cold smokestacks and wood frame houses. . . . This is the Cleveland Clinic, a medical complex that has gained international fame . . . and now stands as a graphic symbol of the city's transition from a manufacturing to a service economy. With 9,134 employees, the clinic is the city's largest private employer, a plateau it achieved when it passed LTV Steel, the nation's No. 2 steelmaker, which is mired in bankruptcy proceedings. . . . "It's not a healthy sign for a hospital to be the No. 1 employer in a city as big as Cleveland," said . . . the clinic's chief executive. (Hundely, in the *Chicago Tribune,* June 20, 1988)

The Urban Poor

Sooner or later, most attempts at improving, revitalizing, or saving our central cities lead us back to considering the urban poor. A great number of the problems considered to be big-city problems are bound up with the presence there of millions mired in poverty. During the 1980s, much thought but little policy action was given to the plight of the urban poor. There are numerous explanations for this inaction. One is an emotional weariness that followed the great expenditure of civic and policy energies on Great Society programs, along with disappointment over the perceived failures of those programs. A second is a national swing to the conservative right, as signalled by Ronald Reagan's election. A third explanation centers around a spiraling national deficit that crowds out new domestic policy initiatives. And, most telling of all, inaction can be explained by a widespread sense (and a fear) that, as far as poverty is concerned, nothing really works.

As the 1990s begin, the public temperament may be changing. Concern for the poor, both rural and urban, seems to be climbing back onto the national policy agenda. Journals of intellectual opinion pull our memories back to the riots of the 1960s and remind us of what can befall a society in which the Kerner Commission's "two nations" stand separated and intact. Many such journals have begun to make an inventory of "poverty programs that work." Many of these are of the small-scale variety, relying on local rather than federal initiatives: for example, a Chicago bank that makes mortgage loans

453

to inner-city borrowers; an Allegheny County program that created a community college offering job training to former steel workers; the promise of a privately funded, college education to inner-city youth who finish high school. The purpose of such inventories is not only to provide a pool of future policy alternatives, it is also to keep alive a public view that poverty programs can be made to work (e.g., *Washington Monthly,* June 1988).

In framing future poverty programs, policymakers are likely to invoke two long-standing ideas, one liberal, the other conservative.[7] The liberal idea involves an investment in *human capital,* resting on the belief that public money spent on job training and education is the surest, best way to ensure national prosperity and a rising standard of living (e.g., Reich 1983, Thurow 1980). The conservative idea establishes a distinction between the deserving poor (those who want to work and are able to work) and the undeserving poor (those who are able to work but have little wish to do so). This distinction accords with what many perceive to be traditional American values (a work ethic, a success ethic); and it also accords with a widely held belief that no one has an inherent right to an income—that "workfare" (i.e., government-subsidized employment) is preferable to welfare.

Thus, future poverty programs are likely to be grounded on the idea of an investment in human capital: job training, education to overcome illiteracy, and workshop experience that instills habits of work-force discipline. (To the extent that present policy is forerunner of future policy, we should note that Congress' welfare reform legislation of 1988—the Family Security Act—embodies these same principles.)

Time was, not long ago, that any distinction between the deserving and the undeserving poor would have given rise to fierce ideological debate. For conservatives, all who received public money were to be regarded as recipients of charity, and charity was a gift to be reserved for the deserving. For liberals, a commitment to equality of outcomes was sufficient to make the idea of charity demeaning to the human spirit and an affront to the idea of income as a social right. For them, there could be no easily established distinction between the deserving and the undeserving poor.

Complicating matters have been accusations of racism and elitism. Is a distinction between the deserving and the undeserving poor only a disguised racism, a way of doing nothing to assist poor Hispanics and blacks? Is it a way of blaming the slums on those who live there—in short, a way of blaming the victim?

However, a national belief may now be emerging that this distinction does have validity, and that the deserving poor ought to be saved from

_____

7. This, again, reaffirms a long-standing political tradition: In difficult decisions, no side is likely to leave empty-handed.

what a journal of liberal opinion has recently called a "destructive ghetto culture" (*New Republic,* June 13, 1988). It is a culture, says Christopher Jencks, of "sane, healthy adults who refuse to follow norms of behavior that most of society endorses," a culture that "approves (or at least fails to disapprove) of idleness, single parenthood, theft, and violence" (*New Republic,* June 13, 1988).

However, to identify and thus characterize a destructive ghetto culture is not to be unmindful of its many causes and sources (e.g., Wilson 1987, Auletta 1982), not least of which may be a social and economic system that has driven jobs and good housing out of urban centers; the manifold inheritances of what the Kerner Commission called white racism; and the propensity of contemporary America to see the inner city as a sandbox. But even when these things are said, it is a destructive ghetto culture that gives greatest worry to those concerned about the future of American cities (liberals and conservatives alike), for it is a culture that stubbornly resists attempts to change it.

This growing national consensus is likely to target future poverty programs toward the deserving poor. But with this in mind, we should reexamine the statistics on poverty (taken from chapter 17), which tell the story of an underclass that is, for the most part, deserving. Consider the following statistics:

- Over 50 percent of the families living in poverty have one or more members in the work force, most of whom work at least part time on a continuing basis.
- Children under seventeen account for approximately 42 percent of the people living in poverty, with the elderly accounting for another 13 percent.
- Nearly one-quarter of those heads of households who do not work are ill or disabled, with another 40 percent caring for children and/or keeping house.

Providing these deserving poor with the opportunity to escape the pathology of the ghetto represents an ideal that both liberals and conservatives applaud. Given society's commitment to a market economy, this opportunity will most likely come in the private sector, in the form of government-subsidized jobs and training programs. But it will also be costly. For example, job opportunities for mothers with small children make little sense in the absence of day-care programs. And even more critical, few families can survive on the $7,000 annual salary that many new service jobs are paying; therefore, workfare may need to be supplemented with other forms of income. But whatever its form, a rethinking of the assumptions (both liberal and conservative) about poverty may be necessary if the poverty of the cities is to be overcome. Success will require not only patience and policy inventiveness, but also a public willingness to account even small successes as major accomplishments.

A National Urban Policy?

In the years to come, Congress will no doubt enact many programs designed to assist American cities. And many policy entrepreneurs are likely to suggest that the United States follow Europe's lead in establishing government programs that work at revitalizing entire regions, not single cities. (Examples include Germany's assistance to the heavy industries of the Ruhr valley and Britain's system of incentives to persuade business firms to move northward, away from the overcrowded "home counties.") Others are likely to suggest that the national government create something on the order of an Urban Development Bank, making long-term, low-cost loans to business firms willing to build (or stay) in central cities.

Still others may push for a grant-in-aid program to the states—framed with Europe's experiences in mind—to encourage the states to enact statewide controls over land development and land use, and perhaps even create a special government authority over each of the state's metropolitan areas. (Sweden, for example, has given the city of Stockholm the authority to buy up extensive tracts of land all around the city, and the city has developed a ring of satellite suburbs which are famous for their orderly planning and high quality of urban amenities; see Heidenheimer et al. 1975.)

Perhaps most visionary of all will be those who push for a comprehensive national urban policy. That policy, if it is to be truly national and truly comprehensive, would most likely authorize some form of national control over the locational and investment decisions of private business, controlling where they are to be located and the purposes for which they are to be permitted to invest their capital (e.g., Smith 1979, Kantor 1988, Moynihan 1969b).

Of all these possible policies, only some form of an Urban Reconstruction Bank seems even remotely likely. Although economic Conservatives are likely to oppose it, an Urban Reconstruction Bank does have historic precedent (the Reconstruction Finance Corporation of the Great Depression), and it is in some degree ideologically compatible with our society's attachment to a market economy (see, for example, the writings of investment banker Felix Rohatyn 1981). In contrast, a regional development plan would run counter to the highly developed sense of localism that lies at the heart of our system of congressional government. Thus Congress is likely to be wary of any proposal to assist one region of the country at the expense (or so it will be presumed) of other parts of the nation.

Statewide controls over land use and metropolitan development run counter to our tradition of local governments as republics in miniature—not to mention our long history of land development as opportunity for the business entrepreneur and the strength of our belief that land and buildings are commodities to be bought and sold for profit.

As to the idea of a comprehensive national urban policy, its realization seems remotest of all. It, after all, strikes at almost everything held sacred by protectors of a market economy: the rights of a business to locate where it wishes and to decide how and for what purposes it is to invest its capital. And perhaps even more important as an impediment to the development of a national urban policy is the fact that as a society we have no consistent vision of what it is that we wish our cities to be, nor have we arrived at a consensus concerning the role that cities are to play in our national life. Our vision of cities is clouded by an ambivalent regard: We see them as symbols of accomplishment and as creators of culture and wealth, but we also see them as places of violence and evil that are merely to be endured. Side by side, both visions work to constrain our policy options. What, then, lies in store for our cities?

The Future of American Cities

As those who read science and social fiction well know, cities have traditionally played a central role in futurist writings. From Plato onward to the early twentieth century, what was imagined as a utopian future was usually set in the city, for the city was characteristically seen as the instrument of human progress. Then, in our own century, futurist writing became darker and more pessimistic. The city remained as the place where the future was imagined; but now mankind's fate was seen to be painful and problematic. And the city was not utopia, but *dystopia*—the symbol and instrument of human suffering and political repression.[8]

If present trends continue—barring war or a wrenching economic depression—what the future holds for many American central cities is probably something between the antipodes of utopia and dystopia. They will remain places of disheartening poverty, crime, drugs, and physical decay, but also places that will continue to fulfill many of our dreams of the good urban life: places of visual and architectural variety; places of economic opportunity and productivity; places for the stroller's enjoyment, with thronging sidewalks and (it is to be hoped) safe passage; and above all, centers of culture and creativity.

If all the above sounds familiar, there is good reason: The future is already here. It is embedded in the present, for as Shakespeare continues to remind us,

> . . . in such indexes . . .
> . . . there is seen
> The baby figure of the giant mass
> Of things to come.

---

8. This pessimistic view not only pervades twentieth century fiction, but also art and films. See, for example, George Grosz's painting *Metropolis* (1917) and films such as Fritz Lang's *Metropolis* (1926) and Martin Scorsese's *Taxi Driver* (1976).

References

Adams, Herbert B. *The Germanic Origin of New England Towns.* Baltimore, MD: Johns Hopkins University Studies (in Historical and Political Science), 1882.

Adrian, Charles R. and Press, Charles. *Governing Urban America.* 5th edition. New York: McGraw-Hill, 1977.

Advisory Commission on Intergovernmental Relations. *City Financial Emergencies: The Intergovernmental Dimension.* Washington, DC: U.S. Government Printing Office, 1973.

Advisory Commission on Intergovernmental Relations. *Citizen Participation in the American Federal System.* Washington, DC: U.S. Government Printing Office, 1980.

Advisory Commission on Intergovernmental Relations. *Fiscal Disparities: Central Cities and Suburbs, 1981.* Washington, DC: U.S. Government Printing Office, 1984.

Advisory Commission on Intergovernmental Relations. *Local Revenue Diversification: User Charges.* Washington, DC: U.S. Government Printing Office, 1985.

Alexander, K.A.; Cook, M.; and McDill, E.L. "Curriculum Tracking and Educational Stratification: Some Further Evidence." *American Journal of Sociology,* 1978, *43,* 47-66.

459

Alford, Robert R. and Lee, Eugene C. "Voting Turnout in American Cities." *American Political Science Review*, 1968, *62*, 796-813.

Alinsky, Saul D. *Reveille for Radicals*. Chicago: University of Chicago Press, 1946.

Alinsky, Saul D. *Rules for Radicals: A Practical Primer for Realistic Radicals*. New York: Random House, 1971.

Altshuler, Alan. *Community Control*. New York: Pegasus, 1970.

Ambrose, P. and Colenutt, B. *The Property Machine*. Harmondsworth, England: Penguin, 1975.

Anderson, Martin. *The Federal Bulldozer: A Critical Analysis of Urban Renewal*. Cambridge, MA: MIT Press, 1964.

Andrews, Wayne. *Battle for Chicago*. New York: Harcourt, Brace, 1946.

Arkes, Hadley. *The Philosopher in the City: The Moral Dimensions of Urban Politics*. Princeton, NJ: Princeton University Press, 1981.

Armor, David. "School and Family Effects on Black and White Achievement: A Reexamination of the USOE Data." In Frederick Mosteller and Daniel P. Moynihan (eds.), *On Equality of Educational Opportunity*. New York: Random House, 1972.

Aronson, J. Richard and Hilley, John L. *Financing State and Local Governments*. Washington, DC: Brookings, 1986.

Auletta, Ken. *The Underclass*. New York: Random House, 1982.

Bachrach, Peter. *The Theory of Democratic Elitism: A Critique*. Boston: Little, Brown, 1967.

Bachrach, Peter and Baratz, Morton S. "Two Faces of Power." *American Political Science Review*, 1962, *54*, 947-952.

Bachrach, Peter and Baratz, Morton. *Power and Poverty*. New York: Oxford, 1970.

Badger, Lee W.; Jones, L. Ralph; and Parlour, Richard R. "*Wyatt v. Stickney*: Context and Consequence." In L. Ralph Jones and Richard R. Parlour (eds.), *Wyatt v. Stickney: Retrospect and Prospect*. New York: Grune and Stratton, 1981.

Baltzell, E. Digby. *Philadelphia Gentlemen: The Making of a National Upper Class*. Glencoe, IL: Free Press, 1958.

Banfield, Edward C. *Political Influence*. New York: Free Press, 1961.

Banfield, Edward C. *The Unheavenly City*. Boston: Little Brown, 1970.

Banfield, Edward C. *The Unheavenly City Revisited*. Boston: Little Brown, 1974.

Banfield, Edward C. and Wilson, James Q. *City Politics*. Cambridge, MA: Harvard University Press, 1963.

Baron, Harold M. "Race and Status in School Spending: Chicago, 1961-1966." *Journal of Human Resources*, 1971, *6*, 1-24.

Baskin, John. *New Burlington: The Life and Death of an American Village*. New York: Norton, 1976.

Bayley, David and Mendelsohn, Harold. *Minorities and the Police: Confrontation in America*. New York: Free Press, 1969.

Beer, Thomas. *The Mauve Decade: American Life at the End of the Nineteenth Century*. New York: Vintage, 1961.

Bellah, Robert N.; Madsen, Richard; Sullivan, William M.; Swidler, Ann; and Tipton, Steven M. *Habits of the Heart: Individualism and Commitment in American Life*. New York: Harper and Row, 1985.

Bellman, Richard F. "Report on the Question of Zoning." In *A Sheltered Crisis: The State of Fair Housing in the Eighties*. Washington, DC: U.S. Commission on Civil Rights, 1983.

Bender, Leslie. "Home Rule Revisited." *Journal of Legislation*, 1983, *10*.

Benton, J. Edwin. "American Federalism's First Principles and Reagan's New Federalism Policies." *Policy Studies Journal*, 1985, *13*, 568-575.

Berger, Thomas and Luckman, Peter. *The Social Construction of Reality*. Garden City, NY: Anchor, 1967.

Berkeley, George E. and Fox, Douglas M. *80,000 Governments: The Politics of Subnational America*. Boston: Allyn and Bacon, 1978.

Bernstein, Richard J. *The Restructuring of Social and Political Theory*. New York: Harcourt, Brace, and World, 1961.

Bienen, Henry. *Violence and Social Change: A Review of Current Literature*. Chicago: University of Chicago Press, 1968.

Bingham, Richard D.; Hawkins, Brett W.; and Hebert, F. Ted. *The Politics of Raising State and Local Revenue*. New York: Praeger, 1978.

Bisgaier, Carl. "Notes on Implementation." In Jerome G. Rose and Robert E. Rothman (eds.), *After Mount Laurel: The New Suburban Zoning*. New Brunswick, NJ: Center for Urban Policy Research, Rutgers University, 1977.

Bisgaier, Carl. "Statement." In *A Sheltered Crisis: The State of Fair Housing in the Eighties*. Washington, DC: U.S. Commission on Civil Rights, 1983.

Bish, Robert L. *Public Economy of Metropolitan Areas*. Chicago: Markham, 1971.

Black, J. Thomas; Howland, Libby; and Rogel, Stuart L. *Downtown Retail Development: Conditions for Success and Project Profiles*. Washington, DC: Urban Land Institute, 1983.

Block, Peter B. *Equality of Distribution of Police Services: A Case Study of Washington, DC*. Washington, DC: Urban Institute, 1974.

Bluestone, Barry and Bennet, Harrison. *The Deindustrialization of America: Plant Closings, Community Abandonment, and the Dismantling of Basic Industry*. New York: Basic, 1982.

Boesel, David and Rossi, Peter H. *Cities Under Seige: An Anatomy of the Ghetto Riots*. New York: Basic, 1971.

Bolland, John M. "The Limits to Pluralism: Power and Leadership in a Nonparticipatory Society." *Power and Elites*, 1984, *1*, 69-88.

Bolland, John M. "Perceived Leadership Stability and the Structure of Urban Agenda-Setting Networks." *Social Networks*, 1985a, 7, 153-172.

Bolland, John M. "Political Power and Public Policy: A Cognitive Interpretation." Paper presented at the annual meeting of the Midwest Political Science Association, Chicago, 1985b.

Bolland, John M. and Herson, Lawrence J.R. "Reputations and Reality: A Note on the Interpretation of Community Power Structures." Unpublished manuscript, University of Alabama, 1989.

Bolland, John M. and Redfield, Kent D. "The Limits to Citizen Participation in Local Education: A Cognitive Interpretation." *Journal of Politics*, 1988, *50*, 1033-1046.

Bolland, John M. and Selby, John. "Race and Agenda-Setting Networks in the New South." Paper presented at the annual meeting of the American Political Science Association, Washington, 1988.

Bollens, John C. *American County Government*. Beverly Hills, CA: Sage, 1969.

Bollens, John C. and Schmandt, Henry J. *The Metropolis: Its People, Politics, and Economic Life*. 4th edition. New York: Harper and Row, 1982.

Bolotin, Fredric N. and Cingranelli, David L. "Equity and Urban Policy: The Underclass Hypothesis Revisited." *Journal of Politics*, 1983, *45*, 209-219.

Boorstin, Daniel J. *The Americans: The Colonial Experience*. New York: Vintage, 1974.

Boots, Andrew J.; Dawson, Grace; Silverman, William; and Hatry, Harry P. *Inequality in Local Government Services: A Case Study of Neighborhood Roads*. Washington, DC: Urban Institute, 1972.

Boyer, Richard and Savageau, David. *Places Rated Almanac: Your Guide to Finding the Best Places to Live in America*. Chicago: Rand McNally, 1985.

Boyte, Harry C. *The Backyard Revolution: Understanding the New Citizen Movement*. Philadelphia: Temple University Press, 1980.

Branch, Taylor. *Parting the Waters: America in the King Years 1954-1963*. New York: Simon and Schuster, 1988.

Brewer, Gary D. and deLeon, Peter. *The Foundations of Policy Analysis*. Chicago: Dorsey, 1983.

Bridenbaugh, Carl. *Cities in the Wilderness: The First Century of Urban Life in America (1625-1742)*. New York: Ronald, 1938.

Bridenbaugh, Carl. *Cities in Revolt: Urban Life in America (1743-1776)*. New York: Capricorn, 1955.

Bridges, Amy. *A City in the Republic: Antebellum New York and the Origins of Machine Politics*. New York: Cambridge University Press, 1984.

Brown, Lawrence D.; Fossett, James W.; and Palmer, Kenneth T. *The Changing Politics of Federal Grants*. Washington, DC: Brookings, 1984.

Browning, Rufus P.; Marshall, Dale Rogers; and Tabb, David H. *Protest Is Not Enough: The Struggle of Blacks and Hispanics for Equality in Urban Politics*. Berkeley: University of California Press, 1984.

Bryan, John H. and Picard, Raymond (eds.). *Managing Fire Services*. Washington, DC: International City Management Association, 1979.

Bryce, James B. *The American Commonwealth*. 2nd edition, rev. London: Macmillan, 1889.

Buckwalter, Doyle W. "Dillon's Rule in the 1980's: Who's in Charge of Local Affairs?" *National Civic Review*, 1982, *71*, 399-406.

Buenker, John D. *Urban Liberalism and Progressive Reform*. New York: Norton, 1973.

Burke, James. *Connections.* Boston: Little, Brown, 1978.

Burnham, Walter Dean. *Critical Elections and the Mainsprings of American Politics.* New York: Norton, 1970.

Cain, Glen G. and Watts, Harold W. "Problems in Making Policy Inferences from the Coleman Report." In Peter H. Rossi and Walter Williams (eds.), *Evaluating Social Programs: Theory, Practice, and Politics.* New York: Academic, 1972.

Campbell, Angus and Schuman, Howard. "Racial Attitudes in Fifteen American Cities." In National Advisory Commission on Civil Disorders, *Supplemental Studies.* Washington, DC: U.S. Government Printing Office, 1968.

Caro, Robert A. *The Power Broker: Robert Moses and the Fall of New York.* New York: Knopf, 1974.

Carver, Joan. "Responsiveness and Consolidation: A Case Study." *Urban Affairs Quarterly,* 1973, *9,* 211-250.

Castells, Manuel. *The Urban Question: A Marxist Approach.* Cambridge, MA: MIT Press, 1977.

Charles, Michael T. *Policing the Streets.* Springfield, IL: Thomas, 1986.

Childs, Richard S. *Civic Victories: The Story of an Unfinished Revolution.* New York: Harper, 1952.

Chudacoff, Howard P. *The Evolution of American Urban Society.* Englewood Cliffs, NJ: Prentice-Hall, 1975.

Cigler, Allan J. and Loomis, Burdett A. *Interest Group Politics.* Washington, DC: CQ Press, 1986.

Clark, Kenneth. *The Nude: A Study of Ideal Art.* Princeton, NJ: Princeton University Press, 1956.

Clark, Terry N. and Ferguson, Lorna C. *City Money: Political Processes, Fiscal Strain, and Retrenchment.* New York: Columbia University Press, 1983.

Clark, W.A.V. "Residential Segregation in American Cities: A Review and Interpretation." *Population Research and Policy Review,* 1986, *5,* 95-127.

Cleaveland, Frederick N. (ed.). *Congress and Urban Problems: A Casebook on the Legislative Process.* Washington, DC: Brookings, 1973.

Cobb, Roger and Elder, Charles D. *Participation in American Politics: The Dynamics of Agenda-Building.* 2nd edition. Boston: Allyn and Bacon, 1983.

Cohen, Joshua and Rogers, Joel. *On Democracy.* Harmondsworth, England: Penguin, 1983.

Coleman, James S. *Community Conflict.* Glencoe, IL: Free Press, 1957.

Coleman, James S. "Destructive Beliefs and Potential Policies in School Desegregation." In John W. Smith (ed.), *Detroit Metropolitan City-Suburban Relations.* Dearborn, MI: Henry Ford Community College Occasional Papers, 1979.

Coleman, James S.; Campbell, E.Q.; Hobson, C.F.; McPortland, J.; Mood, A.M.; et al. *Equality of Educational Opportunity.* Washington, DC: Department of Health, Education, and Welfare, Office of Education, 1966.

Coleman, James S. and Kelly, Sara. "Education." In William Gorham and Nathan Glazer (eds.), *The Urban Predicament*. Washington, DC: The Urban Institute, 1976.

Committee for Economic Development. *Modernizing Local Government to Secure a Balanced Federalism: A Statement on National Policy*. New York: Committee for Economic Development, 1966.

Conlin, Joseph R. *The Morrow Book of Quotations in American History*. New York: Morrow, 1984.

Connery, Donald S. *One American Town: A Relic of the Past—A Model for the Future*. New York: Simon and Schuster, 1972.

Converse, Philip E. "The Nature of Belief Systems in Mass Publics." In David Apter (ed.), *Ideology and Discontent*. New York: Wiley, 1964.

Converse, Philip E.; Miller, Warren E.; Rusk, Jerrold G.; and Wolfe, Arthur C. "Continuity and Change in American Politics: Parties and Issues in the 1968 Election." *American Political Science Review*, 1969, *63*, 1083-1105.

Conyers, John. "The Real Problem Is Poverty." *Nation*, January 24, 1976, p. 84.

Cook, Stuart W. "The 1954 Social Science Statement and School Desegregation: A Reply to Gerard." *American Psychologist*, 1984, *39*, 819-832.

Cook, Thomas D. and Campbell, Donald T. *Quasi-Experimentation: Design and Analysis Issues for Field Settings*. Boston: Houghton Mifflin, 1979.

Coser, Lewis A. *The Functions of Social Conflict*. Glencoe, IL: Free Press, 1956.

Coser, Lewis A. "The Sociology of Poverty." *Social Problems*, 1965, *13*, 140-148.

Coulter, Philip B. "Equity and Efficiency in Fire Protection." Paper presented at the annual meeting of the American Society for Public Administration, Phoenix, 1978.

Coulter, Philip B. "Measuring the Inequality of Urban Public Services: A Methodological Discussion With Applications." *Policy Studies Journal*, 1980, *8*, 683-698.

Coulter, Philip B. *Political Voice: Citizen Demand for Urban Public Services*. Tuscaloosa: University of Alabama Press, 1988.

Cox, Kevin R. *Conflict, Power and Politics in the City: A Geographic View*. New York: McGraw-Hill, 1973.

Cox, Kevin R. *Urbanization and Conflict in Market Societies*. New York: Metheun, 1978.

Crain, Robert L.; Katz, Elihu; and Rosenthal, Donald. *The Politics of Community Conflict: The Fluoridation Decision*. Indianapolis, IN: Bobbs–Merrill, 1969.

Crenson, Matthew. *The Unpolitics of Air Pollution: A Study of Non-Decision Making in the Cities*. Baltimore, MD: Johns Hopkins University Press, 1971.

Crewe, Ivor. "Electoral Participation." In David Butler, Howard Penniman, and Austin Ranney (eds.), *Democracy at the Polls: A Comparative Study of National Elections*. Washington, DC: American Enterprise Institute, 1981.

Croly, Herbert. *The Promise of American Life*. New York: Macmillan, 1909.

Cuomo, Mario. *Forest Hills Diary: The Crisis of Low Income Housing*. New York: Vintage, 1975.

Dahl, Robert A. *Who Governs? Democracy and Power in an American City*. New Haven: Yale University Press, 1961.

Dahl, Robert A. and Lindblom, Charles E.. *Politics, Economics, and Welfare: Planning and Politico-Economic Systems Resolved into Basic Social Processes.* New York: Harper and Row, 1953.

Danielson, Michael N. *The Politics of Exclusion.* New York: Columbia University Press, 1976.

Darden, Joe T. "Population Growth and Spatial Distribution." In *A Sheltered Crisis: The State of Fair Housing in the Eighties.* Washington, DC: U.S. Commission on Civil Rights, 1983.

Davies, Don. "School Administrators and Advisory Councils: Partnership or Shotgun Marriage?" *NASSP Bulletin,* 1980, *64,* 62–66.

Davis, Edward M. and Knowles, Lyle. "An Evaluation of the Kansas City Patrol Experiment." *The Police Chief,* June 1975, 22–27.

Davis, Morris and Weinbaum, Marvin G. *Metropolitan Decision Processes: An Analysis of Case Studies.* Chicago: Rand McNally, 1969.

de Grazia, Alfred. *Political Behavior.* New York: Free Press, 1965.

De Vise, Pierre. *Misused and Misplaced Hospitals and Doctors: A Locational Analysis of the Urban Health Care Crisis.* Washington, DC: Association of American Geographers, 1973.

deHaven-Smith, Lance and Van Horn, Carl. "Subgovernment Conflict in Public Policy." *Policy Studies Journal,* 1984, *12,* 627–642.

DeMott, Benjamin. *Supergrow: Essays and Reports on Imagination in America.* New York: Dutton, 1969.

Department of Commerce, Bureau of the Census. *Geographical Mobility: March, 1982–March, 1983.* Washington, DC: U.S. Government Printing Office, 1984.

Department of Commerce, Bureau of the Census. *Poverty in the United States 1985.* Washington DC: U.S. Government Printing Office, 1987.

Department of Health, Education, and Welfare. *Towards a Comprehensive Health Policy for the 1970s.* Washington, DC: U.S. Government Printing Office, 1971.

Department of Health, Education, and Welfare. *Prevalence of Chronic Conditions of the Genitourinary, Nervous, Endocrine, Metabolic, and Blood-Forming System and of Other Selected Chronic Conditions, United States—1973.* Rockville, MD, 1977.

Department of Health and Human Services. *Health Status of the Disadvantaged: Chartbook 1986.* Washington, D.C.: U.S. Government Printing Office, 1986.

Dickstein, Morris. *The Gates of Eden: American Culture in the Sixties.* New York: Basic, 1977.

Dillon, John. *Commentaries on the Law of Municipal Corporations.* 1872 edition. Boston: Little, Brown, 1911.

Dimond, Paul R. *A Dilemma of Local Government: Discrimination in the Provision of Public Services.* Lexington, MA: Lexington, 1978.

Domhoff, G. William. *Who Really Rules? New Haven and Community Power Reexamined.* New Brunswick: Transaction, 1978.

Domhoff, G. William. *Who Rules America Now? A View for the 80's*. Englewood Cliffs, NJ: Prentice-Hall, 1983.

Dornbush, Sanford M. and Ritter, Philip L. "Parents of High School Students: A Neglected Resource." *Educational Horizons*, 1988, *66*, 75-77.

Downes, Bryan T. "A Critical Reexamination of the Social and Political Characteristics of Riot Cities." *Social Science Quarterly*, 1970, *51*, 349-360.

Downs, Anthony. *Opening up the Suburbs: An Urban Strategy for America*. New Haven: Yale University Press, 1973.

Downs, Anthony. *Neighborhoods and Urban Development*. Washington, DC: Brookings, 1981.

Dusek, Jerome. "Do Teachers Bias Children's Learning?" *Review of Educational Research*, 1975, *45*, 661-684.

Dye, Thomas R. "Metropolitan Integration by Bargaining Among Sub-Areas." *American Behavioral Scientist*, 1962, *5*, 11.

Dye, Thomas R. "Urban Political Integration: Conditions Associated with Annexation in American Cities." *Midwest Journal of Political Science*, 1964, *8*, 430-446.

Dye, Thomas R. *Politics in States and Communities*. Englewood Cliffs, NJ: Prentice-Hall, 1969a.

Dye, Thomas R. "Community Power Studies." In James A. Robinson (ed.), *Political Science Annual* (Volume 2). Indianapolis, IN: Bobbs-Merrill, 1969b.

Dye, Thomas R. *Who's Running America? The Conservative Years*. Englewood Cliffs, NJ: Prentice-Hall, 1986.

Dye, Thomas R. and Zeigler, L. Harmon. *The Irony of Democracy: An Uncommon Introduction to American Politics*. 3rd edition. North Scituate, MA: Duxbury, 1975.

Easton, David. *The Political System: An Inquiry into the State of Political Science*. New York: Knopf, 1953.

Edelman, Murray J. *The Symbolic Uses of Politics*. Urbana: University of Illinois Press, 1964.

Editors of Fortune. *The Exploding Metropolis*. Garden City, NY: Doubleday Anchor, 1958.

Eisinger, Peter K. "The Conditions of Protest Behavior in American Cities." *American Political Science Review*, 1973, *67*, 11-28.

Eisinger, Peter K. "Black Mayors and the Politics of Racial Economic Advancement." In Harlan Hahn and Charles H. Levine (eds.), *Urban Politics: Past, Present, & Future*. New York: Longman, 1984.

Emerson, Robert M. *Judging Delinquents: Context and Process in Juvenile Courts*. New York: Aldine, 1969.

Eyestone, Robert. *From Social Issues to Public Policy*. New York: Wiley, 1978.

Fangen, Timothy J. and McGarrell, Edmund F. (eds.). *Sourcebook of Criminal Statistics, 1985*. Washington, D.C.: Department of Justice, Bureau of Justice Statistics, 1986.

Farley, Reynolds. "Racial Integration in the Public Schools, 1967 to 1972: Assessing the Effects of Governmental Policies." *Sociological Focus*, 1975, *8*, 3-26.

Farley, Reynolds. "Components of Suburban Population Growth." In Barry Schwartz (ed.), *The Changing Face of Suburbs*. Chicago: University of Chicago Press, 1976.

Fay, Brian. *Social Theory and Political Science*. London: Allen and Unwin, 1975.

Feagin, Joe R. and Hahn, Harlan. *Ghetto Revolts: The Politics of Violence in American Cities*. New York: Macmillan, 1973.

Feiock, Richard C. "The Political Economy of Urban Service Distribution: A Test of the Underclass Hypothesis." *Journal of Urban Affairs*, 1986, *8*, 31-42.

Fenno, Richard. *Congressmen in Committees*. Boston: Little, Brown, 1973.

Finley, M.I. *The Ancient Greeks*. Harmondsworth, England: Penguin, 1966.

Fischer, Claude S.; Baldassare, M.; Gerson, K.; Jackson, R.M.; Jones, L.M.; and Steuve, C.A. *Networks and Places: Social Relations in the Urban Setting*. New York: Free Press, 1977.

Fogelson, Robert M. *Violence as Protest: A Study of Riots and Ghettos*. Garden City, NY: Doubleday, 1971.

Fogelson, Robert M. and Hill, Robert B. *Who Riots? A Study of Participation in the 1967 Riots*. National Advisory Commission on Civil Disorders, Supplemental Studies. Washington, DC: U.S. Government Printing Office, 1968.

Ford, Paul L. (ed.). *The Works of Thomas Jefferson*. New York: Putnam, 1914.

Fox, Douglas M. *The New Urban Politics: Cities and the Federal Government*. Pacific Palisades, CA: Goodyear, 1972.

Franklin, Grace A. and Ripley, Randall B. *CETA: Politics and Policy 1973-1982*. Knoxville: University of Tennessee Press, 1984.

Fried, Marc. "Social Differences in Mental Health." In John Kosa, Aaron Antonovsky, and Irving K. Zola (eds.), *Poverty and Health: A Sociological Analysis*. Cambridge, MA: Harvard University Press, 1975.

Friedman, Milton and Friedman, Rose. *Freedom to Choose*. New York: Avon, 1981.

Frug, Gerald. "The City as a Legal Concept." In Lloyd Rodwin and Robert M. Hollister (eds.), *Cities of the Mind: Images and Themes of the City in the Social Sciences*. New York: Plenum, 1984.

Fullinwider, Robert K. *The Reverse Discrimination Controversy: A Moral and Legal Analysis*. Totowa, NJ: Rowman and Littlefield, 1980.

Galaskiewicz, Joseph. *Exchange Networks and Community Politics*. Beverly Hills, CA: Sage, 1979.

Gale, Dennis E. *Neighborhood Revitalization and the Postindustrial City: A Multinational Perspective*. Lexington, MA: Lexington, 1984.

Gardiner, John A. "Police Enforcement of Traffic Laws: A Comparative Analysis." In James Q. Wilson (ed.), *City Politics and Public Policy*. New York: Wiley, 1968.

Gardiner, John A. and Lyman, Theodore R. *Decisions for Sale*. New York: Praeger, 1978.

Gardiner, John A. and Olson, David J. (eds.). *Theft of the City: Readings on Corruption in Urban America*. Bloomington: Indiana University Press, 1974.

Gelfand, Mark. *A Nation of Cities: The Federal Government and Urban America.* New York: Oxford University Press, 1975.

Gibson, Quentin B. *The Logic of Social Enquiry.* London: Routledge and Keagan Paul, 1960.

Gilbert, Claire W. "Community Power and Decision Making: A Quantitative Examination of Previous Research." In Terry N. Clark (ed.), *Community Structure and Decision Making: Comparative Analyses.* San Francisco: Chandler, 1968.

Gilder, George. *Wealth and Poverty.* New York: Basic, 1981.

Glaab, Charles N. and Brown, A. Theodore. *A History of Urban America.* 2nd edition. New York: Macmillan, 1976.

Glazer, Nathan. "Housing Problems and Housing Politics." *The Public Interest,* 1967, 7, 21–51.

Glazer, Nathan. *Affirmative Discrimination: Ethnic Inequality and Public Policy.* New York: Basic, 1975.

Goldman, Eric F. *Rendezvous with Destiny: A History of Modern American Reform.* New York: Vintage, 1956.

Goldman, Howard H. and Morrissey, Joseph P. "The Alchemy of Mental Health Policy: Homelessness and the Fourth Cycle of Reform." *American Journal of Public Health,* 1985, 75, 727-731.

Goodlad, John I. *A Place Called School: Prospects for the Future.* New York: McGraw-Hill, 1984.

Goodnow, Frank S. *Municipal Home Rule: A Study in Administration.* New York: Macmillan, 1895.

Gordon, Mitchell. *Sick Cities.* Baltimore, MD: Penguin, 1966.

Gould, Stephen Jay. *The Mismeasure of Man.* New York: Norton, 1981.

Gove, Samuel K. and Masotti, Louis H. (eds). *After Daley: Chicago Politics in Transition.* Urbana: University of Illinois Press, 1987.

Government of the District of Columbia. *Tax Burdens in Washington, D.C. Compared with Those in the Nation's Thirty Largest Cities, 1977.* Department of Finance and Revenue, 1979.

Government of the District of Columbia. *Tax Rates and Tax Burdens in the District of Columbia: A Nationwide Comparison.* Department of Finance and Revenue, 1988.

Grant, Madison. *The Passing of the Great Race: Or, The Racial Basis of European History.* New York: Scribner's, 1916.

Gratz, Roberta B. *The Living City: Thinking Big in a Small Way.* New York: Simon and Schuster, 1989.

Green, Constance M. *American Cities in the Growth of the Nation.* London: Athlene, 1957.

Green, Robert L. *The Urban Challenge—Poverty and Race.* Chicago: Follett, 1977.

Green, Roy E. and Reed, B.J. "Occupational Stress and Mobility among Professional Local Government Managers: A Decade of Change." In *The Municipal Yearbook.* Washington, DC: ICMA, 1988.

Greenawalt, R. Kent. *Discrimination and Reverse Discrimination.* New York: Random House, 1983.

Greer, Scott A. *Governing the Metropolis.* New York: Wiley, 1962.

Greer, Scott A. *Urban Renewal and American Cities: The Dilemma of Democratic Intervention.* Indianapolis, IN: Bobbs–Merrill, 1965.

Griswold, Alfred Whitney. *Farming and Democracy.* New York: Harcourt, Brace, 1948.

Grumm, J.G. and Murphy, R.D. "Dillon's Role Reconsidered." *Annals of the American Academy of Political and Social Science,* 1974, *416,* 120.

Gunn, J.A.W. *Politics and the Public Interest in the 17th Century.* London: Routledge and Kegan Paul, 1969.

Gurr, Ted Robert (ed.). *Violence in America.* Newbury Park, CA: Sage, 1989.

Haar, Charles M. *Between the Idea and the Reality: A Study in the Origin, Fate, and Legacy of the Model City Program.* Boston: Little, Brown, 1975.

Hale, Dennis. "The Evolution of the Property Tax: A Study of the Relation between Public Finance and Political Theory." *Journal of Politics,* 1985, *47,* 382–404.

Hale, George E. and Palley, Marian L. *The Politics of Federal Grants.* Washington, DC: CQ Press, 1981.

Hall, Peter G. *The World Cities.* New York: McGraw–Hill, 1966.

Hall, Peter G. *The World Cities.* 3rd edition. London: Weidenfeld and Nicholson, 1984.

Hamilton, Alexander. "Federalist 9: The Utility of the Union as a Safeguard Against Domestic Faction and Insurrection." In Alexander Hamilton, James Madison, and John Jay (eds.), *The Federalist Papers.* New York: Mentor, 1961.

Hamm, Keith E. "The Role of 'Subgovernments' in U.S. State Policy Making: An Exploratory Analysis." *Legislative Studies Quarterly,* 1986, *11,* 321–352.

Handlin, Oscar. *The Uprooted: The Epic Story of the Great Migration That Made the American People.* Boston: Little, Brown, 1973.

Handlin, Oscar and Handlin, Mary F. *The Wealth of the American People: A History of American Affluence.* New York: McGraw–Hill, 1975.

Hanson, Norwood. *Patterns of Discovery: An Inquiry into the Conceptual Foundations of Science.* Cambridge, England: Cambridge University Press, 1958.

Hanson, Russell L. *The Democratic Imagination in America: Conversations with the Past.* Princeton, NJ: Princeton University Press, 1985.

Harrigan, John. *Political Change in the Metropolis.* 3d edition. Boston: Little, Brown, 1985.

Harrigan, John. *Political Change in the Metropolis.* 4th edition. Boston: Little, Brown, 1989.

Harrington, Michael. *The Other America: Poverty in the United States.* New York: Macmillan, 1962.

Hartman, Chester W. *Housing and Social Policy.* Englewood Cliffs, NJ: Prentice–Hall, 1975.

Haskell, Thomas L. *The Emergence of Professional Social Science: The American Social Science Association and the Nineteenth Century Crisis of Authority.* Urbana: University of Illinois Press, 1977.

Hawkins, Brett W. *Nashville Metro: The Politics of City-County Consolidation.* Nashvillle, TN: Vanderbilt University Press, 1966.

Hays, Samuel P. "The Politics of Reform in Municipal Government in the Progressive Era." *Pacific Northwest Quarterly,* 1964, *55,* 157-169.

Heidenheimer, Arnold J.; Heclo, Hugh; and Adams, Carolyn T. *Comparative Public Policy: The Politics of Social Choice in Europe and America.* New York: St. Martin's, 1975.

Henderson, Anne T. "Parents Are a School's Best Friends." *Phi Delta Kappan,* 1988, *70,* 148-153.

Henig, Jeffrey R. *Public Policy and Federalism: Issues in State and Local Politics.* New York: St. Martin's, 1985.

Hennessey, Timothy M. "Problems in Concept Formation: The Ethos 'Theory' and the Comparative Study of Urban Politics." *Midwest Journal of Political Science,* 1970, *14,* 537-564.

Hersey, John R. *The Algiers Motel Incident.* New York: Knopf, 1968.

Hershkowitz, Allen. "Burning Trash: How It Could Work." *Technology Review,* July 1987, *90,* 26-34.

Herson, Lawrence J.R. "The Lost World of Municipal Government." *American Political Science Review,* 1957, *51,* 330-345.

Herson, Lawrence J.R. "In the Footsteps of Community Power." *American Political Science Review,* 1961, *55,* 820-835.

Herson, Lawrence J.R. "Pilgrim's Progress: Reflections on the Road to Urban Reform." In *Political Science and State and Local Government.* Washington, DC: The American Political Science Association, 1973.

Herson, Lawrence J.R. "The Liberal Arts Considered." *National Journal of Teacher Education,* 1980, *31,* 3.

Herson, Lawrence J.R. *The Politics of Ideas: Political Theory and American Public Policy.* Homewood, IL: Dorsey, 1984.

Herson, Lawrence J.R. "Shooting the Messenger: Thoughts on Bureaucratic Reform." In Donald Calista J. (ed.), *Bureaucratic and Governmental Reform.* Greenwich, CT: JAI Press, 1986.

Herson, Lawrence J.R. and Hofstetter, Richard. "Tolerance, Consensus, and the Democratic Creed: A Contextual Comparison." *Journal of Politics,* 1975, *37,* 1007-1032.

Hill, Richard C. "Fiscal Crisis, Austerity Politics, and Alternative Urban Policies." In William K. Tabb and Larry Sawyers (eds.), *Marxism and the Metropolis: New Perspectives in Urban Political Economy.* New York: Oxford University Press, 1984.

Hirsch, Fred. *Social Limits to Growth.* Cambridge, MA: Harvard University Press, 1976.

Hirschman, Albert O. *Exit, Voice, and Loyalty: Responses to Decline in Firms, Organizations, and States.* Cambridge, MA: Harvard University Press, 1970.

Hofstadter, Richard. *The Age of Reform: From Bryan to FDR.* New York: Knopf, 1955a.

Hofstadter, Richard. *Social Darwinism in American Thought.* Boston: Beacon, 1955b.

Hofstadter, Richard. *The Progressive Historians: Turner, Beard, Parrington.* New York: Knopf, 1968.

Holden, Matthew, Jr. "The Governance of the Metropolis as a Problem in Diplomacy." *Journal of Politics*, 1964, *26*, 627-647.

Hollingshead, August B. *Elmtown's Youth: The Impact of Social Class on Adolescents.* New York: Wiley, 1949.

Homans, George C. *The Human Group*. New York: Harcourt, Brace, 1950.

Horton, John. "Order and Conflict Theories of Social Problems as Competing Ideologies." *American Journal of Sociology*, 1966, *71*, 701-713.

Howe, Frederick. *The City: The Hope of Democracy.* New York: Scribner's, 1905.

Huckfeldt, Robert and Sprague, John. "Networks in Context: The Social Flow of Political Information." *American Political Science Review*, 1987, *81*, 1197-1216.

Huckshorn, Robert J. and Young, C.E. "A Study of Voting Splits on City Councils in Los Angeles County." *Western Political Quarterly*, 1960, *13*, 479-497.

Hunter, Floyd. *Community Power Structure: A Study of Decision Makers.* Chapel Hill: University of North Carolina Press, 1953.

Huntley, Robert J. and Macdonald, Robert J. "Urban Managers: Organizational Preferences, Managerial Styles, and Social Policy Roles." In *The Municipal Yearbook*. Washington, DC: ICMA, 1975.

Hyneman, Charles S. *The Study of Politics: The Present State of American Political Science.* Urbana: University of Illinois Press, 1956.

Isaak, Alan C. *Scope and Methods of Political Science: An Introduction to the Methodology of Political Inquiry.* 4th edition. Homewood, IL: Dorsey, 1984.

Jackson, Kenneth T. *Crabgrass Frontier: The Suburbanization of the United States.* New York: Oxford University Press, 1985.

Jacobs, Alan H. "Volunteer Firemen: Altruism in Action." In W. Arens and Susan P. Montague (eds.), *The American Dimension: Cultural Myths and Social Realities.* Port Washington, NY: Alfred, 1976.

Jacobs, Jane. *The Death and Life of Great American Cities.* New York: Random House, 1961.

Jacobs, Jane. *The Economy of Cities.* New York: Random House, 1970.

Janis, Irving L. *Groupthink.* 2nd edition. Boston: Houghton Mifflin, 1982.

Johnston, R.J. *Residential Segregation, The State and Constitutional Conflict in American Urban Areas.* London: Academic, 1984.

Jones, Bryan D. *Service Delivery in the City: Citizen Demand and Bureaucratic Rules.* New York: Longman, 1980.

Jones, Bryan D. *Governing Urban America: A Policy Focus.* Boston: Little, Brown, 1983.

Jones, Charles O. *An Introduction to the Study of Public Policy.* 3rd edition. Monterey, CA: Brooks Cole, 1983.

Jones, E. Terrence. "The Distribution of Urban Services in a Declining City." In Richard C. Rich (ed.), *The Politics of Urban Public Services.* Lexington, MA: Lexington, 1982.

Judd, Dennis R. *The Politics of American Cities: Private Power and Public Policy.* 2nd edition. Boston: Little, Brown, 1984.

Judd, Dennis R. *The Politics of American Cities: Private Power and Public Policy.* 3rd edition. Boston: Little, Brown, 1988.

Kammerer, Gladys. *Florida City Managers, Profile in Tenure.* Gainesville: University of Florida Public Administration Clearing House, 1961.

Kantor, Paul. *The Dependent City: The Changing Political Economy of American Urban Politics Since 1789.* New York: Scott Foresman, 1988.

Kaplan, Abraham. *The Conduct of Inquiry: Methodology for Behavioral Science.* Scranton, PA: Chandler, 1964.

Kaplan, Harold. *Urban Renewal Politics: Slum Clearance in Newark.* New York: Columbia University Press, 1963.

Katz, Daniel; Gutek, Barbara A.; Kahn, Robert L.; and Barton, Eugenia. *Bureaucratic Encounters: A Pilot Study in the Evaluation of Government Service.* Ann Arbor, MI: Institute for Social Research, 1975.

Keech, William R. *The Impact of Negro Voting: The Role of the Vote in the Quest for Equality.* Chicago: Rand McNally, 1968.

Kelley, Robert. *The Shaping of the American Past.* 3rd edition. Englewood Cliffs, NJ: Prentice-Hall, 1982.

Kelly, Alfred H. and Harbison, Winfred A. *The American Constitution: Its Origins and Development.* Revised edition. New York: Norton, 1955.

Key, V.O., Jr. *Southern Politics.* New York: Knopf, 1950.

Key, V.O., Jr. "A Theory of Critical Elections." *Journal of Politics,* 1955, *17,* 3-18.

King, Martin Luther. "Letter from a Birmingham Jail." In M.L. King, *Why We Can't Wait.* New York: Harper and Row, 1964.

Kingdon, John. *Agendas, Alternatives, and Public Policies.* Boston: Little, Brown, 1984.

Kingsbury, F.J. "The Tendency of Men to Live in Cities." *Journal of Social Science,* 1895, *33,* 1-19.

Kirby, Ronald F.; De leeuw, Frank; and Silverman, William. *Residential Zoning and Equal Housing Opportunities: A Case Study in Black Jack, Missouri.* Washington, DC: Urban Institute, 1972.

Kitto, H.D.F. *The Greeks.* Harmondsworth, England: Penguin, 1951.

Klepper, Christine. "America's Blind Spot: The Devastating Impact of Residential Segregation." In *A Sheltered Crisis: The State of Fair Housing in the Eighties.* Washington, DC: U.S. Commission on Civil Rights, 1983.

Knights, Peter R. *The Plain People of Boston 1830-1860: A Study in City Growth.* New York: Oxford University Press, 1971.

Koehler, David H. and Wrightson, Margaret T. "Inequality in the Delivery of Urban Services: A Reconsideration of the Chicago Parks." *Journal of Politics,* 1987, *49,* 80-99.

Kolstad, Andrew J. and Owings, Jeffrey A. *High School Students Who Change Their Minds about School.* Washington, DC: Center for Statistics, U.S. Department of Education, 1986.

Kotler, Milton. *Neighborhood Government: The Local Foundations of Political Life.* Indianapolis, IN: Bobbs-Merrill, 1969.

Kotter, John P. and Lawrence, Paul R. *Mayors in Action: Five Approaches to Urban Governance.* New York: Wiley, 1974.

Kozol, Jonathan. *Death at an Early Age: The Destruction of the Hearts and Minds of Negro Children in the Boston Public Schools.* New York: New American Library, 1985.

Kraus, S. "Water, Sewers, and Streets: The Acquisition of Public Utilities in Austin, Texas, 1875-1930." Unpublished thesis, University of Texas, 1973.

Kristol, Irving. *Two Cheers for Capitalism.* New York: Basic, 1978.

Kurian, George T. *The New Book of World Rankings.* New York: Facts on File, 1984.

Kuyper, Adrian. "Intergovernmental Cooperation: An Analysis of the Lakewood Plan." *Georgetown Law Journal,* 1970, *58,* 777-798.

Lake, Robert W. *Real Estate Tax Delinquency: Private Disinvestment and Public Response.* New Brunswick, NJ: Center for Urban Policy Research, Rutgers University, 1979.

Lasswell, Harold D. *Politics: Who Gets What, When, and How.* New York: McGraw-Hill, 1936.

Laumann, Edward O. *Bonds of Pluralism: The Form and Substance of Urban Social Networks.* New York: Wiley, 1973.

Laumann, Edward O.; Marsden, Peter V.; and Galaskiewicz, Joseph. "Community-Elite Influence Structures: Extension of a Network Approach." *American Journal of Sociology,* 1977, *83,* 594-631.

Laumann, Edward O. and Pappi, Franz U. *Networks of Collective Action: A Perspective on Community Influence Systems.* New York: Academic, 1976.

Leach, Richard H. *American Federalism.* New York: Norton, 1970.

Lee, Susan P. and Passell, Peter. *A New Economic View of American History.* New York: Norton, 1979.

Leigland, James and Lamb, Robert. *WPP$$: Who Is to Blame for the WPPSS Disaster.* Cambridge, MA: Ballinger, 1986.

Leuchtenburg, William. *Franklin D. Roosevelt and the New Deal, 1932-1940.* New York: Harper and Row, 1963.

Levine, Charles H. "More on Cutback Management: Hard Questions for Hard Times." In Charles H. Levine (ed.), *Managing Fiscal Stress: The Crisis in the Public Sector.* Chatham, NJ: Chatham House, 1980.

Levine, Charles H.; Rubin, Irene S.; and Wolohojian, George G. *The Politics of Retrenchment: How Local Governments Manage Fiscal Stress.* Beverly Hills, CA: Sage, 1981.

Levine, Erwin L. and Wexler, Elizabeth M. *PL 94-142: An Act of Congress.* New York: Macmillan, 1981.

Levitan, Sar A. and Taggart, Robert. *The Promise of Greatness.* Cambridge, MA: Harvard University Press, 1976.

Levitan, Sar A. and Taggart, Robert. "The Great Society Did Succeed." *Political Science Quarterly,* 1977, *91,* 601-618.

Levy, Frank; Meltsner, Arnold J.; and Wildavsky, Aaron. *Urban Outcomes: Schools, Streets, and Libraries.* Berkeley: University of California Press, 1974.

Lewis, Oscar. *Five Families: Mexican Case Studies in the Culture of Poverty.* New York: Basic, 1959.

Lewis, Oscar. *La Vida: A Puerto Rican Family in the Culture of Poverty—San Juan and New York.* New York: Random House, 1965.

Liebow, Elliot. *Tally's Corner: A Study of Negro Streetcorner Men.* Boston: Little, Brown, 1967.

Lindblom, Charles E. *The Intelligence of Democracy: Decision Making Through Mutual Adjustment.* New York: Free Press, 1965.

Lindblom, Charles E. *Politics and Markets: The World's Political Economic Systems.* New York: Basic, 1977.

Lindblom, Charles E. *The Policy Making Process.* 2nd edition. Englewood Cliffs, NJ: Prentice-Hall, 1980.

Lindblom, Charles E. and Cohen, David K. *Useable Knowledge: Social Science and Social Problem Solving.* New Haven: Yale University Press, 1979.

Lineberry, Robert L. *Equality and Urban Policy.* Beverly Hills, CA: Sage, 1977.

Lineberry, Robert L. "Mandating Urban Equality: The Distribution of Municipal Public Services." In Harlan Hahn and Charles H. Levine (eds.), *Readings in Urban Politics: Past, Present, and Future.* 2nd edition. New York: Longman, 1984.

Lineberry, Robert L. and Fowler, Edmund P. "Reformism and Public Policies in American Cities. *American Political Science Review,* 1967, *61,* 701-716.

Lineberry, Robert and Sharkansky, Ira. *Urban Politics and Public Policy.* 3rd edition. New York: Harper and Row, 1978.

Lipset, Seymore M. *Political Man: The Social Bases of Politics.* Garden City, NY: Doubleday, 1960.

Lipsky, Michael. "Toward a Theory of Street-Level Bureaucracy." In Willis D. Hawley and Michael Lipsky (eds.), *Theoretical Perspectives in Urban Politics.* Englewood Cliffs, NJ: Prentice-Hall, 1976.

Lipsky, Michael. *Street-Level Bureaucracy: Dilemmas of the Individual in Public Services.* New York: Russell Sage, 1980.

Lockard, Duane. *The Politics of State and Local Government.* New York: Macmillan, 1963.

Lockwood, Charles and Leinberger, Christopher B. "Los Angeles Comes of Age." *The Atlantic,* 1988, *261(1),* 31-56.

Long, Norton. *The Unwalled City: Reconstituting the Urban Community.* New York: Basic, 1972.

Lord, J.D. "Spatial Perspectives on School Desegregation and Busing." Washington, DC: Commission on College Geography, American Association of Geographers, 1977.

Lotz, Aileen. "Metropolitan Dade County." In Advisory Commission on Intergovernmental Relations, *Substate Regionalism and the Federal System (Volume II: Case Studies).* Washington, DC: U.S. Government Printing Office, 1973.

Lowi, Theodore J. "American Business, Public Policy, Case Studies, and Political Theory." *World Politics,* 1964a, *16,* 677-715.

Lowi, Theodore J. *At the Pleasure of The Mayor: Patronage and Power in New York City 1898-1958.* New York: Free Press, 1964b.

Lowi, Theodore J. *The End of Liberalism: Ideology, Policy, and the Crisis of Public Authority.* New York: Norton, 1969a.

Lowi, Theodore J. "Machine Politics—Old and New." *The Public Interest*, 1969b, *9*, 83–92.

Lubell, Samuel. *The Future of American Politics.* Revised edition. New York: Harper, 1956

Lubin, Roger. "How Should Managers Be Paid? Some Public and Private Sector Comparisons." *Public Management*, 1981, *63(10)*, 2–6.

Lucas, Charles Prestwood. *The Beginnings of English Overseas Enterprise: A Prelude to the Empire.* Oxford: Clarendon, 1917.

Lucie-Smith, Edward and Dars, C. *How the Rich Lived.* New York: Paddington, 1976.

Lucier, Richard L. "Gauging the Strength and Meaning of the 1978 Tax Revolt." In Charles H. Levine (ed.), *Managing Fiscal Stress: The Crisis in the Public Sector.* Chatham, NJ: Chatham House, 1980.

Lueck, Marjorie; Orr, Ann C.; and O'Connell, Martin. *Trends in Child Care Arrangements for Working Mothers.* Washington, DC: U.S. Government Printing Office, 1982.

Lukas, J. Anthony. *Common Ground.* New York: Knopf, 1985.

Lynch, Kevin. *The Image of the City.* Cambridge, MA: MIT Press, 1960.

Lynd, Robert S. and Lynd, Helen M. *Middletown: A Study in American Culture.* New York: Harcourt, Brace, 1929.

Lynd, Robert S. and Lynd, Helen M. *Middletown in Transition: A Study in Cultural Conflicts.* New York: Harcourt, Brace, 1937.

McFeeley, Neil D. "Special District Governments: The New Dark Continent Twenty Years Later." *Midwest Review of Public Administration*, 1978, *12*, 211–245.

McGehee, Scott and Watson, Susan (eds.). *Blacks in Detroit.* Detroit: The Free Press, 1977.

McGrath, Dennis. "Who Must Leave? Alternative Images of Urban Revitalization." *Journal of the American Planning Association*, 1982, *48*, 196–203.

MacIver, Robert M. *Social Causation.* New York: Ginn, 1942.

MacManus, Susan A. "Special District Governments: A Note on Their Use as Property Tax Relief Mechanisms in the 1970's." *Journal of Politics*, 1981, *43*, 1207–1214.

Macpherson, C.B. *The Life and Times of Liberal Democracy.* New York: Oxford University Press, 1977.

Madison, James. "Federalist 10: The Utility of the Union as a Safeguard Against Domestic Faction and Insurrection (Continued)." In Alexander Hamilton, James Madison, and John Jay (eds.), *The Federalist Papers.* New York: Mentor, 1961.

Madison, James. "Federalist 51: The Meaning of the Maxim, Which Requires a Separation of the Departments of Power, Examined and Ascertained (Continued and Concluded)." In Alexander Hamilton, James Madison, and John Jay (eds.), *The Federalist Papers.* New York: Mentor, 1961.

Magleby, David B. *Direct Legislation: Voting on Ballot Propositions in the United States*. Baltimore, MD: Johns Hopkins University Press, 1984.

Mandelker, D.R. "Racial Discrimination and Exclusionary Zoning: A Perspective on Arlington Heights." *Texas Law Review*, 1977, *55*, 1217-1253.

Mannheim, Karl. *Ideology and Utopia*. New York: Harcourt, Brace, 1936.

Mansbridge, Jane J. *Beyond Adversary Democracy*. New York: Basic, 1980.

Marcuse, Herbert. *One Dimensional Man: Studies in the Ideology of Advanced Industrial Society*. Boston: Beacon, 1964.

Marris, Peter and Rein, Martin. *Dilemmas of Social Reform: Poverty and Community Action in the United States*. 2nd edition. Chicago: Aldine, 1973.

Marshall, Foster, Jr. "Urban Homesteading in Columbus: Success in the Politics of Perception." Unpublished Honors Thesis, The Ohio State University, 1985.

Martin, Lowell A. *Library Response to Urban Change: A Study of the Chicago Public Library*. Chicago: American Library Association, 1969.

Martin, Roscoe C.; Munger, Frank J.; Burkhead, Jesse; and Birkhead, Guthrie S. *Decisions in Syracuse*. Bloomington: Indiana University Press, 1961.

Mayer, Martin. *The Builders: Houses, People, Neighborhoods, Governments, Money*. New York: Norton, 1978.

Meehan, Eugene J. *Theory and Method of Political Analysis*. Homewood, IL: Dorsey, 1965.

Meehan, Eugene J. *Public Housing Policy: Convention versus Reality*. New Brunswick, NJ: Rutgers University Press, 1975.

Mencken, H.L.. *The American Language: An Inquiry into the Development of English in the United States*. 1st abridged edition. New York: Knopf, 1963.

Merget, Astrid and Wolff, William. "The Law and Municipal Services: Implementing Equity." *Public Management*, 1976, *58*, 2-8.

Merton, Robert K. *Social Theory and Social Structure*. Glencoe, IL: Free Press, 1957.

Meyer, John R. and Quigley, John M. *Local Public Finance and the Fiscal Squeeze: A Case Study*. Cambridge, MA: Ballinger, 1977.

Meyerson, Martin and Banfield, Edward C. *Politics, Planning and the Public Interest: The Case of Public Housing in Chicago*. Glencoe, IL: Free Press, 1955.

Miles, Rufus. *Awakening from the American Dream: The Social and Political Limits to Growth*. New York: Universe, 1976.

Mill, John Stuart. *On Liberty*. New York: Macmillan, 1926.

Miller, Delbert C. "Industry and Community Power Structure: A Comparative Study of an American and an English City." *American Sociological Review*, 1958, *23*, 9-15.

Miller, Zane. *The Urbanization of Modern America: A Brief History*. New York: Harcourt, Brace, Jovanovich, 1973.

Mills, C. Wright. *The Power Elite*. New York: Oxford University Press, 1956.

Mladenka, Kenneth. "Citizen Demand and Bureaucratic Response: Direct Dialing Democracy in a Major American City." *Urban Affairs Quarterly*, 1977, *12*, 273-290.

Mladenka, Kenneth and Hill, Kim Quaile. "The Distribution of Benefits in an Urban Environment." *Urban Affairs Quarterly*, 1977, *13*, 73-94.

Mollenkopf, John H. *The Contested City*. Princeton, NJ: Princeton University Press, 1983.

Mollenkopf, John. "New York: The Great Anomaly." *PS*, 1986, *19*, 591-597.

Molotch, Harvey. "The City as a Growth Machine: Toward a Political Economy of Place." *American Journal of Sociology*, 1976, *82*, 309-332.

Morris, Charles R. *The Cost of Good Intentions: New York and the Liberal Experiment 1960-1965*. New York: Norton, 1980.

Morris, Richard S. *Bum Rap on American Cities: The Real Causes of Urban Decay*. Englewood Cliffs, NJ: Prentice-Hall, 1980.

Mowbray, A.Q. *Road to Ruin*. Philadelphia: Lippencott, 1969.

Moynihan, Daniel Patrick. *Maximum Feasible Misunderstanding: Community Action in the War on Poverty*. New York: Free Press, 1969a.

Moynihan, Daniel Patrick. "Toward a National Urban Policy." *The Public Interest*, 1969b, *17*, 3-20.

Muir, William Ker. *Police: Streetcorner Politicians*. Chicago: University of Chicago Press, 1977.

Mumford, Lewis. *The Culture of Cities*. New York: Harcourt, Brace, 1938.

Mumford, Lewis. *The City in History: Its Origins, Its Transformations, and Its Prospects*. New York: Harcourt, Brace, World, 1961.

Muñoz, Carlos, Jr. and Henry, Charles. "Rainbow Coalitions in Four Big Cities: San Antonio, Denver, Chicago, and Philadelphia." *PS*, 1986, *19*, 598-609.

Munro, William B. *The Government of American Cities*. 3rd edition. New York: Macmillan, 1920.

Murray, Charles A. *Losing Ground: American Social Policy 1950-1980*. New York: Basic, 1984.

Mushkin, Selma J. and Vehorn, Charles L. "User Fees and Charges." In Charles H. Levine (ed.), *Managing Fiscal Stress: The Crisis in the Public Sector*. Chatham, NJ: Chatham House, 1980.

Naipaul, Shiva. *North of South: An African Journey*. New York: Simon and Schuster, 1979.

National Advisory Commission on Civil Disorders. *Report*. New York: Bantam, 1968.

National Center for Education Statistics. *The Condition of Education 1985*. Washington, DC: U.S. Department of Education, 1985.

National Institute for Mental Health. *Mental Health, United States, 1985*. Washington, DC: U.S. Government Printing Office, 1985.

National Municipal League. *A Model City Charter, With Home Rule Provisions Recommended for State Constitutions*. 6th edition. New York, 1964.

National Training and Information Center, Federal Housing Administration. *The American Nightmare*. Chicago: NTIC, 1976.

Neenan, William B. *Political Economy of Urban Areas*. Chicago: Markham, 1972.

Nelson, Dale C. "Ethnicity and Socioeconomic Status as Sources of Participation: The Case for Ethnic Political Culture." *American Political Science Review*, 1979, *73*, 1024-1038.

Nelson, Richard R. "Intellectualizing about the Moon-Ghetto Metaphor: A Study of the Current Malaise of Rational Analysis of Social Problems." *Policy Sciences*, 1974, *5*, 378-414.

Nelson, William E., Jr. "Cleveland: The Evolution of Black Political Power." In Michael B. Preston, Lenneal J. Henderson, and Paul L. Puryear (eds.), *The New Black Politics: The Search for Political Power.* 2nd edition. New York: Longman, 1987.

New York City Office of Management and Budget. "Message of the Mayor." 1988.

Newman, Oscar. *Defensible Space: Crime Prevention Through Urban Design.* New York: Collier, 1972.

Niederhoffer, Arthur and Smith, Alexander. *New Directions in Police-Community Relations: From Conciliation to Confrontation.* Corte Monte, CA: Rinehart, 1974.

Nivola, Pietro S. "Distributing a Municipal Service: A Case Study of Housing Inspection." *Journal of Politics*, 1978, *40*, 59-81.

Nordlinger, Eric A. *Decentralizing the City: A Study of Boston's Little City Halls.* Cambrige, MA: MIT Press, 1972.

O'Neill, Thomas P. *Man of the House: The Life and Political Memoirs of Speaker Tip O'Neill.* New York: Random House, 1987.

Oldenquist, Andrew. *The Non-Suicidal Society.* Bloomington: Indiana University Press, 1986.

Olson, Mancur, Jr. *The Logic of Collective Action: Public Goods and the Theory of Groups.* New York: Schocken, 1968.

Orbell, John and Uno, Toro. "A Theory of Neighborhood Problem Solving: Political Action vs. Residential Mobility." *American Political Science Review*, 1972, *66*, 471-489.

Ostrom, Elinor. "On the Meaning and Measurement of Output and Efficiency in the Provision of Urban Police Services." *Journal of Criminal Justice*, 1973, *1*, 93-112.

Ostrom, Vincent; Tiebout, Charles M.; and Warren, Robert. "The Organization of Government in Metropolitan Areas: A Theoretical Inquiry." *American Political Science Review*, 1961, *55*, 831-842.

Owen, Wilfred. *The Metropolitan Transportation Problem.* Washington, DC: Brookings, 1956.

Palley, Marian Lief and Palley, Howard A. *Urban America and Public Policies.* Lexington, MA: Heath, 1981.

Park, Robert E.; Burgess, Ernest W.; and Makenzie, Roderick D. *The City.* Reprint of the 1925 edition. Chicago: University of Chicago Press, 1967.

Parkes, Henry Bamford. *The United States of America: A History.* New York: Knopf, 1959.

Paul, Diane B. *The Politics of the Property Tax.* Lexington, MA: Lexington, 1975.

Pearce, Diana. "Black, White, and Many Shades of Gray: Real Estate Brokers and Their Racial Practices." Unpublished Ph.D. dissertation, University of Michigan, 1976.

Pearce, Diana. "A Sheltered Crisis: The State of Fair Housing Opportunity in the Eighties." In *A Sheltered Crisis: The State of Fair Housing in the Eighties.* Washington, DC: U.S. Commission on Civil Rights, 1983.

Pellegrin, Roland J. and Coates, Charles H. "Absentee-Owned Corporations and Community Power Structure." *American Journal of Sociology,* 1956, *61,* 413–419.

Perry, David C. and Watkins, Alfred J. (eds.). *The Rise of the Sunbelt Cities.* Beverly Hills, CA: Sage, 1977.

Perry, Huey L. and Stokes, Alfred. "Politics and Power in the Sunbelt: Mayor Morial of New Orleans." In Michael B. Preston, Lenneal J. Henderson, and Paul L. Puryear (eds.), *The New Black Politics: The Search for Political Power.* 2nd edition. New York: Longman, 1987.

Persell, Caroline H. *Education and Inequality: A Theoretical and Empirical Synthesis.* New York: Free Press, 1977.

Peterson, George E. (ed.). *Property Tax Reform.* Washington, DC: Urban Institute, 1973.

Peterson, George E.; Soloman, Arthur P.; Madjid, Hadi; and Apgar, William C. *Property Taxes, Housing, and the Cities.* Lexington, MA: Lexington, 1973.

Peterson, John E. "Big City Borrowing Costs and Credit Quality." In Robert W. Burchell and David Listokin (eds.), *Cities Under Stress: The Fiscal Crisis of Urban America.* New Brunswick, NJ: Rutgers University Press, 1981.

Peterson, Paul E. *City Limits.* Chicago: University of Chicago Press, 1981.

Pfiffner, James P. "Inflexible Budgets, Fiscal Stress, and the Tax Revolt." In Alberta M. Sbragia (ed.), *The Municipal Money Chase: The Politics of Local Government Finance.* Boulder, CO: Westview, 1983.

Phillips, Christopher. "The Friendly Supper Club." *Parade,* August 3, 1986, p. 10.

Pirenne, Henri. *Medieval Cities: Their Origins and the Revival of Trade.* Translated by Frank D. Halsey. Princeton, NJ: Princeton University Press, 1925.

Piven, Frances Fox and Cloward, Richard. *Regulating the Poor: The Functions of Public Welfare.* New York: Pantheon, 1971.

Platt, Anthony M. *The Politics of Riot Commissions.* New York: Collier, 1971.

Polsby, Nelson W. "How to Study Community Power: The Pluralist Alternative." *Journal of Politics,* 1960, *22,* 474–484.

Polsby, Nelson W. *Community Power and Political Theory: A Further Look at Problems of Evidence and Inference.* 2nd edition. New Haven: Yale University Press, 1980.

Poole, Robert W. *Cutting Back City Hall.* New York: Universe, 1980.

Popper, Karl R. *The Logic of Scientific Discovery.* New York: Basic, 1959.

Popper, Karl R. *The Open Society and Its Enemies.* 2nd edition. Princeton, NJ: Princeton University Press, 1963.

Powledge, Fred. *Model City: A Test of American Liberalism.* New York: Simon and Schuster, 1970.

Pressman, Jeffrey L. "Preconditions of Mayoral Leadership." *American Political Science Review*, 1972, *66*, 511-524.

Pressman, Jeffrey L. and Wildavsky, Aaron. *Implementation: How Great Expectations in Washington Are Dashed in Oakland*. Berkeley: University of California Press, 1973.

Preston, Michael B. "The Election of Harold Washington: An Examination of the SES Model in the 1983 Chicago Mayoral Election." In Michael B. Preston, Lenneal J. Henderson, and Paul L. Puryear (eds.), *The New Black Politics: The Search for Political Power*. 2nd edition. New York: Longman, 1987.

Prewitt, Kenneth and Nowlin, William. "Political Ambitions and the Behavior of Incumbent Politicians." *Western Political Quarterly*, 1969, *22*, 298-308.

Quante, Wolfgang. *The Exodus of Corporate Headquarters from New York City*. New York: Praeger, 1976.

Rabinowitz, Francine. *City Politics and Planning*. New York: Atherton, 1969.

Rabkin, Judith G. "Public Attitudes Toward Mental Illness: A Review of the Literature." *Schizophrenia Bulletin*, 1974, *10*, 9-33.

Rainwater, Lee. "The Lessons of Pruitt-Igoe." *The Public Interest*, 1967, *8*, 116-126.

Rakove, Milton. *Don't Make No Waves—Don't Back No Losers*. Bloomington: Indiana University Press, 1975.

Ransom, Bruce. "Black Independent Electoral Politics in Philadelphia: The Election of Mayor W. Wilson Goode." In Michael B. Preston, Lenneal J. Henderson, and Paul L. Puryear (eds.), *The New Black Politics: The Search for Political Power*. 2nd edition. New York: Longman, 1987.

Ravitch, Diane. *The Great School Wars, New York City, 1805-1973: A History for the Public Schools as a Battlefield of Social Change*. New York: Basic, 1974.

Rawls, John. *A Theory of Justice*. Cambridge, MA: Harvard University Press, 1971.

Reagan, Michael D. *The New Federalism*. New York: Oxford University Press, 1972.

Reich, Robert B. *The Next American Frontier*. New York: New York Times, 1983.

Rein, Martin. *Social Science and Public Policy*. New York: Penguin, 1976.

Renner, Tari. "Municipal Election Processes: The Impact on Minority Representation." In *The Municipal Yearbook*. Washington, DC: International City Management Association, 1988.

Rice, Roger L. "Residential Segregation by Law, 1910-1917." *Journal of Southern History*, 1968, *34*, 179-199.

Rich, Richard C. "The Political Economy of Urban-Service Distribution." In Richard C. Rich (ed.), *The Politics of Urban Public Services*. Lexington, MA: Lexington, 1982.

Rich, Wilbur C. "Coleman Young and Detroit Politics: 1973-1986." In Michael B. Preston, Lenneal J. Henderson, and Paul L. Puryear (eds.), *The New Black Politics: The Search for Political Power*. 2nd edition. New York: Longman, 1987.

Riedel, John. "Boss and Faction." *The Annals of the American Academy of Political and Social Science.* 1964, *353*, 14–26.

Riesman, David. *The Lonely Crowd: A Study of the Changing American Character.* New Haven: Yale University Press, 1950.

Rifkind, Carole. *Main Street: The Face of Urban America.* New York: Harper and Row, 1977.

Riis, Jacob A. *How the Other Half Lives: Studies among the Tenements of New York.* New York: Hill and Wang, 1957.

Riker, William. *Federalism: Origin, Operation, Significance.* Boston: Little, Brown, 1964.

Riordan, William. *Plunkitt of Tammany Hall: A Series of Very Plain Talks on Very Practical Politics.* New York: Dutton, 1963.

Ripley, Randall B. and Franklin, Grace. *Congress, the Bureaucracy, and Public Policy.* 4th edition. Homewood, IL: Dorsey, 1987.

Rivlin, Alice M. *Systematic Thinking for Social Action.* Washington, DC: Brookings, 1971.

Roethlisberger, F.J. and Dickson, William J. *Management and the Worker: An Account of a Research Program Conducted by the Western Electric Company, Hawthorne Works, Chicago.* Cambridge, MA: Harvard University Press, 1939.

Rohatyn, Felix. "Reconstruction of America." *New York Review of Books,* March 5, 1981.

Rose, Richard. "The Making of a Do-It-Yourself Tax Revolt." *Public Opinion,* 1980, *3*, 13–18.

Rosenbaum, J. *Making Inequality: The Hidden Curriculum of High School Tracking.* New York: Wiley, 1976.

Rosenthal, Robert and Jacobson, Lenore. *Pygmalion in the Classroom: Teacher Expectation and Pupils' Intellectual Development.* New York: Holt, Rinehart, and Winston, 1968.

Ross, Bernard H. and Stedman, Murray S., Jr. *Urban Politics.* 3rd edition. Itasca, IL: Peacock, 1985.

Rossell, Christine H. "School Desegregation and White Flight." *Political Science Quarterly,* 1976, *90*, 675–695.

Royko, Mike. *Boss: Richard J. Daley of Chicago.* New York: Dutton, 1971.

Ryan, William. *Blaming the Victim.* Revised edition. New York: Vintage, 1976.

Safire, William. *Safire's Political Dictionary: The New Language of Politics.* New York: Random House, 1978.

Sale, Kirkpatrick. *Power Shift: The Rise of the Southern Rim and Its Challenge to the Eastern Establishment.* New York: Random House, 1975.

Sale, Kirkpatrick. *The Human Scale.* New York: Coward, McCann, and Geoghegan, 1980.

Salisbury, Robert H. "Urban Politics: The New Convergence of Power." *Journal of Politics,* 1964, *26*, 775–797.

Sanders, Heywood T. "Urban Renewal and the Revitalized City: A Reconsideration of Recent History." In Donald Rosenthal (ed.), *Urban Revitalization.* Beverly Hills, CA: Sage, 1980.

Savas, E.S. "Solid Waste Collection in Metropolitan Areas." In Elinor Ostrom (ed.), *The Delivery of Urban Services: Outcomes of Changes.* Beverly Hills, CA: Sage, 1976.

Saxton, Lloyd and Kaufman, Walter (eds.). *The American Scene: Social Problems of the 1970's.* Belmont, CA: Wadsworth, 1971.

Sayre, Wallace S. and Kaufman, Herbert. *Governing New York City: Politics in the Metropolis.* New York: Sage, 1960.

Sbragia, Alberta M. "Politics, Local Government, and the Municipal Bond Market." In Alberta M. Sbragia (ed.), *The Municipal Money Chase: The Politics of Local Government Finance.* Boulder, CO: Westview, 1983.

Scarborough, George. "A Council of Governments Approach." *National Civic Review,* 1982, *71,* 358-361.

Schattschneider, E.E. *The Semi-Sovereign People: A Realist's View of Democracy in America.* New York: Holt, Rinehart, and Winston, 1960.

Schlesinger, Arthur M., Jr. *The Age of Jackson.* Boston: Little, Brown, 1945.

Schlesinger, Arthur M., Jr. *The Crisis of the Old Order.* Boston: Houghton Mifflin, 1957.

Schlesinger, Arthur M., Jr. *The Coming of the New Deal.* Boston: Houghton Mifflin, 1959.

Schlesinger, Arthur M., Sr. *The Rise of the City 1878-1898.* New York: Macmillan, 1933.

Schulze, Robert O. "The Bifurcation of Power in a Satellite Community." In Morris Janowitz (ed.), *Community Political Systems.* Glencoe, IL: Free Press, 1961.

Schumacher, F.E. *Small Is Beautiful: A Study of Economics As If People Mattered.* New York: Harper and Row, 1973.

Schumaker, Paul D. "Policy Responsiveness to Protest Group Demands." *Journal of Politics,* 1975, *37,* 488-521.

Schumaker, Paul D. "The Scope of Political Conflict and the Effectiveness of Constraints in Contemporary Urban Protest." *The Sociological Quarterly,* 1978, *19,* 168-184.

Schumaker, Paul D. *Critical Pluralism, Democratic Performance, and Community Power.* Lawrence: University of Kansas Press, 1990.

Schumaker, Paul D.; Bolland, John M.; and Feiock, Richard C. "Economic Development Policy and Community Conflict: A Comparative Issues Approach." *Research in Urban Policy,* 1986, *2,* 25-46.

Schumpeter, Joseph. *Capitalism, Socialism, and Democracy.* New York: Harper, 1947.

Schwartz, John. *America's Hidden Success: A Reassessment of Twenty Years of Public Policy.* New York: Norton, 1983.

Scott, W.R. *The Constitution and Finance of English, Scottish, and Irish Joint Stock Companies to 1720.* Oxford, England: Oxford University Press, 1910-1912.

Sears, Bill. "How the Dome Miracle Became Reality." *Kingdome Magazine,* March 1976, p.8.

Sears, David O. and Citrin, Jack. *Tax Revolt: Something for Nothing in California.* Cambridge, MA: Harvard University Press, 1982.

Sennett, Richard and Cobb, Jonathan. *The Hidden Injuries of Class.* New York: Knopf, 1972.

Shafritz, Jay M. *The Dorsey Dictionary of American Politics.* Chicago: Dorsey, 1988.

Sharp, Elaine B. "Citizen-Initiated Contacting of Government Officials and Socioeconomic Status: Determining the Relationship and Accounting for It." *American Political Science Review,* 1982, 76, 109-115.

Sheehan, Susan. *A Welfare Mother.* New York: Mentor, 1977.

Shefter, Martin. "National-Local Interaction and the New York City Fiscal Crisis." In Douglas E. Ashford (ed.), *National Resources and Urban Policy.* New York: Methuen, 1980.

Shefter, Martin. "Images of the City in Political Science: Communities, Administrative Entities, Competitive Markets, and Seats of Chaos." In Lloyd Rodwin and Robert M. Hollister (eds.), *Cities of the Mind: Images and Themes of the City in the Social Sciences.* New York: Plenum, 1984.

Shin, Doh C. "Subjective Indicators and Distributional Research on the Quality of Public Services." In Richard C. Rich (ed.), *Analyzing Urban-Service Distributions.* Lexington, MA: Lexington, 1982.

Sigelbaum, Harvey C. "Poor Medical Care Is Poor Public Policy." *New York Times,* Sept. 18, 1988.

Silberman, Charles E. *Criminal Violence, Criminal Justice.* New York: Random House, 1978.

Silver, Allan. "Official Interpretations of Racial Riots." In Robert H. Connery (ed.), *Urban Riots.* New York: Vintage, 1968.

Sisk, Dorothy A. *Creative Teaching of the Gifted.* New York: McGraw-Hill, 1987.

Sitkoff, Harvard. *The Struggle for Black Equality 1954-1980.* New York: Hill and Wang, 1981.

Skolnick, Jerome H. *The Politics of Protest: A Report.* New York: Simon and Schuster, 1969.

Smith, Christopher J. "Neighborhood Effects on Mental Health." In D.T. Herbert and R.J. Johnston (eds.), *Geography and the Urban Environment: Research in Progress and Applications,* Volume 5. New York: Wiley, 1980.

Smith, Marshall S. "Evaluation Findings in Head Start Planned Variation." In Alice M. Rivlin and P. Michael Timpane (eds.), *Planned Variation in Education: Should We Give Up or Try Harder?* Washington, DC: Brookings, 1975.

Smith, Michael P. *The City and Social Theory.* New York: St. Martin's, 1979.

Snyder, Richard C.; Bruck, H.W.; and Sapin, Burton. "Decision-Making as an Approach to the Study of International Politics." In Richard C. Snyder, H.W. Bruck, and Burton Sapin (eds.), *Foreign Policy Decision-Making: An Approach to the Study of International Politics.* New York: Free Press, 1962.

Sofen, Edward. *The Miami Metropolitan Experiment.* Bloomington: Indiana University Press, 1963.

Sonenshein, Raphe. "Biracial Coalition Politics in Los Angeles." *PS,* 1986, *19,* 582-590.

Stanley, Harold W. *Voter Mobilization and the Politics of Race: The South and Universal Suffrage, 1952-1984.* New York: Praeger, 1987.

Stauber, R.L. and Kline, Mary. "A Profile of City Commissioners in Kansas."
  Your Government, April 15, 1965.
Steffens, Lincoln. *The Autobiography of Lincoln Steffens.* New York: Harcourt
  Brace, 1931.
Stein, Maurice R. *The Eclipse of Community: An Interpretation of American Studies.*
  Princeton, NJ: Princeton University Press, 1960.
Stephan, W.G. "School Desegregation: An Evaluation of Predictions Made in
  Brown v. Board of Education." *Psychological Bulletin,* 1978, *85,* 217-238.
Sternlieb, George. "The City as Sandbox." *The Public Interest,* 1971, *25,* 14-21.
Stevens, Barbara J. "Service Arrangement and the Cost of Refuse Collection."
  In E.S. Savas (ed.), *The Organization and Efficiency of Solid Waste Collection.*
  Lexington, MA: Lexington, 1977.
Stevenson, Charles L. *Facts and Values: Studies in Ethical Analysis.* New Haven:
  Yale University Press, 1963.
Stewart, Frank M. *A Half Century of Municipal Reform: The History of the National
  Municipal League.* Berkeley: University of California Press, 1950.
Stinchcombe, J.L. *Reform and Reaction: City Politics in Toledo.* Belmont, CA:
  Wadsworth, 1968.
Stone, Clarence N. "Systemic Power in Community Decision Making: A
  Restatement of Stratification Theory." *American Political Science Review,*
  1980, 74, 978-990.
Stone, Clarence N.; Whelen, Robert K.; and Murin, William J. *Urban Policy and
  Politics in a Bureaucratic Age.* Englewood Cliffs, NJ: Prentice-Hall, 1979.
Stone, Clarence N.; Whelen, Robert K.; and Murin, William J. *Urban Policy and
  Politics in a Bureaucratic Age.* 2nd edition. Englewood Cliffs, NJ: Prentice-
  Hall, 1986.
Sundquist, James L. *Making Federalism Work: A Case Study of Program Coordination
  at the Community Level.* Washington, DC: Brookings, 1969.
Swanson, Cheryl and Bolland, John M. "Judgment Policy and the Exercise of
  Police Discretion." In Stuart Nagel, Erika Fairchild, and Anthony
  Champagne (eds.), *The Political Science of Criminal Justice.* Springfield, IL:
  Thomas, 1983.
Swisher, Carl B. *American Constitutional Development.* Edited by Edward M. Sait.
  2nd edition. Boston: Houghton Mifflin, 1954.
Tabb, William K. "The New York City Fiscal Crisis." In William K. Tabb and
  Larry Sawers (eds.), *Marxism and the Metropolis: New Perspectives in Urban
  Political Economy.* 2nd edition. New York: Oxford, 1984.
Taylor, Charles. "Neutrality in Political Science." In Peter Laslett and W.G. Run-
  ciman (eds.), *Philosophy, Politics, and Society: A Collection* (third series).
  Oxford: Blackwell, 1967.
Thernstrom, Stephan. *Poverty and Progress: Social Mobility in a Nineteenth Century
  City.* Cambridge, MA: Harvard University Press, 1964.
Thomas, Lewis. *The Youngest Science: Notes of a Medicine Watcher.* New York:
  Viking, 1983.
Thompson, Wilbur R. *Preface to Urban Economics.* Baltimore, MD: Johns
  Hopkins University Press, 1968.

Thurow, Lester C. *The Zero Sum Society: Distribution and the Possibilities for Economic Change.* New York: Basic, 1980.

Tiebout, Charles M. "A Pure Theory of Urban Expenditures." *Journal of Political Economy*, 1956, *64*, 416-424.

Tisdale, William R. "Housing Discrimination: A New Technology." In *A Sheltered Crisis: The State of Fair Housing in the Eighties.* Washington, DC: U.S. Commission on Civil Rights, 1983.

Toqueville, Alexis de. *Democracy in America.* Henry Reeve text, edited by Phillips Bradley. New York: Knopf, 1945.

Trounstine, Philip J. and Christensen, Terry. *Movers and Shakers: The Study of Community Power.* New York: St. Martin's, 1982.

Truman, David B. *The Governmental Process: Political Interests and Public Opinion.* New York: Knopf, 1951.

Tucker, Harvey and Zeigler, L. Harmon. *Professionals Versus the Public.* New York: Longman, 1980.

Van Dyke, Vernon. *Political Science: A Philosophical Analysis.* Stanford, CA: Stanford University Press, 1960.

Verba, Sidney and Nie, Norman H. *Participation in America: Political Democracy and Social Equity.* New York: Harper and Row, 1972.

Vidich, Arthur J. and Bensman, Joseph. *Small Town in Mass Society: Class, Power, and Religion in a Rural Community.* Princeton, NJ: Princeton University Press, 1958.

Vose, Clement E. *Caucasians Only: The Supreme Court, the NAACP, and the Restrictive Covenant Cases.* Berkeley: University of California Press, 1959.

Waldo, Dwight. *The Administrative State: A Study of the Political Theory of American Public Administration.* New York: Ronald, 1948.

Walker, David B. *Toward a Functioning Federalism.* Cambridge, MA: Winthrop, 1981.

Wallach, Michael; Kogan, Nathan; and Bem, Daryl J. "Group Influence on Individual Risk-Taking." *Journal of Abnormal and Social Psychology*, 1962, *65*, 75-86.

Walton, John. "Substance and Artifact: The Current Status of Research on Community Power Structure." *American Journal of Sociology*, 1966, *71*, 430-438.

Walzer, Michael. *The Revolution of the Saints: A Study in the Origins of Radical Politics.* Cambridge, MA: Harvard University Press, 1965.

Wanniski, Jude. *The Way the World Works: How Economics Fail and Succeed.* New York: Simon and Schuster, 1978.

Warner, Sam Bass, Jr. *The Urban Wilderness: A History of the American City.* New York: Harper and Row, 1972.

Warner, William Lloyd. *Democracy in Jonesville: A Study in Quality and Inequality.* New York: Harper, 1949.

Watts, T.D. "Three Traditions in Social Thought on Alcoholism." *The International Journal of the Addictions*, 1982, *17*, 1231-1239.

Weber, Max. *The Theory of Social and Economic Organization.* Translated by A.M. Henderson and Talcott Parsons. New York: Free Press, 1947.

Weber, Max. *From Max Weber: Essays in Sociology.* Translated and edited by H.H. Gerth and C. Wright Mills. New York: Oxford University Press, 1946.

Welch, Susan. "The Impact of Urban Riots on Urban Expenditures." *American Journal of Political Science*, 1975, *19*, 741-760.

Wellman, Barry. "The Community Question: The Intimate Networks of East Yorkers." *American Journal of Sociology*, 1979, *84*, 1201-1231.

Wells, William. "Fantasy Obscures Facts of City Crime." *Detroit Free Press*, July 6, 1975, p. 10A.

White, Morton and White, Lucia. *The Intellectual Versus the City: From Thomas Jefferson to Frank Lloyd Wright*. Oxford, England: Oxford University Press, 1977.

White, Sheila C. "Work Stoppages of Government Employees." In J. Joseph Loewenberg and Michael H. Moskow (eds.), *Collective Bargaining in Government: Readings and Cases*. Englewood Cliffs, NJ: Prentice-Hall, 1972.

Whitlock, Brand. *Forty Years of It*. New York: Appleton, 1914.

Wicker, Tom. "Clouds Loom for Economy." Tuscaloosa *News*, August 8, 1987, p. 4.

Wikstrom, Nelson. *Councils of Governments: A Study of Political Incrementalism*. Chicago: Nelson-Hall, 1985.

Wilburn, York. "Unigov: Local Government Reorganization in Indianapolis." In Advisory Commission on Intergovernmental Relations, *Substate Regionalism and the Federal System, Volume II: Case Studies*. Washington, DC: U.S. Government Printing Office, 1973.

Wildavsky, Aaron. *Leadership in a Small Town*. Totowa, NJ: Bedminster, 1964.

Wildavsky, Aaron. *Speaking Truth to Power*. Boston: Little, Brown, 1979a.

Wildavsky, Aaron. *The Politics of the Budgetary Process*. 3rd edition. Boston: Little, Brown, 1979b.

Williams, Linda. "Black Political Progress in the 1980s: The Electoral Arena." In Michael B. Preston, Lenneal J. Henderson, and Paul L. Puryear (eds.), *The New Black Politics: The Search for Political Power*. 2nd edition. New York: Longman, 1987.

Williams, Oliver P. "A Typology for Comparative Local Government." *Midwest Journal of Political Science*, 1961, *5*, 150-164.

Williams, Oliver P. *Metropolitan Political Analysis: A Social Access Approach*. New York: Free Press, 1971.

Williams, Oliver P. and Adrian, Charles R. *Four Cities: A Study of Comparative Making*. Philadelphia: University of Pennsylvania Press, 1963.

Wilson, Edmund. *The American Earthquake: A Documentary of the Twenties and Thirties*. Garden City, NY: Doubleday, 1958.

Wilson, James Q. *The Amateur Democrat: Club Politics in Three Cities*. Chicago: University of Chicago Press, 1962.

Wilson, James Q. (ed). *The Metropolitan Enigma: Inquiries into the Nature and Dimensions of America's Urban Crisis*. Garden City, NY: Doubleday, 1970.

Wilson, James Q. *Varieties of Police Behavior: The Management of Law and Order in Eight Communities*. Garden City, NY: Doubleday, 1972.

Wilson, James Q. *Thinking About Crime*. New York: Basic, 1975.

Wilson, James Q. and Banfield, Edward C. "Public-Regardingness as a Value Premise in Voting Behavior. *American Political Science Review*, 1964, *58*, 876–887.

Wilson, William J. *The Truly Disadvantaged: The Inner City, the Underclass, and Public Policy*. Chicago: University of Chicago Press, 1987.

Wirt, Frederick; Walter, Benjamin; Rabinowitz, Francine; and Hensler, Deborah R. *On the City's Rim: Politics and Policy in Suburbia*. Lexington, MA: D.C. Heath, 1972.

Wirth, Louis. "Urbanism as a Way of Life." *American Journal of Sociology*, 1938, *44*, 1–24.

Wirth, Louis. *Louis Wirth on Cities and Social Life: Selected Papers*. Edited by Albert J. Reiss, Jr. Chicago: University of Chicago Press, 1964.

Wolch, Jennifer R. "Spacial Consequences of Social Policy: The Role of Service-Facility Location in Urban Development Patterns." In Richard C. Rich (ed.), *The Politics of Urban Public Services*. Lexington, MA: Lexington, 1982.

Wolfinger, Raymond E. "Why Political Machines Have Not Withered Away and Other Revisionist Thoughts." *Journal of Politics*, 1972, *34*, 365–398.

Wolfinger, Raymond E. *The Politics of Progress*. Englewood Cliffs, NJ: Prentice-Hall, 1974.

Wood, Robert C. *Suburbia: Its People and Their Politics*. Boston: Houghton Mifflin, 1959.

Wood, Robert C. *1400 Governments: The Political Economy of the New York Metropolitan Region*. Garden City, NY: Doubleday, 1964.

Wright, Deil S. *Federal Grants in Aid: Perspectives and Alternatives*. Washington, DC: American Enterprise Institute, 1968.

Wright, Quincy. "Political Science and World Stabilization." *American Political Science Review*, 1950, *44*, 1–13.

Yates, Douglas. "Service Delivery and the Urban Political Order." In Willis D. Hawley and David Rogers (eds.), *Improving the Quality of Urban Management*. Beverly Hills, CA: Sage, 1974.

Yates, Douglas. *The Ungovernable City: The Politics of Urban Problems and Policy Making*. Cambridge, MA: MIT Press, 1977.

Zeigler, L. Harmon and Jennings, M. Kent. *Governing American Schools: Political Interaction in Local School Districts*. North Scituate, MA: Duxbury, 1974.

Zeigler, L. Harmon and Tucker, Harvey. "Who Governs American Education: One More Time." In Don Davies (ed.), *Communities and Their Schools*. New York: McGraw-Hill, 1981.

Zimmerman, Joseph F. "The New England Town Meeting: Pure Democracy in Action?" In *The Municipal Yearbook*. Washington, DC: International City Management Association, 1984.

Zink, Harold. *City Bosses in the United States: A Study of Twenty Municipal Bosses*. Durham, NC: Duke University Press, 1930.

Zisk, Betty H. *Local Interest Politics: A One-Way Street*. Indianapolis, IN: Bobbs-Merrill, 1973.

Name Index

Adams, Carolyn T., 456
Adams, Herbert B., 109
Adrian, Charles R., 99, 103, 107, 116,
    117, 118, 119, 120, 125, 132, 133,
    351, 352
Alexander, K. A., 403
Alford, Robert R., 113, 140, 144, 198
Alinsky, Saul D., 163, 173, 174
Altshuler, Alan, 270
Ambrose, P., 248n
Anderson, Martin, 297, 299
Andrews, Wayne, 276
Apgar, William C., 420
Aristotle, 149
Arkes, Hadley, 405, 405n
Armor, David, 425
Aronson, J. Richard, 341
Auletta, Ken, 455

Bachrach, Peter, 181, 187, 206n, 220n
Badger, Lee W., 369

Baldassare, M., 149
Baltzell, Digby E., 183
Banfield, Edward C., 63n, 100n, 128,
    127, 171, 172, 177, 181, 188, 191,
    230, 249, 298, 439n, 442, 447,
    448, 451n
Baratz, Morton S., 181, 187, 220n
Baron, Harold M., 419
Barton, Eugenia, 148
Baskin, John, 49n
Bayley, David, 429
Beer, Thomas, 56n
Bellah, Robert N., 7n, 49, 156n, 451n
Bellman, Richard F., 408
Bem, Daryl J., 146
Bender, Leslie, 278n
Bennet, Harrison, 452
Bensman, Joseph, 49n, 106, 268
Benton, J. Edwin, 287
Berger, Thomas, 39, 218
Berkeley, George E., 289

__ Subject Index _____